GW00367059

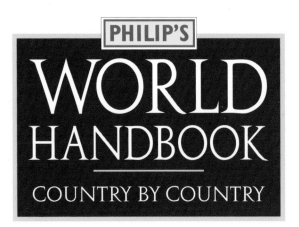

PHILIP'S

WORLD HANDBOOK

COUNTRY BY COUNTRY

PHILIP'S

WORLD
HANDBOOK

COUNTRY BY COUNTRY

EXECUTIVE EDITOR
Caroline Rayner

EDITOR
Kara Turner

EXECUTIVE ART EDITOR
Alison Myer

COVER DESIGN
Stewart Cocking

WORLD FLAGS
Bosse Norrgård

WORLD STATISTICS
Typeset by eMC Design, Bromham,
Bedford, UK

Published in Great Britain in 1995
by George Philip Limited,
an imprint of Reed Books,
Michelin House, 81 Fulham Road, London SW3 6RB,
and Auckland, Melbourne, Singapore and Toronto

Cartography by Philip's

ISBN 0–540–05891–2 (Paperback)
ISBN 0–540–05892–0 (Hardback)

A CIP catalogue record for this book is available
from the British Library

Printed in Great Britain

CONTENTS

See also contents lists for individual sections

GENERAL NOTES

World Gazetteer Statistical Tables

In the country fact-files certain terms have been used which may require some explanation.

AREA The area of the whole country, including inland water areas.

POPULATION The 1994 United Nations official population estimate is given, which is based on the latest censuses. The population of the cities is taken from the most recent census or the latest estimate (whichever is the more recent), and as far as possible is for the urban agglomeration rather than the strictly defined city proper.

ETHNIC GROUPS Only the main ethnic groups are listed and percentages are given wherever

possible. The figures are usually taken from the latest available census results.

LANGUAGES The official languages are listed together with any other major languages, with percentages given wherever possible. The figures are usually taken from the latest available census results.

RELIGIONS The principal religions are listed, with a breakdown of the main demoninations and percentages provided wherever possible.

CURRENCY The currency of each country is given in the format one pound equals 100 pence. Where a country does not have its own currency, the name is given of the country whose currency is used.

World Statistics Section

In the last few years, some countries have broken up to form separate states while others have united to make a single country. Some statistical data have already been published for these new countries, or, alternatively, interpretations have been drawn from the information that had previously been available. All available figures have been used in the listings, but data for the former larger countries – USSR, Czechoslovakia, Ethiopia and Yugoslavia – have sometimes also been given. The form of names for the new countries follows the convention used in Philip's world atlases, but the region that is generally called Serbia is listed under Yugoslavia (Serbia) and Bosnia-Herzegovina is abbreviated to Bosnia.

The world lists include as many countries and territories as possible. For certain countries, the English conventional names have been used rather than some newly-adopted name forms: Burma for Myanmar, Ivory Coast (Côte d'Ivoire) and Surinam (Suriname). Many of the statistics for Belgium include

those of Luxembourg, and any historic figures for Pakistan for 1950 will also contain those for Bangladesh.

Wherever possible, in the world statistics, the world total is given, followed by the countries in alphabetical order. Historic data are given for 1950 or 1970 (depending on data availability) as well as figures for the latest available year. All data are taken from official sources. The production statistics include all countries that have at some point produced over one-thousandth part of the world total. The top-ten producers are also indicated, together with their percentage of the world total.

The measure 'tonnes' is used and it is spelled in this way to indicate that the figures shown are in metric tons. The symbol ... indicates that the relevant figures are not available or that they are not applicable to a particular country. The symbol – means that although there was production for a particular year, it was very small.

WORLD MAPS

Symbols

—————— Principal railways   ▬ ▬ ▬ ▬ Internal boundaries
════════ Motorways
—————— Principal roads   4125   Heights (m)
▬▬▬▬▬▬ International boundaries   ☼   Principal airports

Height of Land

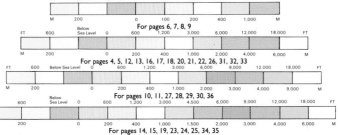

For pages 6, 7, 8, 9

For pages 4, 5, 12, 13, 16, 17, 18, 20, 21, 22, 26, 31, 32, 33

For pages 10, 11, 27, 28, 29, 30, 36

For pages 14, 15, 19, 23, 24, 25, 34, 35

WORLD : Political

Queen Elizabeth Is.
Victoria I.
Baffin I.
GREENLAND (Den.)
ICELAND
Alaska (U.S.)
Anchorage
Aleutian Is. (U.S.)
Churchill
Hudson Bay
NORTH
Edmonton
UNITED KINGDOM
Glasgow
IRELAND
London
Vancouver
CANADA
Calgary
Winnipeg
Seattle
Quebec
Montreal
Newfoundland
FRANCE
AMERICA
Chicago
Detroit
Toronto
Boston
San Francisco
Denver
St. Louis
New York
Washington
PORTUGAL
Madrid
SPAIN
UNITED STATES
Azores (Port.)
Lisbon
Los Angeles
Dallas
Casablanca
MOROCCO
Hawaiian Islands (U.S.)
Tropic of Cancer
Houston
Gulf of Mexico
Miami
Canary Is. (Sp.)
ALG
W. SAHARA
Mexico
Havana
CUBA
BAHAMAS
ATLANTIC
F
West Indies
MEXICO
JAMAICA HAITI
DOMINICAN REP.
Puerto Rico (U.S.)
MAURITANIA
MALI
BELIZE
GUATEMALA HONDURAS
Caribbean Sea
Guadeloupe (Fr.)
Martinique (Fr.)
C. VERDE IS.
SENEGAL
GAMBIA
EL SALVADOR NICARAGUA
BARBADOS
GUINEA-BISSAU
GUINEA
Palmyra Is. (U.S.)
COSTA RICA PANAMA
Caracas
TRINIDAD & TOB.
SIERRA LEONE
IVORY COAST
BURKINA FASO
PACIFIC
VENEZUELA
LIBERIA
Bogota
GUYANA
OCEAN
COLOMBIA
SURINAM
FR. GUIANA
Equator
Galapagos Is. (Ecuador)
Quito
ECUADOR
Belém
KIRIBATI
Manaus
SOUTH
Tokelau Is. (N.Z.)
Marquesas Is. (Fr.)
PERU
BRAZIL
Recife
Ascension (Br.)
W. SAMOA
U.S. Samoa
OCEAN
Lima
AMERICA
St. Helena (Br.)
Cook Is. (N.Z.)
Society Is. (Fr.)
Tahiti (Fr.)
French Polynesia
La Paz
Brasília
Salvador
TONGA
BOLIVIA
Tubuai Is. (Fr.)
Tropic of Capricorn
Pitcairn (Br.)
Easter I. (Chile)
PARAGUAY
Rio de Janeiro
São Paulo
Asunción
Kermadec Is. (N.Z.)
CHILE
ARGENTINA
URUGUAY
Montevideo
Santiago
Buenos Aires
Tristan da Cunha (Br.)
Chatham Is. (N.Z.)
Falkland Is. (Br.)
Tierra del Fuego
S. Georgia (Br.)
FALKLAND IS. DEPENDENCIES (Br.)
ANTARCTICA
ROSS DEPENDENCY
BRITISH ANTARCTIC TERRITORY
NORWEG
West from Greenwich

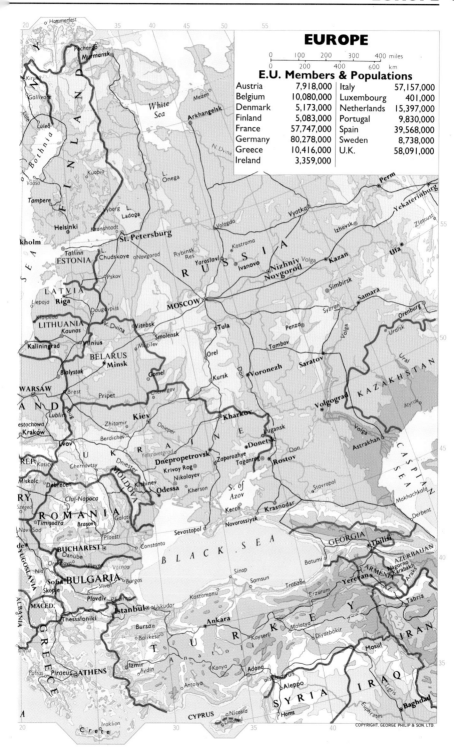

EUROPE

	miles	
0 100 200 300 400		
0 200 400 600 km		

E.U. Members & Populations

Austria	7,918,000	Italy	57,157,000
Belgium	10,080,000	Luxembourg	401,000
Denmark	5,173,000	Netherlands	15,397,000
Finland	5,083,000	Portugal	9,830,000
France	57,747,000	Spain	39,568,000
Germany	80,278,000	Sweden	8,738,000
Greece	10,416,000	U.K.	58,091,000
Ireland	3,359,000		

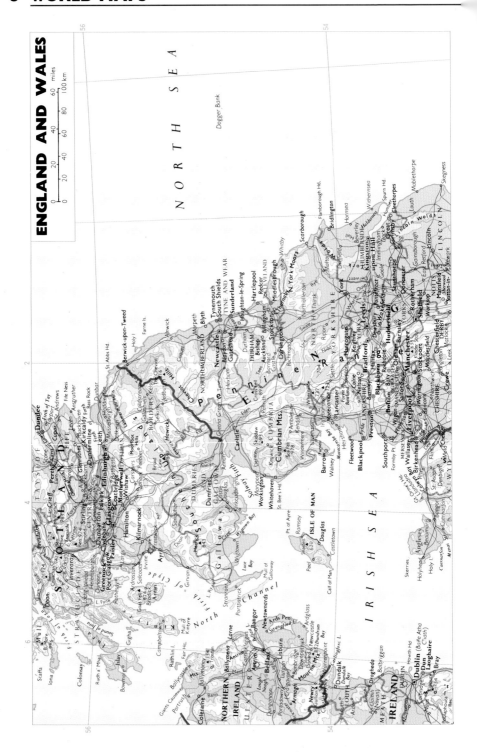

ENGLAND AND WALES

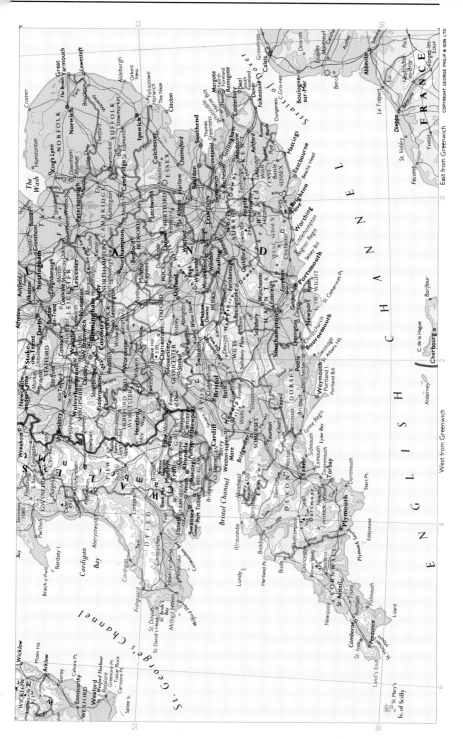

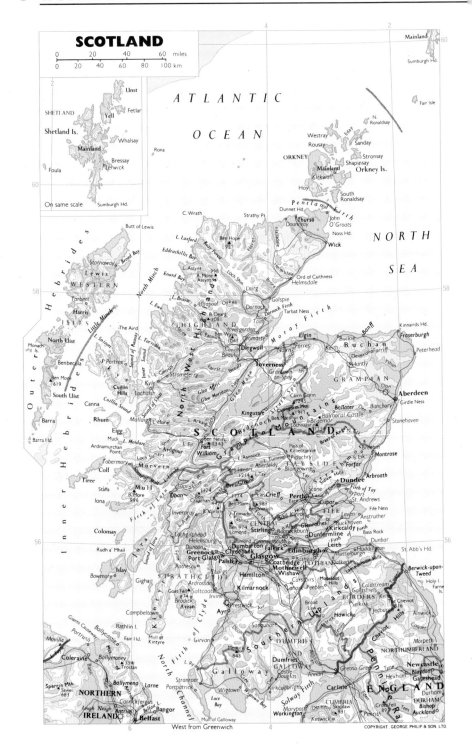

SCOTLAND

0   20   40   60 miles
0 20 40 60 80 100 km

SHETLAND

Unst
Fetlar
Yell
Shetland Is.
Whalsay
Mainland
Bressay
Lerwick
Foula
On same scale   Sumburgh Hd.
Rona

Mainland
Sumburgh Hd.
Fair Isle

A T L A N T I C

O C E A N

Westray
Rousay
ORKNEY
Mainland
Kirkwall
Hoy
South
Ronaldsay

N. Ronaldsay
Eday
Sanday
Stronsay
Shapinsay
Orkney Is.

Pentland Firth
C. Wrath   Strathy Pt   Dunnet Hd.
Thurso
Dunceay
John
O'Groats
Noss Hd.
Wick

N O R T H

S E A

Butt of Lewis
Stornoway Broad Bay
Lewis
WESTERN
Tarbert
Harris
ISLES
The Aird
North Uist
Monach
Is.
Benbecula
Ben More
619
South Uist
Canna
Barra
Barra Hd.

L. Laxford
Ben Hope
Eddrachillis Bay
Reay Forest
L. Assynt 998
B. More
Assynt
Enard Bay
L. Broom
L. Ewe
Ullapool
B. Dearg
1081
L. Maree
Ben Wyvis
Fannich 1045
Conon
Beauly

L. Shin
Luirg
Oykell
Dornoch Firth
Tain

Ben Hee
Loch Naver
Helmsdale
Ord of Caithness
Golspie
Dornoch
Tarbat Ness

Kinnairds Hd.
Fraserburgh
Buchan
Deverandturriff
Peterhead

H I G H L A N D
Invergordon
Cromarty
Dingwall
Inverness
Farrar
Glen Affric
Glen Moriston
L. Arkaig
Fort
William
Ardgour

Moray Firth
Elgin
Nairn
Forres
Keith
Banff
Buckie

GRAMPIAN
Grantown-
on-Spey
Cairn Gorm
Cairn Toul
1291
Loch Laggan
Kingussie
Badenoch
Braemar
Balmoral Castle
Ballater
Banchory

Aberdeen
Girdle Ness
Stonehaven

North West
Mallaig
Skye
Cuillin
Hills
Lochalsh
Kyle
Stromeferry
Portree
Sound of Sleat
L. Tarridon
Inner Sound
Sound of Rasay
L. Alsh

S C O T L A N D
Grampian Mountains
Ben Nevis
1343
Pass of
Killiecrankie
Aberfeldy
Rannoch
Ben Lawers
1214
Tummel
L. Tay
Crieff
Breadalbane

Braco of Angus
Brechin
S. Esk
Forfar
Montrose
Arbroath
Dundee

Mull
B. More
996
Staffa
Iona
Tobermory
Morvern
Coll
Tiree

Oban
Ben
Cruachan
1174
B. More
983
Ben Vorlich
Trossachs
Ben 974
Lomond

Earn
Perth
Carse
Scone
Auchterarder
Tayport
St. Andrews
Fife Ness
Anstruther
Cupar
FIFE
Leven
Buckhaven
Kirkcaldy
Glenrothes
Dunfermline
Forth
Bass Rock
Dunbar

Colonsay
Rudh a' Mhail
Islay
Bowmore
Gigha

Lochgilphead
Helensburgh
Dumbarton
Dunoon
Greenock
Port Glasgow
Clydebank
Paisley
Rothesay
Glasgow
STRATHCLYDE
Ardrossan
Saltcoats
Irvine
Kilmarnock
Prestwick
Ayr

Stirling
Falkirk
CENTRAL
Bannockburn
Alloa
Grangemouth
Bo'ness
Edinburgh
Leith
Musselburgh
Haddington
LOTHIAN
Salkirk
Motherwell
Wishaw
Hamilton
Coatbridge
Carstairs
Lanark
Moffat
Moorfoot
Hills
Peebles
Lammermuir Hills
St. Abb's Hd.
Berwick-upon-
Tweed
Holy I.
Farne
Is.

Rathlin I.
Fair Hd.
Mull of
Kintyre
Campbeltown
Giants Causeway
Ballycastle
Portrush
Moville
Coleraine
Ballymoney
Ballymena
Larne
Spergin Mts
Sawel
683
Antrim
Lough Neagh
NORTHERN
IRELAND
Belfast
Bangor
Carrickfergus
Newtownards

Goat Fell
874
Brodick
Arran
Ailsa Craig
Sanquhar
Girvan
Cairnryan
Stranraer
Portpatrick
Luce
Bay
Mull of Galloway

Southern
Uplands
Broad
Law
Hawick
Jedburgh
Selkirk
Galashiels
Gretna Green
Dumfries
AND
GALLOWAY
Castle
Douglas
Kirkcudbright
Annan
Wigtown
Solway Firth
Carlisle
CUMBRIA
Skiddaw
931
Keswick
Workington
Maryport
Derwent
Cockermouth

Kelso
Coldstream
The Cheviot
816
Cheviot Hills
Pennine
Alnwick
Coquet
Morpeth
NORTHUMBERLAND
Newcastle
Blaydon
Gateshead
Hexham
Tyne
E N G L A N D
Durham
DURHAM
Bishop
Auckland
Cross Fell
893
Tees

58

56

60

2

4

COPYRIGHT. GEORGE PHILIP & SON. LTD.

IRELAND

| 0 | 20 | 40 | 60 miles |
| 0 | 20 | 40 | 60 | 80 | 100 km |

ATLANTIC

OCEAN

SCOTLAND

Tiree
Staffa
B. More
994
Mull
Oban
Iona
Colonsay
Lochgilphead
Rudh a' Mhail
Islay
Bowmore
Gigha
Arran
Campbeltown
Mull of Kintyre

Malin Hd.
Giant's Causeway
Rathlin I.
Ballycastle
Portrush
Fair Hd.
Tory I.
Sheep Haven
Lough Swilly
Inishowen Pen.
Moville
Buncrana
Coleraine
Ballymoney
554
Trostan
Horn Hd.
Bloody Foreland
Errigal
752
Derryveagh Mts.
Londonderry
Ballymena
Larne
Aran I.
Letterkenny
DONEGAL
Sperrin Mts.
Sawel
683
Carrickfergus
Gweebarra B.
Glenties
Finn
Lifford
Strabane
Antrim
Bangor
Loughros More B.
676
Bluestack
Omagh
L. Neagh
Belfast
Newtownards
Rossan Pt.
Killybegs
Donegal
Ballyshannon
NORTHERN
IRELAND
Lisburn
Rathlin O'Birne I.
Donegal Bay
Lower
Erne
Dungannon
Portadown
(Craigavon)
Lurgan
Broad Haven
Killala Bay
Sligo B.
Sligo
Enniskillen
Blackwater
Armagh
Banbridge
Downpatrick
Ardglass
Erris Hd.
Upper
Erne
MONAGHAN
Monaghan
Newry
Newcastle
Mullet Peninsula
Ballina
L. Allen
LEITRIM
CAVAN
Slieve Gullion
573
Castleblaney
852
Mourne Mts.
Dundrum Bay
Blacksod Bay
SLIGO
Leitrim
Cootehill
Warrenpoint
Achill Head
L. Conn
Nephin
806
MAYO
Boyle
Carrick-on-Shannon
Carlingford L.
Louth
Dundalk
Achill I.
Castlebar
ROSCOMMON
L. Gowna
Ardee
LOUTH
Dundalk Bay
Clare I.
Clew Bay
Westport
Claremorris
Longford
L. Sheelin
Ceanannus Mor
(Kells)
Drogheda
Killary Harbour
Croagh Patrick
765
Mweelrea
819
CONNACHT
Roscommon
LONGFORD
An Uaimh
(Navan)
Balbriggan
Inishbofin
L. Mask
L. Corrib
Tuam
L. Ree
MEATH
Twelve Pins
Boyne
Slyne Hd.
Connemara
GALWAY
Athlone
WESTMEATH
Mullingar
Maynooth
DUBLIN
Howth Hd.
Galway
REPUBLIC
Celbridge
Dublin (Baile Atha Cliath)
Kilkieran
Athenry
Ballinasloe
Clare
Tullamore
OFFALY
Allen
Naas
Kippure
754
Dun Laoghaire
Inishmore
Galway Bay
Gort
Loughrea
OF
Birr
Slieve Bloom
Portlaoise
Poulaphouca Res.
Bray
Aran Is.
Slieve Aughty
L. Derg
Mountmellick
KILDARE
Wicklow
Liscannor Bay
Mal Bay
CLARE
IRELAND
Roscrea
LAOIS
Lugnaquilla
925
WICKLOW
Ennis
Nenagh
ULSTER
Arklow
Kilkee
Keeper
894
Thurles
CARLOW
Muine Bheag
Gorey
Loop Hd.
Kilrush
Shannon
Foynes
Limerick
TIPPERARY
Kilkenny
Mt. Leinster
796
Cahore Pt.
Brandon Hd.
Tralee B.
Fenit
Listowel
LIMERICK
Rathkeale
Rath Luirc
(Charleville)
Galtee Mts.
Galtymore
920
KILKENNY
Tipperary
Sl. Naman
Enniscorthy
WEXFORD
Great Blasket
Dingle
Sl. Mish
Tralee
MUNSTER
Caher
Carrick-on-Suir
New Ross
Wexford
Wexford Harbour
Rosslare
Greenore Pt.
Dingle Bay
KERRY
Mitchelstown
Knockmealdown Mts.
Clonmel
Comeragh Mts.
Waterford
Tramore
Tuscar Rock
Carnsore Pt.
Macgillycuddy's Reeks
Killarney
Mallow
Blackwater
Fermoy
WATERFORD
Dungarvan
Dungarvan Bay
Saltee Is.
Valentia Harbour
Carrantuohill
1040
Lakes of Killarney
CORK
Youghal
Ballinskelligs B.
Cahirciveen
Caha Mts.
Macroom
Lee
Midleton
Cobh
Youghal Harbour
Valentia
Kenmare River
Bandon
Cork
Castletown Berehaven
Bantry
Clonakilty
Cork Harbour
Crow Head
Bantry Bay
Dunmanus Bay
Old Head of Kinsale
Mizen Hd.
Baltimore
Galley Hd.
Clonakilty Bay
Clear I.
C. Clear
Fastnet Rock

North Channel

St. George's Channel

FRANCE

0 20 40 60 80 100 miles
0 40 80 120 160 km

Swansea Newport LONDON Southend
Cardiff Bristol Bath Swindon Margate
Taunton ENGLAND Dover Calais
Southampton Brighton Folkestone Hastings C. Gris Nez
Exeter Exmouth Portsmouth Chichester Newhaven Boulogne
Torquay Weymouth Bournemouth Ryde Montreuil
St. Ives Truro Dartmouth Portland Somme
Land's End Falmouth Plymouth Eddystone Le Tréport
Penzance Dieppe
ENGLISH CHANNEL St. Valery Fécamp Caux Yvetot S.Me.
C. de la Hague Cherbourg Pte. de Barfleur Barbec Rouen Bray
Alderney Valognes Le Havre Beauvais
Guernsey St. Peter Port Sark Trouville Honfleur Lisieux Elbeuf Vexin
Channel Is. (Br.) Jersey Bessin Bayeux St. Lo Caen C. Evreux Seir Vernon
St. Helier N Bocage Lisieux Mantes Versailles
Ushant Morlaix Granville Mt. St. Michel Vire Falaise Or. Dreux Yv.
Brest Mts. Guingamp St. Brieuc St. Malo Dinard Avranches Perche E.L.
Pte. de St. Mathieu Bd Arrée Dinan Fougères Alençon Chartres
F R I C.A. Mayenne Beauce
Mts. Noire Rennes MAINE Orléans
Quimper I.V. Laval May. Le Mans O.R.L.E.
Pte. du Raz Mo. Vannes L.C. Blois Romo
Pte. de Penmarch Quimperlé Lorient Vilaine Châteaubriant Loir Sologne
Carnac Quiberon Angers Tours Amboise I.L. Loches Vierzo
Belle I. C.A.F. M.L. R TOURAINE I.
St. Nazaire Nantes Saumur Chinon I.L. Châteauroux I.
Ile de Noirmoutier Cholet Loire Châtellerault Creuse
Ile de Yeu Ven Bocage D.S. Châteauroux
La Roche POITOU Poitiers MARCH
Les Sables d'Olonne Vel. Fontenay Catinau Vi. Vienne Guéret
B A Y Niort H.V.
Ile de Ré La Rochelle Limoges
O F Rochefort AUNIS Creuse
Ile d' Oléron Saintes ANGOUMOIS Angoulême Co.
B I S C A Y Royan Cognac Ch. LIMOU
Le Verdon Grimne Périgueux Tu
Médoc Paulliac D. Perigord
Libourne Dordogne Sarlat
Bordeaux Gi. Garonne Bergerac GUYEN Lot
Arcachon Gr. L.G. Cahors
Agen T.G. Montaub
L. Mont-de-Marsan GASCONY
Gulf of Armagnac Auch Ge. Toulouse
Gascony Biarritz Adour P.A. Pau G.H.
Gijón Llanes Guecho Fuenterrabia Bayonne Orthez Tarbes Garonne Corcas
Oviedo Picos de Europa 2648 Sestao Santander Santona Guernica Lourdes H.P. Pyrenees Ari.
Bilbao Durango San Sebastián BEARN Bigorre Foix
León Sa. de Alba Reinosa Tolosa Vitoria Roncesvalles Lourdes Pic du Midi 2885 Andorra
Saldaña Miranda Pamplona 2885 Canfranc Pt. 1631 Mt. Perdu 3355 La Perche 1609
Astorga Pancorbo P. S Jaca 1609
Sahagún Burgos P A Logroño Tafalla N
Ebro

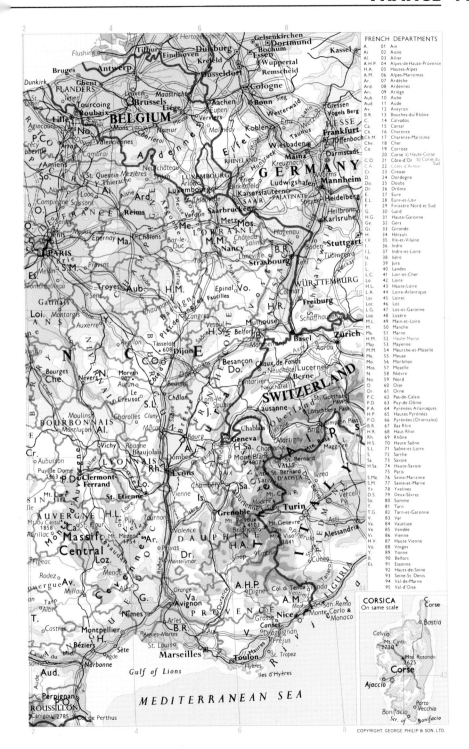

NETHERLANDS

| 0 | 10 | 20 | 30 | 40 | 50 miles |
| 0 | 20 | 40 | 60 | 80 km |

East from Greenwich

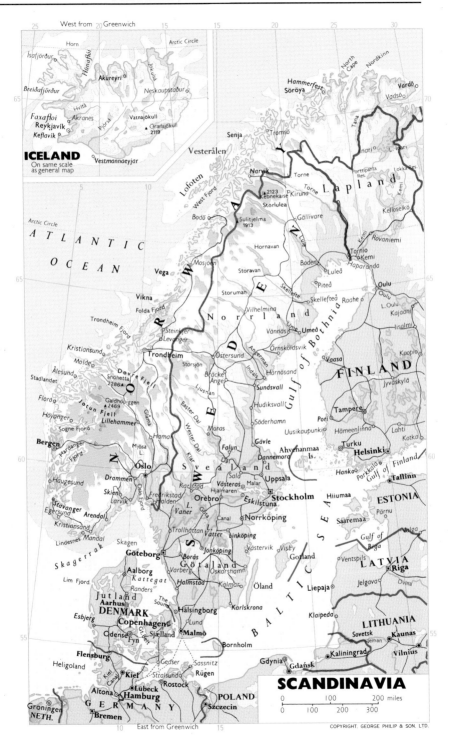

ICELAND
On same scale
as general map

SCANDINAVIA

0	100	200 miles

0   100   200   300

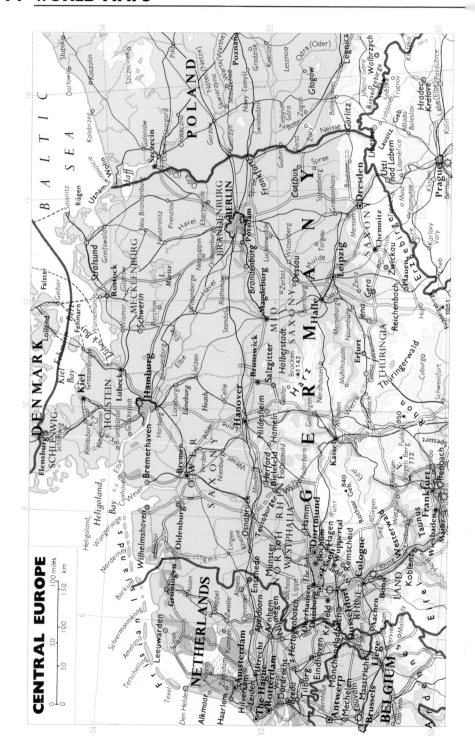

CENTRAL EUROPE

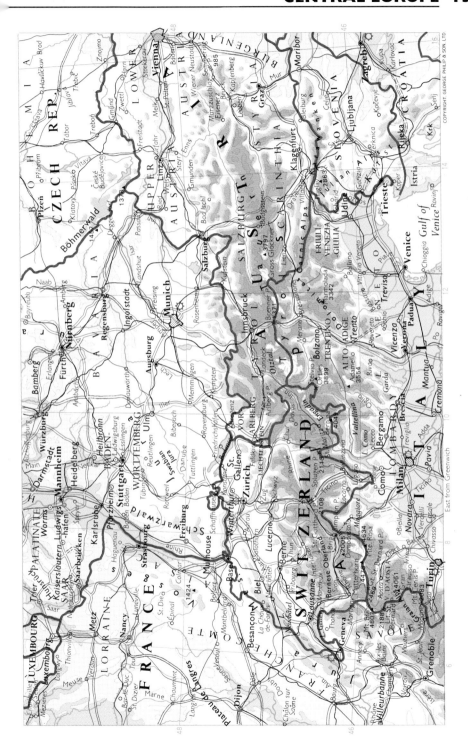

ITALY AND
S.E. EUROPE

0   50   100   150   200 miles
0   100   200   300 km

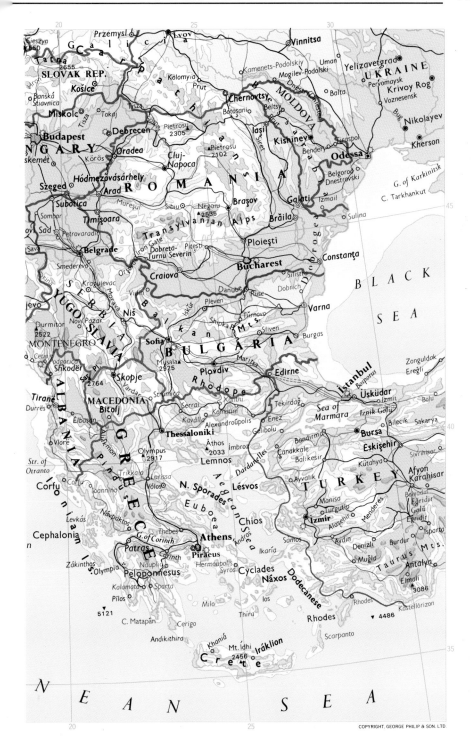

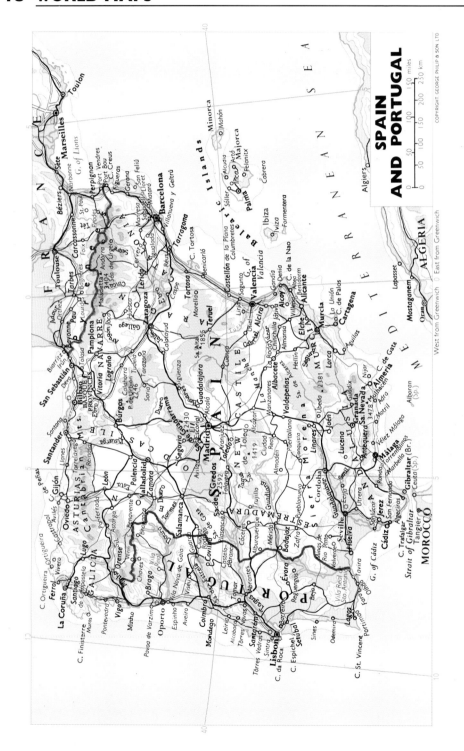

SPAIN
AND PORTUGAL

COPYRIGHT GEORGE PHILIP & SON LTD

West from Greenwich   East from Greenwich

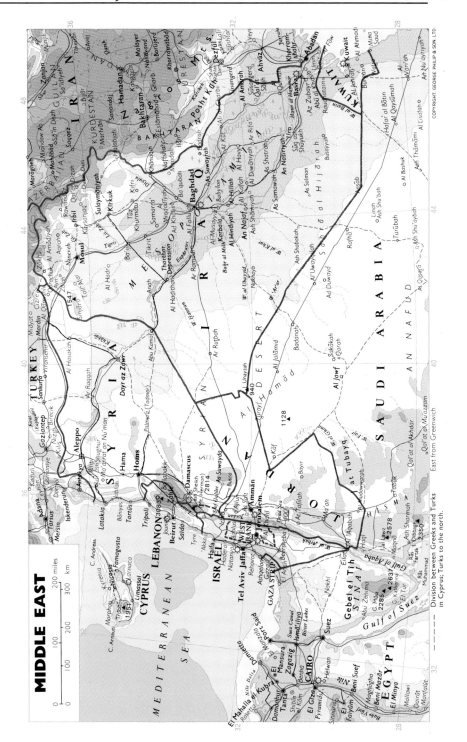

MIDDLE EAST

- - - - - Division between Greeks and Turks
in Cyprus; Turks to the north.

East from Greenwich

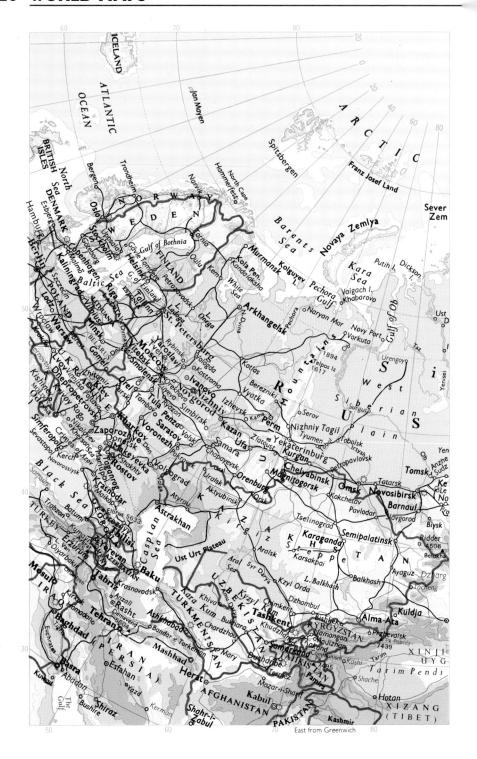

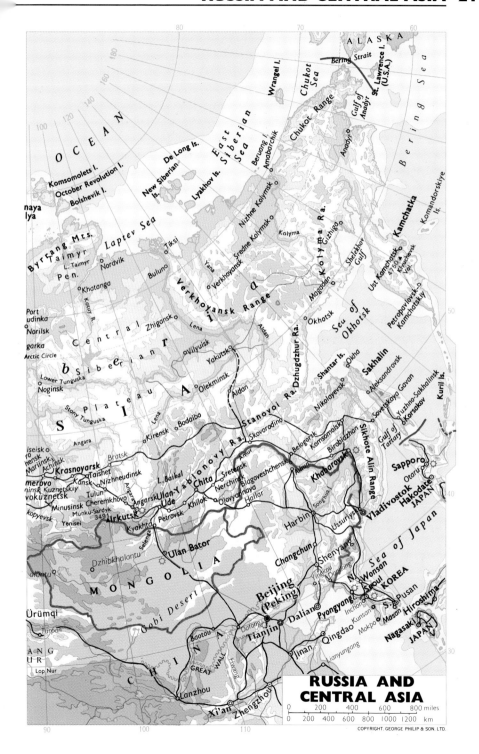

RUSSIA AND CENTRAL ASIA

| 0 | 200 | 400 | 600 | 800 miles |

| 0 | 200 | 400 | 600 | 800 | 1000 | 1200 | km |

COPYRIGHT. GEORGE PHILIP & SON. LTD.

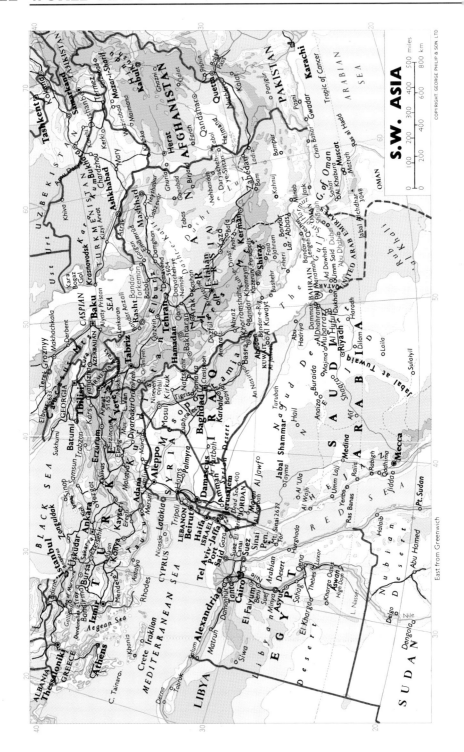

S.W. ASIA

COPYRIGHT GEORGE PHILIP & SON LTD

| 0 | 100 | 200 | 300 | 400 | 500 miles |

| 0 | 200 | 400 | 600 | 800 km |

East from Greenwich

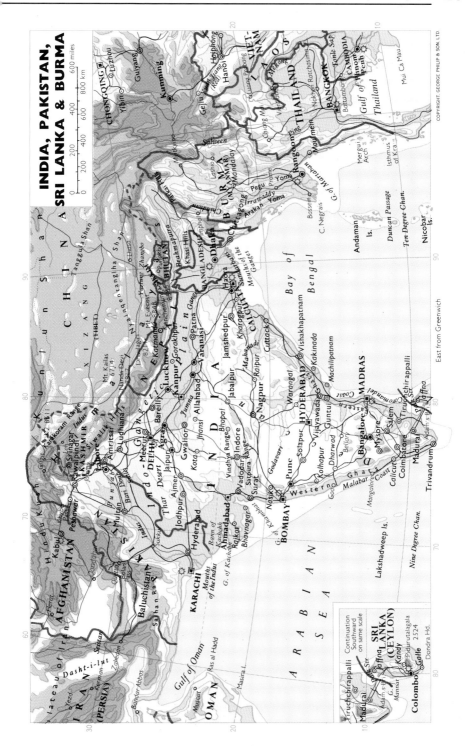

INDIA, PAKISTAN, SRI LANKA & BURMA

SRI LANKA (CEYLON)

Continuation Southward on same scale

COPYRIGHT GEORGE PHILIP & SON, LTD.

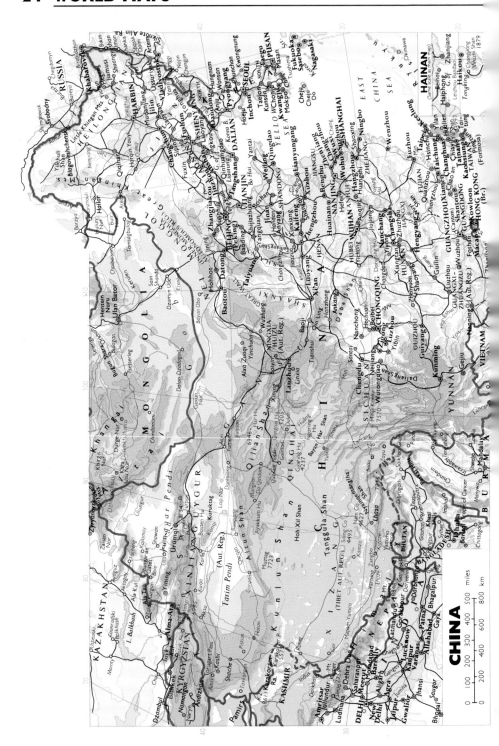

CHINA

JAPAN

0	50 100 150 200 miles
0	50 100 150 200 250 300 km

REFERENCE TO PREFECTURES

HOKKAIDO DISTRICT
1 Hokkaido

TOHOKU DISTRICT
2 Aomori
3 Akita
4 Iwate
5 Yamagata
6 Miyagi
7 Fukushima

CHUBU DISTRICT
8 Niigata
9 Ishikawa
10 Toyama
11 Fukui
12 Gifu
13 Nagano
14 Yamanashi
15 Aichi
16 Shizuoka

KANTO DISTRICT
17 Gumma
18 Tochigi
19 Saitama
20 Ibaraki
21 Tokyo
22 Chiba
23 Kanagawa

KINKI DISTRICT
24 Hyogo
25 Kyoto
26 Shiga
27 Osaka
28 Nara
29 Mie
30 Wakayama

CHUGOKU DISTRICT
31 Tottori
32 Okayama
33 Shimane
34 Hiroshima
35 Yamaguchi

SHIKOKU DISTRICT
36 Kagawa
37 Tokushima
38 Ehime
39 Kochi

KYUSHU DISTRICT
40 Fukuoka
41 Saga
42 Nagasaki
43 Kumamoto
44 Oita
45 Miyazaki
46 Kagoshima

East from Greenwich

COPYRIGHT. GEORGE PHILIP & SON. LTD.

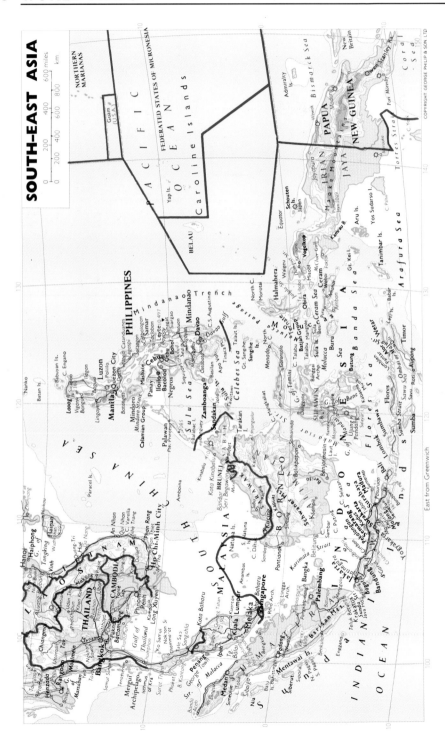

SOUTH-EAST ASIA

NORTHERN MARIANAS

FEDERATED STATES OF MICRONESIA

Guam (U.S.A.)

Caroline Islands

BELAU

Yap Is.

P A C I F I C

O C E A N

Equator

Schouten Is.

IRIAN JAYA

PAPUA NEW GUINEA

Maoke Mountains

Admiralty

Bismarck Sea

New Britain

Owen Stanley Ra.

Port Moresby

Torres Strait

C o r a l S e a

Aru Is.

Kai Is.

Arafura Sea

Tanimbar Is.

Babar

Wetar

Timor

Banda Sea

Ceram Sea

Halmahera

Morotai

Molucca Sea

I N D O N E S I A

Celebes Sea

Sulu Sea

Mindanao Trench

PHILIPPINES

Luzon

Manila Quezon City

Mindoro

Palawan

Calamian Group

Masbate

Panay

Negros

Cebu

Bohol

Leyte

Samar

Mindanao

Davao

Zamboanga

Sandakan

Kota Kinabalu

BRUNEI

Bandar Seri Begawan

S A B A H

SARAWAK

B O R N E O

Natuna Is.

KALIMANTAN

S O U T H

C H I N A S E A

Parasel Is.

Hainan

Haiphong

Hanoi

Ho Chi-Minh City

Phan Rang

V I E T N A M

L A O S

CAMBODIA

Phnom Penh

THAILAND

Bangkok

Gulf of Thailand

Kuala Lumpur

Melaka

Singapore

Kota Baharu

Penang George Town

Str. of Malacca

M A L A Y S I A

Medan

Palembang

Bangka

Belitung

Karimata Strait

Pontianak

Jakarta

Bandung

Yogyakarta

S U M A T R A

Barisan Mts.

Mentawai Is.

Padang

Nias

J A V A

Bali

Lombok

Sumbawa

Flores

Sumba

Java Sea

Flores Sea

I N D I A N

O C E A N

East from Greenwich

SALWEEN

COPYRIGHT GEORGE PHILIP & SON LTD

km

600 miles

800

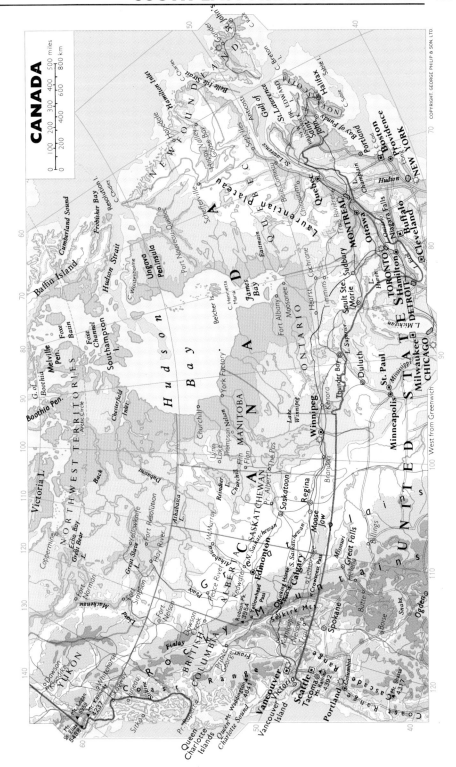

CANADA

Scale: 0 100 200 300 400 500 miles
0 200 400 600 800 km

Projection: Bonne

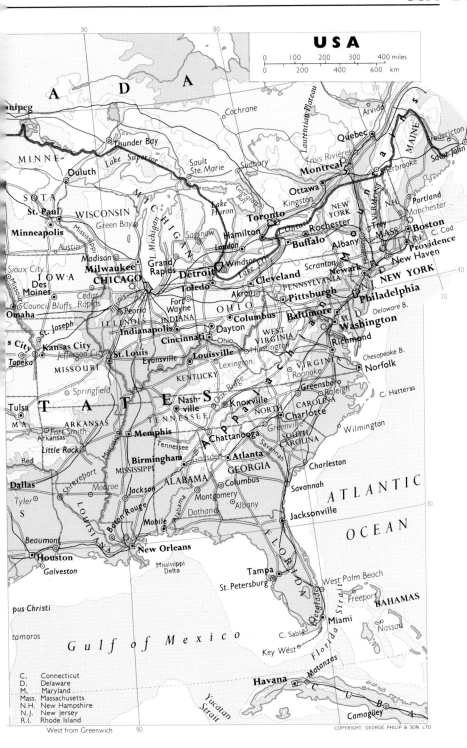

USA

0	100	200	300	400 miles
0	200	400	600	km

C A N A D A

Winnipeg
Cochrane
Arvida
90
80
70

Laurentian Plateau

Quebec
Trois Rivières
Fredericton

Thunder Bay
MINNE-
Duluth
Lake Superior
Sault Ste. Marie
Sudbury
Montreal
Sherbrooke
Saint John
MAINE

SOTA
St. Paul
WISCONSIN
Green Bay
Ottawa
Kingston
NEW YORK
N.H. Portland
Manchester
VERMONT

Minneapolis
Mississippi
MICHIGAN
Lake Huron
Georgian Bay
Toronto
Rochester
Troy
Albany
MASS. Boston
R.I. C. Cod
Providence

Austin
Madison
Saginaw
Hamilton
London
Ontario
Buffalo
Scranton
Newark
New Haven
NEW YORK

Sioux City
IOWA
Milwaukee
Gl. Rapids
Grand Rapids
Windsor
Lake Erie
Cleveland
PENNSYLVANIA
Pittsburgh
Philadelphia
Delaware B.
40

Des Moines
CHICAGO
Detroit
Toledo
Akron
70

Council Bluffs
Cedar Rapids
Fort Wayne
Columbus
OHIO
Ohio
Baltimore
M.D.
Washington

Omaha
Peoria
ILLINOIS
INDIANA
Dayton
WEST VIRGINIA
Huntington
Richmond
Chesapeake B.

St. Joseph
Indianapolis
Cincinnati
Louisville
Lexington
VIRGINIA
Roanoke
Norfolk

Kansas City
St. Louis
Jefferson City
Evansville
KENTUCKY
Blue Ridge
C. Hatteras

Topeka
MISSOURI
Springfield
Nash-ville
Knoxville
NORTH CAROLINA
Greensboro
Raleigh
Wilmington

Tulsa
S T A T E S
TENNESSEE
APP
Chattanooga
Charlotte
Greenville
SOUTH CAROLINA

M.A.
ARKANSAS
Fort Smith
Arkansas
Memphis
Tennessee
Gadsden
Atlanta
Savannah
Charleston

Little Rock
Red
Shreveport
Birmingham
MISSISSIPPI
ALABAMA
Columbus
GEORGIA

Dallas
Tyler
Monroe
Jackson
Alabama
Montgomery
Albany
Savannah

S
LOUISIANA
Baton Rouge
Dothan
Jacksonville
ATLANTIC

Beaumont
Mobile
30

Houston
Galveston
New Orleans
Mississippi Delta
FLORIDA
OCEAN

pus Christi
Tampa
St. Petersburg
West Palm Beach
Freeport
BAHAMAS

tamoros
Gulf of Mexico
C. Sable
Miami
Nassau

Key West
Florida Strait

Havana
Matanzas
C U B A
Camagüey

Yucatan Strait

C. Connecticut
D. Delaware
M. Maryland
Mass. Massachusetts
N.H. New Hampshire
N.J. New Jersey
R.I. Rhode Island

MEXICO AND THE CARIBBEAN

ATLANTIC OCEAN

PACIFIC OCEAN

Caribbean Sea

Gulf of Mexico

Gulf of California

Lower California

UNITED STATES

MEXICO

Tropic of Cancer

West from Greenwich

United States places: Charleston, Savannah, Jacksonville, Atlanta, Columbus, Montgomery, Birmingham, Mobile, Jackson, Baton Rouge, New Orleans, Houston, Dallas, Fort Worth, Austin, San Antonio, Corpus Christi, El Paso, Tampa, Miami

Mexico places: Mexicali, Nogales, Hermosillo, Guaymas, Chihuahua, Ciudad Juárez, Torreón, Durango, Mazatlán, Aguascalientes, Guadalajara, León, San Luis Potosí, Saltillo, Monterrey, Nuevo Laredo, Piedras Negras, Matamoros, Tampico, MEXICO CITY, Puebla, Veracruz, Oaxaca, Acapulco, Villahermosa, Tuxtla Gutiérrez, Coatzacoalcos, Salina Cruz, Mérida

Mountains/features: Eastern Sierra Madre, Western Sierra Madre, Popocatépetl 5452, C. San Lucas, C. Corrientes, C. Catoche, C. Sable, Rio Grande, Revilla Gigedo Is. (Mexico)

Central America: BELIZE, Belmopan, GUATEMALA, Guatemala, EL SALVADOR, San Salvador, HONDURAS, Tegucigalpa, NICARAGUA, Managua, Chinandega, L. Nicaragua, COSTA RICA, San José, PANAMA, Panama, Colón, G. of Darién, G. of Panama, C. Gracias à Dios

Caribbean: BAHAMAS, Nassau, Havana, CUBA, Sta. Clara, Camagüey, Holguín, Santiago de Cuba, Cayman Is. (Br.), JAMAICA, Kingston, HAITI, Port au Prince, DOMINICAN REP., Santo Domingo, Hispaniola, PUERTO RICO, San Juan, Virgin Is. (Br.), ANGUILLA, ST. KITTS–NEVIS, ANTIGUA & BARBUDA, GUADELOUPE (Fr.), DOMINICA, MARTINIQUE (Fr.), ST. LUCIA, ST. VINCENT & THE GRENADINES, BARBADOS, GRENADA, TRINIDAD & TOBAGO, Tobago, Port of Spain, NETH. ANTILLES, Curaçao, Aruba, Turks & Caicos Is., Yucatan Strait, Florida Strait, Florida

South America: VENEZUELA, CARACAS, Maracaibo, G. of Venezuela, Barquisimeto, Ciudad Bolívar, Mérida, COLOMBIA, Cúcuta, Bucaramanga, Barranquilla, Cartagena, Medellín, Sa. Nevada de S. Marta 5800, Caura, Caroní, Orinoco, Apure, Meta, Magdalena, Sa. Pacaraima

Yucatan

Gulf of Campeche

Gulf of Honduras

G. of Tehuantepec

Greater Antilles

Lesser Antilles

0   100   200   300   400   500 miles
0   200   400   600   800 km

SOUTH AMERICA

0   200   400   600   800 miles
0 200 400   800   1200 km

CARIBBEAN SEA

Hispaniola
Sierra Maestra
Santiago de Cuba   HAITI   DOM.
JAMAICA   Port au REP.   S. Juan
    Prince   PUERTO RICO
Kingston   (U.S.)
    Leeward Is.

Windward Is.

BARBADOS
NICARAGUA   G.of Venezuela   Curaçao (Neth.)   Port of Spain
Barranquilla   Maracaibo   TRINIDAD AND TOBAGO
COSTA CANAL ZONE   G. of   La Guaira
RICA   U.S.   Darién   Cartagena   Barquisimeto   Cumaná   Mata la Cruz
PANAMA   Panama   Bucaramanga   Caracas   Santo Tomé
    Sa. de Mérida   Ciudad Bolívar   Georgetown   Paramaribo
Medellín   VENEZUELA   Roraima   GUYANA   SURINAM   FR. GUIANA
Manizales   2810   Demerara
Bogotá   Sa. Pacaraima   Tumucumaque   Cayenne
Pereira   COLOMBIA   Orinoco   Casiquiare
Cali
Pasto   Papayán   Equator
ECUADOR   Quito   Macapá   Amazon   Pará
Chimborazo   Cotopaxi   Putumayo   Japurá   Negro   Belém
6267   5897   Guayaquil   Manaus   São Luis
Cuenca   Marañón   Iquitos   Benjamin Constant   Amazon   Santarém   Teresina   Fortaleza
C. Pariña   Piura   S.   Purus   Madeira   Xingu   Imperatriz   Parnaíba   Natal   C. de São Roque
Chiclayo   S. Antonio   l   v   Roosevelt   Tapajós   Tocantins   João Pessoa   C. Branco
Trujillo   Falls   a   Araguaia   Paulistana   Recife
PERU   Branco   s   BRAZIL   São Francisco   Maceió   Aracaju
Callão   Huancayo   Cuzco   Guaporé   Plateau of   Barreiros   Salvador   Alagoinhas
Lima   Illampú 6550   Mato Grosso   Brasília   Ilhéus
Pisco   Juliaca   BOLIVIA   Cuyabá   Goiânia   Montes   Vitória da
Arequipa   La Paz   Claros   Conquista
Mollendo   Cochabamba   Santa Cruz   Pirapora   Caravelas
Arica   Oruro   Sucre   Corumbá   Liberdade   Belo
Iquique   Potosí   Horizonte
Tropic of Capricorn   Paraguay   Ribeirão   Campos
Antofagasta   Pilcomayo   PARAGUAY   Prêto   Niterói
Taltal   Campinas   C. Frio
La Serena   Asunción   São Paulo   Rio de Janeiro
Tucumán   Corrientes   Curitiba   Santos
Santiago   Iguaçu   Blumenau
Aconcagua   del Estero   Uruguaiana   Santa
Viña del Mar   Córdoba   ARGENTINA   Santa Fé   Uruguay   Maria   Pôrto Alegre
Valparaíso   Mendoza   Rosario   Paraná   Pelotas   Lagoa dos Patos
Santiago   URUGUAY   Bagé   Rio Grande do Sul
Talca   Mercedes   Rocha
Concepción   Buenos   Montevideo   ATLANTIC
    Aires   Rio de la Plata
    Santa   Azul   Mar del Plata
Valdivia   Rosa   Pta. Mogotes
Osorno   Negro   Bahía Blanca
Puerto Montt   Piedma   OCEAN
Chiloé   G. of San Matías
Chonos   Chubut   Rawson
Arch.   Comodoro
    Rivadavia   G. of San Jorge
PACIFIC   Rio Gallegos   Falkland Is.
    Punta   (Br.)
    Arenas   Stanley
OCEAN   Magellan's Str.   South Georgia
    Tierra del Fuego   (Br.)
    Staten I.
C. Froward   C. Horn
Drake Passage
Juan
Fernández
(Chile)

West from Greenwich

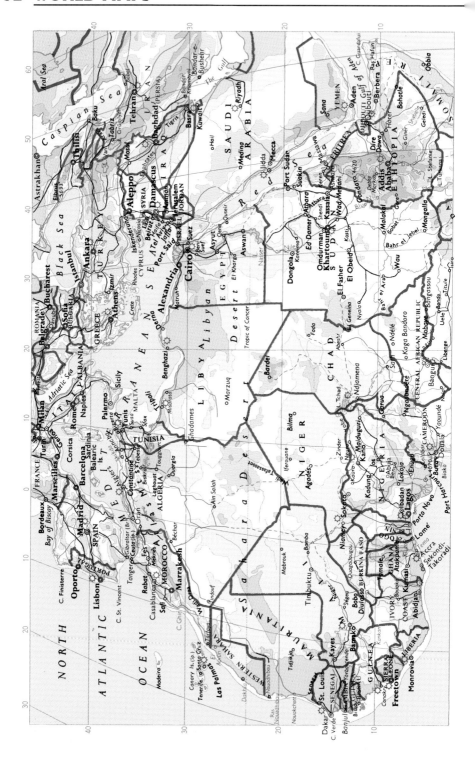

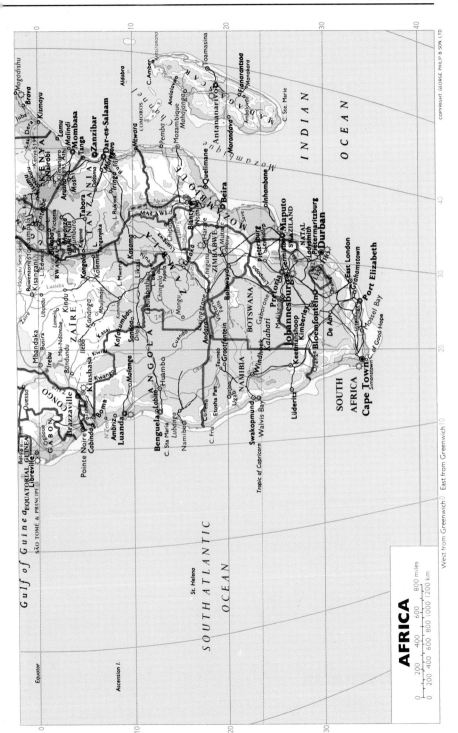

AFRICA

0	200	400	600	800 miles
0	200	400	600	800	1000	1200 km

West from Greenwich 0   East from Greenwich 10

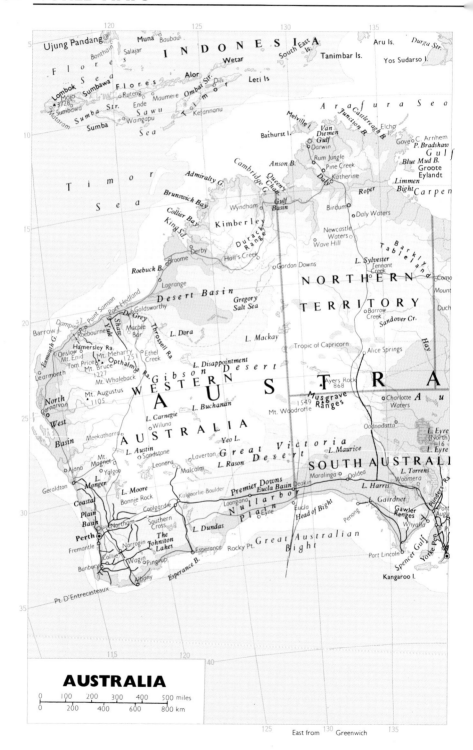

AUSTRALIA

0	100	200	300	400	500 miles
0	200	400	600	800 km	

East from Greenwich

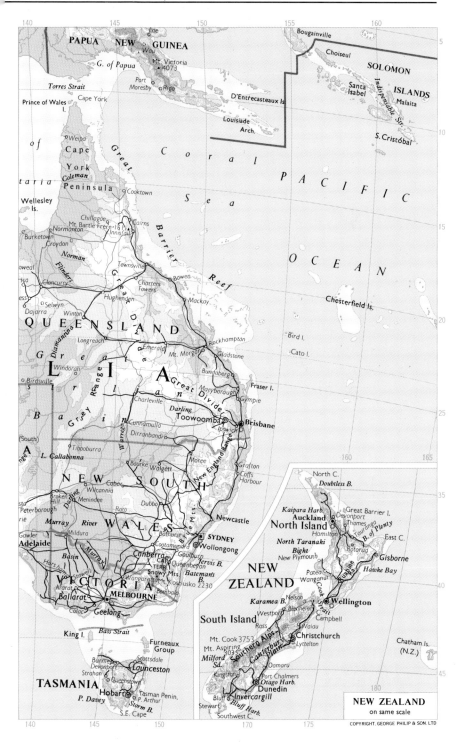

PAPUA NEW GUINEA
Ide
Wau
G. of Papua
Mt. Victoria
4073
Port
Moresby
Rigo
Torres Strait
Prince of Wales I.
Cape York
D'Entrecasteaux Is.
Louisiade Arch.
Bougainville
Choiseul
SOLOMON
Santa Isabel
Malaita
ISLANDS
S. Cristóbal
Indispensable Str.

of
Cape
York
Peninsula
Weipa
Coleman
Cooktown
taria
Wellesley Is.

Coral
Sea

P A C I F I C

O C E A N

Chesterfield Is.
Bird I.
Cato I.

Chillagoe
Mt. Bartle Frere Is.
Normanton
Burketown
Croydon
Cairns
Innisfail
Townsville
Charters Towers
Bowen
Mackay
Hughenden
oweal
Iss
Selwyn
Dajarra
Winton
Cloncurry
Norman
Flinders
Longreach
Emerald
Mt. Morgan
Rockhampton
Gladstone
Bundaberg
Maryborough
Fraser I.
Gympie

Q U E E N S L A N D
Great
Diamantina
Windorah
Birdsville
(South)
A
L. Callabonna
Tibooburra
N E W
S O U T H
Broken Hill
Peterborough
rie
Gawler
Adelaide
Basin
Mildura
Wilcannia
Cobar
Menindee
Dubbo
Rato
Murray River
W A L E S
Bathurst
SYDNEY
Wollongong
Newcastle
Grafton
Coffs Harbour
Moree
Bourke Walgett

Charleville
Darling
Cunnamulla
Dirranbandi
Charleville
Toowoomba
Ipswich
Brisbane
Great Divide
Grey Range
Warrego
New England Range

V I C T O R I A
Ballarat
MELBOURNE
Colac
Geelong
Ararat
Stawell
Horsham
Wangaratta
Mt. Kosciusko 2230
Snowy Mts.
Bombala
Canberra
CAP. TERR.
Goulburn
Queanbeyan
Cootamundra
Jervis B.
Bateman's B.

King I.
Bass Strait
Furneaux Group

TASMANIA
Burnie
Devonport
Strahan
Scottsdale
Launceston
Queenstown
Hobart
Tasman Penin.
P. Arthur
P. Davey
Storm B.
S.E. Cape

North C.
Doubtless B.
Kaipara Harb.
Auckland
Devonport
Great Barrier I.
Thames
Hamilton
Tauranga
B. of Plenty
Rotorua
East C.
North Island
North Taranaki Bight
New Plymouth
Patea
Wanganui
Gisborne
Hawke Bay
Ruahine
NEW ZEALAND
Karamea B.
Nelson
Blenheim
Campbell
Wellington
Cook Strait
South Island
Westport
Ross
Waiau
Mt. Cook 3753
Mt. Aspiring
3035
Milford Sd.
Southern Alps
Canterbury Plains
Christchurch
Lyttelton
Oamaru
Kingston
Port Chalmers
Otago Harb.
Dunedin
Bluff
Invercargill
Bluff Harb.
Stewart
Southwest C.
Chatham Is. (N.Z.)

NEW ZEALAND
on same scale

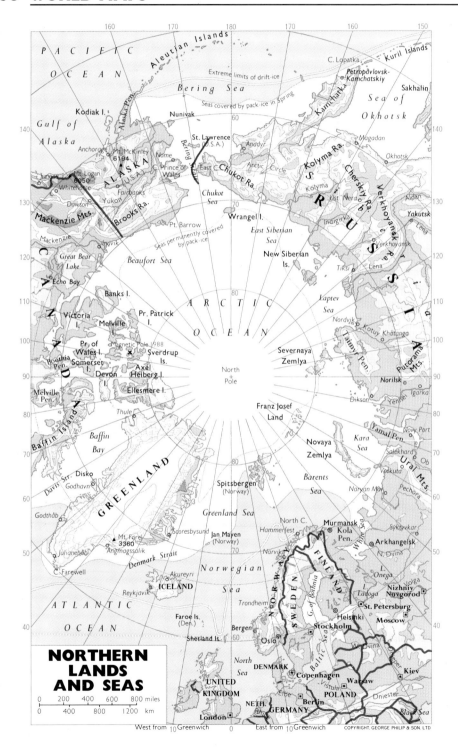

PACIFIC OCEAN

Aleutian Islands

Extreme limits of drift-ice

Bering Sea

Seas covered by pack-ice in spring

C. Lopatka

Petropávlovsk-Kamchatskiy

Kuril Islands

Sakhalin

Sea of Okhotsk

Kodiak I.

Nunivak

Magadan

Okhotsk

Gulf of Alaska

St. Lawrence (U.S.A.)

Anadyr

Anchorage

Mt. McKinley 6194

Nome

ALASKA (U.S.A.)

C. Prince of Wales

East C.

Chukot Ra.

Arctic Circle

Kolyma Ra.

Cherskiy Ra.

Verkhoyansk Ra.

Juneau

Mt. Logan 6050

Fairbanks

Bering Str.

Chukot Sea

Kolyma

Ust' Nera

Aldan

Yakutsk

Whitehorse

Yukon

Brooks Ra.

Wrangel I.

Indigirka

Verkhoyansk

Lena

Dawson

Mackenzie Mts.

Pt. Barrow

East Siberian Sea

New Siberian Is.

R U S S I A

Mackenzie

Inuvik

Seas permanently covered by pack-ice

Tiksi

Lena

Great Bear Lake

Beaufort Sea

Laptev Sea

Nordvik

Kotuy

Khatanga

Taimyr Pen.

Putorana Mts.

Echo Bay

Banks I.

Victoria I.

Melville I.

Pr. Patrick I.

A R C T I C

O C E A N

Severnaya Zemlya

Norilsk

Yenisey

Igarka

Pr. of Wales I.

Magnetic Pole 1988

Sverdrup Is.

North Pole

Dikson

Novy Port

Boothia Pen.

Somerset I.

Axel Heiberg I.

Devon I.

Franz Josef Land

Kara Sea

Yamal Pen.

Salekhard

Ob

Melville Pen.

Ellesmere I.

Thule

Novaya Zemlya

Volta

Ural Mts.

C A N A D A

Baffin Island

Baffin Bay

GREENLAND

Spitsbergen (Norway)

Barents Sea

Pechora

Naryan Mar

Disko

Davis Str.

Godhavn

Greenland Sea

North C.

Hammerfest

Murmansk

Kola Pen.

White Sea

Syktyvkar

Arkhangelsk

Godthåb

Mt. Forel 3360

Angmagssalik

Scoresbysund

Jan Mayen (Norway)

N. Dvina

Julianehåb

Denmark Strait

Narvik

N O R W A Y

S W E D E N

F I N L A N D

L. Onega

Nizhniy Novgorod

C. Farewell

Akureyri

ICELAND

Norwegian Sea

Trondheim

G. of Bothnia

L. Ladoga

St. Petersburg

Moscow

Reykjavik

Bergen

Helsinki

Stockholm

ATLANTIC OCEAN

Faroe Is. (Den.)

Shetland Is.

Oslo

Baltic Sea

W. Dvina

North Sea

DENMARK

Copenhagen

Warsaw

Kiev

UNITED KINGDOM

NETH.

GERMANY

Berlin

POLAND

Dniester

Black Sea

London

Elbe

Vistula

NORTHERN LANDS AND SEAS

0 200 400 600 800 miles

0 400 800 1200 km

West from Greenwich   East from Greenwich

WORLD
FLAGS

See pages 43–58 for detailed explanations of each flag's meaning and origin.

AFGHANISTAN

ALBANIA

ALGERIA

AMERICAN SAMOA

ANDORRA

ANGOLA

ANGUILLA

ANTIGUA & BARBUDA

ARGENTINA

ARMENIA

ARUBA

ASCENSION

AUSTRALIA

AUSTRIA

AZERBAIJAN

AZORES

BAHAMAS

BAHRAIN

BANGLADESH

BARBADOS

BELARUS

BELGIUM

BELIZE

BENIN

BERMUDA

BHUTAN

BOLIVIA

BOSNIA-HERZEGOVINA

BOTSWANA

BRAZIL

BRUNEI

BULGARIA

BURKINA FASO

BURMA (MYANMAR)

BURUNDI

CAMBODIA

CAMEROON

CANADA

CANARY ISLANDS

CAPE VERDE

CAYMAN ISLANDS

CENTRAL AFRICAN REP

CHAD

CHILE

CHINA

COLOMBIA

COMOROS

CONGO

COSTA RICA

CROATIA

CUBA

CYPRUS

CZECH REPUBLIC

DENMARK

DJIBOUTI

DOMINICA

DOMINICAN REPUBLIC

ECUADOR

EGYPT

EL SALVADOR

EQUATORIAL GUINEA

ERITREA

ESTONIA

ETHIOPIA

FALKLAND ISLANDS

FAROE ISLANDS

FIJI

FINLAND

FRANCE

FRENCH GUIANA

FRENCH POLYNESIA

GABON

GAMBIA, THE

GEORGIA

GERMANY

GHANA

GIBRALTAR

GREECE

GREENLAND

GRENADA

GUADELOUPE

GUAM

GUATEMALA

GUINEA

GUINEA-BISSAU

GUYANA

HAITI

HONDURAS

HONG KONG

HUNGARY

ICELAND

INDIA

INDONESIA

IRAN

IRAQ

IRELAND

ISRAEL

ITALY

IVORY COAST

JAMAICA

JAPAN

JORDAN

KAZAKHSTAN

KENYA

KIRIBATI

KOREA, NORTH

KOREA, SOUTH

KUWAIT

KYRGYZSTAN

LAOS

LATVIA

LEBANON

LESOTHO

LIBERIA

LIBYA

LIECHTENSTEIN

LITHUANIA

LUXEMBOURG

MACAU

MACEDONIA

MADAGASCAR

MADEIRA

MALAWI

MALAYSIA

MALDIVES

MALI

MALTA

MARSHALL ISLANDS

MARTINIQUE

MAURITANIA

MAURITIUS

MEXICO

MICRONESIA, FED. STATES

MOLDOVA

MONACO

MONGOLIA

MONTSERRAT

MOROCCO

MOZAMBIQUE

NAMIBIA

NAURU

NEPAL

NETHERLANDS

NETHERLANDS ANTILLES

NEW CALEDONIA

NEW ZEALAND

NICARAGUA

NIGER

NIGERIA

NORTHERN MARIANAS

NORWAY

OMAN

PAKISTAN

PALAU

PANAMA

PAPUA NEW GUINEA

PARAGUAY

PERU

PHILIPPINES

PITCAIRN ISLANDS

POLAND

PORTUGAL

PUERTO RICO

QATAR

RÉUNION

ROMANIA

RUSSIA

RWANDA

ST CHRISTOPHER & NEVIS

ST HELENA

ST LUCIA

ST VINCENT & THE GRENADINES

SAN MARINO

SÃO TOMÉ & PRÍNCIPE

SAUDI ARABIA

SENEGAL

SEYCHELLES

SIERRA LEONE

SINGAPORE

SLOVAK REPUBLIC

SLOVENIA

SOLOMON ISLANDS

SOMALIA

SOUTH AFRICA

SPAIN

SRI LANKA

SUDAN

SURINAM

SWAZILAND

SWEDEN

SWITZERLAND

SYRIA

TAIWAN

TAJIKISTAN

TANZANIA

THAILAND

TOGO

TONGA

TRINIDAD & TOBAGO

TRISTAN DA CUNHA

TUNISIA

TURKEY

TURKMENISTAN

TURKS & CAICOS ISLANDS

TUVALU

UGANDA

UKRAINE

UNITED ARAB EMIRATES

UNITED KINGDOM

UNITED STATES OF AMER

URUGUAY

UZBEKISTAN

VANUATU

VATICAN CITY

VENEZUELA

VIETNAM

VIRGIN ISLANDS, BRITISH

VIRGIN ISLANDS, US

WALLIS & FUTUNA ISLANDS

WESTERN SAMOA

YEMEN

YUGOSLAVIA

ZAÏRE

ZAMBIA

ZIMBABWE

UNITED NATIONS

AFGHANISTAN

After many changes since the late 1970s, a new flag was introduced in 1992 based on the colours used by the Mujaheddin during the civil war. The flag bears the new national arms which show wheatsheaves and the *shahada*, the Muslim statement of faith, above a mosque.

ALBANIA

The name of the country means 'land of the eagle'. Following the formation of a non-communist government in March 1992, the star that had been placed above the eagle's head in 1946 was removed.

ALGERIA

Featuring traditional Islamic symbols and colours, this design dates back to the early 19th century. Used by the liberation movement that fought against French rule after 1954, it was adopted on independence in 1962.

AMERICAN SAMOA

A flag was introduced in 1960 for this American dependency. It shows the American eagle holding two typically Samoan objects: a war-club and a fly-whisk, both symbols of a chief's authority. The colours used on the flag are those of the American flag.

ANDORRA

Andorra is traditionally said to have been granted independence by Charlemagne in the 9th century, after the Moorish Wars. The flag, adopted in 1866, sometimes features the state coat of arms on the obverse in the yellow band.

ANGOLA

The flag is based on that of the Popular Movement for the Liberation of Angola during the struggle for independence from Portugal (1975). The emblem, incorporating a half gearwheel and a machete, symbolizes Angola's socialist ideology.

ANGUILLA

This flag came into use in 1993 and, since Anguilla is a British dependency, the British Blue Ensign is flown. The three dolphins depicted on the shield represent strength, unity and endurance, while the white stands for peace and the blue for the sea.

ANTIGUA AND BARBUDA

The design of the flag was decided in a competition in 1967. The V depicted in the design denotes victory and the golden sun symbolizes the dawning of a new era. The black represents African heritage and the soil, blue is for hope and red for the dynamism of the people.

ARGENTINA

The 'celeste' and white stripes, symbol of independence since 1810 around Buenos Aires, became the national flag in 1816 and influenced other Latin American countries. A yellow May Sun, only used on the state flag, was added two years later.

ARMENIA

The flag used in the period 1918–22 was re-adopted on 24 August 1990. The colours represent the blood shed in the past (red), the land of Armenia (blue) and the unity and courage of the people (orange).

ARUBA

The flag of this Dutch overseas territory was introduced in 1976. The four points of the star represent the area's four main language groups.

ASCENSION

As a dependency of St Helena, Ascension uses her flag, which shows the shield from her coat of arms in the fly of the British Blue Ensign.

AUSTRALIA

Showing its historical link with Britain, Australia's flag, adopted in 1901, features the British Blue Ensign. The five stars in the fly represent the Southern Cross constellation and the larger star, known as the Commonwealth Star, symbolizes the six states and the territories.

AUSTRIA

According to legend, the flag's colours date from the battle of Ptolemais in 1191, when the only part of the Duke of Bebenberg's tunic not bloodstained was under his swordbelt. The design was officially adopted in 1918.

AZERBAIJAN

This flag was instituted on 5 February 1991. The blue stands for the sky, the red for freedom and the green for the land and the Islamic religion; the crescent and star symbolize Islam, and the points of the star represent the eight races of Azerbaijan.

AZORES
The flag dates from 1979 and shows the hawk (*açor*) after which the islands are named, below an arc of nine stars (one for each island).

BAHAMAS
The black hoist triangle symbolizes the unity of the Bahamian people and their resolve to develop the island's natural resources. The golden sand and blue sea of the islands are depicted by the yellow and aquamarine stripes.

BAHRAIN
The flag dates from about 1932, with the white section a result of the British request that it be included in the flags of all friendly Arab states around the Arabian Gulf. Red is the traditional colour of Kharijite Muslims. The serrated edge was added to distinguish between the colours.

BANGLADESH
Bangladesh adopted this flag in 1971 following the break from Pakistan. The green represents the fertility of the land, while the red disc, as the sun of independence, commemorates the blood shed in the struggle for freedom.

BARBADOS
The flag was adopted on independence in 1960. The trident had been part of the colonial badge of Barbados and was retained as the centre to its flag, maintaining the link between old and new. The gold stripe represents the beaches and the two blue stripes sea and the sky.

BELARUS
On 19 September 1991 the old flag of Belarus, previously adopted in 1917, was restored. The white and red derive from the ancient coat of arms, also used by Latvia.

BELGIUM
The colours of Belgium's flag derive from the arms of the province of Brabant which rebelled against Austrian rule in 1787. It was adopted as the national flag in 1830 when Belgium gained independence from the Netherlands.

BELIZE
The badge shows loggers bearing axes and oars, tools employed in the industry responsible for developing Belize. The motto underneath reads '*Sub Umbra Floreo*' ('flourish the shade') and the tree is a mahogany, the national tree.

BENIN
This flag, showing the red, yellow and green Pan-African colours, was first used after independence from France in 1960 and has now been readopted. While Benin was a Communist state after 1975, another flag, showing a red Communist star, was used.

BERMUDA
Instead of the customary British Blue Ensign, the Red Ensign with the shield from Bermuda's badge is on the fly. The shield depicts a red lion holding another shield in which the shipwreck of the *Sea Venture* in 1609 is shown.

BHUTAN
The striking image on Bhutan's flag is explained by the name of this Himalayan kingdom in the local language, *Druk Yil*, which means 'land of the dragon'. The saffron colour stands for royal power and the orange-red for Buddhist spiritual power.

BOLIVIA
Dating from liberation in 1825, the tricolour has been used as both national and merchant flag since 1888. The red stands for Bolivia's animals and the army's courage, the yellow for mineral resources and the green for its agricultural wealth.

BOSNIA-HERZEGOVINA
The flag was adopted when independence was declared in April 1992 and has a shield recalling the ancient Bosnian monarchy of pre-Turkish times. The fleur-de-lis is thought to be derived from the lily specific to Bosnia, *Lilium bosniacum*.

BOTSWANA
Botswana's flag dates from independence

om Britain in 1966. The white-black-white
zebra stripe represents the racial harmony of
the people and the coat of the zebra, the
national animal. The blue symbolizes the
country's most vital need – rainwater.

BRAZIL

The sphere bears the motto 'Order and
Progress' and its 27 stars, arranged in the pattern
of the night sky over Rio de Janeiro, represent
the states and federal district. Green
symbolizes the nation's rainforests, and the
yellow diamond represents its mineral wealth.

BRUNEI

The yellow background represents the flag of
the Sultan, with the black and white stripes
standing for his two main advisers (*wazirs*).
The arms contain the inscription in Arabic
Brunei, Gate of Peace' and a crescent, the
symbol of Islam.

BULGARIA

The Slav colours of white, green and red were
used in the Bulgarian flag from 1878. The
national emblem, incorporating a lion (a symbol
of Bulgaria since the 14th century), was
first added to the flag in 1947, but the crest is
now only added for official occasions.

BURKINA FASO

Formerly Upper Volta, this country adopted a
new name and flag in 1984, replacing those
used since independence from France in
1960. The colours are the Pan-African shades
of Burkina Faso's neighbours, representing
the desire for unity.

BURMA (MYANMAR)

The colours were adopted following independence
from Britain in 1948. The socialist symbol,
added in 1974, includes a ring of 14 stars
for the country's states. The gearwheel represents
industry and the rice plant agriculture.

BURUNDI

Burundi adopted this unusual design when it
became a republic in 1966. The three stars
symbolize the nation's motto 'Unity, Work,
Progress'. Green represents hope for the
future, red the struggle for independence, and
white the desire for peace.

CAMBODIA

As well as being associated with Communism
and revolution, red is the traditional colour of
Cambodia. The silhouette is the historic temple
of Angkor Wat. The blue symbolizes the
water resources which are so vital.

CAMEROON

Cameroon's flag employs the Pan-African
colours, as used by many former African
colonies. The design, with the yellow liberty
star, dates from 1975 and is based on the tricolour
adopted in 1957 before independence
from France in 1960.

CANADA

The British Red Ensign was used from 1892
but became unpopular with Canada's French
community. After many attempts to find a
more acceptable design, the present flag –
featuring the simple maple leaf emblem – was
finally adopted in 1965.

CANARY ISLANDS

As a Spanish Autonomous Region, the Canary
Islands have their own arms and flag. This flag
was adopted in 1982 on the basis of colours
used by the dominant political movement.
The arms can be added in the centre.

CAPE VERDE

This new flag was adopted in September 1992
to replace the red-yellow-green one adopted in
1975. The flag was adopted to symbolize the
end of the rule of the *Partido Africano da
Independencia de Cabo Verde* and the election of
the Movement for Democracy.

CAYMAN ISLANDS

As a British Dependency, the Cayman Islands
fly the Blue Ensign with a white roundel,
depicting the islands' coat of arms in the fly.
The coat of arms shows an English heraldic
lion, with the blue and white wavy lines representing
the sea.

CENTRAL AFRICAN REPUBLIC

The national flag of the Central African
Republic, adopted in 1958, combines the
green, yellow and red of Pan-African unity
with the blue, white and red of the flag of
the country's former colonial ruler, France.

CHAD

Adopted in 1959, Chad's colours are a compromise between the French and Pan-African flags. Blue represents the sky, the streams of the south and hope, yellow the sun and the Sahara Desert in the north, and red represents national sacrifice.

CHILE

Inspired by the US 'Stars and Stripes', the flag was designed by an American serving with the Chilean Army in 1817 and adopted that year. White represents the snow-capped Andes, blue the sky and red the blood of the patriots.

CHINA

Red, the traditional colour of both China and Communism, was chosen for the People's Republic flag in 1949. The large star represents the Communist Party programme; the small stars represent the four principal social classes.

COLOMBIA

The colours – showing the (yellow) land of the nation separated by the (blue) sea from the tyranny of Spain, whose rule the people fought with their (red) blood – are shared by Ecuador and Venezuela. It was first used in 1806.

COMOROS

Since independence in 1975 a flag depicting a crescent and four stars has been flown. This latest design, adopted in 1978, shows the crescent representing the Muslim faith, and the stars representing the four islands, on a plain green background, representing Islam.

CONGO

The People's Republic of the Congo was created in 1970, ten years after it achieved independence from France, becoming Africa's first Communist state. Marxism was officially abandoned in 1990 and this new flag was adopted.

COSTA RICA

Dating from 1848, Costa Rica's national flag is based on the blue-white-blue sequence of the flag of the Central American Federation (*see Guatemala*), which is itself based on the Argentinian flag, but with an additional red stripe in the centre.

CROATIA

The red, white and blue flag was originally adopted in 1848. During the Communist period a red star appeared in the centre, but this was replaced by the present arms, which symbolize the various parts of the country.

CUBA

First designed in 1849, Cuba's flag, the 'Lone Star' banner, was not officially adopted until the island finally gained its independence from Spain in 1901. The red triangle represents the people's bloody struggle for independence.

CYPRUS

Featuring a map of the island with two olive branches, this has been the official state flag since independence from Britain in 1960. However, Cyprus is now divided and the separate communities fly the Greek and Turkish flags.

CZECH REPUBLIC

On independence in January 1993, the Czech Republic adopted the flag of the former Czechoslovakia. It features the red and white of Bohemia with the blue of Moravia and Slovakia, the colours of Pan-Slavic liberation.

DENMARK

The Dannebrog ('the spirit of Denmark') flag is said to represent King Waldemar II's vision of a white cross against a red sky before the Battle of Lyndanisse in 1219, and is possibly the oldest national flag in continuous use.

DJIBOUTI

Djibouti's flag was adopted on independence from France in 1977, though its use by the independence movement had begun five years earlier. The colours represent the two principal peoples in the country: the Issas (blue) and the Afars (green).

DOMINICA

Dominica adopted its flag on independence from Britain in 1978 and slightly amended it in 1981. The parrot, from the coat of arms, is the national bird, the sisserou, and the stars represent the ten island parishes.

DOMINICAN REPUBLIC

This flag dates from 1844, when the country

nally gained its independence from both
Spain and Haiti. The design developed from
Haiti's flag, adding a white cross and re-
arranging the position of the colours.

ECUADOR

Shared in different proportions by Colombia
and Venezuela, Ecuador's colours were used
in the flag created by the patriot Francisco de
Miranda in 1806 and flown by Simón Bolívar,
whose armies also liberated Peru and Bolivia.

EGYPT

Egypt has flown a flag of red, white and black
(Pan-Arab colours) since 1958 but with various emblems in the centre. The present design,
with the gold eagle emblem symbolizing the
Arab hero Saladin, was introduced in 1984.

EL SALVADOR

The original flag, the 'Stars and Stripes', was
replaced in 1912 by the current one. The blue
and white stripes are a common feature of
the flags of Central American countries that
gained their independence from Spain at the
same time in 1821.

EQUATORIAL GUINEA

Equatorial Guinea's flag dates from independence from Spain in 1968. Green represents
the country's natural resources, blue the sea,
red the nation's struggle for independence and
the white stands for peace.

ERITREA

The new flag was hoisted on 24 May 1993 to
celebrate independence from Ethiopia. It is a
variation on the flag of the Eritrean People's
Liberation Front, and shows an olive wreath
which featured on the flag of the region between 1952 and 1959.

ESTONIA

Used for the independent republic of
1918–40, the Estonian flag was readopted in
June 1988. The colours are said to symbolize
the country's blue skies, its black earth and the
snows of its long winter.

ETHIOPIA

Ethiopia's tricolour was first flown as three
separate pennants, one above the other. The

combination of red, yellow and green dates
from the late 19th century and appeared in
flag form in 1897. The present sequence was
adopted in 1941.

FALKLAND ISLANDS

The white roundel in the flag contains the
islands' badge which shows the ship *Desire*,
which discovered the islands in 1592, and a
sheep, representing the main farming activity.

FAROE ISLANDS

In 1948 the Faroe Islands, which are part of
Denmark, adopted a flag combining the local
arms with the Danish arms. The cross, like
that on other Scandinavian flags, is slightly
off-centre. Red and blue are ancient Faroese
colours and the white represents the sea's foam.

FIJI

The Fijian flag, based on the British Blue
Ensign, was adopted in 1970 after independence from Britain. The state coat of arms
shows a British lion, sugar cane, a coconut
palm, bananas and a dove of peace.

FINLAND

Finland became an independent republic only
in 1917 after separation from Russia, then in
the throes of the Revolution, and the present
flag was adopted soon after. The colours symbolize Finland's blue lakes and white snow.

FRANCE

The colours of the French flag originated during the Revolution of 1789. The red and blue
are said to represent Paris and the white the
monarchy. The present design, adopted in
1794, symbolizes republican principles.

FRENCH GUIANA

The official flag flown over 'Guyane' is the
French tricolour. A French possession since
1676 (apart from 1809–17), the territory is
treated as part of mainland France, sending
representatives to the Paris parliament.

FRENCH POLYNESIA

The flag was adopted in 1984 and is in the
traditional colours of Tahiti, but can only be
flown in conjunction with the French tricolour
since it is still a French territory. The emblem

in the centre is a native canoe (*pirogue*) against the background of a rising sun over the sea.

GABON
Gabon's tricolour was adopted on independence from France in 1960. The yellow, now representing the sun, used to be thinner to symbolize the Equator on which the country lies. The green stands for Gabon's forests and blue for the sea.

GAMBIA, THE
The blue stripe in the flag represents the River Gambia that flows through the country, while the red stands for the sun overhead and the green for the land. The design was adopted on independence from Britain in 1965.

GEORGIA
The flag was first adopted in 1917 and lasted until 1921. The colours represent the good times of the past and the future (wine-red), the period of Russian rule (black) and the hope for peace (white). It was readopted on independence in 1990.

GERMANY
The red, black and gold, dating back to the Holy Roman Empire, are associated with the struggle for a united Germany from the 1830s. The horizontal design was officially adopted for the FRG in 1949, and accepted by 'East Germany' on reunification.

GHANA
Adopted on independence from Britain in 1957, Ghana's flag features the colours first used by Ethiopia, Africa's oldest independent nation. Following Ghana's lead, other ex-colonies adopted them as a symbol of black Pan-African unity.

GIBRALTAR
The official flag is the Union Jack but this flag has been in use unofficially (on land only) since about 1966. It is a banner of the city arms granted to Gibraltar in 1502 by Spain; the key symbolizes Gibraltar's strategic importance as the gateway to the Mediterranean.

GREECE
Blue and white became Greece's national

colours during the war of independence. Finally adopted in 1970, the stripes represent the battle cry '*Eleutheria i thanatos*' ('Freedom or Death') used during the struggle against Ottoman (Turkish) domination in the war of 1821–9.

GREENLAND
The flag was introduced in 1985 after a competition to decide a design and can be used on land and at sea. The design is in the Danish colours, with the red depicting the midsummer sun rising over the (white) polar ice.

GRENADA
Each star represents one of Grenada's seven parishes. The country's traditional cash crop, nutmeg, is depicted in the hoist triangle. The people are represented by the colours red (for unity) and yellow (for friendliness and the sunshine), and the island by the colour green.

GUADELOUPE
As an overseas department of France, Guadeloupe uses the French tricolour for its flag.

GUAM
The flag was adopted in 1917. The badge in the centre is based on the island seal and depicts the mouth of the Agana River and a *prao* sailing off Point Ritidian. Guam has been a dependency of the USA since 1898 and flies its flag only with the US 'Stars and Stripes'.

GUATEMALA
The simple design of Guatemala's flag was adopted in 1871, but its origins date back to the Central American Federation (1823–39) formed with Honduras, El Salvador, Nicaragua and Costa Rica after the break from Spanish rule in 1821.

GUINEA
Guinea's Pan-African colours, adopted on independence from France in 1958, represent the three words of the national motto, *Travail, Justice, Solidarité*: Work (red), Justice (yellow) and Solidarity (green). The design is based on the French tricolour.

GUINEA-BISSAU
This flag, using the Pan-African colours, was

dopted on gaining independence from
ortugal in 1973. It is based on the one used
by the PAIGC political party that led the
truggle from 1962, who in turn based it on
he flag of Ghana, the first of the African
olonies to gain independence.

GUYANA

This striking design, adopted by Guyana
on independence from Britain in 1966, has
colours representing the people's energy
building a new nation (red), their persever-
nce (black), minerals (yellow), rivers (white),
nd agriculture and forests (green).

HAITI

Although the colours, first used in 1803, are
said to represent the country's two communities (the blacks [blue] and the mulattos [red]),
the design of Haiti's flag derives from that
of France, to which it once belonged. The
present version was first used in 1843 and
restored in 1986.

HONDURAS

Officially adopted in 1949, the Honduras flag
is based on that of the Central American
Federation (*see Guatemala*). Honduras left the
organization in 1838, but in 1866 added the
five stars to the flag to express a hope for a
future federation.

HONG KONG

Hong Kong has flown the Blue Ensign since
1841 when it became a British dependent territory. The coat of arms dates from 1959,
and includes the British lion and the Chinese
dragon. In 1997 Hong Kong will revert to
Chinese government control.

HUNGARY

The tricolour became popular in the European
revolutions of 1848, though the colours had
been in the Hungarian arms since the 15th
century. Adopted in 1919, the design was
amended in 1957 to remove the state emblem,
which had been added in 1949.

ICELAND

Dating from 1915, the flag became official on
independence from Denmark in 1944. It uses
the traditional Icelandic colours of blue and

white and is in fact the same as the Norwegian
flag, but with the blue and red reversed.

INDIA

India's flag evolved during the struggle for
freedom from British rule. The orange represents the Hindu majority, green the country's
many Muslims and white peace. The Buddhist
wheel symbol, the blue *charka*, was added on
independence in 1947.

INDONESIA

While the colours date back to the Middle
Ages, they were adopted by political groups in
the struggle against the Netherlands in the
1920s and became the national flag in 1945,
when Indonesia proclaimed its independence.

IRAN

Iran's flag has been in use since July 1980 after
the fall of the Shah and the rise of the Islamic
Republic. Along the edges of the stripes is the
legend '*Allah Akbar*' ('God is Great') repeated
22 times; in the centre is the new national
emblem, representing *Allah* (God).

IRAQ

Using the four Pan-Arab colours, Iraq's flag
was adopted in 1963 at the time of the proposed federation with Egypt and Syria. Iraq
retained the three green stars, symbolizing the
three countries, even though the union failed
to materialize.

IRELAND

The Irish flag was first used by nationalists in
1848 in the struggle for freedom from Britain
and adopted in 1922 after independence.
Green represents the Roman Catholics and
orange the Protestants, with white representing the desire for peace between the two.

ISRAEL

The blue and white stripes on Israel's flag are
based on the *tallit*, a Hebrew prayer shawl. In
the centre is the ancient six-pointed Star of
David. The flag was designed in America in
1891 and officially adopted by the new Jewish
state in 1948.

ITALY

When Napoleon invaded Italy in 1796, the

French Republican National Guard carried a military standard of vertical green, white and red stripes. After many changes, it was finally adopted as the national flag after the unification of Italy in 1861.

IVORY COAST (CÔTE D'IVOIRE)
On independence from France in 1960 this former colony adopted a compromise between the French tricolour and the colours of the Pan-African movement. Orange represents the northern savannas, white peace and unity, and green the forests and agriculture.

JAMAICA
Jamaica's distinctive flag dates from independence from Britain in 1962. The gold stands for the country's natural resources and sunshine, the green for its agriculture and hope for the future, and black for the nation's hardships.

JAPAN
The geographical position of Japan in the East is expressed in the name of the country, *Nihon-Koku* (Land of the Rising Sun), and in the flag. Officially adopted in 1870, the simple design had been used by Japanese emperors for many centuries.

JORDAN
Green, white and black are the colours of the three tribes who led the Arab Revolt against the Turks in 1917, while red is the colour of the Hussein dynasty. The star was added in 1928 with its seven points representing the first seven verses of the Koran.

KAZAKHSTAN
This flag was adopted on 4 June 1992. The soaring eagle and the golden sun represent the love of freedom and the blue represents the cloudless skies. There is also a hoist-based vertical strip of golden ornamentation.

KENYA
The Kenyan flag, which dates from independence from Britain in 1963, is based on the flag of the Kenya African National Union, which led the colonial struggle. The Masai warrior's shield and crossed spears represent the defence of freedom.

KIRIBATI
The flag is a banner of the arms granted to the Gilbert and Ellice Islands in 1937 and was adopted on independence in 1979. Kiribati is the sole Commonwealth country to use an armorial banner; that is, a flag whose design corresponds exactly to the shield of its arms.

KOREA, NORTH
The Korean Democratic People's Republic has flown this flag since the country split into two separate states in 1948. The colours are those of the traditional Korean standard, but in a new Communist design with a red star.

KOREA, SOUTH
Adopted in 1950, South Korea's flag is the traditional white of peace. The central emblem signifies nature's opposing forces: the black symbols stand for the four seasons, the points of the compass and the Sun, Moon, Earth and Heaven.

KUWAIT
Kuwait's national flag dates from 1961, when the country ceased to be a British protectorate and gained its independence. The flag features the four Pan-Arab colours, the black portion having an unusual trapezium shape.

KYRGYZSTAN
The flag was adopted in March 1992 and depicts a bird's-eye view of a *yurt* within a radiant sun. The *yurt* stands for the ancient nomadic way of life and the rays of the sun for the 40 traditional tribes.

LAOS
Since 1975 Laos has flown the flag of the Pathet Lao, the Communist movement which won the long struggle for control of the country. The blue stands for the Mekong River, the white disc represents the Moon, and the red is for the unity and purpose of the people.

LATVIA
The burgundy and white Latvian flag, revived after independence from the USSR in 1991, dates back to at least 1280. According to one legend, it was first made from a white sheet stained with the blood of a Latvian hero who was wrapped in it.

LEBANON
Adopted on independence in 1943, Lebanon's colours are those of the Lebanese Legion in World War I. The cedar tree, many of which grow in the country's mountains, has been a Lebanese symbol since biblical times.

LESOTHO
In 1987 this succeeded the flag adopted on independence from Britain in 1966. The white, blue and green represent peace, rain and prosperity – the words of the national motto. The emblem comprises a shield, knobkerrie and ostrich feather sceptre.

LIBERIA
Liberia was founded in the early 19th century as an American colony for freed black slaves. The flag, based on the US flag, was adopted on independence in 1847, with its 11 red and white stripes representing the 11 men who signed the declaration of independence.

LIBYA
The simplest of all world flags, Libya's flag represents the nation's quest for a green revolution in agriculture. Libya flew the flag of the Federation of Arab Republics until 1977, when it left the organization.

LIECHTENSTEIN
The colours of Liechtenstein's flag originated in the early part of the 19th century. The gold crown, often rotated 90° so that the flag can be hung vertically, was added in 1937 to avoid confusion with the flag then used by Haiti.

LITHUANIA
The flag was created in 1918, at the birth of the independent republic; it was suppressed after the Soviet annexation in 1940, and restored in November 1988. The colours represent Lithuania's rich forests and agricultural wealth.

LUXEMBOURG
Luxembourg's colours are taken from the Grand Duke's 14th-century coat of arms. The Grand Duchy's flag is almost identical to that of the Netherlands, but the blue stripe is a lighter shade and the flag itself is longer.

MACAU
Portugal declared Macau independent from China in 1849, and a century later proclaimed it an overseas province. Macau uses the flag of Portugal.

MACEDONIA
The emblem in the centre of the flag is the device from the war-chest of Philip of Macedon, and is one reason why Greece refuses to recognize independent Macedonia. The flag was introduced in August 1992.

MADAGASCAR
Madagascar's colours are those of historical flags of South-east Asia, from where the island's first inhabitants came before AD 1000. The present flag was adopted in 1958 when the country first became a republic after French rule.

MADEIRA
The emblem in the flag is the cross of the Order of Christ, which inspired the colonization of the islands in the 15th century. The flag was adopted in 1978.

MALAWI
The colours in Malawi's flag come from the flag adopted by the Malawi Congress Party in 1953. The rising sun symbol, representing the beginning of a new era for Malawi and Africa, was added when the country gained independence from Britain in 1964.

MALAYSIA
The red and white bands date back to a revolt in the 13th century. The star and crescent are symbols of Islam; the blue represents Malaysia's role in the Commonwealth. This flag was first flown after federation in 1963.

MALDIVES
The Maldives used to fly a plain red flag until the Islamic green panel with white crescent was added early this century. The present design was officially adopted in 1965, after the British left the islands.

MALI
Adopted on independence from France in 1960, Mali's flag uses the Pan-African

colours, employed by the African Demo-
cratic Rally, and symbolizing the desire for
African unity. Its design is based on the
French tricolour.

MALTA
The colours of Malta's flag, adopted on independence in 1964, are those of the Knights of
Malta, who ruled the islands from 1530 to
1798. The George Cross was added in 1943
to commemorate the heroism of the Maltese
people during World War II.

MARSHALL ISLANDS
The flag dates from 1 May 1979 and has two
rays which represent the two chains of islands:
Ratik (Sunrise) is in orange and Ralik (Sunset)
is in white. The 24 points on the star represent
the municipalities of the area, all set against
the blue of the Pacific Ocean.

MARTINIQUE
As an overseas department of France, Martinique uses the French tricolour for its flag.

MAURITANIA
The Mauritanian Islamic Republic's flag features the star and crescent, traditional symbols
of the Islamic religion, as is the colour green.
It was adopted in 1959, the year before the
country gained its independence from France.

MAURITIUS
The flag of this small island state was adopted
on independence from Britain in 1968. Red
stands for the struggle for independence, blue
for the Indian Ocean, yellow for the bright
future, and green for the lush vegetation.

MEXICO
The stripes on the Mexican flag were inspired
by the French tricolour and date from 1821.
The emblem of the eagle, snake and cactus is
based on an ancient Aztec legend about the
founding of Mexico City. The design was
adopted for the Olympic year, 1968.

MICRONESIA, FED. STATES OF
The flag was adopted in 1978 when the country broke away from the US Trust Territory of
Micronesia and became the Federated States
of Micronesia. The four stars stand for the

four states (Kosrai, Pohnpei, Truk and Yaj
that remained in the federation.

MOLDOVA
The flag and the eagle are based on those (
pre-Communist Romania, and the bull's hea
is the distinctive emblem of Moldova. The fla
was adopted in 1990. According to the offici;
description, the tricolour represents 'the pas
present and future' of Moldova.

MONACO
An independent state since AD 980, Monac
has been ruled by the Grimaldi family sinc
1297. The colours of the flag, officially adopt
ed in 1881, come from the Prince of Monaco'
coat of arms, which dates to medieval times.

MONGOLIA
On Mongolia's flag the blue represents th
country's national colour. In the hoist is th
Golden Soyonbo, a Buddhist symbol, repre
senting freedom. Within this, the flame is seer
as a promise of prosperity and progress.

MONTSERRAT
The flag is the British Blue Ensign with the
arms in a white roundel in the fly. The shielc
dates from 1909 and shows a black Passion
cross rising from the (brown) ground, grasped
in the right arm of a female figure in a green
robe, representing the Irish origin of the
island's immigrants.

MOROCCO
A red flag had been flown in Morocco since
the 16th century and the star-shaped green
pentagram, the Seal of Solomon, was added
in 1915. This design was retained when
Morocco gained independence from French
and Spanish rule in 1956.

MOZAMBIQUE
The green stripe represents the fertile land, the
black stripe Africa and the yellow stripe mineral wealth. The badge on the red triangle
contains a rifle, hoe, cogwheel and book,
which are all Marxist symbols of the struggle
against colonialism.

NAMIBIA
Namibia adopted its flag after independence

...m South Africa in 1990. The red and white colours symbolize human resources, while the green, blue and the gold sun represent the natural resources, mostly minerals.

NAURU

The flag represents the geographical location of Nauru, south of the Equator in the middle of the Pacific Ocean. The 12 points of the star stand for the traditional tribes, and the flag was adopted on independence in 1968.

NEPAL

This Himalayan kingdom's uniquely shaped flag was adopted in 1962. It came from the joining together in the 19th century of two triangular pennants – the royal family's crescent moon emblem and the powerful Rana family's sun symbol.

NETHERLANDS

The Dutch national flag dates from 1630, during the long war of independence from Spain that began in 1568. The tricolour became a symbol of liberty and inspired many other revolutionary flags around the world.

NETHERLANDS ANTILLES

The flag was originally introduced in 1959 with six white stars in the centre, but these were reduced to five in 1986 when Aruba became a separate territory. Each star represents one of the five islands that make up the territory.

NEW CALEDONIA

New Caledonia has been a French possession since 1853. It became a French Overseas Territory in 1958 and therefore uses the French tricolour as its flag.

NEW ZEALAND

Like Australia, New Zealand flies a flag based on the British Blue Ensign. Designed in 1869 and adopted in 1907 on acquiring Dominion status, it displays four of the five stars of the Southern Cross constellation.

NICARAGUA

Nicaragua's flag, adopted in 1908, is identical to that of the Central American Federation to which it once belonged. Except for a differ-ence in the shading of the blue and the motif, it is the same as the flag of El Salvador.

NIGER

Niger's flag was adopted shortly before independence in 1960. The circle represents the sun, the orange stripe the Sahara Desert in the north, the green stripe the grasslands of the south, divided by the (white) River Niger.

NIGERIA

This design was selected after a competition to find a new national flag in time for independence in 1960. The green represents the country's forests and the white is for peace.

NORTHERN MARIANAS

The sea-blue flag of this island group shows a grey latte stone, a Polynesian *taga*, surrounded by a wreath of flowers and shells. The flag was originally adopted in 1972 and the wreath was added in 1989. The latte stone represents the old traditions of the Chamorro people.

NORWAY

Norway's flag has been used since 1898, though its use as a merchant flag dates back to 1821. The design is based on the Dannebrog flag of Denmark, which ruled Norway from the 14th century to the early 19th century.

OMAN

Formerly Muscat and Oman, the state's flag was plain red – the traditional colour of the people who lived in the area. When Oman was established in 1970, the state arms of sword and dagger were added with stripes of white and green.

PAKISTAN

This flag was adopted when Pakistan gained independence from Britain in 1947. The green, the crescent moon and five-pointed star are traditionally associated with Islam. The white stripe represents the other religions.

PALAU (BELAU)

The flag dates from 1980 when Palau became a republic and depicts a full moon over the blue Pacific Ocean. The moon stands for national unity and destiny and the blue sea for the achievement of independence.

PANAMA
The Panamanian flag dates from the break with Colombia in 1903. Blue stands for the Conservative Party, red for the Liberal Party and white for the hope of peace. The red star represents law and order and the blue star represents 'public honesty'.

PAPUA NEW GUINEA
When Papua New Guinea became independent from Australia in 1975 it adopted a flag which had been used for the country since 1971. The design includes a local bird of paradise, the *kumul*, in flight and the stars of the Southern Cross constellation.

PARAGUAY
Paraguay's tricolour is a national flag with different sides. On the obverse the state emblem, illustrated here, displays the May Star to commemorate liberation from Spain (1811); the reverse shows the treasury seal – a lion and staff, with the words 'Peace and Justice'.

PERU
Flown since 1825, the flag's colours are said to have come about when the Argentine patriot General José de San Martin, arriving to liberate Peru from Spain in 1820, saw a flock of red and white flamingos flying over his army.

PHILIPPINES
The eight rays of the large sun represent the eight provinces that led the revolt against Spanish rule in 1898 and the three smaller stars stand for the three main island groups. The flag was adopted on independence from the USA in 1946.

PITCAIRN ISLANDS
A flag for local use was granted to Pitcairn in 1984. The flag is the British Blue Ensign with the whole arms in the fly. The arms were first used in 1969.

POLAND
The colours of Poland's flag were derived from the 13th-century coat of arms of a white eagle on a red field, which still appears on the Polish merchant flag. The flag's simple design was adopted when Poland became a republic in 1919.

PORTUGAL
Portugal's colours, adopted in 1910 when became a republic, represent Henry the Navigator (green) and the monarchy (red). The armillary sphere – an early navigation instrument – reflects Portugal's leading role in world exploration.

PUERTO RICO
Puerto Rico fought with Cuba for independence from Spain and their flags are almost identical (the red and blue colours are transposed). The island is a dependent territory of the USA and the flag, adopted in 1952, flown only with the US 'Stars and Stripes'.

QATAR
The flag was adopted in 1971. The maroon colour is said to result from the natural effect of the sun on the traditional red banner, while the white was added after a British request in 1820 that white should be included in the flag of friendly states in the Arabian Gulf.

RÉUNION
As a French Overseas Department, Réunion uses the French tricolour as its flag.

ROMANIA
Romania's colours come from the arms of the provinces that united to form the country in 1861, and the design was adopted in 1948. The central state coat of arms, added in 1965, was deleted in 1990 after the fall of the Communist Ceausescu regime.

RUSSIA
Distinctive Russian flags were first instituted by Peter the Great, based on those of the Netherlands. This flag became the official national flag in 1799 but was suppressed in the Bolshevik Revolution. It was restored in 1991.

RWANDA
Adopted in 1961, this tricolour in the Pan-African colours features the letter 'R' to distinguish it from Guinea's flag. Red represents the blood shed in the 1959 revolution, yellow for victory over tyranny, and green for hope.

ST CHRISTOPHER AND NEVIS
The colours represent fertility (green), sun-

ine (yellow), the independence struggle (red)
ad the African heritage (black); the two stars
and for hope and liberty. The flag was adopted on independence from Britain in 1983.

T HELENA
ince 1984 the British dependent territory of
i Helena, with its dependencies of Ascension
land and the Tristan da Cunha group, has
sed the shield from its new coat of arms in
ae fly of the British Blue Ensign. The main
art of the shield shows a ship sailing towards
ae island.

T LUCIA
'his Caribbean island became an Associated
tate of Great Britain in 1967, and adopted
nis modern-looking flag. It is a symbolic
epresentation of St Lucia itself: the black
olcanic hills of the island rising steeply from
he blue ocean.

T VINCENT AND THE GRENADINES
On independence from Britain in 1979, St
Vincent adopted this tricolour, but with the
slands' coat of arms in the centre. In 1985
his was replaced by the present three green
diamonds representing the islands as the
gems of the Antilles'.

SAN MARINO
The tiny republic of San Marino, enclosed
completely within the territory of Italy, has
been an independent state since AD 885. The
flag's colours – white for the snowy mountains
and blue for the sky – derive from the state
coat of arms.

SÃO TOMÉ AND PRÍNCIPE
Adopted on independence from Portugal in
1975, this variation of the familiar Pan-African
colours had previously been the emblem of the
national liberation movement. The two black
stars represent the two islands that comprise
the country.

SAUDI ARABIA
The inscription on the Saudi flag above the
sword means 'There is no God but Allah, and
Muhammad is the Prophet of Allah'. The only
national flag with an inscription as its main
feature, the design was adopted in 1938.

SENEGAL
Apart from the green five-pointed star, which
symbolizes the Muslim faith of the majority
of the population, Senegal's flag is identical
to that of Mali. It was adopted in 1960
when the country gained its independence
from France.

SEYCHELLES
The flag dates from 1977 following a *coup
d'état* by the People's Progressive Front, and
diagrammatically shows the Indian Ocean (in
white) surrounding the islands of the group
and the resources contained in it. Green represents agriculture and red stands for revolution and progress.

SIERRA LEONE
The colours of Sierra Leone's flag, adopted on
independence from Britain in 1961, come
from the coat of arms. Green represents the
country's agriculture, white stands for peace
and blue for the Atlantic Ocean.

SINGAPORE
Adopted in 1959, this flag was retained when
Singapore broke away from the Federation of
Malaysia in 1963. The crescent stands for the
nation's ascent and the stars for democracy,
peace, progress, justice and equality.

SLOVAK REPUBLIC
The horizontal tricolour which the Slovak
Republic adopted in 1992 dates from 1848.
The red, white and blue colours are typical of
Slavonic flags. The three blue mounds in the
shield represent the traditional mountains of
Slovakia: Tatra, Matra and Fatra.

SLOVENIA
The Slovene flag, based on the flag of Russia,
was originally adopted in 1848. During the
Communist period a red star appeared in the
centre. This was replaced in June 1991 after
independence, with the new emblem showing
an outline of Mt Triglav.

SOLOMON ISLANDS
Adopted on independence in 1978, the five
white stars represent the five main islands,
while the colours stand for the forests (green)
and waters (blue) lit by the sun (yellow).

SOMALIA
In 1960 British Somaliland united with Italian Somalia to form present-day Somalia and the flag of the southern region was adopted. It is based on the colours of the UN flag with the points of the star representing the five regions of East Africa where Somalis live.

SOUTH AFRICA
This new flag was adopted in 1994, after the country's first multiracial elections were held. The colours are a combination of the ANC colours (black, yellow and green) and the traditional Afrikaner ones (red, white and black).

SPAIN
The colours of this flag date back to the old kingdom of Aragon in the 12th century. The present design, in which the central yellow stripe is twice as wide as each of the red stripes, was adopted during the Civil War in 1938.

SRI LANKA
This flag was adopted in 1951, three years after 'Ceylon' gained independence from Britain. The lion banner represents the ancient Buddhist kingdom and the stripes the island's minorities – Muslims (green) and Hindus (orange).

SUDAN
The design of Sudan's flag is based on the flag of the Arab revolt used in Syria, Iraq and Jordan after 1918. Adopted in 1969, it features the Pan-Arab colours and an Islamic green triangle symbolizing material prosperity and spiritual wealth.

SURINAM
Adopted on independence in 1975, Surinam's flag features the colours of the main political parties, the yellow star symbolizing unity and a golden future. The red is twice the width of the green, and four times that of the white.

SWAZILAND
The kingdom has flown this distinctive flag, whose background is based on that of the Swazi Pioneer Corps of World War II, since independence from Britain in 1968. The emblem has the weapons of a warrior – ox-hide shield, two *assegai* (spears) and a fighting stick.

SWEDEN
While this national flag has been flown sin the reign of King Gustavus Vasa in the ea 16th century, it was not officially adopt until 1906. The colours were derived from t ancient state coat of arms dating from 1364

SWITZERLAND
Switzerland's square flag was officially adop ed in 1848, though the white cross on a re shield has been the Swiss emblem since th 14th century. The flag of the Internation Red Cross, based in Geneva, derives from th Swiss flag.

SYRIA
In the Pan-Arab colours, the flag of Syria the one adopted in 1958 by the former Unite Arab Republic. At various times in their hi tory Egypt and Syria have shared the sam flag, but since 1980 Syria has used this desig

TAIWAN
In 1928 the Nationalists adopted this desig as China's national flag and used it in th struggle against Mao Tse-tung's Communis army. When forced to retreat to Taiwan (the Formosa) in 1949, the flag went with them.

TAJIKISTAN
The new flag was adopted early in 1993 an denotes a gold crown of unusual design unde an arc of seven stars.

TANZANIA
In 1964 Tanganyika united with the islanc of Zanzibar to form the United Republic o Tanzania and a new flag was adopted. The colours represent agriculture (green), minerals (yellow), the people (black), water and Zanzibar (blue).

THAILAND
The two red-and-white stripes are all that remains of Thailand's traditional red-on-white elephant emblem, removed from the flag in 1916. The blue stripe was added in 1917 to show solidarity with the Allies in World War I.

TOGO
Togo's Pan-African colours stand for agriculture and the future (green), mineral wealth

...d the value of hard work (yellow), and the ...ood shed in the struggle for independence ...om France in 1960 (red), with the white star ...r national purity.

...ONGA
...ntroduced in 1862 by Taufa'ahau Tupou, the ...rst king of all Tonga, the flag represents the ...hristian faith of the islanders. The red cross, ...milar to the methodist badge and the Red ...ross flag, illustrates the Tongans' adherence ...o the Christian religion.

...RINIDAD AND TOBAGO
...he islands of Trinidad and Tobago have ...own this flag since independence from ...ritain in 1962. Red stands for the people's ...armth and vitality, black for their strength, ...nd white for their hopes and the ocean surf.

...RISTAN DA CUNHA
...he flag is the British Blue Ensign with the ...hield from the arms in the fly. A new coat of ...rms was introduced in 1984.

...UNISIA
...he Tunisian flag features the crescent moon ...nd five-pointed star, traditional symbols of ...slam. It originated in about 1835 when the ...country was still officially under Turkish rule ...nd was adopted after independence from ...France in 1956.

TURKEY
Although the crescent moon and the five-pointed star are symbols of Islam, their presence on Turkey's flag dates from long before the country became a Muslim state. The flag was officially adopted when the republic was founded in 1923.

TURKMENISTAN
The flag dates from 1992 and depicts a typical Turkmen carpet design and a crescent and five stars. The stars and the five elements of the carpet represent the country's traditional tribes.

TURKS AND CAICOS ISLANDS
In the British Blue Ensign is a gold roundel containing the islands' badge which shows a conch shell, a spiny lobster and a turks head cactus, all of which are found on the islands.

TUVALU
The flag is based on the British Blue Ensign, but in a lighter blue, and has nine yellow stars representing the geographical position of the nine main islands. It was adopted on independence in 1978.

UGANDA
Adopted on independence in 1962, Uganda's flag is that of the party which won the first election. The colours represent the people (black), the sun (yellow), and brotherhood (red); the country's emblem is a crested crane.

UKRAINE
The colours of the Ukraine flag, first adopted in 1848, are heraldic in origin. The flag was used in the period 1918–20 and was re-adopted in 1991.

UNITED ARAB EMIRATES
When seven small states around the Gulf combined to form the United Arab Emirates in 1971, this flag was agreed for the new nation. It features the Pan-Arab colours, first used in the Arab revolt against the Turks from 1916.

UNITED KINGDOM
The first Union flag, combining England's cross of St George and Scotland's cross of St Andrew, dates from 1603 when James VI became James I of England. The Irish emblem, the cross of St Patrick, was added in 1801 to form the present flag.

UNITED STATES OF AMERICA
The 'Stars and Stripes' has had the same basic design since 1777, during the War of Independence. The 13 stripes represent the original colonies that rebelled against British rule, the 50 stars the present states of the Union.

URUGUAY
Displayed since 1830, the stripes represent the nine provinces of Uruguay on independence from Spain two years earlier. The blue and white and the May Sun derive from the flag originally employed by Argentina.

UZBEKISTAN
This flag replaced the Soviet-style flag on 18 November 1991. The blue recalls the blue flag

of Timur (a former ruler), the white peace, the green nature and the red vitality. The crescent moon is for Islam and the 12 stars represent the months of the Islamic calendar.

VANUATU
The device in the triangle is a boar's tusk surrounding two crossed fern leaves, the emblems of war and peace. The flag is in the colours of the Vanuaaku Pati, the dominant political party at the time of independence in 1980.

VATICAN CITY
Since the 13th century, the emblem on the flag has represented the Vatican's role as the headquarters of the Roman Catholic Church. Consisting of the triple tiara of the Popes above the keys of heaven given to St Peter, it was adopted in 1929.

VENEZUELA
The seven stars on the tricolour represent the provinces forming the Venezuelan Federation in 1811. The proportions of the stripes are equal to distinguish it from the flags of Colombia and Ecuador.

VIETNAM
First used by the forces of Ho Chi Minh in the liberation struggle against Japan in World War II, this was adopted as the national flag of North Vietnam in 1945. It was retained when the two parts of the country reunited in 1975.

VIRGIN ISLANDS, BRITISH
In the British Blue Ensign is the green badge of the islands, which shows a vestal virgin dressed in white and carrying a lamp. On either side of her are rows of lamps. Below the shield is a gold scroll bearing the motto *Vigilate* ('Be Alert').

VIRGIN ISLANDS, US
The flag was adopted in 1921 and is based on the seal of the USA. The three arrows grasped by the eagle stand for the three main islands. The emblem appears between the initial letters of the islands' name, 'V' and 'I', in blue.

WALLIS AND FUTUNA ISLANDS
As a French Overseas Territory, the Wallis

and Futuna Islands use the French tricolour their flag.

WESTERN SAMOA
The red and white are traditional colours us in Samoan flags of the 19th century. T design of the flag, in use since 1948 (14 yea before independence), links Samoa with oth nations of the southern hemisphere by inclusion of the Southern Cross constellatio

YEMEN
The design of Yemen's flag, incorporating th Pan-Arab colours, dates from 1990 when th Yemen Arab Republic (in the north and wes united with the People's Democratic Republ of Yemen (in the south and east).

YUGOSLAVIA
Only the republics of Serbia and Montenegr now remain in Yugoslavia. The same fla is still used with its colours identifying it a a Slavic state which was once part of th Austro-Hungarian empire. It used to hav a red star in the centre, but this was droppe in 1992.

ZAÏRE
The Pan-African colours of red, yellow anc green were adopted for Zaïre's flag in 1971 The central emblem symbolizes the revolu tionary spirit of the nation.

ZAMBIA
The flag's colours are those of the Unitec Nationalist Independence Party, which led th struggle against Britain. The flying eagle rep resents freedom. The design was adopted or independence in 1964.

ZIMBABWE
Adopted in 1980, Zimbabwe's flag is based or the colours of the ruling Patriotic Front. Within the white triangle is the soapstone bird national emblem and a red star, symbolizing the party's socialist policy.

UNITED NATIONS
Adopted in 1947, this flag bears the UN emblem in white, which is a map of the world as viewed from above the North Pole, surrounded by olive branches of peace.

WORLD
GAZETTEER

CONTENTS

Numbers in brackets refer to the World Maps page on which the country is principally named. Where a nation is too small to appear on the maps at the chosen scales, its position may be determined by the locator map accompanying the text.

AFGHANISTAN

Nearly three-quarters of Afghanistan is mountainous, comprising most of the Hindu Kush and its foothills, with several peaks over 6,400 m [21,000 ft], and much of the rest is desert or semi-desert. However, the restoration of the Helmand canals has brought fertility to the far south-west, and the sweet waters of the Hamun support fish and cattle; the plains of the north, near the borders with Turkmenistan, Uzbekistan and Tajikistan, yield most of the country's limited agriculture.

ECONOMY AND RESOURCES

The most profitable crop may well be opium, from poppies grown in the hills of the Pathans adjoining Pakistan's North-West Frontier province. With the Islamic Revolution in Iran and the crackdown in the 'Golden Triangle' of Laos, Burma and Thailand, Pakistan became the world's biggest source of heroin (the derivative drug); but while US pressure saw the Pakistani government start to control production on its side of the border, it could do little to stem the flow from Afghanistan – a prime source of revenue for the Mujaheddin's fight against occupying Soviet forces in the 1980s.

The war, which cost over a million Afghanis their lives, left what was an already impoverished state almost totally crippled. Before the Soviet invasion Afghanistan had one of the world's poorest records for infant mortality, literacy, women's rights and a host of other measurements, but the occupation also reduced the economy to ruins. Before the 1978 Marxist revolution Afghanis abroad sent home remittances worth some $125 million, and tourism brought in about $50 million; now all that had gone. Based on natural gas, exports were not helped by the decision of the USSR to cap the wells in 1989.

The greatest problem, however, was the one of refugees. Some 2 million people had moved into crowded cities and towns to avoid the Russian shelling, but far more – somewhere between 3 million and 5 million, by most accounts, but nearer 6 million according t the UN Commissioner – fled the country alt gether, predominantly to Pakistan. This latt estimate, the UN stated in 1990, was aroun 42% of the world total of displaced persons.

HISTORY AND POLITICS

Landlocked Afghanistan has always been in critical position in Asia: the Khyber Pass wa both the gateway to India and the back door t Russia. Since earliest times it has been in vaded by Persians, Greeks, Arabs, Mongol Tartars and the British, who finally failed i their attempts to create a buffer state betwee India and Russia and bowed to Afghan inde pendence after the Third Afghan War in 1921 The latest invaders, entering the country o Christmas Day 1979, were 80,000 men of th Soviet army.

The Russian forces were sent in support o a Kremlin-inspired coup that removed a revo lutionary council set up after the ousting of th pro-Soviet government of Mohammed Dau Khan. Killed in that 1978 coup – the Sau Revolution – Daud Khan had been in powe since 1953, first as prime minister and then after he toppled the monarchy in 1972, a founder, president and prime minister of a fiercely pro-Soviet single-party republic.

The Saur Revolution and subsequent Soviet occupation led to a bitter and protracted civil war, the disparate Muslim tribes uniting behind the banner of the Mujaheddin ('holy warriors') to wage an unrelenting guerrilla war financed by the US and oiled with the co-operation of Pakistan. Despite their vastly superior weaponry and resources, the Soviet forces found it impossible to control the mountain-based rebels in a country the size of Texas, and Afghanistan quickly threatened to turn into an unwinnable war – Moscow's 'Vietnam'.

President Gorbachev began moves to end the conflict soon after coming to power in 1985, and in 1988 a cease-fire was agreed involving both Afghanistan and Pakistan, its main overt ally. In February 1989 the Soviet troops withdrew, leaving the cities in the hands of the pro-Moscow government and the countryside under the control of the Mujaheddin; the civil war intensified, however, fuelled by internecine and traditional

uds as well as the battle for the country's
government, before a fragile cease-fire was
agreed in 1991 with a view to talks the following year. However, the divisions remained and
the nation returned to its familiar patchwork
pattern of feuding tribal fiefdoms, with little
control over the countryside being exercised
from Kabul. In the spring of 1992, after a
prolonged onslaught by the Mujaheddin,
the government in Kabul finally surrendered,
bequeathing an uncertain future to the
country. [*Map page 22*] ■

AREA 652,090 sq km [251,772 sq mls]
POPULATION 18,879,000
CAPITAL (POPULATION) Kabul (1,424,400)
GOVERNMENT Islamic republic
ETHNIC GROUPS Pashtun ('Pathan') 52%,
Tajik 20%, Uzbek 9%, Hazara 9%, Chahar
3%, Turkmen 2%, Baluchi 1%
LANGUAGES Pashto, Dari (Persian), both
official
RELIGIONS Islam (Sunni Muslim 74%, Shiite
Muslim 25%)
CURRENCY Afghani = 100 puls

ALBANIA

By far Europe's poorest country, Albania is
also one of the most isolated, separated
physically and culturally from even its closest
neighbours, Greece and Yugoslavia. The
Albanian language has no close affinities with
other European languages, and until 1990 the
political system, priding itself on being the last
fortress of true Marxism-Leninism, emphasized the country's remoteness.

Geographical obstacles have reinforced
Albania's linguistic and political isolation.
The mountainous interior forms a barrier to
penetration from the east. The main ranges,
which rise to almost 2,000 m [6,500 ft] are
continuations of the Dinaric Alps; these run
from north-west to south-east, rising steeply
from the coastal lowlands that border the
Adriatic Sea.

ECONOMY AND RESOURCES

Limestone is the most common type of rock,
although in the central area there are igneous
masses rich in mineral ores, including copper,
iron, nickel and chrome. Albania relies heavily
on exports of chrome for foreign exchange,
and is the world's eighth largest producer,
contributing 2.8% of the total in 1993.

Although the country has adequate energy
resources – including petroleum, brown coal
and hydroelectric potential as well as useful
minerals – Albania remains one of the least
industrialized countries in Europe, and transport is poorly developed. Horses and mules
are widely used in rural areas, and there are no
rail links with other countries. Most people
still live by farming, with maize, wheat, barley,
sugar beet and fruits predominant, though the
country has always found it a difficult task
feeding a population with a growth rate of
2.1% – the highest in Europe.

HISTORY AND POLITICS

Albania declared independence in 1912, after
five centuries under the rule of the Ottoman
Turks. A legacy of this period is the fact that,
until the government closed all religious establishments in 1967, some 70% of Albanians
were Muslims. Though not official, the figure
is likely to be the same today.

At the end of World War II, an Albanian
People's Republic was formed under the
Communist leadership who had led the partisans against the Germans. Pursuing a modernization programme on rigid Stalinist lines,
the regime of Enver Hoxha has at various
times associated politically and often economically with Yugoslavia (up to 1948), the USSR
(1948–61) and China (1961–77) before following a fiercely independent policy.

Hoxha's successor, Ramiz Alia, continued
the dictator's austere policies after his death
in 1985, but by the end of the decade even
Albania was affected by the sweeping changes
in Eastern Europe, and in 1990 the more
progressive wing of the Communist Party (led
by Alia) won the struggle for power. They
instituted, somewhat reluctantly, a wide programme of reform, including the legalization
of religion, the encouragement of foreign
investment, the introduction of a free market
for peasants' produce, and the establishment

of pluralist democracy. A president and the 140-member Assembly are elected under a system of proportional representation by universal adult suffrage, for a period of four years.

In the elections of April 1991, the Communists comfortably retained their majority, but two months later the government was brought down by a general strike and an interim coalition 'national salvation' committee took over; this fragile 'government of stability' in turn collapsed after six months, when the Democrats withdrew their support. Elections in the spring of 1992 brought to an end the last Communist regime in Europe when Dr Sali Berisha, the Democratic Party leader, was elected by parliament as Albania's first non-Communist president.

Meanwhile, the country had descended into chaos and violence, triggered by food shortages. Tens of thousands of unwelcome refugees fled the civil unrest to Greece and Italy, and in some places control rested with local bandits and brigands. In neighbouring Yugoslavia (itself in the throes of disintegration), the large Albanian population in the 'autonomous province' of Kosovo were in conflict with the Serbian authorities.

After a lifetime of Orwellian state control, a backward country was being catapulted without real government into modern industrialized Europe – and towards a Western world preoccupied with recession. At the end of 1993, a UN report put the annual income per capita figure for Albania at around US$820 – alongside many a struggling nation in what is still called the Third World. [*Map page 17*] ∎

AREA 28,750 sq km [11,100 sq mls]
POPULATION 3,414,000
CAPITAL (POPULATION) Tirana (251,000)
GOVERNMENT Multiparty republic
ETHNIC GROUPS Albanian 98%, Greek 1.8%, Macedonian, Montenegrin, Gypsy
LANGUAGES Albanian (official)
RELIGIONS Many people say they are non-believers; of the believers, 65% follow Islam, and 33% Christianity (Orthodox 20%, Roman Catholics 13%)
CURRENCY Lek = 100 qindars

ALGERIA

After Sudan, Algeria is the biggest politic unit in the Middle East and Africa, an the world's 11th largest nation. However, ove 90% of the country's 27.3 million inhabitant live in the Mediterranean coastlands. The vas Saharan territories, covering over 2 millio sq km [772,200 sq mls], or about 85% c the total area, are very sparsely populated most of the inhabitants are concentrated in th oases, which form densely-populated 'islands separated by vast empty areas. The majorit of the population speak Arabic, but there i a significant Berber-speaking indigenous min ority in the mountainous north-east.

ECONOMY AND RESOURCES

European settlers acquired over a quarter o the cultivated land, mainly in north-wester Algeria, and rural colonization transformed the plains, producing cash crops.

Oil was discovered in the Algerian Sahara in 1956 and Algeria's natural gas reserves are among the largest in the world. The country's crude-oil refining capacity is the biggest in Africa. Since independence in 1962, revenues from oil and gas, which provide 65% of all revenue and account for over 90% of exports, have enabled the government to embark on an ambitious economic development programme, with rapid industrialization. Industrial developments include iron and steel plants, food processing, chemicals and textiles, while Algeria is one of the few African nations to have its own car-manufacturing facility, producing about a third of its commercial vehicles. In addition there is an array of production allied to the oil and gas reserves: oil refineries, petrochemical plants and gas liquefaction units. While most of the larger industries are nationalized, much of the light industry remains under private control.

Though agriculture has suffered by comparison, about 30% of Algerians are farmers. Arable land accounts for only 3% of the total land area, but the rich northern coastlands

THE ATLAS MOUNTAINS

Extending from Morocco into northern Algeria and Tunisia, the Atlas is a prominent range of fold mountains. Its highest peak and the highest in North Africa, Jebel Toubkal (4,165 m [13,670 ft]), is one of a jagged row – the High Atlas – in central Morocco; the lesser ranges cluster on either side and to the east, generally with a north-east to south-west trend.

In Morocco there are the Anti-Atlas in the south-west, the Middle Atlas in the centre of the country, and the Er Rif mountains near the Mediterranean coast. In Algeria the range includes the Saharan Atlas and, further north, the Tell or Maritime Atlas. Heavily glaciated during the Ice Age, the highest Atlas ranges are now capped with patches of permanent snow and alpine tundra. North-facing slopes receive good winter rainfall, and are forested with pines, cedars, and evergreen and cork oaks. Tablelands between the ranges provide high pastures and rich soils for farming. The southern and eastern ranges are drier and covered with semi-desert scrub, providing rough pastures and poor cultivation.

Formerly linked to Spain during short spells of geological history, the Atlas Mountains support both European and African plants and animals. While the Algerian bear and wild ass and the Barbary lion, once plentiful, are now extinct, small populations of deer, closely akin to European red deer, graze with Barbary sheep and Dorcas gazelles among the high peaks, and Barbary apes may steal crops.

produce wheat, barley, vines and olives – as well as early fruit and vegetables for the European markets, notably France and Italy. Further south, dates are an important product, but in the mountains the primary occupation of the Berber population is the rearing of sheep, cattle and goats.

HISTORY AND POLITICS

Like its neighbours Morocco and Tunisia, Algeria experienced French colonial rule and settler colonization. Algeria was the first Maghreb country to be conquered by France and the last to receive independence, following years of bitter warfare between nationalist guerrillas and the French armed forces.

In January 1992, with the Islamic fundamentalist FIS on course for electoral victory, the government cancelled the second round and declared a state of emergency, effectively ending Algeria's four-year flirtation with Western-style democracy. In June 1992 the FIS assassinated President Boudiaf and has since been waging a relentless terrorist campaign (including the murder of foreigners) which has led to the death of over 3,000 people. [*Map page 32*] ∎

AREA 2,381,700 sq km [919,590 sq mls]
POPULATION 27,325,000
CAPITAL (POPULATION) Algiers (1,722,000)
GOVERNMENT Socialist republic
ETHNIC GROUPS Arab, Berber, French
LANGUAGES Arabic (official), Berber, French
RELIGIONS Sunni Muslim 98%, Christianity (mainly Roman Catholic)
CURRENCY Algerian dinar = 100 centimes

AMERICAN SAMOA

American Samoa is a group of five volcanic islands and two atolls covering a land area of 200 sq km [77 sq mls] in the South Pacific, with Tutuila the largest. Swain Island to the north also comes under its administration, taking the total population to about 53,000. More than twice that number of American Samoans live in the US. Though the US naval base at Pago Pago closed in 1951, the American influence in the territory is still vital, giving substantial grants and taking 90% of exports, almost exclusively canned tuna. Most of the land is bush or jungle, and agriculture is limited.

The Samoan Islands were divided in 1899, with British consent, between Germany and the US along a line 171° west of Greenwich. American Samoa is now a self-governing 'unincorporated territory of the US'. While Pago Pago – the recipient of about 5,000 mm [200 in] of rain a year – is the capital, the seat of government is to the east at Fagatogo. There is little prospect of Samoan reunification: the American islands enjoy a standard of living some ten times as high as their neighbours in Western Samoa. [*Map page 2*] ∎

AREA 200 sq km [77 sq mls]
POPULATION 53,000
CAPITAL (POPULATION) Pago Pago (3,519)
GOVERNMENT Self-governing 'unincorporated territory of the US'
ETHNIC GROUPS Samoan 90%, Caucasian 2%, Tongan 2%
LANGUAGES Samoan, English
RELIGIONS Christianity
CURRENCY US currency

ANDORRA

Perched near the eastern end of the high central Pyrenees, Andorra consists mainly of six valleys (the Valls) that drain to the River Valira. These deep glaciated valleys lie at altitudes of 1,000–2,900 m [3,280–9,500 ft]. In the north a lofty watershed forms the frontier with France and is crossed by a road over the Envalira Pass at 2,400 m [7,870 ft]; to the south the land falls away down the Valira Valley to the Segre Valley in Spain, again followed by the same vital highway. In the colder months the Envalira Pass often becomes snowbound.

The climate is severe in winter and pleasantly cool in summer when, because the valleys lie in a rain-shadow, slopes above 1,400 m [4,600 ft] often suffer from drought and need irrigation. Some agriculture is possible on the slopes: sheep and cattle are grazed, and crops grow in terraced fields.

Andorra has five main sources of income: stock rearing and agriculture, especially tobacco; the sale of water and hydroelectricity to Catalonia; fees from radio transmission ser-

vices; tourism, based in winter on skiing; and the sale of duty-free goods and of postage stamps. Of these, tourism and duty-free sales are by far the most important – every year up to 10 million visitors come to Andorra to shop, and to witness this rare surviving example of a medieval principality.

The rights of the co-principality or *seigneurs* have been shared since 1278 between the Spanish Bishop of Urgel and the French Comte de Foix. The latter's lordship right passed to the French government, now represented by the prefect of the adjoining *département* of the Eastern Pyrenees. The Andorran pay a small annual sum to the bishop and the prefect, and each co-prince is represented in their Council by a *viguier*; but in most other respects the co-principality governs itself. In 1993, a new democratic constitution was adopted. [*Map page 18*] ∎

AREA 453 sq km [175 sq mls]
POPULATION 65,000
CAPITAL (POPULATION) Andorra la Vella (20,437)
GOVERNMENT Co-principality
ETHNIC GROUPS Spanish 46%, Andorran 28%, Portuguese 11%, French 8%, British 2%
LANGUAGES Catalan (official)
RELIGIONS Christianity (Roman Catholic 90%)
CURRENCY French and Spanish currency

ANGOLA

More than 13 times the size of its former colonial ruler, Portugal, Angola is southern Africa's largest state, extending through 13° of latitude. Most of the country is part of the huge plateau which makes up the interior of southern Africa. In the west is a narrow coastal plain, and in the northeast, several rivers flow northwards to the Zaïre (Congo) River. In the south, some rivers, including the Cubango (Okavango) and Cuanda, flow south-eastwards into the interior of Africa.

There is a strong cooling effect from the old offshore Benguela Current, and climate and vegetation vary from desert on the south coast to equatorial and montane conditions in the centre and north.

ECONOMY AND RESOURCES

Potentially, Angola is one of Africa's richest countries. The country has exceptionally varied agricultural output, while the coastal waters are rich in fish. Oil reserves are important both on the coast and offshore near Luanda and in the enclave of Cabinda (which is separated from Angola by a strip of land belonging to Zaïre), and hydroelectric power and irrigation developments are substantial. Diamonds, a major export (Angola is one of the world's largest producers), come from the north-east, and there are unexploited reserves of copper, manganese and phosphates. The country has a growing manufacturing sector.

HISTORY AND POLITICS

Bantu-speaking peoples from the north settled in Angola around 2,000 years ago. In the late 15th century, Portuguese navigators, seeking a route to Asia around Africa, explored the coast and, in the early 16th century, the Portuguese set up bases. Portugal established Luanda in 1575, and Angola's capital is the oldest European-founded city in Africa south of the Sahara. As a centre of the slave trade, some 3 million captives from Angola passed through it to the Americas, and the depopulation dislocated local life for many generations.

After the decline of the slave trade, Portuguese settlers began to develop the land, and the Portuguese population increased greatly in the 20th century. In the 1950s, local nationalists began to demand independence, and in 1956 the MPLA (Popular Movement for the Liberation of Angola) was founded with support from the Mbundu and mestizos. The MPLA led a revolt in Luanda in 1961, but this was put down by Portuguese troops.

Other opposition groups now developed. In the north, the Kongo set up the FNLA (Front for the Liberation of Angola), while, in 1966, the people of the south, including many Ovimbundu, formed UNITA (National Union for the Total Independence of Angola). The Portuguese agreed to grant indepen-

dence to Angola in 1975, but the rival nationalist forces began a struggle for power. The MPLA formed the government, but UNITA troops, opposed to the MPLA's socialist policies, and with support from South Africa, began a long civil war, which continued into the 1990s. A peace treaty was signed in 1991 and elections were held in 1992. But after a victory for the MPLA, which had renounced its socialist policies, the civil war broke out again. [*Map page 33*] ■

AREA 1,246,700 sq km [481,351 sq mls]
POPULATION 10,674,000
CAPITAL (POPULATION) Luanda (1,544,000)
GOVERNMENT Multiparty republic
ETHNIC GROUPS Ovimbundu 37%, Mbundu 22%, Kongo 13%, Luimbe-Nganguela 5%, Nyaneka-Humbe 5%, Chokwe, Luvale, Luchazi
LANGUAGES Portuguese (official)
RELIGIONS Christianity (Roman Catholic 69%, Protestant 20%), traditional beliefs 10%
CURRENCY Kwanza = 100 lwei

ANGUILLA

Deriving its name from its 'discovery' in 1493 by Columbus – *anguil* is Spanish for eel – Anguilla is indeed long and thin, a low coral atoll covered with poor soil and scrub, measuring 96 sq km [37 sq mls].

Of the 8,000 population – largely of African descent, English-speaking and of various Christian denominations – nearly a quarter live in the capital of The Valley. The main source of revenue is now tourism, though lobster accounts for half of exports, while many Anguillans send home earnings from the UK and USA. Sadly, 80% of the island's coral has now disappeared through the effects of tourism – namely, pollution and the sale of coral as souvenir items.

First colonized by Britain in 1690 and long administered with St Kitts and Nevis, the island was subject to intervention by British troops in 1969 to restore legal government following its secession from the self-governing federation in 1967. Its position as a separate UK dependent territory was confirmed in 1971 and formalized in 1980. [*Map page 30*] ■

AREA 96 sq km [37 sq mls]
POPULATION 8,000
CAPITAL (POPULATION) The Valley (2,000)
GOVERNMENT British dependency
ETHNIC GROUPS Mainly of African descent
LANGUAGES English and Creole
RELIGIONS Christianity
CURRENCY Eastern Caribbean dollar

ANTIGUA AND BARBUDA

A ntigua is untypical of the Leeward Islands in that despite its height – rising to 405 m [1,328 ft] – it has no rivers or forests; Barbuda, by contrast, is a well-wooded low coral atoll.

Both islands rely heavily on tourism, though some attempts at diversification (notably Sea Island cotton) have been successful. Other activities include livestock rearing, mixed market gardening and fishing. Antigua's white-owned sugar industry – accounting for most of exports in the 1960s – was closed down in 1971. Only 1,400 people live on the game reserve island of Barbuda, where lobster fishing is the main occupation, and none on the rocky island of Redondo. Antigua and Barbuda are strategically situated islands linked by Britain after 1860; gaining internal self-government in 1967 and independence in 1981. [*Map page 30*] ■

AREA 440 sq km [170 sq mls]
POPULATION 65,000
CAPITAL (POPULATION) St John's (36,000)
GOVERNMENT Multiparty constitutional monarchy
ETHNIC GROUPS Mainly of African descent
LANGUAGES English, local dialects
RELIGIONS Christianity
CURRENCY Eastern Caribbean dollar

ARGENTINA

L argest of the Spanish-speaking countries of Latin America, but still less than a third of the size of Brazil, Argentina forms a wedge-shaped country from the Tropic of Capricorn to Tierra del Fuego. The western boundary lies high in the Andes, including basins, ridges and peaks of 6,000 m [19,685 ft] in the north. South of latitude 27°S the ridges merge into a single high cordillera, the highest point being Aconcagua at 6,960 m [22,834 ft], the tallest mountain in the western hemisphere; south of 39°S the Patagonian Andes are lower, but include glaciers and volcanoes. Eastern Argentina is a series of alluvial plains, stretching from the Andean foothills to the sea. The Gran Chaco in the north slopes gradually towards the valley of the Paraná River, from the high desert in the foothills to lowland swamp forest.

Further south are the extensive pampas grasslands, damp and fertile near Buenos Aires, drier but still productive elsewhere. Southwards again the pampas give way to the less hospitable plateaus of Patagonia, areas of mixed volcanic, alluvial and glacial debris that form a harsh, windswept landscape. The climate varies dramatically from hot and humid in the north of the country to bitterly cold, damp and stormy in the extreme south.

ECONOMY AND RESOURCES

Argentina is one of the richest of South America's countries in terms of natural resources, and its population – though remarkably urban, with 85% living in towns and cities – is not growing at anything like the rates seen in most of Africa and Asia. The population, predominantly European and mainly middle class, nevertheless relies on an economic base that is agricultural: Argentina's farming industry exports wheat, maize, sorghum and soya beans as well as enormous quantities of meat, and produces sugar, oilseed, fruit and vegetables for home consumption. The chief industries, too, are based ɪ food products, and the government aims switch to manufacturing from agricultural ʳocessing. The manufacturing base is around ʙuenos Aires, where more than a third of ᴛe population live, and there is a strong computer industry.

Minerals are largely undeveloped, though ᴄal and natural gas are exploited and the ᴄountry is approaching self-sufficiency in ᴘetroleum production, mainly from Patagonia ᴎd the north-west. Other areas yet to be explored are the mining of copper and uranium ᴀnd, on a more rural level, fishing and forestry.

HISTORY AND POLITICS

ᴸormerly a dependency of Peru, Argentina ('land of silver') was settled first in the north-ᴡest around Salta and San Miguel de ᴛucumán with strong links to Lima. This area ɪs unusual today in retaining a largely mestizo (mixed Indian and Spanish) population, a ʀemnant of colonial times. In 1776 Argentina, Uruguay, Paraguay and southern Bolivia were ᴅisengaged from Peru to form a separate ʏiceroyalty, with its administrative centre in ᴮuenos Aires. After a long war of independence the United Provinces of the Rió de la ᴘlata achieved self-government under Simón ᴮolívar, but Uruguay, Bolivia and Paraguay ᴛeparated between 1814 and 1828; it took ᴍany years of warfare and turbulence before ᴧrgentina emerged as a national entity in ◄816, united and centred on Buenos Aires.

Early prosperity, based on stock-raising and ꜰarming, was boosted from 1870 by a massive ᴎflux of European immigrants, particularly ꜰtalians and Spaniards for whom the Argentine ᴡas a real alternative to the USA. They settled ꜰands recently cleared of Indians and often organized by huge land companies. Britain provided much of the capital and some of the immigrants; families of English and Welsh sheep farmers, still speaking their own languages, are identifiable in Patagonia today. Development of a good railway network to the ports, plus steamship services to Europe and refrigerated vessels, helped to create the strong meat, wool and wheat economy that carried Argentina through its formative years and into the 20th century.

A military coup in 1930 started a long period of military intervention in the politics

THE PAMPAS

Pampa is a South American Indian word describing a flat, featureless expanse: the pampas of South America are the broad, grassy plains – equivalent to the temperate grasslands of the North American prairies, the Central Asian steppes or the South African veld – that stretch between the eastern flank of the Andes and the Atlantic Ocean. Geologically, they represent outwash fans of rubble, sand, silt and clay, washed down from the Andes by torrents and redistributed by wind and water. Fine soils cover huge expanses of pampas, providing good deep soils in the well-watered areas, but scrub and sandy desert where rainfall and groundwater are lacking.

Originally the pampas were covered with indigenous bunch-grasses, with scattered stands of trees in the well-watered areas. Pampas deer, guanaco, viscachas and cavys were the main grazers, and the pampas fauna included the maned wolf, hairy armadillo and a wealth of bird life including the rhea, the South American ostrich.

Early Spanish settlers introduced horses and cattle, and later the best areas of pampas were enclosed for cattle ranching and cultivation. Now the pampas are almost entirely converted to rangelands growing turf grasses (vehicles have mostly replaced the gauchos) or to huge fields producing alfalfa, maize, wheat and flax.

of the country. The period from 1976 – the so-called 'dirty war' – saw the torture, wrongful imprisonment and murder ('disappearance') of up to 15,000 people by the military, and up to 2 million people fled the country. In 1982 the government, blamed for the poor state of the economy, launched an ill-fated invasion of the Falkland Islands (Islas Malvinas), a territory they had claimed since 1820. Britain regained possession later that year by sending an expeditionary force, and President Galtieri resigned. Constitutional rule was restored in 1983 under President Raúl Alfonsín, though the military remained influential.

The country's economic problems – with

their classic Latin American causes of reliance on certain commodities, big borrowing ($62 billion foreign debt) and maladministration – were inherited by his Peronist successor, Carlos Menem, in 1989. His austerity programme took Argentina through inflation rates of 3,084% and 2,314% down to 85% in 1991 – stable money by previous standards. His policies of economic liberalization and reduction of state involvement may work. [*Map page 31*] ∎

AREA 2,766,890 sq km [1,068,296 sq mls]
POPULATION 34,182,000
CAPITAL (POPULATION) Buenos Aires (11,256,000)
GOVERNMENT Federal republic
ETHNIC GROUPS European 85%, Mestizo, Amerindian
LANGUAGES Spanish (official)
RELIGIONS Christianity (Roman Catholic 92%, Protestant 2%)
CURRENCY Peso = 10,000 australs

ARMENIA

The smallest of the 15 republics of the former Soviet Union, Armenia was also one of the weakest. It is a rugged, wooded and mountainous country landlocked between traditionally hostile neighbours. Most of Armenia consists of a rugged plateau, criss-crossed by long faults and subject to earthquakes. Fast-flowing rivers have cut deep gorges in the plateau. The highest point is Mt Aragats, at 4,090 m [13,419 ft] above sea level. The lowest land is in the north-west, where the capital Yerevan is situated, and the north-east. The largest lake is Ozero (Lake) Sevan.

The height of the land – which averages 1,500 m [4,920 ft] above sea level – helps to give Armenia severe winters and cool summers. The highest peaks are snow-capped, but the total yearly rainfall is generally low, between about 200 mm and 800 mm [8 in to 31 in].

ECONOMY AND RESOURCES

Armenia has few natural resources (though lead, copper and zinc are mined), limited industry, and registered the poorest agricultural output per head in the Union; the country's main products are wine, tobacco, olives and rice, the main occupation the rearing of livestock. Much of the west is recovering from the devastating earthquake of 1988, in which some 55,000 people died. Its vulnerability is heightened by the lack of support for its conflict with Azerbaijan over the area of Nagorno-Karabakh, and its heavy reliance for energy on the other former Soviet republics.

HISTORY AND POLITICS

Originally a much larger independent kingdom centred on Mt Ararat, the legendary resting place of Noah's Ark, Armenia had already been established for more than 1,000 years when it became the first country in the world to make Christianity (Armenian Apostolic) the official state religion in the 4th century. Later, the area came under first Arab and then Turkish control. By the early 16th century, Armenia was part of the Turkish Ottoman empire.

In the 19th century, Armenians suffered great hardships under Turkish rule, and in the 1890s the Turks slaughtered hundreds of thousands of Armenians. Then, during World War I, 600,000 Armenians were killed and 1.75 million deported to Syria and Palestine by the Turks, who feared the Armenians would support Russia.

At the end of World War I, in 1918, an independent Armenian republic was set up in the area held by Russia, though the western part of historic Armenia remained in Turkey, and another area was held by Iran. In 1920, Armenia became a Communist republic and, in 1922, it became, with Azerbaijan and Georgia, part of the Transcaucasian Republic within the Soviet Union. However, in 1936, the three territories became separate Soviet Socialist Republics.

Armenia has long disputed the status of an area called Nagorno-Karabakh, which lies inside Azerbaijan, because the majority of the people there were Armenians. After the break-up of the Soviet Union in 1991, fighting broke

t between Armenia and Azerbaijan, and in
'92 Armenia occupied the land between
eastern border and Nagorno-Karabakh.
ne fierce fighting led to large movements
Armenians and Azerbaijanis. A cease-fire
as finally agreed in 1994, with Armenia in
ntrol of about 20% of Azerbaijan's land
ea. [*Map page 22*] ■

AREA 29,800 sq km [11,506 sq mls]
POPULATION 3,548,000
CAPITAL (POPULATION) Yerevan
(1,254,000)
GOVERNMENT Multiparty republic
ETHNIC GROUPS Armenian 93%, Azerbaijani
3%, Russian 2%, Kurd 2%
LANGUAGES Armenian (official)
RELIGIONS Christianity (mainly Armenian
Apostolic)
CURRENCY Dram = 100 couma

ARUBA

A dry, flat limestone island and the most
western of the Lesser Antilles, Aruba
measures 193 sq km [75 sq mls]. The country
has a population of 62,000, a third living
in the capital of Oranjestad. About half the
people are of Arawak Indian stock; on most
Caribbean islands, the Amerindian population
was extirpated by genocide, disease or transportation.

While tourism and the production of petrochemicals and fertilizers are important, over
half of the country's export earnings still come
from beverages and tobacco, while foodstuffs
account for over half of imports.

Incorporated into the Netherlands Antilles
in 1845, and part of the self-governing federation from 1954, Aruba held a referendum
in 1977, which supported autonomy. The
1983 Constitutional Conference agreed that
Aruba's separate status should least for ten
years from 1986, after which time the islands
would become fully independent. In March
1994 this decision was overturned when

Aruba decided it would remain within the
Kingdom of the Netherlands ■

AREA 193 sq km [75 sq mls]
POPULATION 69,000
CAPITAL (POPULATION) Oranjestad (20,000)
GOVERNMENT Self-governing Dutch
territory
ETHNIC GROUPS Mixed European/Caribbean
Indian 80%
LANGUAGES Dutch, Papiamento, English,
Spanish
RELIGIONS Christianity
CURRENCY Aruban florin = 100 cents

ASCENSION

A scension stands in isolation on the Mid-
Atlantic Ridge, a triangular volcanic
island of 88 sq km [34 sq mls], with a single
high peak, Green Mountain (859 m [2,817 ft]),
surrounded by hot low-lying ash and lava
plains. The island is 1,130 km [700 mls]
north-west of St Helena and is famous for
turtles, which land on the beaches from
January to May to lay their eggs.

The mountain climate is cool and damp
enough to support a farm, which supplies
vegetables for the local community. Administered from St Helena since 1922, its inhabitants are British, St Helenian or American,
many of them involved in telecommunications, satellite research and servicing an
important mid-ocean airstrip. [*Map page 33*] ■

AREA 88 sq km [34 sq mls]
POPULATION 1,500
CAPITAL (POPULATION) Georgetown
(1,500)
GOVERNMENT Dependent territory of the
UK
ETHNIC GROUPS No native ones
LANGUAGES English
RELIGIONS Christianity
CURRENCY St Helena pound = 100 pence

AUSTRALIA

Whether Australia is the world's largest island or its smallest continental land mass – or both, or neither, depending on the school of geography – it is primarily a land of low to medium altitude plateaux that form monotonous landscapes extending for hundreds of kilometres. The edges of the plateaux are more diverse, particularly in the east where deep gorges and waterfalls create rugged relief between the Great Divide and the coast. In the north-west, impressive gorge scenery is found in the Hamersley Range and Kimberley area.

The western half of Australia is formed of ancient rocks. Essentially an arid landscape of worn-down ridges and plateaux, with depressions occupied by sandy deserts and occasional salt lakes, this area has little surface water.

The eastern sixth of the continent, including Tasmania, forms the Eastern Highlands, the zone of greatest relief, greatest rainfall, most abundant vegetation and greatest population. Peaks in this region include Mt Kosciusko, at 2,230 m [7,316 ft] Australia's highest. Much of this area shows signs of volcanic activity in the relatively recent geological past, and these young basalts support nutrient-rich soils in contrast to the generally well-weathered, nutrient-poor soils of nearly all the remainder of Australia.

Between the western plateaux and Eastern Highlands lie the Carpentaria, central and Murray lowlands. The central lowlands drain to the great internal river systems supplying Lake Eyre, or to the Bulloo system, or through great inland deltas to the Darling River. The parallel dune ridges of this area form part of a great continent-wide set of dune ridges extending in a huge anti-clockwise arc, eastwards through the Great Victoria Desert, northwards through the Simpson Desert and westwards in the Great Sandy Desert. All these, though inhospitable, are only moderately arid, allowing widespread if sparse vegetation cover.

Vegetation

On the humid margins of the continent a luxuriant forests. These include the gre jarrah forests of tall eucalyptus hardwoods the extreme south-west of Western Australi the temperate rainforests with the Antarc beech found in Tasmania and on hum upland sites north through New South Wal to the Queensland border; and the tro ical and subtropical rainforests found in tl wetter areas along the east coast, from tl McIllwraith Range in the north to the vicini of Mallacoota Inlet in the south. Some these rainforest areas are maintained as ma aged forests, others are in national park but most of the original cover has been cleare for agriculture, particularly for dairying an cattle-fattening, and for sugar and banana cu tivation north of Port Macquarie.

The most adaptable tree genus in Australi is the *Eucalyptus*, which ranges from the ta flooded gum trees found on the edges of th rainforest to the dry-living mallee specie found on sand plains and interdune areas Acacia species, especially the bright-yellow flowered wattles, are also adapted to a wide range of environments. Associated with thi adaptation of plants is the wide variety o animal adaptations, with 277 different mam mals, about 400 species of reptiles and some 700 species of birds.

Aborigines arriving from Asia over 40,00C years ago brought the dingo, which rapidly replaced the Tasmanian wolf, the largest mar supial predator, and preyed on smaller animals. Fires, lit for hunting and allowed to burn uncontrolled, altered much of the vegetation, probably allowing eucalyptus forests to expand at the expense of the rain forest. However, the Aborigines understood their environment, carefully protecting vital areas of natural food supply, restricting the use of certain desert waterholes which tradition taught would be reliable in a drought, and developing a resource-use policy which was aimed at living with nature.

European settlement after 1788 upset this ecological balance, through the widespread clearing of coastal forests, overgrazing of inland pastures and introduction of exotic species, especially the destructive rabbit. But Europeans also brought the technology which

...abled the mineral, water and soil resources Australia to be developed.

ECONOMY AND RESOURCES

Much of Australia's growth since the beginning of European settlement has been closely related to the exploitation of mineral resources, which has led directly to the founding, growth and often eventual decline of the majority of inland towns. Broken Hill and Mount Isa are copper-, lead-, zinc- and silver-producing centres, while Kalgoorlie, Bendigo, Ballarat and Charters Towers all grew in the 19th-century gold rushes. Today, less glamorous minerals support the Australian economy. In Western Australia, the great iron-ore mines of Mount Tom Price, Mount Newman and Mount Goldsworthy are linked by new railways to special ports at Dampier and Port Hedland. Offshore are the oil and gas fields of the north-west shelf.

In the east, the coal mines of central Queensland and eastern New South Wales are linked by rail to bulk loading facilities at Sarina, Gladstone, Brisbane, Newcastle, Sydney and Port Kemble, which enable this high-grade coking coal to be shipped to worldwide markets and by 1986 had made Australia the biggest exporter (15% of export earnings). Bauxite mining has led to new settlements at Nhulunby and Weipa on the Gulf of Carpentaria, with associated refineries at Kwinana, Gladstone and Bell Bay.

Rum Jungle, south of Darwin, became well known as one of the first uranium mines, but now deposits further east in Arnhem Land are being developed. Meanwhile, new discoveries of ore bodies continue to be made in the ancient rocks of the western half of Australia. Natural gas from the Cooper Basin, just south of Innamincka on Cooper Creek, is piped to Adelaide and Sydney, while oil and gas from the Bass Strait and brown coal from the Yallourn-Morwell area have been vital to the industrial growth of Victoria. Fossil fuels are supplemented by hydroelectric power from major schemes in western Tasmania and the Snowy Mountains and smaller projects near Cairns and Tully in north Queensland.

Australia's mineral wealth is phenomenal. In 1993 it produced over 40% of the world's diamonds, around 13% of gold and iron ore,

THE GREAT BARRIER REEF

When coral is alive it sways gently in the sea's currents, but when it dies it forms hard coral 'limestone' rock. The beautiful Great Barrier Reef, off the coast of Queensland in the Coral Sea and the world's biggest, is a maze of some 2,500 reefs exposed only at low tide, ranging in size from a few hundred hectares to 50 sq km [20 sq mls], and extending over an area of 250,000 sq km [100,000 sq mls].

The section extending for about 800 km [500 mls] north of Cairns forms a discontinuous wall of coral through which narrow openings lead to areas of platform or patch reefs. South of Cairns, the reefs are less continuous, and extend further from the coast. Between the outer reef and the coast are many high islands, remnants of the mainland; coral cays, developed from coral sand on reefs and known locally as low islands, are usually small and uninhabited, exceptions being Green Island and Heron Island.

A major tourist attraction comprising over 400 types of coral and harbouring more than 1,500 species of fish, the modern reefs have evolved in the last 20,000 years, over older foundations exposed to the atmosphere during former low sea levels. Coral is susceptible to severe damage from tropical cyclones and, increasingly, to attack by the crown-of-thorns starfish. Much is now protected as the Great Barrier Reef Marine Park (the world's largest protected sea area), but the existence of oil around and beneath the reef is a great long-term threat to its ecological stability.

8% of silver, 7% of aluminium, nickel, magnesium and uranium, 5% of zinc and lead (down from 14% in 1989), and was the world's biggest exporter of mineral sands. Inspite of these statistics however, by 1991 the country was experiencing its worst recession since the 1920s.

Agriculture

Apart from the empty and largely unusable desert areas in Western Australia and the Simpson Desert, extensive cattle or sheep production dominates all of Australia north and west of a line from Penong in South Australia, through Broken Hill in New South Wales to Bundaberg in Queensland, and east of a line from Geraldton to Esperance in Western Australia. Cattle and sheep populations in this zone are sparse, individual pastoral holdings are large, some over 400,000 hectares [1 million acres], and towns are both small and far apart.

Some Aborigines retain limited tracts of land in Arnhem Land and on the fringes of the deserts where they live by hunting and gathering, but nearly all Aborigines now live close to government settlements or mission stations. Many are employed as stockmen and seasonal agricultural workers, while thousands of others have migrated to country towns and the major cities.

The intensive pastoral and agricultural zones support the bulk of the sheep and cattle of Australia, and wool, mutton and beef production is still the basic industry. The country is the world's largest producer of wool and third in lamb and mutton. Wheat is cultivated in combination with sheep raising over large tracts of the gentle inland slopes of the coastal ranges.

Along the east coast are important cattle-fattening, dairy and sugar-cane industries, the latter significant on the east coast from Brisbane to Cairns. Irrigated areas also support cotton, rice, fruit and vegetable crops, largely for consumption within Australia. Wine production around Perth, Adelaide, central Victoria and eastern New South Wales has expanded in recent decades, producing vintages of international renown.

HISTORY AND POLITICS

European settlement in Australia began in 1788 as a penal colony in New South Wales, spreading quickly to Queensland and Tasmania. During the 19th century the continent became divided into the states of New South Wales, Queensland (1859), South Australia (1836), Tasmania (1825), Victoria (1851) and Western Australia (1829), with the area now forming the Northern Territory being under the control of South Australia. During this colonial period the state seaport capitals of Sydney, Brisbane, Adelaide, Hobart, Melbourne and Perth became established as

MARSUPIALS

Marsupials are mammals that give birth to their young at an early stage of development and attach them to their milk glands for a period, often inside a pouch (*marsupium*). Once widespread around the world, they have mostly been ousted by more advanced forms, but marsupials of many kinds continue to flourish in the isolation of Australia, New Guinea and South America.

Best known are the big red and grey kangaroos that range over the dry grasslands and forests of Australia. Standing up to 2 m [6.5 ft] tall, they are browsers and grazers that now compete for food with cattle and sheep; many hundreds are killed each year. Bounding at speed they can clear fences of their own height. Wallabies – small species of the same family – live in the forests and mountains.

Australia has many other kinds of marsupials, though several have died out since the coming of Europeans. Tree-living koalas live exclusively on eucalyptus leaves. Heavily-built wombats browse in the undergrowth like large rodents, and the fierce-sounding Tasmanian Devils are mild scavengers of the forest floor. There are also many tiny mouse-like, shrew-like, and mole-like species that feed on insects, seeds or honey.

the dominant manufacturing, commercial administrative and legislative centres of their respective states – a position none of them has since relinquished.

In 1901, the states came together to create the Commonwealth of Australia with a federal constitution. Trade between the states became free, and external affairs, defence and immigration policy became federal responsibilities, though health, education, transport, mineral, agricultural and industrial development remained firmly in the hands of each state. Only gradually did powers of taxation give the federal government the opportunity to develop national policies.

The federal capital established at Canberra, in the new Australian Capital Territory, grew from a tiny settlement in 1911 to become a

...eat seat of administration and learning, and ...e largest inland regional commercial centre. ...he federal government's territorial respon-...bilities also include the Northern Territory, ...lf-governing since 1978.

Immigration has changed the ethnic charac-...r of Australia since about 1960. Australian ...ciety now has Greek, Italian, Yugoslav, ...urkish, Lebanese and South-east Asian com-...unities alongside the longer-established ...boriginal, British, Irish, Chinese, Dutch ...d German communities, though the culture ...mains strongly British in flavour. Almost ...)% of the total Australian population live ... Sydney, Melbourne, Adelaide, Brisbane, ...erth and Hobart. Migration within the states ...om inland rural areas to capital cities or ...astal towns leaves many rural communities ...ith an ageing population, while the new min-...g centres have young populations. The most ...apid growth outside new mining centres is ...ccurring in coastal towns through migration ...n retirement and attempts to establish an ...lternative lifestyle by leaving the big cities.

Soon after 1788, small-scale manufacturing ...egan to supply domestic goods and mach-...ery to the colonial community. Inevitably ...anufacturing grew in the colonial seaport ...apitals, especially Sydney and Melbourne, ...hich now have over 60% of all manufactur-...g industry (though only 40% or so of the ...otal population).

Under the Australian Constitution, the fed-...ral government has control over interstate ...nd overseas transport, with the state govern-...ments responsible for regulation within their ...wn borders. Seven railway systems thus exist, ...ach state system focusing on its capital city, ...with the Commonwealth Railways responsible ...or the Trans-Australian, Central Australian ...nd Northern Territory routes. The notorious ...differences in gauges between the states have ...been partially overcome by the construction ...of the standard-gauge links from Brisbane to ...Sydney, Sydney to Melbourne, and Sydney ...to Perth via Broken Hill. The completion of ...the Tarcoola-Alice Springs route will provide ...the basic strategic standard-gauge rail network ...for Australia.

Railways are vital for bulk freight, especially ...mineral ores, coal and wheat. Among the ...busiest of the railways are the iron-ore lines

AUSTRALIAN TERRITORIES

Australia is responsible for a number of terri-tories outside the seven states. In the Indian Ocean Britain transferred to Canberra sover-eignty of Heard Island and McDonald Island (both 1947), and further north the Cocos (Keeling) Islands (1955) and Christmas Island (1958). The federal government also has jurisdiction over the Ashmore and Cartier Islands in the Timor Sea, the Coral Sea Islands Territory, and Norfolk Island in the south-west Pacific – while Lord Howe Island and Macquarie Island are administered by New South Wales and Tasmania respectively. Of all these, only the Cocos Islands (700), Christmas Island (2,300), Norfolk Island (2,000) and Lord Howe Island (300) have per-manent populations.

Australia is also in charge of the largest sector of Antarctica, a continent protected from military and nuclear pollution under international agreement since 1991. A mem-ber of ANZUS since 1951, Australia has re-viewed its own defence position since New Zealand banned US Navy nuclear warships in 1985.

in the north-west of Western Australia. Most cattle and sheep, however, are carried by 'road trains' – a powerful unit pulling several trailers. A rapidly improving highway system links all major cities and towns, providing easy mobility for a largely car-owning population. Some journeys are still difficult, especially when floods wash away sections of road or sand-drifts bury highways. Although 90% of all passenger transport is by road, air services cope with much interstate travel.

Australia is also well served by local broad-casting and television. The radio remains a lifeline for remote settlements dependent on the flying doctor or aerial ambulance, and for many others when floods or bush fires threaten isolated communities.

The worldwide economic depression of the late 1980s was mirrored in Australia by a de-terioration in the country's hitherto buoyant export of agricultural products and its worst unemployment for 60 years. It was against this background that the Labour Prime Minister, Bob Hawke, was elected for an unprecedented fourth term, but in 1991 the worsening economic situation forced his replacement by Paul Keating. Under Keating's administration the key issue of Australia's trade relations, following the extension of the European Community and the success of the Pacific Rim economies, came to the fore, as did the associated question of the country's national identity. With Britain joining the EEC, Australia had looked increasingly to the Pacific Rim countries, and especially to Japan, for its trade. However, fears of a flood of Japanese investment cloaked deeper concerns for many ordinary 'Aussies'. [*Map pages 34–5*] ■

AREA 7,686,850 sq km [2,967,893 sq mls]
POPULATION 17,847,000
CAPITAL (POPULATION) Canberra (310,000)
GOVERNMENT Federal constitutional monarchy
ETHNIC GROUPS White 95%, Aboriginal 1.5%, Asian 1.3%
LANGUAGES English (official)
RELIGIONS Christianity (Roman Catholic 26%, Anglican 24%, other 20%), Islam, Buddhism, Judaism
CURRENCY Australian dollar = 100 cents

AUSTRIA

A mountainous country, more Alpine even than Switzerland and with over 35% forested, Austria has two-thirds of its territory and rather less than a third of the population within the eastern Alps, which extend in a series of longitudinal ridges from the Swiss border in the west almost to Vienna in the east. The longitudinal valleys between the ridges accommodate much of the Alpine population, but are less effective than might be expected as routes of internal communication. Transverse routes, for example the Linz-Klagenfurt and Vienna-Semmering, are vital internal links across the eastern Alps to

the valleys and basins of Steiermark a[nd] Kärnten. The rail and motorway routes ov[er] the 1,371 m [4,500 ft] Brenner Pass are mo[st] intensively used, but these benefit neighbo[urs] rather than Austria.

ECONOMY AND RESOURCES

Austria's lowlands include a section of t[he] northern Alpine foreland, which narrows ea[st]wards towards Vienna and contains t[he] Danube basin. This is Austria's most impo[r]tant east-west route with rail, motorway a[nd] river navigation leading through Vienna [to] Budapest and beyond. Another importa[nt] lowland is the Burgenland, a rich farming are[a] bordering the eastern Alps and facing sout[h]east towards Hungary.

Unlike Switzerland, Austria has importa[nt] heavy industries based in large part on i[n]digenous resources. The mountains are [a] major source of hydroelectric power. O[il] and natural gas occur predominantly in th[e] Vienna Basin and are supplemented b[y] imports from the former Soviet republics an[d] from German refineries. Germany, sharin[g] many cultural links as well as languag[e] remains by far the most important tradin[g] partner. Minerals occur in the eastern Alp[s] notably iron ore in Steiermark (Styria); iro[n] and steel production is located both a[t] Donawitz (near Leoben) in the mountain[s] and also in the Alpine foreland which ha[s] become a major centre of metal, chemica[l] engineering and vehicle manufacturing indus[t]ries. Various industrial plants are also estab[lished around Vienna.

The capital stands at a major Europea[n] crossroads where the Danube is joined b[y] the Moravian Gate route from the north[ern lowlands of Europe, and by the Alpine route through the Semmering Pass. A cit[y] of political as well as cultural and artisti[c] importance, Vienna is home to OPEC, th[e] International Atomic Energy Agency and th[e] UN Industrial Development Organization[, among others, and contains one-fifth o[f] Austria's population.

HISTORY AND POLITICS

A federal republic comprising nine states (*Länder*) – including the capital, Vienna – Austria's present boundaries derive from the

rsailles Treaty of 1919, which dissolved the
astro-Hungarian Empire. It was absorbed
the German Reich in 1938, occupied by
e Allies in 1945 and recovered its full in-
pendence in 1955.

Like most European countries, Austria
perienced low population growth or even
slight reduction in the 1960s and 1970s.
'ithin the country, decline has been greatest
the east, while the west has gained from a
gher birth rate, and also from the settlement
refugees and the industrialization of the
irol since World War II.

Austria's neutrality was enshrined in the
onstitution in 1955, but unlike Switzerland it
as not been frightened to take sides on cer-
in issues. A member of EFTA since 1960, in
994 two-thirds of the population voted in
vour of joining the EU and on 1 January
995 Austria, along with Finland and Sweden,
ecame a member. The EU now has15 mem-
er countries. [*Map page 15*] ■

AREA 83,850 sq km [32,374 sq mls]
POPULATION 7,918,000
CAPITAL (POPULATION) Vienna (1,560,000)
GOVERNMENT Federal republic
ETHNIC GROUPS Austrian 93%, Yugoslav 2%,
Turkish, German
LANGUAGES German (official)
RELIGIONS Christianity (Roman Catholic
78%, Protestant 6%), Islam
CURRENCY Schilling = 100 Groschen

AZERBAIJAN

The Azerbaijani Republic is a country,
facing the Caspian Sea to the east, in
south-western Asia. It includes an area called
the Nakhichevan Autonomous Republic (population 300,000), which is completely cut off
from the rest of Azerbaijan by Armenian
territory. The Caucasus Mountains border
Russia in the north. Another highland region,
including the Little Caucasus Mountains and
part of the rugged Armenian plateau, is in the

south-west. Between these regions lies a broad
plain drained by the River Kura which flows
into the Caspian Sea.

Azerbaijan has hot summers and cool winters. The rainfall is low on the plains, ranging
from about 130 mm to 380 mm [5 in to 15 in]
per year. The annual rainfall is much higher in
the highlands and on the subtropical south-
eastern coast.

ECONOMY AND RESOURCES

Though much of Azerbaijan is semi-arid –
there is also a large tract below sea level – it
nevertheless grows crops such as cotton,
grains, rice and grapes, with fishing also
important, though the Caspian Sea has
become increasingly polluted. With its economy in disarray since the break-up of the
Soviet Union, Azerbaijan now ranks among
the world's 'lower-middle-income' countries.

Oil is still the mainstay of Azerbaijan's revenue. It was being collected by the Caspian
Sea near Baku over 1,000 years ago, and
burning natural gas leaking from the ground
gave the area its name, 'Land of eternal fire'.
Today, along with industries both traditional
(carpets, timber, iron) and modern (cement,
aluminium, chemicals), it makes the country's
economy a viable one. Under Communism,
most property and economic activity were
under government control, but the government is now encouraging private enterprise.

HISTORY AND POLITICS

In ancient times, the area which is now
Azerbaijan was invaded many times. In AD
642, Arab armies introduced Islam. But most
modern Azerbaijanis are descendants of
Persians and Turkic peoples, who migrated to
the area from the east by the 9th century. The
area later came under Mongol rule between
the 13th and 15th centuries, and then the
Persian Safavid dynasty.

In the 18th century, Russia began to
expand. By the early 19th century, Azerbaijan
was under Russian rule. After the Russian
Revolution of 1917, attempts were made to
form a Transcaucasian Federation made up of
Armenia, Azerbaijan and Georgia. When this
failed, Azerbaijanis set up an independent
state. But Russian forces occupied the area in
1920. In 1922, the Communists set up a

Transcaucasian Republic consisting of Armenia, Azerbaijan and Georgia under Russian control, then in 1936 the three areas became separate Soviet Socialist Republics within the Soviet Union.

In the late 1980s, the government of the Soviet Union began to introduce reforms, giving the people more freedom, and when the Soviet Union was voted out of existence in 1991, Azerbaijan became an independent nation.

Since independence, economic progress has been slow, partly because of civil unrest in Nagorno-Karabakh, a region within Azerbaijan, where the majority of the people are Christian Armenians. In 1992, Armenia occupied the area between its eastern border and Nagorno-Karabakh, while ethnic Armenians took over Nagorno-Karabakh. This conflict led to large migrations of Armenians and Azerbaijanis. A cease-fire was agreed in 1994, with about 20% of Azerbaijan territory under Armenian control. [*Map page 22*] ■

AREA 86,600 sq km [33,436 sq mls]
POPULATION 7,472,000
CAPITAL (POPULATION) Baku (1,149,000)
GOVERNMENT Federal multiparty republic
ETHNIC GROUPS Azerbaijani 83%, Russian 6%, Armenian 6%, Lezgin, Avar, Ukrainian, Tatar
LANGUAGES Azerbaijani (official)
RELIGIONS Islam
CURRENCY Manat = 100 gopik

AZORES

Part of the Mid-Atlantic Ridge, the Azores are nine large and several small islands situated about 1,200 km [745 mls] west of Lisbon. They can be divided into three widely separated groups: São Miguel (759 sq km [293 sq mls] out of a total area of 2,247 sq km [868 sq mls]) and Santa Maria are the most easterly; 160 km [100 mls] to the north-west is the central cluster of Terceira, Graciosa,

São Jorge, Pico and Faial; another 240 k [150 mls] to the north-west are Flores and t most isolated significant island of Corvo.

Of relatively recent volcanic origin, t islands are mostly mountainous, with hi cliffs and narrow beaches of shell gravel dark volcanic sand. The highest mounta (and Portugal's highest) is Pico Alto, a vc canic cone of 2,351 m [7,713 ft].

The name Azores means 'islands of tl hawks' and birds of prey are a common sigh

ECONOMY AND RESOURCES
Well watered with an equable, temperate cl mate and fertile soils, the economy of tl Azores is based predominantly on agricultur although tourism is playing an increasing important part. All flat or slightly sloping lan is cultivated with with food crops or vine Small-scale farming and fishing are the mai occupations, with fruit, wine, tea, tobacco an canned fish exported (mostly to Portugal).

HISTORY AND POLITICS
The islands were discovered in the 15th cer tury by Portuguese navigators and were late settled by Flemish knights. There were n indigenous people and the present populatio of 238,000 is mostly of Portuguese stock although later settlers of Moorish origin fron the Algarve and the Alentejo, Jewish farmer from the Minho and Bretons have all left thei cultural mark on the islands. Since 1976 the have been governed as three districts of Port ugal – Angra do Heroísmo, Ponta Delgada an Horta – making up an autonomous region rep resented by five members in the Portugues Parliament. The capital is Ponta Delgada or the island of São Miguel, which hosts mor than half the total population. [*Map page 2*] ■

AREA 2,247 sq km [868 sq mls]
POPULATION 238,000
CAPITAL (POPULATION) Ponta Delgada (21,000)
GOVERNMENT Portuguese Autonomous Region
ETHNIC GROUPS Portuguese
LANGUAGES Portuguese
RELIGIONS Christianity
CURRENCY Portuguese currency

BAHAMAS

BAHRAIN

The Bahamas consists of a coral-limestone archipelago of 29 inhabited low-lying lands, plus over 3,000 uninhabited cays, reefs and rocks, centred on the Grand Bahama Bank off eastern Florida and Cuba. The island of San Salvador was the first landfall in the New World of Christopher Columbus on 12 October 1492.

Over 90% of its 3.6 million visitors a year are Americans, and tourism now accounts for more than half the nation's revenues, involving over 40% of the total workforce. Offshore banking, financial services and a large 'open registry' merchant fleet also offset the imports (including most foodstuffs), giving the country a relatively high standard of living. Nassau and Freeport have commercial shipping ports and international airports, Freeport being the country's leading industrial centre. The remainder of the non-administrative population works mainly in traditional fishing and agriculture, notably citrus fruit production, but fresh vegetables, meat and eggs are produced for the domestic market. Rum is produced for export in the distillery on the island of New Providence.

Though the Bahamas is an independent democracy, it is also élitist. It has developed close ties with the USA since independence from Britain in 1973. However, relations with the USA were strained when the country was used as a tax haven for drug traffickers in the 1980s, with government ministers implicated in drug-related corruption. [Map page 30] ■

AREA 13,880 sq km [5,359 sq mls]
POPULATION 272,000
CAPITAL (POPULATION) Nassau (172,196)
GOVERNMENT Constitutional monarchy
ETHNIC GROUPS Black 73%, Mulatto 14%, White 13%
LANGUAGES English, English Creole 80%
RELIGIONS Christianity 95%
CURRENCY Bahamian dollar = 100 cents

The country is made up of 35 small islands, the largest of which is called Bahrain, located in the Arabian Gulf close to the coast of Saudi Arabia. Bahrain island is about 48 km [30 mls] long and 16 km [10 mls] wide at its broadest.

This relatively liberal state led the region in developing oil production after discovery in 1932. When production waned in the 1970s it diversified into other sectors: its aluminium-smelting plant is the Gulf's largest non-oil industrial complex, and the moves into banking, communications and leisure came when the cosmopolitan centre of Beirut was plunging into chaos. Banking now accounts for some 15% of GDP, while oil takes as much as 20% – though far more of government revenues. Most of the land is barren, but soil imports have created some fertile areas.

Bahrain does have problems, however. Tension between the Sunni and majority Shiite population (the latter favouring an Islamic republic) has been apparent since before independence, and during the First Gulf War Iran responded to Bahrain's support for Iraq by reiterating its claims to the territory. In 1986 a rumbling dispute began with Qatar over claims to a cluster of oil-rich islands, reefs and sandbars; the disagreement was taken by Qatar to the International Court of Justice in 1991. [Map page 22] ■

AREA 678 sq km [262 sq mls]
POPULATION 549,000
CAPITAL (POPULATION) Manama (or Al Manamah, 152,000)
GOVERNMENT Monarchy (emirate) with a cabinet appointed by the Emir
ETHNIC GROUPS Bahraini Arab 68%, Persian, Indian and Pakistani 25%, other Arab 4%, European 3%
LANGUAGES Arabic
RELIGIONS Islam 85%, Christianity 7%
CURRENCY Bahrain dinar = 1,000 fils

BANGLADESH

Battered by a relentless cycle of flood and famine, and plagued by political corruption and a succession of military coups, Bangladesh is perhaps Asia's most pitiful country, once known as Golden Bengal (Sonar Bangla) for its treasures but gradually plundered and now pushed near to the bottom of the Third World pile. It is – apart from statistically irrelevant city-states and small island countries – the most crowded nation on Earth: the 1994 figure was a density of some 818 people per sq km [2,119 per sq ml], well ahead of the next realistic rival Taiwan (574 per sq km [1,486 per sq ml]) and far greater than Europe's contender Belgium (330 per sq km [854 per sq ml]), which in any case has a much larger urban proportion. The world's tenth biggest population – a figure expected to increase by another 30 million or more by the year 2000 – lives on an area of precarious flat lowlands smaller than the US states of Illinois or Iowa.

Apart from a south-eastern fringe of forested ridges east of Chittagong, Bangladesh consists almost entirely of lowlands – mainly the (greater) eastern part of the large delta formed jointly by the Ganges and Brahmaputra. The western part (now West Bengal, in India) is largely the 'dying delta' – its land a little higher and less often flooded, its deltaic channels seldom flushed by floodwaters. In contrast, the heart of Bangladesh, following the main Ganges channel and the wide Brahmaputra, is the 'active delta'. Frequently flooded, with changing channels that are hazardous to life, health and property, the rivers also renew soil fertility with silt washed down from as far away as the mountains of Nepal and Tibet. Indeed, while deforestation in the Himalayan foothills has caused enough silt to form new 'islands' for the burgeoning Bangladeshi population, it has also led to the blocking of some waterways (60% of the country's internal trade is carried by boat), danger to fish stocks, and the increased risk of flooding.

ECONOMY AND RESOURCES

The alluvial silts of the 'active delta' yield u to three rice crops a year as well as the world best jute, and though Bangladesh is no only the third largest producer in a declinir market, high-quality fibre is exported t India; jute and cotton are processed als in post-independence mills, for example ; Narayanganj. There is a large hydroelectr plant at Karnaphuli reservoir, and a moder paper industry using bamboo from the hill Substantial reserves of coal await exploitatior but a more realistic development may be th construction of a canal 320 km [200 mls] lon to transfer water from the flooding Brahma putra to the Ganges, in order to increase sup plies to India's drought-affected areas. Th scheme, like so many others, has run into th political problems and mutual suspicion tha dog the area.

HISTORY AND POLITICS

Bangladesh was until 1971 East Pakistan, the oriental wing of the Muslim state set up by the partition of British India in 1947. Separatec by 1,600 km [1,000 mls] of India from the politically-dominant, Urdu- and Punjabi speaking western province, the easterners fel the victims of ethnic and economic discrimi nation. In 1971 resentment turned to war when Bengali irregulars, considerably aidec and abetted by Indian troops, convened the independent state of 'Free Bengal', with Sheikh Mujibur Rahman as head of state.

The Sheikh's assassination in 1975 – during one of four military coups in the first 11 years of independence – led finally to a takeover by General Zia Rahman, who created an Islamic state before himself being murdered in 1981. General Ershad took over in a coup the following year and resigned as army chief in 1986 to take up the civilian presidency, lifting martial law; but by 1990 protests from supporters of his two predecessors toppled him from power and, after the first free parliamentary elections since independence, a coalition government was formed in 1991.

The new authority faced not only the long-term problems of a debt-ridden, aid-reliant country where corruption is a way of life: it also had to deal with the consequences of the worst cyclone in living memory and, from

THE DELTA CYCLONES

Most of Bangladesh is almost unbelievably low and flat, and the people of the coastal fringes are all too familiar with the cyclones from the Bay of Bengal. Even so, 1991 brought the worst in memory: the official death toll was a staggering 132,000 (it may well have been higher), and more than 5 million people, almost all of them poor peasants already living on or below the poverty line, were made homeless.

The cyclone caused inestimable damage to the area around Chittagong: crops and fields were inundated with sea water; herds of cattle and goats and flocks of poultry were decimated; dykes were breached and trees ripped up; wells filled up with salt water. The struggling survivors were victims of dysentery and cholera, dehydration and malnutrition. However generous, aid rarely reached the most needy, as it was sifted and filtered down the line despite the efforts of charity administrators. Corrupt practices, like cyclones, are endemic to Bangladesh; funds allocated for concrete cyclone-proof shelters, for example, were appropriated by individuals and government officials.

As with most natural disasters – earthquakes, volcanic eruptions, tidal waves, landslips – the cyclones usually affect countries that are least equipped to deal with them and least able to withstand the losses inflicted.

widespread. However, Bangladesh's biggest problem remains a single one: it has far too many people. [*Map page 23*] ■

AREA	144,000 sq km [55,598 sq mls]
POPULATION	117,787,000
CAPITAL (POPULATION)	Dhaka (6,105,000)
GOVERNMENT	Multiparty republic
ETHNIC GROUPS	Bengali 98%, tribal groups
LANGUAGES	Bengali (official)
RELIGIONS	Islam 87%, Hinduism 12%, Buddhism, Christianity
CURRENCY	Taka = 100 paisas

BARBADOS

The most eastern Caribbean country, and first in line for the region's seasonal hurricanes, Barbados is underlain with limestone and capped with coral. Mt Hillaby (340 m [1,115 ft]), the highest point, is fringed by marine terraces marking stages in the island's emergence from the sea. The wet season stretches from June to November, but annual rainfall varies spatially – the higher interior receiving the most. Soils are fertile and deep, easily cultivated except in the eroded Scotland district of the north-east.

Sugar production, using African slave labour, began soon after Barbados became British in 1627. Cane plantations take up most of the cropped land (over half the total), but at 17% now contributes far less than previously to exports. Manufactures now constitute the largest exports, though tourism is the growth sector and the leading industry (432,000 visitors in 1990, 28% from the US and 23% from the UK), and is the most likely future for this relatively prosperous but extremely overcrowded island; at 607 per sq km [1,535 per sq ml], it is one of the most densely populated rural societies in the world (45% urban).

Despite political stability (the island became an independent state within the Commonwealth in 1966) and advanced welfare and education services, emigration (as from many

1992, the increasing prospect of war with Burma, triggered by Rangoon's treatment of the Rohingyas, its Muslim minority. As far back as 1978 Bangladesh took in some 300,000 Rohingyas fleeing persecution, and while most went back, the emigrants of the 1990s are unlikely to follow suit.

Meanwhile, both nations amassed troops on a border that snakes its way through misty hills, mahogany forests and rubber plantations. Defence spending is already too high, and funds should go on other areas: for example, Bangladesh's hospital capacity (one bed for each 5,000 population) is the world's worst. As in West Bengal, an urban educated élite holds the real power, and corruption is

West Indian countries) is high, notably to the US and UK. [*Map page 30*] ■

AREA 430 sq km [160 sq mls]
POPULATION 261,000
CAPITAL (POPULATION) Bridgetown (6,700)
GOVERNMENT Constitutional monarchy
ETHNIC GROUPS Black 92%, White 3%, Mulatto 3%
LANGUAGES English (official), Creole
RELIGIONS Christianity (Protestant 65%, Roman Catholic 4%)
CURRENCY Barbados dollar = 100 cents

BELARUS

The Republic of Belarus ('White Russia') is a landlocked country in Eastern Europe, formerly part of the Soviet Union. The land is low-lying and mostly flat. In the south, much of the land is marshy. This area contains Europe's largest marsh and peat bog, the Pripet (Prypyat) Marshes. A hilly region extends from north-east to south-west through the centre of the country, which includes the highest point in Belarus, situated near the capital, Minsk. This hill reaches a height of only 346 m [112 ft] above sea level.

Forests cover about a third of the country, but farmland and pasture have replaced most of the original forest. The colder north has such trees as alder, birch and pine, whereas ash, oak and hornbeam grow in the warmer south. The climate of Belarus is affected by the moderating influence of the Baltic Sea and continental conditions to the east. Winters are cold and the summers are warm.

ECONOMY AND RESOURCES

The World Bank classifies Belarus as an 'upper-middle-income' economy. Like other former republics of the Soviet Union, it faces many problems in working to turn a government-run economy into a free-market one. Though mainly agricultural – 46% of the land is used efficiently for flax, potatoes,

cereals, dairying, pigs and peat digging – also has the largest petrochemical complex Europe and the giant Belaz heavy-truc plants; these, however, like its many lig industries, are heavily reliant on Russia f electricity and raw materials, including stec More relentlessly integrated into the Sovi economy than any republic, Belarus was al the most dependent on trade, at nearly 70%

HISTORY AND POLITICS

Slavic people settled in what is now Belar about 1,500 years ago. In the 9th century, th area became part of the first East Slavic stat Kievan Rus. Mongol armies overran the are in the 13th century, and, later, Belarus be came part of Lithuania. In 1569, Lithuani including Belarus, became part of Polanc In the 18th century, Russia took over mos of eastern Poland, including Belarus, yet th people kept their individuality. Belarus be came an independent republic in 1918, bu Russia invaded the country and in 1919 Communist state was set up. In 1922, Belaru became a founder republic of the USSR.

Most observers were surprised when thi most conservative and Communist-dominatec of parliaments declared independence on 2⁵ August 1991, forcing the Party president tc stand down. The quiet state of the Europeai Soviet Union, it played a supporting role in it deconstruction and in the creation of the CIS the latter's first meeting was in Minsk – nov its capital. However, in a referendum in May 1995, the people voted for economic inte gration with Russia and adopted Russian as ar official language. It was also agreed that the former Soviet flag for Belarus would eventu ally be restored. [*Map page 5*] ■

AREA 207,600 sq km [80,154 sq mls]
POPULATION 10,163,000
CAPITAL (POPULATION) Minsk (1,613,600)
GOVERNMENT Multiparty republic
ETHNIC GROUPS Belarussian 80%, Russian 13%, Polish 4%, Ukrainian 3%, Jewish 1%
LANGUAGES Belarussian, Russian
RELIGIONS Christianity (mainly Belarussian Orthodox, with Roman Catholics in the west and Evangelicals in the south-west)
CURRENCY Belarussian rouble = 100 kopeks

BELGIUM

Physically Belgium may be divided into the uplands of the Ardennes and the lowland plains, which are drained by the Meuse to the Rhine through the Netherlands, and by the Schelde through Antwerp to the North Sea. The Ardennes, rising in Belgium to about 700 m [2,296 ft] at the highest point, is an area predominantly of moorland, peat bogs and woodland.

Lowland Belgium has varied soils, including some poor-quality sands in the Campine (Kempenland) area near the Dutch frontier, supporting only heaths and woodland. But in general careful cultivation, sound husbandry and attention to drainage have provided good soils; lowland farming is prosperous, with a strong emphasis on grain crops, potatoes and other vegetables, hops, sugar and fodder beet, with hay.

Few hedges exist in the farmed landscape and the holdings are small with intensive cultivation. Traditionally many factory workers of the towns also had a smallholding. There is a small area of polders near the coast, in all less than 500 sq km [200 sq mls], which is rich agricultural land. Outside the towns the density of rural settlement is high.

ECONOMY AND RESOURCES
No minerals other than coal exist in significant quantities and the Belgian emphasis on manufacturing is based on the import of raw materials. The Ardennes includes the country's most productive coalfield (the Campine) in the Sambre-Meuse Valley, centred on the cities of Charleroi and Liège. Charleroi is a coal-mining and metallurgical city while Liège is the centre of the iron industry. The Campine coalfield continues into the Netherlands and Germany, but production has declined in recent years as uneconomic mines have been closed.

Still of major importance, however, is the textile industry, which has existed in the towns of Flanders from medieval times and in its

THE GREAT DIVIDE

Belgium has always been an uneasy marriage of two peoples: the majority Flemings, speaking a very close relative of Dutch, and the Walloons, who speak French (rather than the old Walloon variation of French). The dividing line between the two communities runs east-west, just south of Brussels, with the capital itself officially bilingual.

Since the inception of the country, the Flemings have caught up and overtaken the Walloons in cultural influence as well as in numbers of people. In 1932 the Belgian government was designated bilingual, and in 1970 the country was effectively splintered into four parts. In the far eastern frontier areas German is the official language; Brussels remained bilingual but its province of Brabant divided; and the other eight provinces were split into four Fleming and four Walloon – with only the dominant language being official.

Belgium has three governments: the national authority in Brussels, and regional assemblies for both Flanders and Wallonia. During the 1980s, as power gradually devolved from the centre to the regions in crucial aspects of education, transport and the economy, the tension between the 'Germanic' Flemings and the 'Latin' Walloons increased in government.

The various coalitions of Dutch- and French-speaking Christian Democrats and Socialists – which had held together for more than a decade under the astute stewardship of Prime Minister Wilfried Martens – was seriously undermined by the results of the emergency election of November 1991, with many experts predicting the break-up of the national state into two virtually independent nations before the end of the century – leaving Brussels (ironically the focal point of European integration) as a political island.

modern form includes a wide range of products. It is associated particularly with Ghent and Bruges, though these are equally renowned for their medieval architecture. Industry has been diversified and some manufactures, such as glass, are well known in the international market.

It is this part of the country that makes Belgium not only one of Europe's most crowded nations – with 330 people per sq km [856 per sq ml] – but the most 'urban' of any reasonably sized independent state, with an official figure of 97%.

Belgium's main port is Antwerp, much modernized since 1956. The main industrial centres are served by ship canals, including one of 29 km [18 mls] from Ghent to Terneuzen. Constructed in 1825–7, it can take ships of as much as 61,000 tonnes in capacity. There are canals to Bruges from the North Sea at Zeebrugge, and also to Brussels, both completed in 1922. Barges of 1,372 tonnes capacity can use the 125 km [79 mls] Albert Canal to Liège, opened in 1939, and the Meuse and Sambre are being widened or deepened to take barges of similar capacity. Comparable improvements are being made in the River Schelde between Antwerp and Ghent, and in the Brussels-Charleroi Canal. The North Sea ports of Ostend and Zeebrugge cater for overseas trade.

Now, as in past centuries, the lowlands of Belgium, and particularly the city of Brussels (headquarters of the European Union, of which Belgium was a founder member), remain a major focus of commercial and political life in Europe.

HISTORY AND POLITICS

Throughout a chequered and stormy history as the 'cockpit of Europe', Belgium's fine cities, including Brussels, Ghent and Bruges, have maintained their churches and public buildings, though some have been rebuilt after wars. Following the Napoleonic Wars, from 1815, Belgium and the Netherlands were united as the 'Low Countries', but in 1830, a famous year of ferment in Europe, a National Congress proclaimed independence from the Dutch and in 1831 Prince Leopold of Saxe-Coburg was 'imported from Germany' to become king.

At the Treaty of London in 1839 (which the Netherlands also signed), Britain, France and Russia guaranteed the independence of Belgium – and the famous 'scrap of paper' was upheld when Germany invaded Belgium in August 1914. For nearly four years th fields of Flanders became the battlefield c Europe.

The division between Belgium and th Netherlands rests on history and sentimen rather than on any physical features. Belgiun is predominantly a Roman Catholic coun try, while the Netherlands is traditionall Protestant (though about 34% of the popu lation are Roman Catholic). Both were neutra in foreign policy, but in 1940 they were in vaded by Nazi Germany and remained unde occupation until September 1944.

Since the end of World War II economi progress has been marked, for the geographi cal advantages Belgium possesses have given i a position of significance in Europe, especiall in the EU. The unity of the people, however is less secure, and in the early 1990s ther were growing signs that the fragile alliance which had preserved the nation for so long – and under such arduous circumstances – was beginning to crack.

Of the country's universities, Louvain (Catholic and Belgium's oldest, dating from 1426) provides courses in both Flemish and French; of the universities founded in the 19th century, Ghent (1816) is Flemish and Liège (1817) is French-speaking. At Brussels' Free University (founded in 1834) the courses are mainly in French, but provision is made for Flemish speakers. Gradually, the griev ances of the Flemish speakers have been removed and in 1974 regional councils were established for Flanders, Wallonia and the Brussels district. [*Map page 11*] ∎

AREA 30,510 sq km [11,780 sq mls]
POPULATION 10,080,000
CAPITAL (POPULATION) Brussels (Bruxelles or Brussel, 954,000)
GOVERNMENT Federal constitutional monarchy
ETHNIC GROUPS Belgian 91% (Fleming 55%, Walloon 32%), Italian, French, Dutch, Turkish, Moroccan
LANGUAGES Dutch, French, German (all official)
RELIGIONS Christianity (Roman Catholic 86%), Islam
CURRENCY Belgian franc = 100 centimes

BELIZE

Larger than El Salvador but with only a fraction of its population, Belize is a sparsely populated enclave on the Caribbean coast of Central America, whose head of state is Britain's monarch. A governor-general represents the monarch, while an elected government, headed by a prime minister, actually rules the country.

Behind the swampy coastal plain in the south, the land rises to the low Maya Mountains, which reach a height of 1,120 m [3,674 ft] at Victoria Peak. Northern Belize is mostly low-lying and swampy. The main river, the River Belize, flows across the centre of the country. Offshore lies the world's second biggest coral reef after the Great Barrier Reef.

Belize has a humid tropical climate. Temperatures are high throughout the year and the average yearly rainfall ranges from 1,300 mm [51 in] in the north to over 3,800 mm [150 in] in the south, with February to May the driest months. Hurricanes may sometimes hit the coast, and it was the hurricane damage to Belize City in 1961 that led to the decision to move the capital to Belmopan in 1970.

ECONOMY AND RESOURCES
The World Bank classifies Belize as a 'lower-middle-income' developing country. Its economy is based on agriculture, and sugar cane is the chief commercial crop and export. Other crops include bananas, beans, citrus fruits, maize and rice. Forestry, fishing and tourism are other important activities, but there are few manufacturing industries.

HISTORY AND POLITICS
Between about 300 BC and AD 1000, Belize was part of the Maya empire, which extended into Mexico, Guatemala, Honduras and El Salvador. But this civilization had declined long before Spanish explorers reached the coast in the early 16th century.

Spain claimed the area, although no Spaniards settled there. Instead, Spain ruled the area as part of Guatemala. Shipwrecked British sailors founded the first European settlement in the area in 1638. Over the next 150 years, Britain gradually took control of Belize, using slaves to open up the territory. Spain's last attempt to reassert its rule by force was defeated in 1798. In 1862, the area, then known as British Honduras, became a British colony. The country was renamed Belize in 1973 and it became fully independent in 1981.

Guatemala, which had claimed Belize since the early 19th century, objected to the country becoming independent and British troops remained in the country to prevent a possible invasion. In 1983, Guatemala reduced its claim to the southern fifth of Belize, and in the early 1990s improvements in relations with Guatemala, which finally agreed to recognize Belize's independence in 1992, led Britain to announce its decision to withdraw its troops by the end of 1993. [*Map page 30*] ■

AREA 22,960 sq km [8,865 sq mls]
POPULATION 210,000
CAPITAL (POPULATION) Belmopan (5,000)
GOVERNMENT Constitutional monarchy
ETHNIC GROUPS Mestizo (Spanish-Indian) 44%, Creole (mainly African American) 30%, Mayan Indian 11%, Garifuna (Black-Carib Indian) 7%, White 4%, East Indian 3%
LANGUAGES English (official)
RELIGIONS Christianity (Roman Catholic 58%, Protestant 29%), Hinduism 2%
CURRENCY Belize dollar = 100 cents

BENIN

Previously called Dahomey (the name of an old cultured kingdom centred on Abomey), Benin, one of Africa's smallest countries, extends some 620 km [390 mls] north to south, although the coastline is a mere 100 km [62 mls] long. Lagoons line the coast, and the country has no natural harbours. The harbour at Cotonou, Benin's main port and chief commercial centre, is artificial.

Behind the lagoons is a flat plain partly covered by rainforests. About 80 km [50 mls] inland, there is a large marshy depression. In central Benin, the land rises to low plateaus. The highest land is in the north-west. Northern Benin is covered by savanna (grassland with scattered trees), the habitat of such animals as buffaloes, elephants and lions. The north has two national parks, the Penjari and the 'W', which Benin shares with Burkina Faso and Niger.

ECONOMY AND RESOURCES
Today's dominant tribe in Benin is the Fon, who (with the Yoruba) occupy the more populous and fertile south, mostly as subsistence farmers, growing yams, cassava, sweet potatoes and vegetables. In the central parts and some of the north are the Bariba, renowned for their horsemanship, and the Somba, while some Fulani still follow the increasingly precarious nomadic lifestyle in the far north, the least populated of the regions.

Benin has little to sell, its main exports being palm-oil produce, cotton and groundnuts, with the timber from the central rainforest belt depleting rapidly. Fees from Niger's transit trade through Cotonou are an important additional source of revenue, but illegal trade with Nigeria is also rife. Offshore oil began production in 1982, but output peaked three years later and the industry has since been hampered by low prices.

HISTORY AND POLITICS
After the Dutch expelled the Portuguese from the Gold Coast in 1642, they established their West African headquarters at Ouidah where, until 1961, there was a tiny Portuguese enclave. Several million slaves were shipped from here, mainly to Brazil, where Dahomean customs survive today among blacks there. Because of early European contact, and through returned ex-slaves, coastal Benin early acquired an educated élite, as did Senegal, Sierra Leone and Gabon.

Rival tribal kingdoms flourished in this part of Africa for centuries until the French began establishing their presence from around 1850, creating a colony (Dahomey) in 1892 and formally making the country part of French West Africa in 1904. Before that, from the

13th century, the area had been the wester part of the kingdom (or empire) of Benin centred on the Nigerian city of that nam and famous for its life-size brass heads an plaques and for its ruler, the Oba, from th 15th century. Situated east of Lagos, Benin City is now capital of the Nigerian state c Bendel.

Following independence from France i 1960, the country experienced a series o coups and power struggles, going through 1 changes of government in 12 years. Then during the military single-party regime o General Mathieu Kerekou, who in 197 introduced 'scientific socialism' (and the fol lowing year dropped the name Dahomey) Benin found itself sitting awkwardly as a Marxist state between the market-oriente economies of Togo and Nigeria. Kerekou offi cially abandoned his path in 1989, and in 1990 he was forced to concede multiparty elections in a referendum. He was roundly beaten in March 1991, when the country enjoyed a relatively peaceful return to democ racy for the first time in nearly two decades. [*Map page 32*] ■

AREA 112,620 sq km [43,483 sq mls]
POPULATION 5,246,000
CAPITAL (POPULATION) Porto-Novo (179,000)
GOVERNMENT Multiparty republic
ETHNIC GROUPS Fon, Adja, Bariba, Yoruba, Fulani, Somba
LANGUAGES French (official)
RELIGIONS Traditional beliefs 60%, Christianity 23%, Islam 15%
CURRENCY CFA franc = 100 centimes

BERMUDA

Comprising about 150 small islands, the coral caps of ancient submarine volcanoes rising over 4,000 m [13,000 ft] from the ocean floor, Bermuda is situated 920 km [570 mls] east of Cape Hatteras in North arolina. Some 20 are inhabited, the vast majority of the population living on the biggest land of Great Bermuda, 21 km [13 mls] long nd connected to the other main islands y bridges and causeways. The capital, Hamilton, stands beside a deep harbour on Great Bermuda.

ECONOMY AND RESOURCES

The pleasant climate, coral sand beaches, historic buildings and pastel-coloured townships attract nearly 505,500 tourists each year, mainly from the USA; but if tourism is the mainstay of the economy, the islands are also a tax haven for overseas companies and individuals. Food and energy needs dominate imports, while (legal) drugs and medicines account for over 50% of exports – though services are the main earners, offsetting a large deficit and giving the islanders an annual per capita income of US$27,800 (1994), the third highest in the world.

HISTORY AND POLITICS

Uninhabited when discovered by the Spaniard Juan Mermúdez in 1503, the islands were taken over by the British more than a century later (following a shipwreck) and slaves brought in from Virginia to work the land. Today over 60% of the population is of African descent.

Bermuda remains Britain's oldest colony, but with a long tradition of self-government; the parliament dates from 1603. Ties with the US are strong, however, and in 1941 part of the islands was leased for 99 years by Washington for naval and air bases. The government is in regular discussions with the US, UK and Canada over constitutional change, but public opinion continues to oppose moves towards independence ■

AREA 53 sq km [20 sq mls]
POPULATION 63,000
CAPITAL (POPULATION) Hamilton (3,440)
GOVERNMENT British dependency
ETHNIC GROUPS Black 61%, White 37%
LANGUAGES English
RELIGIONS Christianity (Anglican 37%, Roman Catholic 14%, other Christian 25%)
CURRENCY Bermuda dollar = 100 cents

BHUTAN

Geographically, a smaller and even more isolated version of Nepal, the remote mountain kingdom of Bhutan faces many of the same problems and hopes for many of the same solutions – notably the harnessing of hydroelectric power from the Himalayas: India has already built one plant and commissioned two more from King Jigme Singye Wangchuk.

The world's most 'rural' country (less than 6% of the population live in towns and over 90% are dependent on agriculture), Bhutan produces mainly rice and maize as staple crops and fruit and cardamom as cash crops. Timber is important, too, though outweighed by cement and talcum in earning foreign exchange. Despite these activities, plus tourism and stamps, the World Bank ranks Bhutan as one of the world's poorest countries. Aircraft and diesel fuels are its main imports, supplying crucial contacts.

Like Nepal, Bhutan was subject to a series of pro-democracy demonstrations in 1990, but because the protesters were mainly Hindus there has been little political progress in this predominantly Buddhist country. The Hindu minority, mostly Nepali-speakers, maintain they are the victims of discrimination, denied basic rights such as religious freedom and the ownership of property. The monarch is head of both state and government, though foreign affairs are under Indian guidance following a treaty of 1949. [*Map page 23*] ■

AREA 47,000 sq km [18,147 sq mls]
POPULATION 1,614,000
CAPITAL (POPULATION) Thimphu (30,340)
GOVERNMENT Constitutional monarchy
ETHNIC GROUPS Ngalops, Sharchops, Nepalese
LANGUAGES Dzongkha (official, a Tibetan dialect), Sharchop, Bumthap, Nepali and English
RELIGIONS Buddhism 75%, Hinduism 25%
CURRENCY Ngultrum = 100 chetrum

BOLIVIA

By far the larger of South America's two landlocked countries, Bolivia is made up of a wide stretch of the Andes and a long, broad Oriente – part of the south-western fringe of the Amazon basin. The western boundary is the High Cordillera Occidental, crowned by Sajama at 6,542 m [21,464 ft] and many other volcanic peaks. To the east lies the Altiplano, a high plateau which in prehistoric times was a great lake. Eastwards again rises the Cordillera Real, where Illimani, a glacier-covered peak of 6,462 m [21,200 ft], forms a backdrop to La Paz (The Peace), the world's highest capital. In the transmontane region to the north and east lies the huge expanse of the Oriente – foothills and plains extending from the semi-arid Chaco of the south-east through the savanna-like *llanos* of the centre to the high, wetter forests of the northern plains.

ECONOMY AND RESOURCES
Today Bolivia is the poorest of the South American republics, though it has abundant natural resources with large reserves of petroleum, natural gas and many mineral ores. Lack of investment both in these areas and in the agricultural sector does not help the comparatively poor development, but new irrigation schemes in the south-western Oriente may improve local production of staple foods. Over half the working population is engaged in agriculture, but mining still contributes significantly to the country's wealth. However, Bolivia, once the world's leading tin producer, now ranks fifth with 7.6% of the total. Today's main export may well be coca and refined cocaine; the government, with US help and cooperation with neighbours, is trying to stifle the growing industry.

The collapse of the tin market was linked to the record inflation of 1985 – figures vary between 12,000% and over 20,000%, and the 1980–8 average was the world's worst at 483% – though the rates were more stable by the end of the decade.

THE ALTIPLANO

A high, rolling plateau 3,600 m [12,000 ft] above sea level on the Peruvian border of Bolivia, the Altiplano stretches 400 km [250 mls] north to south between the eastern and western cordilleras of the Andes. Surrounded by high, snow-capped peaks, at its north end lies Lake Titicaca, the highest navigable body of water in the world and according to Indian legend the birthplace of the Inca civilization. To the south are smaller lakes, and extensive salt flats representing old lake beds. Though tropical in latitude the Altiplano is cold, windswept and bleak, by any standards a harsh environment, yet over half the population of Bolivia, including a high proportion of native Indians, make it their home.

The natural vegetation is grassland merging at high levels to *puna* – small bushes and trees forming a harsh scrubland. Summer rains and winter snows bring enough moisture to support grass, and the Altiplano is grazed by guanaco and vicuña as well as many smaller herbivores – chinchillas, viscachas and guinea-pigs. Llama and alpaca, domesticated from guanaco-like ancestors, are herded to provide meat and wool for the peasant farmers. Small and tough, the local people are physiologically adapted for life at high altitude, with more blood, more oxygen-carrying haemoglobin and more efficient lungs than the Indians of the foothills.

HISTORY AND POLITICS
In pre-Conquest days Bolivia was the homeland of the Tiahuanaco culture (7th to 11th centuries AD) and was later absorbed into the Inca empire; Quechua, the Inca language, is still spoken by large Amerindian minorities that constitute the highest proportion of any South American country. Famous for its silver mines, the high Andean area was exploited ruthlessly by the Spanish *conquistadores*; the mine at Potosí, discovered in 1545, proved the richest in the world, and Upper Peru (today's highland Bolivia) was for two centuries one of the most densely populated of Spain's American colonies. In 1824 the local population seized their independence, naming

ᴻe country after Simón Bolívar, hero of other ᴼouth American wars of independence. When ᴹe era of silver passed, the economy flagged ᴺd the country began to lose ground to its ᴺeighbours. The Pacific coast was lost to Chile ᴺnd Peru in 1884 and large tracts of the ᴼriente were ceded to Brazil (1903) and ᴾaraguay (1935). Bolivia is renowned for its ᴾolitical volatility: it has suffered 192 coups in 56 years from independence to 1981. Since 982, however, it has had democratically ᴸlected governments. [*Map page 31*] ■

AREA 1,098,580 sq km [424,162 sq mls]
POPULATION 7,237,000
CAPITAL (POPULATION) La Paz (1,126,000)
GOVERNMENT Multiparty republic
ETHNIC GROUPS Mestizo 31%, Quechua 25%, Aymara 17%, White 15%
LANGUAGES Spanish, Aymara, Quechua (all official)
RELIGIONS Christianity (Roman Catholic 94%)
CURRENCY Boliviano = 100 centavos

BOSNIA-HERZEGOVINA

The Republic of Bosnia-Herzegovina is one of the five republics to emerge from the former Federal People's Republic of Yugoslavia. Much of the country is mountainous or hilly, with an arid limestone plateau in the south-west. The River Sava, which forms most of the northern border with Croatia, is a tributary of the River Danube. Because of the country's odd shape, the coastline is limited to a short stretch of 20 km [13 mls] on the Adriatic coast.

Mediterranean conditions, with sunny, dry summers and mild, moist winters, prevail only near the coast. Inland, the weather becomes more severe, with hot, dry summers and bitterly cold, snowy winters. The north has the most severe weather, where forests of beech, oak and pine are found. The south has bare limestone landscapes, interspersed with farm-land and pasture, which together cover nearly half of the country.

ECONOMY AND RESOURCES
The economy of Bosnia-Herzegovina, the least developed of the six republics of the former Yugoslavia apart from Macedonia, was shattered by the war in the early 1990s. Before the war, manufactures were the main exports, including electrical equipment, machinery and transport equipment, and textiles, while farm products included fruits, maize, tobacco, vegetables and wheat. There are reserves of coal and iron ore.

HISTORY AND POLITICS
Slavs settled in the area that is now Bosnia-Herzegovina around 1,400 years ago. In the late 15th century, the area was taken by the Ottoman Turks. Austria-Hungary gained temporary control over Bosnia-Herzegovina in 1878, formally taking over the area in 1908. In 1914, World War I began when Austria-Hungary's Archduke Francis Ferdinand was assassinated in Sarajevo.

In 1918, Bosnia-Herzegovina became part of the Kingdom of the Serbs, Croats and Slovenes, which was renamed Yugoslavia in 1929. Germany occupied the area during World War II. But from 1945, Communist governments ruled Yugoslavia as a federation containing six republics, one of which was Bosnia-Herzegovina. In the 1980s, the country faced problems as Communist policies proved unsuccessful and differences arose between the country's ethnic groups.

In 1990, free elections were held in Bosnia-Herzegovina and non-Communists won a majority. A Muslim, Alija Izetbegovic, was elected president. In 1991, Croatia and Slovenia, other parts of the former Yugoslavia, declared themselves independent. In 1992, Bosnia-Herzegovina held a vote on independence – most Bosnian Serbs boycotted the vote, while the Muslims and Bosnian Croats voted in favour.

Many Bosnian Serbs, opposed to independence, now started a war against the non-Serbs. They soon occupied more than two-thirds of the land. In their 'ethnic cleansing' campaign, heavily-equipped Bosnian Serb militias drove Muslims from towns they had long inhabited. By early 1993, the Muslims controlled less than a third of the former federal republic, and even the capital, Sarajevo, was disputed territory under constant shellfire. The war was later extended when Croat forces seized other parts of the country.

In 1993 and 1994, the United Nations tried to find a way of ending the war by dividing Bosnia-Herzegovina into self-governing provinces, under a unified, multi-ethnic central government. But attempts to produce a map of provincial boundaries met with failure. [*Map page 16*] ■

AREA 51,129 sq km [19,745 sq mls]
POPULATION 3,527,000
CAPITAL (POPULATION) Sarajevo (525,980)
GOVERNMENT Transitional
ETHNIC GROUPS Muslim 49%, Serb 31%, Croat 17%
LANGUAGES Serbo-Croatian
RELIGIONS Islam 40%, Christianity (Serbian Orthodox 31%, Roman Catholic 15%, Protestant 4%)
CURRENCY Dinar = 100 paras

BOTSWANA

More than half of the land area is occupied by the Kalahari Desert, with much of the rest taken up by saltpans and swamps. Although the Kalahari extends into Namibia and South Africa, Botswana accounts for the greater part of this vast dry upland. It is, however, not a uniform desert: occasional rainfall allows growth of grasses and thorny scrub, enabling the area's sparse human population of about 100,000 – mostly nomadic Bantu herdsmen – to graze their cattle.

ECONOMY AND RESOURCES
When it became independent in 1966, Botswana was one of the world's poorest countries, with cattle as the only significant export. The country was transformed by the mining of vast diamond resources, starting at

Orapa in 1971, and, despite a protracte drought, expanding output in the 1980s mac the economy the fastest growing in su Saharan Africa, paving the way for wid ranging social programmes. Indeed, by 199 Botswana was producing some 15% of th world's total.

Politically stable under Seretse Khama, th country's main target became diversificatio not only to reduce dependence on diamonc (85% of export earnings) and on Sout African imports, but also to create jobs for rapidly expanding population. Copper ha been mined at Selebi-Pikwe since 1974, bu the emphasis in the 1990s is on tourism: 17% of Botswana's huge area (the world's highes figure) is assigned to wildlife conservation an game reserves, and more than half a millio visitors a year are drawn to them.

HISTORY AND POLITICS
The earliest inhabitants of the region were th San, who are also called Bushmen. They hac a nomadic way of life, hunting wild animal and collecting wild plant foods. The Tswana who speak a Bantu language, now form th majority of the population. They are cattle owners, who settled in eastern Botswana more than 1,000 years ago. Their arrival led the San to move into the dry Kalahari region. Today the San form a tiny minority of the population. Most of them live in permanent settlements and work on cattle ranches.

Britain ruled the area as the Bechuanaland Protectorate between 1885 and 1966. When the country became independent, it adopted the name of Botswana. Since then, unlike many African countries, Botswana has been a stable multiparty democracy. [*Map page 33*] ■

AREA 581,730 sq km [224,606 sq mls]
POPULATION 1,443,000
CAPITAL (POPULATION) Gaborone (133,470)
GOVERNMENT Multiparty republic
ETHNIC GROUPS Tswana 75%, Shona 12%, San (Bushmen) 3%
LANGUAGES English (official), Setswana (national language)
RELIGIONS Traditional beliefs 50%, Christianity 50%
CURRENCY Pula = 100 thebe

BRAZIL

By any standard Brazil is a big country. Fifth largest in the world, it covers nearly 8% of South America. Structurally, it has two main regions. In the north lies the vast Amazon basin, once an inland sea and now drained by a river system that carries one-fifth of the Earth's running water. In the centre and south lies the sprawling bulk of the Brazilian Highlands, a huge extent of hard crystalline rock deeply dissected into rolling uplands. This occupies the heartland (Mato Grosso), and the whole western flank of the country from the bulge to the border with Uruguay.

The Amazon River rises in the Peruvian Andes, close to the Pacific Ocean, and many of its tributaries are of similar origin. Several are wide enough to take boats of substantial draught (6 m [20 ft]) from the Andean foothills all the way to the Atlantic – a distance of 5,000 km [3,000 mls] or more.

The largest area of river plain lies in the upper part of the basin, along the frontier with Bolivia and Peru. Downstream the flood plain is relatively narrow, shrinking in width to a few kilometres where the basin drains between the Guiana Highlands in the north and the Brazilian Highlands in the south. Overall only 1–2% of the Amazon Valley is alluvial flood plain; away from this the soils are heavily leached and infertile, and liable to be washed away by tropical rainstorms if the protective canopy of forest is felled: this, unfortunately, is happening at an increasingly alarming rate.

The undulating plateau of the northern highlands also carries poor soils; here rainfall is seasonal, and the typical natural vegetation is a thorny scrub forest, used as open grazing for poor cattle herds. Further south scrub turns to wooded savanna – the *campo cerrado* vegetation that covers 2 million sq km [770,000 sq mls] of the interior plateau. It extends into the basin of the Paraná River and its tributaries, most of which start in the coastal highlands and flow west, draining ultimately into the Plate estuary. The Mato Grosso, on the border with Bolivia, is part of this area and still largely unexplored. The north-eastern uplands are poor farming country; dry for at least half the year, they occasionally suffer long periods of drought.

Conditions are better in the south, with more reliable rainfall. The south-east includes a narrow coastal plain, swampy in places and with abundant rainfall throughout the year; behind rises the Great Escarpment (820 m [2,700 ft]), first in a series of steps to the high eastern edge of the plateau. Over 60% of Brazil's population live in four southern and south-eastern states that account for only 17% of the total area.

ECONOMY AND RESOURCES

For many decades following the early settlements, Brazil was mainly a sugar-producing colony, with most plantations centred on the rich coastal plains of the north-east. Later the same areas produced cotton, cocoa, rice and other crops. In the south, colonists penetrated the interior in search of slaves and minerals, especially gold and diamonds; the city of Ouro Prêto in Minas Gerais was built, and Rio de Janeiro grew as the port for the region.

During the 19th century São Paulo state became the centre of a huge coffee-growing industry; and while the fortunes made in mining helped to develop Rio de Janeiro, profits from coffee were invested in the city of São Paulo. Immigrants from Italy and Germany settled in the south, introducing farming into the fertile valleys in co-existence with the cattle ranchers and gauchos whose herds dominated the plains.

The second half of the 19th century saw the development of the wild rubber industry in the Amazon basin, where the city of Manaus, with its world-famous opera house, served as a centre and market; though Manaus lies 1,600 km [1,000 mls] from the mouth of the Amazon, rubber collected from trees in the hinterland could be shipped out directly to world markets in ocean-going steamers. Brazil enjoyed a virtual monopoly of the rubber trade until the early 20th century, when Malayan plantations began to compete, later with massive success.

Vast mineral resources exist, particularly in Minas Gerais and the Amazon area; they include bauxite, tin, iron ore, manganese,

THE AMAZON

Though not the world's longest river – 6,430 km [3,990 mls] – the Amazon is easily the mightiest, discharging some 180,000 cu m/sec [6,350,000 cu ft/sec] into the Atlantic, more than four times the volume of its nearest rival, the Zaïre. The flow is so great that silt discolours the water up to 200 km [125 mls] out to sea, and the river accounts for a fifth of the world's total river discharge into the oceans.

The Amazon starts its journey in the Andes of Peru – only 150 km [95 mls] from the Pacific – at Lake Villafro, head of the Apurimac branch of the Ucayali, which then flows north to join the other main headstream, the Marañón. Navigable to ocean-going vessels of 6,000 tonnes up to the Peruvian jungle port of Iquitos, some 3,700 km [2,300 mls] from the sea, it then flows east, briefly forming the Peru-Colombian border – before entering Brazil. Here it becomes the Solimões before joining the Negro (itself 18 km [11 mls] wide) at Manaus, where river levels can vary by over 15 m [50 ft] in a year.

Along with more than 1,000 significant tributaries, seven of which are more than 1,600 km [1,000 mls] long, the Amazon drains the largest river basin in the world – about 7 million sq km [2.7 million sq mls] – nearly two-fifths of South America and an area more than twice the size of India. This vast river system provides a crucial network of communications through the otherwise impenetrable jungle: the total is around 43,000 km [27,000 mls].

For nearly half its length the Amazon flows through the world's largest and most important rainforest (*selva*) – a mantle of 6.5 million sq km [2.5 million sq mls] covering an area larger than the whole of Western Europe.

chrome, nickel, uranium, platinum and industrial diamonds. Brazil is the world's leading exporter of iron ore and there are reserves of at least 18,000 million metric tons including the world's biggest at Carajás. Discoveries of new reserves of minerals are frequently being made. The world's largest tin mi is situated in the Amazon region, 50% of world's platinum is in Brazil, and 65% the world's supply of precious stones are pr duced within the country.

The demand for energy has increas rapidly over the years and over a quarter imports are for crude petroleum. An alte native energy was developed from 1976 ma from sugar cane and cassava called ethan (combustible alcohol) with the aim of redu ing demand for petroleum, and in the eig years to 1987, some 3.5 million cars we manufactured to take this fuel; falling prices later made this uneconomic. Larg investments have been made in hydroele tricity – 93% of the country's electricity now from water – and the Itaipú HEP statio on the Paraná, shared with Paraguay, is th world's largest.

Brazil is one of the world's largest farmin countries, and agriculture employs 35% of th population and provides 40% of her export The main agricultural exports are coffe sugar, soya beans, orange juice concentrate beef, cocoa, poultry, sisal, tobacco, maize an cotton. While Brazil is no longer the leadin exporter of coffee – a position now held b Colombia – the country is the world's bigges producer, as it is for sugar cane, bananas oranges, sisal and castor oil.

The manufacturing industry includes th production of steel, chemicals, machinery vehicles, pharmaceuticals, cement, timber paper, shipping and consumer goods. There i also offshore oil production, and nearly 70% of the country's output comes from the conti nental shelf. The Amazon basin is gradually being opened for the controversial exploita tion of forests and mines, with Santarém a new focus of agriculture in a frontier land. There are 35 deep-water ports in Brazil, and the two main oil terminals at São Sebastião and Madre de Jesus are being expanded. Though river transport now plays only a minor part in the movement of goods, for many years rivers gave the only access to the interior, and there are plans to link the Amazon and the Upper Paraná to give a navigable waterway across central Brazil.

A network of arterial roads is being added and these are replacing the 19th-century railways which have been used to take primary products to markets on the coast. Road transport now accounts for 70% of the movement of freight and 97% of passenger traffic.

POPULATION

In 1872 Brazil had a population of about 10 million. By 1972 this had increased almost tenfold, and 1994 saw a figure of 159.1 million Brazilians – with a projected increase to 179.5 million by the end of the century. Of the economically active population (55 million in 1985), 15 million were engaged in agriculture, 9 million in the service industries, 8 million in manufacturing, 5 million in the wholesale and retail trade, and 3 million in construction.

On 21 April 1960, Rio de Janeiro ceased to be the capital and inland the new city of Brasília, built from 1956 onwards, in many ways encapsulated both the spirit and the problems of contemporary Brazil – a sparkling, dramatic, planned city, deliberately planted in the unpopulated uplands of Goiás as a gesture of faith; modern, practical and beautiful, but still surrounded by the shanties of poverty and – beyond them – the challenge of an untamed wilderness.

So much of the nation's wealth is still held by the élites of the cities, particularly those of the south-east, and despite grandiose development plans aimed at spreading prosperity throughout the country, the interior remains poor and underpopulated.

Although possessing great reserves, Brazil has not made the big jump from developing to developed country. The boom of 'the miracle years' from 1968 to 1973, when the economy grew at more than 10% per annum, was not sustained. Indeed, falls in commodity prices and massive borrowing to finance large and often unproductive projects have combined to make Brazil the world's biggest debtor nation; despite paying back $69 billion between 1985 and 1991 – a huge drain on any economy – there was still over $120 billion owed. Inflation during 1990 was nearly 3,000% – down to under 400% in 1991 – and mismanagement and corruption still afflicted administration. In August 1993, an attempt to control the monthly inflation of over 30% was made by the introduction of a new currency, the Cruzeiro real. While Brazil does not have

THE AMAZON RAINFOREST

The world's largest and ecologically most important rainforest was still being destroyed at an alarming rate in the late 1980s, with somewhere between 1.5% and 4% disappearing each year in Brazil alone. Opening up the forest for many reasons – logging, mining, ranching, peasant resettlement – the Brazilian authorities did little in real terms when confronted with a catalogue of indictments: decimation of a crucial world habitat; pollution of rivers; destruction of thousands of species of fauna and flora, especially medicinal plants; and the brutal ruination of the lives of the last remaining Amerindian tribes.

Once cut off from the world by impenetrable jungle, hundreds of thousands of Indians have been displaced in the provinces of Rondonia and Acre, principally by loggers and landless migrants, and in Para by mining, dams for HEP and ranching for beef cattle. It is estimated that five centuries ago the Amazon rainforest supported some 2 million Indians in more than 200 tribes; today the number has shrunk to a pitiful 50,000 or so, and many of the tribes have disappeared altogether.

A handful have been relatively lucky – the Yanomani, after huge international support, won their battle in 1991 for a reserve three times the size of Belgium – but for the majority their traditional lifestyle has vanished forever.

the huge population growths of many African and Asian countries, it does have poverty on a large scale.

HISTORY AND POLITICS

Brazil was 'discovered' by Pedro Alvarez Cabral on 22 April 1500 and gradually penetrated by Portuguese settlers, missionaries, explorers and prospectors during the 17th and 18th centuries. Many of the semi-nomadic Indians indigenous to the country were enslaved for plantation work or driven into the interior, and some 4 million African slaves were introduced, notably in the sugar-growing areas of the north-east.

RIO DE JANEIRO & SÃO PAULO

Much of Brazil's population is concentrated in a relatively small and highly developed 'corner' in the south-east of the country. Rio de Janeiro, discovered by the Portuguese in 1502, lies in a magnificent setting, stretching for 20 km [12 mls] along the coast between mountain and ocean, its superb harbour overlooked by Sugar Loaf Mountain and, on Corcovado, the famous statue of Christ. Though no longer the capital, it remains the focus of Brazil's cultural life, attracting visitors with the world's greatest pre-Lent festival at carnival time.

São Paulo, its early growth fuelled by the coffee boom of the late 19th century, is the most populous city in the southern hemisphere and rivals Mexico City as the world's fastest growing and largest conurbation. Estimates state that the 1985 total of 15.5 million will increase to 22.1 million by the year 2000. In both cities the yawning gap between rich and poor is all too evident, the sprawling shanty towns (*favelas*) on the fringes standing in sharp contrast to sophisticated metropolitan centres.

Little more than a group of rival provinces, Brazil began to unite in 1808 when the Portuguese royal court, seeking refuge from Napoleon, transferred from Lisbon to Rio de Janeiro. The eldest surviving son of King Joãs VI of Portugal was chosen as 'Perpetual Defender' of Brazil by a national congress. In 1822 he proclaimed the independence of the country and was chosen as the constitutional emperor with the title Pedro I. He abdicated in 1831 and was succeeded by his son, Pedro II, who ruled for nearly 50 years and whose liberal policies included the gradual abolition of slavery (1888).

A federal system was adopted for the United States of Brazil in the 1881 constitution and Brazil became a republic in 1889. Until 1930 the country experienced strong economic expansion and prosperity, but social unrest in 1930 resulted in a major revolt and from then until 1945 the country was under the control of President Vargas, who estab-

lished a strong corporate state similar to tha of fascist Italy, although Brazil entered Worl War II on the side of the Allies. Democracy often corrupt, prevailed from 1956 to 196 and from 1985; between were five militar presidents of illiberal regimes.

A new constitution came into force i October 1988 – the eighth since independenc from the Portuguese in 1822 – which trans ferred powers from the president to congres and paved the way for a return to democrac in 1990. Today the country comprises 2: states, each with its own directly elected gov ernor and legislature, three territories and th Federal District of Brasília. [*Map page 31*] ∎

AREA 8,511,970 sq km [3,286,472 sq mls]
POPULATION 159,143,000
CAPITAL (POPULATION) Brasília (1,596,000)
GOVERNMENT Federal republic
ETHNIC GROUPS White 53%, Mulatto 22%, Mestizo 12%, African American 11%, Japanese 1%, Amerindian 0.1%
LANGUAGES Portuguese (official)
RELIGIONS Christianity (Roman Catholic 88%, Protestant 6%)
CURRENCY Cruzeiro real = 100 centavos

BRUNEI

Comprising two small enclaves on the coast of northern Borneo, Brunei rises from humid plains to forested mountains over 1,800 m [6,000 ft] high along the Malaysian border.

Formerly a British protectorate, and still a close ally of the UK, the country was already rich from oil (discovered by Shell in 1929) when it became independent in 1983. Today oil and gas account for 70% of GDP and even more of export earnings – oil 41%, gas 53% – though income from the resultant investments overseas exceeds both. Imports are dominated by machinery, transport equipment, manufactures and foodstuffs. Brunei is, however, currently undergoing a drive towards agricultural

lf-sufficiency. The revenues have made
ultan Hassanal Bolkiah (crowned 1968)
legedly the world's richest man, and given
s people the second highest income
er capita in Asia after Japan. There is no
come tax system in Brunei and citizens
njoy free cradle-to-the-grave welfare. All
overnment employees (two-thirds of the
orkforce) are banned from political activity,
nd the Sultan and his family retain firm
ontrol. [*Map page 26*] ∎

AREA 5,770 sq km [2,228 sq mls]
POPULATION 280,000
CAPITAL (POPULATION) Bandar Seri
Begawan (46,000)
GOVERNMENT Absolute monarchy with an
advisory council
ETHNIC GROUPS Malay 69%, Chinese 18%,
Indian
LANGUAGES Malay and English (both official),
Chinese
RELIGIONS Islam 63%, Buddhism 14%,
Christianity 10%
CURRENCY Brunei dollar = 100 cents

BULGARIA

The Balkan Mountains (Stara Planina),
which rise to heights of over 2,000 m
[6,500 ft], stretch across the centre of the
country, from the eastern coastal areas bordering the Black Sea to the west, separating
two lowland areas: the Danubian lowlands to
the north and the Maritsa Valley to the south.
The climate is one of hot summers and fairly
cold winters.

ECONOMY AND RESOURCES

With fertile soils but few natural resources,
Bulgaria's economy has a distinct agricultural
bias, with half the population still earning their
living from the land. The most productive
agriculture occurs in the two lowland areas –
the hills sloping down to the Danube, where
wheat, barley and maize are the chief crops,
and the warmer central valley of the River
Maritsa, where grains, cotton, rice, tobacco,
fruits and vines are grown.

In the south-facing valleys overlooking the
Maritsa plains, the main crops are plums, vine
and tobacco. A particular feature of this area
is the rose fields of Kazanluk, from which
attar of roses is exported worldwide to the cos-
metics industry.

South and west of the Maritsa Valley are the
Rhodopi Mountains, containing lead, zinc and
copper ores. There are also rich mineral veins
of both iron and non-ferrous metals in the
Stara Planina, north of the capital and chief
industrial city, Sofia.

HISTORY AND POLITICS

The most subservient of the former Eastern
bloc satellites, Bulgaria's links with Russia
date back to 1878, when the Tsar's forces liberated the country from five centuries of
Ottoman (Turkish) rule. In the period after
World War II, and especially under President
Zhivkov from 1954, Bulgaria became all too
dependent on its overseer; nearly two-thirds
of its trade (much of it subsidized) was conducted with the USSR – including most of
its energy requirements.

Predictably, Bulgaria was the last and least
publicized of the Eastern European countries
to fall. In 1990 the Communist Party held on
to power under increasing pressure by ousting
Zhivkov, renouncing its leading role in the
nation's affairs, making many promises of
social and economic reform and changing its
name to the Socialist Party before winning the
first free elections since the war – unconvinc-
ingly and against confused opposition. With
better organization the Union of Democratic
Forces defeated the old guard the following
year and began the unenviable task of making
the transition from central planning to a free-
market economy.

The new government inherited a host of
problems – inflation, food shortages, rising
unemployment, strikes, large foreign debt,
limited Western interest, a declining traditional manufacturing industry, reduced demand at
home and abroad, increased prices for vital
raw materials, and a potential drop in the
recently growing revenue from tourism. In
addition there was the nagging worry of a size-

able Turkish minority disaffected with mismanaged attempts at forced assimilation. [Map page 17] ■

AREA 110,910 sq km [42,822 sq mls]
POPULATION 8,818,000
CAPITAL (POPULATION) Sofia (1,221,000)
GOVERNMENT Multiparty republic
ETHNIC GROUPS Bulgarian 86%, Turkish 10%, Gypsy 3%, Macedonian 3%, Armenian, Romanian, Greek
LANGUAGES Bulgarian (official)
RELIGIONS Christianity (Eastern Orthodox 87%), Islam 13%
CURRENCY Lev = 100 stotinki

BURKINA FASO

As large as Italy, and with just over 10 million inhabitants, landlocked Burkina Faso ('land of upright men') is nevertheless overpopulated: low, seasonal and erratic rainfall, thin, eroded soils, desertification and a dearth of other natural resources combine to keep it one of the poorest and most agrarian states in the world, heavily reliant on aid.

ECONOMY AND RESOURCES
The Mossi people, who are the majority tribe, live around Ouagadougou, the capital; another major group, the Bobo, dwell around the second city of Bobo Dioulasso. Both grow cotton and millet, guinea corn (sorghum) and groundnuts for food, and collect shea nuts for cooking oil. Nomadic Fulani keep cattle. Though small surpluses of all these products are sold overseas and to the better-off countries to the south, especially the Ivory Coast, remittances sent home by migrants working in those countries probably provide most of Burkina Faso's foreign income. Manganese mining could be developed in the far northeast, though this would necessitate an extension, 340 km [210 mls] long, to the railway from Abidjan which is already 1,145 km [715 mls] long. Another hope lies in eliminating the

simulium fly, whose bite causes blindnes. This would permit settlement and farming the valleys, which have the most fertile an best watered lands. Among these is the 'W national park, shared with Niger and Benin.

HISTORY AND POLITICS
Burkina Faso (known until 1984 as Uppe Volta) is the successor to Mossi, an early Wes African state dating from 1100. Plagued b numerous coups and political assassination the country tasted democracy in Decembe 1991 for the first time in more than a decad when the military regime of Blaise Compaor granted elections. However, 20 oppositio parties combined to produce a boycott involv ing 76% of the electorate (claiming that i was a ploy to legitimize the military rule), and the government registered a hollow victory [Map page 32] ■

AREA 274,200 sq km [105,869 sq mls]
POPULATION 10,046,000
CAPITAL (POPULATION) Ouagadougou (634,000)
GOVERNMENT Multiparty republic
ETHNIC GROUPS Mossi 48%, Mande 9%, Fulani 8%, Bobo 7%
LANGUAGES French (official)
RELIGIONS Traditional beliefs 45%, Islam 43%, Christianity 12%
CURRENCY CFA franc = 100 centimes

BURMA (MYANMAR)

Geographically, the country has three main regions. The core area is a great structural depression, largely drained by the Chindwin and Irrawaddy rivers. Its coastal zone has a wet climate, but the inner region between Prome and Mandalay constitutes a 'dry zone', sheltered from the south-west monsoon and with an annual rainfall of less than 1,000 mm [40 in].

To the west lie the fold mountains of the Arakan Yoma, while to the east rises the great han Plateau. In the south-east, running down he isthmus that takes Burma on to the Malay Peninsula, are the uplands of the Tenasserim, with hundreds of islands dotted along the oast of the Andaman Sea.

ECONOMY AND RESOURCES

Once a green and gentle land, rich in agriculture and timber and blessed with many natural resources from precious stones to oil, Burma has become one of the three poorest countries in Asia.

More than 60% of the country is forested, rubber plantations augmenting the indigenous teak. In the dry zone, which was the original nucleus of the Burmese state, small-scale irrigation has long been practised in the narrow valleys, and rice, cotton, jute and sugar cane are important crops. Until 1964 Burma was the world's leading exporter of rice, and the crop still accounts for more than 40% of Burma's meagre export earnings. This central area was also the base of Burmah Oil, hosting the small fields that once made the country the British Empire's second largest producer. Even today it has sufficient oil and gas to meet most of Burma's needs.

HISTORY AND POLITICS

British since 1895, Burma was separate from India as a crown colony in 1937. A battleground for Japanese and British troops in World War II, it became an independent republic in 1948 and left the Commonwealth. Military dictatorship came in 1962 and a one-party state in 1974, both headed by General Ne Win, leader of the Burma Socialist Programme Party.

The party's rigid combination of state control, Buddhism and isolation, under the banner 'The Burmese Way to Socialism', had disastrous results, the country plunging quickly from prosperity to poverty. Politically, too, Burma was in a perilous state, with over a third of the country in rebel hands.

In the south-east the guerrillas of two Karen liberation movements control large tracts of mountains near the Thai border; in the north and east the Burmese Communist Party holds sway in most of Kachin and a good deal of Shan; here also, at the western end of the 'Golden Triangle', the authorities try to con-

tain the local warlords' trafficking in opium. Another flashpoint is in the west, where Rohinya, the Muslim minority, have been persecuted by the army and repeatedly pushed over the border with Bangladesh in tens of thousands.

Burma spends more than 35% of its budget on 'defence' – much of it on the brutal suppression of political opposition and of human rights. In 1990, the coalition NLD won over 80% of the votes in a multiparty election conceded by the regime following violent demonstrations, but the ruling junta simply refused to accept the result – keeping its leader, Nobel Peace Prize winner Aung San Suu Kyi, under house arrest until July 1995. The powerless opposition were forced to renounce the result and agree to a new and no doubt again ineffective agenda for a return to democracy.

Meanwhile, the country continued to crumble, if with great charm; despite the hideous regime a black market flourishes behind the crumbling colonial façade of Rangoon, once a rival to Bangkok and Singapore. Though some visitors make the trips round the attractions of Rangoon, Mandalay and Pagan, tourism is hardly encouraged by the suspicious government, and most of the country is still closed to foreigners.

A change of name – the title Union of Myanmar was officially adopted in 1989 – has not changed the political complexion of a desperate nation. Burma remains an anomaly, holding out almost friendless against the tide of democratic and diplomatic changes that swept the world in the late 1980s and early 1990s. It seems that, even with some form of conciliation, it will not long survive as a geopolitical entity. [*Map page 23*] ∎

AREA 676,577 sq km [261,228 sq mls]
POPULATION 45,555,000
CAPITAL (POPULATION) Rangoon (or Yangon, 2,513,000)
GOVERNMENT Military regime
ETHNIC GROUPS Burman 69%, Shan 9%, Karen 6%, Rakhine 5%, Mon 2%, Chin 2%
LANGUAGES Burmese (official)
RELIGIONS Buddhism 89%, Christianity 5%, Islam 4%
CURRENCY Kyat = 100 pyas

BURUNDI

The Republic of Burundi is the fifth smallest country on the mainland of Africa. It is also the second most densely populated after its northern neighbour Rwanda. Part of the deep Great Rift Valley, which runs throughout eastern Africa into south-western Asia, lies in western Burundi. It includes part of Lake Tanganyika.

East of the Rift Valley are high mountains, reaching 2,670 m [8,760 ft], composed partly of volcanic rocks. In central and eastern Burundi, the land descends in a series of step-like grassy plateaux.

Grasslands cover much of the country. The land was formerly mainly forest, but farmers have cleared most of the trees. Soil erosion is a serious problem, and in some areas new forests are being planted to protect the soil against the rain and wind.

ECONOMY AND RESOURCES
Burundi is one of the world's ten poorest countries. About 92% of the people are farmers, who mostly grow little more than they need to feed their families. The main food crops are beans, cassava, maize and sweet potatoes. Cattle, goats are sheep are raised, while fish, caught in Lake Tanganyika, are an important supplement to the diets of local people. The main cash crops are coffee, which accounts for over 80% of the exports, tea and cotton. Manufacturing is on a small scale, with most of the factories based in Bujumbura.

HISTORY AND POLITICS
The Twa, a pygmy people, were the first known inhabitants of Burundi. About 1,000 years ago, the Hutu, a people who speak a Bantu language, gradually began to settle the area, pushing the Twa into remote areas. From the 15th century, the Tutsi, a cattle-owning people from the north-east, gradually took over the country. The Hutu, although greatly outnumbering the Tutsi, were forced to serve the Tutsi overlords.

Germany conquered the area that is now Burundi and Rwanda in the 1890s. The area called Ruanda-Urundi, was taken by Belgium during World War I. In 1961, the people of Urundi voted to become a monarchy, while the people of Ruanda voted to become a republic. The two territories became fully independent as Burundi and Rwanda in 1962.

After 1962, the rivalries between the Hutu and Tutsi led to periodic outbreaks of fighting. The Tutsi monarchy was overthrown in 1966 and Burundi became a republic. But massacres of thousands of people still occurred as the Tutsi and Hutu fought for power. The worst recent manifestation was in 1972, when the murder of the deposed king in an attempted coup led to the massacre of more than 100,000 Hutu, but some 20,000 were also killed in 1988. As in Rwanda, the indigenous pygmoid Twa people now comprise a tiny proportion of a burgeoning population. The first democratic presidential election, which a Hutu won, took place in 1993. [Map page 33] ■

AREA 27,830 sq km [10,745 sq mls]
POPULATION 6,209,000
CAPITAL (POPULATION) Bujumbura (235,000)
GOVERNMENT Republic
ETHNIC GROUPS Hutu 85%, Tutsi 14%, Twa (pygmy) 1%
LANGUAGES French and Kirundi (both official)
RELIGIONS Christianity 85% (Roman Catholic 78%), traditional beliefs 13%
CURRENCY Burundi franc = 100 centimes

CAMBODIA

The heartland of Cambodia is a wide basin drained by the Mekong River, in the centre of which lies the Tonlé Sap ('Great Lake'), a former arm of the sea surrounded by a broad plain. From November to June, when rains are meagre and the Mekong low, the lake drains to

e south and away to the sea. During the
iny season and period of high river water in
ne to October the flow reverses, and the lake
ore than doubles its area to become the
rgest freshwater lake in Asia.

To the south-west stand low mountain
ains, while the northern rim of the country
bounded by the Phanom Dangrek uplands,
ith a prominent sandstone escarpment.
hree-quarters of the country is forested, and
0% of the population live on the fertile
ains, mostly in small village settlements;
hnom Penh, the capital of Cambodia, is the
nly major city.

ECONOMY AND RESOURCES

he wealth of 'the gentle kingdom' rested on
bundant fish from the lake and rice from the
ooded lowlands, for which an extensive sys-
em of irrigation channels and storage reser-
oirs was developed.

In a short period of stability during the late
950s and 1960s the country developed its
mall-scale agricultural resources and rubber
lantations – it has few workable minerals or
ources of power – remaining predominantly
ural but achieving self-sufficiency in food,
vith some exports. However, civil war and the
Khmer Rouge regime have left Cambodia dev-
stated.

HISTORY AND POLITICS

The Tonlé Sap lowlands were the cradle of the
great Khmer Empire, which lasted from 802 to
1432; its zenith came in the reign of
Suryavarman II (1113–50), who built the
great funerary temple of Angkor Wat: together with Angkor Thom, the 600 Hindu
temples form the world's largest group of
religious buildings.

Cambodia was under French rule from
1863 as part of French Indo-China, achieving
independence in 1954. This was followed by
years of internal political struggles, involvement in the Vietnam War, a destructive civil
war and a four-year period of ruthless Khmer
Rouge dictatorship, under which Pol Pot
ordered the genocide of somewhere between
1 million and 2.5 million people. After the
overthrow of Pol Pot in 1979 by Vietnam
there was a civil war between their puppet
government of the People's Republic of
Kampuchea (Cambodia) and the government
of Democratic Kampuchea, a coalition of
Prince Sihanouk – deposed by a US-backed
coup in 1970 – Son Sann's Khmer People's
Liberation Front and the Khmer Rouge, who
from 1982 claimed to have abandoned their
Communist ideology. It was this strange tripartite government in exile that was recognized by the United Nations.

Denied almost any aid, Cambodia continued to decline, but it was only the withdrawal of Vietnamese troops in 1989, sparking
a fear of a Khmer Rouge revival, that forced
a settlement. In October 1991, following
numerous failures, a UN-brokered peace plan
for elections by 1993 was accepted by all
parties concerned, and a glimmer of real
hope returned to the beleaguered people of
Cambodia. However, peace was fragile and
there was the massive problem of hundreds of
thousands of refugees camped over the border
in Thailand – itself plunged into turmoil in the
spring of 1992. [*Map page 26*] ■

AREA 181,040 sq km [69,900 sq mls]
POPULATION 9,968,000
CAPITAL (POPULATION) Phnom Penh
(800,000)
GOVERNMENT Constitutional monarchy
ETHNIC GROUPS Khmer 94%, Chinese 3%,
Cham 2%, Thai, Lao, Kola, Vietnamese
LANGUAGES Khmer (official)
RELIGIONS Buddhism 88%, Islam 2%
CURRENCY Riel = 100 sen

CAMEROON

H alf the size of neighbouring Nigeria,
Cameroon has only a seventh of the
population. It is, nevertheless, a remarkably
diverse country, stemming from more than
160 ethnic groups (each with their own language) and a colonial past involving several
European countries. The mountainous borderlands between Nigeria and Cameroon lie
on a line of crustal weakness dating from the

break-up of the supercontinent, Gondwana-land. Mostly volcanic, the mountains include Mt Cameroon (4,070 m [13,350 ft]) which is occasionally active. There is desert to the north, dense tropical rainforest in the south and dry savanna in the intermediate area.

ECONOMY AND RESOURCES
Despite oil production passing its peak in the 1980s and likely to stop before the end of the century, and despite patchy industrial development, Cameroon is one of tropical Africa's better-off nations, with an annual income per person of $850 and rare self-sufficiency in food. This relative prosperity rests partly on diverse but well-managed agriculture, with extensive plantations of palm, rubber, bananas and other crops in the south-west dating from colonial times. Douala is Cameroon's main port for exports of cocoa, coffee (the chief cash crops) and aluminium, and for the transit trade of neighbours, while Kribi exports timber. Aluminium is produced at Edéa, using hydroelectric power generated from the Sanaga River, and a railway is being built to the north.

HISTORY AND POLITICS
The word Cameroon is derived from the Portuguese *camarões* – prawns fished by Portuguese explorers' seamen in coastal estuaries – but European contact dates mainly from German rule as a protectorate after 1884. After World War I the country was divided according to League of Nations mandates between France (mainly) and Britain. The French Cameroons became independent in 1960, while following a 1961 plebiscite the north of the British Cameroons voted to merge with Nigeria and the south federated with the new independent state; this became unitary in 1972 and a republic in 1984. Though Cameroon is officially bilingual, the government and public sector are dominated by French-speakers – a fact that continues to upset the rest of the population.

The austerity programme of President Paul Buja, initiated in 1987, appeared to reap rewards by the end of the decade, but there was widespread unrest at the repressive regime (one-party politics was introduced in 1966 by Buja's mentor and predecessor Ahmadou

Ahidjo, who had been president since independence). Elections were held in 1992, but disputes over the results led Buja to declare a state of emergency. [*Map page 32*] ∎

AREA 475,440 sq km [183,567 sq mls]
POPULATION 12,871,000
CAPITAL (POPULATION) Yaoundé (750,000)
GOVERNMENT Multiparty republic
ETHNIC GROUPS Fang 20%, Bamileke and Mamum 19%, Duala, Luanda and Basa 15%, Fulani 10%
LANGUAGES French and English (both official)
RELIGIONS Christianity (Roman Catholic 35%, Protestant 18%), traditional beliefs 25%, Islam 22%
CURRENCY CFA franc = 100 centimes

CANADA

A vast confederation of ten provinces and two territories, Canada is the world's second largest country after Russia, and with an even longer coastline (250,000 km [155,000 mls]). Sparsely populated, it has huge areas of virtually unoccupied mountains, forests, tundra and polar desert in the north and west.

To the east lie the Maritime provinces of Newfoundland, Nova Scotia, New Brunswick and Prince Edward Island, and the predominantly French-speaking province of Québec, clustered about the Gulf of St Lawrence, they are based on ancient worn-down mountains – the northern extension of the Appalachians – and the eastern uptilted edge of the even older Canadian Shield. The central province of Ontario borders the Great Lakes, extending north across the Shield to Hudson Bay. Further to the west come the prairie provinces of Manitoba, Saskatchewan and Alberta; like Québec and Ontario, these include fertile farmlands in the south, where most of the population is to be found, and lake-strewn forest on the subarctic wastelands to the north.

South-western Alberta includes a substan-
al block of the Rocky Mountains, with peaks
rising to over 4,000 m [13,120 ft] in Banff,
oho and Kootenay National Parks. The
esternmost province of British Columbia is
mountainous, a land of spectacular forests,
akes and fjords, with sheltered valleys
arbouring rich farmland. The huge northern
rea includes the relatively small and mountainous Yukon Territory in the west, border-
ag Alaska, and the much more extensive
Northwest Territories stretching from the
0th parallel to the northern tip of Ellesmere
sland.

CONOMY AND RESOURCES

Though the population of Canada expanded
apidly from Confederation onwards, it
emained predominantly rural for many gener-
tions; only in recent decades have Canada's
cities grown to match those of the USA. At
Confederation in 1867 about 80% was rural,
and only Montréal had passed the 100,000
population mark, with just six towns over
25,000. Not until the end of World War II did
he rural and urban elements stand in balance,
and today the situation is reversed: 76% of
Canada's population is urban.

The metropolitan areas of Toronto and
Montréal jointly contain a quarter of the total,
and together with Vancouver account for over
30% of the entire population. By contrast the
urban centres of Newfoundland and the
Maritimes have been relatively stable.

Agriculture and industry

Although farming settlements still dominate
the landscape, if not the economy, abandon-
ment of farmland is a serious problem in the
eastern provinces, where the agrarian economy – except in such favoured areas as the
Annapolis Valley, Nova Scotia – has always
been marginal. Through the St Lawrence lowlands and Ontario peninsula farms are more
prosperous and rural populations are denser,
thinning again along the north shores of the
Great Lakes. On the prairies mechanization of
grain farming long ago minimized the need for
labour, so population densities remain low;
the mixed farming communities on the forest
margins are often denser. The Pacific coast
population is generally concentrated in such

SAINT-PIERRE ET MIQUELON

The last remaining fragment of the once-
extensive French possessions in North
America, Saint-Pierre et Miquelon comprises
eight islands (total area 242 sq km [93 sq
mls]) off the south coast of Newfoundland.

The population of 6,300 (the vast majority
of whom live on Saint-Pierre, the rest on
Miquelon) depend mainly on fishing – the
cause of territorial disputes with Canada.

Settled by Frenchmen in the 17th century
and a colony from 1816, it became an overseas department in 1976, thus enjoying – like
Martinique, Guadeloupe, Guiana and Réunion
– the same status as the departments in
Metropolitan France. In 1985, however, it
became a 'territorial collectivity' (a status
already held by Mayotte in the Indian Ocean),
sending one representative to the National
Assembly in Paris and one to the Senate.

rich farming areas as the Okanagan and lower
Frazer River basins.

Industry, often dependent on local development of power resources, has transformed
many remote and empty areas of Canada.
Newfoundland's Labrador iron-ore workings
around Schefferville are powered by the huge
hydroelectric plant at Churchill Falls, one of
the largest of its kind in the world. Cheap
hydroelectric power throughout Québec and
Ontario, coupled with improved transmission
technology, has encouraged the further development of wood pulp and paper industries,
even in distant parts of the northern forests,
and stimulated industry and commerce in the
south. Canada is by far the world's leading
producer and exporter of paper and board.
Mining, too, has helped in the development of
these provinces; Sudbury, Ontario, supplies
about 20% of the Western world's nickel,
while Canada is one of the leading producers
of zinc and uranium.

In the prairie provinces, small marketing,
distribution and service centres have been
transformed by the enormous expansion of
the petrochemical industry; the mineral-rich
province of Alberta produces 90% of the
country's oil output, and the boom towns

of Alberta, Edmonton and Calgary have far outpaced the growth of the eastern cities during recent decades. By contrast – lacking hydrocarbons, depending mainly on farming, logging and pulping for their prosperity – the settlements of Pacific Canada have on the whole grown slowly, with the notable exception of Vancouver.

The northlands

Canada's northlands, virtually uninhabited apart from small Inuit communities, have an immense, though localized, potential for development. Though the soils are poor and the climate is unyielding, mineral wealth is abundant under the permanently frozen subsoils. Already a major producer of uranium, zinc and nickel, the north also holds vast reserves of copper, molybdenum, iron, cadmium, and other metals of strategic importance; sulphur, potash and asbestos are currently being exploited, and natural gas and petroleum await development beyond the Mackenzie River delta.

Much of this immense mineral wealth will remain in the ground until the high costs of extraction and transportation can be justified. Also, pressure for legislation to protect the boreal forest and tundra against unnecessary or casual damage is rapidly growing – a trend which one day may also curb the massive timber industry.

HISTORY AND POLITICS

Norse voyagers and fishermen were probably the first Europeans briefly to visit Canada, but John Cabot's later discovery of North America, in 1497, began the race to annex lands and wealth, with France and Britain the main contenders.

Jacques Cartier's discovery of the St Lawrence River in 1534 gave France a head start; from their settlements near Québec explorers, trappers and missionaries pioneered routes deeply penetrating the northern half of North America. With possible routes to China and the Indies in mind, Frenchmen followed the St Lawrence and Niagara rivers deep into the heartland of the continent, hoping for the riches of another El Dorado.

Discovering the Great Lakes, they then moved north, west and south in their search

for trade. From the fertile valley of the upper St Lawrence, French influence spread north beyond the coniferous forests and over the tundra. To the west and south they reached the prairies – potentially fertile farming country – exploring further to the Rockies and down the Ohio and Mississippi rivers. By 1763, after the series of wars that gave Britain brief control of the whole of North America, French-speaking communities were already scattered widely across the interior. Many of the southern settlements became American after 1776, when the USA declared independence from Britain, and the northern ones became a British colony.

British settlers had long been established on the Atlantic coast, farming where possible with supplementary fishing. In the 1780s a new wave of English-speaking settlers – the United Empire Loyalists – moved north from the USA into Nova Scotia, New Brunswick and Lower Canada. With further waves of immigration direct from Britain, English speakers came to dominate the fertile lands between Lakes Huron and Erie. From there they gradually spread westwards.

Restricted to the north by intractable coniferous forests and tundra, and to the south by the USA, the settlers spread through Québec into Upper Canada – now Ontario, the only province along the Canadian shores of the Great Lakes. Mostly English-speaking and retaining British traditions, they continued westwards to establish settlements across the narrow wedge of the northern prairie, finally crossing the Rockies to link with embryo settlements along the Pacific coast. So the fertile lowlands of the St Lawrence basin and the pockets of settlement on the Shield alone remained French in language and culture. The bulk of Canada, to east and west, became predominantly British.

Canada's varied topography and immense scale inhibited the development of a single nation; to promote Canadian unity across so wide a continent has been the aim of successive governments for more than two centuries. The union of British Upper Canada and French Lower Canada was sealed by the Confederation of 1867, when as the newly-named Provinces of Ontario and Québec they were united with the Maritime core of Nova

THE TUNDRA

Beyond their habitable southern rim, the northlands of Canada and Alaska are bleak and bare; in the subarctic zone conifers stretch across the continent, but northwards the boreal forest thins and dies out, replaced with tundra. Glaciation has scoured the rocks bare, and soils have had insufficient time to form; the surface thaws in summer, but sub-soils remain frozen. Winters are long and bit-terly cold, summers brief and cool. Even in the south the season of plant growth is only 70–80 days. Precipitation is light – usually less than 250 mm [10 in] a year, and most of it snow; except where it drifts, the snow seldom lies deep, but it provides cover for vegetation and burrowing animals. The tundra is covered with low grasses, lichens, mosses and spindly shrubs, providing food for migrat-ing reindeer and resident hares, voles, lem-mings and other small browsers and grazers. Their numbers are augmented each summer by hosts of migrant birds that fly in from temperate latitudes to feed on the vegetation and insects.

Scotia and New Brunswick. Three years later the settlement on the Red River entered the Confederation as Manitoba, and in the follow-ing year the Pacific colonies of Vancouver Island and British Columbia, now united as a single province, completed the link from sea to sea. Prince Edward Island joined in 1873, the prairie provinces of Alberta and Saskatchewan in 1905, and Newfoundland in 1949.

Though self-governing in most respects from the time of the Confederation, Canada remained technically subject to the British Imperial parliament until 1931, when the cre-ation of the British Commonwealth made the country a sovereign nation under the crown.

With so much of the population spread out along a southern ribbon of settlement, 4,000 km [2,500 mls] long but rarely more than 480 km [300 mls] wide, Canada has struggled constantly to achieve unity. Transcontinental communications have played a critical role. From the eastern provinces the Canadian Pacific Railway crossed the Rockies to reach

Vancouver in 1885. Later a second rail route, the Canadian National, was pieced together, and the Trans-Canada Highway links the extreme east and west of the country symboli-cally as well as in fact. Transcontinental air routes link the major centres, and local air traffic is especially important over trackless forests, mountains and tundra. With radio and telephone communications, all parts of the confederation are now linked, though the vast-ness is intimidating and the country spans six time zones: at noon in Vancouver it is already 3:00 pm in Toronto, and 4:30 pm in St Johns, Newfoundland.

A constant hazard to Canadian nationhood is the proximity of the USA. Though benign, with shared if dwindling British traditions, the prosperous giant to the south has often seemed to threaten the very survival of Canada through economic dominance and cultural annexation. The two countries have the largest bilateral trade flow in the world.

A real and growing threat to unity is the per-sistence of French culture in Québec province – a lasting political wedge between the western prairie and mountain provinces and the east-ern Maritimes. Urbanization and 'American-ization' have fuelled a separatist movement that seeks to turn the province into an inde-pendent French-speaking republic. This issue may obscure a wider and more fundamental division in Canadian politics, with the devel-opment of a Montréal-Toronto axis in the east, and a Vancouver-Winnipeg axis in the west. [*Map page 27*] ■

AREA 9,976,140 sq km [3,851,788 sq mls]
POPULATION 29,141,000
CAPITAL (POPULATION) Ottawa (921,000)
GOVERNMENT Federal multiparty constitutional monarchy
ETHNIC GROUPS British 34%, French 26%, German 4%, Italian 3%, Ukrainian 2%, Native American (Amerindian/Inuit) 1.5%, Chinese, Dutch
LANGUAGES English and French (both official)
RELIGIONS Christianity (Roman Catholic 47%, Protestant 41%, Eastern Orthodox 2%), Judaism, Islam, Hinduism, Sikhism
CURRENCY Canadian dollar = 100 cents

CANARY ISLANDS

The Canary Islands comprise an archipelago of seven large islands and numerous small volcanic islands situated in the Atlantic off southern Morocco, the nearest within 100 km [60 mls] of the mainland. The 'inshore' islands of Lanzarote and Fuerteventura are low-lying, while the western group, including Gran Canaria and Tenerife, are more mountainous, the volcanic cone of Pico de Teide rising to 3,718 m [12,198 ft]. The islands, totalling 7,273 sq km [2,807 sq mls] in area, have a subtropical climate, pleasantly dry at sea level but damp on higher ground.

ECONOMY AND RESOURCES
Soils are fertile, supporting farming and fruit growing, mainly by large-scale irrigation. Bananas, sugar, coffee and citrus fruits are the main crops at lower levels, and temperate cereals, potatoes, tomatoes and vines grow in the cooler, damper air of the hills. Much of the produce is exported to Western Europe for the early spring market. The principal industries include food and fish processing, boat-building and crafts.

Known to ancient European civilizations as the Fortunate Islands, the picturesque Canaries are today a major destination for both winter and summer tourists. The average January temperature being 17.9°C [64°F] rising to 24.4°C [76°F] in July. There are four national parks on the islands, noted for their interesting Mediterranean and African flora and volcanic formations.

HISTORY AND POLITICS
Claimed by Portugal in 1341, the Canary Islands were ceded to Spain in 1479 and since 1927 have been divided into two provinces under the name of their respective capitals, Las Palmas de Gran Canaria (with a population of 342,000 Spain's eighth biggest city) and Santa Cruz de Tenerife. The former province (56% of the area) comprises Gran Canaria, Lanzarote, Fuerteventura and

numerous islets, and the latter (44%) comprises the islands of Tenerife, La Palma, Gomera and Hierro. [*Map page 32*] ■

AREA 7,273 sq km [2,807 sq mls]
POPULATION 1,494,000
CAPITAL (POPULATION) Las Palmas (342,000)/Santa Cruz (189,300)
GOVERNMENT Spanish autonomous region
ETHNIC GROUPS Spanish
LANGUAGES Spanish
RELIGIONS Christianity (mainly Roman Catholic)
CURRENCY Spanish currency

CAPE VERDE

An archipelago of ten large and five small islands, divided into the Barlavent (windward) and Sotavento (leeward) groups Cape Verde lies 560 km [350 mls] off Dakar in Senegal. They are volcanic and mainly mountainous, with steep cliffs and rocky headlands; the highest, Fogo, rises to 2,829 m [9,281 ft] and is active. The islands are tropical, hot for most of the year and mainly dry at sea level.

ECONOMY AND RESOURCES
Higher ground is cooler and more fertile, producing maize, groundnuts, coffee, sugar cane, beans and fruit when not subject to the endemic droughts that have killed 75,000 people since 1900. Poor soils and lack of surface water prohibit development.

Cape Verde's meagre exports comprise mainly bananas and tuna fish, but it has to import much of its food. The only significant minerals are salt and *pozzolana*, a volcanic rock used in making cement. Much of the population's income comes from foreign aid and remittances sent home by the 600,000 Cape Verdeans who work abroad – nearly twice the native population; in the last severe drought (1968–82), some 40,000 emigrated to Portugal alone. Tourism is still in its infancy –

ly 2,000 visitors a year – lagging well behind e Azores, Madeira and the Canaries.

The economic problems experienced by the ape Verdeans are compounded by tens of ousands of Angolan refugees.

HISTORY AND POLITICS
ortuguese since the 15th century – and used iefly as a provisioning station for ships and n assembly point for slaves in the trade from West Africa – the colony became an overseas erritory in 1951 and independent in 1975. inked with Guinea-Bissau in the fight against olonial rule, its Socialist single-party govern- ment flirted with union in 1980, but in 1991 he ruling PAICV was soundly trounced in he country's first multiparty elections by a newly legalized opposition, the Movement for Democracy. [*Map page 32*] ■

AREA 4,030 sq km [1,556 sq mls]
POPULATION 381,000
CAPITAL (POPULATION) Praia (61,800)
GOVERNMENT Multiparty republic
ETHNIC GROUPS Mulatto 71%, Black 28%, White 1%
LANGUAGES Portuguese (official), Crioulo
RELIGIONS Christianity (Roman Catholic 97%, Protestant 2%)
CURRENCY Cape Verde escudo = 100 centavos

CAYMAN ISLANDS

The Cayman Islands comprise three low-lying islands covering 259 sq km [100 sq mls], south of Cuba, with the capital George Town (population 14,000, in a total of 30,000) on the biggest, Grand Cayman.

The main activities used to be farming and fishing until the 1960s, when an economic revolution transformed them into the world's biggest offshore financial centre, offering a secret tax haven to 18,000 companies and 450 banks. The flourishing luxury tourist industry (predominantly from US sources)

now accounts for more than 70% of its official GDP and foreign earnings, while a property boom has put beachfront prices on Grand Cayman among the world's highest. An immi-grant labour force, chiefly Jamaican, consti-tutes about a fifth of the population – similar to European and black groups; the rest are of mixed descent.

A Crown Colony since 1959, the Cayman Islands are a dependent territory of Britain. [*Map page 30*] ■

AREA 259 sq km [100 sq mls]
POPULATION 30,000
CAPITAL (POPULATION) George Town (14,000)
GOVERNMENT British dependency
ETHNIC GROUPS Mulatto 40%, White 20%, Black 20%
LANGUAGES English (official)
RELIGIONS Christianity
CURRENCY Cayman Is dollar = 100 cents

CENTRAL AFRICAN REPUBLIC

The Central African Republic is a remote, landlocked country enclosed by Chad, Sudan, Zaïre, Congo and Cameroon. It lies on an undulating plateau, which is mostly between 600 m and 800 m [1,970 ft to 2,620 ft] above sea level. This plateau divides the headwaters of two river systems. In the south, the rivers flow into the navigable Ubangi (Oubangi) River. This river itself flows into the Zaïre (Congo) River. The Ubangi and its tributary the Bomu form much of the country's southern border. In the north, most rivers are headwaters of the Chari (Shari) River. This river flows into Lake Chad to the north.

Rainforest is confined to the south-west, with tongues of forest extending along the rivers. But wooded savanna covers much of the country, with more open grasslands in the north. The country has many forest and savanna animals, including buffaloes, elephants, lions, leopards and many kinds of birds. About 6% of the land is protected in national parks and reserves. But tourism is on a small scale, because of the remoteness of the country.

ECONOMY AND RESOURCES

The World Bank classifies Central African Republic as a 'low-income' developing country. More than 80% of the people are farmers, and most of them produce little more than they need to feed their families. The main food crops are bananas, maize, manioc, millet and yams. Coffee, groundnuts, cotton, timber and tobacco are produced for export, mainly on commercial plantations.

Diamonds, the only major mineral resource, are the most valuable single export. Manufacturing is on a small scale, with products including beer, cotton fabrics, footwear, leather, soap and sawn timber. Central African Republic's development has been impeded by its remote position, its poor transport system and its untrained workforce. The country depends heavily on aid, especially from France.

HISTORY AND POLITICS

Little is known of the early history of the area. Between the 16th and 19th centuries, the population was greatly reduced by the slave trade and the country is still thinly populated today. Although it is larger than France, France has 18 times as many people.

France set up an outpost at Bangui in 1899 and ruled the country as a colony from 1894. Known as Ubangi-Shari, France ruled the country for most of the time as part of French Equatorial Africa, a vast area which also included Chad, Congo and Gabon. The country became fully independent in 1960.

Central African Republic became a one-party state in 1962, but army officers seized power in 1966. The head of the army, Jean-Bedel Bokassa, made himself emperor in 1976. The country was renamed the Central African Empire, but after a brutal and tyrannical reign, he was overthrown by a military group in 1979. The monarchy was abolished and the country again became a republic.

In March 1981, the country became a multiparty democracy, but the army took over

in September and banned all political partie The country adopted a new, multiparty con stitution in 1991, and elections were held i 1993. [*Map page 32*] ■

AREA 622,980 sq km [240,533 sq mls]
POPULATION 3,235,000
CAPITAL (POPULATION) Bangui (597,000)
GOVERNMENT Multiparty republic
ETHNIC GROUPS Banda 29%, Baya 25%, Ngbandi 11%, Azande 10%, Sara 7%, Mbaka 4%, Mbum 4%
LANGUAGES French (official), Sango (the most common language)
RELIGIONS Traditional beliefs 57%, Christianity 35%, Islam 8%
CURRENCY CFA franc = 100 centimes

CHAD

Chad is Africa's largest landlocked coun try, and twice the size of France, it former ruler. In the Saharan northern third o the country, a sparse nomadic Arabic popu lation lives in a harsh, hot desert containing extensive tracts of mobile dunes (Erg du Djourab), and the volcanic Tibesti Mountains. The wetter southern portions of the country are covered by wooded savanna.

ECONOMY AND RESOURCES

Chad is a sprawling, strife-torn, desperately poor state with no industries except for the processing of agricultural products. Over 90% of the population make a living from crop cultivation, notably cotton, or by animal herding.

In the south, crops of cotton, groundnuts, millet and sorghum are grown – drought permitting – by settled black cultivators. A central bank of thorn bush (Sahel) provides pasturage for migratory cattle and herds of game, though drought and desertification have combined to wreak havoc here in recent years.

Lake Chad is the focal point of much of the country's drainage, affecting two-thirds of the country. However, most water feeding the

ke comes from the rivers Chari and Logone,
e only large perennial water courses in the
untry and now only streams. Agriculture
d population are concentrated along their
lleys and in the vicinity of Lake Chad, now
rinking fast – some estimates state that the
ater area is only 20% of its size in 1970,
d the levels much lower; and while fishing
locally important, catches are less each
ar. Dried fish is still exported, but sales
cotton, meat and other animal products
rovide most exports.

HISTORY AND POLITICS
ince independence Chad has been plagued
y almost continuous civil wars, primarily
etween the Muslim Arab north and the
hristian and animist black south, but also
ith many subsidiary ethnic conflicts. In 1973
olonel Gaddafi's Libya, supporters of the
rab faction, occupied the mineral-rich Aozou
trip in the far north and has held it virtually
ver since.

Libya tried incursions further south in 1983
to back the forces of the previously separate
tate of Bourkou-Ennedi-Tibesti – and in
987, to support one of many abortive coups
gainst a succession of repressive governments
n Ndjamena; the former ended in agreement
n 'joint withdrawal', the latter in crushing
ictory for French and Chadian forces.

Diplomatic relations were restored with
Libya in 1988, but Chad's massive commit-
ments in maintaining control in the drought-
fflicted country as well as on several of its
orders – in addition to an impossible foreign
debt – make it one of the terminally ill nations
of Africa. [*Map page 32*] ∎

AREA 1,284,000 sq km [495,752 sq mls]
POPULATION 6,183,000
CAPITAL (POPULATION) Ndjamena
(530,000)
GOVERNMENT Transitional
ETHNIC GROUPS Bagirmi, Kreish and Sara
31%, Sudanic Arab 26%, Teda 7%, Mbum 6%
LANGUAGES French and Arabic (both
official)
RELIGIONS Islam 40%, Christianity 33%,
traditional beliefs 27%
CURRENCY CFA franc = 100 centimes

CHILE

Extending in an extraordinary shape down
the west coast of South America from
latitude 17° 30'S, well inside the tropics, to
55° 50'S at Cape Horn, Chile falls into three
parallel zones based on the longitudinal folding of the Andes, whose high peaks form the
boundaries with Bolivia and Argentina. It is
the world's 'thinnest' country, 25 times as
long as it is wide.

From the Bolivian border in the north down
as far as 27°S runs an extension of the high
plateau of Bolivia. Several volcanic peaks of
more than 6,000 m [19,680 ft] mark the edge
of the western cordilleras. South of Ojos del
Salado the ranges narrow and steepen, then
gradually reduce in height as they approach
Cape Horn.

The parallel coastal ranges create a rolling,
hilly belt, rising to 3,000 m [10,000 ft] or
more in the north but generally much lower.
Between this belt and the Andes runs the
sheltered and fertile central valley, most
clearly marked southwards from Santiago;
over 60% of the population live in a stretch of
land 800 km [500 mls] long here. Punta
Arenas (population 125,000 in 1991), on the
Straits of Magellan, is the southernmost city in
the world.

Climatically Chile divides readily into a
desert north (the Atacama Desert, where no
recorded rain fell for almost 400 years), a
warm-temperate centre and a cool-temperate
south.

ECONOMY AND RESOURCES
Chile's economy continues to depend on agriculture, fishing and, particularly, mining:
the country is the world's second largest
copper producer (13% of total) and copper
accounts for nearly half of all export earnings.
Magellanes, the southernmost region that
includes Cape Horn and Tierra del Fuego
(shared with Argentina), has oilfields that
produce about half the country's needs. When
the military took over in 1973 inflation was

running at about 850%, despite government controls, and Pinochet reintroduced a market economy and abandoned agricultural reform. Economic decline began in 1981 – brought about, in part, by low world prices for minerals and primary products in general – but with great application the situation has improved. Though there is still political tension and manufacturing industry remains subject to heavy competition, there were encouraging signs of a full recovery as the country entered the 1990s.

HISTORY AND POLITICS

A Spanish colony from the 16th century, Chile developed as a mining enterprise in the north and a series of vast ranches, or *haciendas*, in the fertile central region. After Chile finally freed itself from Spanish rule in 1818 mining continued to flourish in the north, and in the south Valparaiso developed as a port with the farmlands of the southern valley exporting produce to the settlers of California and Australia.

The first Christian Democrat president was elected in 1964, but in 1970 he was replaced by President Allende; his administration, the world's first democratically elected Marxist government, was overthrown in a CIA-backed military coup in 1973 and General Pinochet took power as dictator, banning all political activity in a strongly repressive regime. A new constitution took effect from 1981, allowing for an eventual return to democracy, and free elections finally took place in 1989. President Aylwin took office in 1990, but Pinochet secured continued office as commander-in-chief of the armed forces. [*Map page 31*] ■

AREA 756,950 sq km [292,258 sq mls]
POPULATION 14,044,000
CAPITAL (POPULATION) Santiago (5,343,000)
GOVERNMENT Multiparty republic
ETHNIC GROUPS Mestizo 92%, Amerindian 7%
LANGUAGES Spanish (official)
RELIGIONS Christianity (Roman Catholic 81%, Protestant 6%)
CURRENCY Chilean peso = 100 centavos

CHINA

By far the most populous country in the world, the People's Republic of China also ranks as the third largest country after Russia and Canada, being marginally bigger than the USA. Before the development of modern forms of transport, the vast size of China often hampered efficient communication between the centre of the country and the peripheries. Distances are huge. By rail, the distance from Beijing (Peking) to Guangzhou (Canton) is 2,324 km [1,450 mls].

One of the main determining influences on the evolution of Chinese civilization had been the geographical isolation of China from the rest of the world. Surrounded to the north west and south by forests, deserts and mountain ranges, and separated from the Americas by the vast expanse of the Pacific Ocean, China until modern times was insulated from frequent contact with other civilizations, and its culture and society developed along highly individual lines.

Landscape and relief

The Chinese landscape is like a chequerboard in which mountains and plateaux alternate with basins and alluvial plains. There are two intersecting systems of mountain chains, one trending from north-north-east to south-south-west, the other from east to west. Many mountain areas have been devastated by soil erosion through indiscriminate tree-felling. The agricultural wealth of China is all in the lowlands of the east – where the vast majority of the population lives.

The chequerboard pattern includes an extraordinary variety of landscapes. Manchuria, in the far north, comprises a wide area of gently undulating country, originally grassland, but now an important agricultural area. The loess lands of the north-west occupy a broad belt from the great loop of the Huang He (Hwang Ho) into Shanxi and Henan provinces. Here, valley sides, hills and mountains are blanketed in loess – a fine-grained nstratified soil deposited by wind during the ιst glaciation. Within this region, loess deposits occur widely in the form of plateaux ιat are deeply incised by gorges and ravines.

By contrast with the loess lands, the landcape of the densely populated North China Plain is flat and monotonous. Settlement is concentrated in walled villages while large ields are the product of post-1949 land conolidation schemes. Further south the Yangtze delta is a land of large lakes. Water is a predominant element of the landscape – the lowying alluvial land with its irrigated ricefields is traversed by intricate networks of canals and other man-made works, many of which date back several centuries.

Far inland in the Yangtze basin, and separated from the middle Yangtze valley by precipitous river gorges, lies the Red basin of Sichuan (Szechwan). To the north, west and south, the basin is surrounded by high mountain ranges. The mountains of the Qin Ling ranges, in particular, protect the basin from cold winter winds. With its mild climate and fertile soils, the Red basin is one of the most productive and densely populated regions of China. Ricefields, often arranged in elaborate terraces, dominate the landscape.

Other distinctive landscapes of southern China include those of north-eastern Guizhou province, where limestone spires and pinnacles rise vertically above small, intensively cultivated plains, and the Guangdong coastal lowlands, with their villages in groves of citrus, bananas, mangoes and palms.

The Huang He and the Yangtze

The two major rivers of China are the Huang He and the Yangtze Kiang (Chang Jiang), the world's seventh and third longest. The Huang He, or Yellow River (so called from the large quantities of silt which it transports), is 4,840 km [3,005 mls] long. Also known as 'China's Sorrow', it has throughout history been the source of frequent and disastrous floods. In 1938, dykes along the Huang He were demolished in order to hamper the advance of the Japanese army into northern China, and the river was diverted so as to enter the sea to the south of the Shandong peninsula. In the catastrophic floods which followed, nearly 900,000 lives were lost and

TIBET

With an average elevation of 4,500 m [14,750 ft] – almost as high as Europe's Mont Blanc – and an area of 1.2 million sq km [460,000 sq mls], Tibet is the highest and most extensive plateau in the world. It is a harsh and hostile place, and most of its population of just over 2 million people live in the relatively sheltered south of the country, where the capital, Lhasa, is situated.

Since the 7th century, Tibet has been deeply influenced by Buddhist beliefs, and for much of its history was ruled by Buddhist priests – lamas – as a theocracy. The Dalai Lama, a title passed on in successive incarnations from a dying elder to a newborn junior, usually dominated from Lhasa. Between 1720 and 1911 Tibet was under Chinese control, and in 1950 Tibet was reabsorbed by a resurgent Red China; after an unsuccessful uprising in 1959, the Dalai Lama fled to Delhi and a brutal process of forced Chinese acculturation began: in 1961, a report of the International Commission of Jurists accused China of genocide. An 'Autonomous Region of Tibet' was proclaimed in 1965, but during the 1966–76 Cultural Revolution, many Tibetan shrines and monasteries were destroyed.

54,000 sq km [21,000 sq mls] of land was inundated. Since 1949, the incidence of flooding has declined sharply, largely as a result of state investment in flood-prevention schemes.

The Yangtze, China's largest and most important river, is 6,380 km [3,960 mls] long, and its catchment basin is over twice as extensive as that of the Huang He. Unlike the Huang He, the Yangtze is navigable. During the summer months, ocean-going vessels of 10,000 tonnes may reach Wuhan, and 1,000-tonne barges can go as far upstream as Chongqing. Despite the post-1949 improvement of roads and railways, the Yangtze remains an important transport artery.

Climate and weather

Although the Chinese subcontinent includes a wide variety of relief and climate, it can be divided into three broad regions. Eastern

China is divided into two contrasting halves, north and south of the Qin Ling ranges, while the third region comprises the mountains and arid steppes of the interior.

Northern China: Rainfall is light and variable throughout northern China, and is generally insufficient for irrigated agriculture. In winter, temperatures fall to between –1°C and –8°C [30°F and 18°F] and bitterly cold winds blow eastwards across the North China Plain from the steppes of Mongolia. The summer temperatures, by contrast, are little different from those of southern China, and may reach a daily average of 28°C [82°F]. The growing season diminishes northwards and in northern Manchuria only 90 days a year are free of frost.

Southern China: The area to the south of the Qin Ling ranges receives heavier and more reliable rainfall than the north, and winter temperatures are generally above freezing point. Summer weather, especially in the central Yangtze valley, is hot and humid. At Nanjing, temperatures as high as 44°C [111°F] have been recorded. The far south of China, including Guangdong province and the island of Hainan, lies within the tropics.

The interior: While the Qin Ling ranges are an important boundary between the relatively harsh environments of the north and the more productive lands of the south, a second major line, which follows the Da Hinggan Ling mountains and the eastern edge of the high Tibetan plateau, divides the intensively cultivated lands of eastern China from the mountains and arid steppes of the interior. In the north, this boundary line is marked by the Great Wall of China. Western China includes the Dzungarian basin, the Turfan depression, the arid wastes of the Takla Makan Desert, and the high plateau of Tibet.

ECONOMY AND RESOURCES

Northern China: Despite advances in water conservation since World War II, aridity and unreliability of rainfall restrict the range of crops that can be grown. Millet, maize and winter wheat are the staple crops of the North China Plain, while coarse grains and soya beans are cultivated in Manchuria.

Southern China: Inland, the mild climate and fertile soils of the Red basin make this an important agricultural region. Rice production is dominant but at lower altitudes the climate is warm enough to allow the cultivation of citrus fruits, cotton, sugar cane and tobacco of which China is the world's biggest producer. The far south enjoys a year-round growing season. Irrigated rice cultivation is the economic mainstay of southern China. Double cropping (rice as a main crop followed by winter wheat) is characteristic of the Yangtze valley; along the coast of Guangdong province two crops of rice can be grown each year, and in parts of Hainan Island the annual cultivation of three crops of rice is possible the country produces more than 35% of the world total. Crops such as tea, mulberry and sweet potato are also cultivated, and in the far south sugar cane, bananas, and other tropical crops are grown.

The interior: Although aridity of climate has hampered agriculture throughout most of western China, oasis crops are grown around the rim of the Takla Makan Desert, and farming settlements also exist in the Gansu corridor to the north of the Qilian mountains.

Communist China

Under Communist rule the mass starvation, malnutrition and disease which afflicted China before World War II were virtually eliminated, and living standards greatly improved, particularly in the countryside. One of the salient features of the centrally planned economy was the organization of the rural population into 50,000 communes – self-sufficient units of varying size which farm the land collectively. Communes also ran rural industries, and are responsible for the administration of schools and clinics. Through the communes, labour has been organized on a vast scale to tackle public works schemes such as water conservation, flood control and land reclamation.

Living standards improved markedly, with life expectancy doubling and education improving, though the GNP per capita figure remained that of a poor Third World nation – some 1.5% that of Japan. The agricultural communes were not notably successful, and since peasants have been freed from petty bureaucracy, harvests of grain crops went up by over 40% in the decade from 1976.

Although food supply has generally kept

reast of population growth, the size and owth rate of the Chinese population has ways given cause for concern. By the early 980s, the population was growing at 1.3% er year, a net annual increase of about 13 million people; government penalties and acentives over the size of family have met with ome success, but between 1988 and 2000 it as expected to grow by 187 million – slightly ess than the prediction for India, but more an the 1988 totals for Indonesia or Brazil.

Only 10% of the land area of China is cul-vable, but environmental constraints are uch that there is little prospect of meeting acreased food demand by reclaiming land for griculture. Future growth in food supply nust come from continued intensification of and use and gains in yields.

Although China is an agricultural country, government planners, especially since the death of Mao Tse-tung in 1976, have empha-ized the need to industrialize. China has suf-icient resources in coal, iron ore and oil o support an industrial economy, but it is deficient in capital and industrial technology.

Beijing, the capital city of China, is a gov-ernmental and administrative centre of prime mportance. Several buildings of outstanding architectural interest, such as the former im-perial palace complex (once known as the Forbidden City) and the Temple and Altar of Heaven, have been carefully preserved and are now open to the public. In the 19th and early 20th centuries, with a large community of foreign merchants, Shanghai grew rapidly as a major banking and trading centre. Since 1949, the city has lost its former commercial importance, but it remained China's largest and has emerged as a major centre for the manufacture of iron and steel, ships, textiles and a wide range of engineering products.

HISTORY AND POLITICS

Early Chinese civilization arose along the inland margins of the North China Plain, in a physical setting markedly harsher (especially in terms of winter temperatures) than the en-vironments of the other great civilizations of the Old World. The Shang dynasty, noted for its fine craftsmanship in bronze, flourished in northern China from 1630 to 1122 BC. Shang civilization was followed by many centuries of

THE GREAT WALL OF CHINA

The world's longest fortification, the Great Wall was begun in the 3rd century BC and extended throughout Chinese history; most of the present wall was constructed during the Ming Dynasty, between 1368 and 1644. Its purpose was ostensibly to protect the Chinese Empire from northern nomadic raiders, though (like Egypt's pyramids) it also served as a make-work project for hun-dreds of thousands of otherwise unemployed labourers.

The wall's total length is at least 6,400 km [4,000 mls]; recently, archaeologists discov-ered what may be another 1,000 km [600 mls]. Only a few small sections, renovated largely as tourist attractions, remain in good repair. Contrary to legend, the Great Wall is not visible from the Moon, nor even from very high altitudes. Despite its great length, its flat top is no more than 4 m [13 ft] wide.

political fragmentation, and it was not until the 3rd century BC that China was unified into a centrally administered empire. Under the Ch'in dynasty (221 to 206 BC) the Great Wall of China was completed, while Chinese armies pushed southwards beyond the Yangtze, reaching the southern Chinese coast in the vicinity of Canton.

In succeeding centuries there was a gradual movement of population from the north to the warmer, moister, and more productive lands of the south. This slow migration was greatly accelerated by incursions of barbarian nomads into north China, especially during the Sung dynasty (AD 960 to 1279). By the late 13th century the southern lands, including the Yangtze valley, probably contained around 75% of the Chinese population.

During the Han, T'ang and Sung dynasties, a remarkably stable political and social order evolved within China. The major distinguish-ing features of Chinese civilization came to include Confucianism, whereby the individual was subordinated to family obligations and to state service, the state bureaucracy, members of which were recruited by public examina-tion, and the benign rule of the emperor – the

'Son of Heaven'. Great advances were made in the manufacture of porcelain, silk, metals and lacquerware, while gunpowder, the compass, and printing were among several Chinese inventions which found their way to the West in medieval times. Nevertheless, the economy of pre-modern China was overwhelmingly agricultural, and the peasant class accounted for most of the population.

Despite the geographical diversity and great size of its territory, China during pre-modern times experienced long periods of unity and cohesion rarely disturbed by invasion from outside. Two important dynasties, the Yuan (1279–1368) and the Ch'ing (1644–1912), were established by the Mongols and Manchus respectively, but, almost invariably, alien rulers found it necessary to adopt Chinese methods of government, and the Chinese cultural tradition was preserved intact.

In the 18th century, China experienced a rapid acceleration in the rate of population growth, and living standards began to fall. By the early 19th century, the government was weak and corrupt, and the country suffered frequent famines and political unrest. British victory in the Opium War (1839–42) was followed by the division of China into spheres of influence for the major Western imperialist powers, and by the establishment of treaty ports, controlled by Western countries, along the Chinese coast and the Yangtze.

Meanwhile, the disintegration of imperial China was hastened by peasant uprisings such as the Taiping rebellion (1850–64), and by the defeat of China in the Sino-Japanese War of 1894–5. Belated attempts were made to arrest the decline of the Chinese empire, but in 1912, and following an uprising in Wuhan, the last of the Chinese emperors abdicated and a republic was proclaimed.

Although the republican administration in Beijing was regarded as the legitimate government, real power rested with army generals and provincial governors. Rival generals, or warlords, raised private armies and plunged China into a long and disastrous period of internal disorder. Alternative solutions were offered by two political parties – the Kuomintang (or Chinese Nationalist Party) formed by Sun Yat-sen and later led by Chiang Kai-shek, and the Communist Party.

In 1931, Japan seized Manchuria, and in 193 full-scale war broke out between the tw countries. In the bitter fighting which fo lowed, the Communists, under Mao Tse tung, gained the support of the peasantry an proved adept practitioners of guerrilla warfar

The defeat of Japan in 1945 was followe by a civil war which cost 12 million lives: th Communists routed the Kuomintang armie forcing them to take refuge on the island c Taiwan, and the People's Republic of Chin was officially proclaimed on 1 October 1949.

Communist China

The establishment and consolidation of th Communist regime were carried at a hug human cost: it is now estimated that about on million so-called 'counter-revolutionaries' wer executed in 1949 and 1950. The Great Leap Forward, the radical economic programm started in 1958, which emphasized ideologica purity, ended in failure. In 1966 Mao Tse tung initiated the Great Proletarian Cultura Revolution, another attempt to reassert revol utionary principles: students calling them selves Red Guards took to the streets, de nouncing and often persecuting officials and intellectuals. Eventually order had to be restored by the Army and after Mao's death in 1976, more pragmatic policies were adopted. Under the leadership of Deng Xiaoping, far reaching economic reforms were implemented and China opened itself to foreign investment. However, pressure for political reforms has been resisted and pro-democracy student demonstrations were brutally crushed in Tiananmen Square in 1989. [*Map page 24*] ■

AREA 9,596,960 sq km [3,705,386 sq mls]
POPULATION 1,208,841,000
CAPITAL (POPULATION) Beijing (or Peking, 9,750,000)
GOVERNMENT Single-party Communist Republic
ETHNIC GROUPS Han (Chinese) 92%, 55 minority groups
LANGUAGES Mandarin Chinese (official)
RELIGIONS More than half the people say they are atheists; Buddhism, Taoism, Islam
CURRENCY Renminbi yuan = 10 jiao or 100 fen

COLOMBIA

The Andes cross Colombia from south to north, fanning out into three ranges with two intervening valleys. In the west the low Cordillera Occidental rises from the hot, forested Pacific coastal plain. Almost parallel to it, and separated by the Cauca Valley, is the much higher Cordillera Central; the high peaks of this range, many of them volcanic, rise to over 5,000 m [16,400 ft].

To the east, across the broad valley of the Magdalena River, lies the more complex Cordillera Oriental, which includes high plateaux, plains, lakes and basins; the capital city, Bogotá, is situated on one of the plateaux, at a height of 2,610 m [8,563 ft]. North-west of the mountains lies the broad Atlantic plain, crossed by many rivers. The Andean foothills to the east, falling away into the Orinoco and Amazon basins and densely covered with rain-forest (albeit rapidly diminishing), occupy about two-thirds of the total area of the country. Less than 2% of the population, mainly cattle rangers and Indians, live east of the mountains.

ECONOMY AND RESOURCES

Little of the country is under cultivation, but much of the land is very fertile and is coming into use as roads improve. The range of climate for crops is extraordinary and the agricultural colleges have different courses for 'cold-climate farming' and 'warm-climate farming'. The rubber tree grows wild and fibres are being exploited, notably the *fique*, which provides all the country's requirements for sacks and cordage. Colombia is the world's second biggest producer of coffee, which grows mainly in the Andean uplands, while bananas, cotton, sugar and rice are important lowland products. Colombia imports some food, though the country has the capacity to be self-sufficient. Drugs, however, may be the biggest industry: it was reported in 1987 that cocaine exports earn Colombia more than its main export, coffee.

Industry

Colombia was the home of El Dorado, the legendary 'gilded one' of the Chibcha Indians, but today the wealth is more likely to be coal or oil. The country has the largest proven reserves of coal in Latin America (18 billion tonnes) and is South America's biggest exporter. Gold, silver, iron ore, lead, zinc, mercury, emeralds (90% of world production) and other minerals are plentiful, and hydro-electric power is increasingly being developed. Petroleum is an important export and source of foreign exchange; large reserves have been found in the north-eastern areas of Arauca and Vichada. Early in 1992 BP stepped up its exploration programme among speculation that its new finds, north-east of Bogotá, were among the world's biggest.

There is compulsory social security funded by employees, employers and the government, but the benefits are far from evenly spread. Education spending accounts for nearly 20% of the national budget.

Attempts are being made to broaden the industrial base of the economy to counter the decline in domestic demand and the recession being experienced by Colombia's neighbours. Foreign investment will be essential, but to achieve this the Liberal government – convincing winners in the 1991 elections – must first defeat the drug barons and the habitual violence that pervades the nation.

HISTORY AND POLITICS

Christopher Columbus sighted the country that would bear his name in 1499, and the Spanish conquest of the territory began ten years later. The nation gained independence from Spain following a decade of conflict in 1819, and since the 19th century the two political parties, the pro-clerical, centralizing Conservatives and the anti-clerical, federal-oriented Liberals, have regularly alternated in power. Their rivalry led to two brutal civil wars (1899–1902 and 1949–57), in which some 400,000 people lost their lives: the 1950s conflict, known as *La Violencia*, claimed 280,000 of them. In 1957 the two parties agreed to form a coalition, and this fragile arrangement – threatened by right-wing death squads, left-wing guerillas and powerful drug cartels – lasted until the Liberal President

THE DRUGS TRADE

Colombia is notorious for its illegal export of cocaine, and several reliable estimates class the drug as the country's most lucrative source of foreign exchange. In addition to the indigenous crop, far larger amounts of leaf are smuggled in from Bolivia and Peru for refining, processing and 're-export'. US agencies estimated that in 1987 retail sales of South American cocaine totalled $22 billion – earning about $2 billion in foreign exchange for the producers to reinvest in their own countries, often in property. Violence, though focused on the drug capitals of Medellín and Cali, is endemic, with warfare between rival gangs and between producers and the authorities an almost daily occurrence.

In 1990, as part of US President George Bush's $10.6 billion 'war on drugs', the governments of Colombia, Bolivia and Peru joined forces with the US Drug Enforcement Agency in a concentrated attempt to clamp down on the production and distribution of cocaine. But while early results from Bolivia were encouraging – voluntary eradication quadrupled in a month in Chapare, where over 80% of the country's crop was grown – the situation in Colombia if anything hardened, despite the brave attempts of politicians, administrators and police in many areas to break the socio-economic stranglehold of the drug cartels. A major problem was the support the warlord barons received from their peasant tenant farmers, who knew that no 'legal' crop or occupation would produce the revenue guaranteed by coca, no matter what initial incentives were offered. In addition, the growers of the Upper Huallaga Valley, the world's biggest coca-growing area, enjoyed the protection of the left-wing 'Shining Path' guerrillas.

Virgilio Barco Vargas was elected by a record margin in 1986. Even by the violent standards of South America, however, Colombia remains politically unstable. [*Map page 31*] ■

AREA 1,138,910 sq km [439,733 sq mls]
POPULATION 34,545,000
CAPITAL (POPULATION) Bogotá (4,921,000)
GOVERNMENT Multiparty republic
ETHNIC GROUPS Mestizo 58%, White 20%, Mulatto 14%, Black 4%, mixed Black/Indian 3%, Amerindian 1%
LANGUAGES Spanish (official)
RELIGIONS Christianity (Roman Catholic 93%)
CURRENCY Peso = 100 centavos

COMOROS

The Comoros are three large mountainous islands and several smaller coral islands, lying at the northern end of the Mozambique Channel. Njazidja (formerly Grande Comoro) rises to an active volcano; Nzwami (Anjouan) is a heavily eroded volcanic massif; Mwali (Mohéli) is a forested plateau.

With fertile though porous soils, the islands were originally forested; now they are mostly under subsistence agriculture and produce cash crops such as coconuts, coffee, cocoa and spices, vanilla accounting for 78% of exports.

Formerly French, the Comoros became independent (without the agreement of France) following a referendum in 1974. One of the world's poorest countries, it is plagued by lack of resources and political turmoil.

Mayotte, the easternmost of the large islands (population 101,000), voted to remain French in the 1974 referendum, and in 1976 became a Territorial Collectivity. [*Map page 33*] ■

AREA 2,230 sq km [861 sq mls]
POPULATION 630,000
CAPITAL (POPULATION) Moroni (22,000)
GOVERNMENT Federal Islamic republic
ETHNIC GROUPS Mainly mixture of Arab, Bantu and Malagasy peoples
LANGUAGES Arabic (official), Comorian (Swahili and Arabic dialect), French
RELIGIONS Islam 86%, Roman Catholic 14%
CURRENCY CFA franc = 100 centimes

CONGO

The Republic of Congo is located on the River Congo (Zaïre) in west-central Africa. The Equator runs through the centre of the country. Congo has a narrow coastal plain on which its main port, Pointe Noire, stands. Behind the plain are uplands through which the River Niari has carved a fertile valley. The central part of the country consists of high plains. The north contains large swampy areas in the valleys of rivers that flow into the River Congo and its large tributary, the Oubangi (Ubangi).

Although astride the Equator, only the near-coastal Mayombe ridges and the east-central and northern parts of the Congo basin have a truly equatorial climate and vegetation. The areas around Brazzaville, the capital, and those north and west of it are drier, with savanna vegetation except where tributaries of the River Congo flood widely.

ECONOMY AND RESOURCES
Because of the huge areas of dense forest more than half the population live in towns – a high proportion for Africa – though subsistence agriculture, mainly for cassava, occupies a third of the fast-growing workforce. Oil is by far the country's main source of income (as Africa's fifth largest producer). Palm-oil produce and timber are valuable exports but the timber industry, in relative decline, has always been hampered by poor transport – despite the spectacular Congo-Ocean railway from Brazzaville (formerly the capital of French Equatorial Africa) to Pointe Noire, the nation's only significant port.

HISTORY AND POLITICS
Between the 15th and 18th centuries, part of Congo probably belonged to the huge Kongo kingdom, whose centre lay to the south. But the Congo coast became a centre of the European slave trade. The European exploration of the interior took place in the late 19th century, and the area came under French protection in 1880. It was later governed as part of a larger region called French Equatorial Africa and the country remained under French control until 1960.

Congo became a one-party state in 1964 and a military group took over in 1968. In 1970, Congo became Africa's first declared Communist state, but its Marxist-Leninist ideology did not prevent the government seeking Western help in exploiting the vast off-shore oil deposits. Marxism was abandoned in 1990 and the regime announced the planned introduction of a multiparty system. Following a referendum in favour of a new constitution, elections were held in 1992 and Pascal Lissouba was elected president. Other elections were held in 1993. [*Map page 33*] ∎

AREA 342,000 sq km [132,046 sq mls]
POPULATION 2,516,000
CAPITAL (POPULATION) Brazzaville (938,000)
GOVERNMENT Multiparty republic
ETHNIC GROUPS Kongo 52%, Teke 17%, Mboshi 12%, Mbete 5%
LANGUAGES French (official)
RELIGIONS Christianity (Roman Catholic 54%, Protestant 25%, African Christian 14%), traditional beliefs 5%
CURRENCY CFA franc = 100 centimes

COSTA RICA

Three mountain ranges form the skeleton of the country. In the south-east the Talamanca ranges rise to 3,837 m [12,585 ft] in Chirripo Grande; further north and west the Central Cordillera includes volcanic Irazú (3,432 m [11,260 ft]) and Poas (2,705 m [8,875 ft]), both active in recent decades; Miravalles (2,020 m [6,627 ft]) is one of four active volcanoes in the Cordillera de Guanacaste.

ECONOMY AND RESOURCES
Agriculture is the mainstay of the economy,

the most important crop being coffee, which has been grown in the interior since 1850; in this century bananas have become a second major resource, and together they supply nearly half of Costa Rica's overseas earnings. Timber and fishing are also important. The capital, San José, stands in the fertile Valle Central, in the economic heartland of the country. Drier Guanacaste, in the far northwest, is an important cattle-raising region.

HISTORY AND POLITICS
Christopher Columbus reached the Caribbean coast in 1502 on his fourth and final voyage to the Americas and rumours of treasure (Costa Rica means 'rich coast') soon attracted many Spaniards to settle in the country. Spain ruled the country until 1821, when the Spanish Central American colonies broke away to join Mexico in 1822. In 1823, the Central American states broke with Mexico and set up the Central American Federation. Later, however, this large union broke up and Costa Rica became fully independent in 1838.

From the late 19th century, Costa Rica experienced a number of revolutions, with periods of dictatorship and periods of democracy. In 1948, following a revolt, the armed forces were abolished. Since 1948, Costa Rica has enjoyed a long period of stable democracy, which many in Latin America admire and envy – of the republics of the isthmus, it has the best educational standards, a long life expectancy, the most democratic system of government, the highest per capita gross domestic product, and the least disparity between the poor and the rich. Its neutral stance has enabled the country to play the role of broker in many regional disputes. [*Map page 30*] ■

AREA 51,100 sq km [19,730 sq mls]
POPULATION 3,347,000
CAPITAL (POPULATION) San José (296,625)
GOVERNMENT Multiparty republic
ETHNIC GROUPS White 85%, Mestizo 8%, Black and Mulatto 3%, East Asian (mostly Chinese) 3%
LANGUAGES Spanish (official)
RELIGIONS Christianity (Roman Catholic 81%)
CURRENCY Colón = 100 céntimos

CROATIA

The Republic of Croatia was one of the six republics that made up the former Communist country of Yugoslavia, until it became independent in 1991. The region bordering the Adriatic Sea, with many islands offshore, is called Dalmatia. It includes the coastal ranges, which contain large areas of bare limestone, reaching 1,913 m [6,276 ft] at Mt Troglav. Other highlands lie in the north-east. Most of the rest of the country consists of the fertile Pannonian plains, which are drained by Croatia's two main rivers, the Drava and the Sava.

The coastal area has a typical Mediterranean climate, with hot, dry summers and mild, moist winters. Inland, the climate becomes more continental. Winters are usually bitterly cold, while temperatures often soar to 38°C [100°F] in the summer months.

ECONOMY AND RESOURCES
The wars of the early 1990s disrupted Croatia's economy, which had been quite prosperous before the disturbances. Tourism on the Dalmatian coast had been a major industry. Croatia also had major manufacturing industries, and manufactures remain the chief exports, including cement, chemicals, refined oil and oil products, ships, steel and wood products. Major farm products include fruits, livestock, maize, soya beans, sugar beet and wheat.

HISTORY AND POLITICS
Slav people settled in the area around 1,400 years ago. In 803, Croatia became part of the Holy Roman Empire and the Croats soon adopted Christianity. Croatia was an independent kingdom in the 10th and 11th centuries, but in 1102 the king of Hungary also became king of Croatia, creating a union that lasted 800 years.

In 1526, part of Croatia and Hungary came under the Turkish Ottoman empire, while the rest of Croatia came under the Austrian absburgs. In 1699, however, all of Croatia ame under Habsburg rule. In 1867, the Habsburg empire became the dual monarchy f Austria-Hungary.

Following the defeat of Austria-Hungary in World War I, Croatia became part of the new Kingdom of the Serbs, Croats and Slovenes, which was renamed Yugoslavia in 1929. Germany occupied Yugoslavia during World War II – Croatia was proclaimed independent, but it was really ruled by the invaders.

After the war, the Communists took power with Josip Broz Tito as the country's leader. Despite ethnic differences between the people, Tito held Yugoslavia together until his death in 1980. In the 1980s, economic and ethnic problems, including a deterioration in relations with Serbia, threatened the country's stability. Then, in the 1990s, Yugoslavia split up into five separate nations, one of which was Croatia, officially declaring its independence in 1991.

After Serbia supplied arms to Serbs living in Croatia, war broke out between the two republics, causing great damage and loss of life. The vital tourist industry (Croatia accounted for 80% of the Yugoslav total in 1990) was also devastated, with the fine medieval city of Dubrovnik on the Dalmatian coast a prime casualty. As a result of the fighting, Croatia lost more than 30% of its territory. But in 1992, the United Nations sent a peacekeeping force to Croatia, which effectively ended the war with Serbia.

In 1992, when war broke out in Bosnia-Herzegovina, Croatian troops at first gave support to the Muslims against Serbian attacks. But, later, Croatian forces took some areas of Bosnia-Herzegovina, expelling Muslims from the areas they occupied. [*Map page 16*] ■

AREA 56,538 sq km [21,824 sq mls]
POPULATION 4,504,000
CAPITAL (POPULATION) Zagreb (931,000)
GOVERNMENT Multiparty republic
ETHNIC GROUPS Croat 78%, Serb 12%,
Bosnian, Hungarian, Slovene
LANGUAGES Serbo-Croatian
RELIGIONS Christianity (Roman Catholic
77%, Eastern Orthodox 11%), Islam 1%
CURRENCY Kuna = 100 lipas

CUBA

As large as all the other Caribbean islands put together, Cuba is only 193 km [120 mls] across at its widest, but stretches for over 1,200 km [750 mls] from the Gulf of Mexico to the Windward Passage. Though large, it is the least mountainous of all the Greater Antilles. The plains run the length of the island from Cape San Antonio in the far west to Guantánamo Bay in the south-east (site of an anomalous US naval base), broken by three sets of mountains which occupy no more than a quarter of the country.

ECONOMY AND RESOURCES
The undulating fringes of the mountainous areas provide some of the best tobacco lands, while the higher areas also produce coffee as a cash crop. Sugar cane, however, remains by far the most important cash crop, as it has done throughout the century, and Cuba is the world's third largest producer behind the giants of Brazil and India, producing 74 million tonnes in 1991. It uses over 1 million hectares [2.5 million acres], more than half the island country's cultivated land, and accounts for more than 75% of exports.

Before the 1959 revolution, the cane was grown on large estates, many of them owned by US companies or individuals, but after these were nationalized the focus of production shifted eastwards to Guayabal, with the Soviet Union and Eastern European countries replacing the USA as the main market. Cattle raising and rice cultivation have also been encouraged to help diversify the economy, while Cuba is also a significant exporter of minerals, notably nickel. In 1993, oil production satisfied 40% of domestic requirements.

HISTORY AND POLITICS
Cuba, apart from a brief occupation by the British in 1762–3, remained a Spanish colony from its discovery by Columbus in 1492 (he thought it was part of India) until 1898. It was then under American military

rule until independence in 1902. Since the revolution that deposed the right-wing dictator Fulgencio Batista and brought Fidel Castro to power in 1959 – when 600,000 people fled the island, many of them to Florida – rural development has been fostered in a relatively successful bid to make the quality of life more homogeneous throughout the island. Havana, the chief port and capital, was particularly depopulated.

Cuba's relationship with the US, which secured its independence from Spain but bolstered the corrupt regimes before the revolution, has always been crucial. In 1961, US-backed 'exiles' attempted to invade at the Bay of Pigs, and relations worsened still further the following year when the attempted installation of Soviet missiles on Cuban soil almost led to global war. A close ally of the USSR, Castro has encouraged left-wing revolutionary movements in Latin America and aided Marxist governments in Africa, notably in Angola, while emerging as a Third World leader.

The rapid political changes in Eastern Europe and the USSR from 1989 to 1991 left Cuba isolated as a hardline Marxist state in the Western Hemisphere, and the disruption of trade severely affected the economy of a country heavily dependent on subsidized Soviet oil and aid. Early in 1992 Cuban state radio called for an end to the 30-year-old trade embargo imposed by the US government. Economic difficulties have forced the government to introduce free-market reforms to guard against worsening shortages of food and fuel, but despite the political uncertainty Fidel Castro was re-elected as President of the Council of State for a further five-year term in 1993. [*Map page 30*] ■

AREA 110,860 sq km [42,803 sq mls]
POPULATION 10,9602,000
CAPITAL (POPULATION) Havana (2,119,000)
GOVERNMENT Socialist republic
ETHNIC GROUPS White 66%, Mulatto 22%, Black 12%
LANGUAGES Spanish (official)
RELIGIONS Christianity (Roman Catholic 40%, Protestant 3%)
CURRENCY Cuban peso = 100 centavos

CYPRUS

A small but strategically situated Mediterranean island, Cyprus is a detached fragment of the mainland mountains to the east. In the south, the broad massif of Troodos, rich in minerals, is a classic example of an ophiolite, or intrusive dome of ancient suboceanic rocks. The northern coast is backed by the long limestone range of Kyrenia.

ECONOMY AND RESOURCES

The central plain between Morphou and Famagusta is fertile and well irrigated and grows fruits, flowers and early vegetables. The former forests were cut mainly in classical times to fuel the copper smelteries; *Kypros* is the Greek for copper.

The Greek Cypriot sector has prospered from tourism, British bases, invisible earnings and specialized agriculture, as well as increased manufacturing. The more agriculturally based north has done rather less well: the 'Turkish Republic of Northern Cyprus' is recognized only by Ankara and relies heavily on financial aid from Turkey.

HISTORY AND POLITICS

Turks settled in the north of the island during Ottoman rule, from 1571 to 1878, when Cyprus came under British administration. In the 1950s Greek Cypriots, led by Archbishop Makarios (later President), campaigned for union with Greece (Enosis), while the Turks favoured partition. After a guerrilla campaign by EOKA a power-sharing compromise was reached and in 1960 the island became a republic.

This fragile arrangement broke down in 1963, however, and the following year the UN sent in forces to prevent more intercommunal fighting. In 1968 the Turkish Cypriots set up an 'autonomous administration' in the north, but in 1974, following a coup by Greek-born army officers that deposed Makarios, Turkey invaded the mainland and took control of the northern 40% of the country, displacʒ 200,000 Greek Cypriots. The UN has ᵃce supervised an uneasy partition of the ᵃnd. All attempts at federation have failed. *1ap page 19]* ■

AREA 9,250 sq km [3,571 sq mls]
POPULATION 734,000
CAPITAL (POPULATION) Nicosia (or Lefkosia,169,000)
GOVERNMENT Multiparty republic
ETHNIC GROUPS Greek Cypriot 81%, Turkish Cypriot 19%
LANGUAGES Greek and Turkish (both official)
RELIGIONS Christianity (Greek Orthodox), Islam
CURRENCY Cyprus Pound = 100 cents

CZECH REPUBLIC

With 61% of the total land area of the former Czechoslovakia, the Czech Republic is the larger of its two successor states. ᵑ the west, Bohemia is a diamond-shaped ᵃrea, surrounded by ranges of mountains ᵗhat enclose a basin drained by the River Elbe ᵃnd its tributaries. In the centre lies Prague, ᵗhe historic capital city. Moravia, in the middle ᵒf the country, is divided from Bohemia by ᵖlateau land known as the Moravian Heights. Ǝentral Moravia is a lowland, with the industrial city of Brno, home of the Bren gun, at ᵗts heart.

ECONOMY AND RESOURCES

The Czech Republic is the most highly industrialized of the former Soviet satellites, but agriculture remains strong and well developed, with high yields of most crops suited to the continental climate, including barley, fruit hops, maize, potatoes, sugar beet, vegetables and wheat. Food-processing industries, including brewing, are important in the western provinces. The mountains are rich in minerals, including iron ore, lead, zinc and uranium, while in western Bohemia there are also reserves of hard coal and lignite. Manufactures include such products as chemicals, iron and steel and machinery, but the country also has light industries making such things as glassware and textiles for export.

HISTORY AND POLITICS

Created after World War I and reorganized as a federation in 1969, Czechoslovakia was formally broken up on 1 January 1993, when the eastern Slovak Republic became independent in its own right. The Czech Republic is itself composed of two units, both Czech-speaking, mainly Protestant in religion and with a common history as provinces of the Austrian part of the Austro-Hungarian empire, ruled from Vienna.

Czechoslovakia's 'velvet revolution' of 1989 was Eastern Europe's smoothest transition, toppling the old Communist regime by 'people power' and soon replacing it with a multiparty system that elected a government headed by President Vaclav Havel, the country's best-known playwright and noted dissident (with Charter 77, part of the coalition Civic Forum). It was all very different from 1968, when in the 'Prague Spring' Soviet forces suppressed an uprising supporting Alexander Dubcek's brave attempts at rekindling democracy and breaking the stranglehold of the party bosses.

As elsewhere in Central and Eastern Europe, the road to a free-market economy was not easy. The burdens that plagued the former Soviet satellites were all too obvious – large budget deficit, over-reliance on other Communist countries for trade, increasingly obsolete industrial capacity – and so were the immediate results: inflation, falling production, strikes and unemployment.

Politically, too, there were difficulties. Pragmatic concerns soon dulled the euphoria of democratization and indeed Civic Forum split over the pace of economic reform. Principles of the new constitution were still the subject of controversy in 1992, when resurgent Slovak nationalism forced the parliamentary vote that ended the old Czechoslovak federation – unnecessarily, according to most Czechs and a substantial minority of Slovaks. But the Czech economy, with a serviceable foreign debt and a skilled and adaptable workforce, was in far better shape than that of, say, Poland, while the break-up was, for the most part, amicable. Border adjustments were negligible and negotiated calmly; after the separation, Czechs and Slovaks maintained a customs union and other economic ties, and there was no sign of the bitter hatreds that were causing so much bloodshed in Yugoslavia. [*Map page 16*] ∎

AREA 78,864 sq km [30,449 sq mls]
POPULATION 10,295,000
CAPITAL (POPULATION) Prague (or Praha, 1,216,000)
GOVERNMENT Multiparty republic
ETHNIC GROUPS Czech 81%, Moravian 13%, Slovak 3%, Polish, German, Silesian, Gypsy, Hungarian, Ukrainian
LANGUAGES Czech (official)
RELIGIONS Christianity (Roman Catholic 39%, Protestant 4%)
CURRENCY Czech koruna = 100 halura

DENMARK

The smallest of the Scandinavian countries (but the second largest in population), Denmark consists of the Jutland (Jylland) peninsula, which is an extension of the North German Plain, and an archipelago of 406 islands, of which 89 are inhabited. The coastline – about 7,300 km [4,500 mls] – is extremely long for the size of the country. The largest and most densely populated of the islands is Zealand (Sjaelland), which lies close to the coast of southern Sweden. In the early 1990s this will be connected to the most important island – Fünen (Fyn) – by the Storebaelttunnel. Copenhagen (København), the capital city, lies on the narrow strait, The Sound, which leads from the Kattegat to the Baltic Sea.

Structurally, Denmark is part of a low-lying belt of sedimentary rocks extending from north Germany to southern Sweden, which are geologically much younger than the rest

of Scandinavia. The surface is almost entire covered by glacial deposits, but the unde lying strata are exposed as the 122 m [400 chalk cliffs on the island of Møn. Nowhe in Denmark, however, is higher than 173 [568 ft] and the country averages just 98 [30 ft]. Along the west coast of Jutland, facir the North Sea, are lines of sand dunes wi shallow lagoons behind them.

ECONOMY AND RESOURCES

Denmark has few mineral resources and n coal, though there is now some oil and natu ral gas from the North Sea. A century ago th was a poor farming and fishing country, bu Denmark has now been transformed into on of Europe's wealthiest industrial nations. Th first steps in the process were taken in the lat 19th century, with the introduction of co operative methods of processing and distribut ing farm produce, and the development c modern methods of dairying and pig- an poultry-breeding. Denmark became the mair supplier of bacon, eggs and butter to the grow ing industrial nations of Western Europe Most of the natural fodder for the animal is still grown in Denmark – three-quarters o the land is cultivated and more than 60% i arable – with barley as the principal crop.

Although less than 5% of the workin population is actively engaged in farming, th scientific methods used and the efficient co operative marketing system ensure that outpu remains high. Over a third of Denmark's ex ports are of food products, with Britain and Germany the chief customers.

From a firm agricultural base, Denmark has developed a whole range of industries. Some – brewing, meat canning, fish processing, pot tery, textiles and furniture-making – use Danish products, while others – shipbuilding, oil refining, engineering and metal-working – depend on imported raw materials. The famous port of Copenhagen is also the chief industrial centre and draw for more than a million tourists each year. At the other end of the scale there is Legoland, the famous minia ture town of plastic bricks, built at Billand, north-west of Vejle in eastern Jutland. It was here, in a carpenter's workshop, that Lego was created before it went on to become the world's best-selling construction toy – and a ominent Danish export. The country is also e world's biggest exporter of insulin.

ISTORY AND POLITICS

ontrol of the entrances to the Baltic – the reat and Little Belts and The Sound – contributed to the power of Denmark in the liddle Ages, when the kingdom dominated s neighbours and expanded its territories to nclude Norway, Iceland, Greenland and the aroe Islands. The link with Norway was roken in 1814, and with Iceland in 1944, ut Greenland and the Faroes retain connecions with Denmark. The granite island of Sornholm, off the southern tip of Sweden, lso remains a Danish possession.

Denmark is a generally comfortable mixture f striking social opposites. The Lutheran radition and the cradle of Hans Christian Andersen's fairy-tales co-exist with open attitudes to pornography and one of the aighest illegitimacy rates in the West (44%). A reputation for caring and thorough welfare ervices – necessitating high taxation – is lented somewhat by the world's highest ecorded suicide rate.

It is, too, one of the 'greenest' of the advanced nations, with a pioneering Ministry of Pollution that has real power to act: in 1991 at became the first government anywhere to fine industries for emissions of carbon dioxide, the primary 'greenhouse' gas. At the same time, Danes register Europe's highest rate of deaths from lung cancer.

Denmark gets on well with its neighbours and partners. On 1 January 1973, along with Britain and Ireland, it joined the EEC – the first Scandinavian country to make the break from EFTA – but it still co-operates closely on social, cultural and economic matters with its five Scandinavian partners in the Nordic Council. Having voted by a slender majority to reject the treaty of Maastricht in 1992, the Danes reversed this decision in a second referendum held in May 1993.

Bornholm is a Danish island well away from the rest of the country and far nearer to the southern tip of Sweden (40 km [25 mls]) than to Copenhagen (168 km [104 mls]). A separate administrative region, it was occupied by Germany in World War II but liberated by the Russians, who returned it to Denmark in 1946.

Measuring 558 sq km [227 sq mls], Bornholm is composed mainly of granite and has poor soils, but deposits of kaolin (china clay) spawned a pottery industry. The principal town and ferry port is Rønne, the fishing port Neksø. Fishing and fish processing, agriculture (mainly cattle rearing) and tourism are the main sources of income – the last-named reliant partly on the island's fine examples of fortified churches. [*Map page 13*] ■

AREA 43,070 sq km [16,629 sq mls]
POPULATION 5,173,000
CAPITAL (POPULATION) Copenhagen (1,337,000)
GOVERNMENT Parliamentary monarchy
ETHNIC GROUPS Danish 97%
LANGUAGES Danish (official)
RELIGIONS Christianity (Lutheran 91%, Roman Catholic 1%)
CURRENCY Danish krone = 100 øre

DJIBOUTI

The Republic of Djibouti is a small country in eastern Africa, occupying a strategic position where the Red Sea meets the Gulf of Aden, which leads into the Indian Ocean. Djibouti lies around an inlet of the Gulf of Aden, called the Gulf of Tadjoura. Behind the coastal plain on the northern side of the Gulf of Tadjoura is a highland region, the Mabla Mountains, rising to 1,783 m [5,850 ft] above sea level. Djibouti also contains, at Lake Assal, the lowest point on land in Africa (155 m [509 ft] below sea level).

Djibouti has one of the world's hottest and driest climates. Summer days are exceptionally hot, with temperatures regularly exceeding 42°C [100°F]. The sparse rainfall on the coast is most likely to occur in winter. On average, it rains only on 26 days every year. Inland, where the rainfall is slightly higher on highland areas, rain is more likely between April and October.

A few areas of woodland occur in the mountains north of the Gulf of Tadjoura, where the average annual rainfall reaches about 500 mm [20 in]. But the main vegetation in Djibouti is scrub or dry grassland. The shortage of pasture and surface water makes life difficult for the people, most of whom are nomads who wander in search of pasture.

ECONOMY AND RESOURCES
Djibouti is a poor country. Its economy is based mainly on money it gets for use of its port and the railway that links it to Addis Ababa. Djibouti is a free trade zone and it also has an international airport. The country has no major resources and manufacturing is on a very small scale. The only important activity is livestock raising and half of the people are pastoral nomads. Most of the food the country needs has to be imported.

HISTORY AND POLITICS
Islam was introduced into the area which is now Djibouti in the 9th century AD. The conversion of the Afars led to conflict between them and the Christian Ethiopians who lived in the interior. By the 19th century, the Issas, who are Somalis, had moved north and occupied much of the traditional grazing land of the Afars. France gained influence in the area in the second half of the 19th century and, in 1888, they set up a territory called French Somaliland. The capital of the territory, Djibouti, became important when the Ethiopian emperor Menelik II decided to build a railway to it from Addis Ababa. This made Djibouti the main port handling Ethiopian trade, though Djibouti lost trade when Eritrea was federated with Ethiopia in 1952, giving Ethiopia another port, Assab, on the Red Sea.

In 1967, the people voted to retain their links with France, though most of the Issas were opposed and favoured independence. The country was renamed the French Territory of the Afars and Issas, but it was named Djibouti when it became fully independent in 1977.

Djibouti became a one-party state in 1981, but a new constitution was introduced in 1992, permitting four parties which must maintain a balance between the ethnic groups

in the country. However, in 1992 and 199 tensions between the Afars and Issas flare up when Afars launched an uprising whic was eventually put down by governmer troops. [*Map page 32*] ■

AREA 23,200 sq km [8,958 sq mls]
POPULATION 566,000
CAPITAL (POPULATION) Djibouti (290,000)
GOVERNMENT Multiparty republic
ETHNIC GROUPS Issa 47%, Afar 37%, Arab 6%
LANGUAGES Arabic and French (both official)
RELIGIONS Islam 96%, Christianity 4%
CURRENCY Djibouti franc = 100 centimes

DOMINICA

Dominica is a mountainous, forested island of 751 sq km [290 sq mls] volcanic in origin, with an indented coastline edged with steep cliffs. The climate is tropica with heavy rainfall.

The population of 71,000 is over 90% African and 6% mixed, with small Asian and white minorities and a settlement of about 500 mainly mixed-blood Carib Indians. Predominantly Christian (75% Roman Catholic), most people speak the local French *patois*, though English is the official language. Nearly 30% of the islanders live in the capital, Roseau, and its suburbs.

Though rich soils support dense vegetation, less than 10% is cultivated; bananas and coconut-based soaps and cigars are the chief exports, although fishing, forestry and food-processing industries are being encouraged. Much food is imported, and future prospects for a relatively poor Caribbean island depend a good deal on the development of the island as a luxury tourism destination.

Discovered by Christopher Columbus in 1493, Dominica has been an independent republic (the Commonwealth of Dominica) since 1978, after 11 years as a self-governing

ony of the UK. Britain and France fought
ng over the island, its ownership decided
1805 by a ransom of £12,000 (then
$53,000). [*Map page 30*] ■

REA 751 sq km [290 sq mls]
OPULATION 71,000
:APITAL (POPULATION) Roseau (21,000)
GOVERNMENT Multiparty republic
:THNIC GROUPS Of African descent
.ANGUAGES English (official), French patois
RELIGIONS Christianity (Roman Catholic 75%,
'rotestant 15%)
:URRENCY East Caribbean dollar = 100 cents

DOMINICAN REPUBLIC

Second largest of the Caribbean nations in
both area and population, the Dominican
epublic shares the island of Hispaniola with
Haiti, occupying the eastern two-thirds. Of
he steep-sided mountains that dominate the
land, the country includes the northern
Cordillera Septentrional, the huge Cordillera
Central (rising to Pico Duarte, at 3,175 m
10,417 ft] the highest peak in the Caribbean),
nd the southern Sierra de Bahoruco. Be-
ween them and to the east lie fertile valleys
nd lowlands, including the Vega Real and the
:oastal plains where the main sugar plan-
ations are found. Typical of the area, the
Republic is hot and humid close to sea level,
vhile cooler and fresher conditions prevail in
he mountains; rainfall is heavy, especially
n the north-east.

ECONOMY AND RESOURCES

n the 1980s, growth in industry (exploiting
'ast hydroelectric potential), mining (nickel,
bauxite, gold and silver) and tourism have
ugmented the traditional agricultural economy based on sugar (still a fifth of exports),
coffee, cocoa, tobacco and fruit. There are a
growing number of light processing industries
producing beer, peanut oil, soap, paint, glass
products, textiles and other products.

HISTORY AND POLITICS

Columbus 'discovered' the island and its
Amerindian population (soon to be decimated) on 5 December 1492; the city of Santo
Domingo, now the capital and chief port, was
founded by his brother Bartholomew four
years later and is the oldest in the Americas.
For long a Spanish colony, Hispaniola was initially the centrepiece of their empire but later
it was to become its poor relation. In 1795 it
became French, then Spanish again in 1809,
but in 1821 (then called Santo Domingo) it
won independence. Haiti held the territory
from 1822 to 1844, when on restoring sovereignty it became the Dominican Republic.

Growing American influence culminated in
occupation from 1916 to 1924, followed by
a long period of corrupt dictatorship. Since a
bitter war was ended by US military intervention in 1965, a precarious fledgling democracy has survived violent elections under
the watchful eye of Washington. This highly
Americanized Hispanic society is, however,
far from stable. [*Map page 30*] ■

AREA 48,730 sq km [18,815 sq mls]
POPULATION 7,684,000
CAPITAL (POPULATION) Santo Domingo
(1,601,000)
GOVERNMENT Multiparty republic
ETHNIC GROUPS Mulatto 73%, White 16%,
Black 11%
LANGUAGES Spanish (official)
RELIGIONS Christianity (Roman Catholic 93%)
CURRENCY Peso = 100 centavos

ECUADOR

Ecuador's name comes from the Equator,
which divides the country unequally;
Quito, the capital, lies just within the southern
hemisphere. The country has three distinct
regions – the coastal plain (Costa), the Andean
uplands (Sierra), and the eastern alluvial
plains of the Oriente.

The coastal plain, which averages 100 km

[60 mls] wide, is a hot, fertile area of variable rainfall. Recently cleared of forests and largely freed of malaria, it is now good farmland where banana farms, coffee and cocoa plantations and fishing are the main sources of income, with the country's commercial centre of Guayaquil a flourishing port.

The Andes form three linked mountain ranges across the country, with several of the central peaks rising above 5,000 m [16,400 ft]. Quito, an old city rich in art and architecture from a colonial past, has a backdrop of snow-capped mountains, among them Cotopaxi – at 5,896 m [19,340 ft] the world's highest active volcano – and Chimborazo (6,267 m [20,556 ft]). The Oriente, a heavily forested upland, is virtually unexploited except for recent developments of oil and natural gas.

ECONOMY AND RESOURCES

Ecuador's economy was based on the export of bananas, for which the country was world leader, and is still the biggest exporter, but this changed from 1972 when oil was first exploited with the opening of the trans-Andean pipeline linking with the tanker-loading port of Esmeraldas. Petroleum and derivatives account for about 40% of export earnings, after peaking at 66% in 1985. A shortage of power limits much development in the manufacturing industry – even in the mid-1980s only 60% of the population had use of electricity. During the 1970s, the manufacture of textiles, cement and pharmaceuticals grew, as did food processing, but there is little heavy industry. Fishing has been affected by the warm water current (El Niño) and there is now an emphasis on greater investment and using much more new technology.

Changes in demand for oil and an earth-quake in March 1987, which disrupted much of industry, led the government to suspend payment of interest on its overseas debt, then cancel all debt repayment for the rest of the year. A strict economic recovery programme was put into place and a rescheduling of debt payments agreed in 1989.

HISTORY AND POLITICS

The Inca people of Peru conquered much of what is now Ecuador in the late 15th century, introducing their language, Quechua, which is widely spoken today. But in 1533 Span⋯ forces defeated the Incas and took cont⋯ of Ecuador. The country became independe⋯ in 1822, following the defeat of a Span⋯ force in a battle near Quito. Ecuador th⋯ became part of Gran Colombia, a confede⋯ tion with Panama, Colombia and Venezue⋯ but left in 1830. Between 1830 and 1947 the⋯ were no less than 14 constitutions.

In the 19th and 20th centuries, Ecuad⋯ suffered from political instability, while su⋯ cessive governments failed to tackle the soc⋯ and economic problems of the country.⋯ war with Peru in 1941 led to a loss of ter⋯ tory, but the area taken by Peru is still claim⋯ by Ecuador. After seven years of military ru⋯ elections took place in 1979 and democra⋯ was restored (voting is compulsory for ⋯ literate citizens over the age of 18); civili⋯ governments have ruled since then.

The Galápagos Islands lie scattered acro⋯ the Equator, 970 km [610 mls] west of Ecu⋯ dor (of which they form a province). The⋯ consist of six main islands and over 50 small⋯ ones; all are volcanic, some of them activ⋯ but only four of the islands are inhabited.

Discovered by the Spanish in 1535 b⋯ annexed by Ecuador in 1832, the archipelag⋯ became famous after the visit of Charl⋯ Darwin in 1835, when he collected cruci⋯ evidence for his theory of natural selectio⋯ The islands contain a large variety of uniqu⋯ endemic species of flora and fauna, includin⋯ giant tortoises and marine iguanas. Thoug⋯ 90% of the land area is devoted to a nation⋯ park (which attracted 42,000 visitors in 1992⋯ most of the 10,000 inhabitants derive the⋯ livelihood from fishing and farming. [Ma⋯ page 31] ∎

AREA 283,560 sq km [109,483 sq mls]
POPULATION 11,220,000
CAPITAL (POPULATION) Quito (1,101,000)
GOVERNMENT Multiparty republic
ETHNIC GROUPS Mestizo (mixed White and Amerindian) 40%, Amerindian 40%, White 15%, Black 5%
LANGUAGES Spanish (official)
RELIGIONS Christianity (Roman Catholic 92%)
CURRENCY Sucre = 100 centavos

EGYPT

But for the River Nile, which brings the waters of the East African and Ethiopian Highlands to the Mediterranean, Egypt would scarcely be populated, for 96% of the present population lives in the Nile Valley and its rich delta.

The vast majority of the country, away from the Nile, is desert and semi-desert. Egypt's deserts are not uniform, but offer varied landscapes. Beyond the Gulf of Suez and the Suez Canal the Sinai Peninsula in the south is mountainous and rugged; it contains the highest of Egypt's mountains – Gebel Katherina (2,637 m [8,650 ft]) – and is almost entirely uninhabited. The Eastern Desert, between the Nile and the Red Sea, is a much dissected area and parts of the Red Sea Hills are over 2,000 m [6,560 ft]; water is obtained from the slight rainfall, from occasional springs, and from beneath dry stream beds. Except for a few mining settlements along the coast, this area is not suitable for permanent settlement and is occupied mostly by nomads.

The Western Desert includes almost three-quarters of Egypt and consists of low vales and scarps, mainly of limestones. Over its stony and sandy surfaces great tank battles were fought in World War II. A number of depressions in the desert surface fall below sea level, the most notable being the Qattâra Depression (–133 m [–435 ft]) – a waste of salt lakes and marshes. There are a number of oases, the most important being Khârga, Dakhla, Farâfra, Baharîya and Siwa. By drawing on deep-seated artesian waters, it is hoped to expand the farming area of the first four of these as a contribution to the solution of Egypt's present population problem. Except at the oases, the desert is virtually uninhabited.

ECONOMY AND RESOURCES

The Nile Valley was one of the cradles of civilization, and Egypt has the longest-known history of any African country. The dependable annual flooding of the great river each summer and the discovery of the art of cultivating wheat and barley fostered simple irrigation techniques and favoured co-operation between the farmers. Stability and leisure developed arts and crafts, city life began and the foundations were laid of writing, arithmetic, geometry and astronomy. Great temples and pyramid tombs within the valley remain as memorials to this early civilization – and a magnet for nearly 2 million tourists every year.

Today, even more than in the past, the Egyptian people, living within a desert, depend almost entirely on the waters of the Nile. These are extremely seasonal, and control and storage have become essential during this century. For seasonal storage the Aswan Dam (1902) and the Jebel Awliya Dam in Sudan (1936) were built. The Aswan High Dam (1970), sited 6.4 km [4 mls] above the Aswan Dam, is the greatest of all. Built with massive Soviet aid, it holds back 25 times as much as the older dam and permits year-round storage. Through this dam the Egyptian Nile is now regulated to an even flow throughout the year. The water that has accumulated behind the dam in Lake Nasser (about 5,000 sq km [1,930 sq mls]) is making possible the reclamation of more desert land, the intensification of agriculture and the cultivation of crops that need more water, such as rice for export. The dam is also a source of hydroelectric power and aids the expansion of industry. However, 50,000 Nubians had to be resettled and the regulation of the river's flow has led to some unforeseen environmental problems.

Industry

The traditional Egypt of the *galabiyah*-clad peasant toiling on his tiny plot of land is slowly changing. Pressure of population on the limited amount of farmland is leading to an expansion of industry as an alternative way of life, and Egypt is today one of the most industrialized countries of Africa.

Most of this industrial development has come about since World War II. Textiles, including the spinning, weaving, dyeing and printing of cotton, wool, silk and artificial fibres, form by far the largest industry. Other manufactures derive from local agricultural and mineral raw materials, and include sugar refining, milling, oil-seed pressing, and the manufacture of chemicals, glass and cement. There are also iron-and-steel, oil-refining and car-assembly industries, and many consumer goods such as radios, TV sets and refrigerators are manufactured. The main cities of Cairo and Alexandria – the capital is the largest city in Africa – are also Egypt's major industrial centres.

The Suez Canal, which opened in 1869 and is 173 km [107 mls] long, is still an important trading route. Though it cannot take the large modern cargo vessels, oil tankers and liners, it still carries around 17,500 vessels a year between the Mediterranean and the Red Sea.

HISTORY AND POLITICS
The British-built Suez Canal was nationalized in 1956 by the Egyptian president, Gamal Abdel Nasser, who from 1954 until his death in 1970 was the leader of Arab nationalism. In 1952 the army had toppled the corrupt regime of King Farouk, the last ruler of a dynasty dating back to 1841. Egypt had previously been part of the Ottoman empire (from 1517), though British influence was paramount after 1882 and the country was a British protectorate from 1914 to 1922, when it acquired limited independence.

Egypt was involved in two wars against Israel (in 1967 and 1973) but Nasser's successor broke with the rest of the Arab world to sign a peace treaty with Israel in 1979. He was assassinated in 1981. Egypt joined the allied forces against Saddam Hussein in the 1991 Gulf War. In recent years, the country has experienced a rising tide of Islamic fundamentalism which has included terrorist attacks on foreign tourists. [*Map page 22*] ■

AREA 1,001,450 sq km [386,660 sq mls]
POPULATION 61,636,000
CAPITAL (POPULATION) Cairo (or El Qâhira, 6,800,000)
GOVERNMENT Republic
ETHNIC GROUPS Egyptian 99%
LANGUAGES Arabic (official), French, English
RELIGIONS Islam (Sunni Muslim 94%), Christianity (mainly Coptic Christian 6%)
CURRENCY Egyptian pound = 100 piastres

EL SALVADOR

The only Central American country without a Caribbean coast, El Salvador is also the smallest and the most densely populated. Pressure on agricultural land, combined with civil war, has led to widespread emigration. The Pacific coastal plain is narrow and backed by a volcanic range averaging about 1,200 m [4,000 ft] in altitude. El Salvador has over 20 volcanoes, some of which are still active, and crater lakes occupying a fertile central plain 400 m to 800 m [1,300 ft to 2,600 ft] above sea level. Urban and rural population in this belt together account for 60% of the country's total.

ECONOMY AND RESOURCES
This fertile zone also produces 90% of the coffee and tobacco, and most of the maize and sugar – the foundations of the agricultural economy, with coffee usually accounting for over half the total value of exports. The towns are centres of manufacturing for the domestic market. In May 1992 El Salvador, Guatemala and Honduras created a fre trade zone.

Inland, the frontier with Honduras is marked by mountain ranges which reach heights of 2,000 m [6,560 ft]; previously forested and empty, they are now attracting migrants desperate for agricultural land.

HISTORY AND POLITICS
El Salvador was plagued by conflict from the early 1970s and by full-blown civil war from 1980, when the political left joined revolutionary guerrillas against the US-backed extreme right-wing government. During the next 12 years, more than 75,000 people were killed (most of them civilians) and hundreds of thousands were made homeless as the regime received $4 billion in aid from the US in abetting the 55,000-strong Salvadorean Army and notorious death squads.

After 19 months of UN-mediated talks, the two sides agreed complicated terms at the end of 1991. A cease-fire took effect in February

'92, but the country remained in disarray, ₃th unemployment, for example, standing more than 50% of the workforce. [*Map ₃ge 30*] ■

AREA 21,040 sq km [8,124 sq mls]
POPULATION 5,641,000
CAPITAL (POPULATION) San Salvador (1,522,000)
GOVERNMENT Republic
ETHNIC GROUPS Mestizo (mixed White and Amerindian) 89%, Amerindian 10%, White 1%
LANGUAGES Spanish (official)
RELIGIONS Christianity (Roman Catholic 94%)
CURRENCY Colón = 100 centavos

EQUATORIAL GUINEA

The Republic of Equatorial Guinea consists of a mainland territory which makes ₃p 90% of the land area, called Mbini (or Rio Muni), between Cameroon and Gabon, and ive offshore islands in the Bight of Bonny, the ₃argest of which is Bioko. The island of Anno₃on lies 560 km [350 mls] south-west of Mbini.

Mbini consists mainly of hills and plateaux ₃ehind the coastal plains. Its main river, the ₃olo (formerly Mbini), rises in Gabon and ₃lows across Mbini. Bioko is a volcanic island ₃with fertile soils; Malabo's harbour is part of a ₃submerged volcano.

The climate is hot and humid. Bioko is ₃mountainous, with the land rising to 2,850 m [9,350 ft] and hence it is particularly rainy, ₃though there is a marked dry season between December and February. Mainland Mbini has a similar climate, though the rainfall diminishes inland. The dense rainforests contain valuable trees, including mahogany, okoumé and African walnut, while mangrove forests border much of the coast. Bioko is more varied, with grasslands at higher levels.

ECONOMY AND RESOURCES
Plantations of coffee and cocoa have been established on the mountainous and volcanic islands, similar to many Caribbean islands.

Mainland Mbini, which accounts for over 90% of the country's land area, is very different, lower and thinly peopled, less developed, and with fewer foreign enterprises, except in forestry (especially okoumé and mahogany production) and palm oil. Coffee and cocoa are also grown, though the economy relies heavily on foreign aid.

HISTORY AND POLITICS
At the turn of the 15th century the Papacy awarded Africa and Asia to Portugal, and the Americas west of 50°W to Spain. The latter sought a source of slaves in Africa, and in 1778 the Portuguese ceded the islands of Fernando Poó (Bioko) and Annobon (Pagalu), together with rights on the mainland, Mbini (Rio Muni), against Spanish agreement to Portuguese advance west of 50°W in Brazil.

Guinea, a name which derives from an ancient African kingdom, was once used to describe the whole coastal region of West Africa. Equatorial Guinea was granted partial autonomy from Spain in 1963, and gained full independence in 1968. Thanks to its cocoa plantations, Equatorial Guinea once boasted the highest per capita income in West Africa. But after independence, the bloody 11-year dictatorship of President Francisco Macías Nguema left the economy in ruins. He was overthrown in 1979 and a group of officers, led by his nephew, Lt.-Col. Teodoro Obiang Nguema Mbasago, set up a Supreme Military Council to rule the country. In 1991, the people voted to set up a multiparty democracy and elections were held in 1993. [*Map page 33*] ■

AREA 28,050 sq km [10,830 sq mls]
POPULATION 389,000
CAPITAL (POPULATION) Malabo (37,000)
GOVERNMENT Multiparty republic (transitional)
ETHNIC GROUPS Fang 83%, Bubi 10%, Ndowe 4%
LANGUAGES Spanish (official)
RELIGIONS Christianity (mainly Roman Catholic) 89%, traditional beliefs 5%
CURRENCY CFA franc = 100 centimes

ERITREA

ESTONIA

Eritrea consists of a low coastal plain in the south and mountain ranges in the north. It was Ethiopia's third largest province but only seventh in terms of population. However, the capital, Asmara (Asmera), was the country's second city (358,000) after Addis Ababa.

The economy was devastated by the war of independence. Industries such as textiles and footwear are being rebuilt and so are the ports of Massawa and Assab (Aseb). The main crops are cotton, coffee and tobacco.

The far northern province of Ethiopia bordering the Red Sea, Eritrea was an Italian colony from the 1880s until 1941, when it passed to British military administration. In accordance with a UN resolution, it was given to Ethiopia in 1952, becoming an autonomous region within the Federation of Ethiopia and Eritrea. This became a unitary state ten years later, when the region was effectively annexed by Haile Selassie.

The Eritrean People's Liberation Front (EPLF) then pressed for independence with an unrelenting guerrilla campaign in what became Africa's longest war. Like their counterparts in Tigre and the Oromo movement in Wollo and Gondar, they held large tracts of the countryside for years while government forces occupied the towns. With the fall of the Mengistu regime in 1991, the EPLF gained agreement on independence for Eritrea, guaranteeing access to the Red Sea by making Assab a free port. Independence was formally declared on 24 May 1993. [*Map page 32*] ■

AREA 94,000 sq km [36,293 sq mls]
POPULATION 3,437,000
CAPITAL (POPULATION) Asmera (358,000)
GOVERNMENT Military government
ETHNIC GROUPS Tigre, Afar, Beja, Saho, Agau
LANGUAGES Arabic, English, Tigrinya, Tigre, Saho, Agail, Afar
RELIGIONS Coptic Christianity 50%, Islam 50%
CURRENCY Ethiopian birr = 100 cents

Smallest of the three Baltic states, and the least populous of any of the 15 former Soviet republics, Estonia is bounded on the north by the Gulf of Finland and on the west by the Baltic Sea. The country comprises mostly flat, rock-strewn, glaciated lowland with over 1,500 lakes, and has more than 800 offshore islands, by far the biggest being Saaremaa and Hiiumaa. The largest lake Chudskoye Ozero (Lake Peipus), forms much of the border with Russia in the east.

ECONOMY AND RESOURCES

Over a third of the land is forested, and the timber industry is among the country's most important industries, alongside metal working, shipbuilding, clothing, textiles, chemicals and food processing. The last is based primarily on extremely efficient dairy farming and pig breeding, but oats, barley and potatoes suit the cool climate and average soils. Fishing is also a major occupation.

Like the other two Baltic states, Latvia and Lithuania, Estonia is not endowed with natural resources, though its shale is an important mineral deposit: enough gas is extracted by processing to supply St Petersburg, Russia's second largest city.

HISTORY AND POLITICS

The ancestors of the Estonians, who are related to the Finns, settled in the area several thousand years ago. German crusaders, known as the Teutonic Knights, introduced Christianity in the early 13th century, and by the 16th century, German noblemen owned much of the land in Estonia. In 1561, Sweden took the northern part of the country and Poland the south. From 1625, Sweden controlled the entire country, until it was handed over to Russia in 1721.

Estonian nationalists campaigned for their independence from around the mid-19th century. Finally, Estonia was proclaimed independent in 1918. In 1919, the govern-

ent began to break up the large estates and
istribute land among the peasants.

Then, in 1939, Germany and the Soviet
Union agreed to take over parts of eastern
Europe. In 1940, Soviet forces occupied
Estonia, but they were driven out by the
Germans in 1941. Soviet troops returned in
1944 and Estonia became one of the 15 Soviet
Socialist Republics of the Soviet Union. The
Estonians strongly opposed Soviet rule and
many were deported to Siberia.

Political changes in the Soviet Union in
the late 1980s led to renewed demands for
freedom. In 1990, the Estonian government
declared the country independent and, finally,
the Soviet Union recognized this act in
September 1991, shortly before the Soviet
Union was dissolved. Estonia adopted a new
constitution in 1992, when multiparty elections were held for a new national assembly. In
1994, Russia completed the withdrawal of its
troops from Estonia. [*Map page 13*] ■

AREA 44,700 sq km [17,300 sq mls]
POPULATION 1,541,000
CAPITAL (POPULATION) Tallinn (499,000)
GOVERNMENT Multiparty republic
ETHNIC GROUPS Estonian 62%, Russian 30%,
Ukrainian 3%, Belarussian 2%, Finnish 1%
LANGUAGES Estonian (official)
RELIGIONS Christianity (Lutheran, with
Orthodox and Baptist minorities)
CURRENCY Kroon = 100 sents

ETHIOPIA

E thiopia's main feature is a massive block
of volcanic mountains, rising to 4,620 m
[15,150 ft] and divided into Eastern and
Western Highlands by the Great Rift Valley.
Steep escarpments face each other across the
rift, opening northwards to form the southern
and eastern boundaries of the high Welo
plateau. The Eastern Highlands fall away
gently to the south and east. The Western
Highlands, generally higher and far more
extensive and deeply trenched, are the sources

of the Blue Nile and its tributaries. Off their
north-eastern flank, close to the Red Sea, lies
the Danakil Depression, an extensive desert
that falls to 116 m [380 ft] below sea level.

Giant thistles, red-hot pokers and lobelia
are characteristic of the montane vegetation.
In the desert of the Rift Valley the Danakil
tend their diminishing herds, as do the Somali
pastoralists on the dry Ogaden plain to the
south-east.

ECONOMY AND RESOURCES

In the lower areas of both highlands tropical
cereals, oil seeds, coffee and cotton were the
dominant crops before the wrecking of the
rural economy, while at higher altitudes temperate cereals, pulses and fruits are produced.

Ethiopia was thrust before the attention of
the world late in 1984 by unprecedented television pictures of starving millions – victims
not only of famine but also of more than two
decades of civil war and a Marxist government
determined to enforce hardline economic and
social policies. While that regime was finally
toppled in 1991, and aid continued to pour in
from the richer nations, the accumulative
effects of drought (beginning in 1972, but
with three merciless ones in the 1980s) combined with administrative mismanagement
had left the nation destitute.

HISTORY AND POLITICS

Coptic Christianity reached the northern kingdom of Aksum in the 4th century, surviving
there and in the mountains to the south when
Islam spread through the rest of north-east
Africa. These core areas also survived colonial
conquest; indeed Ethiopia (previously known
as Abyssinia) itself became a colonial power
between 1897 and 1908, taking Somali and
other peoples into its feudal Empire. Invaded
by Italy in 1935, Ethiopia became independent again six years later when British troops
forced the Italians out.

Emperor Haile Selassie ('the Lion of
Judah'), despite promising economic and social
reforms following a two-year drought, was
deposed after his 44-year rule by a revolutionary military government in 1974. A month
later, Ethiopia was declared a socialist state:
foreign investments and most industries were
nationalized and a programme of land collec-

tivization was started, sweeping away the feudal aristocracy. Though the ideology changed, it was still centralized, bureaucratic despotism, proving to be as inefficient as the old system.

By 1977 President Mengistu had assumed control, and with massive Soviet military and financial aid pursued interlocking policies of eliminating rival left-wing groups, suppressing secessionist movements (in Eritrea, Tigre, Wollo, Gondar and Ogaden) and instituting land reform, including the forced resettlement of millions from their drought-afflicted homelands. His period of 'Red Terror' killed tens of thousands of innocent people. Collectivist agriculture failed to cope with deforestation, overgrazing and the effects of drought, while for 14 years more than 60% of the national budget was spent on defence and 'security'. The Marxist government, plagued by Somali incursions (into Ogaden in 1978, and lasting for ten years), as well as internal rebellions, drained vital resources from the economy.

After a decade of unparalleled disaster driven by drought, Mengistu was finally put to flight in 1991 as Addis Ababa was taken by forces of the EPRDF (Ethiopian People's Revolutionary Democratic Front) – an unstable alliance of six separate rebel organizations. The EPRDF announced a caretaker coalition government and plans for multiparty elections, but the administration faced one of the most daunting tasks in the Third World. Relief organizations estimated that of the 25 million people facing starvation in Africa, some 6 million were Ethiopians. In 1993, Eritrea became independent of Ethiopia. [*Map page 32*] ■

AREA 1,128,000 sq km [435,521 sq mls]
POPULATION 53,435,000
CAPITAL (POPULATION) Addis Ababa (2,213,000)
GOVERNMENT Transitional regime
ETHNIC GROUPS Amhara 38%, Galla (Oromo) 35%, Tigre 9%, Gurage 3%, Ometo 3%
LANGUAGES Amharic (official)
RELIGIONS Christianity (Ethiopian Orthodox 53%, other Christian 5%), Islam 31%, traditional beliefs 11%
CURRENCY Birr = 100 cents

FALKLAND ISLANDS

Comprising two main islands and over 200 small islands, the Falkland Islands lie 480 km [300 mls] from South America. Windswept, virtually treeless, covered with peat moorland and tussock grass, the rolling landscape rises to two points of about 700 m [2,300 ft] – Mt Usborne in East Falkland and Mt Adam in West Falkland. Over half the population lives in (Port) Stanley, the capital situated in a sheltered inlet on East Falkland.

ECONOMY AND RESOURCES
The economy is dominated by sheep farming, almost the only industry, with over 40% of exports comprising high-grade wool, mostly to Britain. The UK government is also funding a fishing development programme and helping with tourism: the islands are rich in subarctic wildlife, including penguins, seals and numerous birds, notably the albatross. Since the war with Argentina there has been a large British garrison.

HISTORY AND POLITICS
Discovered in 1592 by the English navigator John Davis, the Falklands were first occupied nearly 200 years later – by the French (East) in 1764 and the British (West) in 1765. The French interest, bought by Spain in 1770, was assumed by Argentina when it gained independence in 1806, and the Argentinians retained their settlements there. The British, who had withdrawn on economic grounds back in 1774, had never relinquished their claim, and in 1832 they returned to the islands to dispossess the Argentine settlers and start a settlement of their own – one that became a Crown Colony in 1892.

The prospect of rich offshore oil and gas deposits from the 1970s aggravated the long-standing dispute, and in 1982 Argentine forces invaded the islands (*Islas Malvinas* in Spanish) and expelled the governor. Two months later – after the loss of 725

rgentinians and 225 Britons – the UK
egained possession. Anglo-Argentine diplomatic relations were restored in 1990, but
the UK refuses to enter into discussions on
overeignty.

outh Georgia and **South Sandwich Island**,
the east, ceased to be Falklands dependen-
ies in 1985, though they are administered via
tanley. They have had no permanent popu-
ation since the closure of the whaling station
t Leith in 1966. [*Map page 31*] ■

AREA 12,170 sq km [4,699 sq mls]
POPULATION 2,120
CAPITAL (POPULATION) Stanley (1,557)
GOVERNMENT British dependency
ETHNIC GROUPS British
LANGUAGES English
RELIGIONS Christianity
CURRENCY Falkland pound = 100 pence

FAROE ISLANDS

The Faroes are a group of rocky islands
situated in the North Atlantic 450 km
[280 mls] from Iceland, 675 km [420 mls]
from Norway and 300 km [185 mls] from the
Shetlands. Like Iceland, they are composed
mainly of volcanic material. They were dramatically moulded by glacial action and the
landscape forms a forbidding setting for the
Faroese farming and fishing settlements. Away
from the villages and scattered hamlets, high
cliffs are home to millions of seabirds. Winters
are mild for the latitude but the summers
are cool. It is usually windy and often over-
cast or foggy. The people speak Faroese,
a Scandinavian language official (alongside
Danish) since 1948. Of the 22 islands, 17
are inhabited.

ECONOMY AND RESOURCES
Sheep farming on the poor soils is the principal occupation but salted, dried, processed
and frozen fish, fishmeal and oil – from cod,

whiting, mackerel and herring – comprise
the chief exports. Faroese motor vessels are
found in all the deep-sea fishing grounds of
the North Atlantic and the capital, Tórshavn,
has ship-repairing yards. Denmark, Norway
and Britain are the country's main trading
partners.

Since 1940 the currency has been the
Faroese króna, which is freely interchangeable
with the Danish krone.

HISTORY AND POLITICS
The Faroe Islands have been part of the
Danish kingdom since 1386 and from 1851
they sent two representatives to the Danish
parliament. Their own elected assembly,
dating from 1852, secured a large degree of
self-government as a region within the Danish
realm in 1948.

The islands left the European Free Trade
Association (EFTA) when Denmark switched
membership to the European Economic
Community (EEC) on 1 January 1973, but
did not join the community – though they
do have a special associate status allowing for
free industrial trade. [*Map page 4*] ■

AREA 1,400 sq km [541 sq mls]
POPULATION 47,000
CAPITAL (POPULATION) Tórshavn (14,601)
GOVERNMENT Danish self-governing region
ETHNIC GROUPS Of Scandinavian descent
LANGUAGES Faroese (official), Danish
RELIGIONS Christianity (mainly Lutheran)
CURRENCY Danish currency & Faroese króna

FIJI

By far the most populous of the Pacific
nations, Fiji comprises more than 800
Melanesian islands, of which the larger ones
are volcanic, mountainous and surrounded by
coral reefs, while the rest are low coral atolls.
About 100 islands are permanently inhabited.
Easily the biggest are Viti (10,430 sq km
[4,027 sq mls]), with the capital of Suva on

its south coast, and Vanua Levu, which is just over half the size of the main island.

ECONOMY AND RESOURCES

The islands' economy is basically agricultural, with sugar cane (45% of exports), copra and ginger the main cash crops, and fish and timber also exported. However, nearly 20% of revenues are generated by sales of gold. The main trading partners are the UK and Australia for exports, and the US, New Zealand and Australia for imports.

HISTORY AND POLITICS

Fiji suffers today from its colonial past. It was a British colony from 1874 until 1970, when it became an independent state and a member of the Commonwealth. The Indian workers brought in by the British for the plantations in the late 19th century now outnumber the native Fijians, but have been until recently second-class citizens in terms of electoral representation, economic opportunity and land ownership. The constitution adopted on independence in 1970 was intended to ease racial tension, but two military coups in 1987 overthrew the recently elected (and first) Indian-majority government, suspended the constitution and set up a Fijian-dominated republic outside the British Commonwealth.

The country finally returned to full civilian rule in 1990; but with a new constitution guaranteeing Melanesian political supremacy, many Indians had already emigrated before the elections of 1992, taking their valuable skills with them. The turmoil of the late 1980s also had a disastrous effect on the growing tourist industry – and by the time the situation stabilized, most of the Western countries that provide the foreign visitors were already in deep recession. [*Map page 3*] ∎

AREA 18,270 sq km [7,054 sq mls]
POPULATION 771,000
CAPITAL (POPULATION) Suva (71,600)
GOVERNMENT Republic
ETHNIC GROUPS Indian 49%, Fijian 46%
LANGUAGES English, Bauan, Hindustani
RELIGIONS Christianity 53%, Hinduism 38%, Islam 8%
CURRENCY Fiji dollar = 100 cents

FINLAND

Located almost entirely between latitude 60°N and 70°N, Finland is the most northerly state on the mainland of Europe though Norway's county of Finnmark actually cuts it off from the Arctic Ocean. A third of its total area lies within the Arctic Circle, a far higher proportion than for its two large Scandinavian partners.

The climate of the northern province of Lappi (Lapland) is not as severe as in places which lie in similar latitudes, such as Canada and Siberia, because of the North Atlantic Drift. This influence keeps the Arctic coasts of Europe free from ice all year round.

Finland enjoys a short but warm summer with average July temperatures at Helsinki of 17°C [63°F] and 13°C [55°F] in Lapland. Because of the high latitudes, summer days are extremely long; indeed, in the Arctic region there is virtually no night throughout the month of June.

Winters are long and cold (Helsinki's January average is –6°C [21°F]) and the days are short. In severe winters the sea freezes for several miles offshore and ice-breakers have to be used to keep the ports open. Snowfall is not heavy, however, and rail and road transport is seldom badly disrupted, even in Lapland.

Landscape

Geologically, Finland is made up of a central plateau of ancient crystalline rocks, mainly granites, schists and gneisses, surrounded by lowlands composed of recent glacial deposits. In the 600 million years between the formation of these ancient rocks and the last Ice Age, the surface of the land was worn down to a peneplain, and most of central and southern Finland is below 200 m [650 ft]. However, the roots of an old mountain system running north-west to south-east can still be traced across Lapland and along Finland's eastern border with Russia. Peaks of over 1,000 m [3,000 ft] occur in northern Lapland, near the Swedish and Norwegian borders.

A tenth of the land surface is covered by lakes. Concentrated in the central plateau, they are in most cases long, narrow and shallow, and aligned in a north-west to south-east direction, indicating the line of movement of the ice-sheet which scoured out their basins. The number of lakes varies from 60,000 to 85,000, depending on the source of the information and the definition used; but whatever the exact figure may be, they dominate the landscape of the southern half of Finland and contribute to its austere beauty. The Saimaa area in the south-east, near the Russian frontier, is Europe's largest inland water system.

Although under increasing threat from pollution caused by wood processing and fertilizers as well as acid rain, the lakes are still rich in fish – mainly trout, salmon, pike and perch - and provide a prime source of recreation for large numbers of Finnish people.

ECONOMY AND RESOURCES

More than two-thirds of Finland is covered by lakes and forest – a fact that accounts for almost everything from the composition of its exports to the brilliance of its rally car drivers. Forests occupy almost 60% of the land surface, the main trees being pine, spruce and birch. Forest-based products – wood pulp, sawn timber, paper and board – still constitute 40% of Finland's exports, but since World War II engineering, shipbuilding and metallurgical industries have greatly expanded. Whilst a member of EFTA, Finland saw its economy grow at a faster rate than that of Japan during the 1980s. In 1992 Finland formally applied to become a member of the European Union, and in 1994 the Finnish people voted in favour of membership of the EU on 1 January 1995.

HISTORY AND POLITICS

Between 1150 and 1809 Finland was under Swedish rule, and one of the legacies of this period is a Swedish-speaking minority of 6.5% of the total population. In some localities on the south and west coasts, Swedish speakers are in a majority and Åland, an island closer to the Swedish coast than to Finland, is a self-governing province. Many towns in Finland use both Finnish and Swedish names; for

THE LAPPS

Hunters, fishermen and herdsmen living in Arctic Europe, approximately 35,000 Lapps are scattered between Norway (with 20,000), Sweden and Finland, with a small group in Russia. Physically, the short, dark Lapps – or Samer, as they call themselves – are noticeably different from other Scandinavians, though their language, Saarme, is related to Finnish. They probably originated in northern Russia at least 2,000 years ago, and may have been the original inhabitants of Finland. Until the 17th century, when they first learned to domesticate reindeer, they lived entirely by hunting and fishing; thereafter, many followed a semi-nomadic life, driving their herds each summer from their winter settlements at the edge of the forest to the high pastureland.

Industrialization, especially mining and hydroelectric development and the associated roads, has badly affected nomadic herding, and it now occupies only about 10% of Lapps. Most live in fixed settlements in coastal areas, and a steady trickle migrate south, assimilating themselves into modern Scandinavian society.

example, Helsinki is Helsingfors and Turku is Åbo in Swedish. Finnish bears little relation to Swedish or any Scandinavian language, and is closest to Magyar, the native tongue of Hungary. Since 1945, Finland has managed to retain its neutrality and played an important role in the setting up of the CSCE. Finnish politics are dominated by multiparty coalitions. [Map page 13] ∎

AREA 338,130 sq km [130,552 sq mls]
POPULATION 5,083,000
CAPITAL (POPULATION) Helsinki (977,000)
GOVERNMENT Multiparty republic
ETHNIC GROUPS Finnish 93%, Swedish 6%
LANGUAGES Finnish and Swedish (both official)
RELIGIONS Christianity (Evangelical Lutheran 88%)
CURRENCY Markka = 100 penniä

FRANCE

Although replaced by the Ukraine as Europe's biggest 'country' in 1991, France remains a handsomely proportioned runner-up, well ahead of Spain and more than twice the area of the entire United Kingdom. Yet the nation possesses space as well as size, and while the growth of cities in the years since World War II has been spoken of in terms of crisis (*la crise urbaine*), urban expansion is a problem only in a few special areas, notably Paris and its immediate surroundings. In general, France has stayed predominantly rural.

Frontiers

Frontiers are a natural concern of continental European countries, but of France's 5,500 km [3,440 mls] almost half consists of sea coast and another 1,000 km [620 mls] winds through the mountains of the Pyrenees and the Alps. In general the Pyrenees frontier follows the crest line of the major hills, rather than the watershed between rivers flowing north into France or south into Spain. There are few easy crossings through the Pyrenees into Spain, but good coastal routes exist on the west from Bayonne into the Basque country, and on the east from Perpignan to Gerona.

In the south-east of France, Savoie and the county of Nice were ceded by Italy at the Treaty of Turin in 1860 and in the following year the Prince of Monaco gave Menton and a neighbouring area to France. The cession of Savoie meant that France's territory extended to the summit of Mont Blanc, the highest mountain in Europe outside the Caucasus.

It also gave France part of the shores of Lake Geneva. Geneva itself is Swiss, but French territory lies within walking distance, and special customs arrangements exist so that people from the French countryside may use the city's trading facilities. North of Geneva the frontier runs through the Jura Mountains to Basle on the Rhine where France, Germany and Switzerland meet. Though Basle itself is in Switzerland, its airport is in France. North

of Basle, for 160 km [100 mls] the border between France and Germany follows the Rhine. Alsace and Lorraine, west of the river, were sought by both countries for centuries and after the Franco-Prussian War in 1870–1 the whole of Alsace and part of Lorraine were returned to Prussia. This frontier remained until the Treaty of Versailles following World War I, but in World War II it was violated again by the Germans – their third invasion of France in 70 years. The frontiers from the Rhine to the North Sea were defined in their present form during the 18th century. Local government in France was reorganized during the French Revolution. In 1790 Turgot defined the *départements* as areas in which everyone could reach the central town within one day.

Landscape

Highland France: Most of France lies less than 300 m [1,000 ft] above sea level, but there are several distinctive upland areas. The most impressive are the Alps and the Pyrenees, but they also include the ancient massifs of Brittany and the Central Plateau, the Vosges and that part of the Ardennes which is within France.

The Alps are formed of complex folded rocks of intricate structure, with relief made even more complicated by the successive glaciations of the Ice Age. Areas of permanent snow exist on Mont Blanc and many other high peaks, and visitors to the upper Arve valley at Chamonix, St-Gervais and other holiday centres have easy access to glaciers. The Alps are visited by tourists throughout the year – in winter for skiing, and in summer for walking on the upland pastures (the original 'alps'). In the French Alps, as in the other alpine areas, hydroelectricity has become universal both for general home use and for industry. The Pyrenees, though comparable to the Alps, lack arterial routes.

The Breton massif includes part of Normandy and extends southwards to the neighbourhood of La Rochelle. In general physical character it is a much dissected hilly area. The Massif Central is more dramatic: it covers one-sixth of France between the Rhône-Saône valley and the basin of Aquitaine, and its highest summits rise to more than 1,800 m

,900 ft]; striking examples are Mont du
.antal and Mont Dore (1,866 m [6,200 ft]).
olcanic activity of 10–30 million years ago
ppears in old volcanic plugs. Earlier rocks
nclude limestones, providing poor soils for
griculture, and coal measures which have
een mined for more than a century at St-
tienne and Le Creusot. The Vosges and the
.rdennes are forested areas of poor soil.

.owland France: Although France has strik-
ng mountain areas, 60% of the country is less
han 250 m [800 ft] above sea level. Fine
ivers, including the Rhône, Garonne, Loire
nd Seine, along with their many tributaries,
Irain large lowland areas. From the Mediter-
anean there is a historic route northwards
hrough the Rhône-Saône valley to Lyons and
Dijon. North-westwards there is the famous
oute through the old towns of Carcassonne
.nd Toulouse to Bordeaux on the Gironde
:stuary, into which the Garonne and the
Dordogne flow. This is the basin of Aquitaine,
ordered by the Massif Central to the north
.nd the Pyrenees to the south. It is not a uni-
orm lowland – there are several hilly areas and
on the coast a belt of sand dunes, the Landes,
:xtending for 200 km [125 mls] from Bayonne
:o the Gironde estuary.

From Aquitaine there is an easy route to the
north, followed by the major railway from
Bordeaux to Poitiers, Tours, Orléans and
Paris. This lowland is called the Gate of
Poitou, though in place of the word 'gate' the
French say *seuil* or 'threshold', which is perhaps more appropriate. Crossing the threshold
brings the traveller to the Paris basin, in the
heart of which is the great city itself.

The ancient centre of Paris lies on the Ile de
la Cité, where the Seine was easily crossed.
The Paris basin is a vast area floored by sedimentary rocks. Those that are resistant to erosion, including some limestones and chalks,
form upland areas. The Loire, with its many
tributaries in the south-west of the basin, and
the Seine, with its numerous affluents (notably
the Yonne, Aube, Marne, Aisne and Oise),
offer easy routes between the upland areas.

ECONOMY AND RESOURCES

The lowlands of France are warmer than those
of England in summer; the cooler winters of
the north, with more frost and snow than on

the lowlands of England, have little adverse
effect on agriculture. Rainfall is moderate,
with a summer maximum in the north and a
winter maximum in the areas of Mediterranean climate to the south.

Modern improvements in agriculture include the provision of irrigation during the
summer in the south. This has transformed
many areas in the Rhône and Durance valleys,
and also the coastal lands such as the Crau,
south-east of Arles. Without irrigation this
was a stony, steppe-like area; now it supports
vast flocks of sheep and has fine hay crops,
cut three times a year. Further west in the
Camargue, on the Rhône delta, rice is grown
with the help of irrigation and there are other
areas of rice production close to the Mediterranean. Water comes either from canals,
leading into ditches through the fields, or by
sprinkler systems from a network of underground pumps; one water point can supply
4 hectares [10 acres].

France's agricultural revolution is far from
complete. There are areas where modern technology has made large reclamation schemes
possible, but there are still many independent
peasant farmers, making a living that is a
meagre reward for the labour expended, even
with the generous terms of the EU's Common
Agricultural Policy (CAP). The younger generation tend to regard emigration to the towns
as a more promising way of life.

Alpine areas: In the alpine areas of France,
including the Pyrenees, farms are far more
numerous on hillslopes having good exposure
to sunlight (the *adret*) than on those less
favoured (the *ubac*). There are fine upland
pastures, apparently retaining their fertility
through centuries of use, which provide summer feed for cattle. Although there is still traditional farming in these areas, many people
have diversified or emigrated. Some find work
in tourist resorts, and many of the old timber-
built houses have been bought by people from
the cities as holiday homes. The future of
peasant farming in mountain areas is a problem that France shares with Switzerland,
Austria and Spain.

Mediterranean France: From the French
Riviera lowlands extend northwards through
the Rhône and Saône valleys and westwards
through Languedoc to the neighbourhood of

Narbonne. This is the area of Mediterranean climate, having most rain in winter, with wheat, vines and olives as the traditional crops. Wheat is well suited to a Mediterranean climate, for it grows best with a cool, moist period followed by one that is warm and dry; in 1993 France was the world's fifth largest producer. Vines need summer warmth – with temperatures of at least 18°C [64°F] for the greater part of the growing season, and dryness, but not to an excessive degree, during the 70 days from the opening of the buds to maturity. The olive is the traditional tree of the Mediterranean climate. Originally a native of Egypt, through the centuries it was planted first in the eastern and later in the western Mediterranean. The ripe, dark purple fruits contain oil, used for cooking; green, unripe olives are commonly used as appetizers.

These three crops are familiar in the south but with them are many more, including maize (the country is the world's fifth largest producer) and a wide range of vegetables. Not all the rural land in Mediterranean France is continuously cultivated for agriculture, for in places it is interspersed with rocky outcrops unsuited to cultivation but covered with *maquis* or pines. Farmers have made fertile the patches of good soil and adequate moisture, and the general landscape is a mixture of rough hills and limestone pavements surrounding rich areas of cultivation.

Aquitaine: To the west, Aquitaine is not a uniform lowland; the agricultural land is interspersed by hills and plateaux that are generally wooded or left as heathland. It is nevertheless a richly productive area, with arable farming for cereal crops, maize and vegetables, and also pastures for cattle. Aquitaine is also a celebrated wine-producing area, with enormous fields laid out as vineyards. Many of the old farms have disappeared, and even whole villages have been abandoned, for example in the Dordogne, as vines have replaced other, less remunerative crops. Much of the wine is consumed on the home market as the normal *vin ordinaire*, mostly red but including some less favoured whites.

The famous claret-producing area around Bordeaux includes the Médoc, between the Gironde estuary and the sea: here also are the districts that produce white table wines,

CORSICA

Annexed by France from Genoa in 1768 – just months before the birth of Napoleon Bonaparte, its most famous son – Corsica is 168 km [105 mls] from France and just 11 km [7 mls] from Sardinia, which is Italian territory. Corsica is divided into two *départements* of France, with its administrative centre at Ajaccio on the west coast. Roughly oval in shape, it is 190 km [118 mls] long and half as wide.

Most of the island is formed of rugged mountains, with more than 40 peaks over 2,000 m [6,500 ft] and some reaching over 2,900 m [9,500 ft]. Varied ancient rocks, much metamorphosed, make up these mountains. Only a quarter of Corsica provides rough grazing for sheep and goats; another quarter is in forests with evergreen oak and cork oak to 650 m [2,000 ft], then chestnuts with beech followed by pines to the treeline, between 1,600 and 2,000 m [5,000–6,000 ft]. In winter there is heavy snow on the mountains, causing severe flooding in the numerous short rivers.

Only 2% of the island is cultivated, mainly in the valleys, on terraced hillsides or on the discontinuous fringe of alluvial lowland along the coasts. Fishing is a primary activity and industries include tunny and lobster canning, chiefly at Ajaccio and Bastia, the two main towns – though tourism is now the main earner. Separatist terrorist movements are still sporadically active in some areas.

such as graves and sauternes. Aquitaine can in fact boast a wide range of red and white wines; several of them, though well known locally, are not exported because the quantity produced is small, and possibly because they do not travel well. Cognac and Armagnac wines are suited to brandy distillation.

Northern France: Northwards from Aquitaine through the lowland Gate (*seuil*) of Poitou, the winters become cooler, with rain in the summer as well as the winter months. Though the summers are cooler in the Paris basin than in Aquitaine, vines flourish on favoured slopes facing south, and many fine

'rench wines come from these northern areas.
As a whole, the Paris basin is agriculturally
rch, with varied soils. The last Ice Age has left
many areas of drifts and wind-blown soils,
here as elsewhere in Europe providing land of
great fertility. Between the valleys of the Paris
basin lie the *pays*, low plateaux, each with its
own characteristic. Some, such as the Beauce,
with fertile soils, are suited to crops; others,
uch as the Sologne, have poor, sandy soils,
hard to cultivate and best suited to forest.
Local farmers have for centuries adjusted their
activity to the qualities of the soil, and now use
their specialized production as a basis both for
trade with other areas, and for sale in the
towns. Despite all the profound changes in
French life, the variety of agriculture and land
use in the Paris basin remains clear – few areas
of the world have so neat a division into units
as the *pays* of France.

Finally, to the west of the Paris basin there
is the area of ancient rocks covering Brittany
and its margins. This area, regarded as ar-
chaic but picturesque, has small farms with
fields divided by wooded hedges to give a
sheltered *bocage* landscape. Rich in medieval
churches, old customs and even costumes, it
was never of great economic significance. Like
Cornwall, in the far south-west of England, it
had its own language (still used) and is part of
the traditional Celtic west of Europe. There is
now increasing pressure for local autonomy in
Brittany, expressed particularly in efforts to
improve agriculture by upgrading pastures,
removing hedges to enlarge fields for animals
and cultivation, developing market gardening,
and encouraging industrial growth in the
towns. Fishing remains a valued resource,
while tourism (both from France and neighbouring Europe) brings additional prosperity
to Brittany.

Agriculture remains a valued resource in the
French economy – for example, France
accounts for almost 6% of the world's barley
and wheat (more of the latter than Canada),
and agriculture contributes 17% of export
earnings – and politicians make this clear both
in Paris and outside France. But there are
many changes. In general these appear to
reflect the opinion of the American geogra-
pher, Isaiah Bowman, that 'man takes the best
and lets the rest go'. Poor land is abandoned,

perhaps for forest, but promising areas are
made rich through investment. Improvements
such as drainage, irrigation and scientific fertilization in some areas counterbalance the
decline in agriculture elsewhere, such as in the
Alps and the Pyrenees. Loss of people from
the land does not indicate a decline in agricultural production but rather an improvement in
agricultural efficiency, and the freedom of
people, no longer tied to the land, to seek, and
generally to find, alternative and more satisfy-
ing employment.

Forests

Forests cover one-fifth of France. Most of
them are on soils of poor quality, including the
sands in parts of the Paris basin, the Vosges
and the Landes between Bordeaux and the
Spanish frontier, the poor limestones of
Lorraine and the clay-with-flints of Normandy. Some of the great forests were planted
by landowners as parts of their estates, like
those of Fontainebleau and Rambouillet near
Paris; others were planted as barriers between
former kingdoms, such as those between
Normandy and Picardy.

The greatest single forested area in France
is the Landes, which covers 10,000 sq km
[3,860 sq mls]. This is mainly coniferous
forest, interspersed only here and there by
farms. Since 1956, attempts have been made
to reclaim and replant the extensive areas
devastated by fire, and to substitute a more
varied rural economy for the exclusive exploitation of the pine forests. In the Alps and the
Pyrenees about a quarter of the land is covered
with forest.

In France, some two-thirds of all the woodlands are comprised of deciduous trees,
compared with less than a third in Germany,
and about 60% of the country's timber
requirements, especially for paper pulp-
making, has to be imported. Since World
War II various laws have been passed to
encourage the production of softwood.

Farms revert to waste when they are no
longer cultivated, and become impenetrable
thickets of vegetation. Through most of
France this vegetation is known as *maquis*,
from the shelter it gives to fugitives: the term
maquis was given in World War II to the resistance forces in hiding. In dry summers the risk

THE VINEYARDS

While behind Italy in production of both grapes and wine, France remains the drink's spiritual home as well as its greatest per capita consumer. Vines are grown south of a line from Nantes to the Ardennes. In the northern areas they occur on sites with specially favourable climatic qualities, notably good southerly exposure to sunshine; in the southern areas the vine covers a high proportion of the agricultural land.

The threat of disease, the need to preserve the quality of particular named vines, and the necessity of maintaining the export trade, all involve government control. Different soils and varying types of grape, combined with local traditions of treating them, produce a wide range of wines, most of which are consumed locally. In the export market clarets from the Bordeaux area, burgundies from the Rhône valley south of Dijon, and champagne, an aerated wine from the *pays* of the same name in the Paris basin, are all well known, but there are many other lesser-known wines of which smaller quantities are exported. The quality of the vintage varies each year according to climatic conditions.

of fire is considerable, especially in the south.

RESOURCES AND INDUSTRY

France is a declining but still significant producer of iron ore (mostly from Lorraine), and several other minerals are also mined, including bauxite, potash, salt and sulphur. There are old coalfields in the north-east, but the output of these does not meet the country's needs. France instead switched to new sources of energy, including experiments with solar power in the Pyrenees and the world's first major tidal power station on the Rance estuary in Brittany, but more significantly utilizing the water of the mountains for hydro-electric power (24% of output) and mined uranium – seventh largest producer in the world, with 5% of world production – to create the most nuclear-based output of any nation (73% by the early 1990s).

Since World War II, the marked industrial expansion in France has been accompanied by a change in the distribution of population. Before the war France was regarded as a country with a fairly even distribution of population between town and country, but from the late 1940s there was a spectacular increase in the urban population. In the first postwar planning period, 1947–53, industrial production rose by 70%, agricultural production by 21% and the standard of living by 30%.

During the following years there was further expansion, particularly in the chemical and electrical industries. In the period of the third plan, 1958–61, the success of export industries became notable, especially in such products as automobiles, aircraft and electrical goods. In this period, too, natural gas was discovered at Lacq, and such industries as chemicals and aluminium smelting prospered. However, traditional industries, such as textiles and porcelain, are still important, and despite technological innovation and success, France is still weak in 'high-tech' areas compared to Japan, the USA and several European rivals.

Nevertheless, the country's postwar transition to a prosperous, dynamic society with more relaxed attitudes has been rapid and pronounced. French life has been, and still is, focused to a remarkable degree on Paris, where traditional luxury industries, such as perfumes, thrive alongside commerce, light industry, heavy industry and services of all kinds. Virtually all the major commercial enterprises of France have their headquarters in Paris – and Paris and district now has almost a fifth of the total population.

The other important industrial centres are on and around the mining areas, and at or near the major ports where imported raw materials are used: Fos, west of Marseilles, for example, and the steel complex at Dunkerque. The aims of modern planning include the development of regional prosperity, based on such centres as Lyons, Marseilles, Toulouse, Nantes, Lille, Nancy and Strasbourg, home to the European parliament. While the industrial attraction of the Paris area remains powerful and population growth continues to exceed that of the second largest urban area, the district around Lyons, the traditional centralization of France is showing signs of weakening

:d governments of both complexions have
:ught to reduce state power both in local
:fairs and the economy.

Modern economic planning in France has
:en pursued at a time of great difficulty,
:hich included the loss of the colonial terri-
:ries in North Africa and South-east Asia,
: well as the period of unrest in the 1960s,
:ot only in the universities but throughout
:e country. Consumer industries have pros-
:ered, but some critics say that there is still
:adequate provision for social services, in-
:uding housing. Since World War II there
:as been agitation about the poor standard
:f housing throughout France, both rural
:nd urban, much of it obsolete and without
:asic amenities. Rapid urban growth, which
:ill continues, has resulted in overcrowding
:nd even the growth of poor shanty towns
: house immigrants, especially those from
:pain and North Africa. The 4 million under-
:rivileged workers from the Maghreb coun-
:ries could prove to be one of the nation's
:most testing problems in the 1990s.

Achieving expansion and prosperity over
:he whole country has not been easy. In
:rance, as in most other countries, there
:emains a disparity between the richer and
:oorer areas; for France this is between the
:ast and the west, the richest of all being in
:losest touch with the great industrial com-
:plexes of Germany and the Benelux countries.
:Though often devastated in European wars,
:his always emerges in peacetime as one of the
:most prosperous corners of France.

HISTORY AND POLITICS

Celtic Gaul was conquered by Caesar in
57–52 BC and was under Roman rule until
Clovis I, king of the Franks, defeated the
Romans in 486. After the death of Charlemagne, whose empire extended over a large
area of Europe, France became a separate
kingdom (843). By the 14th century, however,
nearly half of France belonged to the English
king. This led to the Hundred Years' Wars
(1337–1453), at the end of which the English
were driven out of France. Francis I, in the
16th century, continued to strengthen and
centralize the powers of the crown, and in the
17th century, the French monarchy, under
Louis XIV, experienced its golden age, when
the arts flourished at the court of Versailles.

However, the country's economic problems
and social changes brought about the French
Revolution of 1789 and the abolition of
feudalism. Following a period of corrupt
and inefficient government, Napoleon seized
power in 1799 and eventually crowned himself
'Emperor of the French' in 1804. His rule was
as absolute as that of previous monarchs but
he established a modern and efficient administration. Defeated in foreign wars, Napoleon
had to abdicate in 1814. Constitutional
monarchy, restored in 1814, gave way to the
Second Empire in 1848 and the Third
Republic after France's defeat in the Anglo-
Prussian War in 1871.

France suffered huge human losses during
World War I when the fighting went on incon-
clusively for nearly four years on the western
front. Germany was eventually defeated and
had to sign the Treaty of Versailles which
returned Alsace and Lorraine (ceded in 1871)
to France. In 1939, Hitler invaded Poland and
France and Britain declared war on Germany.
France was soon overrun by German forces
and in June 1940, Marshal Pétain signed an
armistice. He was put in charge of a puppet
government in Vichy, initially controlling less
than half of the country, but by 1942, the
whole of France was occupied.

Meanwhile, General de Gaulle had formed
an alternative 'Free French' government in
London and rallied the various resistance
movements around him. France was liberated
by the Allied forces in 1944. The Fourth
Republic (1946–58) was a period marked by
political instability and colonial wars, first in
Indo-China and then in Algeria. As a result of
the latter, de Gaulle was called back to power
in 1958. He brought in a new constitution
which defined the new institutions of the Fifth
Republic and in particular gave greater powers
to the president. He then proceeded to grant
independence to all remaining colonies and to
modernise the French economy in the context
of the developing European integration
(France was a founder member of the
European Steel and Coal Committee in 1951
and of the EEC in 1957). He also reasserted
the independence of France's foreign policy.
However, growing discontent with the regime
led to a students' and workers' revolt in 1968

and de Gaulle's resignation in 1969. His right-wing successors, Pompidou and Giscard d'Estaing, continued his policies. In May 1981, the French elected François Mitterand as the first Socialist president of the Fifth Republic and he won a second mandate in 1988. Jacques Chirac succeeded him as president following elections in May 1995. [*Map pages 10–11*] ■

AREA 551,500 sq km [212,934 sq mls]
POPULATION 57,747,000
CAPITAL (POPULATION) Paris (9,319,000)
GOVERNMENT Multiparty republic
ETHNIC GROUPS French 93%, Arab 3%, German 2%, Breton 1%, Catalan 1%
LANGUAGES French (official)
RELIGIONS Christianity (Roman Catholic 86%, other Christians 4%), Islam 3%
CURRENCY Franc = 100 centimes

FRENCH GUIANA

The smallest country in South America, French Guiana has a narrow coastal plain comprising mangrove swamps and marshes, alternating with drier areas that can be cultivated; one such is the site of the capital, Cayenne. Inland, a belt of sandy savanna rises to a forested plateau.

ECONOMY AND RESOURCES
The economy is very dependent on France, both for budgetary aid and for food and manufactured goods. The French have also built a rocket-launching station near the coast at Kourou. Timber is the most important natural resource; bauxite and kaolin have been discovered but are largely unexploited. Only 104 sq km [40 sq mls] of the land is under cultivation, where sugar, cassava and rice are grown. Fishing, particularly for shrimps, much of which are exported, is a leading occupation, and tourism, though in its infancy, has as main attractions the Amerindian villages of the interior and the lush tropical scenery.

HISTORY AND POLITICS
A French settlement was established in 160 by a group of merchant adventurers, and afte brief periods of Dutch, English and Portuguese rule the territory finally became permanently French in 1817. In 1946 – a year afte the closure of Devil's Island, the notoriou convict settlement – its status changed to tha of an overseas department of France, and i 1974 it also became an administrative region

An independence movement developed i the 1980s, but most people want to retain the links with France and continue to obtain financial aid in order to develop their territory [*Map page 31*] ■

AREA 90,000 sq km [34,749 sq mls]
POPULATION 141,000
CAPITAL (POPULATION) Cayenne (41,660)
GOVERNMENT Overseas department of France
ETHNIC GROUPS Creole 42%, Chinese 14%, French 10%, Haitian 7%
LANGUAGES French (official)
RELIGIONS Christianity (Roman Catholic 80%, Protestant 4%)
CURRENCY French currency

FRENCH POLYNESIA

French Polynesia consists of 130 islands, totalling only 4,000 sq km [1,544 sq mls] but scattered in five groups over a large area of ocean halfway between Australia and South America. The Society Islands comprise the Leewards, of which the best known is Bora-Bora, and the Windwards, which include Moorea and Tahiti – the largest island and home to the capital of Papeete. Along with the Marquesas, most of the Tubuais and the smaller Gambier islands, these islands are of volcanic origin with steep-sided mountains; the Tuamotus are low-lying coralline atolls.

ECONOMY AND RESOURCES
The relatively high standard of living comes

gely from the links with France, including a ▊bstantial military presence. The other factor ▊ich changed the islands' economy from ▊bsistence agriculture and fishing is tourism; 1988 this earned about half as much as all ▊ible exports. After petroleum re-exports, the ▊ain earners are cultured pearls, vanilla and ▊trus fruits. Almost half the territory's trade is ▊th France, and it shares a currency (the ▊cific franc) with New Caledonia and Wallis ▊d Futuna.

▊STORY AND POLITICS
▊he tribal chiefs of Tahiti eventually agreed ▊ a French protectorate in 1843, and by ▊e end of the century France controlled all ▊ the present islands. They formed an over-▊as territory from 1958, sending two deputies ▊d a senator to Paris, and in 1984 gained ▊creased autonomy with a territorial assem-▊y. There are, however, sporadic calls for ▊dependence. The French government began ▊ationing military personnel there in 1962, ▊nd have carried out nuclear testing at ▊ururoa. [*Map page 2*] ■

AREA 4,000 sq km [1,544 sq mls]
POPULATION 215,000
CAPITAL (POPULATION) Papeete (79,000)
GOVERNMENT Overseas territory of France
ETHNIC GROUPS Polynesian 70%, French 10%, Chinese 7%
LANGUAGES French (official), Tahitian
RELIGIONS Christianity (Protestant 47%, Roman Catholic 40%)
CURRENCY CFP franc = 100 centimes

GABON

The Gabonese Republic lies on the Equator in west-central Africa. In area, it is a little larger than the United Kingdom, with a coastline 800 km [500 mls] long. Behind the narrow, partly lagoon-lined coastal plain, the land rises to hills, plateaux and mountains divided by deep valleys carved by the River Ogooué and its tributaries. The Ogooué, which rises in Congo, reaches the sea near Port Gentil. This seaport lies on an island in the river's estuary near Cape Lopez, Gabon's most westerly point.

Most of Gabon has an equatorial climate, with high temperatures and humidity through-out the year. The rainfall is heavy and the skies are often cloudy. The capital, Libreville, is marginally drier between June and August, when winds blow outwards from the land towards the sea.

Dense rainforest covers about 75% of the country, but, in the east and south, the rainforest gives way to savanna grasslands. The forests contain abundant animals, with antelopes, including the rare bongo and sitatonga, buffaloes, chimpanzees, elephants and gorillas. Gabon has several national parks and wildife reserves.

ECONOMY AND RESOURCES
Figures for GNP suggest that Gabon is one of Africa's richest states, but this is misleading: though rich in natural resources, the country has a small population, to whom the wealth has not yet spread.

With much of the country densely forested, valuable timbers were the main exports until 1962. Since then, minerals have been devel-oped, as so often in Africa, by foreign compa-nies whose profits leave the country. First came oil and gas from near Port Gentil (oil still provides over 65% of export earnings). Then the world's largest deposit of manganese was mined at Mouanda, near Franceville, although originally the ore had to be exported through the Congo by a branch of the Congo-Ocean railway. Gabon is the world's fourth biggest producer of manganese and has about a quarter of the world's known re-serves. Lastly, there is uranium from nearby Mounana; Gabon, Niger and the Central African Republic are France's main sources of uranium. The Trans-Gabon railway was completed in 1987 to provide the country's own outlet for the manganese and uranium, and to open new areas to forestry.

Apart from cocoa and coffee which are grown in the north near Mbini, farming of all kinds is rare and engages only 1% of the land area, the Gabonese preferring to work in other economic activities and the towns. Most food has to be imported.

HISTORY AND POLITICS

The name Gabon is derived from the name given by a Portuguese explorer in the 16th century to an estuary which he thought resembled a hooded and sleeved cloak, *gabão* in Portuguese. In the 19th century the French Navy suppressed the local slave trade, and landed freed slaves at the base called Libreville – where, as in the British counterpart of Freetown, in Sierra Leone, an educated élite established itself.

Gabon became a one-party state in 1968 and though multiparty elections were held in 1990 (the first for 26 years, following widespread demonstrations that required French military intervention), there were allegations of government fraud. The Gabonese Democratic Party, formerly the only party, won a majority in the National Assembly. [*Map page 33*] ■

AREA 267,670 sq km [103,347 sq mls]
POPULATION 1,283,000
CAPITAL (POPULATION) Libreville (418,000)
GOVERNMENT Multiparty republic
ETHNIC GROUPS Fang 36%, Mpongwe 15%, Mbete 14%, Punu 12%
LANGUAGES French (official)
RELIGIONS Christianity (Roman Catholic 65%, Protestant 19%, African churches 12%), traditional beliefs 3%, Islam 2%
CURRENCY CFA franc = 100 centimes

GAMBIA, THE

The Republic of The Gambia is the smallest country in mainland Africa, consisting of a narrow strip of land bordering the River Gambia. The Gambia is almost entirely enclosed by Senegal, except along the short Atlantic coastline. The land is low-lying, and near the sea the land is flat and the soils are salty. The middle river is bordered by terraces,

called *banto faros*, which are flooded after heavy rains. The upper river flows through deep valley which the river has cut into a sandstone plateau.

The Gambia has hot, humid summers, but the winter temperatures (November to May) drop to around 16°C [61°F]. In winter, dry north-easterly winds blow over the country, but in the summer, moist south-westerlies bring rain, which is heaviest on the coast but diminishes inland.

Mangrove swamps line the river banks from the coast through to the centre of the country. But savanna used to cover most of the land until it was largely cleared for farming. The Gambia is rich in birdlife. Crocodiles and hippopotamuses live in the River Gambia.

ECONOMY AND RESOURCES

Except for the capital Banjul, which is also the major port, no town has a population of more than 10,000, and all the large settlements are on the river, which provides the principal means of communication.

Rice is grown in swamps and on the floodplains of the river (though not enough to feed the country's modest population), with millet, sorghum and cassava on the higher ground. Groundnuts still dominate the economy and provide 90% of export earnings, but a successful tourist industry has now been developed: whether northern Europeans looking for sunshine or black Americans tracing their ancestry, the number of visitors rose from a few hundred at independence to more than 90,000 in 1990.

HISTORY AND POLITICS

Portuguese mariners reached The Gambia's coast in 1455 when the area was part of the large Mali empire. In the 16th century, Portuguese and English slave traders operated in the area, and English traders bought rights to trade on the River Gambia in 1588.

In 1664, the English established a settlement on an island in the river estuary, and in 1765 the British founded a colony called Senegambia, which included parts of The Gambia and Senegal. Britain handed this colony over to France in 1783.

In 1816, Bathurst (now Banjul) was founded as a base for Britain's anti-slavery opera-ons. But control of inland areas was made difficult by wars between local Muslims and non-Muslims. In the 1860s and 1870s, Britain and France discussed the exchange of The Gambia for some other French territory, but no agreement was reached and Britain made The Gambia a British colony in 1888. It remained under British rule until it achieved full independence in 1965. In 1970, The Gambia became a republic. But in July 1994, a military group overthrew the president, Sir Dawda Jawara, who fled into exile.

One major political issue concerns relations between the English-speaking Gambians and their French-speaking Senegalese neighbours. In 1981, an attempted coup in The Gambia was defeated with the help of Senegalese troops. In 1982, The Gambia and Senegal set up a defence alliance, the Confederation of Senegambia. But this move towards closer co-operation ended in 1989, when the Confederation was dissolved. [*Map page 32*] ∎

AREA 11,300 sq km [4,363 sq mls]
POPULATION 1,081,000
CAPITAL (POPULATION) Banjul (150,000)
GOVERNMENT Military regime
ETHNIC GROUPS Mandinka (also called Mandingo or Malinke) 40%, Fulani (also called Peul) 19%, Wolof 15%, Jola 10%, Soninke 8%
LANGUAGES English (official)
RELIGIONS Islam 95%, Christianity 4%, traditional beliefs 1%
CURRENCY Dalasi = 100 butut

GEORGIA

Positioned between Russia and Turkey, Georgia comprises four main areas: the Caucasus Mountains (Bolshoi Kavka) in the north, including Mt Elbrus (5,633 m [18,841 ft]) on the Russian border; the Black Sea coastal plain in the west; the eastern end of the mountains of Asia Minor to the south; and a low plateau in the east, protruding into Azerbaijan. Separating the two mountain sections is the crucial Kura valley, in which the capital Tbilisi stands.

The Black Sea plains have hot summers and mild winters, when temperatures seldom drop below freezing point. The rainfall is heavy, but inland Tbilisi has moderate rainfall, with the heaviest rains in spring and early summer. Summers are hot but winters are colder than in the west. Snow covers the highest mountains throughout the year.

ECONOMY AND RESOURCES
The largest of the three Transcaucasian republics, Georgia is rich in citrus fruits and wine (notably in the Kakhetia region), tea (the main crop), tobacco, wheat, barley and vegetables, while perfumes are made from flowers and herbs and, in Imeretia, silk is a flourishing industry. Almost 40% forested, it also has a significant stake in timber. It has large deposits of manganese ore, but despite reserves of coal and huge hydroelectric potential, most of its electricity is generated in Russia and the Ukraine.

HISTORY AND POLITICS
Mostly Orthodox Christians, Georgians have a strong national culture and a long literary tradition based on their own language and alphabet. Land of the legendary 'Golden Fleece' of Greek mythology, the area was conquered by the Romans, Persians and Arabs before establishing autonomy in the 10th century, but Tartars, Persians and Turks invaded before it came under Russian domination around 1800. Renowned for their longevity, the population's most famous product was Josef Stalin, born in Gori, 65 km [40 mls] north-west of Tbilisi.

Always a maverick among the Soviet republics, Georgia was the first to declare independence after the Baltic states (April 1991), but did not officially join the CIS until parliament ratified the decree in March 1994. When Gorbachev resigned, the democratically elected leader of Georgia, Zviad Gamsakhurdia, found himself holed up in Tbilisi's KGB headquarters, under siege from rebel forces representing widespread disapproval of his policies, from the economy to the imprisonment of political opponents. In January he fled the country (now ruled by a military council), returning to lead resistance from his home territory in the west, though to little effect. He committed suicide at the end of 1993. A charismatic, highly individual president, Gamsakhurdia had also been in conflict with the Ossetian minority in one of the republic's three autonomous regions (Abkhazia in the north-west, South Ossetia in north-central Georgia, and Adzharia (Ajaria) in the south-west), who feared being swamped in a new independent nation. In March 1992 former Soviet foreign minister Edvard Shevardnadze agreed to become chairman of the ruling council. [*Map page 22*] ■

AREA 69,700 sq km [26,910 sq mls]
POPULATION 5,450,000
CAPITAL (POPULATION) Tbilisi (1,279,000)
GOVERNMENT Multiparty republic
ETHNIC GROUPS Georgian 70%, Armenian 8%, Russian 6%, Azerbaijani 6%, Ossetian 3%, Greek 2%, Abkhazian 2%, other 3%
LANGUAGES Georgian (official)
RELIGIONS Christianity (Georgian Orthodox 65%, Russian Orthodox 10%, Armenian Orthodox 8%), Islam 11%
CURRENCY Lari

GERMANY

On reunification, West and East Germany moved from the ninth and 15th biggest countries in Europe (in terms of area) to a combined fourth – still much smaller than France, Spain and Sweden – but with the independence of the Ukraine the following year dropped back to fifth. It is, nevertheless, 12th in the world in terms of population.

Germany extends from the North Sea and Baltic coasts in the north to the flanks of the central Alps in the south. The country includes only a narrow fringe of Alpine mountains, with the Zugspitze (2,963 m [9,721 ft]) the country's highest peak. There is, however,

a wide section of the associated Alpine foreland bordering Switzerland and Austria stretching northwards from the foothills of the Alps to the Danube. The foreland is largely covered by moraines and outwash plains which, with many lakes, including the Bodensee (shared with Switzerland), are relics of the glacial age, and are reminders of the many glaciers that once emerged from the Alpine valleys.

The central uplands of Europe are more amply represented, occupying a broad swathe of Germany. Four types of terrain are found. Block mountains are remnants of pre-Alpine fold mountains shattered and reshaped by the later earth movements. The Harz, Thüringer Wald and Erzgebirge (Ore Mountains) massifs rise above a varied scarpland terrain, notably the Thüringian Basin, which has the fertile Erfurt lowland at its heart.

Tectonic uplift was greatest in the south, close to the Alps, producing the Schwarzwald (Black Forest) and Böhmerwald. Between these great blocks of forested mountains are open basins of sedimentary rocks, their resistant bands picked out by erosion as in the magnificent scarp of the Schwäbische Alb, overlooking the Neckar basin.

A third kind of country is provided by down-faulted basins filled with softer deposits of more recent age, notably the Upper Rhine plain between Basle and Mainz. Earth movement and eruptions produced a fourth element, such volcanic mountains as the Vogelsberg and the hot and mineral springs that gave rise to the famous spas. Here is Germany at its most picturesque, with baronial castles on wooded heights, looking down over vineyards to clustered villages of half-timbered houses, whose occupants still cultivate open-field strips as they have done for centuries.

The northern lowlands, part of the great North European Plain, owe their topography mainly to the retreat of the ice-sheets. The most recent moraines, marked by forested ridges that may include good boulder-clay soils, are restricted to Schleswig-Holstein. The rest of the lowland is covered with leached older moraine and sandy outwash, so that in many places soils are poor. The glacial period also left behind loess, windblown dust deposited along the northern edge of the ntral uplands and in basins within them, oviding some of the country's best soils for heat, malting barley and sugar beet. This elt broadens in the lowland of Saxony around alle and Leipzig.

The coast is also the product of glaciation and subsequent changes. The low Baltic shore diversified by long, branching inlets, formed eneath the ice of the glacial period and now eloved by yachtsmen, while inland the most ecent moraines have left behind a confused errain of hills and lakes, but also areas of good oil developed on glacial till. The movement of rater around the edge of the ice-sheets carved cream trenches (*Urstromtäler*), south-east to orth-west; these are now in part occupied by he present rivers, and have also proved con- enient for canal construction. The North Sea s fringed by sandy offshore islands, the prod- cts of a beach bar now breached by the sea.

ECONOMY AND RESOURCES

Over a quarter of Germany is forested, vith particular concentration in the Alps, he massifs of the central uplands, and the poorer areas of the northern lowland. It is amazing that this economically most advanced country has some of Europe's smallest farms, particularly characteristic of southern Ger- many. Most are used for arable-based mixed farming, with minor livestock enterprises. In the warmer basins tobacco, vegetables and, increasingly, maize are grown. Vineyards and orchards clothe the slopes of the Rhine and its tributaries. Much larger wheat and sugar-beet farms with important livestock enterprises are characteristic of the loess soils on the northern edge of the central uplands. The Bavarian Alpine foreland in the south, and Schleswig-Holstein in the north, are other areas of above-average farm size. The sandy northern low-land, which used to support a poor agriculture based on rye, potatoes and pigs, increasingly specializes in intensive meat and poultry pro- duction. Dairy specialization is typical of the milder north-west and the Alpine fringes.

Because of the generally small size of hold- ings many farmers seek a supplementary income outside agriculture – often a halfway stage to giving up agriculture altogether. Persons employed in agriculture, who were a quarter of the employed population of the

FRG in 1950, accounted for well below 10% on reunification four decades later. With this movement out of agriculture, the average size of holding is steadily but all too slowly rising.

In the GDR, by contrast, all agricultural holdings were brought into 'co-operatives', many of over 500 hectares [1,236 acres] and some up to ten times that size. The East German government's version of the collective farm proved much more efficient than the equivalent in many other Communist states, however, and the economic outlook was quite promising prior to reunification.

Minerals and energy

Germany is the most important coal producer of continental Western Europe, though output from the Ruhr, Saar and Aachen fields has dropped since the mid-1950s, owing mainly to competition from oil. Some oil and gas is home-produced, mainly extracted from fields beneath the northern lowland, but most of the oil consumed in Germany is delivered by pipeline from Wilhelmshaven, Europoort and the Mediterranean to refineries in the Rhineland and on the Danube.

Brown coal (lignite) is excavated between Cologne and Aachen, but the former GDR (East Germany) was unique in depending for energy supply on this source of low calorific value, economically mined in vast open pits. The older centre of mining was in the lowland of Saxony, between Halle and Leipzig, but the main area of expansion is now in Niederlausitz, south of Cottbus. Brown coal is increasingly reserved for electricity generation, although atomic plants built on the coast and principal rivers are expected to be of increas- ing importance (at present 34% of the total for the former FRG), with hydroelectric stations concentrated in the Bavarian Alps. Energy needs and feedstock for the important chemi- cal industry around Halle are met by oil brought by pipeline from the former Soviet republics or by tanker through Rostock. The other mineral resource of value is potash, mined south of the Harz; Germany is the world's third largest producer. The non-ferrous metallic ores of the Harz and other massifs of the central uplands are no longer of great significance, while high-grade imported iron ores have proved more economic than the

THE REUNIFICATION

In 1945, a devastated Germany was divided into four zones, each occupied by one of the victorious powers: Britain, France, the USA and the Soviet Union. The division was originally a temporary expedient (the Allies had formally agreed to maintain German unity), but the Russians published a constitution for the German Democratic Republic in 1946. The split solidified when the Russians rejected a currency reform common to all three Western zones. The German Federal Republic – 'West Germany' – was created in 1949.

Throughout the years of the Cold War, as NATO troops faced Warsaw Pact tanks across the barbed wire and minefields of the new frontier, the partition seemed irrevocable. Although both German constitutions maintained hopes of reunification, it seemed that nothing short of the total war both sides dreaded could bring it about. The West, with three-quarters of the population, rebuilt war damage and prospered. The East was hailed as the industrial jewel of the Soviet European empire, though some of its people were prepared to risk being shot to escape westwards.

By the late 1980s it was clear that the Soviet empire was crumbling. In the autumn of 1989, thousands of East Germans migrated illegally to the West across the newly open Hungarian border and mass demonstrations in East German cities followed. At first, the government issued a stream of threats, but when it became clear that there would be no Soviet tanks to enforce its rule, it simply packed up. With the frontiers open, it became clear that the 'successful' East German economy was a catastrophic shambles, a scrapyard poisoned by uncontrolled pollution, with bankruptcy imminent. The choice facing German leaders in 1990 was starkly simple: either unite East and West, or accept virtually the entire Eastern population as penniless refugees.

The West German government acted quickly, often bullying the weaker Easterners. The Western Deutschmark became the common currency and on 3 October 1990 – more than 45 years after Germany had lost the war – the country was formally reunited. The costs of bringing the East up to the standards of the West are high, and Germans will be paying them for years to come. But there had been no other possible choice.

home ores found predominantly in the districts of Siegen and Peine-Salzgitter.

SETTLEMENT AND INDUSTRY

From Neolithic times the core settlement areas of Germany were the fertile lowlands – areas like the northern edge of the central uplands in Lower Saxony and Westphalia, the Upper Rhine plain, the Main and Neckar basins, and the Alpine foreland. From these core areas land-hungry medieval peasants advanced to clear large areas of forest in the uplands, and also streamed eastwards to settle in lands beyond the Elbe and Saale.

The fragmentation of the Holy Roman Empire into a swarm of competing states had a positive side in the founding and fostering by local rulers, large and small, of a dense system of towns, among them future regional capitals like Hanover, Stuttgart or Munich (München). The contrast with the 'French desert' created by Parisian centralization is striking.

When industrial growth came in the 19th century, heavy industry naturally concentrated in the Ruhr and Saar coalfields, but thanks to the railways other production could disperse widely to these existing towns. Since 1945 the Ruhr and Saar coalfields have been undergoing a difficult period of conversion, owing to the problems of the now declining coal, steel and heavy engineering industries. Western Europe's largest industrial region, stretching from Duisburg to Dortmund, the Ruhr ('the forge of Germany') has seen its mines for top-grade coking coal cut from 145 to less than 20 and has been forced to diversify – the western end into petrochemicals based on the Rhine ports and pipelines, the eastern part into lighter and computer-based industry.

By contrast, towns away from the coalfields, especially the great regional capitals of southern Germany, have flourished with the inauguration of modern industries (motor vehicles, electrical equipment, electronics), the growth f administrative and office work, and the division among a number of cities of capital functions formerly concentrated in Berlin.

As an advanced industrial country of Western type, the role of East Germany within the Communist-bloc states was to provide technically advanced equipment, receiving in return supplies of raw materials and semifinished products such as steel. Because of industrial inertia, the location of the important machine-building industry had not greatly changed since capitalist times, being heavily concentrated in and around the southern cities of Leipzig, Chemnitz (then Karl-Marx-Stadt) and Dresden. Other centres were Magdeburg and East Berlin, which was also the leading producer of electrical equipment.

The GDR inherited a traditional strength in precision and optical industries, mostly located in Thüringia (such as the famous Zeiss works at Jena), the base for important developments in industrial instrumentation and electronics. The government tried to steer some major new developments into the rural north and east of the country, including shipbuilding at Rostock – also the site of a new ocean port, to avoid the use of facilities in the FRG – oil refining and chemicals at Schwedt, and iron smelting and steel rolling in the town of Eisenhüttenstadt.

While the inner parts of the greatest cities have tended to lose population, their suburbs and satellites have exploded across the surrounding countryside, forming vast urban areas of expanding population. In the west and south of the country, an axis of high population growth and high density stretches from the Rhine-Ruhr region (largest of all but checked in expansion by the problems of Ruhr industry), through the Rhine-Main (Frankfurt), Rhine-Neckar (Mannheim-Ludwigshafen) and Stuttgart regions to Munich. In the east and north plains the densely populated areas are more isolated, centred on the cities of Nuremberg, Hanover, Bremen, Hamburg, Dresden, Leipzig and, of course, Berlin.

Since 1950 there has been a tendency for the West's population to drift towards the more attractive south. Urban population losses have in part been made up by immigrant workers (nearly 2.5 million at their peak

BERLIN

Like defeated Germany itself, Berlin was formally divided between the four victorious powers – despite the fact that it was located in Prussia, 160 km [100 mls] inside Soviet-occupied eastern Germany. In June 1948, in an attempt to bring the whole city under their control, the Soviets closed all road and rail links with the West. The Western Allies supplied the city by a massive airlift; in October 1949 the blockade was abandoned, but Berlin's anomalous situation remained a potential flashpoint, and provoked a series of diplomatic crises – mainly because it offered an easy escape route to the West for discontented East Germans.

In August 1961, alarmed at the steady drain of some of its best-trained people, the East German authorities built a dividing wall across the city. Over the years, the original improvised structure – it was thrown up overnight – became a substantial barrier of concrete and barbed wire, with machine-gun towers and minefields; despite the hazards, many still risked the perilous crossing, and hundreds of would-be refugees – often youngsters – died in the attempt.

The Berlin Wall, with its few, heavily-guarded crossing points, became the most indelible symbol of the Cold War, the essential background to every spy thriller. When the East German government collapsed in 1989, the Wall's spontaneous demolition by jubilant Easterners and Westerners alike became the most unambiguous sign of the Cold War's ending.

When East Germany joined the West, it was agreed that Berlin would become the formal capital of the unified state in the year 2000 – until that time, both Berlin and the quiet, Rhineland city of Bonn were to be joint capitals.

in the early 1970s, with Turkey the principal source), increasingly joined by their families to supplement a German native population – which at the end of the 1960s entered a period of negative growth.

Germany's wary neighbours, fearing that a

nation suddenly swollen to nearly 80 million through reunification could swamp Europe, could rest easy. According to a report from the Institute of German Economy, published in 1992, there will be 20 million fewer Germans alive than today by the year 2030, and on current trends the number of young people below the age of 15 will drop from 13.7 million in 1990 to 10 million in 2010. The findings suggested that, as a result, the country would need at least 300,000 new immigrants a year to fill the gap in its labour market.

Communications
Germany has the advantage of the superb Rhine waterway, which from its Alpine sources cuts right across the central uplands to the North Sea. A combination of summer snow-melt from the Alps and autumn-spring rainfall in the central uplands gives it a powerful and remarkably even flow – if increasingly polluted. Although traffic is at its most intensive between Rotterdam and the Rhine-Ruhr region, where Duisburg is the largest inland harbour of Europe, standard 1,250-tonne self-propelled barges can reach Basle. The Rhine-Main-Danube waterway has also opened a through route to Eastern Europe and the Black Sea, while for north German traffic the Mittelland Canal, following the northern edge of the central uplands, opens up links to the north German ports and Berlin. Unusually for Europe, Germany's rivers and canals carry as much freight as its roads.

Hamburg is Germany's biggest seaport, followed by Bremen with its outport, Bremerhaven. All German ports suffer by being too far from the main centre of European population and economic activity in the Rhinelands; the Belgian and Dutch ports are at a great advantage being closer.

Germany was the first European country to build motorways (Hitler's *Autobahns*, built in the 1930s), and also enjoys an efficient if highly subsidized railway network. Both are crucial to a country which, on reunification, increased its land borders from nine to ten countries. Air travel, too, both internal and international, is increasingly important.

HISTORY AND POLITICS
The German Empire that was created under Prussian dominance in 1871, comprising four kingdoms, six grand duchies, five duchies and seven principalities, and centred on the great imperial capital of Berlin, was to last for fewer than 75 years. Even at its greatest extent it left large areas of Europe's German-speaking population outside its boundaries, notably in Austria and large parts of Switzerland. Following the fall of Hitler in 1945, a defeated Germany was obliged to transfer to Poland and the Soviet Union 114,500 sq km [44,200 sq mls] situated east of the Oder and Neisse rivers, nearly a quarter of the country's pre-war area. The German-speaking inhabitants were expelled – as were most German-speaking minorities in the countries of Eastern Europe – and the remainder of Germany was occupied by the four victorious Allied powers.

The dividing line between the zones occupied by the three Western Allies (USA, UK and France) and that occupied by the USSR rapidly hardened into a political boundary dividing the country. In 1948 West Germany was proclaimed as the independent Federal Republic of Germany (FRG), with a capital at Bonn (deemed 'provisional' pending hoped-for German reunification), and measuring 248,000 sq km [96,000 sq mls]. East Germany became the German Democratic Republic (GDR), a Soviet satellite of 108,000 sq km [41,700 sq mls]. Berlin was similarly divided, the three western sectors of an enclave of occupation becoming 480 sq km [186 sq mls] embedded in the territory of the GDR, of which the Soviet-occupied East Berlin was deemed to be capital.

Administration
The system of powerful federal states (*Länder*) created in the FRG after World War II remained remarkably stable, though huge disparities of size have remained in spite of various reform proposals. Bavaria has by far the largest area, and North Rhine-Westphalia, with the Rhine-Ruhr region at its heart, has the largest population, over a fifth of the German total. At the other extreme are the 'city states' of Bremen and Hamburg, though Saarland is also small.

In 1990 the ten *Länder* of the FRG (excluding the enclave of West Berlin) were joined by the five rejuvenated old states of the GDR –

andenburg, Mecklenburg-West Pomerania, xony, Saxony-Anhalt and Thüringia – plus e new 'united' Berlin. The East German ganization had been very different, the untry politically divided into 15 adminis- ative districts (*Bezirke*) under the control of e central government in East Berlin.

he cost of unification

he stability of the federal system may well me under considerable strain in the early ars of the reunited Germany. The phenom- al and sustained rise of the FRG from the hes of World War II to become the world's ird biggest economy and its largest exporter the so-called *Wirtschaftswunder*, or 'econ- mic miracle', accomplished with few natural sources – was already levelling out before e financial costs of reunification (such as the wo-for-one' Deutschmark for Ostmark deal r GDR citizens) became apparent.

While East Germany had achieved the high- st standard of living in the Soviet bloc, it was ell short of the levels of advanced EC coun- ries. Massive investment was needed to ebuild the East's industrial base and transport ystem, and that meant increased taxation. In ddition, the new nation found itself fun- elling aid into Eastern Europe (Germany led he EC drive for recognition of its old allies lovenia and Croatia) and then into the for- mer Soviet republics. All this took place against a background of continued downturn n world trade: in February 1992 the German government officially announced the calcula- ion of negative growth – it averaged 8% a year n the 1950s – and the German economy, on paper at least, was 'in recession'.

The costs could be social, too. If Westerners resent added taxes and the burden of the GDR, and if the Easterners resent the over- bearing, patronizing attitudes of the old FRG, there could be cultural as well as economic polarization. In 1992 there was the spectacle – not seen in 18 years – of several public sector strikes. More likely, however, are a revived German sense of identity bordering on hege- mony, even a swing to the 'right', and a revival of Fascism.

Reunification soon appeared in the early 1990s to be the beginning rather than the end of a chapter in German history. At the very

least, it would be a more complicated, expen- sive and lengthy undertaking than anyone was prepared to envisage as the Berlin Wall came crumbling down. [*Map pages 14–15*] ■

AREA 356,910 sq km [137,803 sq mls]
POPULATION 80,278,000
CAPITAL (POPULATION) Berlin
(3,446,000)/Bonn (296,000)
GOVERNMENT Federal multiparty republic
ETHNIC GROUPS German 93%, Turkish 2%,
Yugoslav 1%, Italian 1%, Greek, Polish,
Spanish
LANGUAGES German (official)
RELIGIONS Christianity (Protestant, mainly
Lutheran 45%, Roman Catholic 37%),
Islam 2%
CURRENCY Deutsche Mark = 100 pfennig

GHANA

The Republic of Ghana faces the Gulf of Guinea in West Africa, just north of the Equator. Behind the thickly populated southern coastal plains, which are lined by lagoons, lies a plateau region in the south- west. Northern Ghana is drained by the Black and White Volta rivers which flow into Lake Volta. This lake, which has formed behind the Akosombo Dam, is one of the world's largest artificially created lakes.

Rainforests grow in the south-west. To the north, the forests merge into savanna (tropical grassland with some woodland). More open grasslands dominate in the far north. Tem- peratures and humidity are uniformly high all year round.

ECONOMY AND RESOURCES

The Akosombo Dam below Lake Volta pro- vides power to smelt imported alumina into aluminium, and for the main towns, mines and industries in the Takoradi-Kumasi-Tema triangle, the most developed part of the coun- try. To build the dam, a second deep-water port was developed at Tema, east of Accra, the capital. Tema is now Ghana's main port for imports and for cocoa export.

Cocoa has been the leading export since 1924, and until the late 1970s Ghana was the world's leading producer. However, neighbouring Ivory Coast has now overtaken Ghana both in this and in forestry production. In turn, Ghana has attempted to expand the fishing, tourism and agricultural industries.

Unlike the Ivory Coast, Ghana has long been a producer of minerals – gold has been exploited for a thousand years. The area within a radius of 100 km [60 mls] of Dunkwa produces 90% of Ghana's mineral exports. However, production of most minerals is currently static or declining. The few remaining gold mines, with the notable exception of Obuasi, are now scarcely economic. Manganese production was recently revived to meet a new demand in battery manufacture, but the country's substantial reserves of bauxite remain undeveloped while imported alumina is used in the Tema aluminium smelter. Industrial diamonds contribute modestly to Ghana's economy. Offshore oil was discovered in 1978 but has yet to be commercially developed.

HISTORY AND POLITICS

Formerly known appropriately as the Gold Coast, Ghana's post-colonial name recalls the state which lay north of the upper Niger from the 8th to the 13th centuries, and from whose population some of today's Ghanaians may well be descended.

In 1957 Ghana was the first tropical African country to become independent of colonial rule, and until 1966 was led by Dr Kwame Nkrumah, a prominent Third World spokesman and pioneer of Pan-African Socialism.

Nkrumah's overthrow was followed by a succession of coups and military governments, with Flight-Lieutenant Jerry Rawlings establishing himself as undoubted leader in 1981. While his hardline regime has steadied the economy, political progress has been token: an agreement to change the constitution to a pluralist democracy and set up a consultative assembly (in place of his ruling Provisional National Defence Council) was approved by a referendum in April 1992, but was seen by opponents as merely window-dressing. Only

29% of the electorate voted in the 199 elections and Rawlings, now presiden remains firmly in control. [*Map page 32*] ■

> **AREA** 238,540 sq km [92,100 sq mls]
> **POPULATION** 16,944,000
> **CAPITAL (POPULATION)** Accra (965,000)
> **GOVERNMENT** Multiparty republic
> **ETHNIC GROUPS** Akan 54%, Mossi 16%, Ewe 12%, Ga-Adangame 8%, Gurma 3%
> **LANGUAGES** English (official)
> **RELIGIONS** Christianity 62% (Protestant 28%, Roman Catholic 19%), traditional beliefs 21%, Islam 16%
> **CURRENCY** Cedi = 100 pesewas

GIBRALTAR

The Rock, as it is popularly known, guard the north-eastern end of the Strait o Gibraltar and lies directly opposite the very similar peninsula of Ceuta, one of two remaining Spanish enclaves in Morocco (the other is Melilla). Only 23 km [14 mls] separate Ceuta and Gibraltar. The Rock, 6.5 sq km [2.5 sq mls] in area, occupies a narrow peninsula consisting largely of a ridge thrusting south along the eastern side of Algeciras Bay, terminating in the 30 m [100 ft] cliffs of Europa Point. It shelters a spacious anchorage and harbour from east winds with long artificial break-waters and quays constructed of stone tunnelled from the ridge. On the north there is a low, flat sandy plain used for an airport.

Shrubs, partly wild olives, clothe the more precarious slopes and provide shelter for the only wild monkeys in Europe. Considerable areas of the summit are used as catchments for drinking water, supplemented by diesel-powered seawater distillation.

ECONOMY AND RESOURCES

Houses cover the slope facing the harbour and spread around two flattish beaches on the south, leaving the precipitous eastern slopes

...ninhabited except near Catalan Bay. The ...uilt-up area has an excellent road network ...ut the topography prohibits cultivation and ...he Gibraltarians rely on the port, the ship-...pairing yards, the military and air bases, and ...n tourism for their livelihood. About 2,400 ...erchant ships and numerous pleasure craft ...all at Gibraltar annually and the low import ...uties, excellent tourist facilities and almost ...ainless summers make it a popular shopping ...nd holiday centre.

HISTORY AND POLITICS

...ocal rock carvings demonstrate that Gibral-...ar has been inhabited since Neolithic times. ...reeks and Romans also settled here, but ...he first sure date for colonization is AD 711 ...vhen Tariq ibn Zaid, a Berber chieftain, ...ccupied it. Although taken over by Spaniards ...or a short while in the 14th century, it ...emained Moorish until 1462. An Anglo-...Dutch naval force captured it in 1704 and it ...vas formally recognized as a British posses-...sion at the Treaty of Utrecht in 1713. In spite ...of long sieges and assaults – not to mention ...pressure from Spain – it has remained British ...ever since, becoming a strategically vital ...naval dockyard, a commercial port and a base ...for reconnaissance aircraft.

The 28,000 Gibraltarians are of British, Spanish, Maltese, Portuguese and Genoan descent. Though bilingual in Spanish and English, they remain staunchly pro-British. In 1966, following a long-standing claim, the Spanish government called on Britain to give 'substantial sovereignty' of Gibraltar over to Spain and closed the border (1.2 km [0.74 mls]) to all but pedestrian traffic. In a 1967 referendum the residents voted overwhelmingly to remain under British control, and in 1969 they were granted the status of a self-governing dependency.

Spain closed the frontier completely, preventing thousands of Spaniards from reaching their daily work. The border was reopened fully by Spain in 1985 following British agreement that, for the first time, they would discuss the sovereignty of Gibraltar; but despite being fellow members of NATO (Spain joined in 1982) and the EU (Spain joined on 1 January 1986), there has been no progress towards British compliance with the UN General Assembly's resolution for an end to Gibraltar's 'colonial status' by 1 October 1996. [*Map page 18*] ■

AREA 6.5 sq km [2.5 sq mls]
POPULATION 28,000
CAPITAL (POPULATION) Gibraltar Town (28,000)
GOVERNMENT British dependency
ETHNIC GROUPS British, Spanish, Maltese, Portuguese
LANGUAGES English, Spanish
RELIGIONS Christianity (mainly Roman Catholic)
CURRENCY Gibraltar pound = 100 pence

GREECE

Mainland Greece consists of a mountainous peninsula which projects 500 km [312 mls] into the Mediterranean from the south-west corner of the Balkans, and an 80 km [50 ml] coastal belt along the northern shore of the Aegean Sea.

Nearly a fifth of the total land area of Greece is made up of its 2,000 or so islands, found mainly in the Aegean Sea to the east of the main peninsula but also in the Ionian Sea to the west; only 154 of these islands are inhabited, but they account for over 11% of the population. Some of the islands of the Dodecanese group in the eastern Aegean lie just 16 km [10 mls] off the coast of Turkey, and northern Corfu in the Ionian Islands is separated from the Albanian coast by a narrow channel.

The principal structural feature of Greece are the Pindos Mountains, which extend south-eastwards from the Albanian border to cover most of the peninsula. The island of Crete is also structurally related to the main Alpine fold mountain system to which the Pindos range belongs. Its highest peak, Mt Ida, is 2,456 m [8,057 ft] high. In these ranges limestone rocks predominate, though many of the Aegean Islands are of similar formation to the Rhodopi Massif in the north and made up of crystalline rocks.

ECONOMY AND RESOURCES

With so much of Greece covered by rugged mountains, only about a third of the area is suitable for cultivation, yet 40% of the population depend for their living on agriculture. The average farm size is under 4 hectares [10 acres], though on a few areas of flat land, mostly around the Aegean coasts in Macedonia and Thrace, large estates can be found.

The chief crops are typical of Mediterranean lands – wheat, olives, vines, tobacco and citrus fruits. Most villagers keep a few domestic animals, particularly sheep and goats. The mountain pastures are poor, in the main consisting of scrubland, and many areas have been stripped of what tree cover they once had by goats (notoriously destructive of growing trees), and by the need for wood for ships, house building and charcoal burning.

Greece has been described as a land of mountains and of the sea. Nowhere in Greece is more than 80 km [50 mls] from the sea, and most of the towns are situated on the coast. Greater Athens, which consists of the capital city and its seaport, Piræus, has a third of the total population and has grown six-fold since 1945. Thessaloniki (Salonica), the second city, is also a seaport, serving not only northern Greece but also southern Yugoslavia. Greece's mountainous terrain makes communication on land difficult, but the country has the world's largest merchant fleet (measured by ownership, not national registry), and shipbuilding and repairs are still important industries, while fishing provides a crucial supplement to the diet of a people who have difficulty wresting a living from their poor if beautiful homeland.

Greece is poorly endowed with industrial raw materials. There are deposits of iron ore, bauxite, nickel and manganese, but no coal and very small amounts of oil. The possibilities for hydroelectric development are severely limited because of the irregularity of the streams, many of which dry up entirely during the long summer drought. Thus Greece must import most of its sources of energy – mainly oil and coal. Industrial activity is largely

CRETE

The island of Crete was the home of the sea-faring Minoan civilization, which flourished in the period 3500–1100 BC and left behind a wealth of archaeological sites and artefacts. Most southerly and by far the largest of the Greek islands, Crete has a milder, more maritime climate than the mainland. The rugged, harbourless south coast, backed by steep limestone mountains, is the more inhospitable side, with winter gales adding to the hazards of navigation.

Most of the population of 536,980 live in the lowlands of the north, about a quarter of them in Iráklion (the capital) and Khania. About a quarter of the island is under crops; agriculture, tourism and small-scale mining are the main sources of income. Though Greek-speaking, Cretans differ in outlook and culture from the mainlanders; they suffered long occupation by Venetians and then by Turks, remaining under Turkish rule until 1898, 70 years after mainland Greece had been liberated.

concerned with the processing of agricultural produce – fruit and vegetables, canning, the production of wine and olive oil, cigarette manufacture, textiles and leather processing. Greece is one of the world's major producers of dried fruits; the word 'currant' is derived from the name of the Greek town of Corinth that lies on the narrow isthmus connecting the southern peninsula of the Pelopónnisos to the mainland. A canal, built in 1893 and 4.8 km [3 mls] long, cuts through the isthmus, linking the Gulf of Corinth with the Aegean.

The tourist industry is vital – in 1992 there were nearly 9.8 million visitors. Overseas visitors are attracted by the warm climate, the beautiful scenery, especially on the islands, and also by the historical sites which survive from the days of classical Greece. However, a number of factors have combined to limit the importance of tourism in recent years, including the emergence of cheaper rivals like Turkey and Tunisia, the recession in Western countries and the appalling pollution in Athens – by some measures the most polluted y in Europe outside the former Eastern bloc, with 60% of the nation's total manufacturing capacity.

HISTORY AND POLITICS

In the great days of classical Greece, during the thousand years before Christ, Greek colonies were established all round the shores of the Mediterranean and Black Seas. For a brief period in the 4th century BC, Alexander the Great built an empire which extended from the Danube, through Turkey and the Middle East to the Indus Valley of northern India. Even more important were the great contributions to philosophy, sculpture, architecture and literature made by the early Greeks.

The great epic poems of Greece – the *Iliad* and the *Odyssey* – speak of the exploits of ancient Greek seafarers who travelled around the Mediterranean. Today Greeks are still great seamen and wanderers, and large communities are to be found in the USA, Australia, Canada and Latin America. Since 1960 many Greek migrants have found work in Germany, and the admission of Greece to the EC (on 1 January 1981) has given further opportunities for Greeks to find work in Western Europe. The gap in economic strength and performance between Greece and most of its EU partners remains wide, but the prospect of a single market may help to overcome the traditional obstacles of partisan, often volatile politics, an inflated, slow-moving government bureaucracy, and a notorious 'black economy'. In February 1994 the government imposed a trade embargo on the Former Yugoslav Republic of Macedonia over its alleged territoiral claim on northern Greece. [*Map page 17*] ∎

AREA 131,990 sq km [50,961 sq mls]
POPULATION 10,416,000
CAPITAL (POPULATION) Athens (3,097,000)
GOVERNMENT Multiparty republic
ETHNIC GROUPS Greek 96%, Macedonian 2%, Turkish 1%, Albanian, Slav
LANGUAGES Greek (official)
RELIGIONS Christianity (Eastern Orthodox 97%), Islam 2%
CURRENCY Drachma = 100 lepta

GREENLAND

Recognized by geographers as the world's largest island (the Australian mainland being considered a continental land mass), Greenland is almost three times the size of the second largest, New Guinea. However, more than 85% of the land is covered in continuous permafrost, an ice-cap with an average depth of about 1,500 m [5,000 ft], and though there are a few sandy and clay plains in the ice-free areas, settlement is confined to the narrow rocky coasts. The few towns, including the capital of Godthåb (Nuuk), are on the southwest coast, warmed by the southerly currents of the Atlantic; on the east side, a northerly current from the Arctic chills the pack-ice and makes it inaccessible for most of the year.

ECONOMY AND RESOURCES

The economy still depends substantially on subsidies from Denmark, which remains its chief trading partner. The main rural occupations are sheep rearing and fishing – with shrimps, prawns and molluscs contributing over 60% of exports. The only major manufacturing is fish canning, which has drawn many Eskimos to the towns; few now follow the traditional life of nomadic hunters. Most Greenlanders (a mixture of Inuit Eskimo and Danish extraction) live precariously between the primitive and the modern; in the towns rates of alcoholism, venereal disease and suicide are all high. Yet the nationalist mood prevails, buoyed by abundant fish stocks, lead and zinc from Uummannaq in the north-west, untapped uranium in the south, possible oil in the east – and the increase in organized, often adventure-oriented tourism.

HISTORY AND POLITICS

The first recorded European to visit this barren desert was Eirike Raudi (Eric the Red), a Norseman from Iceland who settled at Brattahlid in 982. It was he who named the place Greenland – to make it sound attractive to settlers. Within four years, more than 30 ships had ferried pioneers there, founding a colony which would last five centuries.

Greenland became a Danish possession in 1380 and, eventually, an integral part of the Kingdom of Denmark in 1953. After the island was taken into the EC in 1973 – despite a majority vote against by Greenlanders – a nationalist movement developed and in 1979, after another referendum, a home rule was introduced, with full internal self-government following in 1981. Then, in 1985, Greenland withdrew from the EC, halving the Community's territory.

Independence is a daunting task, as the Danes point out: the island is nearly 50 times the size of the mother country with only 1% of the population – figures which make Mongolia, the world's least densely populated country, look almost crowded. [*Map page 36*] ■

AREA 2,175,600 sq km [839,999 sq mls]
POPULATION 58,000
CAPITAL (POPULATION) Godthåb (or Nuuk, 12,000)
GOVERNMENT Self-governing division of Denmark
ETHNIC GROUPS Greenlander 86%, Danish 14%
LANGUAGES Eskimo dialects, Danish
RELIGIONS Christianity (mainly Lutheran)
CURRENCY Danish currency

GRENADA

Ｔhe most southern of the Windward Islands, the country of Grenada also includes the Southern Grenadines, principally Carriacou. It is mainly mountainous, with lush vegetation. Grenada is known as 'the spice island of the Caribbean' and is the world's leading producer of nutmeg, its main crop. Cocoa, bananas and mace also contribute to exports, but attempts to diversify the economy from an agricultural base have been largely unsuccessful. In the early 1990s

there were signs that the tourist industry w finally making a recovery after the debilitatir events of 1983.

Formally British since 1783, Grenad became a self-governing colony in 1967 an independent in 1974. Then, in 1979, it wer Communist after a bloodless coup whe Maurice Bishop established links with Cub After Bishop was executed by other Marxis in 1983, the US (supported by some Carit bean countries) sent in troops to restor democracy, and since the invasion the ailin economy has been heavily reliant on America aid. [*Map page 30*] ■

AREA 344 sq km [133 sq mls]
POPULATION 92,000
CAPITAL (POPULATION) St George's (35,700)
GOVERNMENT Constitutional monarchy with a bicameral legislature
ETHNIC GROUPS Black 84%, Mixed 12%, East Indian 3%, White 1%
LANGUAGES English, French patois
RELIGIONS Christianity (Roman Catholic 64%, Protestant 34%)
CURRENCY East Caribbean dollar = 100 cents

GUADELOUPE

Ｓlightly the larger of France's two overseas departments in the Caribbean, Guadeloupe comprises seven islands including Saint-Martin and Saint-Barthélemy to the northwest. Over 90% of the area, however, is taken up by Basse-Terre, which is volcanic – La Soufrière (1,467 m [4,813 ft]) is the highest point in the Lesser Antilles – and the smaller Grande-Terre, made of low limestone; the two are separated by a narrow sea channel called Rivière-Salée (Salt River).

The commercial centre of Pointe-à-Pitre (population 25,300) is on Grande-Terre. Food is the biggest import (much of it from France), bananas the biggest export, followed by wheat flour, sugar, rum and aubergines.

rench aid has helped create a reasonable
andard of living, but despite this and thriving
urism – the majority of it from France and
e USA – unemployment is high.

Though sharing an identical history to
lartinique, Guadeloupe has a far stronger
paratist movement, which sporadically
sorts to acts of terrorism.

t **Martin** is administered as two separate
arts: the northern two-thirds (Saint-Martin,
rench and administered as part of Guad-
loupe), and the southern third (St Maarten,
Dutch and part of the Netherlands Antilles
deration). Located 260 km [162 mls] north
f Guadeloupe, the island is just 88 sq km
34 sq mls] in total. [*Map page 30*] ■

AREA 1,710 sq km [660 sq mls]
POPULATION 421,000
CAPITAL (POPULATION) Basse-Terre
(14,000)
GOVERNMENT Overseas department of
France
ETHNIC GROUPS Mixed (Black and White)
90%
LANGUAGES French
RELIGIONS Christianity (Roman Catholic 95%)
CURRENCY French currency

GUAM

The largest of the Marianas, measuring
541 sq km [209 sq mls], Guam is composed mainly of a coralline limestone plateau,
with mountains in the south, hills in the centre and narrow coastal lowlands in the north of
the island. Though parts are highly developed
along American lines, there are also traditional
villages, beautiful beaches and dense jungles.
Almost half the population of 147,000 are
Chamorro – of mixed Indonesian, Spanish
and Filipino descent – and another quarter
Filipino, but 20% of the total population
is composed of US military personnel and
their families.

ECONOMY AND RESOURCES

Textiles, beverages, tobacco and copra are the
main exports, but most food is imported. As a
Pacific tourist destination, it is second only to
Hawaii; in 1990 visitors' receipts were $550
million. All this helps to give Guamanians a
relatively high standard of living, with an
annual per capita income of over $6,000.

HISTORY AND POLITICS

Populated for over 3,000 years, charted by
Magellan in 1521, colonized by Spain from
1668, but ceded to the US after the 1896–8
war and occupied by the Japanese 1941–4, it is
today – as a 'self-governing unincorporated
territory' – of huge strategic importance to
Washington, and a third of its usable land is
occupied by American naval and airforce
establishments. In 1979, a referendum overwhelmingly backed a return of much of the
military land to civilian use, and a 1982 vote
showed clear support for the Commonwealth
status enjoyed by the Northern Marianas.
[*Map page 26*] ■

AREA 541 sq km [209 sq mls]
POPULATION 147,000
CAPITAL (POPULATION) Agana (50,800)
GOVERNMENT US territory
ETHNIC GROUPS Chamorro 47%, Filipino
25%, American 20%
LANGUAGES Chamorro, English
RELIGIONS Christianity (Roman Catholic 98%)
CURRENCY US currency

GUATEMALA

Most populous of the Central American
countries, Guatemala's Pacific coastline, two and a half times longer than the
Caribbean coast, is backed by broad alluvial
plains, formed of material washed down from
the towering volcanoes that front the ocean.
These include extinct Tajumulco (4,217 m
[13,830 ft]), the highest peak in Central
America.

A heavily-dissected plateau, the Altos, forms the core of the country; beautiful lakes such as the Atitlán mark its junction with the mountains. This area, with comfortable temperatures for living and maize cultivation, is both a focus of dense rural settlement and also the site of the capital – earthquake-prone Guatemala City. The north-eastern third of the country is the Petén, a flat, low-lying limestone wilderness on the Yucatan Peninsula. Once a centre of Mayan civilization, it contains many remarkable archaeological remains, in particular Tikal and Uaxactún.

ECONOMY AND RESOURCES
The plains have been used for commercial-scale agriculture only since the 1950s, when malaria was brought under control and roads were built; cattle and cotton are now more important than the traditional banana crop. Lower mountain slopes, up to about 1,500 m [5,000 ft], yield most of the country's best coffee, above that maize and beans are grown.

HISTORY AND POLITICS
Guatemala was under Spanish rule from 1524 to 1821, when it became independent. The republic is divided into 22 departments. While Indians are in the majority, society and government are run on autocratic, often repressive lines by the mestizos of mixed Indian and European stock. The Indians were the principal victims of the army's indiscriminate campaign against left-wing URNG guerrillas in the early 1980s – the acceleration of a policy in place since the 1950s.

The 'low-intensity' civil war that followed was still smouldering when a UN-mediated cease-fire became operative in neighbouring El Salvador in February 1992. This influence, allied to the government's sudden recognition of Belizean independence in 1991 (Guatemala had claimed the entire territory), would benefit a nation whose 'defence' spending takes 15% of the budget, and whose record on human rights is appalling. As in El Salvador, Washington's stance is vitally important: in keeping with all the Central American republics (except Nicaragua), the US is crucial to the economy – in Guatemala's case, accounting for more than 40% of trade.

In March 1994 a human rights agreement was reached, allowing for the establishment of a UN observer mission in the country [Map page 30] ■

AREA 108,890 sq km [42,042 sq mls]
POPULATION 10,322,000
CAPITAL (POPULATION) Guatemala City (2,000,000)
GOVERNMENT Republic
ETHNIC GROUPS Amerindian 45%, Ladino/Mestizo (mixed Hispanic and Amerindian) 45%, White 5%, Black 2%, others including Chinese 3%
LANGUAGES Spanish (official)
RELIGIONS Christianity (Roman Catholic 75%, Protestant 25%)
CURRENCY Guatemalan quetzal = 100 centavos

GUINEA

The Republic of Guinea faces the Atlantic Ocean in West Africa. A flat, swampy, mangrove-fringed plain borders the coast, behind which the land rises to a plateau region called Fouta Djalon. Dense forests occupy the western foothills of the Fouta Djalon. The Upper Niger plains, named after one of Africa's longest rivers, the Niger, which rises there, are in the north-east. The Sénégal and Gambia rivers also start in north-eastern Guinea. In the south-east lie the Guinea Highlands, which reach 1,752 m [5,748 ft] at Mt Nimba on the border with Ivory Coast and Liberia.

ECONOMY AND RESOURCES
Two-thirds of the population are employed in agriculture and food processing. Bananas, palm oil, pineapples and rice are important crops on the wet Atlantic coastal plain, where swamps and forests have been cleared for agricultural development, while in the drier interior cattle are kept by nomadic herdsmen.

Guinea's natural resources are considerable: it has some of the world's largest reserves high-grade bauxite, and the three large ☐nes account for some 80% of export earn-☐s. The Aredor diamond mine has also been ☐ry profitable since opening in 1984, and ☐ere is great potential for iron-ore mining and ☐droelectric power.

☐ISTORY AND POLITICS

☐uinea was the first independent state of ☐rench-speaking Africa. France granted the ☐oublesome territory independence in 1958 ☐llowing a rise in nationalism after World ☐ar II, and for more than a quarter of a ☐ntury Guinea was ruled by the repressive ☐gime of President Ahmed Sékou Touré, who ☐olated Guinea from the West and leaned ☐wards the Eastern bloc for support.

Though reconciled with France in 1978, it ☐as not until after the military coup following ☐ouré's death in 1984 that economic reforms ☐egan to work (it is estimated that up to a ☐uarter of the population left for neighbouring ☐ountries during Touré's presidency). After ☐is death, military leaders took over. Colonel ☐ansana Conté became president and his gov-☐rnment introduced free enterprise policies. ☐1 1993, Conté won a presidential election. ☐*Map page 32*] ∎

AREA 245,860 sq km [94,927 sq mls]
POPULATION 6,501,000
CAPITAL (POPULATION) Conakry (705,000)
GOVERNMENT Multiparty republic
ETHNIC GROUPS Fulani 40%, Malinke 26%, Susu 11%, Kissi 7%, Kpelle 5%
LANGUAGES French (official)
RELIGIONS Islam 85%, traditional beliefs 5%, Christianity 2%
CURRENCY Guinean franc = 100 cauris

GUINEA-BISSAU

The Republic of Guinea-Bissau is a small country in West Africa, where the land is mostly low-lying, with a broad, swampy coastal plain and many flat offshore islands, including the Bijagós Archipelago. These islands were probably once joined to the mainland but the coast has been submerged in recent geological time – this submergence has created broad river estuaries. The land rises in the east where there are low plateaus, but the highest land (up to 310 m [1,017 ft]) is found near the border with Guinea.

Mangrove forests grow along the coasts and estuaries, while dense rainforest covers much of the coastal plain. Inland, the forests thin out and merge into savanna, with open grassland on the highest ground. The country has a rich birdlife. Wild animals include buffaloes, crocodiles, gazelles and leopards.

ECONOMY AND RESOURCES

Guinea-Bissau is a poor country. Agriculture employs more than 80% of the people, but most farmers produce little more than they need to feed their families. Major crops include beans, coconuts, groundnuts, maize, palm kernels and rice, the staple food.

Fishing is also important – the main port is Bissau – and fish, including shrimps, make up about one third of the country's exports. Groundnuts and coconuts together make up about 40% of the exports. Livestock are raised and some hides and skins are exported. Guinea-Bissau has some undeveloped mineral deposits (there are bauxite deposits in the south), but the country has few manufacturing industries.

HISTORY AND POLITICS

Historians know little of the early history of the area, which lay near the edge of the medieval West African empires of Ghana and Mali. The coast was first visited by Portuguese navigators in 1446. Between the 17th and early 19th centuries, the Portuguese used the coast as a slave-trade base. Some slaves were taken to Brazil and others to the Cape Verde Islands where they were forced to work on Portuguese plantations.

Portugal appointed a governor to administer Guinea-Bissau and the Cape Verde Islands in 1836, but in 1879, the two territories were separated and Guinea-Bissau became a colony, then called Portuguese Guinea. But development was slow, partly because the territory did not attract settlers on the same scale as Portugal's much healthier African colonies of Angola and Mozambique.

In 1956, African nationalists in Portuguese Guinea and Cape Verde founded the African Party for the Independence of Guinea and Cape Verde (PAIGC). Because Portugal seemed determined to hang on to its overseas territories, the PAIGC began a guerrilla war in 1963. By 1968, it held two-thirds of the country. In 1972, a rebel National Assembly, elected by the people in the PAIGC-controlled area, voted to make the country independent as Guinea-Bissau. In 1974, Guinea-Bissau became independent, followed in 1975 by Cape Verde.

In 1974, Guinea-Bissau faced many problems arising from its under-developed economy and its lack of trained people to work in the administration. One objective of the leaders of Guinea-Bissau was to unite their country with Cape Verde. But army leaders overthrew Guinea-Bissau's government in 1980. The Revolutionary Council, which took over, did not favour unification with Cape Verde and instead concentrated on national policies. It followed a socialist programme, introducing some reforms. For example, it reduced adult illiteracy from 97% to 64% between 1974 and 1990. Other reforms concerned women who were now encouraged to play a full part in national development.

In 1991, the country abolished the law making the PAIGC the country's only political party. Opposition parties were then formed, with ten opposition parties legalized since November 1991. Legislative elections to a new 100-seat legislature were held in July 1994 and won by the PAIGC. [*Map page 32*] ■

AREA 36,120 sq km [13,946 sq mls]
POPULATION 1,050,000
CAPITAL (POPULATION) Bissau (125,000)
GOVERNMENT Multiparty republic
ETHNIC GROUPS Balante 27%, Fulani (or Peul) 23%, Malinke (Mandingo or Mandinka) 12%, Mandyako 11%, Pepel 10%
LANGUAGES Portuguese (official)
RELIGIONS Traditional beliefs 54%, Islam 38%, Christianity 8%
CURRENCY Guinea-Bissau peso = 100 centavos

GUYANA

The vast interior, covering 85% of th land area, includes low forest-covere plateaux, the wooded Rupununi savanna meandering river valleys, and the spectacula Roraima Massif on the Venezuela-Braz border. The coastal plain is mainly artificia reclaimed from the tidal marshes and man grove swamps by dykes and canals. It largely uninhabited and 95% of the popu lation live within a few kilometres of the coas leaving the interior virtually empty.

ECONOMY AND RESOURCES
Land reclamation for sugar and cotton plant ing began in the 18th century under Dutc West India Company rule, using slave labour and continued through the 19th century afte the British took over, with indentured Asia labour replacing slaves after emancipation Today sugar remains the main plantatior crop, with production largely mechanized most of it in the lower Demerara River area.

The Asian community, however, whicl makes up about half the total Guyanan popu lation, is involved in rice growing. Bauxite mining and alumina production are well established industries, combining with suga production to provide 80% of the country': overseas earnings. But neither sugar nor rice provide year-round work and unemploymen remains a stubborn problem. The economy which is 80% state-controlled, entered a pro longed economic crisis in the 1970s, and in the early 1980s the situation was exacerbated by the decline in the production and the price of bauxite, sugar and rice.

Following unrest, the government sought to replace Western aid by turning for help to soci alist countries. During the late 1980s Western aid and investment were again sought, but by 1989 the social and economic difficulties had led to the suspension of foreign assistance.

HISTORY AND POLITICS
The 'land of many waters' was settled by the

Dutch between 1616 and 1621. The territory was ceded to Britain in 1814, and in 1831 British Guiana was formed. Independent since 1966, Guyana – the only Englishspeaking country in South America – became a republic in 1970. Forbes Burnham was the first prime minister after independence. Under a new constitution adopted in 1980, the powers of the president were increased, and Burnham became president until his death in 1985. He was succeeded by Hugh Desmond Hoyte, but Hoyte was defeated in presidential elections in 1992 by an Asian Indian Cheddi Jagan, who had been prime minister prior to independence. [*Map page 31*] ▉

AREA 214,970 sq km [83,000 sq mls]
POPULATION 825,000
CAPITAL (POPULATION) Georgetown (188,000)
GOVERNMENT Multiparty republic
ETHNIC GROUPS Asian Indian 49%, Black 36%, Mixed 7%, Amerindian 7%, Portuguese, Chinese
LANGUAGES English (official)
RELIGIONS Christianity (Protestant 34%, Roman Catholic 18%), Hinduism 34%, Islam 9%
CURRENCY Guyana dollar = 100 cents

HAITI

Occupying the western third of Hispaniola, the Caribbean's second largest island, Haiti is mainly mountainous with a long, indented coast. Most of the country is centred around the Massif du Nord, with the narrow Massif de la Hotte forming the southern peninsula. In the deep bight between the two lies the chief port and capital, Port-au-Prince.

ECONOMY AND RESOURCES

Haiti has few natural resources and most of the workforce is engaged on the land, with coffee the only significant cash crop. Two-thirds of the population, however, lives at or below the poverty line, subsisting on small-scale agriculture and fishing. Measures have been taken to increase productivity, such as the Artibonite valley irrigation scheme, and the planting of tropical fruit and vegetables has been encouraged.

HISTORY AND POLITICS

Ceded to France in 1697, a century before the rest of Hispaniola, Haiti developed as a sugar-producing colony. Once the richest part of the Caribbean, it is now the poorest nation in the Western Hemisphere. For nearly two centuries, since a slave revolt made it the world's first independent black state in 1804, it has been bedevilled by military coups, government corruption, ethnic violence and political instability, including a period of US control from 1915 to 1934.

The violent regime of François Duvalier ('Papa Doc'), president from 1957 and declaring himself 'President for Life' in 1964, was especially brutal, but that of his son Jean-Claude ('Baby Doc'), president from 1971, was little better; both used their murderous private militia, the Tontons Macoutes, to conduct a reign of terror. In 1986 popular unrest finally forced Duvalier to flee the country, and the military took over.

After another period of political chaos and economic disaster – not helped by the suspension of US aid between 1987 and 1989 – the country's first multiparty elections were held in December 1990, putting in office a radical Catholic priest, Father Jean-Bertrand Aristide, on a platform of sweeping reforms. But with the partisans of the old regime, including the Tontons Macoutes, still powerful, the military took control in September 1991, forcing Aristide to flee (to the USA) after only seven months of government. Tens of thousands of exiles followed in the ensuing weeks, heading mainly for the US naval base at Guantánamo Bay, in Cuba, in the face of a wave of savage repression, but the American government returned the 'boat people' to Port-au-Prince. Military intervention (as in Panama in 1989) was considered by the Organization of American States, but they instead imposed a trade embargo, inflicting further hardship on an already impoverished Haitian population.

However, in 1994, the US sent in troops to restore democracy and reinstate Aristide as president once again. He returned to Haiti on 15 October 1994. [*Map page 30*] ■

AREA 27,750 sq km [10,714 sq mls]
POPULATION 7,035,000
CAPITAL (POPULATION) Port-au-Prince (1,144,000)
GOVERNMENT Transitional government
ETHNIC GROUPS Black 95%, Mulatto 5%
LANGUAGES French (official) 10%, Haitian Creole 88%
RELIGIONS Christianity (Roman Catholic 75%), Voodoo
CURRENCY Gourde = 100 centimes

HONDURAS

Some 80% of Honduras is mountainous, with peaks of more than 2,500 m [8,000 ft] in the west. The state has a short frontage, 124 km [80 mls] long, on the Pacific Ocean in the Gulf of Fonseca. Most of Honduras has a seasonal climate, relatively dry between November and May.

Second largest of the Central American countries, Honduras has a small population: indeed, it is five times as large as neighbouring El Salvador – its opponent in the 'Soccer War' of 1969, triggered by illegal Salvadorean immigration – but has fewer people.

ECONOMY AND RESOURCES
The mountain ranges are metalliferous: lodes of gold drew the first Spanish *conquistadores* to found Tegucigalpa, the capital, in 1524, and silver is still an important export. Mining contributes more to the economy than it does in any other Central American state.

The limited lowlands around the Gulf form some of the prime cotton lands of the country. Traditional cattle ranching, employing cowboys, is as much in evidence as agriculture. The aromatic pine forests of the east are being consumed by new paper mills on the hot, rain-soaked Caribbean coast. The lower alluvium-filled valleys of the rivers draining into the Caribbean have been reclaimed and the forest replaced by orderly banana plantations. Honduras was the original 'banana republic' – the world's leading exporter in the interwar years. Today it remains an important crop, accounting for nearly a quarter of exports, with production dominated by two US companies, though coffee is now the largest earner. Dependent on these cash crops, the country is the least industrialized in the region.

It is also the most reliant on the US for trade – quite a claim in Central America: 56% of its imports and 49% of its exports are with the Americans.

HISTORY AND POLITICS
After a short civil war in the 1920s a series of military regimes ruled Honduras until 1980, when civilians took over; the country has since had a series of democratically elected pro-American centre-right governments, but with the military retaining considerable influence.

Aid from the US is crucial, partly in return for services rendered; strategically important to Washington, Honduras allowed the US-backed 'Contra' rebels to operate from its territory against the Communist revolutionary Sandinista government in Nicaragua throughout the 1980s, and in 1990 – following the Sandinistas' defeat in the elections – signed a peace agreement with the pro-American government of Violeta Chamorro. Less enthusiastically, the Honduran Army also collaborated with US efforts to defeat left-wing guerillas in El Salvador. [*Map page 30*] ■

AREA 112,090 sq km [43,278 sq mls]
POPULATION 5,493,000
CAPITAL (POPULATION) Tegucigalpa (679,000)
GOVERNMENT Republic
ETHNIC GROUPS Mestizo 90%, Amerindian 7%, Black (including Black Carib) 2%, White 1%
LANGUAGES Spanish (official)
RELIGIONS Christianity (Roman Catholic 85%, Protestant 10%)
CURRENCY Honduran lempira = 100 centavos

HONG KONG

The 1,071 sq km [413 sq mls] that comprise the British colony of Hong Kong consist of Hong Kong Island itself, 235 smaller islands, the Kowloon peninsula on the Chinese province of Guangdong and the 'New Territories' adjoining it. Hong Kong Island is largely hilly, but the highest point in the colony is Tai Mo Shan at 957 m [3,140 ft] in the New Territories. Much land reclamation has taken place along the rugged coast, particularly in the harbour area, where sites backfilled with the island's refuse have provided the foundations for many of the skyscrapers which form Hong Kong's distinctive skyline.

ECONOMY AND RESOURCES

The colony has few natural resources: most of its food, water and raw materials have to be brought in, principally from China. Its prosperity rests on the ingenuity, acumen and hard work of the people.

The economy of Hong Kong is based on manufacturing (textiles, electronics, watches and plastic goods), banking and commerce, with the sheltered waters between Kowloon and Victoria providing one of the finest natural deep-water harbours in the world. Thus, when the Chinese resume control of the colony, they will inherit the world's biggest container port, its biggest exporter of clothes and its tenth biggest trader. Hong Kong's economy has been so successful since World War II that its huge neighbour will be increasing its export earnings by more than a quarter.

Certainly, the entrepreneurial spirit is still strong as time ticks away to the changeover: in 1992 Hong Kong embarked on its scheme for a new airport to replace the dangerous Kai Tak – the world's largest civil engineering project and due for opening in 1997, with final completion in 2040. Nevertheless, with the future still uncertain, the economy has recently shown signs of slowing as some businessmen drifted elsewhere and some services shifted to rivals such as Singapore.

HISTORY AND POLITICS

Hong Kong was acquired by Britain in three stages. The island itself, containing the city of Victoria, was ceded in 1842; Kowloon, on the mainland, came under its control in 1860; and the New Territories, between Kowloon and the Chinese border, were leased in 1898.

On 1 July 1997 the Crown Colony and its possessions will return to the Chinese government. Under a 1984 accord, China agrees to allow the territory to enjoy full economic autonomy and pursue its capitalist path for at least another 50 years. In 1988, a Draft Basic Law, drawn up by an Anglo-Chinese committee, was published for discussion. However, the events of Tiananmen Square in 1989 and the limitations on democratic representation suggested in the basic law have caused anxiety and resentment among many Hong Kong citizens. Negotiations between Britain and China to safeguard the interests of the inhabitants are still continuing. [*Map page 24*] ∎

AREA 1,071 sq km [413 sq mls]
POPULATION 5,838,000
CAPITAL (POPULATION) Victoria (part of Hong Kong Island – population 1,251,000)
GOVERNMENT UK appointed governor
ETHNIC GROUPS Chinese 98%, others 2% (including European)
LANGUAGES English and Chinese (official)
RELIGIONS Buddhism majority, Confucism, Taoism, Christianity, Islam, Hinduism, Sikhism, Judaism
CURRENCY Hong Kong dollar = 100 cents

HUNGARY

Hungary has two large lowland areas – the aptly-named Great Plain (Nagyalföld) which occupies the south-eastern half of the country and is dissected by the country's two main rivers, the Danube and the Tisa, and the Little Plain (Kisalföld) in the north-west. Between them a line of hills runs south-west to north-east from Lake Balaton to the Slovak border. Balaton (72 km [45 mls] long), the largest lake in central Europe, is a favourite holiday resort.

The Hungarian Plains have some of the most fertile agricultural land in Europe, especially in the areas covered by a mantle of loess (a windblown deposit dating from the Ice Age), but there are also infertile areas of marsh, sand and dry steppeland, where crop growing gives way to grazing. In the region to the north-west of the Great Plain, known as Hortobagy and the only remaining steppe in Europe outside the former USSR, it is still possible to see Europe's last remaining cowboys – the *gulyas* – riding on horseback to round up their cattle. But the expanse of dry steppeland where this way of life is practised is dwindling as irrigation schemes are introduced, and ranching gives way to the growing of wheat, tobacco and rice.

The continental climate, with its spring rains, long, hot summers and cold winters, favours crops such as wheat, maize, sunflowers and vines. Rainfall is around 63 cm [25 in] in the west, but falls to under 50 cm [20 in] in the east.

ECONOMY AND RESOURCES

Hungary has reserves of gas, but is poorly endowed with natural resources, bauxite being one of the few plentiful minerals. Industries have been built up on the basis of imported raw materials, mainly from the former USSR. The main industrial centres are in the north, around the towns of Miskolc and Budapest (home to a fifth of the population) where iron and steel, engineering and chemicals predominate. Aluminium is manufactured north of Lake Balaton.

Hungary's move away from the classic Eastern European reliance on heavy industry and agriculture would be easier than, say, that of Poland, and many joint ventures with Western capital were inaugurated in the first months of the new democracy, bringing in not only high-tech expertise but also much-needed managerial skills. Hungary has the edge in tourism, too – by the late 1980s the number of annual visitors was already outstripping its own population.

The lack of energy resources, however, remains a concern, and the government began

THE DANUBE

With around 300 tributaries and a length of 2,850 km [1,750 mls], the Danube is Europe's second longest river. Rising from a source in the Black Forest in south-west Germany, it flows east and south through Austria, the Slovak Republic, Hungary and Yugoslavia, and forms a large part of the Romanian-Bulgarian frontier before entering the Black Sea through a wide, swampy delta on the border between Romania and the Ukraine. Navigable as far upstream as Ulm in Bavaria, the Danube links the three capitals of Vienna, Budapest and Belgrade. It has long been one of Europe's main commercial waterways, and with the ending of the Cold War and the consequent divisions between East and West, it is likely to be of growing importance.

pursuing an ambitious programme to increase its nuclear capacity from the 1988 figure of 49% of electricity generation. Even as a relative success, Hungary's progress has its cost, with inflation around 25–30% and unemployment doubling in 1991 alone to 700,000 – around 14% of the workforce.

HISTORY AND POLITICS

As a large part of the Austro-Hungarian empire, Hungary enjoyed an almost autonomous position within the Dual Monarchy from 1867, but defeat in World War I saw nearly 70% of its territory apportioned by the Treaty of Versailles to Czechoslovakia, Yugoslavia and Romania. Some 2.6 million Hungarians live in these countries today. The government hoped to regain lost land by siding with Hitler's Germany in World War II, but the result was the occupation of the Red Army and, in 1949, the establishment of a Communist state. The heroic Uprising of 1956 was put down by Soviet troops and its leader, Imre Nagy, was executed.

President János Kádár came to power in the wake of the suppression, but his was a relatively progressive leadership, introducing an element of political freedom and a measure of economic liberalism. Before the great upheavals of 1989 Hungary had gone further an any Eastern European Soviet satellite in ecentralization and deregulation.

However, failure to tackle the underlying economic problems led in 1988 to some of his own Socialist Workers Party members exerting pressure for change. In 1989 the central committee agreed to a pluralist system and the parliament, previously little more than a rubber-stamp assembly, formally ended the party's 'leading role in society'. In 1990, in the first free elections since the war, Hungarians voted into office a centre-right coalition headed by the Democratic Forum.

Unlike its more static neighbours, the new government of Prime Minister Jozsef Antall was able to press on with a rapid transition to a full market economy. The region's first stock market was set up, Budapest was chosen as the European Union's first regional office and Hungary – a founder member of the now defunct Warsaw Pact – applied to join NATO. [Map pages 16–17] ∎

AREA 93,030 sq km [35,919 sq mls]
POPULATION 10,161,000
CAPITAL (POPULATION) Budapest (2,016,000)
GOVERNMENT Multiparty republic
ETHNIC GROUPS Magyar (Hungarian) 98%, Gypsy, German, Croat, Romanian, Slovak
LANGUAGES Hungarian (official)
RELIGIONS Christianity (Roman Catholic 64%, Protestant 23%, Orthodox 1%), Judaism 1%
CURRENCY Forint = 100 fillér

ICELAND

Situated far out in the North Atlantic Ocean, Iceland is not only the smallest but also the most isolated of the independent Scandinavian countries. Though politically part of Europe, the island (nearer to Greenland than to Scotland) arises geologically from the boundary between Europe and America – the Mid-Atlantic Ridge. It is indeed a product of the ridge, formed almost entirely by volcanic outpourings at a point where the Earth's crust is opening at a rate measurable in centimetres per year.

A central zone of recently active volcanoes and fissures crosses Iceland from Axarfjörður in the north to Vestmannaeyjar in the south, with a side-branch to Reykjanes and an outlying zone of activity around the Snaefellsnes peninsula in the west. During the thousand years that Iceland has been settled, between 150 and 200 eruptions have occurred in the active zones, some building up substantial volcanic cones. Between 1104 and 1970 Mt Hekla, in the south-west, erupted at least 15 times. Its earliest outpourings of ash devastated local farms, some of which have recently been excavated.

A huge eruption in 1783 destroyed pasture and livestock on a grand scale, causing a famine that reduced the Icelandic population by a quarter. More recent eruptions include the formation of a new island – Surtsey – off the south-west coast in 1963, and the partial devastation of the town of Vestmannaeyjar-Karpstadur, on neighbouring Heimaey, ten years later. Paradoxically, Iceland is also an island of glaciers and ice-sheets, with four large ice-caps occupying 11% of the surface and several smaller glaciers.

ECONOMY AND RESOURCES

Since the country was formerly pastoral, with most of the population scattered in farms and small hamlets, the standard of living depended on the vicissitudes of farming close to the Arctic Circle. Now the economy is based on deep-sea fishing; fish and fish products make up 70% of exports. About a fifth of the land is used for agriculture, but only 1% is actually cultivated for root crops and fodder. The rest is used for grazing cattle and sheep. Self-sufficient in meat and dairy products, Iceland augments its main exports with clothing such as sheepskin coats and woollen products.

Geothermal and hydroelectric power provide cheap energy for developing industries, including aluminium smelting and hot-house cultivation; and most houses and offices in Reykjavik, the capital, are heated geothermally. About a quarter of the workforce is engaged in the production of energy and manufacturing – processing food and fish, making cement and refining aluminium from imported bauxite. The population is concentrated mainly in settlements close to the coast, over half of them in or near Reykjavík. Living standards currently compare with those of other Scandinavian countries. In some respects they are better: Iceland boasts the lowest infant mortality rate in the world and the highest life expectancy outside Japan.

HISTORY AND POLITICS

Colonized by Viking and British farmers in the 9th century, Iceland became a dependency first of Norway, then of Denmark, though mainly self-governing with a parliament (*Althing*) dating from AD 930. This is thought to be the world's first parliament in the modern sense, and is certainly the oldest. Recognized as a sovereign state from 1918, the country was united with Denmark through a common sovereign until 1944, when Iceland became a republic. The Icelandic language has close affinities to Anglo-Saxon and differs little today from when it was introduced in the ninth century. [*Map page 13*] ■

AREA 103,000 sq km [39,768 sq mls]
POPULATION 266,000
CAPITAL (POPULATION) Reykjavík (101,000)
GOVERNMENT Multiparty republic
ETHNIC GROUPS Icelandic 94%, Danish 1%
LANGUAGES Icelandic (official)
RELIGIONS Christianity (Evangelical Lutheran 92%, other Lutheran 3%, Roman Catholic 1%)
CURRENCY Icelandic króna = 100 aurar

INDIA

A diamond-shaped country – the world's seventh largest – India extends from high in the Himalayas through the Tropic of Cancer to the warm waters of the Indian Ocean at 8°N. Almost 919 million people live here in the world's second most populous state – and its largest democracy.

Landscape

Geographically, India can be divided into three parts – the mountainous north, the great alluvial plains of the Brahmaputra and Ganges, and the plateaux and lowlands that occupy the southern area, including the Deccan and most of the peninsula. Each provides an astonishing range of scenery – a picture intensified by the variety of peoples cultures and activities within them.

The mountainous north: The Himalayan foothills make a stunning backdrop for northern India, rising abruptly from the plains in towering ranks. Harsh dry highlands, sparsely occupied by herdsmen, stretch northwards to the everlasting snows of the Karakoram. Below lie alpine meadows, lakes and woodlands, often grazed in summer by seasonally migrant flocks from lower villages. The high plateau of Meghalaya ('abode of the clouds') is damp and cool; nearby Cherrapunji has one of the highest rainfalls in the world.

The plains: The great plains form a continuous strip from the Punjab eastwards. Among the most densely populated areas of India (the state of Uttar Pradesh has a population larger than Nigeria, Pakistan or Bangladesh), these lowlands support dozens of cities and smaller settlements – notably Agra, with its Red Fort and Taj Mahal, and the sacred cities of Allahabad and Varanasi (Benares).

Downstream from Tinpahar ('three hills'), near the Bangladeshi border, the Ganges begins its deltaic splitting into distributary streams, while still receiving tributaries from the north and west. The Sundarbans – mangrove and swamp forests at the seaward margin of the Ganges delta – extend eastwards into Bangladesh.

South-west from the Punjab plains lies the Thar or Great Indian Desert, its western fringes in Pakistan but with a broad tract of dunes in the north-eastern lowlands in Rajasthan, India's largest state. The desert ranges from perennially dry wastelands of shifting sand to areas capable of cultivation in wet years. As the name Rajasthan implies, this state was once (until 1950) a land of rajahs and princes, palaces and temples; some of the buildings – including universities – endowed by these private benefactors remain important in Jodhpur, Jaipur, Ajmer, Udaipur and other

...ies. Rajasthan rises in a series of steps to a ...ged, bare range of brightly coloured sand-...one ridges, the Aravallis, that extend north-...stwards and end at Delhi.

Between the Gulfs of Khambhat and ...achchh is the low peninsular plateau of ...athiawar, whose declining deciduous forests ...ll harbour small groups of tribal peoples, ...d indeed the last of India's native lions. ...etween this and the Pakistan border stretch-...the desert salt marsh of the Rann of ...achchh, once an arm of the Arabian Sea and ...ll occasionally flooded by exceptionally ...avy rains.

South-east of the Aravallis is an area of tran-...ion between the great plains of the north ...d the uplands and plateaux of peninsular ...dia. First come the Chambal badlands ...astelands south of Agra, now partly re-...aimed), then rough hill country extending ...uth-eastwards to Rewa. The River Sone ...ovides a lowland corridor through the hills ...uth of Rewa, and an irrigation barrage pro-...des water for previously arid lands west of ...aya. Eastwards again the hills are forested ...ound Ambikapur and Lohardaga.

Peninsular India: South of the Chambal ...iver and south of Indore (a princely capital ...ntil 1950), the sandy plateau of the north ...ves way to forested hills, split by the broad ...orridors of the Narmada and Tapi rivers. ...ribal lands persist in the Satpura Range, and ...e Ajanta Range to the south is noted for ...rimitive cave paintings near Aurangabad. ...rom here to the south volcanic soils pre-...ominate. The Ghats are edged with granite, ...neiss, sandstone and schist, and clad in heavy ...ainforest.

ECONOMY AND RESOURCES

...n total, around 50% of India is cultivated, ...2% is forested and 20% is classified as desert, ...asteland or urban.

The mountainous north: The fertile Vale of ...Kashmir has emerald-green rice terraces, ...walnut and plane trees, and apple and apricot ...orchards around half-timbered villages. It is ...crossed by ancient trackways once used as ...rade routes by mule and yak trains, now ...military roads to the garrisons of the north. ...The wet, forested eastern Himalayas of Assam ...are ablaze with rhododendrons and magnolias,

KASHMIR

Until Indian independence in August 1947, Kashmir's mainly Muslim population was ruled, under British supervision, by a Hindu maharaja. Independence obliged the maharaja to choose between Pakistan or India; hoping to preserve his own independence, he refused to make a decision. In October, a rag-tag army of Pathan tribesmen invaded from newly created Pakistan. Looting industriously, the Pathans advanced slowly, and India had time to rush troops to the region. The first Indo-Pakistan war resulted in a partition that satisfied neither side, with Pakistan holding one-third and India the remainder, with a 60% Muslim population. Despite promises, India has refused to allow a plebiscite to decide the province's fate. Two subsequent wars, in 1965 and 1972, failed to alter signifi-cantly the 1948 cease-fire lines.

In the late 1980s, Kashmiri nationalists in the Indian-controlled area began a violent campaign in favour of either secession to Pakistan or local independence. India re-sponded by flooding Kashmir with troops and accusing Pakistan of intervention. By 1992, at least 3,000 Kashmiris had died. India stood accused of repression, and there was little sign of a peaceful end to the conflict.

and terraced for buckwheat, barley and rice growing. Tropical oaks and teaks on the forest ridges of Nagaland, Manipur and Mizoram, bordering Burma, alternate with rice patches and small towns; on the hilltops dry culti-vation of rice is practised, in plots cleared for a few years' cultivation and then left fallow.

The plains: Heavily irrigated by canals en-gineered in the late 19th century, the rich allu-vial soils have provided prosperity for Sikh and Jat farmers of the Punjab and Haryana. Here are grown winter wheat and summer rice, cotton and sugar cane with sorghum in the drier areas, the successful agriculture forming a foundation for linked industrial develop-ment. Many small market towns are thriving and the fine plans for the joint state capital of Chandigarh, devised by Le Corbusier, have been fully realized.

Somewhat similar landscapes extend eastwards to the plains surrounding Delhi, India's third largest city on the west bank of the Jumna (Yamuna) River. An ancient site, occupied for over 3,000 years, it now includes the Indian capital New Delhi, designed by Sir Edwin Lutyens and built from 1912. Old city and new lie at a focal point of road and rail links, and like many Indian cities rapidly became overcrowded. To the east again are the lowlands of Uttar Pradesh, crisscrossed by the Ganges and Jumna rivers and their many tributaries. Slightly wetter, but less irrigated, these plains are farmed less for wheat and rice than for spiked millet and sorghum, though maize and rice cultivation increase again in the wetter areas towards the state of Bihar.

Along the Nepal border the *terai* or hillfoot plains, formerly malaria-infested swamp forest, have now been cleared and made healthy for prosperous farming settlements. West Bengal consists largely of the rice- and jute-growing lands flanking the distributary streams that flow south to become the Hooghly, on which Calcutta is built. The Ganges-Kobadak barrage now provides irrigation for the north of this tract, while improving both water supply and navigation lower down the Hooghly. South and west of the Aravallis lie the cotton-growing lands of tropical Gujarat; Ahmadabad is its chief city. Industrial development becomes important around the coalfields of the Damodar Valley, centred on Asansol and the developing steel town of Jamshedpur.

Peninsular India: Bombay, India's second largest city, lies on the coastal lowlands by a broad estuary, among ricefields dotted with low lava ridges. Fishing villages with coconut palms line the shore, while inland rise the stepped, forested slopes and pinnacles of peninsular India's longest mountain chain, the Western Ghats (Sahyadri).

East of the Ghats, on rich black soils well watered by the monsoons, stretch seemingly endless expanses of cotton and sorghum cultivation. Arid in late winter and spring, and parched by May, they spring to life when the rains break in late May or June. The sleepy market towns follow a similar rhythm, full of activity when the agricultural cycle demands,

and relaxing under the broiling sun when t' time for activity is past.

South from the holiday beaches of Goa (fo merly a Portuguese enclave, still Portugue in flavour), past busy Mangalore, Calic and Cochin to the state capital of Kera Trivandrum, the coast becomes a kaleid scope of coconut groves and fishing village ricefields, scrublands, cashew orchards ar tapioca plantations.

To the east the peninsula is drier, wi rolling plateaux given over to the productic of millet, pulses and other dry crops. Suga rice and spices are grown where simple eng neering provides tanks, stopped with earth (masonry dams, to save the summer rains; no canals perform the same task. Bangalore ar Hyderabad, once sleepy capitals of prince' states, are now bustling cities, respective! capitals of Karnataka and Andhra Pradesh.

Communications and development

A vital memorial from colonial times is th railway network – a strategic broad-gauge sys tem fed by metre-gauge subsidiaries, wit' additional light railways, for example to th hill-stations of Simla (in Himachal Pradesh) Darjeeling (between Nepal and Bhutan) an Ootacamund (in Tamil Nadu). Among devel opments since independence are the fast an comfortable intercity diesel-electric trains, bu steam-engines remain the main workhorses ir a coal-rich country.

The road system also has strategic element from the Mogul and British past, now ration alized into a system of national highways Main roads are passable all year round, anc feeder-roads are largely all-weather dirt road taking traffic close to most of India's 650,00C villages. The well-served international airport are linked with good, cheap internal services widely used by passengers from a broad socia' spectrum, including pilgrims and tourists.

At independence India was already estab lished as a partly industrialized country, and has made great strides during a successior of five-year plans that provided explicitly for both nationalized and private industry. The Damodar coalfield around Asansol has been developed, and new fields opened. The Tata family's steel city of Jamshedpur, itself now diversified by other industries, has been comemented by new state plants and planned towns at Durgapur and other places, in collaboration with Britain, Germany and the former Soviet Union. Major engineering factories have been built at Bangalore, Vishakhapatnam and elsewhere (including the ill-fated Bhopal), and oil refineries set up at Barauni in the north-east, and near Bombay for new fields recently developed in the north-west. Several nuclear power stations are in operation, and the massive potential of hydroelectric power is being exploited. Small-scale industry is also being encouraged. Industrial estates have had mixed success, but do well in places like Bangalore where there are enough related industries to utilize interactions.

In the countryside a generation of effort in community and rural development is starting to achieve results, most obviously where the Green Revolution of improved seeds and fertilizers has been successful, for example in the wheatlands of the Punjab and Haryana, or where irrigation has been newly applied and brought success. In such areas it can be argued that the gap between landless labourers and prosperous farmers widens when new methods bring greater yields; but this is one of many social problems that beset a complex, diverse society which appears to be always on the verge of collapse into chaos, but despite its size, burgeoning population and potential for division manages to remain intact.

HISTORY AND POLITICS

India's earliest settlers were widely scattered across the subcontinent in Stone Age times. The first of its many civilizations developed in the Indus Valley about 2600 BC, and in the Ganges Valley from about 1500 BC. By the 4th and 3rd centuries BC Pataliputra (modern Patna) formed the centre of a loosely-held empire that extended across the peninsula and beyond into Afghanistan. This first Indian empire broke up after the death of the Emperor Asoka in 232 BC, to be replaced by many others, both transient and lasting, during the centuries that followed. The Portuguese who crossed the Indian Ocean in the late 15th century, and the British, Danes, French and Dutch who soon followed them, found a subcontinent divided in itself and ripe for plundering.

THE HIMALAYAS

The Earth's highest mountain range, with an average height of 6,100 m [20,000 ft], the Himalayas are structurally part of the high plateau of Central Asia. The range stretches over 2,400 km [1,500 mls] from the Pamirs in the north-west to the Chinese border in the east. There are three main ranges: Outer, Middle and Inner; in Kashmir, the Inner Himalayas divide into five more ranges, including the Ladakh Range and the Karakorams. The world's highest mountain, Mt Everest (8,848 m [29,029 ft]), is on the Tibet-Nepal border; the next highest is K2 (8,611 m [28,251 ft]) in the Karakorams, and there are a further six peaks over 8,000 m [26,250 ft].

The name comes from the Nepalese words *him* ('snows') and *alya* ('home of'), and the mountains are much revered in Hindu mythology as the abode of gods. Recently, the hydroelectric potential of the range has inspired more secular reverence: enormous quantities of energy could be tapped, although certainly at some cost to one of the world's most pristine environments.

As a result of battles fought both in Europe and in India itself, Britain gradually gained ascendancy over both European rivals and local factions within the subcontinent; by 1805 the British East India Company was virtually in control, and the British Indian Empire (which included many autonomous states) was gradually consolidated. Power was transferred from the East India Company to the British Crown after the Sepoy Rebellion in 1857. Organized opposition to Britain's rule began before World War I and reached a climax after the end of World War II. In August 1947 the Indian subcontinent became independent, but divided into the separate states of India, a mainly Hindu community, and Pakistan, where Muslims formed the vast majority. In the boundary disputes and reshuffling of minority populations that followed perhaps a million lives were lost – and events since then have done little to promote good relations between the two states.

Languages and religions

India is a vast country with enormous problems of organization. It has over a dozen major languages, each with a rich literature, and many minor languages. Hindi, the national language, and the Dravidian languages of the south (Tamil, Telugu and Malayalam) are Indo-European; in the north and east occur Sino-Tibetan tongues, and in forested hill refuges are found residual Austric languages. Racial stocks, too, are mixed, with dark tribal folk in forest remnants, Mongoloids in the north and east, and often lighter-coloured skins and eyes in the north-west – and in the higher castes throughout the country.

The mosaic of religion also adds variety – and potential conflict. Hinduism is all-pervasive (though the state is officially secular), and Buddhism is slowly reviving in its country of origin (the Buddha was born on the border of India and Nepal about 563 BC). Buddhism's near-contemporary Mahavira and Jainism, with common elements including stress against destruction of any form of life, are strong in the merchant towns around Mt Abu in the Aravalli hills north of Ahmadabad. Islam contributes many mosques and tombs to the Indian scene; the Taj Mahal is the most famous, but there are many more.

The forts of Delhi, Agra and many other northern cities, and the ghost city of Fatehpur Sikri, near Agra, are also Islamic relics of the Mogul period (1556–1707). Despite the formation of Pakistan, India retains a large Muslim minority of about 76 million. Now it is the turn of the Punjab's militant Sikhs, claiming to represent their population of 13 million, who seek separation. Christian influences range from the elaborate Catholic churches and shrines remaining from Portuguese and French settlement, to the many schools and colleges set up by Christian denominations and still actively teaching; there are also notable church unions in both south and north India. The British period of rule left its own monuments; Bombay and Calcutta both have some notable Victoriana, and New Delhi is a planned city of the Edwardian period.

Recent history

During the Cold War period, under Nehru's leadership, India played a prominent role in the Third World as one of the leading non-aligned nations. This, however, did not prevent a border dispute with China in 1962 during which Chinese troops invaded Indian territory, and in 1965 an undeclared war with Pakistan over Kashmir. Internally India continued to suffer from religious and communal conflict and separatist pressures.

Indira Gandhi (Nehru's daughter), elected as prime minister in 1966, resorted to emergency powers between 1975 and 1977, using press censorship and mass imprisonment of opponents to impose her policies. Defeated in the 1977 elections, she nevertheless managed to regain office in 1980. In June 1984, in response to an increasingly militant campaign for Sikh autonomy, Indian troops stormed the Golden Temple of Amritsar, a holy shrine and centre of Sikh extremism. A few months later Indira Gandhi was assassinated by a Sikh member of her personal guard. Her son, Ranjiv Gandhi, succeeded her as prime minister but lost the 1989 elections following accusations of incompetence and corruption. He too was murdered, during the 1991 electoral campaign.

In recent years autonomous pressures in Kashmir and Punjab have increased, and conflict between Hindus and Muslims has dramatically sharpened. The destruction of a mosque in Ayodhya by Hindu extremists in December 1992 led to widespread rioting and a series of bombings in Calcutta and Bombay during 1993 which killed over 300 people.

Sikkim, after Goa the smallest of India's 25 self-governing states, was a Buddhist kingdom before being ruled by Britain from 1866 and protected by India from 1950 to 1975, when following a plebiscite it joined the Union. On the border with Nepal is Mt Kanchenjunga, at 8,598 m [28,028 ft] the world's third highest peak. The state is the world's biggest producer of cardamom (a spice).

Indian islands. The Andaman and Nicobar Islands, in the Bay of Bengal, became an Indian state in 1950 and now form one of the country's seven Union territories (with a population of 280,660); a similar status is held by the Lakshadweep (Laccadive) Islands, off

: Malabar Coast, where 10 of the 36 coral
►lls are inhabited (population 51,707). [*Map
ge 23*] ∎

AREA 3,287,590 sq km [1,269,338 sq mls]
POPULATION 918,570,000
CAPITAL (POPULATION) New Delhi (part of
Delhi, 294,000)
GOVERNMENT Multiparty federal republic
ETHNIC GROUPS Indo-Aryan (Caucasoid)
72%, Dravidian (Aboriginal) 25%, other
(mainly Mongoloid) 3%
LANGUAGES Hindi 30% and English (both
official), Telugu 8%, Bengali 8%, Marati 8%
Urdu 5% and many others
RELIGIONS Hinduism 83%, Islam (Sunni
Muslim) 11%, Christianity 2%, Sikhism 2%,
Buddhism 1%
CURRENCY Indian rupee = 100 paisa

INDONESIA

With the break-up of the Soviet Union in
1991, Indonesia moved up from the
fifth to the fourth most populous nation on
Earth. It is also the world's largest archipelago,
with 13,677 islands (less than 6,000 of which
are inhabited) scattered over an enormous
area of tropical sea. However, three-quarters
of the area is included in the five main centres
of Sumatra, Java, Kalimantan (southern
Borneo), Sulawesi (Celebes) and Irian Jaya
(the western end of New Guinea), which also
include over 80% of the people; more than
half the population live on Java alone, despite
its being only 7% of the land area.

Most of the big islands stand on continental
shelves and have extensive coastal lowlands,
though Sulawesi and the chain of islands
between Java and Irian Jaya rise from deep
water. All are mountainous, for this is an area
of great crustal activity. Along the arc formed
by Sumatra, Java and the Lesser Sunda Islands
stand over 200 volcanoes, about 70 of which –
including Krakatoa (Pulau Rakata) in the
Sunda Strait – have erupted within the last two

centuries, usually with memorable violence.
Java alone has over 120 volcanoes, 14 of which
exceed 3,000 m [10,000 ft].

The natural vegetation of the tropical lowlands is rainforest, which also spreads up into
the hills. Much of this has now been cleared by
shifting cultivators and replaced by secondary
growth, though forest is still the dominant vegetation on most of the less populated islands.

ECONOMY AND RESOURCES

About a tenth of the land area is under permanent cultivation, mostly rice, maize, cassava and sweet potato, and Indonesia remains
essentially an agricultural nation. There are
also large plantations of rubber, sugar cane,
coffee and tea. Accessible parts of the rainforest are being exploited at an alarming rate
for their valuable timber; native forest in
Sumatra is now virtually restricted to reserves
and national parks, though mountain forests,
less vulnerable because they are more isolated,
still remain over wide areas. Many of the
coasts are lined with mangrove swamps,
and several accessible islands are stunningly
beautiful; tourism is one of the country's
fastest growing sectors.

The population of Indonesia is complex and
varied. There is a wide range of indigenous
peoples, speaking some 25 different languages
and over 250 dialects. Four of the world's
major religions – Islam, Hinduism, Christianity and Buddhism – are well represented,
though followers of Islam are in the great
majority and Indonesia is the world's most
populous Muslim nation.

General Suharto's military regime, with US
technical and financial assistance, has brought
a period of relatively rapid economic growth,
supported by an oil boom that by 1970
accounted for 70% of export earnings – a figure that shrank to less than 50% by 1990. Self-
sufficiency in rice and a degree of population
control also helped raise living standards,
though Java's overcrowding remained a problem, and in 1986 a 'transmigration programme' was initiated to settle large numbers
of Javanese on sparsely populated islands,
notably (and notoriously) on Irian Jaya.

While the Javanese dominate Indonesian
affairs, most of the country's wealth – oil, timber, minerals and plantation crops – comes

EAST TIMOR

Invaded by Indonesian troops in 1975, East Timor has effectively remained its 21st state despite numerous UN condemnatory resolutions. The end of the Cold War has done little to ease the people's plight; Australia still does not recognize their right to self-determination, while the Western powers leave the problem to the ineffectual UN.

East Timor was a neglected, coffee-growing Portuguese colony for 300 years before Lisbon promised independence in 1974. The 1975 free elections were won by Fretilin, the left-wing nationalists who had fought the empire for years, but the following month Indonesia occupied the territory. Their policies of deportation, resettlement, harassment, torture, bombings, summary executions and massacres – including one filmed by a British film crew in 1991 – have resulted in the deaths of a third of the population (still officially 630,000) and the encampment of 150,000 or more, according to Amnesty International. At the same time, 100,000 Indonesians have been settled in a country rich in sandalwood, marble and coffee, with oil reserves of 5 billion barrels.

Fretilin's fighters, who returned to the hills in 1975, have since kept up a sporadic and dispersed campaign, while the population – mostly Catholic – await international help. In practice, however, East Timor stays closed to the world.

from other islands. Establishing better relations with the West and its ASEAN (Association of South-east Asian Nations) neighbours, the government has now deregulated much of the economy.

HISTORY AND POLITICS

The first important empire in the region was centred at Palembang in south-eastern Sumatra. This was the great maritime power of Sri Vijaya, which held sway from the 8th to 13th centuries over the important trade routes of the Malacca and Sunda Straits. During the 14th century it was replaced by the kingdom of Madjapahit, centred on the fertile lands of east-central Java. From the 16th century onwards, European influences grew, the area coming progressively under the dominatic and ruthless exploitation of the Dutch East India Company. Freedom movements starting in the early 20th century found their full expression under Japanese occupation in World War II, and Indonesia declared its independence on the surrender of Japan in 1945. After four years in intermittent but brutal fighting, the Dutch finally recognized the country as a sovereign state in 1949 under Achmed Sukarno, leader of the nationalist party since 1927.

Sukarno's anti-Western stance and repressive policies plunged his country into chaos, while costly military adventures drained the treasury. In 1962 he invaded Dutch New Guinea (Irian Jaya) and between 1963 and 1966 he attempted to destabilize the fledgling Federation of Malaysia by incursions into northern Borneo. Throughout his dictatorship Indonesia seemed to be permanently on the edge of disintegration, government forces fighting separatist movements in various parts of the country. In 1967 Sukarno was toppled by General Suharto, following the latter's suppression of a two-year allegedly Communist-inspired uprising that cost 80,000 lives.

Corruption and nepotism remain rife and power is firmly in the hands of Golkar, the military-backed coalition which thwarts the aspirations of the two permitted political parties. The army, perhaps correctly, continues to regard itself as the only protector of stability in a country that has proved almost impossible to govern. [*Map page 26*] ■

AREA 1,904,570 sq km [735,354 sq mls]
POPULATION 191,170,000
CAPITAL (POPULATION) Jakarta (1980 census = 7,886,000; 1993 estimate = 9,000,000)
GOVERNMENT Multiparty republic
ETHNIC GROUPS Javanese 39%, Sundanese 16%, Indonesian (Malay) 12%, Madurese 4%, more than 300 others
LANGUAGES Bahasa Indonesian (official)
RELIGIONS Islam 87%, Christianity 10% (Roman Catholic 6%), Hinduism 2%, Buddhism 1%
CURRENCY Rupiah = 100 sen

IRAN

The Islamic Republic of Iran is a large country in south-western Asia. The barren central plateau covers about half of the country. It includes the Dasht-e-Kavir (Great Salt Desert) and the Dasht-e-Lut (Great Sand Desert). The Elburz (or Alborz) Mountains north of the plateau contain Iran's highest point, Damavand. West of the plateau are the Zagros Mountains, beyond which the land descends to plains bordering the Gulf. Forests of such trees as beech and oak cover about a tenth of Iran, mainly in the Caspian Sea region and the Zagros Mountains. Much of Iran has a severe, dry climate, with hot summers and cold winters, though the climate in the lowlands is generally milder.

ECONOMY AND RESOURCES
The most populous and productive parts of Iran lie at the four extremities – the fisheries, ricefields and tea gardens of the Caspian shore in the foothills of the earthquake zone to the north, the sugar plantations and oilfields of Khuzestan to the south (target of the Iraqi invasion in 1980), the wheat fields of Azerbaijan in the west, and the fruit groves of oases of Khorasan and Seistan in the east. In between are the deserts of Kavir and Lut, and the border ranges which broaden in the west into the high plateaux of the Zagros, the summer retreats of the tribes of Bakhtiars and Kurds.

The cities of the interior depend on ingenious arrangements of tunnels and channels for tapping underground water, and these have been supplemented by high dams, notably at Dezful. The burgeoning capital of Tehran is the crossing-point of the country's two great railways, the Trans-Iranian from the Gulf to the Caspian and the east-west track from Mashhad to Tabriz.

HISTORY AND POLITICS
Called Persia until 1935, the country retained its Shah – thanks first to British and later American support – until 1979, when the emperor's extravagantly corrupt regime (a single-party affair from 1975) was toppled by a combination of students, middle-class professionals and, above, all, clerics offended by the style and pace of Westernization.

The despotism was replaced with another: that of a radical fundamentalist Islamic republic inspired by the return of exiled leader Ayatollah Khomeini. The revolution created a new threat to the conservative Arabs of the Gulf and beyond, who saw it as a dangerous call to challenge the flimsy legitimacy of their own oil-rich governments. The effect would rumble round the Muslim world: 12 years later, in far-off Algeria, the Islamic Salvation Front won the democratic elections.

Many Arab states were less hostile, however, and despite Iranian backing of a series of international terrorist attacks and hostage-takings linked to the Palestinian issue, their regime won respect for the steadfast way they fought the Iraqis from 1980-8, when hundreds of thousands of zealous young Shiite men died defending their homeland.

The war left Iran's vital oil production at less than half the level of 1979 (though still seventh highest in the world and supported by the largest known gas reserves outside Russia), and the government began to court the Western powers. Its stance during the Second Gulf War (albeit predictable) and a tempering of the militant position to one of peace-broker on international issues – led by President Rafsanjani – encouraged many powers to re-establish closer links with a country whose role took on even greater significance with the Muslim republics of the former Soviet Union to the north gaining independence from Moscow in 1991. [*Map page 22*] ■

AREA 1,648,000 sq km [636,293 sq mls]
POPULATION 65,758,000
CAPITAL (POPULATION) Tehran (6,476,000)
GOVERNMENT Islamic republic
ETHNIC GROUPS Persian 46%, Azerbaijani 17%, Kurdish 9%, Gilaki 5%, Luri, Mazandarani, Baluchi, Arab
LANGUAGES Farsi (or Persian, official)
RELIGIONS Islam 99%
CURRENCY Rial

IRAQ

T he country includes a hilly district in the north-east, and in the west a substantial slice of the Hamad or Syrian Desert; but essentially it comprises the lower valleys and combined deltas of the Tigris and Euphrates. Rainfall is meagre, but the alluvium is fertile and productive when supplied with water. The western desert is nomad country, with good winter grazing, and from here the tribes move in summer with their flocks to the banks of the Euphrates.

ECONOMY AND RESOURCES

The north-east of Iraq includes part of the Zagros Mountains, where fruits and grains grow without the help of irrigation. The Kirkuk oilfield is the country's oldest and largest, and nearby the Lesser Zab River has been impounded behind a high dam. The population here includes many Turks, settled in the times of Ottoman rule, and Kurdish tribes akin to those in Iran.

Upstream of Ramadi and Samarra, the Jazirah stands too high for irrigation, though the swamp of Tharthar is used to store the excess flow of the River Euphrates through a diversionary channel from Samarra. This is dry-farming country or pasture. In the north near the Syrian frontier the block mountain of Sinjar is an oasis of fertility, with an unorthodox Yezidi population (a religious sect).

Downstream of the Jazirah lies Iraq proper, the deltaic plains which, with skill and effort, can be drained and irrigated. The rivers rise rapidly in spring as the snows melt around their sources in Turkey, and are full enough for irrigation throughout the summer. Lower down, a barrage on the Euphrates at Hindiyah and another on the Tigris at Kut control canals which irrigate land reclaimed from the great swamp.

In addition to the Kirkuk oilfield, which exports by pipeline through Syria and Lebanon, there are reserves of oil near Mosul, Khanaqin and Basra. The main seaport,

Basra, is connected to the Gulf by the cruci Shatt-al-Arab Waterway, shared with Iran an the ostensible cause of the First Gulf Wa (Iran-Iraq War).

HISTORY AND POLITICS

Absorbed into the Ottoman (Turkish) empir in the 16th century, Iraq was captured b British forces in 1916 and after World War became a virtual colony as a League o Nations mandated territory run by Britain The Hashemite dynasty ruled an independen kingdom from 1932 (British occupatio 1941–5), but in 1958 the royal family an premier were murdered in a military coup tha set up a republic. Ten years later, after strug gles between the Communists and Pan-Arab Baathists, officers for the latter seized control From 1969 the vice-president of this single party government was Saddam Hussein, who in a peaceful transfer of power became president in 1979. The next year he invaded neighbouring Iran.

The Gulf Wars

Supplied with financial help and arms by the West, the Soviets and conservative Arab countries, all of whom shared a fear of the new Islamic fundamentalism in Iran, Saddam amassed the fourth largest army in the world by 1980. His attack on Iran was meant to be a quick, land-grabbing, morale-boosting victory. Instead it led to an eight-year modern version of Flanders which drained Iraqi resolve (over a million men were killed or wounded, many of them fighting fellow Shiites), and nearly crippled a healthy if oil-dependent economy that had, despite colossal defence spending, financed a huge development programme in the 1970s. Even then, Iraq was still the world's sixth biggest oil producer in 1988, and Saddam's repellent regime continued to enjoy widespread support from Western countries.

If Iraq was hit by this long war, it was decimated by the Second Gulf War. In August 1990 Saddam, having accused Kuwait of wrecking Baghdad's economy by exceeding its oil quota and forcing prices down, ordered the invasion of Kuwait, then annexed it as an Iraqi province. It gave him more oil and far better access to the Gulf. Unlike a decade before, the international community were almost unani-

THE KURDS

With between 15 and 17 million people dispersed across the territories of five countries – Turkey (8 million), Iran, Iraq, Syria and Armenia – the Kurds form the world's largest stateless nation, and they are likely to remain so. The 1920 Treaty of Sévres, a postwar settlement designed to dismember the old Ottoman Empire, proposed a scheme for Kurdish independence, but it was never implemented.

Neither Arab nor Turk, the Kurds are predominantly Sunni Muslims, and in the past have provided more than their fair share of Islam's leaders: indeed, Saladin, the near-legendary nemesis of the Crusaders, was a Kurd. Now, as in the past, the Kurds are an agricultural people; many earn their living by pastoralism, a way of life that pays little attention to borders or the governments that attempt to control them. Since World War II, they have suffered consistent repression by most of their titular overlords. Turkey has regularly used armed force against Kurdish nationalists; an uprising in Iran was put down in 1979–80; and during the Iran-Iraq war of the 1980s, Iraqi forces regularly used chemical weapons – as well as more orthodox brutality – against Kurdish settlements.

The defeat of Iraqi dictator Saddam Hussein by Coalition forces in 1991 inspired another massive uprising; but Saddam's badly weakened army still proved quite capable of murdering Kurdish women and children on a scale that provoked a limited Western intervention. The outcome, though, was upwards of 1.5 million Kurds living in refugee camps, with the dream of an independent Kurdistan no nearer realization.

mous in their condemnation of the invasion, and following the imposition of sanctions a multinational force – led by the USA but backed primarily by Britain, France and Saudi Arabia – was dispatched to the Gulf to head off possible Iraqi moves on to Saudi oilfields.

After Saddam failed to accede to repeated UN demands to withdraw his troops, the Second Gulf War began on 16 January 1991

with an Anglo-American air attack on Baghdad, and in late February a land-sea-air campaign freed Kuwait after just 100 hours, Iraq accepting all the terms of the UN cease-fire and Coalition troops occupying much of southern Iraq. This did not prevent the brutal suppression of West-inspired revolts by Shiites in the south and Kurds in the north, millions of whom fled their homes. International efforts were made to help these refugees, some of whom had fled to Iran and others, less successfully, to Turkey.

Saddam Hussein, though surviving in power, was left an international leper in charge of a pitiful country. Much of the infrastructure had been destroyed in the war, disease was rife and food scarce, trade had virtually ceased and oil production was near a standstill. Sanctions, war damage and mismanagement have combined to cause economic chaos and personal hardship, and normal life is unlikely to return until the establishment of a regime acceptable to the rest of the international community; that, in turn, means the end of Saddam. [*Map page 19*] ∎

AREA 438,320 sq km [169,235 sq mls]
POPULATION 19,925,000
CAPITAL (POPULATION) Baghdad (3,841,000)
GOVERNMENT Republic
ETHNIC GROUPS Arab 77%, Kurdish 19%, Turkmen 2%, Persian 2%, Assyrian
LANGUAGES Arabic (official), Kurdish (official in Kurdish areas)
RELIGIONS Islam 96%, Christianity 4%
CURRENCY Iraqi dinar = 20 dirhams = 1,000 fils

IRELAND

Geographically, Ireland is the whole island west of Britain; the Republic of Ireland (Eire, or the Irish Free State until 1949) comprises the 26 counties governed from Dublin, and Northern Ireland (Ulster) is the six counties that remained part of the United Kingdom from 1921, when the Free State was granted dominion status within the British Commonwealth. Today, the word 'Ireland' is used as political shorthand for the Republic – which occupies some 80% of the island of Ireland.

The original four provinces of Ireland gradually emerged as major divisions from Norman times. Three counties of the present Republic (Donegal, Cavan and Monaghan), together with the six counties which now make up Northern Ireland, formed the old province of Ulster; Connacht, in effect the land beyond the River Shannon, includes the five counties of Leitrim, Sligo, Roscommon, Galway and Mayo; Munster comprises Clare, Limerick, Tipperary, Kilkenny, Waterford, Cork and Kerry; and Leinster consists of the heart of the central lowland and the counties of the southeast (Wicklow, Wexford and Carlow) between Dublin and Waterford harbour.

Physically, the main outlines of Ireland are simple. In the western peninsulas of Donegal and Connacht ancient rocks were folded to form mountain chains running north-east to south-west; good examples are the fine Derryveagh range of Co. Donegal and the Ox Mountains of Co. Sligo. The highest peaks, for example Errigal, 752 m [2,466 ft], are generally of quartzite, a metamorphosed sandstone. The same trend is seen also in the long range, including the Wicklow Mountains, between Dublin Bay and Waterford harbour in the south-east, and in the Slieve Bloom of the central lowland. The fine east-west ranges of the south, extending from Waterford to the western peninsulas, and the islands of Kerry and West Cork, were formed at a later period. Much of lowland Ireland is floored by rocks contemporary with the coal measures in England, and these also form some uplands like those around Sligo. Unfortunately these rocks contain little coal; some is mined in the Castlecomer area of Co. Kilkenny, and near Lough Allen in the upper Shannon Valley.

The basalt lavas that poured out in the north-east of Ireland, forming the desolate Antrim Plateau with its fine scenic cliffs on the famous Coast Road, and the Giant's Causeway, are more recent. Irish soils, however, are largely derived from glacial deposits, and the famous peat bogs result from the drainage patterns that emerged as the ice sheets of the Ice Age dispersed. Peat remains the main indigenous fuel source, but reserve may not last long into the 21st century.

ECONOMY AND RESOURCES

Agriculture has been the traditional support of the Irish people, though fishing, home craft and local labouring have been extra sources of livelihood in the poorer western areas. There is a marked contrast between the richest and the poorest agricultural areas. In the eastern central lowland and the south-east, particularly the lowland areas of Wicklow and Wexford, there are large farms, with pasture supporting fine-quality cattle, sheep and in some areas racehorses. From Wexford, too, rich farmlands extend westwards to the counties of Tipperary and Limerick, and from Waterford to Cork and Killarney. Many of the farms specialize in dairying.

North of the Shannon, in Clare and east Galway, there is intensive sheep and some cattle production. To the north farming is mixed, with dairying, meat production, and in some cases specialization on crops such as potatoes and barley. Little wheat is grown; oats are better suited to the damp summer climate.

Farming in much of Ireland is now relatively prosperous, aided by EU grants. The number of people working on the land continues to decline, but that is due to the introduction of machinery, the union of small farms into larger holdings, and the increased opportunities of finding employment in the towns, with overseas emigration still an alternative. The tradition of emigration dates back to the great famine of 1846–51, when over a million people fled to Britain and the USA.

Ireland is economically far more prosperous than it was in 1845, when the population of the island numbered 8.5 million. Industrialization only really happened in the north-east, especially Belfast, leaving the Free State an agrarian country from the 1920s. As a result, it has something of a 'Third World' profile: rural (though almost 29% of the population lives in and around Dublin), dependent on tourism and, increasingly, high-tech industries such as electronics and pharmaceuticals. Prosperity in the 1960s was followed by a slowdown in growth – when government

pending was high – but with a new spirit of
economic co-operation, the 1990s appeared to
ave reversed the trend.

The poorer western areas have been aided
y government grants and the development of
ocal industries, including the tourist industry.
Some industries flourish, especially tweed
manufacture. The fishing industry, though
never meeting expectations, is increasingly
prosperous. The poor west, known from 1891
as the 'congested areas', is not depopulated as
in some comparable areas of Scotland, though
discarded houses are taken over as holiday
cottages. Many problems have been at least
partially solved and the EU has been a source
of help, making the Republic feel part of a
wider world than the British Isles.

HISTORY AND POLITICS
The Anglo-Irish Treaty of 1921 established
southern Ireland – Eire – as an independent
state, with the six northern Irish counties, and
their Protestant majority, remaining part of
the United Kingdom (though Eire's constitution claimed authority over the whole island).
Northern Ireland (Ulster) was granted local
self-government from the Stormont parliament in Belfast. However, the Protestant
majority (roughly two-thirds of the population) systematically excluded the Catholic
minority from power and often from employment, despite occasional attacks from the
near-moribund IRA – the Irish Republican
Army – which had done most of the fighting
that led to Eire's independence.

In 1968, inspired by the Civil Rights movement in the southern states of the USA, northern Catholics launched a civil rights movement of their own. But Protestant hostility
threatened a bloodbath, and in August 1969
British Prime Minister Harold Wilson
deployed army units to protect Catholics from
Protestant attack.

Within a short period, the welcome given by
Catholics to British troops turned to bitter-
ness; the IRA and many of the Catholic
minority came to see them as a hostile occupying force, and there were deaths on both
sides. Protestant extremists were quick to form
terrorist organizations of their own. In 1971,
the British introduced internment without trial
for suspected IRA terrorists, removing some of

the main security risks from the streets but
provoking violent protest demonstrations. In
1972, British troops killed 13 demonstrators
in Londonderry, claiming to have been fired
upon: the claims were vigorously denied by
the demonstrators.

In an attempt to end the alienation of the
Catholics, Britain negotiated an agreement
with some Protestant politicians to share
power in an executive composed of both communities, but the plan collapsed after dissatis-
fied Protestants staged a general strike. The
British government responded by suspending
the Stormont parliament and ruling Northern
Ireland direct from Westminster. The failure
of power-sharing encapsulated the British policy dilemma in Ulster: the Catholics, or most
of them, wanted to join the Irish Republic; the
Protestants, virtually without exception, did
not. Each side bitterly distrusted the other,
and long years of sectarian killing only
increased the distrust.

The violence continued throughout the
1970s and 1980s, despite a series of political
initiatives that included an Anglo-Irish agreement giving the Republic a modest say in
Ulster's affairs. Among the conflict's victims
over the following years were Earl Mount-
batten and several senior British politicians,
as well as soldiers, policemen, terrorists
and thousands of ordinary men and women.
Armed troops patrolling the streets and almost
daily reports of sectarian murders became
a way of life. But with the increasing war-
weariness of the people, a joint declaration on
Northern Ireland was agreed between the
British and Irish prime ministers in December
1993. This first step towards a lasting peace
was followed in 1994 by a declared cease-fire
by the IRA and Loyalist paramilitary groups.
[*Map page 9*] ■

AREA 70,280 sq km [27,135 sq mls]
POPULATION 3,539,000
CAPITAL (POPULATION) Dublin (1,024,000)
GOVERNMENT Multiparty republic
ETHNIC GROUPS Irish 94%
LANGUAGES Irish and English (both official)
RELIGIONS Christianity (Roman Catholic 93%,
Protestant 3%)
CURRENCY Irish pound (Punt) = 100 pence

ISRAEL

Within the 1949 borders, the country is made up of four areas: the highlands of Galilee in the north, the valleys of Jezreel and the Jordan, the arid hills of Judaea, a thin coastal plain and the Negev Desert. To the east lies part of the Great Rift Valley which runs through East Africa as far south as Mozambique. In Israel, the Rift Valley contains the River Jordan, the Sea of Galilee and the Dead Sea.

In general, the country is most fertile in the north, and becomes progressively more desert-like towards the south.

ECONOMY AND RESOURCES

In the north of Israel, Galilee is rolling hill country with good rainfall and a rich black soil weathered from basalt. Both here and in the hills of Judaea, new pine woods have been established to fix the soil and hold the water. The Upper Jordan Valley is excellent farmland, with rich and fertile soils reclaimed from the swamps of Lake Huleh.

The valley of Jezreel, with a deep alluvial soil washed down from Galilee, is intensively tilled with market gardens. South of the promontory of Carmel, the coastal plain of Sharon is excellent fruit-growing country, but needs irrigation, especially in its southern stretches. Here the drifting dunes have been fixed with grass and tamarisk and reclaimed for pasture.

The Negev Desert

Between Sinai and the Rift Valley, the great wedge of desert plateau known as the Negev accounts for about half the total territory of Israel. Its bedrock is widely covered with blown sand and loess, which will grow tomatoes and grapes in profusion if supplied with fresh water. The object of the Jordan-Western Negev scheme, the most ambitious of Israel's irrigation enterprises, has been to direct through canals and culverts all the water that can be spared from the Upper Jordan and the

JERUSALEM

Though held sacred by all of the world's three great monotheisms, Jerusalem's religious importance has brought the city little peace. King David's capital in the 11th century BC, with the building of the great Temple of Solomon, it became the cult centre of Judaism. The Temple was destroyed by the Assyrians and rebuilt in the 6th century, re-assuming its importance until AD 70, when Jerusalem, Temple and all, was destroyed by Roman legions during the great Jewish Revolt against the Empire. Later, a rebuilt Jerusalem became a great centre of Christian pilgrimage. In the 7th century, the city was captured by the expanding armies of Islam, and for Muslims, too, Jerusalem (al-Quds in Arabic) is also a holy place: it was visited by the Prophet Muhammad during the 'Night Journey' recounted in the Koran, and Muslims also believe that it was from Jerusalem that the Prophet ascended to paradise. The great mosque known as the Dome of the Rock was built on the site of the Jewish Temple.

During the Israeli War of Independence, Arab and Jew fought bitterly for possession of the city: neither could oust the other and until 1967 it was divided by bristling fortifications, with the Wailing Wall, the only surviving part of the old Temple, firmly under Arab control. In the Six Day War, Israeli soldiers at last captured all of the city, to universal Jewish rejoicing and Arab lamentation.

streams and drainage channels of the coastal plain southwards to the desert.

The Negev south of Be'er Sheva is pioneer territory, with new towns mining oil, copper and phosphates, factories using the potash and salt of the Dead Sea, and farms experimenting with solar power and artificial dew. Carob trees have been planted for fodder, and dairy farms and plantations of bananas and dates have been established with the aid of the artesian springs of the rift valley or Araba. Elat on the Gulf of Aqaba is an increasingly successful tourist town and Israel's sea outlet to Africa and most of Asia. From here, a pipeline takes imported oil to the refinery at Haifa.

THE PALESTINIANS

The sorrowful modern history of the Palestinians began in 1948, when the birth of Israel transformed most of their former territory into a foreign state; some 700,000 fled, most finding no better homes than refugee camps in Jordan, Lebanon and Egypt's Gaza Strip. After the 'Six Day War' in 1967, most Palestinians not already refugees found themselves living under enemy occupation. Since 1964, the Palestine Liberation Organization has existed to free them by 'armed struggle', but the PLO's adoption of international terrorism as a tactic alienated many potential allies, as did their alliance with Saddam Hussein during the 1991 Gulf War. The 1987 *intifada* brought much world support, but by late 1991, when peace talks with Israel at last began, almost half the Palestinian population were still classified as refugees. After long and difficult negotiations, Israel and the PLO finally signed a historic treaty in September 1993: the PLO recognized the state of Israel and Israel granted the Palestinians self-rule in the Gaza Strip and Jericho.

To supplement the facilities of Haifa, Israel built a deep-sea port at Ashdod to replace the old anchorage at Jaffa (Yafo).

Industry
Israel has become the most industrialized country in the Near East. Iron is smelted at Haifa and converted to steel at the foundries of Acre. Chemicals are manufactured at Haifa and at plants by the Dead Sea. With the aid of a national electricity grid, factories for textiles, ceramics and other products have been widely established in country towns, including the new foundations of Dimona and Mizpe Ramon in the Negev. Some railways were inherited from the British, but most commercial movement is now along the road network. Despite its expansion, Israel remains vulnerable on many fronts: reliance on huge US aid (the world's biggest per capita movement); terrorism and international pressure over Palestine; hostile neighbours and huge defence spending; massive influx of immigrants, often overqualified and notably now from the former Soviet republics; and a lack of natural resources forcing dependence on imported raw materials.

HISTORY AND POLITICS
In 1948 the new Jewish state of Israel comprised the coastal plain, the vale of Esdraelon (Jezreel) behind Haifa, the foothills in the south, most of the hill country of Samaria, and half of Jerusalem with a corridor to the west. It was also the intention of the UN that Israel should acquire either Galilee in the north or the Negev Desert in the south, but in the event both these regions were included. The rest of Palestine, mainly Judaea and the Rift Valley west of the river, was added to Jordan, but as a result of the Six Day War in 1967, its administration as the 'West Bank' was taken over by Israel along with East Jerusalem. At the same time the Israelis also occupied the Gaza Strip (Egypt) and the Golan Heights (Syria).

In October 1973, Egypt and Syria launched attacks against Israel in an unsuccessful attempt to regain territories. Egypt and Israel eventually signed a peace treaty in 1979: Israel agreed to withdraw from the Sinai and Egypt recognized Israel.

In 1982, Israeli forces invaded Lebanon to destroy PLO strongholds in that country and only left in 1985. From 1987 onwards, Palestinian resistance to Israeli occupation of the Gaza Strip and the West Bank became more and more widespread and violent. In the 1990s, increased international pressure eventually led to the signing of a treaty in 1993 between Israel and the PLO. A framework document for peace with Jordan was signed in July 1994. [*Map page 19*] ■

AREA 26,650 sq km [10,290 sq mls]
POPULATION 5,458,000
CAPITAL (POPULATION) Jerusalem (544,200)
GOVERNMENT Multiparty republic
ETHNIC GROUPS Jewish 82%, Arab and other 18%
LANGUAGES Hebrew and Arabic (both official)
RELIGIONS Judaism 82%, Islam 14%, Christianity 2%, Druse and others 2%
CURRENCY New Israeli shekel = 100 agorat

ITALY

Despite more than a century of common language, religion and cultural traditions, great differences remain in the ways of life of people in different parts of Italy. These can partly be explained in terms of geography. The long, narrow boot-shaped peninsula, with coastal lowlands on either side of the central Apennines, extends so far south that its toe, and the neighbouring island of Sicily, are in the latitudes of North Africa. Southern Sicily is as far south (36°N) as Tunis and Algiers, while the northern industrial city of Milan (45.5°N) is nearer to London than it is to Reggio in Calabria, the extreme south of peninsular Italy. Given their markedly disparate social and historical backgrounds, the long period of isolation that preceded the unification and widely differing climates, it is hardly surprising that northern and southern Italy retain their independence of character and culture.

The Alps and Apennines: Italy's topographical structure is determined mainly by the events of the Alpine period of mountain building, when the main ranges of the Alps and the Apennines were uplifted together. There are traces of earlier periods in the central Alps, between Mont Blanc (4,807 m [15,771 ft]) on the French border and Monte Rosa (4,634 m [15,203 ft]) on the Swiss border, and in the Carnic Alps in the north-east. Here ancient crystalline rocks predominate, although many of the higher peaks are formed from limestone. The Dolomite Alps, famous for their climbing and skiing resorts, have given their name to a particular form of magnesian limestone.

Generally lower than the Alps, the Apennines reach their highest peaks – almost 3,000 m [9,800 ft] – in the Gran Sasso range overlooking the central Adriatic Sea near Pescara. The most frequently occurring rocks are various types of limestone.

Italy is well known for volcanic activity and earthquakes. Three volcanoes are still active – Vesuvius, near Naples, renowned for its burial

VESUVIUS

Rising steeply from the Plain of Campania, behind the Bay of Naples, the massive cone of Vesuvius forms one of a family of southern Italian volcanoes, clustered in an area of crustal weakness. Others include the nearby island of Ischia, Stromboli and Vulcano of the Lipari Islands, and Etna in eastern Sicily.

Ischia's volcanoes last erupted in the 14th century. Stromboli and Vulcano are currently active, emitting lava and gases, and Etna has a long record of eruptions from 475 BC to the present day. In April 1992 an eruption threatened to destroy a village on Etna's slopes.

Vesuvius, which probably arose from the waters of the bay some 200,000 years ago, has been intermittently active ever since; over 30 major eruptions have been recorded since Roman times. However, its slopes are forested or farmed, the fertile volcanic soils producing good crops during the quiescent periods between eruptive spells. There are many settlements on its flanks, and laboratories for volcanic and seismic studies.

The most famous eruption of Vesuvius occurred in AD 79, when the flourishing Roman port of Pompeii and nearby town of Stabiae were engulfed in a rain of ashes. Excavations begun in 1748 have revealed streets, shops, houses, frescos, statues, and many other artefacts of Roman times – even the bread in the bakery.

of Pompeii in AD 79, Etna in Sicily, and Stromboli on an island in the south Tyrrhenian Sea. Traces of earlier volcanism are to be found throughout the country. Ancient lava flows cover large areas, and where they have weathered they produce fertile soils. Mineral deposits, such as the iron ores of Elba and the tin ores of the Mt Annata area, are often associated with earlier volcanic intrusions. Italy is still subject to earthquakes and volcanic eruptions. During the 20th century disasters have occurred at Messina (1908 – the worst in Europe in recent times, with more than 80,000 deaths), Avezzano (1915), Irpinia (1930), Friuli (1976) and Naples (1980).

Lombardy: The great triangular plain of Lombardy, lying between the northern Alps and the Apennines, is drained by the River Po, which flows west to east, rising in the Ligurian Alps near the French frontier and flowing across a delta into the Gulf of Venice.

Central Italy: Between the Po Valley and the River Tiber, Central Italy is a transitional zone between the industrially developed north and the poor, agrarian south. It contains Rome, which has survived as a capital city for over 2,000 years, Florence and Bologna. Almost all Italians are brought up as Roman Catholics; since a 1985 agreement between church and state, Catholic religious teaching is offered, but not compulsory, in schools. The Vatican, in theory an independent state, is in fact an enclave of Rome.

ECONOMY AND RESOURCES

The Apennines: The slopes are covered by thin soils and have been subjected to severe erosion, so that in many areas they are suitable only for poor pasture. Between the mountains, however, are long narrow basins, some of which contain lakes. Others have good soils and drainage and provide a basis for arable farming.

Lombardy: The Lombardy plains are the most productive area of Italy, both agriculturally and industrially. There is no shortage of water, as in the areas further south, although some places are served by irrigation canals. Crops include maize, wheat, potatoes, tomatoes, rice and mulberries – these associated with the development of the silk industry. In the Alpine valleys above the Lombardy plain vines are cultivated.

Industry and urban life in Lombardy is long established. Textiles – silk, cotton, flax and wool – metal-working and food processing all began long before the modern industrial period. Large-scale Italian industry was slower to develop than in Britain and Germany, partly because of the lack of coal, but in Lombardy this has been offset by the availability of hydroelectric power from the Alpine rivers, and by the development of a natural gas field in the area of the Po delta. Oil and gas are also imported by pipeline from Austria. Italy is more dependent on imported energy than any European country, nearly 60% of it oil, though

VENICE

The city of Venice originally grew up on a group of over 100 small islands, lying in a lagoon sheltered from the open Adriatic Sea by a sandbar. It now also includes the mainland industrial suburbs of Mestre and Marghera, where two-thirds of the city's population live. Causeways carry road and rail links to the mainland, but cars are not allowed in the old city. Boats of all types, from the traditional gondolas to the diesel-powered water-buses, use the canals which form the 'streets' of Venice.

Venice was once the capital of an imperial republic which, until overthrown by Napoleon in 1797, controlled much of the trade of the Adriatic and the eastern Mediterranean. The heart of the city is around St Mark's Square, where stand the cathedral and the Palace of the Doges (Dukes) who once ruled the republic.

The unique site and the rich art treasures attract about 2 million tourists a year, providing a living for tens of thousands of Venetians who cater for them; tourists, too, help to support such craft industries as glass-blowing, for which the city is famous. For Expo 2000 the figure is expected to be over 250,000 a day, imposing a massive strain on a city already suffering from erosion, subsidence and pollution.

Algeria remains a major supplier of gas through the Transmed pipeline via Tunisia.

Engineering and metal-working are now the most important industries, centred on Milan and, in Piedmont, on Turin. Lombardy remains dominant, however; the most densely populated region, it accounts for a third of Italy's GDP and some 30% of export earnings, and in the 1992 election the separatist party made huge gains at the expense of established rivals.

Central Italy: The area has a glorious history of artistic and literary achievement, but with its limited resources, steep slopes and difficult communications it has been left behind in economic development by the more favoured lowlands of the north, and relies heavily on tourism for regional income.

SICILY

The triangular-shaped island of Sicily lies in a strategic position between the two basins of the Mediterranean, and has had a stormy history as successive powers wishing to dominate the Mediterranean have sought to conquer it. A beautiful island, with both natural and man-made attractions to interest the millions of tourists, it is nevertheless in a low state of economic development and its people are among the poorest in Europe.

There is some industrial development around the ports of Palermo, Catania, Messina and Syracuse, based on imported materials or on oil and natural gas found offshore during the 1960s. The only other local industrial materials are potash, sulphur and salt. However, a large proportion of the inhabitants still live by peasant farming, supplemented by fishing and work in the tourist industry.

There are few permanent streams on Sicily, as the island experiences an almost total drought in summer, and agriculture is severely restricted by the availability of water. Citrus fruits, vines and olives are among the chief crops. On coastal lowlands such as those around Catania, Marsala and Palermo, wheat and early vegetables are grown. The rapid growth in the population and the strong family ties which exist among Sicilians have, however, led to a situation in which too many people are trying to make a living from tiny parcels of land.

The Mezzogiorno: The south of Italy, known as the Mezzogiorno, is the least developed part of the country. It displays, in less severe form, many of the characteristics of the developing countries of the Third World. Its people depend for their livelihood on Mediterranean crops produced on small peasant farms too small to lend themselves to modern techniques, although there are some large estates.

Over a third of the people are still in agriculture, with unemployment three or more times that of the north. Though the eight regions of the Mezzogiorno cover some 40% of the land area (including Sicily and Sardinia) and contain more than a third of the country' population, they contribute only about a quarter of the GDP.

The birth rate is much higher than in the north, and there is a serious problem of overpopulation which is partly eased by large-scale, often temporary, migration to the cities of the north and to Italy's more developed partners in the EU, as well as more permanent migration overseas. Migration often exacerbates the problems of the Mezzogiorno, however, as it tends to take away the younger, more active members of society, leaving behind an ageing population.

There are also serious urban problems, caused by the rapid growth of cities such as Naples and Reggio as young people leave the rural areas to live in the slums. As one of Italy's major ports, Naples imports oil, coal, iron ore, chemicals and cotton to provide the raw materials for manufacturing industries. In recent years great efforts have been made by a government-sponsored agency, the *Cassa di Mezzogiorno*, to found new factories in the Naples area, but they have had little effect on the mass poverty and unemployment of the region.

HISTORY AND POLITICS
In 1800, present-day Italy was made up of several political units, including the Papal States, and a substantial part of the north-east was occupied by Austria. The struggle for unification – the Risorgimento – began early in the century, but little progress was made until an alliance between France and Piedmont (then part of the kingdom of Sardinia) drove Austria from Lombardy in 1859. Tuscany, Parma and Modena all joined Piedmont-Lombardy in 1860, and the Papal States, Sicily, Naples (including most of the southern peninsula) and Romagna were brought into the alliance. King Victor Emmanuel II was proclaimed ruler of a united Italy in Turin the following year, Venetia was acquired from Austria in 1866, and Rome was finally annexed in 1871. Since that time Italy has been a single state, becoming a republic following the abolition of the monarchy by popular referendum in 1946.

Regions like Tuscany, Umbria and Lazio have retained considerable autonomy from

SARDINIA

ust a little smaller than Sicily, but with less than a third of its population, Sardinia's isolation from the mainstream of Italian life is due partly to its physical position, 480 km [300 mls] from the Italian coast, but the rugged, windswept terrain and lack of resources have also set it apart.

The chief crops on the lowlands are wheat, vines, olives and vegetables, and there are rough pastures for sheep on the scrub-covered hills. Fishing for tuna provides an important source of income for the ports of the west coast. Sardinia is rich in minerals, including lead, zinc, iron ore and lignite, and the island is an increasingly popular tourist destination.

ome, with control over health and education, or example, and other devolved powers. ndeed five regions enjoy more autonomy than he rest: French-speaking Valle d'Aosta, in the orth-west of the country; Trentino-Alto ldige, the largely German-speaking area in he far north; Friuli-Venézia Giulia in the orth-east; and the two island provinces of ardinia and Sicily.

North and south

ince unification the population has doubled, nd though the rate of increase is notoriously low today, the rapid growth of population, n a poor country attempting to develop its esources, forced millions of Italians to migrate during the first quarter of the 20th entury. Italy's short-lived African empire nabled some Italians to settle overseas, but it did not substantially relieve the population ressure. Now there are immigrant Italians to be found on all the inhabited continents. Particularly large numbers settled in the USA, South America and Australia, and more recently large numbers of Italians have moved for similar reasons into northern Europe.

The problems of the Mezzogiorno, including especially those of the Naples area and Sicily, arise partly from geographical limitations and partly from historical circumstances. They are no longer a problem only for Italy,

for the stability and prosperity of Italy is a matter of concern for the rest of Europe, and in particular for the countries of the EU, of which Italy was a founder member. The continuing gulf between north and south has a disturbing effect on the economic and political health of Italy, a country whose people have contributed so much to the civilization of Europe.

Overall, however, Italy has made enormous progress since the devastation of World War II, particularly given its few natural resources. However, social problems, corruption at high levels of society, and a succession of weak coalition governments all contributed to instability. A referendum in April 1993 saw 82% of Italians voting to replace the system of proportional representation for the senate with one of majority voting. In 1994, new political groupings emerged. A right-wing coalition was formed, but its leader, Silvio Berlusconi, a multi-millionaire owner of television and publishing businesses, was forced to resign in December. In 1995, Lamberto Dini, a former banker, was appointed as the new prime minister. [*Map page 16*] ■

AREA 301,270 sq km [116,320 sq mls]
POPULATION 57,157,000
CAPITAL (POPULATION) Rome (2,791,000)
GOVERNMENT Multiparty republic
ETHNIC GROUPS Italian 94%, German, French, Greek, Albanian, Slovene, Ladino
LANGUAGES Italian (official) 94%, Sardinian 3%
RELIGIONS Christianity (Roman Catholic) 83%
CURRENCY Lira = 100 centesimi

IVORY COAST

The Republic of the Ivory Coast is officially known as the Côte d'Ivoire. The south-east coast is bordered by sand bars that enclose lagoons, on one of which the chief port and former capital of Abidjan is situated. But the south-western coast is lined by rocky cliffs. Behind the coast is a coastal plain, but the land rises inland to high plains. The highest land is an extension of the Guinea Highlands in the north-west, along the borders with Liberia and Guinea. The rivers run in a generally north-south direction.

The Ivory Coast has a hot and humid tropical climate, experiencing high temperatures throughout the year. The south has two distinct rainy seasons: May to July, and October to November. Inland, the rainfall decreases. In contrast, northern Ivory Coast has a dry season and only one rainy season.

ECONOMY AND RESOURCES

There are substantial forests in the south where the basic resources of coffee, cocoa and timber are produced, as well as the lesser crops of bananas and pineapples. However, the depletion of the rainforest, as in much of West Africa, has been rapid. The Guinea savanna lands of the centre and north are much less fertile, producing small amounts of sugar, cotton and tobacco that now support developing industries, and food crops important to a rapidly growing market in Abidjan. Like Kenya, which is economically comparable, the Ivory Coast has few worked minerals, but manufacturing industries are developing.

In terms of such indices as GNP and international trade figures, the relatively stable Ivory Coast is one of Africa's most prosperous countries. This show of prosperity was initiated by the Vridi Canal, opened in 1950, which made Abidjan a spacious and sheltered deep-water port – a rarity in an area of Africa renowned for barrier reefs. The Ivory Coast's free-market economy has proved attractive to foreign investors, especially French firms, and France has given much aid, particularly for basic services and education. It has also attracted millions of migrant West African workers. In 1960, the Ivory Coast freed itself economically from support of seven other countries in the French West African Federation. The country is the world's largest exporter of cocoa and Africa's biggest producer of coffee. It has few worked minerals, but its manufacturing industries are developing.

Outward prosperity is visually expressed in Abidjan, but across the country there are great social and regional inequalities. In 1983, the National Assembly agreed to move the capital from Abidjan to Yamoussoukro, site of the world's biggest church (consecrated by Pope John Paul II in 1990) and the president's birthplace. But economic setbacks in the 1980s delayed the completion of the capital and government offices remained in Abidjan until 1990. Further efforts are being made to develop other towns and the relatively backward north. A second port to Abidjan has been developed since 1971 at San Pedro in the west of the country.

HISTORY AND POLITICS

Ivory Coast became a French colony in 1893 and gained independence in 1960. Under the patriarchal rule of President Felix Houphouët-Boigny, it became one of the most prosperous of the tropical African nations. Pressure from demonstrations by students and workers in 1990 led to the country's first multiparty presidential election. Houphouët-Boigny, at the time already Africa's longest-ruling head of state, was returned to power. He died in 1993, and his successor as president was Henri Konan Bédié. [*Map page 32*] ∎

AREA	322,460 sq km [124,502 sq mls]
POPULATION	13,780,000
CAPITAL (POPULATION)	Yamoussoukro (126,000)
GOVERNMENT	Multiparty republic
ETHNIC GROUPS	Akan 41%, Kru 17%, Voltaic 16%, Malinke 15%, Southern Mande 10%
LANGUAGES	French (official)
RELIGIONS	Islam 38%, Christianity 28%, traditional beliefs 17%
CURRENCY	CFA franc = 100 centimes

JAMAICA

Third largest of the Caribbean islands and the most populous in the English-speaking 'West Indies', Jamaica has a central range culminating in Blue Mountain Peak (2,256 m [7,402 ft]), from which it declines estwards. Called Xaymaca ('land of wood and water') by the Arawak Indians, half the country lies above 300 m [1,000 ft] and moist south-east trade winds bring rain to the mountains, windward slopes receiving up to 500 cm [200 in] in a normal year; hurricanes may bring exceptionally heavy rains during the later part of the wet season, which extends from May to October – as well as devastation, as with Hurricane Gilbert in 1988.

The 'cockpit country' in the north-west of the island is an inaccessible limestone area of steep broken ridges and isolated basins. These offered a refuge to escaped slaves prior to emancipation in 1838.

ECONOMY AND RESOURCES

In various parts of the island the limestone has weathered to bauxite, an ore of aluminium. Bauxite overlies a quarter of the island; mined since 1952, most is exported as ore, about one-fifth as alumina, making Jamaica the world's third producer and accounting for over 38% of exports. Tourism and bauxite production, Jamaica's two most important industries, comprise almost two-thirds of foreign earnings. In 1992 the island had over 1.5 million visitors, spending more than US$850 million. Garment manufacture, bananas and illegal marijuana are also important elements of an economy hampered by large foreign debts.

Sugar, a staple product since the island became British in 1655, first made Jamaica a prized imperial possession, and the African slaves imported to work the plantations were the forefathers of much of the present population. But the plantations disappeared and the sugar market collapsed in the 19th century; today sugar contributes only about 10% of the country's foreign earnings.

Michael Manley's democratic socialist experiment in the 1970s was followed by a modest growth in the 1980s; but unemployment and underemployment are currently rife, and many Jamaicans leave their country each year to work abroad, mainly in the USA, Canada and the UK.

HISTORY AND POLITICS

Jamaica gained independence from Britain in 1962. Since then government has been con-

trolled alternatively by the socialist People's National Party and the conservative Jamaican Labour Party (led by Edward Seaga). The PNP won the general election held in March 1993. [*Map page 30*] ■

AREA 10,990 sq km [4,243 sq mls]
POPULATION 2,429,000
CAPITAL (POPULATION) Kingston (588,000)
GOVERNMENT Constitutional monarchy
ETHNIC GROUPS Black 76%, Afro-European 15%, East Indian and Afro-East Indian 3%, White 3%
LANGUAGES English (official), English Creole, Hindi, Spanish, Chinese
RELIGIONS Christianity (Protestant 70%, Roman Catholic 8%)
CURRENCY Jamaican dollar = 100 cents

JAPAN

The Japanese archipelago lies off the Asian mainland in an arc extending from 45°N to 30°N, occupying a latitudinal range comparable to the Atlantic seaboard of the USA from Maine to Florida. Four large and closely grouped islands (Hokkaido, Honshu, Shikoku and Kyushu) constitute 98% of the nation's territory, the remainder being made up of some 4,000 smaller islands, including the Ryukyus, which lie between Kyushu and Taiwan. Japan is a medium-sized country, smaller than France but larger than Italy.

The Japanese islands occupy a zone of instability in the Earth's crust, and earthquakes and volcanic eruptions are frequent. Throughout Japan, complex folding and faulting has produced an intricate mosaic of landforms, in which mountains and forested hills alternate with small inland basins and coastal plains. The pattern of landforms is further complicated by the presence of several volcanic cones and calderas. The highest mountain in Japan, the majestic cone of Fuji-san (3,776 m [12,388 ft]), is a long-dormant volcano which last erupted in 1707.

In the mountains, fast-flowing torrents, fed by snowmelt in the spring and by heavy rainfall during the summer, have carved out a landscape of deep valleys and sharp ridges. In central Japan, dense mixed forests of oak, beech and maple blanket mountain slopes to an altitude of 1,800 m [5,900 ft]; further north in Hokkaido, boreal forests of fir and spruce predominate. In central Honshu, the Japan Alps with their snow-capped ridges provide spectacular mountain scenery.

Small intensively cultivated coastal plains, separated from one another by rugged mountain spurs, make up most of Japan's lowlands. None of the plains is extensive: the Kanto plain, which is the largest, covers an area of only 13,000 sq km [5,000 sq mls]. Most of the coastal plains are formed of material deposited by rivers, but their soils have been altered and improved by centuries of careful cultivation.

ECONOMY AND RESOURCES

Japan is a predominantly mountainous country and only 16% of the land is cultivable. Although Japan lacks extensive habitable areas, the population is nevertheless the eighth largest in the world. A limited area of agricultural land must therefore support many people, and Japan is now one of the most densely populated countries in the world – with an ever-ageing profile.

The main centres of population and industry are concentrated within a narrow corridor stretching from the Kanto plain, through the coastlands of the Setonaikai, to northern Kyushu. This heavily urbanized zone contains nine cities with populations of over a million and three great industrial regions, centring respectively on Tokyo, Osaka and Nagoya. The capital Tokyo, which will be overtaken by Mexico City as the world's most populous metropolis by 2000, forms the nucleus of a large and congested conurbation.

The Japanese boom

In 1945 Japan lay in ruins, with its major cities in ashes – two of them dangerously radioactive. Its smouldering ports were choked with the sunken remnants of its merchant marine, and its people were demoralized. Less than two generations later, the Japanese economy was second only to that of the USA. Its high-tech products dominated world markets, while Japanese banks and private investors owned huge slices of industry and real estate on every continent.

The far-sighted American Occupation authorities deserve some of the credit. Realizing that industrial recovery could only go hand in hand with political development, they wrote Japan a new constitution. As a link with the past, the emperor kept his place, but as a constitutional monarch answerable to a democratically elected Diet, with women given full voting rights for the first time. Trade unions, with the right to strike, were established, and land reform eliminated politically subservient tenants: by 1950, 90% of farmland was owner-cultivated. Great industrial conglomerates were broken into smaller units, and education was enormously expanded.

The Korean War in 1950 gave the slowly recovering Japanese economy a tremendous boost. Japanese factories, well paid in US dollars, provided much of the steel, vehicles and other equipment the war demanded. When the Occupation formally ended in 1952, Japan was clearly on the way up. The US military presence, guaranteed by treaty, continued, but caused no resentment: on the contrary, safe beneath the US defence umbrella, Japan could devote its resources to productive industry, not armaments.

The Japanese owed the first stage of their transformation to the Americans; the rest, they did themselves. Carefully planned economic policies, directed by the Ministry of Trade and Industry – nicknamed 'Japan Inc.'s Corporate Headquarters' – directed investment to key industries. First, the metal, engineering and chemical industries were rationalized and modernized – and in the 1950s and 1960s, efficient Japanese steel-makers consistently undersold their rivals, while producing better-quality steel. 'Made in Japan', once a sneering joke to describe shoddy goods, was taking on an entirely new commercial meaning.

Japan's major weakness was its near-total lack of natural resources; but foresight and planning made up for them. After the 1970s oil crisis, it was clear that the costs of heavy industry were going to rise unprofitably high; besides, the pollution they had brought was reaching dangerous levels. MITI switched sources to automobiles and electronics. soon, Japan began to capture and dominate these markets, too.

By the 1980s, Japan's trading partners were becoming seriously alarmed. Noting that trade with Japan was largely a one-way traffic – Japan's home market is still notoriously hard to penetrate – they built protective walls of tariffs and duties. Japan responded with its usual flexibility: it bought factories within its rivals' walls, and traded from there. The Tokyo stock market even survived a serious 'crash' in the spring of 1992 – testament to the strength of the national economy.

HISTORY AND POLITICS

Early Japan was peopled by immigrants arriving in successive waves from Korea and elsewhere on the Asian mainland. The earliest zone of settlement included northern Kyushu and the coastlands of the Setonaikai (Inland Sea). By the 5th century AD, Japan was divided amongst numerous clans, of which the largest and most powerful was the Yamato. Shinto, a polytheistic religion based on nature worship, had already emerged, as had the Japanese imperial dynasty.

During the next three centuries Chinese cultural and political influences entered Japan. These included Buddhism, the Chinese script, and Chinese methods of government and administration. At a later stage, Confucianism was also imported. Early cities, modelled on the capital of T'ang-dynasty China, were built at Nara (710) and at Kyoto (794); the latter city remained the seat of the imperial court until 1868.

The adoption of the Chinese system of centralized, bureaucratic government was relatively short-lived. From the early 12th century onwards, political power passed increasingly to military aristocrats, and government was conducted in the name of the emperor by warrior leaders known as *shoguns*. Civil warfare between rival groups of feudal lords was endemic over long periods, but under the rule of the Tokugawa *shoguns* (1603–1867), Japan enjoyed a great period of peace and prosperity; society was feudal and rigidly stratified, with military families (the feudal lords and their retainers, or *samurai*) forming a powerful élite.

In the 1630s, Japan embarked on a lengthy phase of enforced isolation from the rest of the world. This policy of seclusion could not be maintained indefinitely. In 1853, Commodore Perry of the US Navy arrived in Japan and demanded that ports be opened to Western trade. The capitulation of the *shogun* to Perry's demands prepared the way for the overthrow of the Tokugawa government, and with the Meiji Restoration of 1868 imperial rule was resumed.

Under Western-style government, a programme of modernization began. Industrialization proceeded swiftly, and after victories in the Sino-Japanese War (1894–5) and the Russo-Japanese War (1904–5), Japan began to build up an overseas empire which included the colonies of Taiwan and Korea. The growing strength of the Japanese military was demonstrated by the army's seizure of Manchuria in 1931. During the 1930s, and especially after the outbreak of war between Japan and China in 1937, militarist control of the government of Japan grew steadily. In 1941, the launching of a surprise attack on the American naval base of Pearl Harbor in Hawaii took Japan – and drew the USA – into World War II.

From its defeat in 1945 to 1952, Japan was administered by US forces. Many liberal reforms were enacted, and under the new constitution the power of the emperor was much reduced, with sovereignty formally vested in the people. The current system of government is a constitutional monarchy with the emperor as head of state and the prime minister as head of government. In spite of recent political scandals, the Liberal Democrats have continued to dominate the Japanese political scene. [*Map page 25*] ■

AREA 377,800 sq km [145,869 sq mls]
POPULATION 124,815,000
CAPITAL (POPULATION) Tokyo (11,927,000)
GOVERNMENT Constitutional monarchy
ETHNIC GROUPS Japanese 99%, Chinese, Korean, Ainu
LANGUAGES Japanese (official)
RELIGIONS Shintoism 93%, Buddhism 74%, Christianity 1% (most Japanese consider themselves to be both Shinto and Buddhist)
CURRENCY Yen = 100 sen

JORDAN

The Hashemite Kingdom of Jordan is an Arab country in south-western Asia. The Great Rift Valley in the west contains the River Jordan and the Dead Sea, which Jordan shares with Israel. The Great Rift Valley runs south through East Africa to Mozambique. East of the Rift Valley is the Transjordan plateau, where most Jordanians live. To the east and south of the county lie vast areas of desert. Jordan has a short coastline on an arm of the Red Sea, the Gulf of Aqaba.

The city of Amman has a much lower rainfall and longer dry season than the Mediterranean lands to the west. The Transjordan plateau, on which Amman stands, is a transition zone between the Mediterranean climate zone to the west and the true desert climate to the east. Parts of the western plateau have a scrub vegetation, much like that in Mediterranean lands. Jordan also has areas of dry grassland, though few plants grow in the eastern deserts.

ECONOMY AND RESOURCES

Jordan is not blessed with the natural resources enjoyed by some Middle East countries – whether oil or water – and a limited agricultural base is supported by mining of phosphates and potash, the main exports. The World Bank classifies Jordan as a 'lower-middle-income' developing country and the country's economy depends substantially on aid. Because of the dry climate, under 6% of the land is farmed or used as pasture. Major crops include barley, citrus fruits, grapes, olives, vegetables and wheat. Jordan has an oil refinery and manufactures include cement, pharmaceuticals, processed food, fertilizers and textiles.

HISTORY AND POLITICS

After World War I, the Arab territories of the Ottoman empire were divided by the League of Nations and the area east of the River Jordan ('Transjordan') was awarded to Britain

as part of Palestine, becoming a separate emirate in 1923. When the mandate ended 1946 the kingdom became independent, Jordan, and two years later (in the first Arab Israeli War) it acquired the West Bank region which was officially incorporated into the state in 1950.

This crucial area, including Arab Jerusalem was lost to Israel in the 1967 war, and Jordan has since carried the burden of Palestinian refugees on its own limited territory. In the 1970s the guerrillas using Jordan as a base became a challenge to the authority of King Hussein's government, and after a short civil war the Palestinian leadership fled the country. In 1988 Hussein suddenly renounced all responsibility for the West Bank – recognition that the PLO, and not long-suffering Jordan, was the legitimate representative of the Palestinian people, though Palestinians nevertheless, still formed a majority of the population.

The country's position was further undermined by the 1991 Gulf War, when despite official neutrality the pro-Iraq, anti-Western stance of the Palestinians did nothing to improve prospects of trade and aid deals with Europe and the US, Jordan's vital economic links with Iraq having already been severed. Another factor was the expulsion and return of large numbers of Palestinians and Jordanians from crucial jobs in Kuwait, Saudi Arabia and other wealthy Gulf states. There were, however, signs of political progress: in 1991 the ban on political parties was removed and martial law was lifted after 21 years. Multiparty elections were held in 1993. In October 1994, Jordan and Israel signed a peace treaty ending a state of war which had been going on for over 40 years. The treaty restored some land in the south to Jordan. [*Map page 19*] ■

AREA 89,210 sq km [34,444 sq mls]
POPULATION 5,198,000
CAPITAL (POPULATION) Amman (1,272,000)
GOVERNMENT Constitutional monarchy
ETHNIC GROUPS Arab 99%, of which roughly half are Palestinians
LANGUAGES Arabic (official)
RELIGIONS Islam 93%, Christianity 5%
CURRENCY Jordanian dinar = 1,000 fils

KAZAKHSTAN

Although a modest second in size behind Russia among the former Soviet republics, Kazakhstan is a colossal country – more than two and a half times the combined area of the other four Central Asian states, over four times the size of Ukraine (Europe's largest 'whole' state), bigger than any nation in Africa and indeed ninth in the world.

This new nation, stretching from near the Volga River in the west to the Altai Mountains in the east, comprises mainly vast plains with a (mineral-rich) central plateau. North to south, the steppe gradually gives way to desert.

ECONOMY AND RESOURCES
Kazakhstan has emerged as a powerful entity, wealthier and more diversified than the other Asian republics. Irrigation schemes have led to the fertilization of large areas between the Aral Sea and Lake Balkhash, a rich fishing ground. Though its agriculture is traditionally associated with livestock rearing, Kazakhstan accounted for 20% of the cultivated area of the Soviet Union and in 1993 produced 6.2% of the world's total barley and wheat output.

Well endowed with oil and gas, it also has good deposits of coal, iron ore, bauxite, copper, nickel, tungsten, zinc, silver and gold. Though not industrialized by Western standards, it is growing in oil refining, metallurgy, engineering, chemicals, food processing and textiles, the last mostly dependent on home-grown cotton and high-quality native wool.

HISTORY AND POLITICS
The first extension of the Russian Empire in Central Asia, the area's *'khanates'* were gradually subdued or bought off from the 18th century, though rural resistance persisted well into the Soviet era. It was Kazakhstan that gave Mikhail Gorbachev his first ethnic problem when, in 1986, nationalist riots erupted after a Russian replaced a Kazakh as the republic's Party leader, and in 1991 it led the Central Asian states into the new Common-

wealth; indeed, the meeting that finally buried the Soviet Union was held in Alma-Ata, testimony to Kazakhstan's rank as number three in the hierarchy – an estimate helped by its 1,800 nuclear warheads.

It was not always so. Successive Soviet regimes used the huge republic as a dumping-ground and test-bed. Stalin exiled Germans and other 'undesirables' there, and Khrushchev experimented with his (largely catastrophic) Virgin Lands Programme; the Soviet missile- and rocket-launching site was located at Baykonur, north-east of the Aral Sea (shrunk by 70% after disastrous Soviet irrigation projects dried up its two feeder rivers), and the USSR's first fast-breeder nuclear reactor was built at Mangyshlak, on the Caspian Sea.

Kazakhstan could provide the 'new order' with a valuable bridge between East and West, between Islam and Christianity; it is the only former Soviet republic where its ethnic population is almost outnumbered by another group (the Russians), and its (Sunni) Muslim revival is relatively muted. Such divisions can of course have the opposite effect, leading to ethnic tensions and cruelties. [*Map page 20*] ■

AREA 2,717,000 sq km [1,049,150 sq mls]
POPULATION 17,027,000
CAPITAL (POPULATION) Alma-Ata (1,147,000)
GOVERNMENT Multiparty republic
ETHNIC GROUPS Kazakh 40%, Russian 38%, German 6%, Ukrainian 5%, Uzbek, Tatar
LANGUAGES Kazakh (official); Russian, the former official language, is widely spoken
RELIGIONS Mainly Islam, with a Christian minority
CURRENCY Tenge

KENYA

Bisected by the Great Rift Valley, the Kenya Highlands were formed by volcanoes and lava flows rising from 1,500 m

[4,900 ft] to the snow-capped peak of Mt Kenya at 5,199 m [17,000 ft]. The greater part of the country, however, comprises plains cut across old crystalline rocks, except where sedimentary strata extend across the Tana Basin and into the Somali Republic.

ECONOMY AND RESOURCES

Some 80% of the people crowd into about 15% of the plains in the south-west of the country, where average rainfalls of over 750 mm [30 in] a year support dense farming populations. Corn meal is the staple diet, but Kenya is one of the few African nations also supporting a dairy industry. The Kikuyu and other tribes practise small-scale farming on the

fertile volcanic soils on the eastern flanks the Highlands from Limuru to Nyeri, Me and Embu.

The western Highlands descend to t equally populous Lake Victoria basin arou Kakamega and Kisii, focusing on Kisum Nakuru and Eldoret are farming centres or inally settled by Europeans. The mode capital city of Nairobi is within this core ar of Kenya, from which derive most of th exports of tea, coffee, pyrethrum and sis with soda ash from the Magadi alkaline lake

A second concentration of populatie occurs along the coast adjacent to Mombas Kenya's second city and a port that also serve Uganda via Nairobi. There are ancient tow

AIDS AND POVERTY IN AFRICA

The Acquired Immune Deficiency Syndrome was first identified in 1981, when American doctors found otherwise healthy young men succumbing to rare infections. By 1984, the cause had been traced to the Human Immunodeficiency Virus (HIV), which can remain dormant for many years and perhaps indefinitely; only half of those known to carry the virus in 1981 had developed AIDS ten years later. By the early 1990s, AIDS was still largely restricted to male homosexuals or needle-sharing drug users in the West. However, the disease is spreading fastest among heterosexual men and women in the Third World.

Africa is the most severely hit. In 1991 a World Health Organization (WHO) conference in Dakar, Senegal, was told that AIDS would kill more than 6 million Africans in the coming decade. In the same period, 4 million children would be born with the disease, and millions more would be orphaned by it. In Uganda, an estimated million people are thought to be carrying the virus. The total number of AIDS cases in adults and children reported to the WHO up to the end of 1994 was 1,025,073, but the WHO estimates the real figure is in excess of 4.5 million, of which an estimated 70% are in Africa. Trained people are desperately needed to help the continent's future development. Africans are also more than usually vulnerable to HIV and AIDS infection, partly because of urbanization and sexual freedom. In addition, most are poor and many are undernourished; many more suffer from various debilitating, non-fatal diseases. Their immune systems are already weak, making them less likely to shrug off exposure to the HIV virus, and more likely to develop AIDS.

Thus in Africa, a pregnant mother with HIV has a one-in-two chance of passing the virus to her child; in the West, the child of a similarly afflicted mother has only one chance in eight of contracting the infection. African poverty also means that victims have virtually no chance of receiving any of the expensive drugs developed to prolong the lives of AIDS sufferers. Even if researchers succeed in developing an AIDS vaccine, it is likely to be well beyond the reach of countries whose health budget is seldom much more than $2 a year for each citizen; there are few refrigerators to store such a vaccine, and few needles to administer it safely.

Africa faces millions of individual human tragedies. Yet even so, AIDS-related deaths are unlikely to impinge significantly on continental population growth. At its current rate of increase – 2.97% per annum – Africa by the year 2000 will have acquired more than 243 million extra people – more than 40 times the number of predicted deaths from AIDS. And AIDS is only the newest scourge Africa must suffer. Malaria, measles, a host of water-borne infections and simple malnutrition will kill far more Africans during the same period.

d ruins, and an Islamic Swahili culture. ese now co-exist with an international urist industry that is Kenya's third biggest urce of foreign exchange. By contrast, the tensive semi-arid interior plains contain dely scattered pastoral peoples such as the asai, Turkana and Galla.

By the standards of tropical Africa, Kenya s a stable and safe economy, even allowing r the traditionally thriving black market d usual reliance on aid. The country could vertheless be in danger from two explosions, e in AIDS and the other, by contrast, in eer numbers of people. Though relatively arse in terms of density, Kenya's extra- dinarily high birth rate of 4.2% is expected produce an increase of 82% in its popu- tion between 1988 and 2000 – a figure xceeded only by Haiti. By 1990 it was already gistering the world's 'youngest' profile, ith more than 52% of the total under 15 ears of age.

HISTORY AND POLITICS

he 1990s brought signs, too, of increasing olitical problems as Daniel arap Moi, the resident since 1978 and successor to the noderate Jomo Kenyatta, found his auth- ritarian one-party regime under threat. In December 1991, after months of pressure and overnment defections, he was forced to con- ede the principle of pluralist democracy – not een since 1969. The president (a Kalenjin n a country whose affairs have always been dominated by the Kikuyu) was re-elected in multiparty elections in December 1992, hough there were many allegations of vote- igging. [Map page 33] ■

AREA 580,370 sq km [224,801 sq mls]
POPULATION 27,343,000
CAPITAL (POPULATION) Nairobi (1,429,000)
GOVERNMENT Multiparty republic
ETHNIC GROUPS Kikuyu 21%, Luhya 14%, Luo 13%, Kamba 11%, Kalenjin 11%
LANGUAGES Swahili and English (both official)
RELIGIONS Christianity (Roman Catholic 27%, Protestant 19%, others 27%), traditional beliefs 19%, Islam 6%
CURRENCY Kenyan shilling = 100 cents

KIRIBATI

The Republic of Kiribati comprises three groups of coral atolls – 16 Gilbert Islands, eight Phoenix Islands and 11 of the Line Islands – plus the higher and volcanic Banaba. Comprising 728 sq km [281 sq mls], they are scattered over 5 million sq km [2 million sq mls] of the Pacific, straddling both the Equator and the International Date Line.

ECONOMY AND RESOURCES
Little of the coral islands rises above 4 m [13 ft], though coconuts, bananas, papayas, and breadfruits are harvested, with taro (babai) laboriously cultivated in deep pits to provide the staple vegetable. Following the exhaustion of Banaba's phosphate deposits in 1980, the main exports are copra (63%), fish and fish preparations (24%), but Kiribati remains heavily dependent on foreign aid.

HISTORY AND POLITICS
Kiribati was known as the Gilbert Islands until independence in 1979. Together with the Ellice Islands (which broke away as Tuvalu in 1975), the Gilberts were a British protectorate from 1892 and a colony from 1916; they were occupied by the Japanese in World War II, and recaptured after the battle for Tarawa in 1943.

The future, both medium-term economic and long-term environmental (due to possible rising sea levels from global warming) is bleak, compounded by an overcrowding problem that has forced the resettlement of some 4,700 people in the 1990s. [Map page 3] ■

AREA 728 sq km [281 sq mls]
POPULATION 77,000
CAPITAL (POPULATION) Tarawa (24,000)
GOVERNMENT Multiparty republic
ETHNIC GROUPS Micronesian
LANGUAGES English (official), Gilbertese
RELIGIONS Christianity (Roman Catholic 48%, Protestant 45%)
CURRENCY Australian currency

KOREA, NORTH

Mountains and rugged hills occupy most of the Korean peninsula, and only 20% of the surface area is suitable for cultivation. The interior of North Korea is a harsh environment, characterized by long and severe winters, during which lakes and rivers regularly freeze over. High forested mountains, cut by river gorges, lie along the borders of North Korea and Manchuria. Further south, a chain of bare, eroded mountains runs for almost the entire length of the peninsula, parallel with and close to the eastern coast.

ECONOMY AND RESOURCES

The most productive land in the peninsula occurs along the southern coast, where winters are relatively mild. While South Korea contains the best rice lands in the peninsula, most mineral resources, including coal – which supplies 70% of the country's energy needs – and iron ore, are concentrated in North Korea. Though the North has nearly 55% of the land area, it has only just over a third of the total Korean population.

While the Communist regime's collectivist agriculture programme has been reasonably successful – around 90% of cultivated land is under the control of co-operative farms – most of its effort went into the development of heavy industry, a decision which, after initial success, left the economy lagging well behind the 'sunrise' countries of the region, which moved quickly into electronics and computers. Defence, too, continues to be a significant drag on the economy.

HISTORY AND POLITICS

The Stalinist regime of North Korea installed by the Soviet Union after World War II – and supported by China during the Korean War of 1950–3 – has been a total dictatorship revolving around the extraordinary and dynastic personality cult of Kim Il Sung and his nominated heir, Kim Jung Il, whom the president also designated his successor as supreme commander of the army. The world's mo durable Communist ruler, Kim Il Sur imposed on North Korea his own brand Marxism-Leninism, resting on the principle of self-reliance and party supremacy, and cr ated a forbidding society virtually closed foreigners and with few international friends

As the Cold War ended and the Sovi satellites strived for a new age, North Kore remained isolated from the momentou events taking place outside. In 1991, howeve there were quite sudden signs of progress (se *South Korea*), with unexpected breakthrough appearing to end confrontation on the penir sula. However, the sudden death of the 'Grea Leader' on 8 July 1994, at a time of increas ing uncertainty surrounding North Korea' nuclear capabilities, cast a cloud of uneas over the region as a whole. [*Map page 24*] ■

AREA	120,540 sq km [46,540 sq mls]
POPULATION	23,483,000
CAPITAL (POPULATION)	Pyongyang (2,639,000)
GOVERNMENT	Single-party people's republic
ETHNIC GROUPS	Korean 99%
LANGUAGES	Korean (official)
RELIGIONS	Traditional beliefs 16%, Chondogyo 14%, Buddhism 2%, Christianity 1%
CURRENCY	North Korean won = 100 chon

KOREA, SOUTH

The Republic of Korea, as South Korea is officially known, occupies the southern part of the Korean peninsula. Mountains cover most of the country apart from the narrow coastal lowlands. The western coastlands, where the capital and main industrial city, Seoul, is situated, is a region of low-lying hills and plains dotted with farms. The southern coast is another major farming region. Many islands are found along the west and south coasts. The largest island is Cheju-do, which contains South Korea's highest peak, rising to 1,950 m [6,398 ft].

Like North Korea, South Korea is chilled winter by cold, dry winds blowing from central Asia. Snow often covers the mountains in the east, but the summers are hot and wet, especially in July and August, when it rains, on average, every other day.

ECONOMY AND RESOURCES

The story of South Korea since the civil war had been a very different one from the North, though it was hardly a Far Eastern oasis of liberalism. While land reform based on small-holdings worked well enough to produce some of the world's highest rice yields (and self-sufficiency in food grains), the real economic miracle came in industrial expansion from the early 1960s. Initiated by a military government – one of several bouts of army rule since the inauguration of the republic – and based on slender natural resources, the schemes utilized cheap, plentiful but well-educated labour to transform the economy and make South Korea one of the strongest countries in Asia. The original manufacturing base of textiles remains important, but South Korea is now a world leader in footwear, shipbuilding, and a host of other activities, including consumer electronics, toys and vehicles.

Seoul, hiding its pollution and housing shortages as best it could, celebrated the country's growth by hosting the 1988 Olympic Games: from a population of 1.4 million in 1950, it had reached 10.5 million by 1985. The dynamism of the country must now be linked to more liberal policies – and less spending on defence. The economy was growing, too: at nearly 9% a year from 1960 to 1990. South Korea has now opened up the possibility of trade links with China, which, though Communist, is desperate to broaden its economic possibilities, while approaches are being made to bodies to recognize the country's achievements and net status. A major breakthrough occurred in 1991 when both North and South Korea were admitted as full members of the United Nations.

HISTORY AND POLITICS

For centuries the Koreans were very much a united people, an independent kingdom – 'Land of the Morning Calm' – knitted together by race, language and culture. Then, in

THE KOREAN WAR

Hastily divided in 1945 between a Soviet-occupied North and an American-occupied South, Korea was considered by most Western strategists an irrelevance to the developing Cold War. But when the heavily-armed North invaded the South in June 1950, US President Truman decided to make a stand against what he saw (mistakenly) as Moscow-organized aggression. A Soviet boycott of the UN allowed American troops – assisted by contingents from Britain, Canada, France and other allies – to fight under the UN flag, and under General Douglas MacArthur they went on the offensive. American seapower permitted a landing far behind North Korean lines, and soon the Northerners were in retreat.

With some misgivings, Truman ordered his forces north of the 38th parallel, the former partition line. But as US troops neared the Chinese frontier in November 1950, hundreds of thousands of Chinese 'volunteers' surged across the Yalu River and threatened to overwhelm them. They retreated far southwards in disarray, until a 1951 counter-attack slowly pushed back up the country and the combatants became entrenched along the 38th parallel in a bitter war of attrition that endured until an armistice was negotiated in 1953. Not until 1991, almost 40 years later, were North and South able to agree to a tentative non-aggression pact.

1910, came annexation by Japan and its harsh colonial rule, followed after World War II with division by the Allied powers into the Soviet (North) and American (South) zones of occupation each side of the 38th parallel. In 1948 the Soviets established a Communist regime in the North, the Americans a republic in the South, and the country – especially after the civil war of 1950–3 – seemed permanently partitioned. With a handful of interruptions, the two governments retained their hostile positions on the artificial frontier for nearly four decades; then, in 1991, the sides began to talk.

They first came together over a combined table-tennis team, yet only ten months later they had signed a full-blown non-aggression pact. In January 1992, following New Year messages from both presidents talking of unification, they signed a nuclear weapons agreement, setting up a joint control committee. While German-style reunification still seems a remote possibility in the near future – deep suspicion remains on both sides, and much depends on the events in North Korea following the death of Kim Il Sung in 1994 – it was a remarkable breakthrough from such institutionalized positions. [*Map page 24*] ■

AREA 99,020 sq km [38,232 sq mls]
POPULATION 44,563,000
CAPITAL (POPULATION) Seoul (or Soul, 10,628,000)
GOVERNMENT Multiparty republic
ETHNIC GROUPS Korean 99%
LANGUAGES Korean (official)
RELIGIONS Buddhism 28%, Christianity (Protestant 19%, Roman Catholic 6%)
CURRENCY South Korean won = 100 chon

KUWAIT

Most of the country is a flat desert, extremely dry and hot. Kuwait has large reserves of oil and natural gas. The impressive if unevenly distributed prosperity built by the ruling Sabah family since oil was first commercially produced in 1946 was suddenly and brutally undermined by the Iraqi invasion of 1990. Occupying troops were soon expelled by a US-led multinational force – but not before they had set fire to more than 500 oil wells (causing unprecedented pollution) and destroyed almost all industrial and commercial installations in Kuwait.

Kuwait's revenge over the devastation was directed mainly at the large contingent of Palestinian, Jordanian and Yemeni immigrant workers (seen as pro-Iraq) on whom the economic progress of the country had been based for more than two decades. Reconstruction for this former British protectorate (the country

gained independence in 1961) was expected to cost hundreds of billions of dollars, but the high proportion of foreign investment made during the good years had produced massive funds to get it under way. Predictably in a country with virtually no meaningful agricultural activity, oil would be the key to recovery. [*Map page 19*] ■

AREA 17,820 sq km [6,880 sq mls]
POPULATION 1,633,000
CAPITAL (POPULATION) Kuwait City (189,000)
GOVERNMENT Constitutional monarchy
ETHNIC GROUPS Kuwaiti Arab 40%, non-Kuwaiti Arab 38%, various Asian 21%
LANGUAGES Arabic 78%, Kurdish 10%, Farsi 4%
RELIGIONS Islam 92%, Christianity 6%
CURRENCY Kuwaiti dinar = 1,000 fils

KYRGYZSTAN

The Republic of Kyrgyzstan, or Kirghizia as it is also known, is a landlocked country between China, Tajikistan, Uzbekistan and Kazakhstan. The country is mountainous, with spectacular scenery. The highest mountain, Pik Pobedy in the Tian Shan range, reaches 7,439 m [24,406 ft] above sea level in the east. Less than a sixth of the country is below 900 m [2,950 ft]. The largest of the country's many lakes is Ozero Issyk-Kul (Ysyk Köl) in the north-east. Its shoreline is 1,609 m [5,279 ft] above sea level.

The lowlands have warm summers and cold winters. But the altitude influences the climate in the mountains, where January temperatures plummet to –28°C [–18°F]. Because of its remoteness from the sea, much of Kyrgyzstan has a low annual rainfall.

ECONOMY AND RESOURCES

Kyrgyzstan has a strong agricultural economy. Much of the lower land is used as pasture for sheep, pigs, cattle, goats, horses and yaks –

astoralism is the traditional livelihood of the Mongoloid Kyrgyz, though few nomads remain – while irrigated land produces a wide range of crops from sugar beet and vegetables to rice, cotton, tobacco, grapes and mulberry trees (for silkworms). The main manufacturing industry is textiles and there are huge reserves of uranium, mercury and gold.

HISTORY AND POLITICS

The area that is now Kyrgyzstan was populated in ancient times by nomadic herders. Mongol armies conquered the region in the early 13th century. They set up areas called *hanates*, ruled by chieftains, or *khans*. Islam was introduced in the 17th century.

China gained control of the area in the mid-18th century, but, in 1876, Kyrgyzstan became a province of Russia. Russia encouraged settlement by Russians, Ukrainians and others, a policy which was resented by the local people whose grazing land was reduced in area. In 1916, Russia put down a rebellion and many local people fled to China.

In 1917, Communist leaders seized control of Russia, and in 1922, when the Soviet Union was formed, Kyrgyzstan became an autonomous *oblast* (self-governing region). In 1936, it became a Soviet Socialist Republic in the Soviet Union, and under Communism, nomads were forced to live on government-run farms. The government tried to suppress some local customs, including religious worship, but Communist rule also led to improvements in such fields as health and education.

Following the break-up of the Soviet Union in 1991, and despite its geographical isolation on the borders of China's Xinjiang provinces and its conventionally strong links with Moscow, Kyrgyzstan has pursued very aggressive 'European' policies towards Western-style capitalist democracy in the period since independence was declared in August 1991. Its young president, Askar Akayev, has introduced rapid privatization, nurtured pluralism, and encouraged trade and investment links with OECD countries. In addition, he has established good relations with China, a suspicious neighbour and potential foe. However, the large Russian minority (in positions of power under the Soviet regime), disenchanted Uzbeks and an influx of Chinese Muslim immigrants have the potential for an ethnic tinderbox. [*Map page 20*] ∎

AREA 198,500 sq km [76,640 sq mls]
POPULATION 4,667,000
CAPITAL (POPULATION) Bishkek (628,000)
GOVERNMENT Multiparty republic
ETHNIC GROUPS Kyrgyz 52%, Russian 22%, Uzbek 13%, Ukrainian 3%, German 2%, Tatar 2%
LANGUAGES Kyrgyz
RELIGIONS Islam
CURRENCY Som = tyiyn

LAOS

The Lao People's Democratic Republic is a landlocked country in South-east Asia. Mountains and plateaux cover much of the country. The highest point is Mount Bia, which reaches 2,817 m [9,242 ft] in central Laos. Most people live on the plains bordering the River Mekong and its tributaries. This river, one of Asia's longest, forms much of the country's north-western and south-western borders. A range of mountains, called the Annam Cordillera, runs along the eastern border with Vietnam.

Laos has a tropical monsoon climate. Winters are dry and sunny, with winds blowing from the north-east. Temperatures rise until April, when the wind directions are reversed and moist south-westerlies reach Laos, heralding the start of the wet monsoon season.

ECONOMY AND RESOURCES

Laos is one the world's poorest countries. Agriculture employs about 76% of the people, as compared with 7% in industry and 17% in services. The River Mekong is the main artery, as the country has no railways. Up to 85% of the sparse population work on collective farms at subsistence level, growing mainly rice, although timber and coffee are both exported. But the most valuable export is electricity, which is produced at hydroelectric power stations on the River Mekong and is exported to Thailand. Laos also produces opium – in the early 1990s, Laos was thought to be the world's third biggest source of this illegal drug.

HISTORY AND POLITICS

From the 9th century AD, Lao and Thai people set up a number of small states ruled by princes. But the area that is now Laos was united in 1353, in a kingdom called Lan Xang ('land of a million elephants'). Around 1700, the region was divided into three separate kingdoms. France made Laos a protectorate in the late 19th century and ruled it as part of French Indo-China, a region which also included Cambodia and Vietnam. Laos became a member of the French Union in 1948 and an independent kingdom in 1954.

After independence, Laos suffered from instability caused by a long struggle power between royalist government forces and a pro-Communist group called the Pathet Lao. Civil war broke out in 1960 and continued off and on into the 1970s. The Pathet Lao finally took control of Laos in 1975 and the king abdicated. Laos was greatly influenced by the dominant Communist government in Vietnam, which had used Laos as a great supply line during the Vietnam War (1957–75).

From the late 1980s, along with other Communist countries, Laos began a programme of economic reforms, including the encouragement of private enterprise and opening up trade links with neighbours (notably China and Japan). But there were few indications that the Communist government was prepared to introduce political reforms and some measure of democracy. [*Map page 26*] ∎

AREA 236,800 sq km [91,428 sq mls]
POPULATION 4,742,000
CAPITAL (POPULATION) Vientiane (377,000)
GOVERNMENT Single-party republic
ETHNIC GROUPS Lao 67%, Mon-Khmer 17%,
Thai 8%, Man 5%
LANGUAGES Lao (official)
RELIGIONS Buddhism 58%, traditional beliefs
34%, Christianity 2%, Islam 1%
CURRENCY Kip = 100 at

LATVIA

The Republic of Latvia is one of thre states on the south-eastern corner of th Baltic Sea which were ruled as parts of th Soviet Union between 1940 and 1991. Latvi consists mainly of flat plains separated by lov hills, composed of glacial moraine deposite in the last Ice Age. The country's highest poin is only 311 m [1,020 ft] above sea level, an small lakes and peat bogs are common. Th country's main river, the Daugava, is als known as the Western Dvina.

Forests cover about 40% of the county Pine and spruce forests are widespread, bu mixed forests with alder, aspen and birch als occur. About 27% of the land is under crops while 13% is used for grazing livestock.

ECONOMY AND RESOURCES

Like its Baltic neighbours, Latvia contains much of the former Soviet Union's less traditional, 'clever' industries, while Ventspils is an important conduit for the export of Russian oil and gas. Latvia is the most urbanized of the Baltic states, with over 70% of the population living in cities and towns.

In the 1990s, however, it faced many problems in transforming its government-run economy into a free-market one. The country lacks any significant natural resources apart from its land and forests, and it has to import many of the materials needed for its most valuable activity, manufacturing. In addition, Latvia produces only about a tenth of the electricity it needs. The rest has to be imported from Belarus, Russia and Ukraine. Manufactured products cover a wide range, including electronic goods, farm machinery, fertilizers, processed food, plastics, radios, vehicles and washing machines.

HISTORY AND POLITICS

The ancestors of most modern Latvians settled in the area about 2,000 years ago. But between the 9th and 11th centuries, the region was attacked by Vikings from the west and

THE BALTIC STATES

The three Baltic republics have always found it hard to establish their nationhood, though their cultures have proved resilient. Estonia and Latvia survived 1,000 years of rule by Danes, Swedes, Lithuanians and Poles before becoming part of the Russian Empire in 1721; Lithuania, once a powerful medieval empire, was united with Poland in 1385 but also came under Russian control in 1795.

Nationalist movements grew in all three countries in the late 19th century, and in 1920, following German occupation, the Soviet Union granted them the status of independent democratic republics. However, all had Fascist coups by the time Hitler assigned them to Stalin in the notorious secret pact of 1939.

After three years of occupation by (Nazi) Germany, incorporation into the USSR was confirmed by plebiscite in 1944. On declaring independence in 1990, the Baltic states claimed this was fraudulent and that their countries were never legally part of the Soviet Union. Referenda supported this view, and on 6 September 1991 the transitional States Council of the Soviet Union recognized them as independent sovereign states. All three were United Nations members by the end of the year.

Under Soviet rule, many Russian immigrants settled in Latvia and many native Latvians (Letts) feared that the Russians would become the dominant ethnic group. In the late 1980s, when reforms were being introduced in the Soviet Union, Latvia's government ended absolute Communist rule and made Latvian the official language. In 1990, it declared the country to be independent, an act which was finally recognized by the Soviet Union in September 1991.

Latvia held its first free elections to its parliament in 1993. Voting was limited only to citizens of Latvia on 17 June 1940 and their descendants. This meant that about 34% of Latvian residents were unable to vote. In 1994, Latvia adopted a law restricting the naturalization of non-Latvians, including many Russian settlers, who are not allowed to vote or to own land. [*Map page 13*] ■

AREA 64,589 sq km [24,938 sq mls]
POPULATION 2,583,000
CAPITAL (POPULATION) Riga (917,000)
GOVERNMENT Multiparty republic
ETHNIC GROUPS Latvian 53%, Russian 34%, Belarussian 4%, Ukrainian 3%, Polish 2%, Lithuanian, Jewish
LANGUAGES Latvian (official)
RELIGIONS Christianity (including Lutheran, Russian Orthodox and Roman Catholic)
CURRENCY Lats = 10 santimi

Russians from the east, while in the 13th century German invaders took over, naming the country Livland, or Livonia in Latin.

From 1561, the area was partitioned between various groups, including Poles, Lithuanians and Swedes. In 1710, the Russian Peter the Great conquered Riga, and Latvia was soon under Russian rule. Nationalist movements developed in the 19th century and, just after the end of World War I (1914–18), Latvia declared itself independent. However, in 1939, Germany and the Soviet Union made a secret agreement to divide up parts of eastern Europe, and in 1940 Soviet troops invaded Latvia, which became part of the Soviet Union. German forces seized Latvia in 1941, but Soviet troops returned in 1944.

LEBANON

The Republic of Lebanon is a country on the eastern shores of the Mediterranean Sea. The country's narrow coastal plain contains the main cities, including Beirut (Bayrut) and Tripoli (Tarabulus). Behind the coastal plain are the rugged Lebanon Mountains, which rise to 3,088 m [10,131 ft]. Another range, the Anti-Lebanon Mountains, form the eastern border with Syria. Between the two ranges is the Beqaa Valley, a fertile farming region.

The coast of Lebanon experiences the hot, dry summers and mild, wet winters that are typical of many Mediterranean lands. Inland, onshore winds bring heavy rain to the western slopes of the mountains in winter, with snow at the higher altitudes. Lebanon was famous in ancient times for its cedar forests in the mountains (as depicted on their flag), but these have been largely cut down. Forest and woodland now cover only about 8% of the land.

ECONOMY AND RESOURCES

Lebanon's economy, devastated by civil war, is gradually being rebuilt. The main agricultural crops include citrus and other fruits, olives, sugar beet and tobacco, and the principal industries are textiles, electrical goods, processed food and chemicals. The previously thriving financial and commercial sectors are being developed once again.

HISTORY AND POLITICS

For three decades after its independence from the French mandate in 1944 Lebanon was a relatively peaceful and prosperous country by Middle East standards. An association with France going back a century – before that the country was part of the Ottoman empire – had bequeathed a distinct Gallic flavour, though with so many racial and religious groups the population was truly cosmopolitan; Beirut, the dominant city, was a centre of international commerce (the Lebanese are descendants of the Phoenicians, legendary traders and businessmen).

All that changed suddenly after March 1975 when this beautiful country saw sporadic conflict spiral into violent civil war between Christians, Muslims and Druses. The complex politics of the next 14 years proved almost unfathomable as Lebanon sank into a seemingly permanent state of ungovernable chaos. Bombing, assassination and kidnapping became routine as numerous factions and private militias – Maronite, Druse, Sunni and Shia groups (including fundamentalists backed by Iran) – fought for control. The situation was complicated by a succession of interventions by Palestinian liberation organizations, Israeli troops, the Syrian Army, Western and then UN forces, as the country became a patchwork of occupied zones and 'no-go' areas.

The core religious confrontation has deep roots: in 1860 thousands of Maronite (aligned to the Catholic Church) were murdered by Druses (so tangential to other Islamic sects that they are now not regarded as Muslims), and Muslim tolerance of Christian power after independence lasted only until 1958. Though not directly involved, Lebanon was destabilized by the Arab-Israeli War of 1967, and the exile of PLO leadership to Beirut in 1970.

By 1990 the Syrian Army had crushed the two-year revolt of Christian rebels against the Lebanese government. Since then, the Lebanese Army has regained control of many areas and the government has been able to start the process of reconstruction. However, Israeli-backed forces continue to occupy the south of the country (claimed to be a base for Palestinian terrorists), while the fundamentalist Hezbollah still controls much of the Beqaa Valley in the north. [*Map page 19*] ∎

AREA 10,400 sq km [4,015 sq mls]
POPULATION 2,915,000
CAPITAL (POPULATION) Beirut (1,500,000)
GOVERNMENT Multiparty republic
ETHNIC GROUPS Arab (Lebanese 80%, Palestinian 12%), Armenian 5%, Syrian, Kurdish
LANGUAGES Arabic (official)
RELIGIONS Islam 58%, Christianity 27%, Druse
CURRENCY Lebanese pound = 100 piastres

LESOTHO

Consisting mainly of a high mountainous plateau deeply fretted by the headwaters of the Orange (Oranje) River, Lesotho declines altitudinally from east to west, with the highest ridges, over 3,000 m [9–10,000 ft], developed on basaltic lavas. This treeless zone with its steep valleys has an excess of water, making it boggy in summer, frozen in winter. It is, nevertheless, overpopulated. All of this ntrasts with the lower narrow western belts the foothills and lowlands, stretching south-ards from Butha-Buthe to Mohale's Hoek. ere the dominant rock is sandstone.

CONOMY AND RESOURCES

he physical environment, and being sur-unded on all sides by South Africa, provides ajor economic problems for the country. lost of the population are involved in subsis-nce agriculture, battling for a living against teep slopes and thin soils. The only urban and ndustrial development lies at Maseru, but the rend is still for people to drift to the small owns or to find employment in the gold and oal mines of South Africa. The country's cenery is conducive to tourism and the alti-ude allows winter sports; however, massive apital investment, especially in roads, would e necessary to develop this potential.

HISTORY AND POLITICS

ormerly a British protectorate (known as Basutoland), Lesotho became independent in 1966, joining the Commonwealth as a consti-utional monarchy. However the constitution was suspended in 1970 and the prime minis-er, Chief Jonathan, was deposed by an army coup in 1986. In 1990 the ruling Military Council replaced King Moshoeshoe II with his son, Letsie III, but its own leader, Major-General Lekhanya, was in turn overthrown by a coup in 1992. This led to the first elections for 23 years being held in 1993. A civilian prime minister was voted in and a new consti-tution restoring multiparty democracy was adopted. The military were opposed to the new government and in August 1994 launched a coup attempt, propelling the country into a constitutional crisis. [Map page 33] ■

AREA 30,350 sq km [11,718 sq mls]
POPULATION 1,996,000
CAPITAL (POPULATION) Maseru (109,000)
GOVERNMENT Constitutional monarchy
ETHNIC GROUPS Sotho 99%
LANGUAGES Sesotho and English (both official)
RELIGIONS Christianity 93% (Roman Catholic 44%), traditional beliefs 6%
CURRENCY Loti = 100 lisente

LIBERIA

L iberia is a sparsely populated country with a swampy and humid coastal strip, 500 km [311 mls] long, bordering the Atlantic Ocean. Behind this the land rises to plateaux and low mountains in the interior with large tracts of inaccessible tropical rainforest. A number of rivers flow across the country gen-erally from the north-east to the south-west. The most important rivers are the Cavally (or Cavalla), which forms the border with Ivory Coast, and the St Paul which reaches the Atlantic Ocean near the capital, Monrovia.

Liberia has a tropical climate with high tem-peratures and humidity throughout the year. Rainfall is abundant, with two especially wet periods, namely May to July and October to November. The rainfall generally increases from east to west across the country.

ECONOMY AND RESOURCES

Liberia is popularly known for its 'flag of con-venience' (used by about one-sixth of the world's commercial shipping), and for large American-owned rubber plantations.

There has been an open-door policy towards foreign entrepreneurs, and the econ-omy has developed rapidly following the exploitation of large iron-ore deposits by for-eign companies, mainly American. Though diamonds and gold have long been worked, iron ore accounts for about half the value of all exports. The economy is a mixture of large foreign-owned corporations operating mines and plantations, and of various indigenous peoples who still exist largely as very poor shifting subsistence cultivators.

HISTORY AND POLITICS

West Africa's oldest independent state, Liberia lacks a legacy of colonial administration. The country was founded in the early 19th century as an American colony for freed black slaves wanting to return to Africa from the USA.

In 1989 Liberia was plunged into vicious civil war when a force led by Charles Taylor invaded from the Ivory Coast. The president, Samuel Doe, who had seized power in 1980, was later assassinated and a jigsaw of conflicts developed between his successor, Amos Sawyer, Taylor and other rebel forces, including those led by Prince Johnson. Peacekeeping troops from five West African countries arrived in October 1990, but despite several agreements fighting continued into 1991. By mid-1993, an estimated 150,000 people had died and hundreds of thousands were homeless. In July 1993, a cease-fire was agreed, but elections scheduled for 1994 were postponed when more fighting occurred. [*Map page 32*] ■

AREA 111,370 sq km [43,000 sq mls]
POPULATION 2,941,000
CAPITAL (POPULATION) Monrovia (425,000)
GOVERNMENT Multiparty republic
ETHNIC GROUPS Kpelle 19%, Bassa 14%, Grebo 9%, Gio 8%, Kru 7%, Mano 7%
LANGUAGES English (official)
RELIGIONS Christianity 68%, Islam 14%, traditional beliefs and others 18%
CURRENCY Liberian dollar = 100 cents

LIBYA

The Socialist People's Libyan Arab Jamahiriya, as Libya is officially called, is a large country in North Africa. Most people live on the Mediterranean coastal plains in the north-east and north-west. The Sahara, the world's largest desert which occupies 95% of Libya, reaches the Mediterranean coast along the Gulf of Sidra (Khalij Surt). The Sahara is mostly uninhabited except around scattered oases, where date palms provide protection from the hot sun. The land rises towards the south, reaching 2,286 m [7,500 ft] at Bette Peak on the border with Chad.

The plains in the north-east and north-west experience a Mediterranean climate, with hot, dry summers and mild winters with some rain. Inland, the average yearly rainfall drops to 100 mm [4 in] or less.

ECONOMY AND RESOURCES

When it became independent in 1951, Libya was one of the poorest countries in the world, with few known natural resources and a largely nomadic population. This bleak picture changed dramatically after 1959 with the discovery of vast reserves of oil and natural gas.

With growing revenues from petroleum and gas exports, important highways were built to link the different regions across the desert, and considerable investment was made in housing, education and health provision. Today the country's income per head is twice that of its nearest rivals on the African continent - Algeria, Gabon and South Africa. But despite a high population growth rate (6.5%), agricultural development and industrialization still rely heavily on immigrant workers.

HISTORY AND POLITICS

A former Turkish possession and Italian colony, the kingdom of Libya gained independence from British and French military administration in 1951. But, in 1969, a military group headed by Colonel Muammar Gaddafi deposed King Idris and set up a military government. Under Gaddafi, the government took control of the economy and used money from oil exports to finance welfare services and development projects.

Gaddafi has attracted international criticism for his support for radical movements, such as the PLO and various terrorist groups. In 1986, his policies led the US to bomb installations in the capital and in Benghazi. Libya has several long-running disputes with its neighbours, notably Chad, where it sent troops to intervene in a civil war. In 1994, the International Court of Justice ruled against Libya's claim for territory in the Aozou Strip in northern Chad. [*Map page 32*] ■

AREA 1,759,540 sq km [679,358 sq mls]
POPULATION 5,225,000
CAPITAL (POPULATION) Tripoli (990,000)
GOVERNMENT Single-party socialist state
ETHNIC GROUPS Libyan Arab and Berber 89%, others 11%
LANGUAGES Arabic (official)
RELIGIONS Islam
CURRENCY Libyan dinar = 1,000 dirhams

LIECHTENSTEIN

LITHUANIA

The tiny state of Liechtenstein stands at the end of the eastern Alps between Austria and Switzerland, where the Rhine cuts its way northwards out of the Alpine chains. The capital, Vaduz, is situated on the Ober-land plateau above the fields and meadows of the Rhine Valley, and rising numbers of tourists (there were as many as 72,000 overnight visitors in 1992) are arriving at its royal castle, intrigued by the notion of this miniature state.

While Liechtenstein is best known abroad for its postage stamps – an important source of income – it is as a haven for international companies, attracted by extremely low taxation and the strictest (most secretive) banking codes in the world, that the state has generated the revenue to produce the highest GDP per capita figure on record. Since World War II there has also been an impressive growth in specialized manufacturing – the product of a judicious mixture of Swiss engineers, Austrian technicians, Italian workers and international capital.

Liechtenstein became an independent principality within the Holy Roman Empire in 1719 and since then has always managed to escape incorporation into any of Europe's larger states. Liechtenstein has been in customs and currency union with Switzerland since 1923, which also provides overseas representation; and although many Swiss regard it as their 27th canton, it retains full sovereignty in other spheres. [Map page 15] ∎

AREA 157 sq km [61 sq mls]
POPULATION 30,000
CAPITAL (POPULATION) Vaduz (4,919)
GOVERNMENT Principality
ETHNIC GROUPS Alemannic 95%
LANGUAGES German, Alemannic dialects
RELIGIONS Christianity (Roman Catholic 87%, Protestant 8%)
CURRENCY Swiss currency

Largest and most populous of the Baltic states, Lithuania is also the most homogeneous, some 80% of its population being staunch Catholics who speak the native language and are proud of their history and culture. The country consists mostly of a low, glaciated but fairly fertile central lowland. In the east, towards the border with Belarus, is an area of forested sandy ridges, dotted with lakes.

ECONOMY AND RESOURCES

Livestock rearing (cattle, pigs and poultry) was highly intensified under the Soviet collective system. Crops grown are very similar to those of Estonia, and although there are also widespread forests and significant peat reserves, Lithuania remains pitifully short of any significant natural resources.

A range of industries, among them many of the most advanced programmes in the former Soviet Union, include timber, metalworking, textiles, building materials, fertilizers, fibres and plastics, computers and instruments and food processing. Craftsmen still make jewellery from amber, a semi-precious fossilized resin found in abundance along the Baltic coast.

HISTORY AND POLITICS

From 1988 it was Lithuania which led the 'Balts' in their drive to shed Communism and regain their nationhood; in March 1990 it became the first of the 15 constituent Soviet republics to declare itself an independent, non-Communist country, resulting in the occupation of much of its capital by Soviet troops and an economic blockade not suffered by the other states of the Union. The successful crusade was led by the emotional president, Vytautas Landsbergis, whose crucial role in the process of 'deconstruction' – and that of his people – was somewhat overshadowed by the figure of Boris Yeltsin and the mighty Russian Federation.

After independence, Lithuania faced numerous problems as it sought to change its Communist-run economy into a private enterprise one. In 1992, the Democratic Labour Party, containing many ex-Communists, won a general election, and in 1993 Algirdas Brazauskas, a former Communist Party chairman, became president. However, Lithuania's strongest links were with Western Europe and finally, in 1993, the last Soviet troops withdrew from the country.

While Lithuania, in concert with the other Baltic states, seeks to establish closer ties with the rest of Europe – a US$2.5 billion highway is planned, linking the three capitals with Warsaw – it also has simmering ethnic problems of its own. Its significant Polish population, largely self-governing under the Soviets, now fear 'Lithuanization', while the majority resent the pro-Union stance taken by Poles and Russians during their fight for freedom. [*Map page 13*] ∎

AREA 65,200 sq km [25,200 sq mls]
POPULATION 3,706,000
CAPITAL (POPULATION) Vilnius (593,000)
GOVERNMENT Multiparty republic
ETHNIC GROUPS Lithuanian 80%, Russian 9%, Polish 7%, Belarussian 2%
LANGUAGES Lithuanian (official)
RELIGIONS Christianity (mainly Roman Catholic)
CURRENCY Litas = 100 centai

LUXEMBOURG

T he Grand Duchy of Luxembourg is one of the smallest and oldest countries in Europe. The north is mountainous, belonging to an upland region which includes the Ardennes in Belgium and Luxembourg, well wooded and famed for its deer and boar. This scenic region contains the country's highest point, at 565 m [1,854 ft] above sea level. The southern two-thirds of Luxembourg is a rolling plateau called the Bon Pays.

Luxembourg has a temperate climate characterized by warm summers and autumns in the south. Winters can sometimes be severe especially in the Ardennes region.

ECONOMY AND RESOURCES
Stock rearing is important, and crops include grains, potatoes, roots and fruit, and vines in the Moselle valley. There is also a prosperous iron and steel industry based on rich iron-ore deposits. Luxembourg also has many high technology industries, producing electronic goods and computers. Other major activities include tourism and financial services.

HISTORY AND POLITICS
Declaring itself a Grand Duchy in 1354, Luxembourg is the only one out of hundreds of independent duchies, which once comprised much of continental Europe, to survive and become a full member of the United Nations.

In 1922, Luxembourg formed an economic union with Belgium, extended in 1944 to include the Netherlands under the composite name of Benelux. Luxembourg is a founder member of NATO (1949) and the EEC (1957), and is perhaps best known to Europeans as the host for the European Investment Bank, the Secretariat of the European Parliament, the European Monetary Co-operation Fund and the Court of the European Communities.

Though Luxembourg's population is barely a thousandth of the EU total, it remains a relatively important player in Western European commerce and politics. [*Map page 11*] ∎

AREA 2,590 sq km [1,000 sq mls]
POPULATION 401,000
CAPITAL (POPULATION) Luxembourg (76,000)
GOVERNMENT Constitutional monarchy (Grand Duchy)
ETHNIC GROUPS Luxembourger 71%, Portuguese 10%, Italian 5%, French 3%, Belgian 3%, German 2%
LANGUAGES Letzeburgish (Luxembourgian – official), French, German
RELIGIONS Christianity
CURRENCY Luxembourg franc = 100 centimes

MACAU

MACEDONIA

Macau (also known as Macao) comprises a peninsula at the head of the Canton (Pearl) River, 64 km [40 mls] west of Hong Kong and connected to China by a narrow isthmus, and the islands of Coloane and Taipa.

One of the principal economic activities is tourism (in 1990 there were nearly 6 million visitors, 81% from Hong Kong), but there is no airport – most visitors arrive via Hong Kong. The territory, with a population that is 98% Chinese, is also heavily reliant on the Chinese mainland for food, water and raw materials. Macau's major industry is textile manufacturing, which accounts for 62% of all exports, but revenue from gambling is also important to the economy.

A Portuguese colony from 1557 and for 200 years one of the great trading centres for silk, gold, spices and opium, Macau was overtaken in importance by Hong Kong in the 19th century. When China re-established diplomatic relations with the colonial power in 1979, the coastal enclave was redefined as 'Chinese territory under Portuguese administration', and in 1987 the powers agreed that the territory will return to China on 20 December 1999 as a Special Administrative Region of that country – an agreement based on the 'one country, two systems' principle used by China and Britain to settle the future of Hong Kong in 1984. Macau will continue to persue capitalist policies after 1999. [*Map page 24*] ■

AREA 16 sq km [6 sq mls]
POPULATION 398,000
CAPITAL (POPULATION) Macau (395,000)
GOVERNMENT Overseas territory of Portugal
ETHNIC GROUPS Chinese 95%, Portuguese 3%
LANGUAGES Cantonese, Portuguese
RELIGIONS Buddhism 45%, Christianity
CURRENCY Pataca = 100 avos

The Former Yugoslav Republic of Macedonia is a country in south-eastern Europe, which was once one of the six republics that made up the former Federal People's Republic of Yugoslavia. Macedonia is landlocked between Albania, Greece and Bulgaria, its northern frontier dangerously contiguous with Serbia's troubled Kosovo region.

Geologically, most of the country forms part of the Balkan Mountains, a well-wooded region of ancient, rounded crystalline rocks. The highest point is Mt Korab, which reaches 2,764 m [9,068 ft] above sea level on the border with Albania. The country suffers periodic earthquakes, the capital Skopje, was devastated as recently as 1963. Most of the country is drained by the River Vardar and its many tributaries. In the south-west, Macedonia shares two large lakes – Ohrid and Prespa – with Albania and Greece.

ECONOMY AND RESOURCES
Already one of the most undeveloped regions of the former Yugoslavia, the new republic has suffered from an economic blockade imposed by Greece. The leading sector of the economy is manufacturing and manufactures dominate the exports. Manufactures include cement, chemicals, iron and steel, textiles and tobacco products. Macedonia mines coal, but it has to import all its oil and natural gas. Chromium, copper, iron ore, lead, manganese, uranium and zinc are also mined.

Agriculture employs under 10% of the population. Major crops include cotton, fruits, maize, tobacco and wheat, and livestock rearing and forestry are also important. The country's farmers fulfil Macedonia's basic food needs.

HISTORY AND POLITICS
Until the 20th century, Macedonia's history was closely tied to that of a larger area, also called Macedonia, which included parts of northern Greece and south-western Bulgaria.

Between the 14th and 19th centuries, Macedonia was ruled by the Turkish Ottoman empire. Between 1912 and 1913, the region was divided between Serbia, which controlled the north and centre, Bulgaria which took a small area in the east, and Greece which gained the south. At the end of World War I (1914–18), Serbian Macedonia became part of the Kingdom of the Serbs, Croats and Slovenes, which was renamed Yugoslavia in 1929. After World War II (1939–45), a Communist government under President Josip Broz Tito took power in Yugoslavia.

Tito died in 1980, and in the early 1990s the country broke up into five separate republics. Macedonia declared its independence in September 1991. Greece, however, objected to the use of the name 'Macedonia' which it considered to be a territorial claim on the Greek province of the same name. It also objected to a symbol on the Macedonian flag, the currency and a reference in the constitution to the desire to reunite the three parts of the old Macedonia.

As a result, Macedonia adopted a new clause in its constitution rejecting any Macedonian claims on Greek territory and, in 1993, the United Nations accepted the new republic as a member under the name of The Former Yugoslav Republic of Macedonia (FYROM). By the end of 1993, all the countries of the European Union, except for Greece, were establishing diplomatic relations with the FYROM. But Greek hostility continued. In early 1994, Greece banned Macedonian use of the Greek port of Thessaloniki, which normally handles 75% of Macedonia's foreign trade and 100% of its vital oil imports. [*Map page 17*] ∎

AREA 24,900 sq km [9,600 sq mls]
POPULATION 2,142,000
CAPITAL (POPULATION) Skopje (563,000)
GOVERNMENT Multiparty republic
ETHNIC GROUPS Macedonian 65%, Albanian 21%, Turkish 5%, Romanian 3%, Serb 2%
LANGUAGES Macedonian
RELIGIONS Christianity (mainly Eastern Orthodox, with Macedonian Orthodox and Roman Catholic communities), Islam
CURRENCY Denar = 100 paras

MADAGASCAR

The world's fourth largest island Madagascar is virtually a semi-continent bigger than France and immensely varied physically, ecologically and culturally. There are extensive rugged areas so that soils are often poor and farming unrewarding, and the coasts are hostile, with little natural shelter. The north and east are hot and wet, and subject to cyclones. The west is drier, and the south and south-west are arid.

Separated from the African mainland for more than 50 million years, Madagascar developed a distinct flora and fauna – over 150,000 plant and animal species are unique to the islands. Before the coming of people some 3,000 years ago, nearly all the island was variously forested, and although up to 90% of it was cleared for agriculture, a strange collection of animals survived in the remnants – among them 40 species of chameleons, pygmy hippos, elephant birds and the renowned lemurs. But with so much of the forest gone, Madagascar is today one of the most eroded places in the world and its unique wildlife is seriously under threat.

ECONOMY AND RESOURCES

Also unique to the island is its mixture of peoples, derived from several continents. Those on the west side are of Bantu origin, drawn from southern Africa via the Comoros Islands 'bridge'. Those of the centre and east (the Merina or Hova people) came first from Indonesia, as early as 2,000 years ago, with later waves arriving during the 7th to 15th centuries. Other Asians followed, all rice growers, reverent to cattle, with language and funeral rites similar to those in South-east Asia. They had a monarchy until French occupation in 1895. In the south, the Betsileo are more mixed Bantu-Indonesian, as are other groups, yet all feel 'Malagasy' rather than African or Asian. Many other immigrant groups, including Europeans, Chinese and Indians, have also settled.

Both landscapes and agriculture (dominant-rice with cattle and pigs) in the central high-nds are south Asian in character; the east ast and northern highlands are more rican, with fallow farming of food crops and ltivation of coffee, sugar, essential oil plants d spices for export – the country produces)% of the world's vanilla. In the dry west and uth nomadic pastoralism is important, and ce is grown by irrigation. Significant minerals e graphite, chromite and mica. Air transport important, with a network of over 60 air-orts and airstrips.

HISTORY AND POLITICS

he government which took power on inde-endence in 1960 continued Madagascar's nks with France, but a resurgence of nation-lism in the 1970s was followed by the emer-ence of Didier Ratsiraka, who seized power in 975 and established a dictatorial one-party ocialist state. Under a new constitution pproved in 1992, Ratsiraka, whose incompe-ence had plunged Madagascar into poverty, vas defeated in elections in 1993 by the oppo-ition leader, Albert Zafy. [*Map page 33*] ■

AREA 587,040 sq km [226,656 sq mls]
POPULATION 14,303,000
CAPITAL (POPULATION) Antananarivo (802,000)
GOVERNMENT Republic
ETHNIC GROUPS Merina 27%, Betsimisaraka 15%, Betsileo 11%, Tsimihety 7%, Sakalava 6%
LANGUAGES Malagasy (official), French, English
RELIGIONS Christianity 51%, traditional beliefs 47%, Islam 2%
CURRENCY Malagasy franc = 100 centimes

MADEIRA

Madeira is the largest of the group of picturesque volcanic islands of that name lying 550 km [350 mls] from the Moroccan coast and 900 km [560 mls] south-west of the Portuguese capital, Lisbon. Porto Santo and the uninhabited Ilhas Selvagens and Desertas complete the group, with a total area of 813 sq km [314 sq mls], of which Madeira itself contributes 745 sq km [288 sq mls].

With a warm temperate climate, adequate rainfall and good soils, Madeira was originally forested, but early settlers cleared the uplands for plantations. Farming is still the main occupation, producing sugar cane, wines, vegetables and both temperate and tropical fruits. The main exports are grapes (mainly for Madeira wine), bananas and sugar. Handi-crafts and, increasingly, tourism are additional sources of revenue.

Known to the Genoese in the 14th century but colonized by the Portuguese from the 15th century onwards, the islands have since 1976 formed an autonomous region of Portugal. [*Map page 32*] ■

AREA 813 sq km [314 sq mls]
POPULATION 253,000
CAPITAL (POPULATION) Funchal (45,000)
GOVERNMENT Portuguese autonomous region
ETHNIC GROUPS Portuguese
LANGUAGES Portuguese
RELIGIONS Christianity (mainly Roman Catholic)
CURRENCY Portuguese currency

MALAWI

The Republic of Malawi is a landlocked country in southern Africa. It includes part of Lake Malawi, which is drained in the south by the River Shire, a tributary of the River Zambezi. Lake Malawi, which is called Lake Nyasa in Tanzania and Mozambique, lies on the floor of the Great African Rift Valley. This huge gash in the Earth's crust extends from Mozambique to south-western Asia. The land is mostly mountainous. The highest peak, Mulanje, reaches 3,000 m [9,843 ft] in the south-east. Malawi's unusual shape (nowhere is it more than 160 km [100 mls] wide) derived from a 19th-century missionaries' and traders' route up the Zambezi, Shire and Lake Nyasa (Malawi).

ECONOMY AND RESOURCES

The country is relatively poor in natural resources, and compared with its neighbours has a high population density, placing excessive pressure on the land. This problem was inflamed during the 1980s, when Malawi became the main host to nearly a million refugees from neighbouring Mozambique, putting an intolerable burden on an already weak economy, despite massive aid packages.

Industrial and urban development are extremely limited. Most of the commercial activity centres on agriculture, which provides over 90% of Malawi's domestic exports. Tea and tobacco, mostly from large estates, are the principal export crops, while basic foodstuffs such as maize are largely derived from small, quasisubsistence peasant holdings which occupy most of the farmland. Malawi has a long history as an exporter of labour migrants, and large numbers of Malawians still work or seek work abroad, notably in South Africa.

HISTORY AND POLITICS

Malawi's recent history has been dominated by one man: Dr Hastings Kumuzu Banda. Already 62 years old, he led the country (formerly Nyasaland) to independence in 1964, and two years later declared a one-party republic with himself as president for life from 1971. His autocratic regime was different from most of black Africa in being conservative and pragmatic, hostile to socialist neighbours but friendly with South Africa.

At first his austerity programme and agricultural policies seemed to have wrought an economic miracle, but the 1980s sealed a swift decline and a return to poverty. As well as a million refugees Malawi faced another immediate problem – the world's worst recorded national incidence of AIDS. Malawi means 'the land lake where the sun is reflected in the water like fire', but the reality for most of the people has been a good deal less romantic.

In June 1993, 63% of voters chose a multiparty system in a referendum, with Dr Banda remaining as president, but in further elections

in May 1994, Banda and his party, the Malawi Congress Party, were defeated. Bakili Muluzi was elected president. [*Map page 33*] ■

AREA 118,480 sq km [45,745 sq mls]
POPULATION 8,823,000
CAPITAL (POPULATION) Lilongwe (223,318)
GOVERNMENT Multiparty republic
ETHNIC GROUPS Maravi (Chewa, Nyanja, Tonga, Tumbuka) 58%, Lomwe 18%, Yao 13%, Ngoni 7%
LANGUAGES Chichewa and English (both official)
RELIGIONS Christianity (Protestant 34%, Roman Catholic 28%), traditional beliefs 21%, Islam 16%
CURRENCY Kwacha = 100 tambala

MALAYSIA

The Malay Peninsula is dominated by folc mountains with a north-south axis. There are seven or eight ranges, with frequently exposed granite cores. The most important is the so-called Main Range, which runs from the Thai border to the south-east of Kuala Lumpur, attaining 2,182 m [7,159 ft] at its highest point, Gunong Kerbau. South of the Main Range lies the flat and poorly drained lowland of Johor, which is punctuated by isolated hills, often rising over 1,060 m [3,500 ft]. The small rivers of Malaya have built up a margin of lowland around the coasts.

Northern Borneo has a mangrove-fringed coastal plain, up to 65 km [40 mls] wide, backed by hill country averaging 300 m [1,000 ft] in height. This is dominated by the east-west fold mountains of the interior, which rise from 1,400 m to 2,300 m [4,500 to 7,500 ft]; the most striking is the granite peak of Mt Kinabalu (4,101 m [13,455 ft]) in Sabah, Malaysia's highest mountain. The natural vegetation of most of Malaysia is lowland rainforest and its montane variants. The Malaysian forests, which are dominated by the dipterocarp family of trees, are the richest in

ecies of all the world's forests. Unfortu-
tely, few undisturbed areas remain, mostly
such national parks such as the Gunong
ulu in Sarawak and the Kinabalu in Sabah.

CONOMY AND RESOURCES

he traditional mainstays of the economy –
ce, plus exports of rubber, palm oil and tin
Malaysia is among the world's biggest pro-
ucers of all three) – have been supplemented
y exploitation of other natural resources,
otably oil and timber, though the pace of the
tter is causing widespread unrest among
vironmentalists. Exports are now safely
verse, from Sarawak's pepper to the new
roton 'national car', and with a growing
ourist industry in support, Malaysia seems set
join Japan and the four 'little dragons' as a
ccess story of postwar eastern Asia.

HISTORY AND POLITICS

he new country of Malaysia was born in
963 by the joining of the Federation of
Malaya (independent from Britain since
957), the island state of Singapore and the
olonies of Sarawak and North Borneo
renamed Sabah). In 1965 Singapore seceded
o become an independent nation, and the
resent federation comprises 11 states and a
ederal territory (Kuala Lumpur) on the
Malay Peninsula, and two states and a federal
erritory (Labuan) in northern Borneo. The
egions are separated by some 650 km
400 mls] of the South China Sea.

An early golden age of Malay political
ower came in the 15th century with the rise
of the kingdom of Malacca, which controlled
he important sea routes and trade of the
region. In 1414, the ruler of Malacca accepted
he Islamic faith, which remains the official
religion of Malaysia today. The country is,
however, characterized by great ethnic, religious and cultural diversity, with Malays of
many different origins, Chinese and Indians
(mainly brought in by the British to work the
tin mines and rubber plantations), Eurasians,
Europeans and a number of aboriginal peoples, notably in Sabah and Sarawak.

This patchwork has caused tensions, particularly between the politically dominant
Muslim Malays and the economically dominant, mainly Buddhist, Chinese, but while

riots did break out in 1969, it has never escalated into serious armed conflict; nor has it
prevented remarkable economic growth that
has, according to World Bank ratings, made
Malaysia an upper middle-income country. By
the early 1990s, it was playing a leading role in
regional affairs, especially through its membership of ASEAN (Association of South-east
Asian Nations). [*Map page 26*] ■

AREA 329,750 sq km [127,316 sq mls]
POPULATION 19,695,000
CAPITAL (POPULATION) Kuala Lumpur
(938,000)
GOVERNMENT Federal constitutional
monarchy
ETHNIC GROUPS Malay and other indigenous
groups 62%, Chinese 30%, Indian 8%
LANGUAGES Malay (official)
RELIGIONS Islam 53%, Buddhism 17%,
Chinese folk religionist 12%, Hinduism 7%,
Christianity 6%
CURRENCY Ringgit (Malaysian dollar) = 100
cents

MALDIVES

The archipelago of the Maldives comprises
over 1,190 small low-lying islands and
atolls (202 of them inhabited), scattered along
a broad north-south line starting 650 km
[400 mls] west-south-west of Cape Comorin.
Coral reefs, probably built on a foundation of
extinct submarine volcanoes, the Maldives are
strategically significant as mid-ocean islands.
Adequately watered and covered with tropical
vegetation, the islands' crops are coconuts,
bananas, mangoes, sweet potatoes and spices,
but much food is imported – as are nearly all
capital and consumer goods. Fish are plentiful
in lagoons and open sea; bonito and tuna are
leading exports together with copra and coir.
Tourism, however, has now displaced fishing
as the mainstay of the economy, though its
future depends much on political stability.

The islands were settled from Sri Lanka

about 500 BC. For a time under Portuguese and later Dutch rule, they became a British protectorate in 1887, administered from Ceylon but retaining local sultanates. Independence was granted in 1965, and the last sultan deposed in 1968. A coup against the authoritarian nationalist government was put down with Indian troops in 1988. [*Map page 3*] ■

AREA 298 sq km [115 sq mls]
POPULATION 246,000
CAPITAL (POPULATION) Malé (55,130)
GOVERNMENT Republic
ETHNIC GROUPS Mixture of Sinhalese, Indian and Arab
LANGUAGES Divehi (Sinhala dialect)
RELIGIONS Islam
CURRENCY Rufiyaa = 100 laaris

MALI

The Republic of Mali is a landlocked country in northern Africa. The land is generally flat, with the highest land in the Adrar des Iforhas on the border with Algeria. This highland region in the northern desert contains many wadis (dry valleys), where rivers once flowed. But today, the only permanent rivers and streams are in the south. The main rivers are the Sénégal, which flows westwards to the Atlantic Ocean, and the Niger, which makes a large turn, called the Niger Bend, in south-central Mali.

Northern Mali is part of the Sahara, with a hot, practically rainless climate, but the south has enough rain for farming. The dry grasslands in central and south-eastern Mali are part of a region called the Sahel. During long droughts, the northern Sahel dries up and becomes part of the Sahara. Southern Mali, which is covered by savanna, is the most densely populated part of the country.

ECONOMY AND RESOURCES

Water (or the lack of it) dominates the life of the people and most of the country's population is concentrated along the Sénégal and Niger rivers, which provide water for stock and irrigation and serve as much-needed communication routes. The Niger and its tributaries support a fishing industry that exports dried fish to neighbouring Ivory Coast, Burkina Faso and Ghana.

With the exception of small areas in the south of the country, irrigation is necessary for all arable crops. The savanna grasslands and highland areas in the Sahelian south-east are free of tsetse fly (carrier of sleeping sickness) and large numbers of sheep and cattle are traditionally kept in the area, though grazing lands have been decimated by a series of catastrophic droughts. Northern Mali is entirely poor desert, inhabited only by Tuareg and Fulani nomads.

Millet, cotton and groundnuts are important crops on the unirrigated lands of the south, while rice is intensively grown with irrigation. A large irrigation scheme has been developed near Ségou which produces rice, cotton and sugar cane, and there are many other smaller schemes. Industry is confined mainly to one commercial gold mine, salt production and embryonic manufacturing – shoes, textiles, beer and matches.

HISTORY AND POLITICS

In the 14th century it was the centre of a huge West African Malinka empire based on the legendary city of Timbuktu (Tombouctou). A French colony between 1893 and 1960, Mali was then governed by a radical Socialist government for the first eight years of independence, before this was overthrown by a bloodless coup under General Moussa Traoré. His repressive military, single-party regime did little for the country – despite successful pressure from aid donor nations to liberalize the planned economy – and in 1987 the World Bank classified Mali as the world's fourth poorest country; they were still in the bottom 20 in 1993. In 1985 the government had been involved in a border dispute with neighbouring Burkina Faso; the International Court of Justice finally granted Mali 40% of its claimed land.

Student-led protests finally ended Traoré's 23-year reign in 1991. Following a referendum in 1992, elections were held, in which Alphar umar Konare became Mali's first democrat-ally elected president. [*Map page 32*] ■

AREA 1,240,190 sq km [478,837 sq mls]
POPULATION 10,462,000
CAPITAL (POPULATION) Bamako (646,000)
GOVERNMENT Multiparty republic
ETHNIC GROUPS Bambara 32%, Fulani (or Peul) 14%, Senufo 12%, Soninké 9%, Tuareg 7%, Songhai 7%, Malinké (Mandingo or Mandinke) 7%
LANGUAGES French (official)
RELIGIONS Islam 90%, traditional beliefs 9%, Christianity 1%
CURRENCY CFA franc = 100 centimes

MALTA

M alta lies in the centre of the Med-iterranean, roughly halfway between Gibraltar and Suez, 93 km [58 mls] south of Sicily and 290 km [180 mls] from North Africa. Its strategic importance arises from its position, and from its possession of magnifi-cent natural harbours – notable among them Grand Harbour and Marsamxett; these lie on either side of the rocky peninsula on which stands the capital, Valletta.

ECONOMY AND RESOURCES

Malta and the neighbouring islands of Comino and Gozo have few natural resources (apart from splendid building stone), and with no rivers and sparse rainfall there are only limited possibilities for agriculture. Yet they constitute one of the world's most densely populated states, with two-thirds of the people living in the 'conurbation' of districts around Valletta. The native islanders are of mixed Arab, Sicilian, Norman, Spanish, English and Italian origin. Maltese and English are spoken, the former universally, although it was not written until the present century.

From the Napoleonic period until after World War II, the Maltese economy depend-ed on agriculture (which still involves nearly

half the workforce), and the existence of British military bases. Before the last garrison left in 1979 Malta had already obtained inde-pendence, and was developing export-oriented industries and 'offshore' business facilities that would replace the income from the military and naval connections. Germany became its chief trading partner ahead of the UK and Italy, though Libya supplies most of its oil.

Year-round tourism, taking advantage of the mild Mediterranean winters and the hot, dry summers, brings over a million visitors annually, of whom 50% are British. The skill of the dockyard workers is still world-famous, however, and with help from overseas, Malta is developing a new port, wharf and storage facilities. The other main industries include electronics, textiles, foodstuffs and clothing.

HISTORY AND POLITICS

A former British colony, Malta became inde-pendent in 1964, and in 1974 it became a republic. In 1979, Britain's military agreement with Malta expired and it ceased to be a military base when all British forces withdrew. In the 1980s, the Maltese people declared their country to be neutral. But in the 1990s, Malta applied to join the EU. [*Map page 4*] ■

AREA 316 sq km [122 sq mls]
POPULATION 364,000
CAPITAL (POPULATION) Valletta (102,000)
GOVERNMENT Multiparty republic
ETHNIC GROUPS Maltese 96%, British 2%
LANGUAGES Maltese and English (both official)
RELIGIONS Christianity (Roman Catholic 99%)
CURRENCY Maltese lira = 100 cents

MARSHALL ISLANDS

T he country comprises over 1,250 islands and atolls – including the former US nuclear testing sites of Bikini and Enewetak – totalling just 181 sq km [70 sq mls]. The pop-ulation, mainly Micronesian, Protestant and

English-speaking, is 52,000, with nearly half living in the capital of Dalap-Uliga-Darrit on Majuro island.

The economy, based on agriculture and tourism, is very heavily supported by aid from the US, which still retains a missile site on the largest island, Kwajalein. Self-governing since 1979, the Marshall Islands became a republic 'in free association with the USA' in 1986, moving from Trust Territory status to a sovereign state responsible for its own foreign policy, but not (until 2001) for its own defence and security. [*Map page 3*] ∎

AREA 181 sq km [70 sq mls]
POPULATION 52,000
CAPITAL (POPULATION) Dalap-Uliga-Darrit (20,000)
GOVERNMENT Republic 'in free association with the USA'
ETHNIC GROUPS Micronesian
LANGUAGES English, Marshallese dialects, Japanese
RELIGIONS Christianity (mainly Protestant)
CURRENCY US currency

MARTINIQUE

Martinique comprises three groups of volcanic hills and the intervening lowlands. The highest peak is Mt Pelée (1,397 m [4,583 ft]), notorious for its eruption of 1902, when in minutes it killed all the inhabitants of St Pierre (estimated at about 28,000) except one – a prisoner who was saved by the thickness of his cell.

ECONOMY AND RESOURCES
Bananas, rum and pineapples are the main agricultural exports, but tourism (mainly French and American) is the biggest earner; transport equipment and food, chiefly from France, are the main imports. The industrial sector includes cement, food processing and oil refining, using Venezuelan crude; oil products account for 14% of exports. French

government expenditure is higher than on Guadeloupe, at some 70% of GDP, helping provide jobs and retain a better standard of living than its northern compatriot.

HISTORY AND POLITICS
Martinique was 'discovered' by Columbus in 1493, colonized by France from 1635 and apart from brief British interludes, has been French ever since. It became an oversea department in 1946 – with the same status and representation as *départements* – and was made an administrative region in 1974. The island has a less vociferous independence movement than Guadeloupe – though in the 1991 elections the separatists made substantial gains, winning 19 of the 41 seats. [*Map page 30*] ∎

AREA 1,100 sq km [425 sq mls]
POPULATION 375,000
CAPITAL (POPULATION) Fort-de-France (100,000)
GOVERNMENT Overseas department of France
ETHNIC GROUPS Of African descent, Mixed, White
LANGUAGES French, Creole patois
RELIGIONS Christianity (mainly Roman Catholic)
CURRENCY French currency

MAURITANIA

The Islamic Republic of Mauritania in north-western Africa is nearly twice the size of France – but France has more than 26 times as many people. Part of the world's largest desert, the Sahara, covers northern Mauritania and most Mauritanians live in the south-east. The land is mostly flat or gently rolling, with low rocky plateaux and areas of drifting sand dunes in the interior. The highest point, Kediet Ijill, reaches 915 m [3,002 ft] above sea level and is rich in the mineral haematite (an iron ore).

The amount of rain and the length of the

ny season increase from north to south. uch of the land is desert, with dry north-east d easterly winds throughout the year. In the mmer, south-westerly winds bring rain to e south of the country.

Savanna vegetation characterizes the far uth. Here, such trees as baobabs and palms ot the landscape. To the north, the savanna erges into the dry grasslands of the Sahel, here trees are rare. But most of Mauritania is esert and plants grow only around oases or in adis (dry valleys) beneath which some water ontinues to flow.

CONOMY AND RESOURCES

part from oasis settlements such as Atar and idjikdja, the only permanent arable agricul-ure is in the south, concentrated in a narrow rip along the Sénégal River. Crops of millet, orghum, beans, peanuts and rice are grown, ften using the natural late-summer floods for rigation. When the Sénégal River Project is omplete, large areas should be developed for rigated crops of rice, cotton and sugar cane.

Many people are still cattle herders who rive their herds from the Sénégal River hrough the Sahel steppelands in tandem with he seasonal rains. In good years the country's ivestock outnumber the human population by bout five to one, but the ravages of drought nd the development of the mining industries n the 1980s – allied to traditional overgrazing - have reduced the nomadic population from hree-quarters to less than a third of the national total.

Off the Atlantic coast, the cold Canaries Current is associated with some of the richest ishing grounds in the world. The national ishing industry is still evolving and over 100,000 tonnes of fish are landed and processed each year, mainly at the major fish-ing port of Nouadhibou (Port Étienne); the potential catch is estimated at 600,000 tonnes.

As the Atlantic coast in the south of the country lacks good harbours, a port and capi-tal city have been constructed at Nouakchott. This now handles a growing proportion of the country's trade, including exports of copper mined near Akjoujt. Exported minerals, particularly high-grade iron ores, worked from the vast reserves around Fdérik, provide the country with most of its foreign revenue,

though animal products, gum arabic and dates are also among the exports. Apart from the main north-south highway and routes associ-ated with mineral developments, land commu-nications consist of rough tracks.

HISTORY AND POLITICS

From the 4th to the 16th centuries, parts of Mauritania belonged to two great African empires – ancient Ghana and Mali. Portu-guese explorers arrived in the 1440s but European contact did not begin in the area until the 17th century when trade in gum arabic, a substance obtained from the acacia tree, became important.

France set up a protectorate in Mauritania in 1903 and the country became a territory of French West Africa and a French colony in 1920. French West Africa was a huge territo-ry, which included present-day Benin, Burkina Faso, Guinea, Ivory Coast, Mali, Niger and Senegal, as well as Mauritania. In 1958, Mauritania became a self-governing territory in the French Union and it became fully inde-pendent in 1960.

In 1961, Mauritania's political parties were merged into one by the president, Mokhtar Ould Daddah, who made the country a one-party state in 1965. In 1976, Spain withdrew from Spanish (now Western) Sahara, a territory bordering Mauritania to the north. Morocco occupied the northern two-thirds of this territory, while Mauritania took the rest. But Saharan guerrillas belonging to POLISARIO (the Popular Front for the Liberation of Saharan Territories) began an armed struggle for independence. In 1978, military leaders overthrew Ould Daddah and set up a military regime.

The rulers in Nouakchott surrendered their claims to the southern part of the Western Sahara in 1979. The following year slavery was formally abolished – though some estimates put the number of 'Haratines' (descendants of black slaves) still in bondage as high as 100,000. Unlike several of the former colonial territories of West and Central Africa, Mauritania was not affected by the wave of democratization that toppled military and single-party regimes from the late 1980s. However, in 1991, the country adopted a new constitution when the people voted to create a multiparty government. Multiparty elections, held in 1992, were won by Maaouiya Sidi Ahmed Taya, former president of the military government. [*Map page 32*] ■

AREA 1,025,220 sq km [395,593 sq mls]
POPULATION 2,217,000
CAPITAL (POPULATION) Nouakchott (393,000)
GOVERNMENT Multiparty Islamic republic
ETHNIC GROUPS Moor (Arab-Berber) 70%, Wolof 7%, Tukulor 5%, Soninke 3%, Fulani 1%
LANGUAGES Arabic and French (both official)
RELIGIONS Islam 99%
CURRENCY Ouguiya = 5 khoums

MAURITIUS

M auritius consists of the main island, Rodruigues (formerly a dependency), situated 800 km [500 mls] to the east of Madagascar, 20 nearby islets and the dependencies of the Agalega Islands and the tiny Cargados Carajas shoals (St Brandon). The beautiful main island, fringed with coral reefs, rises to a high lava plateau. Good rainfall (up to 5,000 mm [200 in] a year) and steep slopes have combined to give fast-flowing rivers, now harnessed for limited hydroelectric power.

Similar to Réunion in climate and soils, its vast plantations produce sugar cane (now declining but with derivatives like molasses still accounting for over 40% of exports), tea and tobacco, while home consumption centres around livestock and vegetables. To some extent the decline in sugar has been offset by the growth in tourism (374,600 visitors in 1993) and the expansion of textiles and clothing (nearly half of exports), especially woollen knitwear.

French from 1715 and British from 1810, the colony gained independence within the Commonwealth in 1968. The islands suffer from increasing tensions between the Indian majority – descended from contract workers

brought in to tend the plantations after the en of slavery in 1834 – and the Creole (mixe Afro-French) minority. The country became republic in March 1992. [*Map page 3*] ■

AREA 1,860 sq km [718 sq mls]
POPULATION 1,104,000
CAPITAL (POPULATION) Port Louis (144,000)
GOVERNMENT Republic
ETHNIC GROUPS Indian 56%, Creole 30%, European 4%
LANGUAGES English, Creole, French
RELIGIONS Hinduism 52%, Christianity 26%, Islam
CURRENCY Mauritius rupee = 100 cents

MEXICO

M exico is a land of great physical variety The northern, emptier, half is open basin-and-range country of the Mesa Central The land rises southwards from the Ric Grande (Rio Bravo del Norte) at the US border, averaging about 2,600 m [8,500 ft] above sea level in the middle, where it is crowned by many snow-capped volcanic cones, Orizaba (5,750 m [18,865 ft]) in the east being the highest. Though an active earth-quake zone, this is the most densely settled part of the country. The Mesa Central ends equally dramatically in the west, where the Sierra Madre Occidental rise to over 4,000 m [13,120 ft], and in the east, where the Sierra Madre Oriental form a backcloth to the modest coastal plain bordering the Gulf of Mexico. In the far north-west is the isolated, 1,220 km [760 ml] mountain-cored peninsula of Baja California.

Mountains dominate southern Mexico, broken only by the low, narrow isthmus of Tehuantepec, which is crossed by railways and roads linking the Gulf ports with Salina Cruz on the Pacific. The flat, low-lying limestone Yucatan peninsula in the south-east is an exception in a country where half the land is ver 1,000 m [3,280 ft] above sea level, and a quarter has slopes of over 25 degrees. Deserts characterize the north-west of the country and tropical rainforest is the natural vegetation of the Tehuantepec region; over 70% of the country is arid or semi-arid and irrigation is mandatory for agriculture.

ECONOMY AND RESOURCES

Agriculture occupies half the population but contributes less than a third of the economic product contributed by manufacturing, with metals also important. Fresh petroleum discoveries during the 1970s from massive reserves in Tabasco and Campeche have turned Mexico into the world's fourth biggest producer, much of it exported to the USA, but the economy is now very diverse with food processing, textiles, forestry and tourism all making significant progress. Only an estimated 15–20% of the nation's mineral wealth has been exploited, with precious metals comprising almost half the value of the total known mineral reserves.

The world's largest and most populous Spanish-speaking nation, Mexico has a faster-growing population than any other big country: between 1960 and 1980 it doubled, growing at an unprecedented 3.5% a year. It is thus an astonishingly young society; the average Mexican is a 17-year-old, and 75% of the people are under 30.

The combination of a stable and very high birth rate (now about 27 per thousand) and a declining and now low death rate (about five per thousand) is the main cause of this population explosion. Mexico City (population 1 million in 1930, 8.7 million in 1970, 15.0 million in 1990) is already the most populous in the Americas and estimated to be the world's largest by 2000, overtaking both Tokyo and São Paulo.

HISTORY AND POLITICS

While the century after independence in 1821 was characterized by political chaos, climaxing in the violent revolution of 1910–21, the post-revolutionary period was steady by Latin American standards, with the PRI in power for more than six decades from 1929 and instituting crucial land reforms in the 1930s. The economy has been dominated by this regime

PRE-COLUMBIAN CIVILIZATIONS

The pre-Columbian civilizations of Central America flourished for centuries before the Spanish conquest and this heritage plays a strong role in fostering Mexican national identity today.

The Olmecs, the classical cultures of Teotihuacan, the Zapotecs and the Toltecs all left remarkable architectural monuments in the Mexican landscape, but the two outstanding cultures were those of the Maya and the Aztecs. The Maya civilization was the most brilliant, flourishing from the 3rd to the 10th centuries in an area extending from the Yucatan peninsula to Honduras. The Maya were mathematically advanced and had a sophisticated calendar.

The Aztec empire was at its height when Mexico succumbed to the Spanish *conquistadores* in 1519. Originally an insignificantly nomadic tribe, the Aztecs invaded the settled lands of central Mexico in the 13th century and founded their island-city of Tenochtitlán in Lake Texcoco in 1325. During the 15th century they conquered neighbouring states and drew tribute from an empire which extended from the Pacific to the Gulf of Mexico and into northern Central America.

Many of the great pre-Columbian centres survive as archaeological sites today. The stepped pyramid, the rectangular courtyard and the symbolic ornamental masonry are particularly characteristic of the architecture.

since oil was nationalized in 1938, enjoying huge growth in the 1970s, when living standards rose considerably, but running into massive debt crises in the 1980s.

Mexico has since pursued the idea of a trading area with Canada and the US, but rural-urban migration and high unemployment remain the biggest domestic problems. Above all, there is the emigration across the world's busiest border: hundreds of thousands of Mexicans cross into the USA each year, many of them staying as illegal immigrants. In June 1993 Mexico joined the OECD, the first new member for some 20 years, and negotiated an economic alliance called NAFTA (North

American Free Trade Agreement) with the United States and Canada, which took effect on 1 January 1994. [*Map page 30*] ■

AREA 1,958,200 sq km [756,061 sq mls]
POPULATION 91,858,000
CAPITAL (POPULATION) Mexico City (15,048,000)
GOVERNMENT Federal republic
ETHNIC GROUPS Mestizo 60%, Amerindian 30%, European 9%
LANGUAGES Spanish (official)
RELIGIONS Christianity (Roman Catholic 90%, Protestant 5%)
CURRENCY Peso = 100 centavos

the USA' – they had been a US Trust Territory since 1947 – and were formally admitted as an independent member of the UN in September 1991. [*Map page 26*] ■

AREA 705 sq km [272 sq mls]
POPULATION 121,000
CAPITAL (POPULATION) Palikir (Pohnpei Island = 33,000)
GOVERNMENT Federal republic
ETHNIC GROUPS Micronesian, Polynesian
LANGUAGES English, local languages
RELIGIONS Christianity
CURRENCY US currency

MICRONESIA

MOLDOVA

Comprising the bulk of the Carolines, the Federation – despite a land area of just 705 sq km [272 sq mls] – stretches across more than 3,200 km [2,000 mls] of Pacific, with the Equator as the southern boundary. The 607 islands divide into four groups and range from mountains to low atolls. Over half the land area is contributed by the main island, Pohnpei, on which Palikir is situated.

The cultures of the 'FSM', both Micronesian and Polynesian, are diverse, and four main languages are spoken in line with the four states of Yap, Truk, Pohnpei and Kosrae – though English is official.

ECONOMY AND RESOURCES
While some areas are highly Americanized, the traditional way of life has survived in others, based on subsistence farming and fishing. Copra is the main crop and phosphate is also exported, while tuna-fishing brings in revenue from American, Japanese and Korean fleets. The FSM remains heavily dependent on US aid however.

HISTORY AND POLITICS
The FSM became a sovereign state in 1986, when they entered into 'free association with

The Republic of Moldova, or Moldavia as it is also called, is a small country sandwiched between Ukraine and Romania. It was formerly one of the 15 republics that made up the Soviet Union. Much of the land is hilly and the highest areas are near the centre of the country, where the highest point, 429 m [1,407 ft] above sea level, is situated. A large plain covers southern Moldova. The main river is the Dniester (Dnestr or Nistru), which flows through the eastern part of the country.

Moldova has warm summers and fairly cold winters, when temperatures dip below freezing point. Forests of hornbeam, oak and other trees grow in the north and centre of the country, and in the drier south the land was originally grassy steppe, though most of this region is now used for farming. Rich pasture lies along the rivers.

ECONOMY AND RESOURCES
Though barred from the Black Sea by an arm of the Ukraine, Moldova is well off. Fertile lands and a tolerant climate provide vines, tobacco and honey as well as more conventional produce, while light industry – based mainly on food processing and household appliances – is expanding. Moldova has no major natural resources and imports materials

d fuels for its industries. Exports include
od, wine, tobacco, textiles and footwear.

▄STORY AND POLITICS
▄ the 14th century, the Moldovans formed a
▄ate called Moldavia, which included parts of
▄omania and Bessarabia. The Ottoman Turks
▄ok the area in the 16th century, but in 1812
▄ussia took over Bessarabia. In 1861,
▄loldavia and Walachia united to form
▄omania. Russia retook southern Bessarabia
▄ 1878.

After World War I (1914–18), all of
▄essarabia was returned to Romania, but the
▄oviet Union did not recognize this act. From
▄944, the Moldovan Soviet Socialist Republic
▄as part of the Soviet Union. In 1989, the
▄loldovans asserted their independence by
▄aking Romanian the official language and, at
▄he end of 1991, when the Soviet Union broke
▄p, Moldova became an independent country.
▄n 1992, however, fighting occurred between
▄loldovans and Russians in Trans-Dniester,
▄he land east of the River Dniester .

Moldova held its first multiparty elections in
▄994. The people also rejected a proposal to
▄nite with Romania. [*Map page 17*] ■

AREA 33,700 sq km [13,010 sq mls]
POPULATION 4,420,000
CAPITAL (POPULATION) Chişinau (or
Kishinev, 667,000)
GOVERNMENT Multiparty republic
ETHNIC GROUPS Moldovan 65%, Ukrainian
14%, Russian 13%, Gagauzi 4%, Jewish 2%,
Bulgarian
LANGUAGES Moldovan (Romanian) – official
RELIGIONS Christianity (Eastern Orthodox)
CURRENCY Leu = 100 bani

increased in size by 20% since its land
reclamation programme began in 1958.
Monaco falls into four districts: vacation-
oriented Monte Carlo; the old town of
Monaco-Ville, with the royal palace and
cathedral; the shops, banks and smart houses
of La Condamine; and the light industries and
marinas of Fontvieille.

A densely populated city-state, Monaco
derives its considerable income almost entirely from services: banking, finance, and above
all tourism; this is based not just on its climate
but also on the famous casino. Monégasques
are not allowed to gamble there, but there is
ample compensation in paying no state taxes.

Monaco has been ruled by the Grimaldi
dynasty since 1297, though in 1815 (with the
Treaty of Vienna) it came under the protection of the kingdom of Sardinia; the greater
part, including Menton, was annexed by
France in 1848 and the remainder came under
its protection in 1861 – a situation that essentially survives today within a customs union.
The present monarch, Prince Rainer III
(ascended 1949), drew up a new liberalizing
constitution in 1962. [*Map page 11*] ■

AREA 1.5 sq km [0.6 sq mls]
POPULATION 31,000
CAPITAL (POPULATION) Monaco (31,000)
GOVERNMENT Constitutional monarchy
under French protection
ETHNIC GROUPS French 47%, Monégasque
16%, Italian 16%
LANGUAGES French, Monégasque
RELIGIONS Christianity (mainly Roman
Catholic)
CURRENCY French currency

MONACO

MONGOLIA

The world's smallest nation outside Rome,
and by far its most crowded, the tiny
principality of Monaco – comprising a rocky
peninsula and a narrow stretch of coast – has

Worthy of its harsh, isolated reputation,
Mongolia is the world's largest landlocked country and the most sparsely populated. Despite its traditional nomads, more than
half the population live in towns, a quarter of

them in Ulan Bator, a modern city built in the postwar Soviet mould. Geographically Mongolia divides into two contrasting regions, north and south of a line joining the mountains of the Altai, Hangayn and Hentiyn ranges.

In the north, pastures support herds of cattle and wheat is grown, especially where black earth soils occur. In the far north-west, boreal forests blanket the slopes. The southern half of the country has a strong continental climate with meagre, variable rainfall. In these semi-desert steppelands, salt lakes occupy shallow depressions, poor scrub eventually giving way to the arid wastes of the Gobi Desert.

ECONOMY AND RESOURCES
Mongolia is a land of nomadic pastoralists – less than 1% of the land is cultivated – and huge herds of sheep, goats, yaks, camels and horses form the mainstay of the traditional economy. Herdsmen's families inhabit *ghers* (*yurts*), circular tents covered in felt, and subsist on a diet of milk, cheese and mutton.

Textiles and food processing were developed, with aid from the USSR and COMECON, and mineral deposits such as flourspar, copper, molybdenum and coking coal were exploited. In the late 1980s minerals overtook the agricultural sector as the country's main source of income.

HISTORY AND POLITICS
Outer Mongolia broke away from China following the collapse of the Ch'ing dynasty in 1911, but full independence was not gained until 1921 – with Soviet support in what was the world's second Socialist revolution. In 1924 a Communist People's Republic was proclaimed and the country fell increasingly under Soviet influence.

In recent years, Mongolia has followed the path of other less remote Soviet satellites, reducing the presence of Soviet troops (1987–9), introducing pluralism (the country's first multiparty elections were held in 1990), launching into privatization and a free-market economy in 1991, and early in 1992 adopting a new constitution eschewing Communism and enshrining democracy. In June 1993, Mongolians voted in their first direct presidential election, electing Pun Salmaagiyn

Ochirbat as president. The pace of change was frantic after seven decades of authoritarian rule – Mongolia still owes Moscow $15 billion – and like the newly independent republics of the former Soviet empire, the Mongolians will not find the transition easy. [*Map page 21*] ∎

AREA 1,566,500 sq km [604,826 sq mls]
POPULATION 2,363,000
CAPITAL (POPULATION) Ulan Bator (575,000)
GOVERNMENT Multiparty republic
ETHNIC GROUPS Khalkha Mongol 79%, Kazakh 6%
LANGUAGES Khalkha Mongolian (official)
RELIGIONS Lamaistic Buddhism was once the main religion; reliable recent information is unavailable
CURRENCY Tugrik = 100 möngös

MONTSERRAT

The Emerald Isle, as it is also known, lies 43 km [26.7 mls] south-west of Antigua. Although tourism is the mainstay of the island's economy (25% of national income), it is well supported by exports of electronic equipment, Sea Island cotton, fruit and vegetables; unusually for the Caribbean, Montserrat is almost self-sufficient in food. Discovered by Columbus in 1493 and colonized from 1632 by Britain, which brought in Irish settlers, Montserrat (though still a UK dependent territory) has been self-governing since 1960 ∎

AREA 102 sq km [39 sq mls]
POPULATION 11,000
CAPITAL (POPULATION) Plymouth (3,500)
GOVERNMENT Dependent territory of the UK
ETHNIC GROUPS Black, European
LANGUAGES English
RELIGIONS Christianity
CURRENCY East Caribbean dollar = 100 cents

MOROCCO

More than a third of Morocco is mountainous. The High (*Haut*) Atlas contains the highest peak, Djebel Toubkal, at 4,165 m [13,665 ft]. Other ranges include the Anti Atlas in the south, the Middle (*Moyen*) Atlas, and the Rif Atlas (*Er Rif*) in the far north. Between the Atlas Mountains and the narrow western coastal plain lies a broad plateau. There are fertile plains in the west and south-west, while in the south-east the country extends into the Sahara Desert. The Sahara region is barren, but cedars, firs and junipers swathe the mountain slopes.

The Atlantic coast of Morocco is cooled by the Canaries Current. Inland, summers are hot and dry, and winters are mild. In winter, between October and April, south-westerlies from the Atlantic bring moderate rainfall, and snow often falls on the High Atlas Mountains.

ECONOMY AND RESOURCES

Since independence a large proportion of the once-important European and Jewish communities have departed. To the difficulties accompanying reunification were added the burdens of a fast-growing population – nearly half the people are under 15 years old – high unemployment and a lack of trained personnel and capital. Yet Morocco has considerable potential for economic development: the country possesses large cultivable areas, abundant water supplies for irrigation and hydro-electric power, and diverse mineral resources including deposits of iron ore, lead and zinc.

Two principal ways of life exist in the mountains – peasant cultivation and semi-nomadic pastoralism. In contrast to these, modern economic development is found in the Atlantic plains and plateaux. The major irrigation schemes created during the colonial period are situated here, resulting in the intensive agricultural production of citrus fruits, grapes, vegetables, wheat and barley. More than half of the population is involved in agriculture.

Phosphates, of which Morocco is the world's leading exporter and third largest producer, are mined around Khouribga as well as in Western Sahara. These are the vital raw material for fertilizers. But the country's modern industry is concentrated in the Atlantic ports, particularly in Casablanca, which is the largest city, chief port and the major manufacturing centre.

The biggest growth industry, however, is tourism, based on the Atlantic beaches, the Atlas Mountains and the rich, international history of cities like Casablanca, Tangier, Agadir, Marrakech, Rabat and Fès (Fez), famed not only for its hat but also as the home of the University of Kairaouin – founded in 859 and the oldest educational institution in the world. Morocco is Africa's biggest tourist destination, attracting more than 3.2 million visitors in 1991.

HISTORY AND POLITICS

The name Morocco is derived from the Arabic *Maghreb-el-Aksa* ('the farthest west'). Over the centuries the country's high mountains have acted as a barrier to penetration, so that Morocco has been much less affected by outside influences than Algeria and Tunisia. Morocco was the last North African territory to succumb to European colonialism; not until 1912 did the Sultan of Morocco accept the French protectorate, in a settlement that gave Spain control of the Rif Mountains and several enclaves along the coast (of which Ceuta and Melilla remain under Spanish administration).

In 1956 France and Spain gave up their protectorate as Morocco became independent, and in 1958 the international zone of Tangier was incorporated in a unified Morocco, which became an independent kingdom. Ruled since 1961 by the authoritarian and nationalistic regime of King Hassan II, Morocco is today one of only three kingdoms left on the continent of Africa, though the king's grip showed signs of slipping during the unsettled 1980s. He has pressed Morocco's claims for Western Sahara, but the cost of the struggle to contain the Saharan nationalist guerrillas has drained the country's resources.

Western Sahara is a former Spanish possession (and the province of Spanish Sahara from

1960) occupying the desert lands between Mauritania and the Atlantic coast; with an area of 266,000 sq km [102,700 sq mls] it is more than half the size of Morocco. Most of the indigenous population are Sahrawis, a mixture of Berber and Arab, almost all of whom are Muslims. The capital is El Aaiún, which has a population of 97,000.

Rich in phosphates – it has the world's largest known deposits of phosphate rock – the country has since the mid-1970s been the subject of considerable conflict, with the Rabat government claiming the northern two-thirds as historically part of 'Greater Morocco'. While Morocco has invested heavily in the two-thirds or so of Western Sahara it controls, the rich earnings from the phosphate exports could finance more economic, social and educational programmes. In 1991, more than 170,000 Sahrawi refugees were living in camps around Tindouf, in western Algeria.

A cease-fire was agreed in 1991 between the Rabat government and the Sahrawi liberation movement, POLISARIO (the Popular Front for the Liberation of Saharan Territories), who are still in dispute over part of Western Sahara. In the early 1990s the peace, overseen by the United Nations, remained fragile. [*Map page 32*] ∎

AREA 446,550 sq km [172,413 sq mls]
POPULATION 26,448,000
CAPITAL (POPULATION) Rabat (893,000)
GOVERNMENT Constitutional monarchy
ETHNIC GROUPS Arab 70%, Berber 30%
LANGUAGES Arabic (official)
RELIGIONS Islam 99%, Christianity 1%
CURRENCY Moroccan dirham = 100 cents

MOZAMBIQUE

The Republic of Mozambique borders the Indian Ocean in south-eastern Africa. The coastal plains are narrow in the north but broaden in the south, making up nearly half of the country. Inland lie plateaux and hills,

which make up another two-fifths o[f] Mozambique, with highlands along the bor[?]ders with Zimbabwe, Zambia, Malawi an[d] Tanzania. The coast is fringed by sand dune[s] and swamps, with coral reefs offshore. Th[e] only natural harbour is at the capital, Maputo[,] in the far south.

Mozambique has a tropical climate, thoug[h] Maputo lies just outside the tropics. Due t[o] the warm, southwards-flowing Mozambiqu[e] (Agulhas) Current, Maputo has hot an[d] humid summers, though winters are mild an[d] fairly dry. Inland, the temperatures and th[e] humidity are a little lower.

Whilst palm trees are common on the coast[,] inland patches of rainforest contain trees such[?] as ebony and ironwood. On the whole however, savanna is the most widespread vegetation type.

ECONOMY AND RESOURCES

Only the inner borderlands are high; because of this and its remoteness from Portugal, Mozambique attracted few European settlers. Agriculture is still based around subsistence crops, such as maize and groundnuts, but in the northern foothills farmers also grow cotton and cashew for export. On the alluvial flats of Mozambique's coastal plains are plantations of coconut, sisal and sugar. There is some light industry based mainly in Beira and Maputo. At the limit of navigation on the River Zambezi is Africa's biggest dam, Cabora Bassa, whose power goes largely to South Africa. Large deposits of coal, copper, bauxite and offshore gas have yet to be exploited.

Mozambique forms a transit route for much of the overseas trade of Swaziland, Zimbabwe and Zambia, involving mainly the ports of Maputo, Beira and Nacala-Velha, just north of the town of Moçambique. Rail, port and handling services provide employment and substantial revenues.

HISTORY AND POLITICS

Like other former ex-Portuguese African countries, Mozambique arose from the search for a route round Africa to the riches of Asia; Vasco da Gama and his successors established forts at Beira (Sofala), Quelimane and Moçambique Island. Dutch conquest of Portuguese Asia in the 17th century, and ubsequent concentration by the Portuguese in the slave trade from West Africa to the Americas, resulted in decay of Mozambique settlements. However, being so little affected by the slave trade, and acting as a refuge in wars, Mozambique was never depopulated to the extent of Angola, and still maintains a higher population on a smaller area.

When the Portuguese rulers and settlers abruptly abandoned Mozambique in 1975 at independence, they left behind a country totally unprepared for organizing itself – the literacy rate, for example, was less than 1%. The Marxist-Leninist government of Samora Machel's FRELIMO movement (Front for the Liberation of Mozambique), which had been fighting the colonial regime for more than a decade, tried to implement ambitious social policies, but erratic administration, along with a series of natural disasters, reduced the economy to ruins by the mid-1980s.

From the 1970s progress was also severely hampered by the widespread activities of the Mozambique National Resistance (MNR, or RENAMO), backed first by Rhodesia and later by South Africa. RENAMO soon controlled huge areas of the countryside – convoys could only cross the 'Tete Corridor' escorted by Zimbabwean and Malawian forces – forcing more than a million refugees to flee, the vast majority of them going to poor Malawi; by 1988 almost half of all Mozambique's population was reliant on external aid.

Well before Machel was mysteriously killed in a plane crash inside South Africa in 1986, his government had been opening up the country to Western investment and influence – a policy continued by his successor, President Joaquim Chissano. In 1989 FRELIMO formally abandoned its Marxist ideology, and the following year agreed to end one-party rule and hold talks with the rebels. Despite South Africa's withdrawal of official assistance, the talks dragged on without a permanent ceasefire and hostilities continued to dog the country. Relief agencies estimated in 1991 that up to 3 million people had been displaced by the war – and that as many again faced starvation. A peace agreement between FRELIMO and RENAMO was finally reached and a cease-fire took effect in October 1992. The demobilization of government and RENAMO forces took place in 1994 and UN troops were stationed in the country. Multiparty elections were held in 1994. [*Map page 33*] ■

AREA 801,590 sq km [309,494 sq mls]
POPULATION 15,527,000
CAPITAL (POPULATION) Maputo (1,070,000)
GOVERNMENT Multiparty republic
ETHNIC GROUPS Makua 47%, Tsonga 23%, Malawi 12%, Shona 11%, Yao 4%, Swahili 1%, Makonde 1%
LANGUAGES Portuguese (official)
RELIGIONS Traditional beliefs 48%, Christianity (Roman Catholic 31%, other 9%), Islam 13%
CURRENCY Metical = 100 centavos

NAMIBIA

Namibia is a country of enormous physical and social diversity. Fringing the southern Atlantic coastline is the arid Namib Desert, virtually uninhabited, separated by a major escarpment from a north-south spine of mountains which culminate in the Khomas Highlands near Windhoek. This rugged spine, built of thick schists and quartzites, rises to 2,483 m [8,150 ft] in the peak of Moltkeblik. To the east, the country occupies the fringes of the Kalahari Desert.

ECONOMY AND RESOURCES
Though 60% of the population is engaged in agriculture, and offshore the Benguela Current feeds some of the Atlantic's richest fishing grounds, over 60% of Namibia's income comes from exports of minerals – notably uranium (3% of the world total) and diamonds (in 1993 the world's seventh largest producer). There are also large gasfields and good prospects for oil.

HISTORY AND POLITICS
Apart from the British enclave of Walvis Bay, Namibia was (as South West Africa) a German protectorate from 1884 before being

occupied by the Union of South Africa at the request of the Allied powers in 1915. Granted a League of Nations mandate in 1920, South Africa refused to place the territory under UN trusteeship after World War II, and in 1966 the mandate was cancelled. However, South Africa continued to exploit Namibia, even though in 1971 the International Court of Justice ruled that its occupation of the country was illegal; the main nationalist movement, SWAPO, began a guerrilla campaign supported by Cuba and Angola, but it was not until March 1990, following increasing international pressure, that the country eventually won its independence and joined the Commonwealth.

The status of Walvis Bay, the crucial deep-water port and military base, was in doubt at independence, but on 28 February 1994 South Africa renounced all claims and it was returned to Namibia. [*Map page 33*] ■

AREA 825,414 sq km [318,694 sq mls]
POPULATION 1,500,000
CAPITAL (POPULATION) Windhoek (115,000)
GOVERNMENT Multiparty republic
ETHNIC GROUPS Ovambo 50%, Kavango 9%, Herero 7%, Damara 7%, White 6%, Nama 5%
LANGUAGES English (official)
RELIGIONS Christianity 90% (Lutheran 51%)
CURRENCY Namibian dollar = 100 cents

NAURU

A low-lying coral atoll of just 21 sq km [8 sq mls] located halfway between Australia and Hawaii, 40 km [25 mls] south of the Equator, Nauru is the world's smallest republic. The climate is hot and wet, though the rains can fail.

ECONOMY AND RESOURCES
A plateau rising to over 60 m [200 ft], surrounded by a belt of fertile, cultivated land, has provided the island with rich deposits of high-grade phosphate rock, exported to the Pacific Rim countries for fertilizer. The industry, nationalized in 1970, accounts for over 98% of exports, and though Nauru is only just inside the world's top 20 producers this is enough to furnish the population with an average national income of US$20,000 – a similar figure to Canada or Denmark – giving them exemption from taxes and free education and welfare. The 7,000 native people – of mixed Micronesian and Polynesian origin, speaking hybrid Nauruan language and predominantly Christian (mainly Protestant) – are supplemented by more than 3,000 migrant workers from less endowed Pacific islands.

Nauru's economic future is, nevertheless, uncertain, since the phosphates are likely to be exhausted by the end of the century. The government is planning to derive new revenue from shipping and air services, as well as developing the island as a Pacific tax haven.

HISTORY AND POLITICS
Discovered by Britain in 1798, the island was under the control of Germany (1888), Australia (1914), Japan (1942) and Australia again (UN trusteeship from 1946) before it gained independence in 1968 ■

AREA 21 sq km [8 sq mls]
POPULATION 11,000
CAPITAL (POPULATION) Yaren District (559)
GOVERNMENT Democratic republic
ETHNIC GROUPS Nauruan 58%, other Pacific groups 26%
LANGUAGES Nauruan, English
RELIGIONS Christianity
CURRENCY Australian currency

NEPAL

O ver three-quarters of Nepal lies in a mountain heartland located between the towering Himalayas, the subject of an inconclusive boundary negotiation with China in 1961, and the far lower Siwalik Range overlooking the Ganges plain. Its innumerable lleys are home to a mosaic of peoples, of .do-European and Tibetan stock, with a wide nge of cultures and religions, and exercising :rce clan loyalties. This heartland, some)0 km [500 mls] from west to east, is divided :tween the basins of three main rivers – the :haghara, Gandak and Kosi. Between the last vo, on a smaller river flanked by lake :posits, stands Katmandu, the royal and :rliamentary capital, surrounded by emerald :cefields and orchards. The provincial centre f Pokhara is in a similar valley tributary to the :andak, north of Nuwakot.

Nepal's most famous assets are the moun- .ins, now an increasing tourist attraction ringing vital revenue to the country. Everest 3,848 m [29,029 ft]) and Kanchenjunga 8,598 m [28,208 ft]) are the tallest peaks of a nagnificent range, giving a backdrop that ominates every vista in Nepal.

:CONOMY AND RESOURCES

:outh of the Siwalik Range, the formerly wampy and malarious *terai*, or hillfoot plain, s now an economic mainstay, with new farm- ng settlements growing rice, wheat, maize, ute and sugar. Development is encouraged by he *terai* section of the Asian Highway and new oads to India and Tibet.

The authorities now hope for more than ncreased tourism. Today's plan is for the Himalayas to be tapped for their colossal hydroelectric potential, to supply the factories of industrial India; Nepal's goal is to become the powerhouse of the region. If the scheme envisaged by the government and the World Bank proceeds, the first stage would be under way by the mid-1990s at Chisapani Gorge. Once completed, the 267 m [878 ft] dam would house the second-largest HEP plant in the world, generating more than the total of Britain's nuclear stations combined. There would be environmental costs, including the displacement of 70,000 people, but the result would be valuable and renewable 'clean' power.

Financing such schemes – at $6 billion Chisapani alone is nearly twice the total gross national product – is a huge problem for a country which ranks alongside Laos as the poorest in Asia. With Chinese Tibet to the north and India to the south, the nation is already heavily reliant on Indian trade and co- operation – a fact emphasized when border restrictions operated in the late 1980s. Devoid of coast, independent trade links and mineral resources, Nepal has remained an undevel- oped rural country, with more than 90% of the adult population (only one in four of whom can read) working as subsistence farmers. In addition, indiscriminate farming techniques have led to deforestation – in turn causing the erosion of precious soils.

HISTORY AND POLITICS

While tourism is now encouraged, it was only in 1951 that Nepal was opened up to foreign- ers. Before that it had been a patchwork of feu- dal valley kingdoms, and though these were conquered by the Gurkhas in the 18th century – forming the present country – local leaders always displayed more allegiance to their clans than to the state. From the mid-19th century these families (notably the powerful Rana) reduced the power of the central king, but in 1951 the monarchy was re-established. A brief period of democracy ended with the return of autocratic royal rule in 1960 under King Mahendra, but after mass demonstrations and riots his son, Birendra, despite attempts at stalling, was forced to concede a new constitu- tion incorporating pluralism and basic human rights in 1990 and the hierarchical system of *panchayats* (rubber-stamping local councils) was over. In May 1991 the first democratic elections for 32 years took place with 10 mil- lion voters, and were won by the left-of-centre Nepali Congress Party. Though the birth- place of Buddha (Prince Siddhartha Gautama, *c.* 563 BC), Nepal remains a predominantly Hindu country. [*Map page 23*] ▪

AREA 140,800 sq km [54,363 sq mls]
POPULATION 21,360,000
CAPITAL (POPULATION) Katmandu (419,073)
GOVERNMENT Constitutional monarchy
ETHNIC GROUPS Nepalese 58%, Bihari 19%, Tharu 4%, Tamang 4%, Newar 3%
LANGUAGES Nepali
RELIGIONS Hinduism 90%, Buddhism 5%, Islam 3%
CURRENCY Nepalese rupee = 100 paisa

NETHERLANDS

Often, and inaccurately, called Holland – this refers only to the two north-western provinces – the Netherlands is the most crowded country of any size in Europe. The daunting figures for density are only an average however: the east and south are relatively sparsely populated, while the figure for the province of Zuid-Holland is 1,080 people per sq km [2,800 per sq ml].

The greatest concentration of population is in the towns and cities of Randstad Holland, a horseshoe of urban areas 50 km [31 mls] in diameter, with Dordecht at the centre of the loop. This area, dominant in the Dutch economy, includes most of the major cities, including (clockwise) Hilversum, Utrecht, Dordecht, Rotterdam, The Hague (home of the International Court of Justice), Leiden, Haarlem and Amsterdam, the last still the centre of Dutch cultural life despite being overtaken in size by Rotterdam. Nearly all of this crucial area, rich in history and culture, lies well below sea level.

To anyone travelling through the Netherlands, the density of people is obvious, for the fields are smaller, the villages more tightly concentrated with small neat houses, and the land is cultivated more intensively. Over much of the countryside rivers are at a higher level than the surrounding farmland, with villages sited above the flood level.

Since 1900 almost 3,000 sq km [1,160 sq mls] have been added to the nation's territory by reclaiming land from the sea. The largest and most famous project has been the reclamation of the Zuiderzee, begun in 1920. The major sea barrage of 32 km [21 mls] was completed in 1932, and by 1967 four large 'island' areas were finished, providing some 1,814 sq km [700 sq mls] of former seabed for both cultivation and for planned towns and villages. A controversial fifth area, Markerwaard, is under way, leaving the Ijsselmeer, a freshwater lake, the only remnant of the original inlet.

Without the protection of dykes and sand dunes along the coast, more than two-fifths of the Netherlands (the 'Low Countries') would be flooded. Constant pumping – formerly by windpumps (as most picturesque 'windmills' were) and steam pumps, but now by automated motor pumps – lifts surplus water from ditches to canals at a higher level, and from canals to the rivers, particularly the rivers Lek and Waal, which take the waters of the Rhine to the sea, and the Maas (Meuse in France and Belgium).

The dunes that line much of the coast are carefully guarded against erosion by planting marram grass and, where possible, trees. There are massive dykes to guard the farmland and towns, but inspite of sea defence systems periodic flooding does affect parts of the country. In 1953 the exceptionally high tides at the end of January broke through coastal dykes and sand dunes, causing widespread devastation. In January 1995, catastrophic flooding once again affected low-lying areas following a period of heavy rainfall and around 250,000 people had to be evacuated.

ECONOMY AND RESOURCES

The use of land in the Netherlands varies. In the west, near Haarlem, the concentration on bulb farming is marked in soils of clay mixed with sand. There, too, glasshouse cultivation combined on many holdings with the growing of flowers and vegetables out-of-doors, is widespread. The Dutch grow and sell more than 3 billion flowers every year. Much of the produce is exported, some of it by air to London and other north European cities. Some soils are better suited to pastoral farming, with milk, cheese and butter production. Gouda has a famous cheese market, and the well-known round, red-coated Edam cheeses come from northern areas. In the areas above sea level, farming is varied, with a combination of cattle and crops, including fruit.

Industry and commerce provide support for the greater part of the Dutch population. Mineral resources include china clay, which is abundant and natural gas from the North Sea. The emphasis of modern industry is on oil, steel, electrical engineering and chemicals.

In the area south of Rotterdam a vast port and industrial area, Europoort, has been developed since 1958. Together with Rotter-

THE DUTCH POLDERS

Polders are artificial farmlands reclaimed from water. The first were formed in Holland and Zeeland about a thousand years ago, when settlers on marshlands found that they could protect their land by building dykes of earth, brushwood (around which mud would accumulate) and stones. The effort was vast, but dry land was created and protected against floods from rivers and high tides. Sluices were made in the dykes to let out surplus water; marshes and peat bogs were gradually drained and the water pumped out to major rivers and canals by windpumps. These were largely replaced in the mid-19th century by steam-pumps.

Today some of the most profitable farmland in the Netherlands is polderland, much of it 6–7 m [about 20 ft] below sea level. Within some of the polders the farmland is divided into hundreds of strips separated by water channels and accessible only by boat. Modern polders, including those of the Zuiderzee, have large fields of great fertility. With modern technology the level of water in each polder can be controlled from central pumping stations. Many older settlements are on dykes, or patches of land known to lie above the highest flood levels. The Dutch engineers have, over the centuries, exported their expertise to many areas, most notably the Fens in eastern England.

dam's own facilities, the complex is the largest and busiest in the world. The Dutch are skilled at languages, to which a considerable part of the teaching time is given even in primary schools. This is essential to the country's prosperity, for now as in past centuries the Dutch control a main outlet for the commerce of Europe in the port of Rotterdam, with the Rhine Valley and a wider area as its hinterland. The main export markets are the EU partners – Germany, Belgium, the UK and France – while strong trade links with Indonesia recall the Dutch colonial age.

HISTORY AND POLITICS

The country came into being as the United Provinces of Netherlands when it declared its independence from Spain in 1581. In the 17th century, the Dutch republic experienced a golden era of economic prosperity, naval pre-eminence, religious tolerance and artistic achievement. It succeeded in building an empire with colonies in the Americas, Africa and Asia. But it became part of the Napoleonic Empire and had to reassert its independence in 1813.

The constitution of 1814 instituted a hereditary constitutional monarchy which is still in place today. The country maintained its neutrality during World War I, but in 1940 was invaded by German forces. In 1949 the Netherlands abandoned its neutrality and joined NATO.

Since the end of World War II, it has been at the heart of European construction, as a founder member of Benelux, the ECSC and the EEC. The granting of independence to its former colonies has led to large-scale immigration to the Netherlands with all the attendant social and economic problems. The Dutch political system (based on proportional representation) encourages the existence of numerous political parties. [*Map page 12*] ∎

AREA 41,526 sq km [16,033 sq mls]
POPULATION 15,397,000
CAPITAL (POPULATION) Amsterdam (1,091,338)
GOVERNMENT Constitutional monarchy
ETHNIC GROUPS Netherlander 95%, Indonesian, Turkish, Moroccan, German
LANGUAGES Dutch (official)
RELIGIONS Christianity (Roman Catholic 34%, Dutch Reformed Church 17%, Calvinist 8%), Islam 3%
CURRENCY Guilder (florin) = 100 cents

NETHERLANDS ANTIILLES

The Netherlands Antilles consists of two very different island groups – Curaçao and Bonaire, off the coast of Venezuela, and

Saba, St Eustatius and the southern part of St Maarten, at the northern end of the Leeward Islands, some 800 km [500 mls] away. Curaçao is the largest island, accounting for nearly 45% of the total of 993 sq km [383 sq mls] and 80% of the population.

The people – mainly mulatto, Catholic and Creole-speaking – are well off by Caribbean standards, enjoying the benefits of an economy buoyed by tourism, offshore banking and oil refining from Venezuela (mostly for export to the Netherlands), more than the traditional orange liqueur. The soil is generally too poor however, to permit large-scale agriculture.

With Aruba, the Netherlands Antilles formed part of the Dutch East Indies, in 1954 attaining internal self-government as constitutional equals with the Netherlands and Surinam. Curaçao is politically dominant in the federation ■

AREA 993 sq km [383 sq mls]
POPULATION 197,000
CAPITAL (POPULATION) Willemstad (50,000)
GOVERNMENT Self-governing Dutch territory
ETHNIC GROUPS Of African descent 85%, European
LANGUAGES Dutch, Papiamento (a dialect of Spanish, Portuguese, Dutch and English), English
RELIGIONS Christianity
CURRENCY Guilder = 100 cents

NEW CALEDONIA

Most southerly of the Melanesian countries, New Caledonia comprises the main island of Grande Terre and the dependencies of the Loyalty Islands (Iles Loyauté), Ile des Pins and the Bélep archipelago. The remaining islands (many of them coral atolls) are all small and uninhabited.

ECONOMY AND RESOURCES
New Caledonia's economy is dominated by a single commodity, nickel, which accounts for

over 83% of export earnings. The world largest producer in the 1960s, it has slipped sixth place – though still with a healthy 5% the total world share and with reserves est mated at more than a third of the known wor total. Other exports are copra and coffee.

HISTORY AND POLITICS
A French possession since 1853 and oversee territory from 1958, New Caledonia today ha a fundamental split on the question of inde pendence from Paris. The Kanaks, the indige nous Melanesian people (but numberin under half the total), on the whole support i the less numerous French settlers (many c whom fled Algeria after it gained indepen dence) are passionately against it. An agree ment for increased autonomy – supposedl leading to independence – has helped to eas tension between the two camps, but the futur of the former colony looks cloudy. Anothe independence referendum (one was held i 1987) has been promised for 1998. Much ma depend on finance: France provides a third o the government budget, but separatists have purchased (from its French owner) the islands' largest nickel mine. [*Map page 3*] ■

AREA 19,000 sq km [7,334 sq mls]
POPULATION 178,000
CAPITAL (POPULATION) Nouméa (98,000)
GOVERNMENT French overseas territory
ETHNIC GROUPS Melanesian 43%, European 37%
LANGUAGES French, Melanesian and Polynesian dialects
RELIGIONS Christianity (Roman Catholic 60%, Protestant 30%)
CURRENCY CFP franc = 100 centimes

NEW ZEALAND

Geologically part of the Circum-Pacific Mobile Belt of tectonic activity, New Zealand is mountainous and partly volcanic. Many of the highest mountains – the Southern r example – were thrust up from the seabed the past 10 to 15 million years, representing only the latest in a long series of orogenies. Much of the North Island was formed by volcanic action even more recently, mainly in the past 1 to 4 million years. Minor earthquakes are common, and there are several areas of volcanic and geothermal activity, especially in the North Island.

Its youth makes New Zealand a rugged country with mountains always in sight and about 75% of the total land area above the 200 m [650 ft] contour. The North Island has many spectacular but low ranges with peaks of 1,200 to 1,500 m [4,000 to 5,000 ft], made up of folded sedimentary rocks that form good soils. The Coromandel Range and hilly Northland peninsula are softer and more worn, with few peaks over 800 m [12,600 ft].

Overlying these older rocks in the centre and north are massive spreads of lava, pumice and volcanic tuffs, formed during the past 1 to 3 million years. The great central plateau is dominated by three slumbering volcanoes – Ruapehu (2,797 m [9,176 ft], the North Island's highest peak), Ngauruhoe and Tongariro. Further north, extensive fields of lava and ash cones lie across the base of the Northland peninsula, forming a firm, rolling site for the suburbs of Auckland, New Zealand's largest city.

The far larger South Island is also mainly mountainous, with an alpine backbone extending obliquely from north-east to south-west. The highest peaks form a central massif, the Southern Alps, clustered around Mt Cook, at 3,764 m [12,349 ft] New Zealand's highest mountain. From this massif, which is permanently ice-capped, glaciers descend on either flank, and on the east the outwash fans of glacier-fed rivers form the Canterbury Plains – South Island's only extensive lowland. In the far south-west (Fjordland), the coast is indented by deep, steeply-walled sounds that wind far into the forested mountains.

ECONOMY AND RESOURCES

From 1844, when the first Merinos were introduced from Australia, New Zealand became predominantly a land of sheep, the grassy lowlands (especially in the South Island) providing year-round forage. Huge flocks were

NEW ZEALAND TERRITORIES

New Zealand comprises not just the two main islands, Stewart Island, Chatham Island and a number of uninhabited outlying islands, but also territories further out in the Pacific, including the Kermadec Islands (with an isolated meteorological station) and Tokelau (population 2,000); formerly part of the Gilbert and Ellice Islands – now called Kiribati – and transferred from Britain to New Zealand in 1926, the group became part of the country in 1949. The Cook Islands (population 19,000) became an internally self-governing state in 'free association' with New Zealand in 1965; Niue (population 2,000) has had the same status since 1974. These Polynesian islanders have full citizenship, while Wellington controls defence and foreign affairs. The main exports are citrus fruits and juices, copra, bananas and honey.

built up, mainly for wool and tallow production. From the lowlands they expanded into the hills – the 'high country' which was cleared of native bush and sown with European grasses for pasture. More than half the country is still covered with evergreen forest. The North Island proved more difficult to turn into productive farmland, only later proving its value for dairying.

New Zealand's early prosperity was finally established when the export of frozen mutton and lamb carcasses began in 1882. Soon a steady stream of chilled meat and dairy products – and later of fruit – was crossing the oceans to established markets in Britain, and the country is still the world's second biggest producer of lamb. Wheat and other cereals were also grown. High productivity was maintained by applications of fertilizers, mainly based on rock-phosphate mined on Nauru.

New Zealand is a prosperous country, with a high standard of living for a refreshingly harmonious multiracial population. Since 1907 a self-governing Dominion, it long relied on British markets for the export of agricultural produce, and has generally strong ties and affinities with Britain. Though agricultural products are still the main exports, the economy has diversified considerably since World War II, including fish, timber and wood pulp. Iron ores, coal and small amounts of gold are among the few valuable minerals, recently boosted by natural gas and petroleum. Geothermal and hydroelectric power are well developed, and timber and forest products are finding valuable overseas markets. Despite the country's isolation, a promising tourist industry is also developing, based on the scenic beauty, abundance of game animals, and relatively peaceful and unhurried way of life.

However, the idyll was showing signs of cracking from the 1970s, beginning when the UK joined the EEC and New Zealand's exports to Britain shrank from 70% to 10%. Along with a re-evaluation of its defence position, the country has had to rethink its previous 'safe' economic strategy – cutting subsidies to farmers, privatization, seeking new markets in Asia – and, like Australia and most fellow members of the OECD, find a way to survive the recession of the late 1980s and early 1990s.

HISTORY AND POLITICS
New Zealand was discovered by Abel Tasman in 1642 and charted thoroughly by James Cook in 1769–70. Both explorers recorded the presence of Maoris – Polynesians who hunted and farmed from well-defended coastal settlements, who were themselves relatively recent arrivals on the islands. Sealing gangs and whalers were New Zealand's first European inhabitants, closely followed by missionaries and farmers from Britain and Australia. By the early 1830s about 2,000 Europeans had settled there.

In 1840 Britain took possession, in a treaty which gave rights and privileges of British subjects to the Maori people. The following decades saw the arrival of thousands of new settlers from Britain, and by mid-century there were over 30,000. Though their relationships with the Maoris (who at this stage outnumbered them two to one) were generally good, difficulties over land ownership led to warfare in the 1860s. Thereafter the Maori population declined while European numbers continued to increase.

New Zealand fought in World War I as an ally of Britain, and during World War II

THE MAORIS

'Strong, raw-boned, well-made, active people, rather above than under the common size ... of a very dark brown colour, with black hair, thin black beards, and ... in general very good features.' So Captain James Cook described the Maoris he met in New Zealand in 1770. Of Polynesian stock, the Maoris settled (mainly in North Island) from about AD 800 to 1350. A warlike people, living in small fortified settlements, they cultivated kumaras (sweet potatoes) and other crops, hunted seals and moas (large flightless birds, now extinct) and gathered seafoods.

The Maoris befriended the early European settlers; readily accepting British sovereignty, Christianity and pacification, they rebelled only as more and more of their communal land was bought for the settlers' use. Given parliamentary representation from 1876, they eventually integrated fully. Now Maoris form about 9% of New Zealand's population, still living mostly in North Island. Though socially and politically equal in every way to whites, they are still over-represented in the poorer, unskilled sections of the population, separated more by poverty and lack of opportunity than by colour from the mainstream of national life.

forged close links with Australia and the USA. Although it sent troops to support the Americans in the Vietnam war, the country has since adopted a much more independent foreign policy. [*Map page 35*] ∎

AREA 270,990 sq km [104,629 sq mls]
POPULATION 3,531,000
CAPITAL (POPULATION) Wellington (326,000)
GOVERNMENT Constitutional monarchy
ETHNIC GROUPS New Zealand European 74%, New Zealand Maori 10%, Polynesian 4%
LANGUAGES English and Maori (both official)
RELIGIONS Christianity (Anglican 21%, Presbyterian 16%, Roman Catholic 15%, Methodist 4%)
CURRENCY New Zealand dollar = 100 cents

NICARAGUA

argest and least densely populated of the Central American countries, Nicaragua's astern half is almost empty. With over 50 cm [300 in] of rain in some years, it is rested and rich in a tropical fauna including rocodiles, turtles, deer, pumas, jaguars and monkeys. Cut off from the populous west f Nicaragua, it was for two centuries the British protectorate of the Miskito Coast, with Bluefields (San Juan del Norte) as the largest ettlement.

Inland, the plain gives way to mountain anges broken by basins and fertile valleys. In the west and south they overlook a great depression which runs from the Gulf of Fonseca south-eastwards and contains lakes Managua and Nicaragua. Nicaragua (8,264 sq km [3,191 sq mls]) is the largest lake in Central America; though only 20 km [12.5 mls] from the Pacific, it drains to the Caribbean by the navigable San Juan River and formed an important route across the isthmus before the Panama Canal was built.

Forty volcanoes, many active, rise above the lakes; San Cristóbal (1,745 m [5,725 ft]) is the highest, still-smoking Momotombo the most spectacular. Earthquakes are common and the capital Managua was vitually destroyed in 1931 and 1972.

ECONOMY AND RESOURCES
In the early 1990s, Nicaragua faced many problems in rebuilding its shattered economy. Agriculture is the main activity, employing nearly half of the people. Coffee, cotton, sugar and bananas are grown for export, while rice is the main food crop. The country has some copper, gold and silver, but mining is underdeveloped. Most manufacturing industries are based in and around Managua.

HISTORY AND POLITICS
Christopher Columbus reached Nicaragua in 1502 and claimed the land for Spain, which ruled Nicaragua until 1821. In the mid-19th century, Nicaragua was ravaged by civil war, but by the early 20th century the United States had considerable influence in the country, and in 1912 US forces entered the country. From 1927 to 1933, rebels under General Augusto César Sandino tried to drive the US forces out of the country. In 1933, the US marines set up a Nicaraguan army, called the National Guard. Its leader, Anastasio Somoza Garcia, had Sandino murdered in 1934. From 1937, Somoza ruled Nicaragua as a dictator.

In the mid-1970s, many people began to protest against the Somoza dictatorship, and in 1979, after a 17-year campaign, the long domination of the corrupt Somoza family (who controlled 40% of the economy) was ended by a popular uprising led by the Sandinista National Liberation Front (named after General Sandino), which went on to win democratic power in 1985. Meanwhile, the US government, which opposed the Sandinista regime, claiming that it was a Communist dictatorship, trained and supplied Contra guerrillas from bases in Honduras and imposed a trade embargo, pushing Nicaragua into increasing dependence on Cuba and the former Soviet Union.

A cease-fire agreed in 1989 was followed the next year by electoral defeat for Daniel José Ortega Saavedra's Sandinistas at the hands of the US-backed coalition of Violeta Barrios de Chamorro. But while the two sides were forced into working uneasily together to try and put the country back on its feet with the benefit of conditional US aid, fighting frequently broke out between former Contra rebels and ex-Sandinistas, most notably away from the capital. Some progress towards peace and disarmament had been made by the summer of 1994. [*Map page 30*] ■

AREA 130,000 sq km [50,193 sq mls]
POPULATION 4,275,000
CAPITAL (POPULATION) Managua (682,000)
GOVERNMENT Multiparty republic
ETHNIC GROUPS Mestizo 77%, White 10%, Black 9%, Amerindian 4%
LANGUAGES Spanish (official)
RELIGIONS Christianity (Roman Catholic 91%, others 9%)
CURRENCY Córdoba = 100 centavos

NIGER

The title Niger, derived from the Tuareg word *n'eghirren* (meaning 'flowing water') is something of a misnomer for the country that bears the river's name. West Africa's great waterway runs through only the extreme south-west of what is, apart from its fertile southern strip, a desolate territory of hot, arid sandy and stony basins.

The monotony of the northern 60% of the country is broken by the jagged peaks of the Aïr Mountains, rising to 2,022 m [6,634 ft] from the desert plains; here rainfall is sometimes sufficient to permit the growth of thorny scrub. The southern part of the country includes the most fertile areas of the Niger basin around Lake Chad.

ECONOMY AND RESOURCES

In the north, severe droughts since the 1970s have crippled the traditional lifestyle of the nomads in the area, grazing their camels, horses, cattle and goats, and whole clans killed as the Sahara slowly makes its way south.

The same period has seen the growth of uranium mining by the government in conjunction with the French Atomic Energy Commission, and this has now overtaken groundnuts as Niger's chief export, despite the drop in world demand during the 1980s. Tin and tungsten are also mined here, but reserves of other minerals, including iron ore, manganese and molybdenum, remain largely untouched. Over 95% of Niger's population however still derive their living from agriculture and trading.

The southern part of the country has also been affected by drought; but here desertification, linked to overgrazing, climbing temperatures as well as water shortage, is a wider problem. The crucial millet and sorghum crops – often grown by slash-and-burn techniques – have repeatedly failed, and migration to the already crowded market towns and neighbouring countries is widespread. The capital, Niamey, a mixture of tra-

ditional African, European colonial and modern Third World, is the prime destination for migrants travelling in search of food and work.

South of Niamey is the impressive 'W' national park, shared with Burkina Faso and Benin. The wooded savanna landscape – offering protection to elephants, buffaloes, crocodiles, cheetahs, lions and antelopes –

THE SAHARA DESERT

The world's biggest desert, the Sahara's 9,065,000 sq km [3,500,000 sq mls] stretch from the Atlantic to the Red Sea and amount to almost a third of the African continent. To the north, it is bordered by the Mediterranean; to the south, it merges with the Sahel, a zone of sparse vegetation and irregular rainfall. On average, the Sahara receives less than 100 mm [4 in] of rain annually, though a scattering of oases fed by underground water support small, sedentary communities and nomadic herdsmen alike; the region as a whole has around a million inhabitants. Daytime shade temperatures frequently reach 50°C [122°F]; at night, because heat quickly escapes through the cloudless skies, temperatures can fall below freezing point. Over 70% of the Sahara's area is covered with coarse gravel and rock, rising in its high central plateau to mountains of 3,000 m [10,000 ft] or more, mostly of volcanic origin. About 15% is made up of plains of shifting sand, including the Great Western Erg, a sand sea of more than 78,000 sq km [30,000 sq mls] in Algeria, where winds of 50 km/h [30 mph] or more regularly whip up sandstorms, dark walls 1.5 km [1 ml] high and up to 500 km [300 mls] wide.

The Sahara was not always a desert: as recently as 15,000 years ago, during the last Ice Age, even the Great Western Erg was green and fertile, well stocked with grazing animals and a paradise for the humans of the era, who left behind numerous cave paintings of successful hunts. At present, though, the Sahara is growing southwards at the expense of the marginal Sahel lands – an expansion caused by long-term drought exacerbated by overpopulation and overgrazing.

intended to attract growing numbers of
tourists in the 1990s.

HISTORY AND POLITICS

Nomadic Tuaregs settled in the Aïr Mountains about 1,000 years ago, and by the 15th
century they had built up an empire based on
Agadez. At around the same time, the Zerma-
Songhai people founded the Songhai empire
along the River Niger. The Songhai conquered
the Tuaregs, but in the late 16th century
Songhai was defeated by a Moroccan army.

Later on, the Hausa and then the Fulani set
up kingdoms in the area. France became
involved in Niger in the late 19th century and
ruled Niger as part of French West Africa from
1900–58. The country became an autonomous republic in 1958, and in 1960 it
became fully independent.

Food shortages and the destruction of the
traditional nomadic lifestyle of some of Niger's
people have caused political instability. In
1974, a group of army officers, led by Lt.-Col.
Seyni Kountché, overthrew the country's first
president, Hamani Diori, and seized control of
the government. Civilian rule was restored in
1989 after Kountché's death. In 1992, a referendum was held, in which 89% of the people
voted for a new, multiparty constitution.
Elections were held in 1993. [*Map page 32*] ■

AREA 1,267,000 sq km [489,189 sq mls]
POPULATION 8,846,000
CAPITAL (POPULATION) Niamey (398,000)
GOVERNMENT Multiparty republic
ETHNIC GROUPS Hausa 53%, Djerma-Songhai
21%, Tuareg 11%, Fulani (or Peul) 10%
LANGUAGES French (official)
RELIGIONS Islam 98%
CURRENCY CFA franc = 100 centimes

NIGERIA

Four times the size of the United Kingdom,
whose influence dates from 1861, Nigeria
is tropical Africa's most important country.

The landscape varies from the savanna of the
north – much of it under threat of desertification – through mountains and tropical rainforests to the coastal lands on the Gulf of
Guinea. The coast has huge expanses of fine
sandy beaches, interspersed with mangrove
swamps where rivers join the ocean. Much of
the country's coast is formed by the Niger
delta, behind which lie thousands of creeks
and lagoons.

ECONOMY AND RESOURCES

Before roads were constructed, the inland
waterways provided crucial transport, and
boats and canoes still carry both people and
cargoes between towns and villages in the area.
Here the heavy rains allow the production of
yams, cassava, maize and vegetables, with rice
grown on the patches of land beside rivers and
on large stretches of irrigated land where
streams do not flood in the wet seasons.

Farther north, in the forest belt, the hills rise
towards the Jos Plateau – famous for its holiday resorts – and in the east towards the steep
valleys and wooded slopes of the Cameroon
Highlands. These areas produce Nigeria's
important tree crops – cocoa, rubber, hardwoods and palm oil. North of the Jos Plateau,
parkland gives way to grassland, but the savanna becomes increasingly dry and some areas
are now little more than semi-arid scrub.

Northern Nigeria is reliant on one precarious wet season, while the south enjoys two.
Poor-quality millet and sorghum are the
staples, with cotton and groundnuts the main
cash crops. Where desertification has not
taken hold, livestock are still important –
enjoying the absence of the tsetse fly that
afflicts the area of moist vegetation in the
south of the country.

Nigeria is unique in Africa south of the
Sahara for the numerous pre-colonial towns of
the south-west (such as Ibadan) and the north
(such as Kano). Domestic trade between these
and Nigeria's very varied regions was developed in pre-colonial days, and is now intense.

The country is in the top 15 producers of
world oil, but there are many other resources
(albeit dwarfed in exports by oil), including
cocoa in the south-west, timber, rubber and
palm oil in the south-centre and east, and
cotton and groundnuts in the north.

THE SAHEL

The Sahel is a wide band of scrub and savanna grassland stretching from Mauritania and northern Senegal in the west through parts of Mali, Burkina Faso, Benin and Niger to southern Chad in the east, and including much of northern Nigeria. To the north is the Sahara, the world's largest desert; to the south are the rainforests of tropical West and Central Africa. Though used mainly for pasture, the whole area has irregular and unpredictable rainfall and suffers frequently from drought and the resultant famine. Attention was first drawn to the desperate plight of the region by the Sahelian famine of 1973, when hundreds of thousands died.

Over the past 30 years, the Sahara has gradually encroached southwards in the world's most blatant example of 'desertification'. The causes are many and interwoven. As well as declining rainfall, there are the pressures of a growing population; herdsmen overgrazing the land with their cattle, sheep and goats; overcultivation by farmers; cutting of ground cover, mainly for fuelwood; and poor or faulty irrigation techniques, where limited water supplies are wasted and the land left too saline or alkaline to support crops.

Ironically, the problem was aggravated in the previous two decades, when above-average rainfall encouraged the expansion of settlement and the cultivation of cash crops into marginal land. Experts estimate that as much as two-thirds of the world's pasture and grazing lands are now in danger from desertification. Africa, and notably the Sahel, is the worst affected: in places the Sahara has advanced more than 350 km [200 mls] in just two decades. The process is containable – even reversible – if the land is allowed to recover and the soil rejuvenated through tree planting, terracing and proper irrigation under careful and consistent management with sufficient funds. But these conditions are rarely found: pressures of population, lack of finance and changing policies all mean that such techniques have not been applied anywhere in the Sahel on a substantial scale.

Nigeria's foreign exchange earnings from oil, the country's prime source of income were halved in a year. Oil production had begun in the 1950s and risen steadily to a peak of 2.4 million barrels a day in the early 1980s. Foreign exchange earnings peaked in 1980 at $26 billion, but by the end of the decade this figure had shrunk to $9 billion. At the same time the foreign debt, constantly shuffled and rescheduled, had blossomed to some $36 billion, easily Africa's largest. In seven years the annual income of the average Nigerian has shrunk from $1,120 (among the top three on the continent) to a meagre $270, a figure below even that of some poor neighbours. In 1991 the World Bank officially reclassified Nigeria as a low-income rather than middle-income country.

In the early 1990s there were, nevertheless, signs of a recovery, with agriculture (50% of the population still rely on farming) and some areas of manufacturing growing quickly.

There are over 88 million Nigerians, making it by far the most populous African state; one in every six Africans is Nigerian. It is also the second most populated country of the Commonwealth, and eleventh in the world. Natural wealth and substantial armed forces give Nigeria a commanding position in Africa, and its oil and gas reserves are a focus of worldwide interest.

HISTORY AND POLITICS
European contact dates back to the 15th century. A federation of 31 states, many of which are larger than most African states, Nigeria includes many tribal groups, the largest being the Yoruba of the south-west, the Ibo of the east, and the Hausa, Fulani and Kanuri of the north. The north is predominantly Muslim, and the Islamic influence is increasing in the south, where most people are pagan or Christian. With so many diversities, including those of religion and a developing social system, Nigeria suffers internal stresses and national unity is often strained.

Though blessed with many natural resources, Nigeria has had an uneasy path since independence in 1960 (becoming a full republic in 1963). Democratically elected governments have found it an impossible task to unify and stabilize an unruly jigsaw of more

an 250 ethnic and linguistic groups, and
vilian administrations have ruled for only ten
ars since the departure of the British.
An unwieldy tripartite federal structure first
troduced in 1954 proved unable to contain
valries after independence and in 1966 the
rst Prime Minister, Abubaka Tafawa Balewa,
nd many other leaders were assassinated in
military coup. A counter-coup brought
eneral Yakubu Gowon to power, but a
cious civil war ensued from 1967 when the
astern Region (Biafra), dominated by the
hristian Ibo, attempted to secede from the
nion after the slaughter of thousands of their
ibe in the north by Muslim Hausa – and
rangles over increasing oil revenues.

DEMOCRACY IN AFRICA

The great flush of liberty that followed decol-
onization in the 1950s and 1960s did not
bring the rewards of peace, prosperity and
self-government that many early African
nationalists had envisaged. Instead, within a
few years, most of the newly-independent
African nations had been transformed into
corrupt and incompetent dictatorships, at
best authoritarian one-party states, usually
heavily reliant on Western or Soviet subsidies
and often plagued by guerrilla fighting and
banditry. Governments were changed, if at
all, by means of a coup d'état.

In the late 1980s, however, new hope
reached the world's poorest continent.
Everywhere, it seemed, dictators were succumbing peacefully to popular demands for
multiparty elections and many long-running
civil wars were coming to an end. By the early
1990s, some form of democracy was in place
in 80% of African nations.

But democracy has no easy answer to
Africa's chronic problem: its poverty, and the
continuing collapse in world prices for most
African commodities. In some instances
Western-style democracy may even prove to
be impossible, as in Algeria, where in 1992
the military intervened to prevent power
passing to elected Islamic fundamentalists,
who had sworn to destroy the system that
would have given them their victory.

Hundreds of thousands died (most from
starvation) before Biafra admitted defeat early
in 1971. The federation was gradually splintered from three to 21 full states (now 31) to
try to prevent one area becoming dominant.
Gowon was overthrown in 1975, but another
attempt at civilian rule (1979-83) also ended
in a military takeover. The latest coup, a
bloodless affair in 1985, brought General
Ibrahim Babangida to office, and he immediately faced the crucial problems of falling oil
prices and mounting foreign debts. In 1989,
Babangida promised to introduce civilian rule
by 1992. Elections did take place in July 1992
though the two permitted parties were both
created by the Armed Forces Ruling Council
and genuine pluralism still seemed a long way
off. However, presidential elections held in
1993 and declared invalid by the military
government did lead to the resignation of
Babangida. A transitional council is preparing
a return to civilian rule. Whatever the regime,
Nigeria's biggest worry could simply be
numbers: on the trends of the 1980s the total
population could be more than 300 million by
the year 2025. [*Map page 32*] ■

AREA 923,770 sq km [356,668 sq mls]
POPULATION 88,515,000
CAPITAL (POPULATION) Abuja (federal
capital, 306,000)
GOVERNMENT Federal republic
ETHNIC GROUPS Hausa 21%, Yoruba 21%,
Ibo (or Igbo) 19%, Fulani 11%, Ibibio 6%
LANGUAGES English (official)
RELIGIONS Christianity (Protestant 26%,
Roman Catholic 12%, others 11%), Islam 45%
CURRENCY Naira = 100 kobo

NORTHERN
MARIANAS

The Northern Mariana Islands comprise all
17 Mariana Islands except Guam, the
most southerly, forming a mountainous and
volcanic chain extending northwards with a
total land area of 477 sq km [184 sq mls].

The population of 47,000 is concentrated on three of the six inhabited islands, with Saipan and the capital town of Susupe accounting for 19,000. Tourism appears to be the key to the future: the number of foreign visitors rose from 130,000 in 1984 to over 435,400 in 1990.

Part of the US Trust Territory of the Pacific from 1947, its people voted in a 1975 UN plebiscite for Commonwealth status in union with the USA. Washington approved the change in 1976, granting US citizenship, and internal self-government followed in 1978. [*Map page 26*] ■

AREA 477 sq km [184 sq mls]
POPULATION 47,000
CAPITAL (POPULATION) Saipan (19,000)
GOVERNMENT Commonwealth in union with the USA
ETHNIC GROUPS Chamorro, Micronesian, Spanish
LANGUAGES English, Chamorro
RELIGIONS Christianity (mainly Roman Catholic)
CURRENCY US currency

NORWAY

One of the world's most distinctly shaped countries, the kingdom of Norway occupies the western part of the Scandinavian peninsula, from North Cape at latitude 71°N to Lindesnes at 58°N, a north-south distance of over 1,600 km [1,000 mls]. It covers an area far larger than Poland, yet has a population of less than 4.4 million, most of whom live in the southern part of the country, where the capital, Oslo, is situated.

Nowhere in Norway is far from the sea. At the widest point it is only 430 km [270 mls] from west to east, and near the Arctic port of Narvik the Swedish border comes to within 6.5 km [4 mls] of the Norwegian coast. A third of Norway lies within the Arctic Circle, but the climate is not as severe as might be expected because the Norwegian coast benefits from th moderating effects of the warm waters of th North Atlantic Drift. Even on the Arctic coas the ports of Hammerfest and Kirkenes rema unfrozen in most winters.

Landscape

Norway is a rugged, mountainous country i which communication is difficult. The No: wegian landscape is dominated by rollin plateaux, the *vidda*, generally 300 m to 900 [1,000 ft to 3,000 ft] high, above which som peaks rise to as much as 1,500 m to 2,500 r [5,000 ft to 8,000 ft] in the area between Osl Bergen and Trondheim. In the far north th summits are around 1,000 m [3,000 ft] lower

The highest areas retain permanent ice fields, as in the Jotunheim Mountains abov Sognefjord. The Norwegian mountains hav been uplifted during three mountain-buildin; episodes during the last 400 million years, an they contain rocks of the earliest geologica periods. Intrusions of volcanic materia accompanied the uplifting and folding, anc there are great masses of granites and gneisse: – the source of Norway's mineral wealth There are few large areas of flat land in th country, but in the east the *vidda* are broke by deep valleys of rivers flowing to the low lands of south-east Norway, focused on Oslo In glacial times the whole country was covered by the great northern ice-cap. When it melted about 10,000 years ago it left behind larg deposits of glacial moraine, well represented around Oslo in the Raa moraines. Soils of better quality are used for crops and meadows, while the less productive sands and gravels remain forested.

The coast and the islands

The configuration of the coast – the longest in Europe – helps to explain the ease with which the Norwegians took to the sea in their early history and why they have remained a seafaring nation since. The *vidda* are cut by long, narrow, steep-sided fjords on the west coast, shaped by the great northern ice-cap. The largest of these, Sognefjord – 203 km [127 mls] long and less than 5 km [3 mls] wide – is the longest inlet in Europe and the best known fjord, though not the most spectacular.

Along the coast there are hundreds of

lands, the largest group of which, the ofoten Islands, lie north of the Arctic Circle. These islands, known as the *skerryguard*, protect the inner coast from the battering of the Atlantic breakers, and provide sheltered leads of water which the coastal ferries and fishing boats can navigate in safety.

Until recently, communications along the coast were easier by boat than by land. Oslo is linked to the south by rail and a line reaches north to Bodö at latitude 67.5°N. Roads are difficult to build and costly to maintain, and are often blocked by snow in winter and spring snow accumulates to March).

There are still several hundred ferries which carry cars across the fjords, but much money has been invested in the building of a north-south trunk road, with bridges across the fjords, to avoid the constant use of ferries. Air transport is of increasing importance and many small airstrips are in use, bringing remote communities into contact with the populated south.

ECONOMY AND RESOURCES

With two-thirds of the country comprising barren mountains, snowfields or unproductive wastes, and one-fifth forested, less than 3% of the land can be cultivated. The barrenness of the soil, the heavy rainfall, winter snows and the short growing season restrict agriculture, especially in the north, though in the long days of summer good crops of hay, potatoes, quick-growing vegetables and even rye and barley are grown. Near the coast, farming is restricted to the limited areas of level or gently-sloping ground beside the sheltered fjords. Cattle and sheep use the slopes above them in the summer but are fed in stalls during the winter. Everywhere fish is caught in the local waters.

The sea has always been a major influence in Norwegian life. A thousand years ago Viking sailors from Norway roamed the northern seas, founding colonies around the coasts of Britain, Iceland and even North America. Today fishing, shipbuilding and the management of merchant shipping lines are of vital importance to the Norwegian economy, and its merchant ships, most of which seldom visit the home ports, earn profits which pay for a third of the country's imports.

Iron and lead ores are found in the north,

copper in central Norway and titanium in the south. The extent of Norway's mineral resources is not fully known, and prospecting is still revealing new deposits. Oil and natural gas deposits in the seabed of the North Sea have made a great contribution to the Norwegian economy in recent years, and comprise more than half of the country's export earnings. Statfjord B (816,000 tonnes) is the world's biggest oil platform. Exploitation of all these reserves provides more than enough for the country's needs.

There is no coal in mainland Norway, although some is found in the islands on the Svalbard archipelago in the Arctic Ocean. The lack of coal has been partly compensated for by the development of hydroelectricity, begun in the early 20th century, when the waterfalls of rivers flowing down the steep slopes above the fjords were first harnessed. Later, inland sites were developed, the greatest concentration is in the Rjukan Valley, 160 km [100 mls] west of Oslo. Today Norway (which owns five of the world's highest waterfalls) derives 99.6% of its electricity from water power.

The availability of cheap electricity made possible the rapid growth of the wood-pulp, paper and chemical industries, and later stimulated the metal-working industries. Many of the industrial sites are on the shores of remote fjords, where cheap electricity and deep-water access for the import of raw materials and for the export of finished products are the determining factors in choosing the location. The aluminium and chemical industries of the south-west coast are typical.

Metal-working has developed in the far north since World War II. After primary treatment iron is exported from Kirkenes to a smelter at Mo-i-Rana, on the coast just south of the Arctic Circle, which uses coal imported from Svalbard. The port of Narvik was connected by rail to the Swedish system in 1903, so that Swedish iron ore could be sent from an ice-free port to supply the iron smelters of Germany and other continental markets. This trade remains important today.

Rapid industrial development since World War II has transformed the Norwegian economy, and has ensured that the Norwegians are among the most prosperous people in Europe. Few people are very wealthy – taxation rates are high – but few are very poor, and an advanced welfare state (common to all the Scandinavian countries) provides good services even to the most isolated or rural communities. The great majority of people own their houses, and many families have second homes on the shores of fjords and lakes. Today's Norwegians are also more generous than their Viking ancestors: the nation is by far Europe's biggest donor of foreign aid per capita, with a figure of 1.1% of GNP – well above the OECD (Organization for Economic Co-operation and Development) target of 0.7%.

The pre-war economy, dependent on forestry, farming, fishing and seafaring, is still important, but the numbers employed in these industries are dwindling as more and more people move into the new industries and services in the growing towns. There are still few large towns, and all six of those with more than 50,000 population are on the coast. The largest are Oslo, Bergen and Trondheim.

HISTORY AND POLITICS

After having been united with Denmark (1381–1814) and Sweden (1814–1905), Norway became independent in 1905. In 1940, although neutral at the time, it was occupied by German troops. At the end of World War II Norway abandoned its neutrality. Unlike its neighbours, Sweden and Finland, which have remained neutral, Norway is a member of NATO (North Atlantic Treaty Organization). However, it refused to join the EEC when Britain, Ireland and Denmark decided to enter (on 1 January 1973), and in November 1994 the Norwegian people again voted against joining the European Union. Norway is, however, a member of the Nordic Council and remains a member of EFTA, along with Iceland, Switzerland and Leichtenstein.

Svalbard is an archipelago of 62,920 sq km [24,295 sq mls] – half as big again as Denmark – sitting halfway between the North Pole and the Arctic Circle. Despite this exposed, northerly position, the climate is tempered by the relatively mild prevailing winds from the Atlantic. By far the largest island is Spitzbergen (or Vestspitzbergen), the former

SCANDINAVIA

There are several possible definitions of the term Scandinavia. In the narrow geographical sense it refers to the peninsula shared by Norway and Sweden; in a broader cultural and political sense it includes the five countries of the Nordic Council – Norway, Sweden, Denmark, Finland and Iceland. All except Finland have related languages, and all have a tradition of parliamentary democracy: Finland and Iceland are republics, while the others are constitutional monarchies.

There are also strong historical links between them, beginning in the 8th century when their ancestors, the Norsemen, colonized large parts of northern Europe. All have at different times been governed together, Sweden and Finland separating in 1809, Norway and Sweden in 1905, and Denmark and Iceland as recently as 1944.

Because of their northerly position, and their exposure to Atlantic weather systems, the Scandinavian states have a cool, moist climate not favourable to crops. However, because of the long hours of daylight in the northern summer, some surprisingly good crops are grown north of the Arctic Circle.

The Scandinavians were once among the poorest peoples of Europe, but during the last century they have become among the richest, making full use of their limited natural resources, and also seizing the opportunities which their maritime position gave them to become major shipping and fishing nations.

also being used as the name of the whole group of islands.

The rival claims on the islands by the Norwegians, the Dutch and the British lost their importance in the 18th century with the decline of whale hunting, but were raised again in the 20th century with the discovery of coal. A treaty signed in Paris by 40 parties in 1920 finally recognized Norwegian sovereignty in return for mining rights, and in 1925 the islands were incorporated officially into the kingdom of Norway.

Coal remains the principal product and main occupation, with mines run by Norway d the former Soviet Union, both of which produce similar amounts of coal. Soviet citizens outnumbered Norwegians by more than to 1 in 1988, when the total population was 646. By 1993 the population was 2,977. Following the success of the North Sea projects, there is now prospecting in Svalbard for oil and natural gas. There are several meteorological stations and a research station, and other residents work on the extensive national parks and nature reserves. An airport opened in 1975 near Longyearbyen, the capital that is named after an American (J.M. Longyear), who in 1905 was the first man to mine coal on Svalbard.

an Mayen is a volcanic island of 380 sq km [147 sq mls], north-north-east of Iceland but actually closer to the east coast of Greenland. Mountainous and partly covered by glaciers, its dominant feature is the volcano of Beerenberg (2,277 m [7,470 ft]), which had been dormant but became active again in 1970.

The island was named in 1614 after the Dutch whaling captain Jan Jacobsz May, but 'discovered' by Henry Hudson in 1608. Though uninhabited, it was used by seal trappers and other hunters, and in 1921 Norway established a meteorological and radio station. In 1929 it was annexed into the kingdom of Norway, and today the only residents are the 30 or so staff at a weather station.

Bjørnøya (Bear Island) lies halfway between Svalbard and the Norwegian mainland, on the cusp of the Norwegian Sea and Barents Sea. Measuring 179 sq km [69 sq mls], it is uninhabited but remains the centre of important cod fisheries; after a long dispute over territorial rights it was internationally recognized as part of Norway in 1925. [*Map page 13*] ■

AREA 323,900 sq km [125,050 sq mls]
POPULATION 4,318,000
CAPITAL (POPULATION) Oslo (746,000)
GOVERNMENT Constitutional monarchy
ETHNIC GROUPS Norwegian 97%
LANGUAGES Norwegian (official), Lappish, Finnish
RELIGIONS Christianity (Lutheran 88%)
CURRENCY Norwegian krone = 100 øre

OMAN

The Sultanate of Oman occupies the south-eastern corner of the Arabian peninsula. It also includes the tip of the Musandam peninsula, overlooking the strategic Strait of Hormuz. This area is separated from the rest of Oman by the United Arab Emirates. A narrow, fertile plain, the Al Batinah, borders the Gulf of Oman in the north. The plain is backed by the Al Hajar Mountains. In the south, the land is barren and rocky and includes part of the bleak Rub 'al Khali desert.

ECONOMY AND RESOURCES
Backward compared to its oil-rich Gulf neighbours to the west until 1970, the country has since been enjoying an expanding economy based on oil reserves far larger than expected when production began modestly in 1967.

Petroleum now accounts for more than 90% of government revenue – and because of Oman's detached situation the industry was not hit by the lack of confidence that afflicted the Gulf states in the 1991 war. Huge natural gas reserves were discovered in 1991 that were equal in size to all the finds of the previous 20 years. There are also some copper deposits.

But agriculture still provides a living for half of the people. Major crops include alfalfa, bananas, coconuts, dates, limes, tobacco, vegetables and wheat. Some farmers raise camels and cattle, and fishing, especially for sardines, is also important. But Oman has to import food to feed its people.

HISTORY AND POLITICS
In ancient times, Oman became an important trading area on the main route between the Gulf and the Indian Ocean. Islam was introduced in the 7th century AD and Arab-Muslim culture remains the unifying force in Oman.

Portuguese sailors captured several seaports in Oman, including Muscat, in 1507, but Arabs expelled the Portuguese in 1650. In the 1740s, the Al Bu Said family took power in Oman, and this family has ruled Oman ever since. In 1798, Oman signed the first of several treaties of friendship with Britain. Then, in the late 19th and early 20th centuries, war broke out between the Sultan's forces and peoples from the interior who wanted a religious leader to take over the government. Conflict broke out again in the 1950s and again, in the south, between 1964 and 1975, but the rebels were put down with the aid of British troops.

Oil was discovered in 1964 and the country became fully independent in 1971. Since Sultan Said bin Taimur was deposed in 1970 by his son, Qaboos bin Said – with British collusion – Oman has made substantial strides, particularly after the end of the civil war against Yemen-backed separatist guerrillas in the southern province of Dhofar (Zufar). An absolute ruler – as his family heads have been since 1749 – Qaboos has tended to forego the usual prestigious projects favoured by wealthy Arab leaders, in favour of social programmes. Even so, by 1992 an estimated 65% of adults could not read or write, and defence and internal security were taking a large proportion of the annual budget. Ties with Britain remain close and Oman is also an ally of the United States, allowing it to use air and naval bases during emergencies. [*Map page 22*] ■

AREA 212,460 sq km [82,031 sq mls]
POPULATION 2,077,000
CAPITAL (POPULATION) Muscat (250,000)
GOVERNMENT Monarchy with a consultative council
ETHNIC GROUPS Omani Arab 74%, Pakistani 21%
LANGUAGES Arabic (official)
RELIGIONS Islam 86%, Hinduism 13%
CURRENCY Omani rial = 1,000 baiza

PAKISTAN

West of the Indus delta, the arid coastal plain of Makran rises first to the Coast Range, then in successive ridges to the north –

stark, arid, deforested and eroded. Between the ridges lie desert basins like that containing the saltmarsh of Hamun-i-Mashkel on the Iranian border. Ridge and basin alternate through Baluchistan and the earthquake zone round Quetta, the *daman-i-koh* ('skirts of the hills') are still irrigated by the ancient tunnels called *karez* or *qanats*, which facilitate the growing of cereals and fruit.

North again stretches the famous North West Frontier province, pushing up between the towering Hindu Kush and Karakoram with K2 on the border with China the world's second highest mountain standing at 8,611 m [28,251 ft]. East of Peshawar lies Kashmir, which Pakistan controls to the west of the 1947 cease-fire line, and India to the east.

ECONOMY AND RESOURCES

As Egypt is the gift of the Nile, so Pakistan is the gift of the Indus and its tributaries. Despite modern industrialization, irrigated farming is vital to this Islamic state, both in Punjab, the 'land of the five rivers' – Indus, Jhelum, Beas, Ravi and Sutlej – and downstream on the dry plains flanking the Indus between Khairpur and Hyderabad. The HEP stations at Tarbela (on the Indus) and Mangla (on the Jhelum) are among the world's biggest earth- and rock-filled dams.

Like most developing countries, Pakistan has increased both mineral exploitation and manufacturing industry. To the small oil and coalfield near Rawalpindi has now been added a major resource of natural gas between Sukkur and Multan. Karachi, formerly the capital and developed in the colonial period as a wheat port, is now a considerable manufacturing centre, principally textiles; so is the cultural centre, Lahore, in the north. The well-planned national capital of Islamabad, begun in the 1960s, is still growing to the north-east of Rawalpindi, with the serrated outline of the Murree Hills – refuge for the wealthier citizens on weekends – as a backdrop to the architecture of the new city.

The world's seventh most populous country, Pakistan is likely to be overtaken by Bangladesh – its former partner separated by 1,600 km [1,000 mls] of India – by the end of the century.

'West' Pakistan's economy has done better

an poor Bangladesh, while reserves of some inerals (notably bauxite, copper, phosphates nd manganese) have yet to be exploited. Yet ere are huge problems: dependence on textes, an increasingly competitive area, and on mittances from Pakistani workers abroad, specially in the Middle East (the main source " foreign income); a chronic trade deficit and ebt burden; massive spending on defence and curity; growing drug traffic through the forth-West Frontier; and the added pressure f some 5 million Afghan refugees who fled ne civil war in their homeland. However, the ll of Kabul to Afghan Mujaheddin rebels in ne spring of 1992 brought the prospect of an nprovement in Pakistan's refugee problem – nough it also raised the possibility of renewed athan nationalism.

HISTORY AND POLITICS

The 1947 cease-fire ended war and appalling nternecine slaughter that followed the grant of ndependence from Britain, when the old ndian empire was divided between India and Pakistan – Hindu and Muslim states. The Kashmir problem was partly religious – a mainly Muslim population ruled by a Hindu maharaja who acceded to India – but there was also an underlying strategic issue: five rivers rising in or passing through Kashmir or the neighbouring Indian state of Himachal Pradesh are vital to Pakistan's economy, and could not be left in the hands of possible enemies.

In 1971, East Pakistan broke away from the western wing of the nation and formed the new state of Bangladesh, following a bitter civil war and Indian military intervention, but neither country state has enjoyed political stability or sound government.

Pakistan has been subject to military rule and martial law for much of its short life, interspersed with periods of fragile democracy resting on army consent. During one such, in 1988, Benazir Bhutto – daughter of the president executed after his government (the country's first elected civilian administration) was overthrown by the army in 1977 – was freely elected prime minister, the first female premier in the Muslim world. Two years later she was dismissed by the president following accusations of nepotism and corruption, but

managed to return to power following her party's success in elections held in October 1993. [*Map page 23*] ■

> **AREA** 796,100 sq km [307,374 sq mls]
> **POPULATION** 136,645,000
> **CAPITAL (POPULATION)** Islamabad (204,000)
> **GOVERNMENT** Federal republic
> **ETHNIC GROUPS** Punjabi 60%, Sindhi 12%, Pushtun 13%, Baluch, Muhajir
> **LANGUAGES** Urdu (official)
> **RELIGIONS** Islam 97%, Christianity, Hinduism
> **CURRENCY** Pakistan rupee = 100 paisa

PALAU (BELAU)

The republic of Palau comprises an archipelago of six Caroline groups, totalling 26 islands and over 300 islets varying in terrain from mountain to reef and totalling 458 sq km [177 sq mls].

Eight of the islands are permanently inhabited, including Peleliu (Beleliu) and Angaur – guarding the passage between the Indian and Pacific Oceans and the scene of fierce battles between American and occupying Japanese forces in World War II. Most of the largely Catholic population speak the official Palauan (Belauan), but English is widely used. The present capital is Koror (population 9,000 – over half the national total), site of one of the few deep-water harbours in the Pacific, on the island of the same name; a new capital is being built in the east of Babelthuap, the largest island, where coastal plains surround a high jungle interior.

ECONOMY AND RESOURCES

Agriculture is still largely at subsistence level, with copra the main export crop, but luxury tourism is growing, based strongly on scuba-diving and sea fishing. The country relies heavily on US aid – indeed Washington has pursued a policy of deliberate indebtedness – and the US government is by far the largest employer on the islands.

HISTORY AND POLITICS

The last remaining member of the four states that comprised the US Trust Territory of the Pacific, established under UN mandate in 1947 – thanks to sustained American skulduggery – Palau (Belau) voted to break away from the Federated States of Micronesia in 1978, and a new self-governing constitution became effective in 1981. The territory then entered into 'free association with the USA', providing sovereign-state status, but in 1983 a referendum rejected the proposal, since Washington refused to accede to a 92% vote in a 1979 referendum that declared the nation a nuclear-free zone. The result was a stalemate with the UN Trusteeship still technically in force, that was until 1 October 1994, when full independence was declared. [*Map page 26*] ■

AREA 458 sq km [177 sq mls]
POPULATION 17,000
CAPITAL (POPULATION) Koror (9,000)
GOVERNMENT Independent republic
ETHNIC GROUPS Palauan (mixture of Polynesian, Melanesian and Malay)
LANGUAGES Palauan (official), English
RELIGIONS Christianity (mainly Roman Catholic)
CURRENCY US currency

PANAMA

Less than 60 km [37 mls] wide at its narowest point, the isthmus of Panama not only links Central and South America but also, via its famous Canal, the Atlantic and Pacific Oceans. Most of the country, including some 750 offshore islands, lies below 700 m [2,300 ft], sweltering daily in tropical heat and high humidity, with heavy downpours marking the May to December rainy season. The mountain ranges trend north-west to south-east slightly against the lie of the country, and fragment the lowlands. The eastern region and the Caribbean coast are covered in dense tropical rainforests.

ECONOMY AND RESOURCES

Basins and valleys between the ranges suppo pockets of agriculture, and rainforests ha been cleared for production of bananas, co fee, cocoa and sugar cane, for cattle ranchir and for subsistence crops of rice, maize ar beans. To the east, in Darien, the thick jung remains largely undisturbed and still home a few indigenous Indian tribes.

Many Panamanians live within about 20 k [12 mls] of the Canal Zone, a quarter them in the capital city and 80% of the cou try's GDP originates here. This includ revenues from free trade, the open-registr merchant fleet (some 12,000 ships), and 'of shore' finance facilities. With exports bananas (25% of total), shrimps (19%) an mahogany, not to mention income fror tourism and substantial US aid, these hav given Panama the highest standard of livir in Central America.

The Panama Canal is 82 km [51 mls] lon from deep water at either end, 65 km [40 mls long from coast to coast. Three sets of locks a each end lift vessels to the elevated centra section 26 m [85 ft] above sea level, which includes Gatun Lake and the Gaillard Cut 13 km [8 mls] through the continental divide

HISTORY AND POLITICS

Though an American-built railway crossed th isthmus in 1855, it was a French compan under Ferdinand de Lesseps that begar cutting the Canal in 1880, but engineerin problems and deaths from disease stoppec operations after ten years. In 1903 the province of Panama declared independence from Colombia and granted the USA rights in perpetuity over a Canal Zone, 16 km [10 mls] wide. Work on the present Canal began a year later, and it was finally opened for shipping in 1914. In 1980 there were some 13,000 transits through the Canal – over 36 ships per day – carrying twice the total cargo of 1960. Now running close to capacity, the Canal cannot take fully-laden ships of over about 80,000 tonnes (thus excluding most large tankers) and an alternative Panama Seaway is under discussion. From 1979 sovereignty of the Canal Zone was restored to Panama, and the Canal itself will follow suit in 1999.

Panama's government has changed many

mes since independence. In 1983, General Manuel Antonio Noriega became Panama's leader. In 1988, two US grand juries in Florida indicted Noriega on charges of drug trafficking. In 1989, Noriega was apparently defeated in a presidential election, but the government declared the election invalid. After the killing of a US marine, US troops entered Panama and arrested Noriega, who was convicted by a Miami court of drug offences in 1992. Elections in 1994 were won by the Democratic Revolutionary Party, led by Pérez Balladares. [*Map page 30*] ■

AREA 77,080 sq km [29,761 sq mls]
POPULATION 2,585,000
CAPITAL (POPULATION) Panama City (584,000)
GOVERNMENT Multiparty republic
ETHNIC GROUPS Mestizo 60%, Black and Mulatto 20%, White 10%, Amerindian 8%, Asian 2%
LANGUAGES Spanish (official)
RELIGIONS Christianity (Roman Catholic 84%, Protestant 5%), Islam 5%
CURRENCY Balboa = 100 cents

PAPUA NEW GUINEA

Forming part of Melanesia, Papua New Guinea is the eastern section of the island of New Guinea, plus the Bismarck Archipelago and the copper-rich island of Bougainville – geographically, though not politically, part of the Solomons. The backbone of the main island is a high cordillera of rugged fold mountains, averaging between 2,500 to 4,600 m [8,000 to 15,000 ft] in height and covered with tropical montane 'cloud' forest.

Isolated valleys and intermontane basins run parallel with the main ranges. Fertile with alluvium and volcanic materials, these are the sites of isolated settlements, even today linked only by light aircraft. The capital city, Port Moresby, is not linked by road to any other major centre, and communication with the highlands depends on the country's 400 airports and airstrips.

ECONOMY AND RESOURCES

The traditional garden crops of the 'highlanders' include kaukau (sweet potato), sugar cane, bananas, maize, cassava and nut-bearing pandans. Pigs are kept mainly for status and ritual purposes. In the lowlands, taro is the staple food, although yams and sago are also important. The main cash crops are coconuts, coffee, cocoa and rubber.

While 80% of the population still live by agriculture, minerals (notably copper, gold and silver) have provided an important share of the country's exports, encouraging 'PNG' to reduce its dependence on Australian aid. Most of the copper comes from the world's biggest mine at Panguna, on Bougainville.

HISTORY AND POLITICS

Although the first European contact came as early as 1526, it was only in the late 19th century that permanent German and British settlements were established. After World War II, the UN Trust Territory of New Guinea and the Territory of Papua were administered by Australia. Self-government came in 1973, with full independence in 1975.

Demands by the Bougainville islanders for a greater share of the earnings from the copper mine spiralled into a separatist struggle by 1989 – followed by the closure of the mine, a declaration of independence by the secessionists and a blockade of the island by the government. Despite a peace accord of 1991, the position was still unchanged after three years – with the 'revolution' passing into the hands of criminal gangs. [*Map page 26*] ■

AREA 462,840 sq km [178,703 sq mls]
POPULATION 4,205,000
CAPITAL (POPULATION) Port Moresby (174,000)
GOVERNMENT Constitutional monarchy
ETHNIC GROUPS Papuan 84%, Melanesian 15%
LANGUAGES English (official)
RELIGIONS Christianity (Protestant 58%, Roman Catholic 33%, Anglican 5%), traditional beliefs 3%
CURRENCY Kina = 100 toea

PARAGUAY

A landlocked nation, Paraguay is bounded mainly by rivers – the Paraná (South America's second longest) in the south and east, the Pilcomayo in the south-west, and the Paraguay and Apa rivers in the north-west. The middle reach of the Paraguay, navigable for vessels of 1,700 tonnes to Asunción, 1,610 km [1,000 mls] from the sea, divides the country unequally. The eastern third, an extension of the Brazilian plateau at a height of 300 m to 600 m [1,000 ft to 2,000 ft] is densely forested with tropical hardwoods. The western two-thirds is the Northern Chaco, a flat, alluvial plain rising gently from the damp, marshy Paraguay river valley to semi-desert scrubland along the western border.

ECONOMY AND RESOURCES

During Stroessner's dictatorship (1954–89), there was considerable economic growth, particularly in the 1970s, and great emphasis was placed on developing hydroelectricity: by 1976 Paraguay was self-sufficient in electric energy and by 1990 the country was producing 99.9% of its electricity from water power. This was achieved by the development of two major projects – Acaray and Itaipú (the world's largest HEP project, inaugurated in 1984). In 1984 another complex on the Paraná river at Yacyreta was begun in conjunction with Argentina, and is due for completion in 1998. Yacyreta has the world's longest dam.

HISTORY AND POLITICS

Paraguay was settled in 1537 by Spaniards attracted by the labour supply of the native Guarani Indians – and the chance of finding a short cut to the silver of Peru. Forming part of the Rio de la Plata Viceroyalty from 1766, Paraguay broke free in 1811 and achieved independence from Buenos Aires in 1813. For over a century the country struggled for nationhood, torn by destructive internal strife and conflict with neighbouring states: in

1865–70, war against Brazil, Argentina and Uruguay cost the country more than half its 600,000 people and much of its territory. At a time when most other South American countries were attracting European settlers and foreign capital for development, Paraguay remained isolated and forbidding. Some territory was regained after the Chaco War against Bolivia in 1929–35, and in 1947 a period of civil war was followed by political and economic stability.

In 1954 General Stroessner seized power and assumed the presidency. His regime was a particularly unpleasant variety of despotism and he ruled with an ever-increasing disregard for human rights during nearly 35 years of fear and fraud before being deposed by his own supporters in 1989. The speeches about reform from his successor, General Andrés Rodríguez, sounded somewhat hollow, but at the end of 1991 Paraguayans did indeed go to the polls to elect a constituent assembly which would frame a new constitution incorporating a multiparty system. Free multiparty elections held in 1993 resulted in the instalment of Juan Carlos Wasmosy, Paraguay's first civilian president since 1954. [*Map page 31*] ■

AREA	406,750 sq km [157,046 sq mls]
POPULATION	4,830,000
CAPITAL (POPULATION)	Asunción (945,000)
GOVERNMENT	Multiparty republic
ETHNIC GROUPS	Mestizo 90%, Amerindian 3%
LANGUAGES	Spanish and Guaraní (both official)
RELIGIONS	Christianity (Roman Catholic 96%, Protestant 2%)
CURRENCY	Guaraní = 100 céntimos

PERU

L argest of the Andean states, Peru spread over coastal plain, mountains and forested Amazon lowlands in the interior.

The coastal plain is narrow and generally

rid, cooled by sea breezes from the offshore Humboldt Current. Occasionally it suffers violent rainstorms, associated with shifts in the pattern of surface waters. Rivers that cut through the foothills provide water for irrigated agriculture, mainly of cotton, rice and sugar cane. The middle slopes of the Andes – the Quechua, at heights of 2,000 m to 3,500 m [6,500 ft to 11,500 ft] – are warm-temperate and fairly well watered. These areas supported the main centres of Indian population in the Inca empire, and are just as well suited to densely populated rural settlements today.

Above stand the higher reaches of the Andes, extending westwards in cold inhospitable tablelands at 4,000 m to 4,800 m [13,000 ft to 15,700 ft], cultivated up to 4,200 m [13,700 ft] by peasant farmers and grazed by their sheep, alpacas, llamas and vicuñas. The snowy peaks of the high Andes rise to over 6,000 m [19,500 ft]. Though close to the Pacific Ocean, most of the rivers that rise here eventually drain into the Amazon. Their descent to the lowlands is through the *montaña*, a near-impenetrable maze of valleys, ridges and plains, permanently soaked by rain and thickly timbered. Beyond extend the Amazon lowlands – hot, wet and clad mainly in dense tropical rainforest. Occupying half the country, they are thinly inhabited by native Indians.

ECONOMY AND RESOURCES

Lima was developed as the Spanish colonial capital, and through its port of Callao passed much of the trade of the Spanish settlers; 19th-century exports included guano (bird-droppings, valuable as an agricultural fertilizer) from the offshore islands, and wild rubber. Peru gained independence from Spain in 1824, but difficulties of communication, political strife, earthquakes and other natural disasters, and a chronically unbalanced economy have dogged the country's development.

Today Peru faces many economic, social and political problems. Agricultural production has failed to keep up with population, so wheat, rice, meat and other staple foods are imported. Cotton, coffee and sugar are exported. Peru is the leading producer of coca, the shrub used in the illegal production of cocaine, and earnings were thought to be in excess of

THE ANDES

Created 200 million years ago by the collision of the Nazca plate and the land mass of South America – and still moving at about 12.5 mm [0.5 in] each year – the Andes mountain system extends along the entire west side of the continent from the coast of the Caribbean to Tierra del Fuego for over 6,400 km [4,000 mls], making it the world's longest chain.

The Andes is the highest mountain range outside the Himalayas and Argentina's Cerro Aconcagua, at 6,960 m [22,834 ft], is the highest peak outside Asia. Argentina shares with Chile four of the ten highest summits. In the middle section there are two main chains and elsewhere three, with the breadth exceeding 800 km [500 mls] to the north of latitude 20°S. Altogether the range has 54 peaks over 6,100 m [20,000 ft].

Many of South America's great rivers, including the Orinoco, Negro, Amazon and Madeira, rise in the Andes, and the range is home to the continent's largest lake, Titicaca, which lies on the Peru-Bolivia border at 3,812 m [12,506 ft]. The Andes contains numerous volcanoes and is subject almost everywhere to violent earthquakes. Many volcanoes are still active and Cotopaxi in north-central Ecuador is usually regarded as the world's highest (5,896 m [19,457 ft]).

The condor, symbol of the mountains and the world's largest vulture, is now down to a few hundred, despite attempts by several Andean countries – backed by the United States – to increase its dwindling numbers.

In 1910 the Andes were tunnelled, linking Chilean and Argentine railways by the tunnel, 3 km [2 mls] long, at an altitude of 3,200 m [10,500 ft], north of Aconcagua.

US$3 billion in the 1980s. An agreement was reached in February 1990 with the USA to stop the planting of coca in some areas and instead to plant oil palms, but success has been limited and much still finds its way to Colombia for processing and re-export.

Peru once had the largest fish catch in the world and there are 70 canning factories. Anchoveta was the main target, but fishing

THE INCA CIVILIZATION

The empire of the Incas, centring on Cuzco in the Peruvian highlands, developed from millennia of earlier Andean civilizations that included the Chavin, the Nazca and the Tiahuanaco. The Incas began their conquests about AD 1350, and by the end of the 15th century their empire extended from central Chile to Ecuador. Perhaps some 10 million people owed allegiance to it when it fell to the Spanish *conquistadores* in 1532.

The empire was military and theocratic, with the sun as the focus of worship. Temples and shrines, built of huge, laboriously shaped, closely fitting but uncemented blocks (the Incas had no metal tools), were created for sun worship; the Sun Temple at Cuzco had a circumference of 350 m [1,148 ft], and many other buildings were equally massive. The people were skilled farmers, using elaborate irrigation systems and terraced fields.

Gold and silver were particularly valued by the Incas for ornamentation. They were prized also by the *conquistadores*, who looted them from every corner of the empire and quickly set the Indians to mining more. The Incas had no written script: buildings and terracing – notably those of 'the lost city' of Machupicchu north-west of Cuzco – and delicate ornaments form their main memorials, though fragments of Inca culture and beliefs remain among the Quechua-speaking peoples of Peru and Bolivia.

was halted from 1976 until 1982 because of depleted stocks. In 1983 a warm current known as 'El Niño' ruined the fishing but recovery followed from 1986.

Several metals are exported, including silver, zinc and lead, with copper the most important earner. However, industrial unrest has reduced production dramatically. Exports of oil are growing, providing much-needed foreign capital for industrial development, now forthcoming after a lull following limited debt repayment in 1985. Peru's inflation rate – a staggering 7,480% in 1990 – settled down to a modest 200% or so in 1991, the year that many state industries were liberalized.

HISTORY AND POLITICS

Amerindian people probably reached the are about 12,000 years ago. Several civilization developed in the Andes region. By about A 1200, the Inca were established in souther Peru. In 1500, their empire extended from Ecuador to Chile. The Spanish adventure Francisco Pizarro visited Peru in the 1520s Hearing of Inca riches, he returned in 1532 By 1533, he had conquered most of Peru.

In 1820, the Argentinian José de Sar Martín led an army into Peru and declared th country to be independent. But Spain still hel large areas. In 1823, the Venezuelan Simór Bolívar led another army into Peru, and i 1824 one of his generals defeated th Spaniards at Ayacucho. The Spaniards surren dered in 1826, but Peru suffered much insta bility throughout the 19th century and into th 20th century.

In 1980, when civilian rule was restored, a left-wing group called the *Sendero Luminoso*, o the 'Shining Path', began guerrilla warfare against the government. In 1990, Alberto Fujimori, son of Japanese immigrants, became president. In 1992, he suspended the constitution and the guerrilla leader, Abimael Guzmán, was arrested, but instability continued. A new constitution was introduced in 1993, giving increased power to the president, who faced many problems in rebuilding the shattered economy.

To add to Peru's problems, the country suffered the worst cholera outbreak in the Americas this century early in 1991, with some 2,500 deaths. Trading partners were reluctant to import vulnerable Peruvian food products. [*Map page 31*] ∎

AREA 1,285,220 sq km [496,223 sq mls]
POPULATION 23,331,000
CAPITAL (POPULATION) Lima (Lima-Callao, 6,415,000)
GOVERNMENT Transitional republic
ETHNIC GROUPS Quechua 47%, Mestizo 32%, White 12%, Aymara 5%
LANGUAGES Spanish and Quechua (both official)
RELIGIONS Christianity (Roman Catholic 93%, Protestant 6%)
CURRENCY New sol = 100 centavos

PHILIPPINES

The Republic of the Philippines consists of 7,107 islands, of which, 2,770 are named and about 1,000 permanently inhabited, with the two largest, Luzon and Mindanao, making up over two-thirds of the total area. The country lacks extensive areas of lowland and most of the islands are characterized by rugged interior mountains, the highest of which are Mt Apo (2,954 m [9,691 ft]) in Mindanao and Mt Pulog (2,929 m [9,610 ft]) in Luzon. There are over 20 active volcanoes in the islands, including Mt Apo and Mt Pinatubo, which erupted violently in 1991.

ECONOMY AND RESOURCES

The most important lowland region is the central plain of Luzon, a key rice-producing area and a major zone of population concentration, including the Manila Bay area. The most impressive man-made sight, however, is the spectacular series of irrigated rice terraces that contour the mountain slopes in the northern interior of Luzon. These have been constructed by Igorot tribesmen, descendants of some of the earliest people to colonize the Philippines. Elsewhere in the islands, and especially on Cebu, Leyte and Negros, maize is the staple foodstuff, reflecting the Philippines' former contacts with Spanish America. Another link is Roman Catholicism; over 80% of the population are Catholic, and named after King Philip II of Spain, the country is the only predominantly Christian nation of any size in Asia.

The economy, lacking any exploitable natural resources, remains weak, and levels of unemployment and emigration among Filipinos are high.

HISTORY AND POLITICS

Following three centuries of harsh Spanish rule the islands were ceded to the US in 1898 after the Spanish-American War. Though the Philippines gained independence from the USA in 1946, ties have remained strong,

notably during the corrupt regime of President Ferdinand Marcos (1965–86), though in 1991 the Philippines government announced the closure of Subic Bay naval base, the largest in Asia, by the end of 1992.

Marcos was overthrown by the 'people power' revolution that brought to office Corazon Aquino, widow of the opposition leader assassinated in 1983. The political situation remained volatile however, with Communist and Muslim Nationalist rebels undermining stability. Mrs Aquino did not stand in the presidential elections in 1992. Her successor was General Fidel V. Ramos. [*Map page 26*] ■

AREA 300,000 sq km [115,300 sq mls]
POPULATION 66,188,000
CAPITAL (POPULATION) Manila (or Metro Manila, 6,720,000)
GOVERNMENT Multiparty republic
ETHNIC GROUPS Tagalog 30%, Cebuano 24%, Ilocano 10%, Hiligaynon Ilongo 9%, Bicol 6%, Samar-Leyte 4%
LANGUAGES Pilipino (Tagalog) and English (both official)
RELIGIONS Christianity (Roman Catholic 84%, Philippine Independent Church or Aglipayan 6%, Protestant 4%), Islam 4%
CURRENCY Philippine peso = 100 centavos

PITCAIRN ISLANDS

A British dependent territory of four islands (48 sq km [19 sq mls]), Pitcairn is situated halfway between New Zealand and Panama in the Pacific Ocean.

Subsistence gardening and fishing are the main activities. The islanders also derive some income from wood carvings and postage stamps, as well as from outside investment.

Uninhabited until 1790, Pitcairn was occupied by nine mutineers from HMS *Bounty* and some men and women from Tahiti. In 1856 some 194 of its people moved at their own request to Norfolk Island, though 43 of them returned between 1859 and 1864. The present population of 70, all living in Adamstown on Pitcairn, come under the administration of the British High Commission in Wellington and use the New Zealand dollar. [*Map page 2*] ■

AREA 48 sq km [19 sq mls]
POPULATION 70
CAPITAL (POPULATION) Adamstown (70)
GOVERNMENT British dependent territory
ETHNIC GROUPS English, Tahitian
LANGUAGES English
RELIGIONS Seventh-Day Adventists
CURRENCY New Zealand currency

POLAND

Poland consists mostly of lowlands that form part of the Northern European Plain. On its southern borders are the Tatra Mountains, a section of the Carpathian range. The geographical location of Poland has had a strong influence on the country's stormy history. On many occasions powerful neighbours – notably Russia and Germany – have found it all too easy to invade and occupy the land. The most recent frontier changes came at the end of World War II – in which the country lost 6 million people, or a massive 17% of the total population – when Poland gave up territory to the USSR, and in compensation gained parts of Germany as far as the River Oder.

ECONOMY AND RESOURCES

As a result of these changes Poland lost poor agricultural land in the east and gained an important industrial region in the west, including, in the south-west, Silesia and the former German city of Breslau (now called Wroclaw), in the north-west the Baltic port of Stettin (now Szczecin), and in the north the other port of Danzig (now Gdansk). Acquisition of a length of Baltic coastline (there was only a narrow access corridor where the Poles developed the port of Gdynia as a competitor with Danzig) gave Poland a chance to develop

maritime interests. Now a major fishing nation, Poland's fleets operate worldwide.

Before World War II Poland was primarily an agricultural country, with 65% of the population dependent on farming, but the postwar industrialization drive under Communism reduced this proportion to about 30%, most of them still on privately owned farms. Poland is still, however, a major supplier of agricultural produce: nearly two-thirds of the land surface is farmed, about half of this area supporting crops of rye and potatoes. Oats, sugar beet, pigs and dairy produce are also important.

Poland's industrial development since World War II has been striking. Coal, lignite, sulphur, lead and zinc are the main mineral products, though Poland is also Europe's top producer of copper and silver. Underground salt deposits form the basis of important chemical industries. Most of Poland's industrial energy is derived from coal, but oil and natural gas are being developed, and hydroelectric power is being produced in increasing amounts from the Carpathians. Heavy industries include manufacture of steel and cement, and many secondary products. Many of Poland's newer industries remain almost wholly reliant on gas and oil from various parts of the former Soviet Union – a difficult position in a changing world.

Poland's reliance on heavy industry, much of it state-controlled and unprofitable, proved to be a major obstacle in the country's 'fast-track' route from Communism to capitalism that followed the pioneering triumph of democratic forces in 1989. The old industries needed drastic measures – re-equipping, restructuring and diversifying – but this could be achieved only with huge assistance from the West; Poland received nearly 70% of all Western credits to Eastern Europe between 1989 and 1991, adding to an already unserviceable foreign debt. Rising inflation (1,000% at one stage) and unemployment however, coupled with a drastic drop in living standards (the economy shrank by 10% in 1991), led to a resurgence of militant unionism.

HISTORY AND POLITICS

Under the banner of the independent trade union Solidarity, based originally in the Gdansk shipyards and led by Lech Walesa, land was the first of the Soviet satellites to allenge and bring down its Communist gime. The example set by the Poles (even ough they were to be the last Eastern ropean country to implement full democ- cy in October 1991), proved an inspiration t only to the other European Socialist states, t it also to the peoples of the Baltic republics. Elected national president a year earlier, ech Walesa found it difficult to form a stable vernment after the 1991 elections – the untry's first truly democratic ballot since fore World War II – with the new constitu- on producing a parliament representing no ss than 29 different parties. Solidarity itself ad not lived up to its name, dividing in 1990 ver personality clashes and the speed of form, seemingly unable to reconcile an nate conflict between its two roles – on the ne hand forming 35% of a government nplementing severe economic measures and, n the other, a trade union trying to protect he interests of its members. Indeed, Poland's ransition to a free market proved more painful han that of Czechoslovakia and Hungary. Despite being the pioneer of the process it eemed weighed down by its very size, a pris- ner of its postwar past. [*Map pages 4–5*] ■

AREA 312,680 sq km [120,726 sq mls]
POPULATION 38,341,000
CAPITAL (POPULATION) Warsaw (1,655,000)
GOVERNMENT Multiparty republic
ETHNIC GROUPS Polish 98%, Ukrainian 1%
LANGUAGES Polish (official)
RELIGIONS Christianity (Roman Catholic 94%, Orthodox 2%)
CURRENCY Zloty = 100 groszy

PORTUGAL

The most westerly of Europe's 'mainland' countries, Portugal occupies an oblong coastland in the south-west of the Iberian peninsula, facing the Atlantic Ocean. Here the Meseta edge has splintered and in part foundered to leave upstanding mountain ranges, particularly in the Serra da Estrêla and its continuation just north of the River Tagus (Tejo), and in the Serra de Monchique.

Portugal has two conurbations with over a million inhabitants. Lisbon, the capital, is the chief centre of the country's financial, com- mercial and industrial concerns and has a fine sheltered harbour in the large Tagus estuary. Oporto, the main centre for the densely- populated north, has an ocean outpost. These two cities still dominate the nation, but during recent decades tourism and rapid residential growth have transformed the subtropical coastline of the Algarve, and have led to a substantial increase in its population.

ECONOMY AND RESOURCES

The mild, moist airflow from the Atlantic encourages good tree growth. Forests reach a height of at least 1,300 m [4,260 ft] in the north and over a quarter of the country is forested. Pines form the most common species, especially on the sandy 'litorals' near the coast, where large plantations provide tim- ber as well as resin and turpentine. Cork oaks abound in the Tagus valley and farther south; Portugal is the world's leading producer of the cork that is derived from their bark.

A wide variety of fruits is cultivated, includ- ing olives, figs and grapes. Portugal is home to some of the world's greatest vineyards and in 1991 ranked eigth in the world, producing 991,000 tonnes of wine. Most of the grapes are grown north of the Tagus, where the most celebrated speciality is port wine from the Douro valley near the Portuguese-Spanish frontier. The grape juice is transported by boat down the Douro to Vila Nova, where it is fortified and stored for export. The lower parts of the Douro and Minho basins produce famous sparkling vinhos verdes, while the vineyards near the Tagus estuary are noted for white table wines and brandy. In the south the Algarve, with its greater sunshine and aridity, specializes more in liqueurs and muscatels.

The Portuguese economy relies heavily on agriculture and fishing, which together employ over a quarter of the national workforce. These industries are mostly undercapitalized and still rather primitive by European stan- dards, although they provide valuable exports.

In the rainy north the pressure of overpopulation has created fragmented and tiny agricultural holdings (*minifundia*); in the drier south large holdings (*latifundia*) tend to create monoculture with below-average yields and seasonal unemployment. Recently there has been some investment in irrigation.

The main general crops are food cereals and vegetables, including a wide variety of the beans that form a frequent and favourite item of the Portuguese diet. Maize and rye predominate in the north, and wheat, barley and oats in the south. Of the many farm animals, the pig deserves special mention as the forager of the heavy yield of acorns from the cork and evergreen oaks.

Portugal's long coastline provides an important supplementary source of livelihood and of foreign tourist currency. The shallow lagoons yield shellfish, especially oysters; the coastal waters supply sardines, anchovy and tunny; the deep-sea fisheries, long frequented by Portuguese sailors, bring hake, mackerel, halibut and, above all, cod.

While much of Portuguese industry is concerned with the products of farming, fishing and forestry, the manufacture of textiles and ceramics is also widespread. Modern engineering, associated with a complete iron and steel plant, has been established at Seixal near Lisbon. There is some small-scale mining for copper ores and wolfram (a tungstate of iron and manganese, from which tungsten is obtained), but a relative shortage of power resources is a problem. A small quantity of poor-quality coal is mined annually, and this is supplemented with foreign imports. Great efforts have been made to develop hydroelectric power stations in the north, but Portugal remains the poorest member of the EU since switching economic allegiance from EFTA on 1 January 1986.

HISTORY AND POLITICS
Portugal first established its independence in 1128. It formed an alliance with England in 1373, which has lasted. In the 15th century, Portugal built an empire with colonies in South America, Africa, India and the Far East, and became a major naval power. Occupied by French forces during the Napoleonic wars, it was liberated by British troops in 1811.

A republic was proclaimed in 1910 and t following two decades saw a great deal political instability. This led to the dictatorsh of Prime Minister Antonio Salazar which w to last from 1932 to 1968. Salazar engaged long and expensive colonial wars again emerging independence movements, partic larly in Angola and Mozambique. General di satisfaction with Salazar's policies (large continued by his successor, Caetano) final culminated in a bloodless coup by left-win army officers on 25 April 1974. They soo granted independence to the former coloni and attempted to establish a radical sociali regime. This was rejected by Portuguese vo ers in the 1976 elections and by 1979 the cen tre right parties were in power and civilia government was fully restored in 1982 Portugal was a founder member of NATO (i 1949) and joined the EC in 1986, at the sam time as Spain. [*Map page 18*] ■

AREA 92,390 sq km [35,672 sq mls]
POPULATION 9,830,000
CAPITAL (POPULATION) Lisbon (2,561,000)
GOVERNMENT Multiparty republic
ETHNIC GROUPS Portuguese 99%, Cape Verdean, Brazilian, Spanish, British
LANGUAGES Portuguese (official)
RELIGIONS Christianity (Roman Catholic 95%, other Christians 2%)
CURRENCY Escudo = 100 centavos

PUERTO RICO

Easternmost of the major Greater Antilles, Puerto Rico is mountainous in the interior, with a narrow coastal plain. Cerro de Punta (1,338 m [4,389 ft]) is the highest peak.

ECONOMY AND RESOURCES
Flat ground for agriculture is scarce, mainly devoted to cash crops like sugar, coffee, bananas and, since the arrival of Cuban refugees, tobacco, as well as tropical fruits, vegetables and various spices.

However, the island is now the most industrialized and urban nation in the Caribbean –
nearly half the population lives in the San Juan
area – with chemicals constituting 36% of
exports and metal products (based on deposits
of copper) a further 17%. Manufacturing,
dominated by US companies attracted by tax
exemptions, and tourism are now the two
growth sectors in a country where the standard
of living (while low in US terms) is nevertheless the highest in Latin America outside the
island tax havens, and rising.

HISTORY AND POLITICS

Puerto Rico ('rich port') was discovered in
1493 by Colombus and was a Spanish possession until ceded to the USA in 1898. It
became a self-governing Commonwealth in
free association with the USA after a referendum in 1952. Though this gave the island a
considerable measure of autonomy, American
influence stretches well beyond its constitutional roles in defence and immigration.

Debate over the exact status of the country
subsided in the 1970s, the compromise apparently accepted as a sensible middle way
between the extremes of being the 51st state of
the US or completely independent, but resur-
faces with the boom years. A referendum in
December 1991 narrowly rejected a proposal
to guarantee 'the island's distinct cultural
identity' – a result interpreted as a move
towards statehood. Meanwhile, free access to
the US has relieved the growing pressure
created by one of the greatest population
densities in the New World, with New York
City traditionally the most popular destination; the immigrants, however, are not always
welcome. [*Map page 30*] ■

AREA 8,900 sq km [3,436 sq mls]
POPULATION 3,646,000
CAPITAL (POPULATION) San Juan (1,816,000)
GOVERNMENT Self-governing Commonwealth
in free association with the USA
ETHNIC GROUPS Spanish 99%, African-
American, Indian
LANGUAGES Spanish, English
RELIGIONS Christianity (mainly Roman
Catholic)
CURRENCY US currency

QATAR

The State of Qatar is an Arab Emirate
which occupies a peninsula jutting out
from the Arabian peninsula into the Gulf. The
low-lying land is mostly stony desert, with
some barren salt flats. Much of the country's
drinking water supply is distilled sea water.

Qatar derives its high standard of living
from oil and gas. Oil was first discovered in
1939 and accounts for about 90% of Qatar's
exports. Money from oil has been used to create manufacturing industries and to develop
agriculture and fishing. But despite diversification into cement, steel and fertilizers, oil and
gas still account for over 80% of revenues. The
economy of the country is heavily dependent
on the immigrant workforce, notably from
India and poorer Middle East states.

Once part of the Ottoman empire, Qatar
signed a protection treaty with Britain in 1916.
Having failed to set up a federation of emerging new states in the area, it declared its
independence in 1971. [*Map page 22*] ■

AREA 11,000 sq km [4,247 sq mls]
POPULATION 540,000
CAPITAL (POPULATION) Doha (217,000)
GOVERNMENT Constitutional absolute
monarchy
ETHNIC GROUPS Southern Asian 34%,
Qatari 20%
LANGUAGES Arabic
RELIGIONS Islam 92%, Christianity, Hinduism
CURRENCY Qatar riyal = 100 dirhams

RÉUNION

Réunion is the largest of the Mascarene
islands, lying east of Madagascar and
south-west of Mauritius and composed of a

rugged, mountainous forested centre surrounded by a fertile coastal plain. The volcanic mountains rise in spectacular scenery to the peak of the sporadically active Piton des Neiges (3,070 m [10,076 ft]). Réunion receives heavy rainfall from the cool south-east trade winds in winter, while the summers can be oppressively hot and humid.

The lowlands are intensely cultivated with huge plantations of sugar cane; providing 75% of exports (plus rum 3%), this remains the island's only significant industry, though vanilla, perfume oils and tea also produce revenue. Local consumption revolves around vegetables, maize and livestock. Tourism is a big hope for the future, following the success of Mauritius, but unemployment is high and France still subsidizes the islands heavily in return for its use as the main military base in the area. The people of the island – which has a very varied and potentially explosive ethnic mix – are divided on its status; as in the other overseas departments (Guadeloupe, Martinique and French Guiana), there is increasing pressure on Paris for independence, especially from the young underprivileged population. In 1991 several people were killed in outbreaks of civil unrest. [*Map page 3*] ■

AREA 2,510 sq km [969 sq mls]
POPULATION 644,000
CAPITAL (POPULATION) Saint-Denis (122,875)
GOVERNMENT French overseas department
ETHNIC GROUPS Mixed 64%, East Indian 28%, Chinese 2%, East African 1%
LANGUAGES French, Creole
RELIGIONS Christianity (mainly Roman Catholic), Islam
CURRENCY French currency

ROMANIA

O n three sides Romania has clearly defined natural boundaries – the Danube in the south, the Black Sea coast, 200 km [125 mls]

long, in the east, and the River Prut in th north-east – but in the west the frontier wi Hungary crosses the Hungarian Plain, cuttin across several tributaries of the River Tisa.

Romania is dominated by a great arc of hig fold mountains, the Carpathians, which curv round the plateaux of Transylvania in th heart of the country. South and east of th Carpathians are the plains of the lowe Danube. The southern arm of the fold moun tains, rising to 2,538 m [8,327 ft], is known a the Transylvanian Alps, the legendary home o Count Dracula. Where these meet th Danube, on the border with Yugoslavia, th river has cut a deep gorge – the Iron Gat (Portile de Fier) – whose rapids over 160 kn [100 mls] long have been tamed by the con struction of a huge barrage. In the east th Danube delta area has more than 3,00 glaciated lakes and some of Europe's most cel ebrated expanses of wetland.

There is a great contrast between the fairy tale landscape of wooded hills in Transylvani and the Carpathians, and the wheat and maize fields of the Danubian lowlands.

ECONOMY AND RESOURCES
Romania is still a strong agricultural country with an export surplus of cereals, timber, fruits and wine, though the agrarian workforce shrank from 75% in 1950 to less than 30% in 1984. In 1991 the country ranked sixth in maize production and tenth in wine.

Under Ceausescu there was a great drive to develop industries, based on the abundant oil and gas resources of areas on the flanks of the Transylvanian Alps. The copper, lead, zinc and aluminium industries use domestic supplies, mainly found in the Bihor Massif in Transylvania, but the iron and steel industry, especially the new plant at Galati at the head of the Danubian delta, relies on imported ores.

Bucharest, the capital, lies between the Danube and the Carpathians. An important industrial centre, its manufactures include vehicles, textiles and foodstuffs.

HISTORY AND POLITICS
Ceausescu's 24-year rule was one of the Communist world's most odious. Corrupt and self-seeking, he had nevertheless won plaudits from the West for his independent stance

ainst Soviet control – including a knight-od from Queen Elizabeth II. Coming to wer in 1965, he accelerated the party policy distancing the country from Moscow's reign aims while pursuing a strict Stalinist proach on the domestic front. The remorse-ss industrialization and urbanization pro-ammes of the 1970s caused a severe debt oblem, and in the 1980s he switched onomic tack, cutting imports and diverting itput to exports. But while Romania hieved the enviable status of a net creditor, s people – brainwashed by incessant propa-anda – were reduced from sufficiency to absidence to shortage, with food and energy oth savagely rationed. Meanwhile, with many f his relatives in positions of power, eausescu built ghetto-like 'agro-industrial' ousing complexes, desecrating some of the ountry's finest architecture and demolishing nousands of villages in the process.

The army-backed revolt of 1989 began in he western province of Transylvania, follow-ng the suppression of demonstrations in Timisoara by the notorious *Securitate* (secret olice). It culminated only days later in the xecution of the dictator Nicolae Ceausescu und his wife on Christmas Day, on charges of genocide and corruption. A provisional gov-rnment of the National Salvation Front founded only on 22 December) took control; much of the old administrative apparatus was dismantled, the Communist Party was dis-solved and religion was re-legalized. In May 1990, under Ion Iliescu, the NSF won Romania's first free elections since the war by a huge majority – a result judged flawed but not fraudulent by international observers.

The NSF, however, contained many old-guard Communists, and its credibility sank further when Iliescu used miners to curb anti-government demonstrations. Strikes and protests continued, not only against the new authorities but also against the effects of a gradual but nevertheless marked switch to a market economy: food shortages, rampant inflation and rising unemployment. In addi-tion, foreign investment was sluggish, deterred by the political instability. During 1991 the struggle between the two factions of the NSF – conservative President Iliescu (a former Ceausescu Politburo member) and reformist

Prime Minister Petre Roman – personified the split that existed right across a country in des-perate need of unity.

Another problem appeared with the new independent status of Moldova. The republic has a vociferous Romanian minority in the large area of Bessarabia, handed over to the USSR as part of the Hitler-Stalin pact of 1940 and not returned by the Red Army in 1945. The new mood in the former Soviet Union rekindled the concept of *Romania Mare* ('Greater Romania').

A new constitution, approved in 1991, made the country a democratic republic. Elections held under this constitution in 1992 again resulted in victory for Ion Iliescu, whose party was renamed the Party of Social Democracy in 1993. In March 1994 a coalition government was formed, but the gov-ernment still faces many problems as it tries to reform the economy. [*Map page 17*] ■

AREA 237,500 sq km [91,699 sq mls]
POPULATION 22,922,000
CAPITAL (POPULATION) Bucharest
(2,064,000)
GOVERNMENT Multiparty republic
ETHNIC GROUPS Romanian 89%, Hungarian
7%, Gypsy 2%
LANGUAGES Romanian (official)
RELIGIONS Christianity (Romanian
Orthodox 87%, Roman Catholic 5%, Greek
Orthodox 4%)
CURRENCY Leu = 100 bani

RUSSIA

It is an indication of the sheer size of the former Soviet Union that, having shed very nearly a quarter of its area with the departure of the 14 republics in 1991, the Russian Federation remains by far the largest country in the world, still getting on for twice the size of Canada, China or the USA. This territorial immensity brings a number of disadvantages – it is awkward to administer, large investments have to be made in the transport system and the long borders are difficult to defend – but set against these are the benefits that derive from the diversity of environments and cultures and the abundance of resources in the country's vast expanses, many of which are relatively untouched.

Landscape

Diversity certainly characterizes Russia's landforms, for within the country's borders are to be found rugged peaks and salt flats, glaciers and deserts, marshes and rolling hills as well as broad level plains. In the west the North European Plain, underlain by the ancient peneplained rocks of the Russian platform, occupies the greater part of European Russia as well as much of Ukraine and all of Belarus and the Baltic nations. On the eastern side of the plain are the Ural Mountains: popularly seen as the divide between Europe and Asia, the Urals are low and rounded with few peaks rising above 1,600 m [5,248 ft]. The eastern slopes of the Urals merge into the West Siberian lowland, the largest plain in the world, with extensive low-lying marshes. Still further to the east the Siberian platform, similar in origin to the Russian platform, underlies the Central Siberian Plateau. The relief of this plateau is a good example of a peneplain, with its rolling uplands rising 500 to 700 m [1,640 to 2,300 ft] and deeply incised river valleys.

The extensive plains of Russia are surrounded on the south and east by mountain ranges of geologically recent origin: the Caucasus, rising to over 5,000 m [16,400 ft] on the borders of Georgia and Azerbaijan; the Altai and Sayan, extending into Mongolia; and, beyond Lake Baykal and the Lena River, the East Siberian ranges at the easternmost tip of the Asian land mass. The Kamchatka peninsula is still geologically unstable – part of the 'Pacific Rim' – and volcanic eruptions and earthquakes occur fairly often. Much of Russia's landscape bears the imprint of the last Ice Age in the form of chaotic drainage systems, extensive marshlands, lakes and moraines in the lowland areas and cirques and U-shaped valleys in the mountains. Today large areas remain ice-bound, while more than half the total area has permafrost – permanently frozen ground which may extend

TRANS-SIBERIAN RAILWAY

The world's longest line, the Trans-Siberian Railway runs for 9,310 km [5,785 mls] from Moscow to Vladivostok and Nakhodka on the Sea of Japan. The Siberian section, beginning at Chelyabinsk in the southern Urals, was built between 1881 and 1905, with an extension round Lake Baykal completed in 1917. The line has played a crucial role in opening up Siberia for settlement and industrialization, and most of the major cities and towns are served by it. Today the lifeline is largely double-track and electrified; the whole journey from capital to coast (involving 92 stops in eight time zones) takes over seven days. A spur of 3,200 km [2,000 mls], opened in 1984, passes north of Lake Baykal to reach Sovetskaya Gavan, opposite the island of Sakhalin.

hundreds of metres in depth. In the permafrost of East Siberia prehistoric woolly mammoths have been found in near-perfect condition.

The rivers that flow across the Russian plains are among the longest and most languid in the world. Drainage in European Russia forms a radial pattern with the hub in the Central Uplands west of Moscow. The Volga flows from this area for 3,700 km [2,300 mls] south to the landlocked Caspian Sea, the world's largest inland body of water. In Siberia the main rivers flow north to the Arctic – among them the Yenisey-Angara, the Ob-Irtysh and the Lena, respectively the fifth, sixth and 11th longest in the world. Shifting channels and irregular flow make these rivers difficult to navigate and they are ice-bound in winter. In the east Lake Baykal (Oz Baykal) acts as a holding reservoir for the Yenisey.

Natural regions

Extending latitudinally across Russia, and corresponding to the major climatic belts, are a series of sharply differentiated natural zones – from north to south the tundra, the taiga, the mixed forests and the steppe. The dominant natural zones can also be seen as vertical bands in the mountainous regions.

Tundra: This zone forms a continuous strip north of the Arctic Circle from the Norwegian border to Kamchatka. Climatic conditions here restrict plant growth and soil formation so that the region well deserves its name 'bald mountain top', the meaning of the word 'tundra' in Lapp. Stunted shrubs, mosses, lichens and berry-bearing bushes growing in thin, infertile soils form the vegetation cover, supporting various hardy creatures – including the herds of reindeer which for centuries have formed the basis of the local tribes' economy.

Taiga: Extending south from the boundary with the tundra and occupying about 60% of the country are the coniferous forests that make up the taiga – larger than the Amazonian rainforest. Different species of tree dominate in different parts of the taiga, but throughout the most common are firs, pines and the silver birch. Soils under the forest are podzols, a Russian term meaning 'ashy-grey underneath'. These soils are acidic and usually unsuitable for cultivation unless fertilized. A major source of wealth in the taiga has always been its large population of fur-bearing animals such as ermine, sable and beaver – and it was the quest for furs that first lured man into this inhospitable environment.

Mixed forest: In the west and east the coniferous forests merge into zones of mixed forest – wide in European Russia but contracting towards the east to form a narrow finger which peters out beyond the Urals. The mixed forest contains both coniferous species and broadleaves such as oak, beech, ash, hornbeam and maple. Today much of the natural vegetation has been cleared for farming, despite the fact that the soils require heavy application of fertilizers to be productive. From early times the mixed forest has been the focus of settlement for the Russians and has supported large numbers of people.

Steppe: Sandwiched between the forests to the north and the semi-deserts and deserts of the Central Asian republics to the south is the steppe zone. Hardly any natural vegetation remains in the steppe today as vast expanses have been brought under the plough. The soils of the steppe are chernozems, black-earths, and they are among the most fertile in the world. Before conversion into farmland the steppe consisted of extensive grasslands which

LAKE BAYKAL

With a lowest point of 1,620 m [5,315 ft], Oz Baykal in southern Siberia is the world's deepest lake. Also the largest in Eurasia – at 636 km [395 mls] long by an average width of 48 km [30 mls] it measures some 31,500 sq km [12,160 sq mls], more than the area of Belgium – it is so deep that it is the world's largest body of fresh water and indeed contains no less than a fifth of the fresh water contained in all the world's lakes. Its volume of 23,000 cu km [5,520 cu mls] is as much as the five Great Lakes of North America combined.

Situated in a deep tectonic basin, and fed by 336 rivers and streams, it acts as a reservoir for only one river: the Angara, which flows north to join the Yenisey. Though renowned for the purity of its water and its endemic lifeforms (65% of its 1,500 animal species and 35% of its plant species are unique to Baykal), industrial plants, including mining but notably cellulose factories at the southern end, have caused increasing pollution since the 1960s.

The graben fault that hosts the arc-shaped lake was caused by gigantic upheavals in the Earth's crust some 80 million years ago. When the climate turned wetter, about 25 million years ago, the lake began to fill – and it is still getting larger. When the *sarma* wind blows from the north-west, it generates waves more than 5 m [16.5 ft] high. Located 80 km [50 mls] from the Mongolian border, Lake Baykal drains an area of 540,000 sq km [208,500 sq mls] – an area 13% greater than that drained by all five of North America's Great Lakes.

in the north were interspersed with trees. The vast majority of the steppeland of the former Soviet Union, however, falls in the Ukraine and Kazakhstan.

ECONOMY AND RESOURCES

Russia's physical environment offers varied opportunities for exploitation. The vast stretches of forest make it the world's largest possessor of softwoods, but although the most extensive stands are found in Siberia, felling has been concentrated in the European part of the country, where the wood is of high quality and is more readily accessible.

The rivers, lakes and seas have yielded marine and freshwater products from early days. In the 11th century fishing villages were already established on the northern coast of European Russia for whaling, sealing and fishing. Today fish catches are large on the Pacific coast while, among the freshwater varieties, the sturgeon continues to be valued for its famous caviar.

Because of the widespread occurrence of poor soils and harsh climatic conditions, agriculture is confined to a relatively small area of the country. Most of the arable is in the steppe and forest-steppe and from the time this was first ploughed it has been used for grains. More than half of the output that made the USSR the world's top producer of barley, oats and rye, and second in wheat, came from Russian land. On the Black Sea coast, subtropical conditions allow the cultivation of crops exotic to the rest of the country, including wines, tea and citrus fruits.

Mineral and energy resources are abundant and formed the basis of the former USSR's powerful industrial economy. The most notable mineral deposits are found on the Kola peninsula by the Barents Sea, in eastern Siberia and the far east where spectacular discoveries of gold, lead, zinc, copper and diamonds have been made. Iron ore is found in most regions – the Soviet Union produced a quarter of the world total – but the most recently opened field is at Kursk, south of Moscow. Energy resources are varied. Estimates show Russia to have sufficient coal to last several hundred years, while oil and natural gas deposits are projected to last for several decades, with the main fields in the Volga-Urals region and western Siberia. Before 'deconstruction' the USSR was by far the world's leading producer of oil and gas, and Russia itself was responsible for over 90% of oil output and nearly 80% of gas. Large hydropower complexes have also been built on many rivers, though the development of nuclear energy remains under review following the tragic disaster of Chernobyl (in the Ukraine) in 1986.

THE KURIL ISLANDS

A chain of 56 windswept volcanically active islands extending 1,200 km [750 mls] between the end of Russia's Kamchatka Peninsula and the tip of Japan's northern island of Hokkaido, the Kurils separate the Sea of Okhotsk from the Pacific Ocean. Totalling 15,600 sq km [6,000 sq mls] but sparsely peopled, they were discovered by the Dutch in 1634, divided between Russia and Japan in the 18th century and ceded to Japan in 1875. At the end of World War II they were seized by Stalin, giving his fleets ice-free northern access to the Pacific. The Japanese, however, still regard the southern section – Etorofu, Kunashir, Shikotan and the Habomai islets – as theirs, referring to them as the 'northern territories' and allotting 7 February as a national day in their honour.

Though there are rich fishing grounds in the territorial waters and the possibility of mineral wealth, it is indeed a matter of honour rather than economics for Tokyo. The Soviets offered to return Shikotan and the Habomai islands in 1956, but the Japanese held out for all four, and the offer was withdrawn. While the advent of Gorbachev and glasnost made little difference, the deconstruction of the Soviet Union has: Boris Yeltsin's Russia, desperate for Japanese aid and co-operation, found the islands a stumbling block to assistance. However, over half the population who have moved there since 1945 are Russian, and in a 1991 poll the islanders voted 4–1 to remain under Moscow's control – even though various bridge-building exercises were being initiated towards Japan.

Population

The state that the Communists inherited in 1917 was not merely large; it was also made up of peoples of very diverse ethnic, religious and cultural backgrounds. Among the varied peoples – speaking over 100 languages – the Slavs, consisting of the Russians, Ukrainians and Belarussians, were the most numerous. Other groups include the Turkik and Persian people of Central Asia, the Caucasians, the altic peoples, Finno-Ugrians, Mongols and any others. Under Soviet rule the ethnic .versity of the state was recognized in the .istence of federal republics (of very disparate ze), and autonomous republics and regions ere set up to recognize smaller ethnic groups.

Although all parts of Russia are inhabited, /en the most remote, the greatest concentra-.on of people has traditionally been in the uropean part of the country. It was here that ■ the centuries before the Revolution the first .ussian towns with their fortresses (*kremlins*) nd onion-domed churches were founded.)utside this settled core there were towns and ■ties which the Russians acquired during their xpansion or themselves established on the :ontiers. In central Asia the Russians took ver what had once been a flourishing urban ivilization, gaining towns such as Bukhara Bukhoro), Samarkand (Samarqand) and Chiva all now in Uzbekistan.

After the Revolution, changes took place in ■he distribution of population so that the ■ormer pattern of a small highly populated ·ore and 'empty' periphery began to break ■own. Today the settled area extends into Siberia and, in a narrow band, across to the Pacific Ocean. As a result, a far higher propor-:ion of the Russian population is to be found ast of the Urals than before the Revolution, :ven before World War II. This redistribution nas been actively encouraged by a regime committed to a policy of developing the east. Migration to the towns and cities has also been marked since 1917 so that the greater part of the Russian population is now urban (in 1990 ■t was 74%). Some of these urban settlements have been built from scratch during Soviet times and are to be found in the more remote regions of the country. Norilsk, for example, was founded in the 1930s north of the Arctic Circle near to important mineral deposits. The most famous city is the capital Moscow (Moskva); like the other cities of the North European Plain, it is a mixture of the old and the new, but it is also a mixture of European and Asian styles and cultures.

While Russian cities and towns have been the site of vigorous building programmes, villages all over the country have changed ittle. In the forests, people still live in the traditional wooden hut (*izba*), while in the

steppe agricultural workers' dwellings are often of wattle and daub. Electricity has been introduced and in most villages a range of other services is now provided, though some still do not have a modern sanitation system or running water.

ECONOMIC DEVELOPMENT

The Soviet government transformed the USSR from an underdeveloped country into the second most powerful industrial nation of the world. At the time of the Revolution (1917) most industrial development was concentrated in a few centres in the European part of the country: Moscow, St Petersburg and, in the Ukraine, the Donbas. Also, much was financed by foreign investment and the development of major industrial sectors was unbalanced. On taking power the Communist Party vowed to develop industry rapidly and to introduce it into the backward regions of the country. As in many other parts of the world, Soviet industrialization was initially based on the iron and steel industry. In Stalin's drive of the 1930s, heavy national investment went into expanding production in the already exist-ing industrial areas of European Russia and establishing the industry in central and eastern Russia; new large integrated steel mills were built in the southern Urals and on the Kuzbas coalfield in western Siberia. Later the industry was introduced into the Kazakh republic on the Karaganda coalfield. Most recently a new plant has been established at Kursk in European Russia.

The shift away from coal as a basis for industrial development to alternative energy sources has taken place later in the countries of the former Soviet Union than in many other countries. Since the 1960s, however, pet-roleum and natural gas industries have begun to develop rapidly and the same is true of industries based on hydroelectricity; HEP has been especially important in building up industry in eastern Siberia, where massive installations on the River Angara provide the energy for aluminium production.

Although the introduction of large-scale industry into formerly backward parts of the country has helped to even out levels of development, regional imbalances in produc-tion in the territories of the old Soviet Union

COMMONWEALTH OF INDEPENDENT STATES

After 74 years, the Union of Soviet Socialist Republics slipped into history a week ahead of schedule on Christmas Day 1991, when Mikhail Gorbachev resigned the leadership of what had become a nation only on paper. His offices in the Kremlin were occupied by Boris Yeltsin, first President of the Russian Federation and driving force behind the 'deconstruction' of the Soviet Union.

Though far from substituted, the USSR was in part replaced by the Commonwealth of Independent States, born in Minsk on 8 December 1991 when Russia, Ukraine and hosts Belarus – between them responsible for 73% of the Soviet population, nearly 80% of its grain production and over 85% of its industrial output – signed a declaration effectively ending the former superpower's life both as a geopolitical entity and as a force in international relations. Two weeks later, in the Kazakhstan capital of Alma-Ata, they were joined by Moldova, Armenia, Azerbaijan and the five Asian republics; missing were the three Baltic states (already *de facto* independent nations), and Georgia: Georgia finally joined in March 1994. Azerbaijani and Moldovan membership effectively lapsed because of non-ratification until September 1993 and April 1994 respectively. The declaration from the 11 governments covered subjects as diverse as international borders, human rights, ethnic minorities, non-interference and international law, while setting up committees on foreign affairs, defence, finance, transport and security.

These remarkable events, spread over less than three weeks, could be traced back to 1985 and the appointment of Gorbachev as General Secretary of the Communist Party. His unprecedented policies of *glasnost* (openness) and *perestroika* (restructuring) were to have a devastating effect in a very short time. The domestic impact was equally dramatic, the republics of the USSR ridding them-selves of doctrinaire Communism, adopting pluralism and declaring themselves independent of Moscow. In 1991, the entire system through which the Soviet Union had functioned for seven decades came crumbling down in the course of one calendar year.

The first signs of actual disintegration of the USSR came in January 1991 in Lithuania, and within weeks all three Baltic states had voted for independence, Georgia following in March. Over the next few months Gorbachev tried continually to establish consensus on a new Union treaty and economic reform, but when Yeltsin became directly elected President of Russia in June, his federation took the lead in opposing the Soviet president's increasingly personal and decree-based rule as he attempted to find a middle way between the old guard and the progressives.

While the new laws had produced far-reaching effects on the political and social lives of Soviet citizens, the parallel restructuring of the economy patently failed – not least because the movement to a market economy was constantly hindered by party bureaucrats, factory managers, collective farm chairmen and many others who were unwilling to see the erosion of their positions.

In August, hardline Communist leaders ousted Gorbachev – detaining him in his Crimean *dacha* – and a small emergency committee took control of the Soviet Union. Resistance, bravely led by Yeltsin, centred on Moscow, and after three days the coup collapsed. Gorbachev returned to his post in the Kremlin, but his already tenuous position, now undermined by events, was further weak-ened by the worst harvest for a decade, an energy crisis that included a coal-miners' strike, and the collapse of the Soviet Central Bank.

On 21 December Gorbachev was told by the Alma-Ata protocol that his services were no longer required; outmanoeuvred by Yeltsin and overtaken by events, he resigned on Christmas Day, and the tricolour flag of Russia replaced the hammer and sickle on the Kremlin. Two days later, the Chamber of Deputies of the Supreme Soviet, the USSR's parliament, formally voted itself out of existence, and the Soviet Union was clinically dead.

remain large. The pre-revolutionary foci of development continued to attract a large pro-portion of available investment and retained their leading position in Soviet industry. This effectively means Russia, and of the regions developed since the Revolution only western

beria can be said to have a well-developed
ature industrial structure today. Other parts
Russia and the former Soviet Union, es-
cially the non-Russian republics in the
uth, still have relatively weak industrial
conomies. For example, in 1989 the Russian
ederation produced nearly 60% of both
ude steel and agricultural machinery. In
oth cases the Ukraine was a respectable
econd (35% and 30%), but the next republic
as below 5%.

While overall industrial production forged
head, agriculture was the 'Achilles' heel' of
he Soviet economy, and in several years from
he middle 1960s foreign grain had to be
mported. Since 1965 there has been a notable
mprovement in yields but even so output and
onsumption per capita can only just keep
head of increases in population. Western
ommentators often ascribed the poor perfor-
nance of agriculture to concentration on
arms which are too large and too impersonal
o be efficient.

Soviet farms were of two types, collective
(kolkhozi) and state (sovkhozi). The former
vere, according to the official definition,
democratically-run producers' co-operatives
vhich, in return for a grant of land, delivered
ome of their produce to the state. In theory
free to run their affairs, they were always sub-
ect to considerable government interference.
The equally large state farms were state owned
and managed. Until the 1950s they were relatively uncommon because they were expensive
to run, but in the last two decades their number increased. While the greater part of total
Soviet agricultural output came from collective and state farms, a large share of market
garden produce and some livestock products
originated on the so-called personal plots of
farm workers.

In both agriculture and industry the Soviet
government pursued large-scale projects.
Campaigns, as they were called in the former
USSR, were at times launched to rapidly
increase the output of chemicals or machinery,
for example. A much-publicized campaign in
agriculture was launched in the 1950s to bring
into cultivation thousands of hectares of
hitherto fallow land east of the Ural Mountains. As a result of this project, much of it in
Kazakhstan and called the Virgin Lands

Campaign, the sown land of the nation
doubled in the space of a few years. Following
some initial difficulties, and the ensuing withdrawal from some of the more marginal land,
the Virgin Lands are now a principal grain-
producing region.

In the drive for economic development, the
Soviet government at first neglected the consumer sector. Growth rates in textiles, food
industries and wood processing, for example,
lagged behind those for iron and steel production. The paucity of consumer goods, often
compounded by gross inefficiencies in the
state distribution system, was obvious in the
size of the queues that formed whenever scarce
products came on sale. Another indication is
the existence of a flourishing black market.

During Stalin's rule a conscious policy to
restrict foreign trade and maximize self-
sufficiency was pursued. With the formation of
Comecon, the Eastern trading block, after
World War II and the realization that much of
Western technology would be useful to its own
continued development, the USSR revised
trade policy. By the 1980s the Soviet Union
was trading with most countries of the world,
although the Soviet share of total turnover was
small. Once again, Russia had the lion's share:
while only 15% of its output went to other
Soviet republics in 1989, the nearest rivals
were Ukraine and Kazakhstan (32%), while
six republics recorded a dependency of more
than 60% and another four a figure of more
than 50%.

HISTORY AND POLITICS

The present size of Russia is the product of a
long period of evolution. In early medieval
times the first Slavic state, Kievan Rus, was
formed at the junction of the forest and steppe
in what is now the Ukraine. As the centuries
wore on other states were formed further to
the north. All were eventually united under the
principality of Muscovy. In the 13th century
Mongol hordes from the east penetrated the
forests and held sway over the Slavic people
there, extracting tribute from them.

It was only in the 16th century that the
Mongol yoke was thrown off as the Slavs,
under Ivan the Terrible, began to advance
across the steppes. This signalled the beginning of a period of expansion from the core

area of Slavic settlement to the south, east and west. Expansion across Siberia was rapid and the first Russian settlement on the Pacific, Okhotsk, was established in 1649. Progress across the open steppe, the realm of tribal horsemen, was slower but by 1696 Azov, the key to the Black Sea, was secured. A series of struggles in the 17th and 18th centuries against the Swedes and Poles resulted in the addition of the Gulf of Finland, the Baltic coast and part of Poland to the growing Russian empire, and in the 19th century the Caucasus, Central Asia and new territories in the Far East were added. In the 20th century the gains and losses of area through war, treaties and secret deals have been comparatively small, if at times dramatic.

Russia has been a centralized state throughout its history. A major landmark in the country's history, and indeed in the history of the world, was the 1917 Revolution, when the Tsarist order was overthrown and a Communist government established under Lenin – replacing one form of totalitarianism with another. The years from 1917 witnessed colossal changes in the political, social and economic structure of the country, the most dramatic and far-reaching of which took place from the 1930s when Stalin instituted central planning of the economy, collectivized agriculture and began a period of rapid industrialization. After Stalin's death in 1953, Soviet leaders modified some policies but they remained true to the general principles of Communism until the radical approach of Gorbachev changed the face of Russia – and in the process most of the Communist world.

A new country

Given its size and resources it may be thought that Russia would not need the Commonwealth of Independent States, its economic strength (properly managed) making it more than viable as a major nation and a natural successor internationally to the Soviet Union; indeed it inherited the USSR's mantle on the UN Security Council and its diplomatic missions worldwide, while applying for membership of CSCE and even NATO.

But Russia, despite its size, fears isolation. With the Eastern European countries and the Baltic states fully independent, the three

Caucasus republics unstable, the Asia republics (whose fast-growing population suggest that by 2000 Russia will lose its majority in the CIS) looking increasingly to the Islamic neighbours, and even Mongolia converting to democracy and the free market Russia has little control of the former 'buffer zones'. Though large and powerful, it has always felt under siege, and better that the buffers were partners rather than opponents In any case, at least in the medium term, the Commonwealth states had to live with the structure created by the Soviet system – an that meant interdependency.

Despite Gorbachev's best and at time brave efforts, the Russian President Bor Yeltsin inherited an economy in crisis, bogged down by lumbering and often obstructive bureaucracy, inept use of resources and cumbersome, inefficient transport system, of which the state airline Aeroflot (the world' largest) was a prime example. Though the West preferred aid, the impressive-sounding amounts were relatively small, and the final solution would have to lie with the Russian themselves.

After the abolition of price controls sent the cost of basic commodities rocketing, 1992 and 1993 saw food shortages worsen and unemployment rise. Like Eastern Europe, the Russians found it difficult to stabilize their economy, its citizens paying a high price for the introduction of Western-style democratic capitalism. However, in spite of these difficulties, the people backed Yeltsin's programme of reforms in a referendum in April 1993. In October 1993, Yeltsin used the army to crush a parliamentary rebellion and in elections held in December 1993 won backing for his proposed new constitution giving the president extensive powers. However, these elections also saw the emergence as a significant political force of Zhironovsky's extreme nationalist party and the bitter struggle between conservatives and reformers showed no sign of abating.

Neither is the nation homogenous. Several autonomous regions – including Karelia, Komi, North Ossetia, Tatarstan, Gorno-Altay, Bashkortostan, Buryatia and the vast Sakha (formerly Yakutia) – declared independence in the last months of Soviet control. They could ell pursue their policy (although some have een dissuaded by the war in Chechenia), ffectively reducing Russia's size and influence i the region. [*Map pages 20–1*] ■

AREA 17,075,000 sq km [6,592,000 sq mls]
POPULATION 147,370,000
CAPITAL (POPULATION) Moscow (8,957,000)
GOVERNMENT Federal multiparty republic
ETHNIC GROUPS Russian 82%, Tatar 4%, Ukrainian 3%, Chuvash 1%, more than 100 other nationalities
LANGUAGES Russian (official)
RELIGIONS Christianity (mainly Russian Orthodox, with Roman Catholic and Protestant minorities), Islam, Judaism
CURRENCY Russian rouble = 100 kopecks

RWANDA

The Republic of Rwanda is a small, land-locked African country, bordered by Uganda, Tanzania, Burundi and Zaïre. Lake Kivu and the River Ruzizi form the boundary in the west. These two features lie in the Great African Rift Valley. Overlooking the valley in western Rwanda are high, volcanic mountains of the Mufumbiro Range, reaching 4,507 m [14,787 ft] above sea level in the north-west.

Kigali stands on the central plateau of Rwanda. Here, temperatures are moderated by the altitude. The rainfall is abundant, but much heavier rain falls on the western mountains. The floor of the Great Rift Valley is warmer and drier than the rest of the country.

Rainforests occur in the west of the country. These forests contain many plant and animal species, including mountain gorillas. Forests once also covered eastern Rwanda, but they have been largely cut down to create farmland. The cleared land has been badly eroded by the heavy rain.

ECONOMY AND RESOURCES
Rwanda is by far the most densely populated state in Africa – in 1994 there were 295 people

per sq km [762 people per sq mls] – and the steep slopes are intensively cultivated. Most people are poor farmers, who produce little more than they need to feed their own families. Some cattle are raised, and food crops include bananas, beans, cassava and sorghum. The country's most valuable crop is coffee, which accounts for more than 70% of Rwanda's exports. Some tea, tungsten, pyrethrum, which is used to make insecticides, and tin are other products which are exported. Rwanda has few manufacturing industries, and when conditions permit there is a large movement into neighbouring countries for employment.

HISTORY AND POLITICS
Rwanda was merged with Burundi by German colonialism in 1899, making Ruanda-Urundi part of German East Africa. Belgium occupied it during World War I, and then administered the territory under a League of Nations mandate, later (1946) a UN trusteeship. In 1959 it was again divided into two, Rwanda finally achieving full independence in 1962, the same year as Burundi.

As in Burundi, there are deep social and cultural divisons between the farming majority and the traditional, nomadic owners of cattle. Several decades of ethnic strife climaxed in 1990 when a rebel force of Tutsi 'refugees' invaded from Uganda and occupied much of the north before being repulsed by French, British and Zaïrian troops brought in by the Hutu-dominated Rwanda government. The problems stem from the revolution of 1959, when the Hutu overthrew the aristocratic Tutsi minority rulers in one of the most violent clashes in modern African history. In February 1991, in return for its neighbours granting Tutsi refugees citizenship, Rwandan leaders agreed to the principle of a return to democracy, but the violence continued into 1992, and erupted again in 1994 with appalling loss of life (500,000 people were massacred in three months), following the dual assassination of the presidents of both Rwanda and Burundi when their aircraft was hit by a rocket as it approached the airport at Kigali. Tens of thousands of refugees fled to neighbouring countries, placing a great strain on those countries' resources as well as the aid agencies trying to remedy the situation. [*Map page 33*] ■

AREA 26,340 sq km [10,170 sq mls]
POPULATION 7,750,000
CAPITAL (POPULATION) Kigali (232,730)
GOVERNMENT Republic
ETHNIC GROUPS Hutu 90%, Tutsi 9%, Twa 1%
LANGUAGES French and Kinyarwanda (both official)
RELIGIONS Christianity 74% (mainly Roman Catholic), traditional beliefs 17%, Islam 9%
CURRENCY Rwandan franc = 100 centimes

ST CHRISTOPHER & NEVIS

The federation comprises two well-watered volcanic islands, mountains rising on both to around 1,000 m [3,300 ft], and about 20% forested.

Thanks to fine beaches, tourism (88,264 visitors in 1992) has replaced sugar, nationalized in 1975 and still producing 57% of exports, as the main exchange earner. Industries include electronic equipment, footwear, batik and sugar derivatives; the main agricultural products are cotton, copra, palm oil, bananas, cocoa and tropical vegetables.

The first West Indian islands to be colonized by Britain (1623 and 1628), St Christopher and Nevis became independent in 1983. St Christopher is usually shortened to St Kitts; Nevis derives its name from Columbus (1493), to whom the cloud-covered peaks were reminiscent of Spanish mountains (*nieves* meaning snow). [*Map page 30*] ■

AREA 360 sq km [139 sq mls]
POPULATION 41,000
CAPITAL (POPULATION) Basseterre (15,000)
GOVERNMENT Constitutional monarchy
ETHNIC GROUPS Of African descent
LANGUAGES English
RELIGIONS Christianity
CURRENCY East Caribbean dollar = 100 cents

ST HELENA

St Helena is an isolated rectangular, slab sided island of old volcanic rocks, well of the main line of the Mid-Atlantic Ridge and measuring 122 sq km [47 sq mls]. A tableland deeply dissected by valleys, it has steep cliff and ridges, and there is relatively little fla ground available. Standing in the trade winds St Helena has a cool tropical maritime climate dry at sea level but moist enough for limite farming on the heights.

The population of about 6,000, mainly o East Indian descent, produce potatoes and other vegetables and raise cattle, sheep and goats on smallholdings. Cultivable land is scarce and many are unemployed.

St Helena, a British colony since 1834 and the administrative centre for six of the UK's South Atlantic islands, is heavily dependent on subsidies. [*Map page 33*] ■

AREA 112 sq km [47 sq mls]
POPULATION 6,000
CAPITAL (POPULATION) Jamestown (1,500)
GOVERNMENT Dependent territory of the UK
ETHNIC GROUPS Mixed European (British), Asian and African
LANGUAGES English
RELIGIONS Christianity
CURRENCY St Helenian pound = 100 pence

ST LUCIA

A mountainous, forested island of extinct volcanoes – graphically represented on its flag – St Lucia boasts a huge variety of plant and animal life. To the south of its highest point of Mt Gimie (949 m [3,114 ft]) lies the Qualibou, an area containing 18 lava domes d seven craters. In the west are the dramatic Pitons, rising to over 750 m [2,460 ft].

Though not poor, St Lucia is still overdependent on bananas, a crop easily hit by hurricane and disease. It is supported by coconuts and cocoa, and the free port of Vieux Fort has attracted modern industries. Cruise liners deliver tourists to Castries, and the Grande Cul de Sac Bay to the south is one of the deepest tanker ports in the Americas, used mainly for trans-shipment of oil.

First settled by the British in 1605, St Lucia changed hands between Britain and France 14 times before finally being ceded formally in 1814. Internally self-governing as 'Associated State of the UK' from 1967, it gained full independence within the Commonwealth in 1979. [*Map page 30*] ■

AREA 610 sq km [236 sq mls]
POPULATION 141,000
CAPITAL (POPULATION) Castries (56,000)
GOVERNMENT Constitutional monarchy
ETHNIC GROUPS Of African descent 90%, Mixed 6%, East Indian 3%
LANGUAGES English, French patois
RELIGIONS Christianity (Roman Catholic 90%, Protestant 7%, Anglican)
CURRENCY East Caribbean dollar = 100 cents

ST VINCENT & THE GRENADINES

St Vincent is a mountainous, volcanic island that boasts luxuriant vegetation. Soufrière (1,178 m [3,866 ft]), which last erupted in 1979, is one of two active volcanoes in the eastern Caribbean – Mt Pelée is the other.

Bananas account for 38% of exports, but the island is also the world's biggest producer of arrowroot (for medicines and computer paper). Less prosperous than its Commonwealth neighbours, there are nevertheless prosperous pockets, notably Mustique and Bequia, where beautifully clean waters have fostered tourism.

St Vincent and the Grenadines comprise the main island (constituting 89% of the area and 95% of the population) and the Northern Grenadines, of which the largest are Bequia, Mustique and Canouan. 'Discovered' in 1498, St Vincent was settled in the 16th century and became a British colony with the Treaty of Versailles in 1783, after a century of conflict with France, often supported by the Caribs – the last of whom were deported to Honduras after the Indian War of 1795–7. The colony became self-governing in 1969 and gained independence as part of the Commonwealth in 1979. [*Map page 30*] ■

AREA 388 sq km [150 sq mls]
POPULATION 111,000
CAPITAL (POPULATION) Kingstown (26,500)
GOVERNMENT Constitutional monarchy
ETHNIC GROUPS Of African descent
LANGUAGES English, French patois
RELIGIONS Christianity
CURRENCY East Caribbean dollar = 100 cents

SAN MARINO

Surrounded by Italy, the tiny independent state of San Marino – the world's smallest republic – lies 20 km [12 mls] south-west of the Adriatic port of Rimini. Most of the territory consists of the limestone mass of Monte Titano (725 m [2,382 ft]), around which are clustered wooded mountains, pastures, fortresses and medieval villages. The republic is named after St Marinus, the stonemason saint who is said to have first established a community here in the 4th century AD.

Nearly all the inhabitants live in the medieval fortified city of San Marino, which is visited by over 2 million tourists a year. The chief occupations are tourism (which accounts for 60% of total revenues), limestone quarrying and the making of wine, textiles, ceramics and paints.

San Marino has a friendship and co-operation treaty with Italy dating back to 1862; the ancient republic uses Italian currency, but issues its own stamps, which contribute a further 10% to state revenues. The *de facto* customs union with Italy makes San Marino an easy conduit for the illegal export of lira and certain kinds of tax evasion for Italians. The state is governed by an elected council and has its own legal system. In 1957 a bloodless takeover replaced the Communist-Socialist regime that had been in power from 1945. It has no armed forces, and police are 'hired' from the Italian constabulary. [*Map page 16*] ■

AREA 61 sq km [24 sq mls]
POPULATION 23,000
CAPITAL (POPULATION) San Marino (2,395)
GOVERNMENT Republic
ETHNIC GROUPS San Marinese, Italian
LANGUAGES Italian (official)
RELIGIONS Christianity (Roman Catholic)
CURRENCY Italian currency & San Marino lira = 100 centisimi

SÃO TOMÉ & PRÍNCIPE

These mountainous, volcanic and heavily forested Atlantic islands some 145 km [90 mls] apart, comprise little more than twice the area of Andorra, with São Tomé the larger and more developed of the two. The highest point is Pico de São Tomé which stands at 2,024 m [6,640 ft].

A Portuguese colony since 1522, the islands were suddenly granted independence in 1975, and the cocoa plantations that formed the platform for the economy quickly deteriorated under a one-party hardline socialist state. Reliance on the Soviet Union was lessened from the mid-1980s and the cocoa industry revived – as well as diversification into palm oil, pepper and coffee and the encouragement of tourism.

In 1990 Marxism was abandoned altogether and, following the lead from many mainland African nations and pressure from Portugal (the main trading partner) and France (the major aid donor), São Tomé held multiparty

elections in 1991 – won by the oppositio [*Map page 33*] ■

AREA 964 sq km [372 sq mls]
POPULATION 130,000
CAPITAL (POPULATION) São Tomé (43,420)
GOVERNMENT Multiparty republic
ETHNIC GROUPS Mainly descendants of slaves
LANGUAGES Portuguese, Fang
RELIGIONS Christianity (mainly Roman Catholic)
CURRENCY Dobra = 100 centimos

SAUDI ARABIA

The heart of the state – the largest in th Middle East but over 95% desert - consists of the province of Najd, within which are three main groups of oases. Najd i enclosed on its east side by a vast arc of sand desert which broadens out into the two grea dune-seas of Arabia, the Nafud in the north and in the south the Rub 'al Khali, or 'Empty Quarter', the largest expanse of sand in the world. Here are found most of the country': Bedouin nomads, still deriving a living as traders and herdsmen.

To the west, Najd is separated from the border hills of the Red Sea by fields of rough basaltic lava. Particularly in its southern section towards the border with Yemen, this coastal strip is quite well supplied with water, and a high storage dam has been built inland from Jizan.

ECONOMY AND RESOURCES
The hills of Asir which back the coastal plain benefit from the summer monsoon, and are extensively terraced to grow grain and orchard trees. For the most part, however, lack of water is a big problem. Saudi Arabia relies heavily on desalination plants and has the world's biggest on the shores of the Gulf – vulnerable to the oil pollution resulting from the 1991 war against Iraq.

The eastern province, by the shores of the

MECCA

The holiest city of Islam, Mecca was an important centre of pilgrimage long before the birth of the Prophet Muhammad. Its chief sanctuary, then as now, was the Ka'ba, a square building housing a remarkable and much venerated black stone of probable meteoric origin, said to have been given to the patriarch Abraham by the Archangel Gabriel.

In 632, shortly before his death, the Prophet undertook his own final pilgrimage to the city; the pilgrimage to Mecca – the Hajj – remains the fifth of the Five Pillars of Islam, and every Muslim is expected to make it at least once in a lifetime. Mecca is also part of the Second Pillar, the duty of prayer, for it is towards the Ka'ba (now enclosed by Mecca's Great Mosque) that the world's Muslims face five times daily when they pray.

At the beginning of the 20th century, Mecca was a provincial town in the Ottoman empire; now, with a population of over 618,000, it is the administrative capital of the Western Province of Saudi Arabia. Its chief business remains, as ever, the Hajj, with upwards of 1.5 million pilgrims visiting annually. Non-Muslims (infidels) are to this day excluded from the city.

Gulf, is known as the Hasa. Near its chief city of Hufuf in particular, the long underground seepage of water from the Hejaz, the western mountains, breaks out in the artesian springs of the oases. This region contains the country's great oilfields including Ghawar, the world's largest. The oil port of Az Zahran is linked with Riyadh by the only railway; asphalt roads and, increasingly, air travel are the country's main means of transport.

The world's largest producer and exporter of oil in 1992, Saudi Arabia used the enormous revenues (peaking at more than $100 billion a year after the 400% price hikes of 1973) to launch a colossal industrial and domestic development programme: some $250 billion was spent on the plan for 1980–5, requiring over a million foreign workers. A strictly Muslim society suddenly boasted some of the most advanced architecture and facilities in the world, as well as introducing an array of social and educational benefits.

HISTORY AND POLITICS

During and shortly after World War I, the Saudis of Najd (central Arabia) extended their territory at the expense of the Rashidis and Hashemites, and consolidated their control over the greater part of the Arabian peninsula. The frontiers with neighbours to the south and east remained ill-defined, but this mattered little until its vast reserves of oil (the world's largest) were tapped after World War II; since then some disputes have been settled, notably the division of the Gulfshore Neutral Zone with Kuwait. Progress has not always been smooth. In the mid-1980s world oil prices slumped dramatically, disrupting many of the projects begun in the boom years. Meanwhile, expenditure on defence is high even by the profligate standards of the region. The country's position as the West's staunchest Middle East ally has often conflicted with its role as the guardian of Islam's holy places – hundreds of thousands make the pilgrimage to Mecca every year – and despite large donations to poorer Arab nations (Saudi Arabia is by far the world's biggest donor by percentage of GNP), its commitment to their cherished cause of a Palestinian state has at times appeared relatively weak.

While supporting Iraq against Shiite Iran in the First Gulf War, Saudi Arabia then invited Western forces in to protect it against possible Iraqi aggression following the invasion of Kuwait in 1990, playing a significant role in the quick victory of the Allies over Saddam Hussein. [*Map page 22*] ■

AREA 2,149,690 sq km [829,995 sq mls]
POPULATION 17,451,000
CAPITAL (POPULATION) Riyadh (or Ar Riyad, 2,000,000)
GOVERNMENT Absolute monarchy with consultative assembly
ETHNIC GROUPS Arab (Saudi 82%, Yemeni 10%, other Arab 3%)
LANGUAGES Arabic (official)
RELIGIONS Islam 99%, Christianity 1%
CURRENCY Saudi riyal = 100 halalas

SENEGAL

The Republic of Senegal is on the north-west coast of Africa. The volcanic Cape Verde (Cap Vert), on which Dakar stands, is the most westerly point in Africa. Plains cover most of Senegal, though the land rises gently in the south-east. Wind-blown sand dunes are common in the north and on the coast. The main rivers are the Sénégal, which forms the northern border, and the Casamance in the south. The River Gambia flows from Senegal into The Gambia, a small country almost enclosed by Senegal.

The capital, Dakar, has a tropical climate with a short rainy season between June and September, when moist winds blow from the south-west. During the dry season, hot north-easterly winds blow from the Sahara. Temperatures are higher inland, while the rainfall is greatest in the south.

Desert and semi-desert cover much of the north-east, but in central Senegal dry grass-lands and scrub predominate. The far south is a region of savanna, with forests along the rivers. Although large areas in the south have been cleared for farming, some areas are protected. The largest sanctuary is the Niokolo-Kobo Wildlife Park, which is rich in animal species. Mangrove swamps border parts of the southern coast.

ECONOMY AND RESOURCES

Dakar, once the administrative centre for France's federation of West African colonies, has large modern docks and is the nation's major industrial centre. In the north-east of the country, Fulani tribesmen eke out a spar-tan existence by keeping herds of cattle on the scrub and semi-desert vegetation. In contrast, in the wetter and more fertile south the savanna bushlands are cultivated and cassava, sorghum and rice are grown. About half of the cultivated land produces groundnuts, a crop that still dominates the country's economy and exports. The only other major exports are phosphates, although tourism is becoming an increasingly important source of revenue.

In an attempt to diversify and stabilize th economy, the government is encouragin; fishing and tourism, and is involved with Ma and Mauritania in a major scheme to increas irrigated crop production.

HISTORY AND POLITICS

The name derives from the Zenega Berbers who invaded from Mauritania in the 14th century, bringing Islam with them. On gainin; independence in 1960, Senegal had a well-planned capital, a good road network and a top-heavy administration, all legacies from its role as the administrative centre for French West Africa. Its first president, Léopold Sédar Senghor, was a noted African poet. He contin-ued in office until 1981, when he was suc-ceeded by the prime minister Abdou Diouf.

One of the few African countries to remain stable and democratic through the 1980s, Senegal nevertheless struggles economically, is prone to drought and reliant on aid. Federations with Mali (1959–60) and Gambia (1981–9) were unsuccessful, and since 1989 there have been violent, though sporadic, clashes with Mauritania, such as the border dispute in 1992.

Senegal was the only African colony where French citizenship was granted to the people, and indeed the Senegalese were encouraged to become 'black Frenchmen'. As a result many of the Wolof – the largest tribe group and traditionally savanna farmers – are now city dwellers in Dakar, dominating the political, economic and cultural life of the country. Strangely, today's quality of life is for most Senegalese little better than their neighbours'. [*Map page 32*] ■

AREA 196,720 sq km [75,954 sq mls]
POPULATION 8,102,000
CAPITAL (POPULATION) Dakar (1,382,000)
GOVERNMENT Multiparty republic
ETHNIC GROUPS Wolof 44%, Fulani-Tukulor 24%, Serer 15%
LANGUAGES French (official)
RELIGIONS Islam 94%, Christianity (mainly Roman Catholic) 5%, traditional beliefs and others 1%
CURRENCY CFA franc = 100 centimes

SEYCHELLES

SIERRA LEONE

The Seychelles are a compact group of four large and 36 small granitic islands, plus a ide scattering of coralline islands (14 of them habited) lying mainly to the south and west the four main islands; 82% of the land area composed of the four main islands which ost 98% of the population, the vast majority a lush and mountainous Mahé.

With a beautiful tropical oceanic climate the eychelles produce copra, cinnamon and tea, ut the islands are not self-sufficient in food nd rice has to be imported. The economy is ased on two activities, fishing and tourism. anned fish account for a third of exports, and eep-sea tuna fishing is carried out by foreign eets under licence. Luxury tourism (the main oreign exchange earner) is growing in impor- ance. In 1990, there were 103,770 visitors to ne islands.

Proclaimed a French territory from 1756 nd British from 1814, the islands gained ndependence in 1976. A year later a political oup set up a one-party Socialist state that sev- ral attempts have failed to remove. But mul- iparty democracy was restored when elections vere held in 1992.

Formerly part of the British Indian Ocean Territory (BIOT), Farquhar, Desroches and Aldabra (famous for its unique wildlife) were eturned to the Seychelles in 1976. BIOT now ncludes only the Chagos Archipelago, with Diego Garcia, the largest island, supporting a US naval base. [Map page 3] ■

AREA 455 sq km [176 sq mls]
POPULATION 73,000
CAPITAL (POPULATION) Victoria (24,325)
GOVERNMENT Multiparty republic
ETHNIC GROUPS Mixture of African, Asian and European
LANGUAGES English, French, Creole
RELIGIONS Christianity (Roman Catholic 90%, Anglican 8%)
CURRENCY Seychelles rupee = 100 cents

The coast of Sierra Leone ('lion moun- tain') contains several deep estuaries in the north, with lagoons in the south. The most prominent feature is the mountainous Free- town (or Sierra Leone) peninsula. North of the peninsula is the River Rokel estuary, West Africa's best natural harbour. Behind the coastal plain with its mangrove swamps, the land rises to plateaux and mountains. The highest peak, Loma Mansa, reaches 1,948 m [6,391 ft] near the north-eastern border.

ECONOMY AND RESOURCES

At independence from Britain in 1961, three- quarters of the population were employed in subsistence agriculture, yet rice had to be imported, and only small surpluses of palm kernel, coffee and ginger were produced.

Revenue from the export of minerals, namely diamonds and iron-ore, has been important since the 1930s, although rutile (titanium ore) is now the country's most important export.

The main centres for the production of coffee, cocoa, and timber products are in the south-east of the country near Kenema. Rice and palm oil are produced throughout Sierra Leone, except in the drier north, where groundnuts and cattle herding are more important. The government has established large-scale mechanized rice cultivation in the bolilands of the north-west, the seasonally- flooded riverine grasslands of the south-east and the mangrove swamps near Port Loko, in an effort to boost rice production.

Apart from mills processing palm oil and rice, most factories are in or near the capital, Freetown. The government is doing all it can to aid Sierra Leone's growing tourist industry and modern hotels have been established along the coast near Freetown.

HISTORY AND POLITICS

Portuguese sailors reached the coast in 1460, and in the 16th century the area became a source of slaves. In 1787, Freetown was founded as a home for freed slaves. The British made the Sierra Leone peninsula a colony in 1808, and in 1896 they declared the interior a protectorate. Sierra Leone became independent in 1961.

After independence, Sierra Leone became a monarchy. Its head of state was the British monarch, who was represented in the country by a governor-general. But after a military government took power in 1968, Sierra Leone was made a republic in 1971. Then, in 1991, a majority of the people voted for the restoration of multiparty democracy. In 1992, a military group overthrew the government and seized power. [*Map page 32*] ■

AREA 71,740 sq km [27,699 sq mls]
POPULATION 4,402,000
CAPITAL (POPULATION) Freetown (470,000)
GOVERNMENT Single-party republic
ETHNIC GROUPS Mende 35%, Temne 37%, Limba 8%,
LANGUAGES English (official)
RELIGIONS Traditional beliefs 51%, Islam 39%, Christianity 9%
CURRENCY Leone = 100 cents

SINGAPORE

Singapore comprises the main island itself and an additional 54 much smaller islands lying within its territorial waters. The highest point on the main island is Bukit Timah (176 m [577 ft]). The position of Singapore at the southernmost point of the Malay Peninsula, controlling the Strait of Malacca, has throughout history been one of enormous strategic importance.

ECONOMY AND RESOURCES
Singapore is one of the world's most remarkable commercial and industrial experiments. It is, in effect, a city-state, its downtown thick with skyscrapers, one of the most densely populated countries in South-east Asia and an economy based on its vast port, manufacturing and commercial and financial services.

The port began its modern expansion as conduit for shipping out tin and rubber from Malaya. Today, easily the world's busiest, handles nearly 70 million tonnes a year, much of it entrepôt (re-export) trade but also involving significant amounts of materials for and from its own thriving industries.

The positive strategy of industrialization first labour- and later skill-intensive, has given Singapore an outstanding average growth of 7% a year and has made it the richest of Asia's four 'little dragons'.

HISTORY AND POLITICS
When Sir Stamford Raffles established British influence in 1819, leasing the island and its muddy Malay fishing village for the East India Company, there were only 150 inhabitants. This had not always been so; 'Singapura' (the city of the lion) was an important settlement in the 14th century, but had been destroyed in the rivalry between the great kingdoms of Madjapahit (Java) and Siam. The modern city, originally planned by Raffles, remained under British rule until self-government in 1959. In 1963, Singapore became part of the Federation of Malaysia, but seceded in 1965 to become a fully independent nation.

The success of Singapore owes much to the vision and dynamism of Lee Kuan Yew, prime minister from independence in 1959 to 1990, who despite having a predominantly Chinese population in a Malay region made his ambitious policies work. The cost, however, was a lack of genuine democracy, his regime increasingly bordering on a one-party dictatorship; his attitude, essentially, was that Singapore could not afford the luxury — or danger — of political debate. Impressive though the new city may be, most Singaporeans live in massive apartment blocks reminiscent of postwar Eastern Europe, with most aspects of their lives rigidly controlled and much of their former culture buried forever beneath a Western façade.

Lee's groomed successor, Goh Chok Tong, seemed set to continue his policies with equal vigour, turning Singapore into the hub of an expanding region. Despite its political stance, it was in the vanguard of nations opening up nks with the reticent Communist countries of Laos, Vietnam and North Korea in the post-*perestroika* era.

The future of his party's wealthy establishment appeared secure, with its sights set on replacing Hong Kong as eastern Asia's second financial and commercial centre after Tokyo. The feeling nevertheless persisted that Singapore's crucial tertiary activity would give it little to fall back on in the face of a deep and lasting world recession. [*Map page 26*] ■

AREA 618 sq km [239 sq mls]
POPULATION 2,821,000
CAPITAL (POPULATION) Singapore City (2,818,000)
GOVERNMENT Multiparty republic
ETHNIC GROUPS Chinese 78%, Malay 14%, Indian 7%
LANGUAGES Chinese, Malay, Tamil and English (all official)
RELIGIONS Buddhism, Taoism and other traditional beliefs 54%, Islam 15%, Christianity 13%, Hinduism 4%
CURRENCY Singapore dollar = 100 cents

SLOVAK REPUBLIC

The Slovak Republic, or Slovakia, is a new nation which emerged on 1 January 1994, following the division of the former Czechoslovakia into two states. The land is mainly mountainous, consisting of part of the Carpathian range that divides it from Poland. The highest peak, reaching 2,655 m [8,711 ft], is on the northern boundary in the scenic Tatra Mountains.

By contrast, the south is a fertile lowland, drained by the River Danube, which forms part of the southern border with Hungary – Bratislava, the new nation's chief city, lies in the south and has become the fourth European capital (Vienna, Budapest and Belgrade are the others) to lie on the river. Several rivers flow from the mountainous north into the Danube river basin.

ECONOMY AND RESOURCES

Before 1948, Slovakia's economy was based on farming, but Communist governments developed manufacturing industries, producing such things as chemicals, machinery, steel and weapons. Since the late 1980s, the non-Communist governments have tried to hand over state-run businesses to private ownership. In mid-1994 the new government speeded up the privatization process.

Manufacturing employs about 33% of the workforce. Bratislava and Kosice are the chief industrial cities, but the armaments industry is based on Martin, in the north-west.

Farming employs about 12% of the people. Major crops include barley, grapes for wine-making, maize, sugar beet and wheat. Cattle, pigs and sheep are also raised.

HISTORY AND POLITICS

While the Czechs prospered and flourished under Austrian rule, Slovakia was subject to Hungarian authority for centuries. Its people suffered from enforced 'Magyarization' and their development was stifled. Divisions were exacerbated from 1939 when, after the proclamation of a pro-German Fascist regime in Slovakia, Hitler's troops invaded the Czech lands of Bohemia and Moravia. But, even in Communist Czechoslovakia, the Slovaks were in no sense a persecuted minority; their post-1989 independence movement was driven more by the desire to revive their distinct culture than by serious ethnic grievances. Elections in 1992 led to a victory for the Movement for a Democratic Slovakia, led by a former Communist and staunch nationalist, Vladimir Meciar. In September 1992, the Slovak National Council voted to create a separate, independent Slovak Republic on 1 January 1994.

Following independence, the new Slovak Republic maintained close links with its former partner: around 400,000 Slovak workers cross the frontier to work each week, while about 200,000 are still resident in the Czech Republic. Conversely, 60,000 Czechs live in Slovakia, but at between 500,000 and 600,000, the nation's most substantial minority is Hungarian. Predictably, Slovak independence has raised national aspirations among its Magyar-speaking community, mostly in its southern regions; such ethnic tensions as exist, though, are likely to be settled pragmatically and not by violence. [*Map page 17*] ■

AREA 49,035 sq km [18,932 sq mls]
POPULATION 5,333,000
CAPITAL (POPULATION) Bratislava (441,450)
GOVERNMENT Multiparty republic
ETHNIC GROUPS Slovak 86%, Hungarian 11%, small groups of Czech, German, Gypsy, Polish, Russian and Ukrainian
LANGUAGES Slovak (official)
RELIGIONS Christianity (Roman Catholic 60%, Protestant 6%, Orthodox 3%)
CURRENCY Slovak koruna = 100 halura

SLOVENIA

The Republic of Slovenia was one of the six republics which made up the former Yugoslavia. The most northern of the republics, much of the land is mountainous, rising to 2,863 m [9,393 ft] at Mt Triglav in the Julian Alps (Julijske Alpe) in the north-west. Central and eastern Slovenia contain hills and plains drained by the Drava and Sava rivers. The central limestone area, called the Karst region, is characterised by underground rivers and deep caves. The Postojna caves near Ljubljana are the largest in Europe.

The short Slovenian coast has a mild Mediterranean climate, but inland the climate is more continental with snow-capped mountains in winter. Eastern Slovenia has cold winters and hot summers.

ECONOMY AND RESOURCES

The reform of the formerly government-run economy and the fighting in areas to the south have caused problems for Slovenia, and in 1992 the World Bank classified Slovenia as an 'upper-middle-income' developing country. Manufacturing is the leading activity and manufactures are the leading exports, including chemicals, machinery and transport equipment, metal goods and textiles. Agriculture

employs 8% of the people. Fruits, maize, potatoes and wheat are major crops, while many farmers raise cattle, pigs and sheep. Other important sources of income are wine making and Alpine tourism (1.4 million tourists in 1991).

Slovenia has access to the Adriatic through the port of Koper, near the Italian border, giving it a flourishing transit trade from landlocked central Europe.

HISTORY AND POLITICS

The ancestors of the Slovenes, the western branch of a group of people called the South Slavs, settled in the area around 1,400 years ago. From the 13th century until 1918, Slovenia was ruled for most of the time by the Austrian Habsburgs. In 1918, Slovenia became part of the Kingdom of the Serbs, Croats and Slovenes. This country was renamed Yugoslavia in 1929. During World War II, Slovenia was invaded and partitioned between Italy, Germany and Hungary, but after the war, Slovenia again became an integral part of Yugoslavia.

From the late 1960s, some Slovenes demanded independence, but the central government opposed the break-up of the country. In 1990, when Communist governments had collapsed throughout Eastern Europe, a non-Communist coalition government was elected. Slovenia subsequently declared itself independent. This led to fighting between Slovenes and the federal army, but Slovenia did not become a battlefield like other parts of the former Yugoslavia. The European Community recognized Slovenia's independence in 1992 and elections were held. A coalition government led by the Liberal Democrats was set up as a result. [*Map page 15*] ■

AREA 20,251 sq km [7,817 sq mls]
POPULATION 1,942,000
CAPITAL (POPULATION) Ljubljana (323,000)
GOVERNMENT Multiparty republic
ETHNIC GROUPS Slovene 88%, Croat 3%, Serb 2%, Bosnian 1%
LANGUAGES Slovene (official)
RELIGIONS Christianity (mainly Roman Catholic)
CURRENCY Tolar = 100 stotin

SOLOMON ISLANDS

The double chain of Pacific islands forming the Solomons (and the southerly exten-sion of Vanuatu) extends for some 2,250 km [1,400 mls] and represents the drowned utermost crustal fold on the borders of the ancient Australian continent. New Caledonia es on an inner fold, nearer the mainland. The main islands, all of volcanic origin, are Guadalcanal, Malaita, New Georgia, San Cristóbal, Santa Isabel and Choiseul.

The northern Solomons have a hot and wet tropical oceanic climate, but further south the islands tend to experience an increasingly long cool season.

ECONOMY AND RESOURCES

The coastal plains are used for the subsistence farming that sustains about 90% of the popu-lation. While coconuts (giving copra and palm oil) and cocoa are important exports, tuna fish is the biggest earner and lumbering the main industry, with Japan the main market for both. Significant phosphate deposits are also mined on Bellona Island and marine shells are exo-ported. Plagued by a population growth of 3.5% – half the total is under 20 – the Solomons' progress is faltering, with develop-ment hampered by the mountainous and densely forested environment of the six main islands; transport is often impossible between scattered settlements. The economy was also hit by a devastating cyclone in 1986.

HISTORY AND POLITICS

Occupied by the Japanese during World War II, the islands were the scene of fierce fighting, notably the battle for Guadalcanal, on which the capital Honiara lies. Known as the British Solomons, the islands won full independence in 1978. The country is a constitutional monarchy, with the Queen as head of state, represented locally by a Governor-General. Though currently a stable parliamentary monarchy, political activity is turbulent, and it is likely that a federal republican structure will

be introduced to the country during the 1990s. [*Map page 35*] ■

AREA 28,900 sq km [11,158 sq mls]
POPULATION 366,000
CAPITAL (POPULATION) Honiara (34,000)
GOVERNMENT Constitutional monarchy
ETHNIC GROUPS Melanesian 94%,
Polynesian 4%
LANGUAGES Many Melanesian languages,
English
RELIGIONS Christianity
CURRENCY Solomon Islands dollar = 100
cents

SOMALIA

Somalia is more than twice as large as Italy (which formerly ruled the southern part of the country). The northern section, formerly British Somaliland and the literal 'Horn of Africa', is the highest and most arid, rising to 2,408 m [7,900 ft]; the mountains are an east-erly projection of the Ethiopian Highlands, wooded with box and cedar. The east and south have some 500 mm [20 in] rainfall on the coast. Dunes have diverted one of the country's two rivers, the Scebeli, to the south, making it available for irrigation. The inland plain is arid with grass and thorn bush.

ECONOMY AND RESOURCES

Most Somali are subsistence farmers or nomadic herdsmen. Expatriate Somali living in southern Djibouti, Ogaden (eastern Ethiopia) and north-east Kenya are mostly pastoralists, who move across borders in an increasingly desperate search for pasture, fuelwood and water. Bananas are a major export, especially to Italy. The country's econ-omy has suffered badly from drought and the effects of the civil war.

HISTORY AND POLITICS

The Somali Republic became independent in 1960. The Somali, though belonging to separate tribes or clans, are conscious of being one people and members of one of Africa's rare nation states. The quest for a reunification of all the Somali peoples led to conflict with neighbouring countries, notably Ethiopia and the Ogaden war of 1978, which has continued intermittently and has caused thousands of Somali refugees to flee across the border.

Somalia relied heavily on Soviet aid until Ethiopia went Marxist and sought massive help from Moscow; the revolutionary socialist government of President Siyad Barre, which had seized power and suspended the constitution in 1969, then became increasingly reliant on Italian support and US aid.

Grievances against the repressive regime, spearheaded by secessionist guerrillas in the north, reached their peak in 1991 with the capture of Mogadishu. Free elections and independence for the north-east part of the country, as the Somaliland Republic, were promised after the cease-fire and Barre's fall from power, but vicious factional fighting continued not only in the capital but also in many rural areas. The Western nations virtually abandoned Somalia to its fate, with thousands dying every week in interclan bloodletting and through starvation. One of the world's poorest countries was plunged into anarchy. The situation deteriorated further into 1992, despite UN attempts at mediation and several cease-fires. Much of Mogadishu was reduced to rubble, violence spread to country areas, and tens of thousands of refugees fled to northern Kenya and eastern Ethiopia. In 1993, the United Nations intervened and sent in a task force of US Marines to protect and oversee the distribution of food aid. The US troops withdrew in 1994. [*Map page 32*] ■

AREA 637,660 sq km [246,201 sq mls]
POPULATION 9,077,000
CAPITAL (POPULATION) Mogadishu (or Muqdisho, 1,000,000)
GOVERNMENT Single-party republic, military dominated
ETHNIC GROUPS Somali 98%, Arab 1%
LANGUAGES Somali and Arabic (both official), English, Italian
RELIGIONS Islam 99%
CURRENCY Somali shilling = 100 cents

SOUTH AFRICA

Geologically very ancient, South Africa ha only scant superficial deposits of sed ments less than 600 million years ol Geological history has had a great effect on a aspects of the country's development – on i landforms, patterns of population, industri growth and agricultural potential.

The country is divisible into two majc natural zones – the interior and the coast fringe – the interior in turn consisting of tw major parts. Most of Northern Cape provinc and the Orange Free State are drained by th Orange River and its important right-ban tributaries which flow with gentle gradient over level plateaux, varying in height fron 1,200–2,000 m [4,000–6,000 ft]. The North ern Transvaal is occupied by the Bushveld, a area of granites and igneous intrusions drained by rivers which flow northwards to th Limpopo river.

The coastal fringe is divided from the in terior by the Fringing Escarpment, a featur that makes communication within the countr very difficult. In the east the massive basalt capped rock wall of the Drakensberg, at it most majestic near Mont-aux-Sources and rising to over 3,000 m [over 10,000 ft], over looks the KwaZulu-Natal and Eastern Cape coastlands. In the west there is a similar divide between the interior plateau and the coast lands, though this is less well developed. The Fringing Escarpment also runs along the south coast, where it is fronted by many independent mountain ranges with an east-west alignment.

South Africa's economic and political devel opment is closely related to these physical components.

ECONOMY AND RESOURCES

Stretching from the Northern Transvaal's western border with Botswana, running in a horseshoe to the north of Pretoria and then southwards through KwaZulu-Natal and Eastern Cape province, are the former so-called 'homelands' – territories occupied

most exclusively by Africans. From the out-
t the Africans operated a form of mixed
griculture, giving them subsistence but little
.ore. The men were cattle-keepers and war-
ors, the women tilled the plots, in a culture
ased on extensive holdings of communal
.nd. European farming was also based on
xtensive holdings but incorporated individual
.nd rights. Not surprisingly, conflict arose
om the juxtapositioning of the two groups,
nd with the discovery of valuable minerals –
old in the Banket deposits of the Wit-
atersrand, diamonds in the Kimberlite pipes
f the Cape, platinum in the Bushveld and
oal in the Northern Transvaal and KwaZulu-
Natal – both were drastically affected.

South Africa still produces over 30% of the
orld's gold, and today chrome, uranium,
ickel and many others may be added to the
st. Exploitation of southern Africa's minerals
ed to trade with overseas markets and the
development of major urban complexes.
ohannesburg grew the fastest; its growth
encouraged the expansion of Durban and to a
arge extent caused Cape Town and Port
Elizabeth to flourish. The appearance of a
capitalist, market-oriented economy caused
even greater divergence between white and
black. The politically-dominant whites repro-
duced a European economy and, after the
transfer of political power, developed strong
links with Britain.

The African farmers gained little from the
mineral boom. With their constant needs for
new grazing grounds, frustrated by the white
farmers, and with taxes to pay, they had little
alternative but to seek employment in the
cities and mines, and on European-owned
farms; the African areas became labour pools.
Migrant labour became the normal way of life
for many men, while agriculture in the Native
Reserves (so designated early in the 20th
century) stagnated and even regressed, with
yields decreasing and soil erosion becoming
widespread and of increasing severity.

Small groups of Africans took up urban life
in 'locations' which became a typical feature of
all towns whatever their size. Separated by a
cordon sanitaire of industry, a river or the railway line from the white settlement, these
townships with their rudimentary housing,
often supplemented by shanty dwellings and
without any real services, mushroomed during
World War II and left South Africa with a
major housing problem in the late 1940s.
Nowhere was this problem greater than in the
Johannesburg area, where it was solved by the
building of a vast complex of brick boxes, the
South-Western Townships (SOWETO).

HISTORY AND POLITICS

The country was first peopled by negroids
from the north, who introduced a cattle-
keeping, grain-growing culture. Entering by
the plateaux of the north-east, they continued
southwards into the well-watered zones
below the Fringing Escarpment of present-day
KwaZulu-Natal and Eastern Cape province.
Moving into country occupied by Bushmanoid
peoples they absorbed some of the latter's
cultural features, especially the 'clicks' so characteristic of the modern Zulu and Xhosa
languages. By the 18th century these Bantu-
speaking groups had penetrated to the south-
east in the region of the Kei and Fish rivers.

Simultaneously with this advance, a group
of Europeans was establishing a victualling
point for the Dutch East India Company on
the site of modern Cape Town. These
Company employees, augmented by Hugue-
not refugees, eventually spread out from Cape
Town, beginning a movement of European
farmers throughout southern Africa and bringing about the development of the Afrikaners.

The advance of the Europeans was chan-
nelled in the south by the parallel coastal
ranges, so that eventually black and white met
near the Kei River. To the north, once the
Fringing Escarpment had been overcome, the
level surface of the plateaux allowed a rapid
spread northwards. From this colonizing
process, aided by an implanting of British
people in the south-east and near Durban, the
present disposition of black-dominated and
white-dominated lands arose.

The contrast in prosperity between South
African whites and blacks is nowhere more
visibly expressed than in their respective urban
areas. The white areas could be 'Anytown' in
North America; skyscrapers, multitrack roads,
large department stores and well-tended
suburbs. The black towns could only be South
African: though rudimentary in what they
offer, they have been rigidly planned.

A further problem is posed by the Coloured people – descendants of mixed-race marriages – and the Asiatics, who are mainly descendants of Indians brought in several generations ago to work in the sugar-cane fields of Natal.

The Rise and Fall of Apartheid

From its 1948 institution, *apartheid* – 'separate development' – meant not only racial segregation but also massive racial discrimination. Over the next generation, a whole body of apartheid law was created. Key measures deprived blacks of political rights except in 'homelands' – modest tracts of poor land. Whites were guaranteed exclusive ownership of most of the country's best land, and most blacks, with no right of residence outside homelands few had ever seen, found themselves foreigners in their own country, obliged to carry passes at all times and subject to the authority of an aggressive police force.

The African National Congress, the main black political organization, was banned, and black opposition was brutally suppressed. South Africa's racial policies led to increasing isolation from the rest of the world, and by the 1980s the country was considered a pariah by other nations.

Changing demographic patterns – the blacks were outnumbering whites by more and more every year – combined with international sanctions made apartheid increasingly unsupportable. The 1989 election of liberal Nationalist President F.W. de Klerk brought dramatic change. In 1990, Nelson Mandela, leader of the banned African National Congress (ANC), was released from jail to the negotiating table, after serving 28 years as a political prisoner, and in 1991 de Klerk announced his intention to dismantle the entire structure of apartheid. In 1992, an all-white referendum gave him a mandate to move quickly towards a multiracial democratic system.

Under a new constitution, the first multi-racial elections were held in April 1994, resulting in a massive victory for the ANC (62.7% of the vote, the National Party in second place gained just 20.4% of the vote) and the election of Nelson Mandela as the country's first black president. The four former provinces of South Africa have been replaced by nine new regions, each with its own Prime Minister. [*Map page 33*] ■

AREA 1,219,916 sq km [470,566 sq mls]
POPULATION 40,555,000
CAPITAL (POPULATION) Cape Town (legislative, 1,912,000), Pretoria (administrative, 1,080,000), Bloemfontein (judicial, 300,000)
GOVERNMENT Multiparty republic
ETHNIC GROUPS Black 76%, White 13%, Coloured 9%, Asian 2%
LANGUAGES Afrikaans, English, Ndebele, North Sotho, South Sotho, Swazi, Tsonga, Tswana, Venda, Xhosa, Zulu (all official)
RELIGIONS Christianity 68%, Hinduism 1%, Islam 1%
CURRENCY Rand = 100 cents

SPAIN

A global position between coastal north-west Europe and Africa, and between the Mediterranean countries of the Old World and the Americas, made Spain a great crossroads. Yet the lofty Pyrenean barrier in the north weakened land contacts with the rest of Europe, while the narrow Strait of Gibraltar in the south encouraged African contacts, lending truth to the old cliché that 'Africa begins at the Pyrenees'.

Landscape

Spain occupies most of the Iberian peninsula. Its chief physical feature is the vast central plateau, the Meseta, which tilts gently towards Portugal. A harsh and often barren area, the plateau is crossed by the Central Sierras, a mountain chain running north-west to south-east. This central divide separates two mountain basins: Old Castile in the north and New Castile in the south.

On the north-eastern and southern edges of the Meseta are large triangular lowlands. In the north these drain to the Ebro, in the south to the Guadalquivir, the largest river wholly in Spain. Beyond the Ebro trough the land rises

BALEARIC ISLANDS

The Islas Baleares group contains five larger islands (Majorca, Minorca, Ibiza, Formentera, Cabrera) and 11 rocky islets, together covering 5,014 sq km [1,936 sq mls] and spread over 350 km [218 mls].

Majorca (Mallorca), by far the largest island, has limestone ridges on the north-west and south-east with a plain covered with flat-bedded, very fertile marine sediments between them. Minorca (Menorca), the second largest, has limestone plains and small outcrops of crystalline rocks, but nowhere rises above 358 m [1,175 ft].

The typical sunny Mediterranean climate supports an equally typical vegetation. Shrub-growth (*matorral* or *garrigue*) still clothes the highest areas and is grazed by sheep and goats. The rainier upper slopes of the hills have been terraced for olives, carobs and vines, while the lower slopes are under market-garden crops. The level lowlands are planted with wheat and barley, usually in rotation with beans. Generally, almonds, apricots and carobs are more important here than vines and citrus fruits. The rural economy is essentially peasant with a high degree of self-sufficiency.

Like most Mediterranean islands the Balearics were settled early. Archaeological remains exist from 1,000 BC (Bronze Age) to the Roman period and include boat-shaped burial mounds (*navetas* or *naus*) and conical stone towers (*talayots*) thought to be refuges from piratical raiding parties. Ibiza town and Port Mahon were originally settled from Carthage. During recent times the islands were repeatedly occupied by the British, French and Spanish and remained finally a province of Spain. Each different occupation has left its mark, and Port Mahon has fine buildings representing all these changes of ownership.

Today the population lives mainly either in agricultural villages some way inland or in small ports around the coast. Power resources and raw materials for manufacture are scarce, apart from agricultural products; textile manufacture (wool and cotton) and food processing are the only widespread factory occupations. Handicrafts flourish in response to the tourism that now dominates the whole economy.

Palma, the capital of Majorca and of the Balearic province, continues to grow rapidly. It has a fine harbour with regular sailings to Barcelona, Alicante and Valencia for passengers and the export of Balearic surpluses of almonds, grain, textiles and vegetables. It is also a regular port of call for Mediterranean cruise ships and its airport, one of the busiest in Spain, deals with well over a million visitors annually. Manacor, the only other large centre on Majorca, is an agricultural market town near limestone caves and subterranean lakes that attract numerous tourists. Port Mahon is the capital of Minorca, and Ibiza town the capital of that small island.

---

to the Pyrenees, which form the Franco-Spanish border, and continue westwards in the Cantabrian Mountains. Similarly, the Mediterranean flank of Andalusia rises to a lofty cordillera (mountain chain) that culminates in the snowy Sierra Nevada (peaking at 3,478 m [11,400 ft]). The Mediterranean side of the Meseta has summits of about 2,000 m [6,560 ft] but then drops sharply to narrow coastal plains.

Spain has perhaps the widest range of climate of any country in Western Europe. The most striking contrast is between the humid north and north-west and the mainly arid remainder of the country. Large areas of the country are barren or steppeland, and about a fifth is covered by *matorral*, a Mediterranean scrub like the French *maquis*.

Vegetation

Spain is unique in Europe for the quantity and variety of her plant species, a reflection of varied local environments, a position as a land bridge between Africa and Europe, and a long colonial history during which time many foreign plants were introduced. Generally, moisture-loving plants flourish north of the Central Sierras and drought-enduring species south of them.

The vegetation falls into three broad categories: forest, *matorral* and steppe. Forests (almost 10% of the land surface) are today mainly confined to the rainier north and north-west, with beech and deciduous oak common. Towards the drier south and east, Mediterranean pines and evergreen oaks take over, and forests resemble open parkland. Widespread clearance for fuel and cultivation and grazing by sheep, goats and cattle have turned large areas into *matorral* or shrub.

This low bush growth, often of aromatic evergreen plants, may be dominated over large tracts by one species, such as rosemary, thyme or broom. Where soils are thin and drought prevalent, *matorral* gives way to steppe, mainly of alfalfa and *esparto* grasses.

Population

The population of Spain is most dense on the coastlands and lowlands around the Meseta. Madrid, in the heart of the tableland, forms a grand exception. The capital stands on the small Manzanares River, a tributary of the Tagus, and has a long history dating from early Roman times. The Moors first provided it with clean drinking water and Philip II made it the seat of the national government in 1561. A fine metropolis, it has flourished during the decades since the Civil War (1936–9) and now accommodates about 10% of the total population of continental Spain. The second Spanish city, Barcelona, is a great commercial and industrial centre; in all ways the core of Catalonia, it was given a huge boost by the staging of the summer Olympics in 1992.

The other major cities include Bilbao, the Basque capital and chief urban area of the north coast, long noted for its metallurgy; Cádiz, an important naval centre; Seville, the river port and regional capital of Andalusia; Valencia and Murcia, the largest of the Mediterranean *huerta* cities; Zaragoza, the expanding centre for the Ebro lowland, noted for food processing and engineering; and Málaga, the fast-growing nucleus of the Costa del Sol. Toledo, which was the national capital before Madrid, ranks far below these conurbations in size, but, protected as a national monument, is the finest medieval city that survives almost intact from the golden age of Spain.

ECONOMY AND RESOURCES

Despite the problems of aridity and poor soils, agriculture occupies nearly a third of the national workforce. Irregular river regimes and deeply incised valleys make irrigation difficult and expensive and, on the higher and drier regions, tracts favourable for cultivation are often isolated by expanses of low fertility where only a meagre livelihood can be wrested from the soil. There are, too, problems connected with the size of farms. In semiarid Spain large estates (*latifundios*) abound with much seasonal employment or share cropping, while in the rainy north-west and north excessive fragmentation of small farms (*minifundios*) has proved uneconomic.

It is against this picture of difficulties that the great progress made since 1939 by the Instituto Nacional de Colonización (INC) must be viewed. The institute, by means of irrigation, co-operative farming schemes, concentration of landholdings, agricultural credit schemes and technical training, has resettled over a quarter of the land needing reorganization and reclamation. But, generally, crop yields are still comparatively modest and agricultural techniques remain backward.

Stock rearing: Large areas of farmland are used solely or partly for pastoral purposes which are of great economic importance. Spain has about 20 million sheep, mainly of the native merino type which produces a fine fleece. The Mesta, an old confederation of sheep-owners, controls the seasonal migrations on to the summer pastures on the high sierras. Areas too rocky and steep for sheep are given over to goats while cattle, apart from working oxen, are mostly restricted to regions with ample grass and water – for example the north and north-west. Pigs are bred in the cattle districts of the north, and are also kept to forage the acorns in the large tracts of evergreen oaks in the south. Many working animals are kept, and fighting bulls are bred on the marshes (*marismas*) at the mouth of the Guadalquivir.

Arable crops: The typical arable crops are the classical Mediterranean trio of wheat, olive and vine, with maize important in rainier districts and vegetables and citrus fruits where there is irrigation water. Wheat occupies a third of the cropland and is usually followed in rotation by leguminous pulses or fallow, grazed and so manured by sheep.

In dry areas barley, oats and rye, grown for fodder, replace wheat, and in the wetter north maize dominates both for grain and feed. Rice is harvested in Murcia, Valencia and the Ebro Valley and Spain follows Italy for rice production in Europe.

Fruit growing: Fruits occupy a high and honoured place in Spain's agricultural economy. The olive crop, mainly from large estates in Andalusia, makes Spain one of the world's chief producers of olive oil. Vines cover about 10% of the cultivated land and only Italy and France exceed the Spanish output of wine. Sherry (from Jérez) is renowned and there are other fine wines such as the vintages of Rioja.

For citrus fruit Spain easily outstrips other European producers, the bulk of the crop being Seville oranges destined largely for Britain for making marmalade. Large quantities of other fruits, especially apricots and peaches, are grown with vegetables in irrigated market gardens (*huertas*) and orchards (*vegas*).

Some of the *huertas* are devoted to industrial crops such as cotton, hemp, flax and sugar beet, while most richer soils in Andalusia are entirely given over to cotton. The poorer steppes yield *esparto* (a strong grass) for papermaking.

Maps of modern Spain clearly indicate the tremendous progress made recently in water reservation and river regulation on all the major rivers. Large new reservoirs have been constructed on the Miño, Duero, Tajo, Guadiana, Guadalquivir and other main rivers as well as numerous dams on the lesser watercourses. The INC, which directs this work, aims at bringing 70,000 hectares [173,000 acres] a year under irrigation as well as undertaking all kinds of land reclamation, drainage, reforestation, settlement schemes and farm co-operative planning.

Mining and Industry

Spain is lamentably short of its own supplies of solid and liquid fuels and in an average year produces only small quantities of poor-quality coal (mainly from Asturias at Oviedo near Gijón), and some lignite from a field south of Barcelona. Small deposits of petroleum found near Burgos and at the mouth of the Ebro have not yet proved economic to develop. Some use is made of nuclear power but the main developments have been in hydroelectricity, especially in Catalonia and the northern coastlands.

In contrast to fossil fuels, workable mineral ores are widespread. High-quality iron ores, with substantial reserves, occur in Vizcaya, Santander and Granada. Bilbao, the chief ore-exporting port, has an important integrated iron and steel plant; so have Oviedo, Gijón and several other towns on the north coast, and smaller enterprises are found at Sagunto and Zaragoza.

Many localities yield non-ferrous ores in sufficient quantity to broaden the base of Spain's metallurgical industries. The chief workings are for copper at Río Tinto, lead and silver at Linares and Peñarroya (near Pueblonovo), and mercury at Almadén; in addition, manganese, titanium and sulphur are produced in small quantities and considerable amounts of potassium salts come from the region of Catalonia.

The major Spanish manufacturing industries are based on agriculture rather than minerals. Textiles, including cotton, wool, silk, jute and linen lead the industrial sector. Barcelona, Catalonia's great industrial, financial and commercial centre, is surrounded by a ring of satellite textile towns, some of which specialize in spinning, as at Manresa and Ribas, and others in weaving, as at Sabadell and Granollers.

Cotton fabrics form the chief single product and supply a wide market, especially at home and in Latin America. Barcelona has a wide variety of light industries, while the heavy metallurgical sectors are located in the cities of the north coast. Madrid has become an important centre for consumer goods, particularly electric appliances.

Food-processing industries are concentrated in the north-east, the chief being flour-milling, sugar refining and oil-pressing. Fish canning and processing are widespread in the coastal towns and the Galicians and Basques are skilled fishermen.

Tourism and communications

The relative absence of closely-packed industrial plants and industrial pollution, the historical attractions of the relics of a long history dating from the Greeks and Arabs, and the dry warm sunny climate of the Mediterranean south and east have fostered tourism, the greatest of all Spain's non-agricultural industries. In 1992 39.6 million people visited Spain and the Costa Brava and Costa del Sol are internationally famous as tourist destinations.

Equally significant is the great increase in the number of those who came to live permanently or for most of the year in the picturesque coastlands with warm winters and subtropical vegetation.

The prime communication routes in Spain focus on Madrid, which has radial links to the peripheral cities. First-class highways radiate to the main ports and good roads connect all the major towns; but minor roads are seldom tarred and for so large a country relatively few vehicles are registered.

Railways likewise converge on Madrid with minor networks round the regional capitals and main ports. The tracks are not of standard European gauge, about 75% being broad gauge and the remainder narrow. The chief land communications with France run at either end of the Pyrenees and are supplemented by several high-level transmontane rail and road routes.

Air travel focuses on Madrid airport and, particularly for tourism, on 40 other civil airports, many of them with busy international services. The large coastal and ocean-going traffic involves 230 Spanish ports, but the bulk of the overseas trade passes through the modernized harbours – in particular Bilbao, Barcelona, Cartagena, Cádiz and Gijón.

HISTORY AND POLITICS

First settled by Iberians, Basques and Celts, Spain later became a Roman province until it was invaded by the Visigoths in the 5th century. They established a Christian kingdom and were only displaced by the Moors in 711. The Christian reconquest, started in 962, eventually led to the unification of the kingdoms of Castile and Aragon in 1469 and the fall of the last Moorish enclave (Granada) in 1492, the year in which Columbus reached America. In the 16th century, Spain extended its colonies in the Americas and the Far East. In the aftermath of the Napoleonic Wars, the Spanish king, Ferdinand VII, was restored by British forces in 1814. By 1830, most of

Spain's American colonies had gained independence and in 1898, Cuba, the Philippine and Puerto Rico were lost to the US as a result of the Spanish-American War.

Spain's neutrality in World War I strengthened support for the republican parties and, in reaction to a period of dictatorship by General Primo de Rivera (1923–30), the elections of 1931 produced a republican majority. This led to the abdication of Alphonso XII and the proclamation of a republic. A left-wing Popular Front government was elected in 1936, which provoked a military rebellion led by General Francisco Franco. The ensuing civil war lasted for three years and cost about a million lives. Backed by fascist Italy and Germany, Franco eventually defeated the republican government forces and went on to establish a dictatorship based on corporatism.

Although officially neutral in World War II, Spain's close relations with the fascist powers caused it to be expelled from the United Nations. In 1969, Prince Juan Carlos was named by Franco as his successor and he became king on Franco's death in 1975. He quickly set about restoring democracy: political parties were legalized in 1976 and an election, the first since 1936, was held in 1977. A new constitution, approved by referendum in 1978, established a democratic parliamentary monarchy, and in the same year Catalonia and the Basque country were granted autonomy. Basque extremists, however, have continued their struggle for full independence. In 1981, Juan Carlos was instrumental in putting down an attempted coup by right-wing army officers. Spain joined NATO in 1982 and the EC in 1986. Felipe González Márquez of the PSOE (Socialist Party) has been prime minister since 1982. [*Map page 18*] ∎

AREA 504,780 sq km ([194,896 sq mls]
POPULATION 39,568,000
CAPITAL (POPULATION) Madrid (3,121,000)
GOVERNMENT Constitutional monarchy
ETHNIC GROUPS Castilian Spanish 72%, Catalan 16%, Galician 8%, Basque 2%
LANGUAGES Castilian Spanish (official), Catalan, Galician, Basque
RELIGIONS Christianity (Roman Catholic 97%)
CURRENCY Peseta = 100 céntimos

SRI LANKA

Known as Ceylon until 1972, when it became a Socialist republic, Sri Lanka has been described as 'the pearl of the Indian Ocean'; the island is also its crossroads.

From its mountain core to the coral strand stretches the 'wet zone' of south-western Sri Lanka, supporting cool, grassy downs, rain-forests and tea-gardens near the ancient religious centre of Kandy, and evergreen forest and palm-fringed beaches in the lowlands from Colombo to east of Galle. White Buddhist shrines and peasant cottages dot the cultivated land among coconut palms, rice paddies, sugar-cane plantations and spice gardens. In contrast are the much drier zones of the north and east.

ECONOMY AND RESOURCES

While light industry has gone some way to diversifying an agricultural base dependent on tea, rubber and coconuts, Sri Lanka's economic progress since independence – when it was a relatively prosperous state – has been plagued by civil war and communal violence.

HISTORY AND POLITICS

First inhabited by forest-dwelling negroid Veddas, it was settled later by brown-skinned Aryans from India. These are now dominant in the population, though diluted by successive waves of incomers. Long-resident Tamils farm in the northern limestone peninsula of Jaffna, and Arab *dhow* sailors and merchants settled in the ports. After Vasco da Gama's contact with India in the 15th century came new traders and colonists – first Portuguese, then Dutch, then British (in control from 1796 to 1948) – and new immigrant Tamils were brought in from south-east India to intensively farm the plantations.

Conflict between the Sinhalese Buddhist majority and the Tamil Hindu minority, has led to disorder in 1958, 1971 and 1977; since 1983 the conflict has been virtually continuous as Tamil guerrillas have fought for an inde-

pendent homeland in the north (Eelam), with Jaffna the capital.

An Indian-brokered cease-fire in 1987 allowed an Indian peacekeeping force in, but it failed to subdue the main terrorist group, the Tamil Tigers, and withdrew in March 1990. Between then and the start of 1992 more than 12,000 people died in renewed clashes between the predominantly Sinhalese government forces and the rebels, despite an agreement on Tamil autonomy. In 1993, the country's president was assassinated by a suspected Tamil separatist. Many civilians, too, have lost their lives, and the conflicts have stemmed the flow of foreign tourists.

In addition, the authorities were dogged by a rumbling rebellion of the left-wing Sinhalese nationalist movement (JVP) in the south. Banned in 1983, the JVP escalated their campaign after the Indo-Sri Lankan pact of 1987, but their guerrillas were virtually broken by an offensive initiated by the new government – elected democratically after a delay of some six years in 1988. [*Map page 23*] ∎

AREA 65,610 sq km [25,332 sq mls]
POPULATION 18,125,000
CAPITAL (POPULATION) Colombo (1,863,000)
GOVERNMENT Multiparty republic
ETHNIC GROUPS Sinhalese 74%, Tamil 18%, Sri Lankan Moor 7%
LANGUAGES Sinhala and Tamil (both official)
RELIGIONS Buddhism 69%, Hinduism 16%, Islam 8%, Christianity 7%
CURRENCY Sri Lankan rupee = 100 cents

SUDAN

The Sudan is the largest state of Africa. It consists essentially of vast clay plains and sandy areas, parts of the Nile basin and the Sahara, but it presents two very different landscapes. The extreme north is virtually uninhabited desert; to the south, where the desert gives way to semi-desert, nomads move over age-old tribal areas. During the rainy season the plain becomes a vast reed-covered swamp and the Nilotic cattle-rearing tribes (Shilluk and Dinka) move to the dry ridges and islands until the floods abate.

The belt across the centre of the country holds most of the population. Here low rainfall, supplemented by wells and small reservoirs for irrigation, allows subsistence farming, but the bulk of the population lives adjacent to the Blue and White Niles. This is the predominantly Arab part of the Sudan, where 70% of the population live.

ECONOMY AND RESOURCES

Near the Blue and White Niles, and relying on them for irrigation, are a number of modern mechanized farming schemes, headed by the famous if fallible Gezira Scheme, one of the first of its kind in the world. Crops grown are cotton and oilseed for export, sugar cane and sorghum for local consumption. Despite once being 'the bread-basket of Africa', schemes like Gezira have failed to realize the full agricultural potential.

HISTORY AND POLITICS

The Sudan, formerly an Anglo-Egyptian Condominium, has suffered from an amalgam of the plagues which, in various combinations, have afflicted of post-colonial Africa. The so-called plagues are ethnic, religious and ideological division; political repression and instability; intermittent civil war, with high spending on 'defence'; economic crisis and massive foreign debt which, to service, would cost three times as much as export earnings; prolonged drought (punctuated by flash floods such as those in 1988, which left 1.5 million people homeless); and an influx of famine-stricken refugees since the 1980s.

The 17-year-old civil war that ended in 1972 was rekindled in 1983 by the (largely effective) pressure from extremists for the reinstatement of fundamental Sharic law. The renewed rivalries of the Arab north and the non-Muslim south – a pattern mirrored in neighbouring Chad, which shares many of Sudan's problems – have caused the deaths of hundreds of thousands of people and the decimation of a traditional way of life in an area already prone to drought and severe food shortages. Despite attempts to restore order the fighting continued into the 1990s.

While the power in the land rests in the north with the military council in Khartoum a city laid out in the pattern of the British fla at the confluence of the White Nile and Blu Nile – there seems little hope of a return t democracy, and the possibility of the sout seceding remains a distinct if distant on [*Map page 32*] ■

AREA 2,505,810 sq km [967,493 sq mls]
POPULATION 27,361,000
CAPITAL (POPULATION) Khartoum (561,000)
GOVERNMENT Military regime
ETHNIC GROUPS Sudanese Arab 49%, Dinka 12%, Nuba 8%, Beja 6%, Nuer 5%, Azande 3%
LANGUAGES Arabic (official)
RELIGIONS Islam 73%, traditional beliefs 17%, Christianity (Roman Catholic 4%, Protestant 2%)
CURRENCY Sudanese dinar = 10 pounds

SURINAM

Surinam has a coastline of 350 km [218 mls] of Amazonian mud and silt, fringed by extensive mangrove swamps. Behind lies an old coastal plain of sands and clays, bordering a stretch of sandy savanna. The heavily forested interior uplands further to the south are part of the Guiana Highlands, whose weathered soils form the basis of the crucial bauxite industry.

ECONOMY AND RESOURCES

Surinam's hot, steamy climate grows an abundance of bananas, citrus fruits and coconuts for export, with rice and many other tropical commodities for home consumption. Plantations were initially worked by African slaves, later by Chinese and East Indian indentured labour. Bauxite and its derivatives, shrimps and bananas are the main exports, but though 92% of the land is covered by forest –

...e world's highest figure – at present little is ...ommercially exploited.

HISTORY AND POLITICS

...lthough Spaniards visited as early as 1499, ...urinam was first settled by British colonists in ...651. In 1667 it was ceded to Holland in ...xchange for Nieuw-Amsterdam, now New ...ork, and was confirmed as a Dutch colony, ...alled Dutch Guiana, in 1816.

Surinam gained independence in 1975 and ...ince then the country has experienced a great ...eal of political instability, mainly due to racial ...ension. In 1980 there was a military coup and ...ater, in 1982, after the execution of 15 oppo- ...ition leaders and the banning of all political ...arties, the Netherlands broke off relations ...nd suspended all aid. Relations were resumed ...n 1988 following elections.

Another military coup occurred in 1990, ...ut further elections were held in 1991, and ...Ronald Venetiaan, leader of a coalition group ...alled the New Front, became president. In ...992, a peace agreement was negotiated with ...he *boschneger*, descendants of African slaves, ...who had launched a struggle against the ...government in 1986. [*Map page 31*] ■

AREA 163,270 sq km [63,039 sq mls]
POPULATION 438,000
CAPITAL (POPULATION) Paramaribo (200,970)
GOVERNMENT Multiparty republic
ETHNIC GROUPS Asian Indian 37%, Creole (mixed White and Black), 31%, Indonesian 14%, Black 9%, Amerindian 3%, Chinese 3%
LANGUAGES Dutch (official)
RELIGIONS Christianity (Roman Catholic 23%, Protestant 19%), Hinduism 27%, Islam 20%
CURRENCY Surinam guilder = 100 cents

SWAZILAND

Although the smallest country in sub-Saharan Africa, Swaziland nevertheless reveals strong scenic contrasts. From west to east the country descends in three altitudinal steps: the Highveld, average altitude 1,200 m [4,000 ft], and the Middleveld, lying between 350 and 1,000 m [1,000 and 3,500 ft], are made of old, hard rocks; the Lowveld, average height 270 m [900 ft], is of softer shales and sandstones in the west, and basalts in the east. Shutting the country in on the east are the Lebombo Mountains (800 m [2,600 ft]). Rivers rising in South Africa completely traverse these belts; their valleys provide communication lines and are sources of perennial water, important for irrigation.

ECONOMY AND RESOURCES

In the late 19th century European colonists settled and today the main economic features result from basic differences in occupational structures between 'black' and 'white' Swazi. Those derived from European stock are involved in commerce, industry and, predominantly, the production of exports such as sugar, citrus fruits and wood pulp as well as cereals and cattle. The majority indigenous Swazi are still mostly engaged in subsistence farming based on maize, with fragmented land-holdings and a dispersed settlement pattern. As a result there are few large towns, but the population remains far better off than in Lesotho, with which it is often compared, somewhat unrealistically.

Swaziland is part of a customs union which includes South Africa, but for overseas trade the country relies largely on the port of Maputo (in Mozambique), to which it is linked by the only railway. During the 1980s this was frequently inoperative because of the war in Mozambique – while Swaziland was also burdened with a flow of refugees. The kingdom would no doubt rather have tourists: there are already more than 258,000 a year.

HISTORY AND POLITICS

According to tradition, in the 18th century, a group of Bantu-speaking people, under the Swazi chief Ngwane II, crossed the Lebombo range and united with local African groups to form the Swazi nation. Under attack from Zulu armies, the Swazi people were forced to seek British protection in the 1840s. Gold was discovered in the 1880s and many Europeans sought land concessions from the king, who did not realize that in doing this he was losing control of the land.

In 1894, Britain and the Boers of South Africa agreed to put Swaziland under the control of the South African Republic (the Transvaal). But at the end of the Anglo-Boer War (1899–1902), Britain took control of the country. In 1968, when Swaziland became fully independent as a constitutional monarchy, the head of state was King Sobhuza II.

In 1973, Sobhuza suspended the constitution and took over supreme power in 1976. He banned political parties in 1978, though the people elected the 80 members of an electoral college, from which are chosen representatives to serve in parliament.

Sobhuza died in August 1982 after a reign of 82 years. In 1983, one of his sons, Prince Makhosetive (born in 1968), was chosen as his heir. In April 1986, he was installed as king, taking the name Mswati III. In 1993, Swaziland held its first-ever multiparty elections. [*Map page 33*] ■

AREA 17,360 sq km [6,703 sq mls]
POPULATION 832,000
CAPITAL (POPULATION) Mbabane (38,300)
GOVERNMENT Monarchy
ETHNIC GROUPS Swazi 84%, Zulu 10%, Tsonga 2%
LANGUAGES Siswati and English (both official)
RELIGIONS Christianity (Protestant 37%, indigenous African churches 29%, Roman Catholic 11%), traditional beliefs 21%
CURRENCY Lilangeni = 100 cents

SWEDEN

The kingdom of Sweden is the largest of the Scandinavian countries in terms of both population and area. It occupies the eastern half of the Scandinavian peninsula, extending southwards to latitude 55°N and having a much smaller Arctic area than either Norway or Finland.

The eastern coast, stretching 1,600 km [1,000 mls] along the shores of the Baltic Se and the Gulf of Bothnia, extends from th mouth of the Torne River, which forms th border with Finland, to Ystad in the soutf Sweden also has a coastline facing west alon the shores of the Kattegat – the strait that sep arates Sweden and the Jutland peninsula which is part of Denmark.

Landscape

Sweden's share of the Scandinavian peninsul is less mountainous than that of Norway. Th northern half of the country forms part of th Baltic or Fenno-Scandian Shield, a stable block of ancient granites and gneisses which extends round the head of the Gulf of Bothnia into Finland. This part of Sweden contain most of the country's rich mineral wealth. The shield land is an area of low plateaux which rise gradually westwards.

South of the plateaux area there is a belt o lowlands between the capital city, Stockholm and the second city, Göteborg (Gothenburg). These lowlands contain several large lakes, the chief of which are Mälar, near Stockholm, and the larger Vänern and Vättern, which are situated in the middle of the lowland belt. These are all that remains of a strait which, in glacial times, connected the Baltic with the Kattegat. Changes in land and water level during the later stages of the Ice Age led to the breaking of this connection. Now linked by canals, these lakes form an important water route across the country.

Sweden's topography was greatly affected by the Ice Age: the long, narrow lakes which fill the upper valleys of many of the rivers of northern Sweden have been shaped by the action of ice. They are the relics of a much larger lake system which was fed by water from the melting ice-sheet and provide excellent natural reservoirs for hydroelectric stations. Some of the most fertile soils in Sweden were formed from material deposited in the beds of such glacial lakes. Elsewhere, glacial moraines and deposits of boulder clay are other reminders of the impact of the Ice Age.

Climate

The high mountains which form the spine of the Scandinavian peninsula shut off the modifying influence of the Atlantic weather systems

om northern Sweden. This area therefore
is colder, drier winters than the seaward side,
but also enjoys warmer and drier summers. On
the Norrland plateau annual rainfall is less
than 508 mm [20 in], July temperatures
average 15°C [59°F] and the long summer
days of the high northern latitudes make sum-
mertime pleasant – although the long winters
are dark and cold. The Gulf of Bothnia is
affected by ice between November and April,
creating problems for shipping.

The southern part of Sweden, between the
Kattegat and the Baltic, is open to Atlantic
influences and has milder winters than the
northern areas, but summers are cooler and
wetter. Göteborg has average winter temperatures of 0°C [32°F], compared with
Stockholm's –3°C [27°F], whilst at Hapar-
anda, at the head of the Gulf of Bothnia, the
coldest month of February has an average
temperature of –12°C [10°F]. In summer,
however, there is little difference between
north and south, most areas having between
15°C and 20°C [59°F to 68°F].

ECONOMY AND RESOURCES

There are extensive coniferous forests
throughout northern Sweden; indeed, half the
country's land area is covered with trees. In
the south the original cover of mixed deciduous woodland has been cleared for agriculture
from the areas of better soil, the typical landscape now being farmland interspersed with
forest. This is usually spruce or pine, often
with birch – the national tree.

There are better opportunities for agriculture in Sweden than elsewhere in Scandinavia.
Cereal crops, potatoes, sugar beet and vegetables are grown for human consumption in
Skåne and in central Sweden, but by far the
greatest area of cultivated land is given over to
the production of fodder crops for cattle and
sheep. Dairy farming is highly developed, and
Sweden is self-sufficient in milk, cheese and
butter production..

Many farmers have left the land since World
War II, attracted by the higher wages and
more modern lifestyle of the towns. Sweden
has been able to create a high standard of
living based on industry – despite the fact that,
apart from the large iron-ore deposits, many of
the essential fuels and raw materials have to be

ÅLAND

Swedish settlers colonized various coastal
tracts of Finland from the 12th century, and
the 6.5% of the Finnish population who are
Swedish-speaking include all the 25,000 people of Åland, the group of more than 6,500
islands situated between the two countries in
the Gulf of Bothnia.

Although the inhabitants voted to secede
to Sweden in a 1917 referendum, the result
was annulled in 1921 by the League of
Nations for strategic reasons and Åland (as
Ahvenanmaa) remains a Finnish province.
However, the islands were granted considerable autonomy and still enjoy a large degree
of 'home rule' with their own flag, postage
stamps and representation at the annual
assembly of the Nordic Council.

Boasting many important relics of the
Stone, Iron and Bronze Ages, the province's
income derives mainly from fishing, farming
and, increasingly, from tourism.

imported: the development of hydroelectricity
however, has made up for the lack of oil and
coal. Most of the iron ore obtained from the
mines at Kiruna and Gällivare in Arctic
Sweden is exported via Narvik and Lulea to
Europe, mainly to Germany.

Sweden is famous for high-quality engineering products such as ball bearings, match-
making machinery, agricultural machines,
motor vehicles (Saab and Volvo), ships, aircraft and armaments (Bofors). In addition to
these relatively new industries, the traditional
forest-based industries have been modernized.
Sweden is among the world's largest exporters
of wood pulp and paper and board – as well as
Europe's biggest producer of softwood.

HISTORY AND POLITICS

The bulk of the population lives in the lake-
land corridor between Stockholm and Göteborg, or around the southern city of Malmö.
These citizens, by virtue of their working hard,
peaceful past, now enjoy a standard of living
that is in many ways the envy of most other
Western countries. Sweden has by far the
highest percentage figure for public spending

in the OECD, with over 70% of the national budget going on one of the widest-ranging welfare programmes in the world.

In turn, the tax burden is the world's highest (some 57% of national income) and some Swedes are beginning to feel that the 'soft' yet paternalistic approach has led to overgovernment, depersonalization and uniformity. The elections of September 1991 saw the end of the Social Democrat government – in power for all but six years since 1932 – with voters swinging towards parties canvassing lower taxation. Other attractive policies appeared to include curbs on immigration and diversion of Third World aid (Sweden spends well above the OECD per capita average each year) to the newly independent Baltic states.

Other changes were in the wind, too. A founder member of the European Free Trade Association (EFTA) – Stockholm played host to the inaugural meetings in 1960 – Sweden nevertheless applied for entry to the EC in 1991. And in 1994 the people voted to join the European Union on 1 January 1995.

Sweden remains the key state in Scandinavia: its long experience of peace and stability, and a wide industrial base built on efficiency and quality, together with its strategically central position and relatively large population, form the most important power among the Nordic nations.

However, it is possible that it will be vulnerable to forces largely beyond its control. Like its neighbours, Sweden suffers from forest-killing acid rain generated mostly by the UK and Germany, and after the shock waves from Chernobyl in 1986 the government was also forced to reconsider its electricity-generating programme, now 52% dependent on nuclear power. [*Map page 13*] ∎

AREA 449,960 sq km [173,730 sq mls]
POPULATION 8,738,000
CAPITAL (POPULATION) Stockholm (1,503,000)
GOVERNMENT Constitutional monarchy
ETHNIC GROUPS Swedish 91%, Finnish 3%
LANGUAGES Swedish (official), Finnish
RELIGIONS Christianity (Lutheran 89%, Roman Catholic 2%)
CURRENCY Swedish krona = 100 öre

SWITZERLAND

Nearly 60% of Swiss territory is in th Alps, of which two notable peaks are o the Italian border: the Matterhorn (4,478 [14,700 ft]) and the Monte Rosa (4,634 [15,200 ft]). The Alps are drained by th upper Rhine tributaries and by the Rhôn Valley via Lac Léman (Lake Geneva) Numerous lakes add to the scenic attraction the permanently snow-capped mountains.

ECONOMY AND RESOURCES

The Alps have become one of the great touris attractions of the world. As a result, aroun 200,000 people work in the hotel and caterin industries. Nationally, unemployment is ver low by world standards.

Despite its lingering image as a predomi nantly pastoral country, Switzerland is a ver advanced country, providing its citizens with per capita income which is by far the highest o the reasonably sized economies, and is out stripped only by neighbouring Liechtenstein The reasons for Switzerland's high standard o living include neutrality in two World Wars plentiful hydroelectric power, a central geo graphical position within Europe and rich mineral deposits, including uranium (40% of the electricity is now nuclear-derived) and iron ore. It would also be unfair, however – as in the case of Germany and Japan – not to include hard work, a sense of purpose and organizational ability in the list of attributes.

Agriculture is efficient, with both arable and pastoral farming; a wide range of produce is grown throughout the country, including maize and other cereals, fruits, vegetables, and grapes for the local wine industry. The mountain pastures are still used for summer grazing, though most of the famous migrations of herds and herders up the mountains in summer no longer take place. Industry is progressive and prosperous, in particular mechanical and electrical engineering, metallurgy, chemicals and textiles. Watch- and clock-making is perhaps the most famed of all Swiss industries,

THE ALPS

Thrust upwards by continental collision 25 or 30 million years ago, the Alps are Europe's principal mountain range. They stretch for over 1,000 km [600 mls] between north-eastern Italy and Austria and include Europe's highest mountain, Mont Blanc (4,807 m [15,771 ft]). The Alpine watershed is the source of many great European rivers, including the Rhine and the Po.

Despite the nine major passes that cross them, the mountains were seen by their pastoralist inhabitants and travellers alike as a troublesome obstacle until the 19th century, when interest in mountaineering, originally an English craze, gave puzzled locals new employment as guides. Six tunnels, including one under Mont Blanc, now make access very easy, and tourism has become a mass industry built around modern winter sports.

Alpine agriculture, once the mainstay of mountain life, is currently in decline, but skiing and summer tourism have brought new prosperity. Throughout the 1980s, the Alps attracted up to 50 million visitors a year, most intent on skiing some of the 40,000 runs that have been created for them. Unfortunately, the impact of mass skiing on the fragile Alpine environment is serious. Thousands of hectares of high forest have been bulldozed to create smooth pistes, denuding the slopes of scarce topsoil as well as creating perfect conditions for massive avalanches: in 1987, more than 60 people were killed by summer mudslides, and almost 50 towns and villages were damaged, some of them severely.

The remaining Alpine forests are under threat from industrial air pollution. Acid rain, formed from dissolved sulphur dioxide, is destroying trees at an alarming rate: in some districts, two-thirds have been affected, and many will never recover. In 1994, the Swiss voted to ban foreign lorries using alpine roads. This will be phased in over 10 years.

and it remains a very important source of income for the national economy.

In addition to agricultural and industrial strength Switzerland also has a world trade in banking and insurance, concentrated particularly in Zürich, while its revenues are boosted both by tourism and its position as the headquarters for numerous international bodies. Geneva alone hosts EFTA, GATT and the International Red Cross (which was first formed there in 1864), as well as ten UN agencies that include WHO, ILO and the High Commission for Refugees, and over 140 others: Basle, for example, is home to the Bank for International Settlements (the central banks' bank).

HISTORY AND POLITICS

Ironically, Switzerland has remained stubbornly outside the UN – a policy reiterated by a referendum held in 1986. As Europe started moving towards greater economic and political union, Switzerland announced in May 1992 that it would be applying to join the EU; but a December 1992 referendum rejected this proposal. However, in June 1993, Switzerland decided to establish by 1995 a 600-man battalion for use in the UN peacekeeping force.

Switzerland is a multilingual patchwork of 26 cantons, each of which has control over housing and economic policy. Six of the cantons are French-speaking, one Italian-speaking, one with a significant Romansch-speaking community (*Graubünden*), and the rest speak German. It nevertheless remains a strongly united country – internationally recognized as a permanently neutral power, politically stable with an efficient reservist army (but no navy), active in good causes, and shrewdly trading with most of the countries of the world. [*Map page 15*] ∎

AREA 41,290 sq km [15,942 sq mls]
POPULATION 7,131,000
CAPITAL (POPULATION) Bern (299,000)
GOVERNMENT Federal republic
ETHNIC GROUPS German 64%, French 19%, Italian 8%, Yugoslav 3%, Spanish 2%, Romansch 1%
LANGUAGES French, German, Italian and Romansch (all official)
RELIGIONS Christianity (Roman Catholic 46%, Protestant 40%)
CURRENCY Swiss franc = 100 centimes

SYRIA

The northern part of the former Ottoman province of the same name, Syria stretches from the Mediterranean to the Tigris, and from the southern edge of the Kurdish plateau in the north to the heart of the Hamad or stony desert in the south.

The Orontes River flows northwards along the Great Rift Valley, through alternating gorges and wide valleys which have been reclaimed by drainage and irrigation. Near Hamah and Hims the ranges of Lebanon and Anti-Lebanon are relatively low, but further south the Anti-Lebanon rises to the Heights of Hermon, whose snows water the gardens of the capital, Damascus, on the eastern side. In the far south, by the frontier with Jordan, the volcanic mass of Mount Hauran supports a group of oases around the town of Suwayda. The Golan Heights, in the south-west, are occupied by Israel.

ECONOMY AND RESOURCES

Aleppo, the second city of Syria, is set in a well-watered agricultural area. Further east the steppe becomes progressively drier. This

THE MIDDLE EAST CONFLICT

Arab-Jewish hostility in the Middle East dates from the so-called Balfour Declaration of 1917, when an embattled British government proposed a 'Jewish national home' in the then Turkish imperial province of Palestine without prejudicing the 'existing rights' of the overwhelmingly Arab (Christian and Muslim) population. After World War I, Palestine became a League of Nations mandate under British control; throughout the 1920s, a trickle of Jewish immigrants inspired rioting without noticeably affecting the population balance. But the rise of Nazism in Europe brought floods of Jewish refugees, and Arab-Jewish violence became endemic.

In 1947 the recently formed United Nations proposed a formal partition of the land, which was accepted by the Jews and rejected by the Palestinians. Even before the British announced they would withdraw in May 1948, 150,000 Arab refugees had fled. On 14 May, the day the British quit, the independence of a new State of Israel was declared. Egypt, Lebanon, Syria, Transjordan and Iraq at once launched an invasion, later joined by Yemen and Saudi Arabia. But by the 1949 cease-fire, Israel had beaten them off and controlled more territory than the UN partition plan had allocated the Jews. Jerusalem remained a divided city, half controlled by Israel, half by the armies of Transjordan, later the kingdom of Jordan. An uneasy peace descended, with sporadic border clashes; hundreds of thousands of Palestinians lost their homes. In 1956, full-scale war erupted once more when Israel joined with Britain and France in an attack on Egypt. Egypt's armies were badly mauled, but Israel's borders remained unchanged. In 1967, Israel responded to an Egyptian maritime blockade – and public threats from Syria and Egypt – with a pre-emptive strike that left it in control of the Sinai peninsula, the Gaza Strip, the 'West Bank' of the Jordan and all of Jerusalem. But real peace was no nearer: Israel had acquired an Arab population of several million. Palestinian freedom fighters – 'terrorists' to their enemies – began a worldwide campaign, including aircraft hijacking, to broadcast their people's plight.

A 1973 Egyptian attack across the Suez Canal, backed by Syria, came close to over-running Sinai, but Israeli counterattacks recovered much of the lost territory. Egypt's partial victory eventually led to the 1979 Camp David accord, by which Israel returned Sinai in exchange for Egyptian recognition of Israel's right to exist. Egypt was excoriated by its former Arab allies, and Palestinian terrorism continued. From 1987 onwards, a low-intensity Palestinian uprising (the *intifada*) began, which was repressed by Israel. Finally, on 13 September 1993, the Israeli prime minister Itzhak Rabin officially recognized the PLO, and Yasser Arafat, leader of the PLO, renounced terrorism and recognized the state of Israel, leading to an agreement signed by both sides in Washington. The agreement provided for limited Palestinian self-rule in the Gaza Strip and in the West Bank city of Jericho.

as traditionally winter pasture for the nomads who moved in from their summer homes in the mountains of Lebanon, but in recent years, thanks to techniques of dry-farming with machinery, it has become a prosperous farming zone, devoted almost exclusively to cotton and cereals. The water from the Euphrates barrage, which produces 70% of the country's electricity, will extend agriculture in this region. Syria has only one large harbour, at Latakia.

Syria has struck oil in the 'panhandle' by the Tigris in the far north-east, and a pipeline has been laid from there to the Mediterranean. Another pipeline crosses the desert further south from the Kirkuk fields in Iraq to the sea-terminal at Baniyas.

HISTORY AND POLITICS
President Assad's repressive but stable regime, in power since 1970, was heavily reliant on Arab aid, but Syria's anti-Iraq stance in the 1991 Gulf War will almost certainly result in greater Western assistance to the improving economy. Though small compared to Egypt or Saudi Arabia, Syria's position (both historical and geographical) makes the country a key player in the complicated power game of Middle East politics. [*Map page 19*] ∎

AREA 185,180 sq km [71,498 sq mls]
POPULATION 14,171,000
CAPITAL (POPULATION) Damascus (or Dimashq, 1,451,000)
GOVERNMENT Multiparty republic
ETHNIC GROUPS Arab 89%, Kurd 6%
LANGUAGES Arabic (official)
RELIGIONS Islam 90%, Christianity 9%
CURRENCY Syrian pound = 100 piastres

TAIWAN

High mountain ranges, which extend for the entire length of the island, occupy the central and eastern parts of Taiwan, and only a quarter of the island's surface area is cultivated. The central ranges rise to altitudes of over 3,000 m [10,000 ft], and carry dense forests of broadleaved evergreen trees such as camphor and Chinese cork oak. Above 1,500 m [5,000 ft], conifers such as pine, larch and cedar dominate.

ECONOMY AND RESOURCES
With its warm, moist climate – the island sits astride the Tropic of Cancer – Taiwan provides a highly favourable environment for agriculture, and the well-watered lands of the western coastal plain produce heavy rice crops. Sugar cane, sweet potatoes, tea, bananas and pineapples are also grown. Recently, however, agriculture has declined as industrial output has risen.

Taiwan produces a wide range of manufactured goods, including colour television sets, electronic calculators, footwear and ready-made clothing, and is the world's leading ship-breaker. Taipei, the capital, is a modern and affluent city, as well as being an important administrative and cultural centre.

Less than half the size of Ireland or Tasmania, but supporting nearly 21 million people, Taiwan has been a remarkable success story, averaging nearly 9% growth every year from 1953 to the 1990s.

HISTORY AND POLITICS
Ceded by the Chinese empire to Japan in 1895, Taiwan was surrendered by the Japanese Army to General Chiang Kai-shek's Nationalist Chinese government in 1945. Beaten by Mao Tse-tung's Communists, some 2 million Nationalists and their leader fled the mainland to the island in the two years before 1949. The influx was met with hostility by the 8 million Taiwanese, and the new regime was imposed with force.

Boosted by US help, Chiang's government set about ambitious programmes for land reform and industrial expansion, the latter taking Taiwan into the world's top 20 nations by 1980 and providing high living standards. The island, nevertheless, remained politically isolated, losing its UN seat to Communist China in 1971, and being diplomatically abandoned by the US in 1979, when Washington switched recognition to Beijing. Though few countries take seriously Taipei's claim to be the sole legitimate government of China, the country administers a number of islands off the mainland, notably Quemoy (Jinmen) and Matsu (Mazu).

In 1987, the authoritarian regime lifted martial law after nearly 40 years, a native Taiwanese became president in 1988, and in 1991 came the country's first full general election. Technically still at war with Beijing, there have been signs that the thaw of the Cold War might reach the island. [*Map page 24*] ■

AREA 36,000 sq km [13,900 sq mls]
POPULATION 20,659,000
CAPITAL (POPULATION) Taipei (2,718,000)
GOVERNMENT Multiparty republic
ETHNIC GROUPS Taiwanese (Han Chinese) 84%, mainland Chinese 14%
LANGUAGES Mandarin Chinese
RELIGIONS Buddhism 43%, Taoism 21%, Christianity 7%, Confucianism
CURRENCY New Taiwan dollar = 100 cents

TAJIKISTAN

The Republic of Tajikistan is one of the five central Asian republics that formed part of the former Soviet Union. Only 7% of the country is below 1,000 m [3,280 ft], while almost all of eastern Tajikistan is above 3,000 m [9,840 ft]. The highest point is Communism Peak (Pik Kommunizma) which reaches 7,496 m [24,593 ft]. The main ranges are the westwards extension of the Tian Shan range in the north and the snow-capped Pamirs in the south-east. Earthquakes are common throughout the country.

Tajikistan is a landlocked country with a continental climate. The summers are hot and dry in the lower valleys, but winters are long and bitterly cold in the mountainous areas.

ECONOMY AND RESOURCES

The World Bank classifies Tajikistan as a 'low-income' developing country. Agriculture,

mainly on irrigated land in the north-we (there are 43,000 km [26,720 mls] of irrig tion channels in total), is the principal activi and cotton is the chief product. Other crop include fruits, grains, vegetables and mulber trees (for silkworms), as well as eucalyptus ar geraniums for the perfume industry. Th country has large hydroelectric pow resources and it produces aluminium. Othe wise, manufacturing is mostly on a small scal The country's main exports are aluminiun cotton, fruits, vegetable oils and textiles.

HISTORY AND POLITICS

The ancestors of the people of Tajikistan wei Persians who had settled in the area by 2,50 years ago. The area was conquered man times; one important group of invaders wer the Arabs via whom Islam was introduced i the 7th century. From the 9th centur onwards, the Tajiks lived under the control c various feudal emirates until, in the late 19tl century, Russia conquered part of Tajikistan and it extended its rule after the Russian Revolution of 1917. By 1920, all of Tajikistan was under Russian control.

In 1924, the area was ruled as part of the Uzbek Soviet Socialist Republic. But in 192 it was expanded, taking in areas containing Uzbeks, and it became the Tajik Sovie Socialist Republic within the Soviet Union Under Communism, all features of Tajik life were strictly controlled and religious worship was discouraged, though certain aspects of life were improved, such as health and education.

While the Soviet Union began to introduce reforms in the 1980s, many Tajiks demanded freedom. In 1989, the Tajik government made Tajik the official language instead of Russian, and in 1990 it stated that its local laws over-ruled Soviet laws. Tajikistan became fully independent in 1991, after the break-up of the Soviet Union. As the poorest of the former Soviet republics, Tajikistan faced many problems in trying to reorganize its economy along free-enterprise lines.

In 1992, civil war broke out between the government, which was run by former Communists, and an alliance of democrats and Islamic forces. The government maintained control, but it relied heavily on aid from the Commonwealth of Independent States, e organization through which most of the rmer republics of the Soviet Union have kept contact, but sporadic fighting continues in any parts. [*Map page 22*] ■

AREA 143,100 sq km [55,520 sq mls]
POPULATION 5,933,000
CAPITAL (POPULATION) Dushanbe (602,000)
GOVERNMENT Transitional democracy
ETHNIC GROUPS Tajik 62%, Uzbek 24%, Russian 8%, Tatar, Kyrgyz, Ukrainian, German
LANGUAGES Tajik (official)
RELIGIONS Islam
CURRENCY Tajik rouble = 100 kopeks

TANZANIA

From the islands of Zanzibar and Pemba, Tanzania extends across the high plateau of eastern Africa, mostly above 1,000 m 3,000 ft], to the rift valleys filled by lakes Tanganyika and Nyasa (Malawi). The North-rn Highlands flank branches of the eastern ift valley, containing the strongly alkaline Lake Natron and lakes Eyasi and Manyara, and dominated by the ice-capped extinct volcano of Kilimanjaro which, at 5,895 m 19,340 ft], is the highest mountain in Africa. The Southern Highlands overlook Lake Nyasa at the southern end of the rift system.

ECONOMY AND RESOURCES

Tanzania's population is dispersed into several concentrations mostly on the margins of the country, separated by sparsely inhabited savanna woodland (*miombo*). Attempts to develop the *miombo* woodlands have been hindered by sleeping sickness, drought and poor soils. Along the coast and on self-govern-ing Zanzibar and other islands are old cities and ruins of the historic Swahili-Arab culture, and the major ports and railway termini of Dar es Salaam and Tanga. Rail connections enable Dar es Salaam to act as a port for Zambia and, by ferry across Lake Tanganyika, for eastern

Zaïre. Local products include sisal and cashew nuts with cloves from Zanzibar and Pemba, and there are some fine beach resorts.

Tanzania received 202,000 visitors in 1992, less than a third of Kenya's total, but there are hopes that this figure will rise. Certainly, the country has many of the prerequisites for a successful tourist industry. There are 17 national parks and reserves – among them the Selous, the largest game reserve in the world; the celebrated Serengeti; and the Ngorongoro crater, renowned for its abundant wildlife. In addition, there are important archaeological sites such as Olduvia Gorge, west of the Serengeti, where in 1964 Louis Leakey, the famous British archaeologist and anthropol-ogist, discovered the remains of humans some million years old.

The Northern Highlands centre on Moshi and support intensive agriculture, exporting coffee, tea and tobacco. This contrasts with the nomadic Masai pastoralists of the sur-rounding plains whose traditional lifestyle is based on shifting cultivation. Tea also comes from the Southern Highlands. South of Lake Victoria is an important cotton-growing and cattle-rearing area, focusing on Mwanza. The most important minerals are diamonds.

HISTORY AND POLITICS

Tanzania was formed in 1964 when mainland Tanganyika – which had become independent from Britain in 1961 – was joined by the small island state of Zanzibar. For 20 years after independence Tanzania was run under the widely admired policies of self-help (*ujamaa*) and egalitarian socialism pioneered by Presi-dent Julius Nyerere. While his schemes produced relatively high levels of education and welfare for Africa, economic progress was stifled not only by lack of resources and falling world commodity prices but also by inefficient state corporations and corrupt bureaucracies. As a result the country ranks little better than war-torn states like Ethiopia and the Somali Republic in terms of income, and is almost as dependent on foreign financial aid.

Nyerere stepped down as president in 1985, but retained the (only) party leadership and considerable influence for another five years. In the meantime his successor, Ali Hassan Mwinyi, was attempting to liberalize the economy – if not the political system. In 1992 he amended the constitution to allow multiparty politics, provided the parties were not formed on tribal or racial grounds. [*Map page 33*] ■

> **AREA** 945,090 sq km [364,899 sq mls]
> **POPULATION** 28,846,000
> **CAPITAL (POPULATION)** Dodoma (203,833)
> **GOVERNMENT** Multiparty republic
> **ETHNIC GROUPS** Nyamwezi and Sukuma 21%, Swahili 9%, Hehet and Bena 7%, Makonde 6%, Haya 6%
> **LANGUAGES** Swahili and English (both official)
> **RELIGIONS** Christianity (mostly Roman Catholic) 34%, Islam 33% (99% in Zanzibar), traditional beliefs and others 33%
> **CURRENCY** Tanzanian shilling = 100 cents

THAILAND

M eaning 'Land of the Free' (*Muang Thai*), and known as Siam until 1939, Thailand is comparable in size to France or Spain. The country is centred on the valley of the River Chao Phraya that flows across the central plain extending from the Gulf of Siam to the foothills of the northern mountains. Bounded in the west by the narrow mountain range that borders Burma, and in the east by lower hills separating the plain from the higher Khorat Plateau (Cao Nguyen Khorat), the central plain is Thailand's rice bowl; it presents long vistas, with extensive ricefields, canals and rivers that provide the main routeways, with villages raised on stilts. Northern Thailand is a region of fold mountains, with agriculturally rich intermontane basins.

The capital city, Bangkok, stands at the southern edge of the plain, near the mouth of the Chao Phraya; with a seaport and international airport is the transport centre of the country. Ornate Buddhist temples stand side by side with modern concrete buildings, and the growing city population is already over a tenth of the total. Founded as a royal capital in

1782, this 'Venice of the East' is rich examples of Thai culture, including fantas statues of Buddha. The name Bangkok refe only to the Thon Buri side of the River Ch Phraya; the proper term is Krung Thep ('ci of angels' – like Los Angeles). Today, it is sprawling metropolis with high levels of traf congestion, struggling to absorb the waves migrants who pour in from rural areas search of work.

ECONOMY AND RESOURCES
The hill forests produce teak and other val able timbers. Thailand's highest mountai Doi Inthanon (2,575 m [8,514 ft]), and th high hills surrounding it are the home of man hill tribes who live by shifting cultivation of d rice and opium poppies; Chiengmai, th beautiful northern capital, lies in this are The Khorat Plateau to the east is a sandston region of poor soils supporting savanna wood lands; glutinous rice and cassava (the countr has overtaken Brazil as the world's leadin producer) are its main crops. The long south ern part of Thailand, linked to the Mala Peninsula by the Isthmus of Kra, is a foreste region of rolling hills, producing tin ore an plantation rubber.

Thailand has long been famous for rice pro duction; though fifth in the world league, it i the biggest exporter and it is still the country' best agricultural earner, despite the increasin importance of several other commoditie including rubber, tapioca products and sugar Wolfram, forest products and fisheries are als being exploited. Offshore oil and gas wer discovered in the late 1970s, and crude oi production began in 1983. Industries remain largely underdeveloped, but manufacturing based on cheap labour is expanding rapidly in textiles, clothing, electrical goods and food processing, contributing more to GDP than agriculture since 1984, while local crafts in the villages help to provide overseas income, as does tourism. In 1992 Thailand received near-ly 5.4 million visitors – Burma received just 11,400 – and since 1982 tourism has been the main foreign exchange earner.

HISTORY AND POLITICS
Thailand is the only South-east Asian country that has not been colonized, or occupied by

reign powers, except in war. An absolute monarchy until 1932, when the king graciously surrendered to a bloodless coup that set up a provisional constitution, Thailand has been a more stable recent history than most of its unfortunate neighbours, though for most of the next 40 years it was dominated by military rulers. Forced into alliance with Japan in World War II, the Thais aligned themselves firmly to the USA after 1945 – a policy that has brought much military, technical and financial aid.

Despite continuing army involvements and interventions – the bloodless coup of 1991, claimed to be protecting King Rama IX and promising a swift return to civilian democracy, was the 17th takeover in half a century – and despite the presence of Cambodian refugees and its use by various camps as a political conduit and military springboard for intentions in South-east Asia, Thailand's subtle and pragmatic approach to life has seen the country prosper. In a system often referred to as 'semi-democracy', constitutional rule propped up by the pillars of military, monarch, bureaucracy and religion, Thailand has managed (not without criticism) to avoid the dreadful events that have afflicted the rest of mainland South-east Asia since the end of World War II – though in May 1992 the unelected leadership found itself under serious pressure. Hundreds died in protests against the takeover as prime minister by the head of the army, and an uneasy peace was restored only after his removal and an appeal for order from the King. Elections were held later in 1992 and a civilian government under Prime Minister Chuan Leekpai took office. The new government has committed itself to reducing the political power of the military. [*Map page 26*] ■

AREA 513,120 sq km [198,116 sq mls]
POPULATION 58,183,000
CAPITAL (POPULATION) Bangkok (5,876,000)
GOVERNMENT Constitutional monarchy
ETHNIC GROUPS Thai 80%, Chinese 12%,
Malay 4%, Khmer 3%
LANGUAGES Thai (official)
RELIGIONS Buddhism 94%, Islam 4%,
Christianity 1%
CURRENCY Baht = 100 statang

TOGO

The Republic of Togo is a long, narrow country in West Africa. From north to south, it extends about 500 km [311 mls], but its coastline on the Gulf of Guinea is only 64 km [40 mls] long and it is only 145 km [90 mls] at its widest point. Crossing the country from south-west to north-east, the Togo-Atacora Mountains in southern Togo, which rise to 986 m [3,235 ft], overlook a plateau. The land descends to a densely populated coastal plain in the south. In the north lies another plateau, which descends northwards to the border with Burkina Faso.

The main wet season is from March to July, with a minor wet season in October and November, but temperatures are high throughout the year. The central mountains are cooler and rainier than the capital Lomé, on the coast, while the far north is hot with a single rainy season.

Behind the sandy coastal plain, with its many palm trees, are areas of grassland with clumps of hardwood trees. Some rainforest grows in central Togo, but the north is savanna country with many animal species, including antelopes, buffaloes, elephants, leopards and lions.

ECONOMY AND RESOURCES

The major forests and cash crops are in the south-west. The railway inland from the coast stops at Blitta, in central Togo, and the road is the only means of keeping the poorer, drier northern parts of this awkwardly shaped country in touch with the more developed areas of the south, including the capital and main port of Lomé and the important phosphate mining area, with its port of Kpémé. Phosphates, coffee and cocoa are the important exports, but major food crops are cassava, yams, maize and sorghum-millets.

HISTORY AND POLITICS

As Togoland, the country was colonized by Germany in 1884 and then occupied by

Franco-British troops during World War I. It was partitioned between the two powers under a League of Nations mandate in 1922, with British Togoland later becoming part of Ghana and the larger eastern French section gaining independence as Togo in 1960.

Local rivalries, especially between northerners and southerners, are important political factors and, in 1963, a group of army officers from the north assassinated the president, a southerner. In 1967, Gnassingbé Eyadéma, one of the officers responsible for the 1963 coup, took power and suspended the constitution, though constitutional government was restored in 1980. Following strikes and protests, the principle of multiparty elections was conceded in March 1991, but by the end of the year there were violent clashes between the army and the new civilian government, with old rivalries between Eyadéma's northern Kabre people and the dominant Ewe tribe re-emerging to block the path to stable democratization. Multiparty elections for parliament took place in 1994 and a coalition government was formed. [*Map page 32*] ■

AREA 56,790 sq km [21,927 sq mls]
POPULATION 4,010,000
CAPITAL (POPULATION) Lomé (500,000)
GOVERNMENT Multiparty republic
ETHNIC GROUPS Ewe-Adja 43%, Tem 4%, Kabre 22%, Gurma 16%
LANGUAGES French (official), Ewe, Kabre
RELIGIONS Traditional beliefs 50%, Christianity 35%, Islam 15%
CURRENCY CFA franc = 100 centimes

Nuku'alofa, site of the royal palace. Vava'u (15,000) in the north is the next most populous. Predominantly Christian, the people speak Tongan, though English is also official.

Most Tongans live off their own produce including coconuts, yams, tapioca, groundnuts and fish. While the government owns all land, men are entitled to rent areas to grow food – a policy now under pressure with burgeoning young population. The main exports are coconut oil products and bananas with New Zealand the main trading partner. Tourism is becoming increasingly important, with 23,000 visitors to the islands in 1992.

Tonga is an absolute monarchy. Since 1965 the ruler has been Taufa'ahau Tupou IV, latest in a line going back a thousand years, who presided over the islands' transition from British protectorate to independent Commonwealth state in 1970. His brother is prime minister on a council that has hereditary chiefs as well as elected representatives; there are no parties. The country has remained peaceful, enhancing the name given by Captain James Cook in the 1770s – the Friendly Islands. [*Map page 2*] ■

AREA 750 sq km [290 sq mls]
POPULATION 98,000
CAPITAL (POPULATION) Nuku'alofa (29,000)
GOVERNMENT Constitutional monarchy
ETHNIC GROUPS Polynesian
LANGUAGES Tongan, English
RELIGIONS Christianity
CURRENCY Pa'anga = 100 seniti

TONGA

TRINIDAD & TOBAGO

The archipelago comprises over 170 islands, 36 of which are inhabited, covering 750 sq km [290 sq mls] in a mixture of low coralline and higher volcanic outcrops that fall into three distinct belts. Nearly two-thirds of the population live on the largest island of Tongatapu, 29,000 of them in the capital of

Furthest south of the West Indies, Trinidad is a rectangular island situated just 16 km [10 mls] off Venezuela's Orinoco delta. Tobago is a detached extension of its Northern Range of hills, lying 34 km [21 mls] to the north-east. Trinidad's highest point is Cerro Aripe (940 m [3,085 ft]) in the rugged, forested Northern Range; the capital, Port of ain (in the county of St George, one of the ght counties of Trindad), nestles behind the lls on the sheltered west coast.

CONOMY AND RESOURCES

oth islands are valued for their agricultural roduce, including sugar, coffee, cocoa, rub-er and citrus fruits, but the main source of come is oil. First exploited in 1867, it has een the lifeblood of the nation's economy, iving the island a relatively high standard of ving, and (with petrochemicals) still accounts or over 70% of exports. Falling prices in the 980s had a severe effect, only partly offset by he growth of tourism and continued revenues rom asphalt, which occurs naturally, and gas.

HISTORY AND POLITICS

'Discovered' by Columbus in 1498, Trinidad vas later planted for sugar production by Spanish and French settlers before becoming British in 1797. Black slaves worked the plantations until emancipation in 1834, when Indian and Chinese indentured labourers were brought in. Tobago came under British con-trol in 1814, joining Trinidad to form a single colony in 1899. Independence came in 1962 and a republic was established in 1976, though Tobago would like internal self-government.

A potentially volatile ethnic mix, often over-crowded, Trinidad experienced a sharp politi-cal change in 1986, when after 30 years the People's National Movement was voted out and the National Alliance for Reconstruction coalition took office. After five years of insta-bility, the PNM was returned by a landslide in December 1991, but it faced mounting economic problems. [*Map page 30*] ∎

AREA 5,130 sq km [1,981 sq mls]
POPULATION 1,292,000
CAPITAL (POPULATION) Port of Spain (51,000)
GOVERNMENT Republic
ETHNIC GROUPS Black 43%, East Indian 40%, Mixed 16%, White 1%, Chinese 1%
LANGUAGES English
RELIGIONS Christianity 49%, Hinduism 24%, Islam 9%
CURRENCY Trinidad and Tobago dollar = 100 cents

TRISTAN DA CUNHA

Tristan da Cunha is the largest of four scat-tered islands towards the southern end of the Mid-Atlantic Ridge, a volcanic cone of 2,060 m [6,760 ft], ringed by a lava plain that drops steeply to the sea; a narrow strip of flat ground accommodates the only settlement of about 330 inhabitants. The climate is mild and damp with frequent storms. The island was evacuated 1961–3 following a volcanic eruption. The Nightingale and Inaccessible Islands are small, uninhabited islands nearby; Gough Island, 400 km [250 mls] to the south-east, is a steep, craggy, forest-covered island some 13 km [8 mls] long; its only settlement is a meteorological and radio station.

The islanders grow potatoes and rear sheep and cattle for their own use.

Like Ascension to the north, all the islands are administered as dependencies of St Helena. [*Map page 2*] ∎

AREA 104 sq km [40 sq mls]
POPULATION 330
CAPITAL (POPULATION) Edinburgh (330)
GOVERNMENT Dependent territory of the UK
ETHNIC GROUPS No native ones
LANGUAGES English
RELIGIONS Christianity
CURRENCY English currency

TUNISIA

Smallest of the three Maghreb countries that comprise north-west Africa, Tunisia consists of the eastern end of the Atlas Mountains together with the central step-pelands to the south, which are separated from the country's Saharan sector by the vast low-lying saltpans of Chott Djerid. In the north the lower Medjerda Valley and the low-lying plains of Bizerte and Tunis were densely colonized.

Mountainous northern Tunisia has a Mediterranean climate, with dry, sunny summers, and mild wet winters. The average yearly rainfall decreases to the south; in the north rainfall can be in excess of 900 mm [36 in], whereas at Gafsa in south-central Tunisia, the average annual rainfall is only 150 mm [6 in].

ECONOMY AND RESOURCES

Agriculture is important to the Tunisian economy, employing 40% of the population. Major irrigation schemes have been carried out in recent years and these lowlands, which produce cereals, vines, citrus fruits, olives and vegetables, represent the country's most important agricultural area. New industries, sometimes coupled with tourism, have transformed a number of coastal towns, including Sfax, Monastir and Sousse. By comparison, the interior has been neglected.

HISTORY AND POLITICS

Tunisia has a long and rich history. It was the first part of the region to be conquered by the Phoenicians, Romans (Carthage is now a suburb of Tunis) and later the Arabs and Turks, and each successive civilization has left a marked impression on the country. Consequently, Tunisia has acquired a distinct national identity and culture, with a long tradition of urban life.

In 1881, France established a protectorate over Tunisia and ruled the country until 1956. The new parliament immediately abolished the monarchy and declared Tunisia to be a republic in 1957, with the nationalist leader, Habib Bourguiba, as president.

In 1975, Bourguiba was elected president for life. His government introduced many reforms, including votes for women. But problems arose, such as unemployment and fears that Western influences, introduced by tourists, might damage traditional Muslim values. Finally, the prime minister, Zine el Abidine Ben Ali, removed Bourguiba from office in 1987 and succeeded him as president. He was elected in 1989 and 1994. His party dominated the Chamber of Deputies, though some seats were reserved for the opposition parties. [*Map page 16*] ■

AREA 163,610 sq km [63,170 sq mls]
POPULATION 8,733,000
CAPITAL (POPULATION) Tunis (1,395,000)
GOVERNMENT Multiparty republic
ETHNIC GROUPS Arab 98%, Berber 1%, French and others
LANGUAGES Arabic (official)
RELIGIONS Islam 99%
CURRENCY Tunisian dinar = 1,000 millimes

TURKEY

Lying in two continents, Turkey comprises the broad peninsula of Asia Minor, together with its 'roots' around Lake Van, and in Europe that part of Thrace (Thraki) which lies to the east of the lower Maritsa River. The straits separating the European part (roughly 5% of the total area of the country) and the Asiatic part of Turkey have been of strategic importance for thousands of years. The Dardanelles, joining the Aegean Sea to the Sea of Marmara, are 1.6 km [1 ml] wide at their narrowest point; the Bosphorus, linking the Sea of Marmara to the Black Sea, measures just 640 m [2,100 ft] at one point and is spanned by two suspension bridges at Istanbul.

ECONOMY AND RESOURCES

The heart of the country is the high karst plateau of Anatolia, semi-desert around the central salt lake, but mainly sheep country. The Taurus ranges afford summer grazing for the plateau flocks, and also timber. The northern Pontic ranges are better wooded, with fertile plains.

The valleys of the Gediz and Cürüksu, which open westwards from the plateau to the Aegean, export tobacco and figs, while the deltaic plain around Adana grows abundant cotton. The very high and thinly-peopled plateaux and ranges to the east of the Euphrates produce chrome (in 1993 Turkey

...as the world's fourth largest producer), ...opper and oil.

Istanbul, the former imperial capital of Byzantium and Constantinople, which con-...rols the straits between the Black Sea and the Mediterranean, is the country's chief port and commercial city, but the function of capital ...as been transferred to the more centrally-...laced town of Ankara. Turkey, with a rapidly ...rowing population, now has one of the best ...ailway networks in the Middle East, and ...hough lacking in large resources of mineral oil ...as built up a thriving industrial economy ...ased on imported oil, on coal (from Zonguldak), and above all on hydroelectric power. Though still important, agriculture has ...een overtaken by manufacturing, particularly ...extiles and clothing.

HISTORY AND POLITICS

Constantinople's huge Ottoman empire had been in decline for centuries when alliance with Germany in World War I ended in the loss of all non-Turkish areas. Nationalists led by Mustafa Kemal – known later as Atatürk ('father of the Turks') – rejected peace pro- posals favouring Greece and after a civil war set up a republic. Turkey's present frontiers were established in 1923, when Atatürk became president, and until 1938 he ruled as a virtual dictator, secularizing and moderniz- ing the traditional Islamic state.

Between 1960 and 1970 the government was overthrown three times by military coups; civilian rule returned in 1983 and since then democracy has been relatively stable, though the country's human rights record remained poor. In June 1993, Turkey's first woman prime minister, Tansu Çiller, was elected. Since 1984 Turkey has been fighting armed guerillas of the Kurdish Workers Party in the south-east of the country where Kurds are the majority population.

The economic progress that partnered political stability in the mid-1980s – growth averaged more than 7% a year – encouraged Turkey to apply for EU membership in 1987, but the response from Brussels was unenthusi- astic. Turkey's disputes with Greece – notably over Ankara's invasion of northern Cyprus in 1974, but also over claims to territory and mineral rights in the Aegean – plus the

country's poor human rights record and low standard of living were all factors. Although Turkey has been a NATO member since 1952, and is an associate member of the EU, this was likely to remain the EU's position for some time – while the emergence of Islamic fundamentalism raised new doubts about Turkey's 'European' identity and stance.

Situated at one of the world's great geo- political crossroads, the nation seemed des- tined to remain sandwiched between Europe and the Middle East. Turkey, nevertheless, has a two-way traffic in people with Western Europe: while tourism was a boom industry in the late 1980s (often at the expense of Greece), with 2.5 million visitors a year visiting the country, these were outnumbered by Turkish men working (or seeking work) in EU cities, the majority of them in Germany. [*Map page 22*] ∎

AREA 779,450 sq km [300,946 sq mls]
POPULATION 60,771,000
CAPITAL (POPULATION) Ankara (3,022,000)
GOVERNMENT Multiparty republic
ETHNIC GROUPS Turkish 86%, Kurdish 11%, Arab 2%
LANGUAGES Turkish (official)
RELIGIONS Islam 99%
CURRENCY Turkish lira = 100 kurus

TURKMENISTAN

The Republic of Turkmenistan is one of the five central Asian republics which once formed part of the former Soviet Union. Most of the land is low-lying, with mountains lying on the southern and south-western bor- ders. In the west lies the salty Caspian Sea. A depression called the Kara Bogaz Gol Bay contains the country's lowest point, at 31 m [102 ft] below sea level. Most of Turk- menistan is arid and the Karakum, Asia's largest sand desert, covers about 80% of the country.

Turkmenistan has a continental climate.

The average annual rainfall varies from 80 mm [3 in] in the desert to 300 mm [12 in] in the southern mountains. The summers are hot, but in winter the temperatures sometimes drop well below freezing point.

The vegetation in Turkmenistan is sparse and practically non-existent in the sandy areas. But plants grow around desert oases and in the mountains, where trees such as almond, fig and walnut can be found.

ECONOMY AND RESOURCES
As much Middle Eastern as Central Asian, the scant population of Turkmenistan is found mainly around irrigated oases and along the Kara-Kum canal, growing cereals, cotton and fruit, and rearing karakul lambs. Apart from astrakhan rugs and food processing, industry is largely confined to mining magnesium, sulphur and salt and the production of natural gas. The country is dependent on trade with other former Soviet republics for more than 75% of its GDP, much of which is subsidized.

HISTORY AND POLITICS
Just over 1,000 years ago, Turkic people settled in the lands east of the Caspian Sea and the name 'Turkmen' comes from that time. Mongol armies conquered the region in the 13th century and Islam was introduced in the 14th century.

Russia took over the area in the 1870s and 1880s. After the Russian Revolution of 1917, came under Communist rule and, in 1924, the area became the Turkmen Soviet Socialist Republic. The Communists strictly controlled all aspects of life, discouraging religious worship in particular, though at the same time they improved such services as education, health, housing and transport.

In the 1980s, when the Soviet Union began to introduce reforms, the Turkmen began to demand more freedom, and in 1990 the Turkmen government stated that its laws overruled Soviet laws. In 1991, Turkmenistan became fully independent after the break-up of the Soviet Union and joined the UN. But the country kept ties with Russia through the Commonwealth of Independent States (CIS) which it joined in January 1994.

In 1992, Turkmenistan adopted a new constitution, allowing for the setting up of political parties, providing that they were no ethnic or religious in character. But, effect ively, Turkmenistan remained a one-part state and in 1992, Saparmurad Niyazov, th former leader of the Communist Party (re named the Democratic Party), was the only candidate. Faced with many economic prob lems, Turkmenistan began to look south rather than to the CIS for support. As par of this policy, it joined the Economic Co-operation Organization which had beer set up in 1985 by Iran, Pakistan and Turkey [*Map page 22*] ■

AREA 488,100 sq km [188,450 sq mls]
POPULATION 4,010,000
CAPITAL (POPULATION) Ashgabat (or Ashkhabad, 407,000)
GOVERNMENT Single-party republic
ETHNIC GROUPS Turkmen 72%, Russian 10%, Uzbek 9%, Kazakh 3%, Tatar
LANGUAGES Turkmen (official)
RELIGIONS Islam
CURRENCY Manat

TURKS & CAICOS IS

A group of 30 islands (eight of them inhabited), lying at the eastern end of the Grand Bahama Bank, north of Haiti, the Turks and Caicos are composed of low, flat limestone terrain with scrub, marsh and swamp providing little agriculture.

Tourism has recently overtaken fishing (chiefly lobsters) as the main industry, with direct flights from Miami feeding the new airport on the main tourist island of Providenciales. Offshore banking facilities are also expanding, though harmed in the mid-1980s by allegations of ministerial drug-trafficking and organized crime.

Previously claimed by France and Spain, they have been British since 1766, administered with Jamaica from 1873 to 1959 and a separate Crown Colony since 1973. Around a third of the 14,000 population, mainly of ıxed Afro-European descent, lives in the ↄpital of Cockburn Town on the island of ːand Turk. [*Map page 30*] ■

AREA 430 sq km [166 sq mls]
POPULATION 14,000
CAPITAL (POPULATION) Cockburn Town 4,000)
GOVERNMENT Dependent territory of the JK
ETHNIC GROUPS Of African descent
LANGUAGES English
RELIGIONS Christianity
CURRENCY US currency

TUVALU

Nⁿone of Tuvalu's nine coral atolls – total area 24 sq km [9 sq mls] – rises more han 4.6 m [15 ft] out of the Pacific, and ːhough the climate is uniformly pleasant, poor ɔoils restrict vegetation to coconut palms, ›readfruit trees and bush. The government ɪas tried to publicize the country's vulner-bility to the possible effects of global varming, namely sea-level rise, which would ɪave a detrimental affect on many Pacific ːsland communities.

The population of 9,000 (a third of whom ɪve on the main island of Funafuti, where the ɔapital Fongafale is situated) survive by ɔubsistence farming, raising pigs and poultry, ːnd by fishing. Copra is the only significant ːxport crop, but most foreign exchange comes ːrom the sale of elaborate postage stamps to ːhe world's philatelists. Tuvalu however, ːemains largely dependent on foreign aid.

The population, once far higher, was ːeduced from about 20,000 to just 3,000 in ːhe three decades after 1850, by Europeans ːbducting the inhabitants to work in the ːlantations of other Pacific island territories. An estimated 1,500 Tuvaluans still work overseas, mainly in Nauru.

Tuvalu became an independent constitu-tional monarchy within the Commonwealth in 1978, three years after separation from the Gilbert Islands – a decision supported by a large majority in a referendum held in 1974. [*Map page 3*] ■

AREA 24 sq km [9 sq mls]
POPULATION 9,000
CAPITAL (POPULATION) Fongafale (2,810)
GOVERNMENT Constitutional monarchy
ETHNIC GROUPS Polynesian
LANGUAGES Tuvaluan, English
RELIGIONS Christianity
CURRENCY Australian currency

UGANDA

Extending from Lake Victoria to the west-ern arm of the Great African Rift Valley and beyond, the Republic of Uganda is a land of lakes (sources of the White Nile) originating from the tilting and faulting associated with the rift valley system. On the western side of the country, the Ruwenzori block has been uplifted to 5,109 m [16,762 ft], while the east-ern frontier bisects the large extinct volcano of Mt Elgon (4,321 m [14,176 ft]).

In the south rainfall is abundant in two seasons, and patches of the original rainforest (covering 25% of land area) remain. To the north, one rainy season each year supports a savanna of trees and grassland.

ECONOMY AND RESOURCES

In the south, most of the forest has been cleared from the densely settled areas, notably in the historic kingdoms of Buganda and Busoga. Here the banana is a staple of diet, and coffee, tea and sugar are cash crops; Uganda is the world's eighth largest coffee producer. Here, too, are the capital Kampala, and the industrial centre of Jinja, adjacent to the huge Owen Falls hydroelectric plant. The western areas, the former kingdoms of Bunyoro, Toro and Ankole, depend more on cattle rearing.

In the north, population is generally less

dense, and farmers grow finger-millet and sorghum, with cotton and tobacco as cash crops. Tsetse fly inhibits cattle-keeping in some areas, which have become game parks, but the dry north-east (Karamoja) supports nomadic pastoralists. Blessed with an equable climate, fertile soils and varied resources, from freshwater fish to copper, Uganda could have lived up to Churchill's colonial description as 'the pearl of Africa'. Instead, independence soon brought two decades of disaster with almost ceaseless internal conflict and a shattered economy.

HISTORY AND POLITICS
Little is known of the early history of Uganda. When Europeans first reached the area in the 19th century, many of the people were organized in kingdoms, the most powerful of which was Buganda, the home of the Baganda people. Britain took over the country between 1894 and 1914 and ruled it until independence in 1962. In 1967, Uganda became a republic and Buganda's Kabaka (king), Sir Edward Mutesa II, was made president. But tensions between the Kabaka and the prime minister, Apollo Milton Obote, led to the dismissal of the Kabaka in 1966.

Between the break from Britain in 1962 and the takeover by Yoweri Museveni in 1986, the country suffered a succession of linked civil wars, violent coups, armed invasions and tribal massacres. The worst of several bad periods was the sordid regime of Idi Amin, who in 1971 ousted Obote – then president of a one-party state – and in an eight-year reign of terror killed up to 300,000 people as all political and human rights were suspended. Amin was finally removed when he tried to annex part of Tanzania and President Nyerere ordered his troops to carry on into Uganda after they had repelled the invaders.

Obote returned to power, but the bloodshed continued and he was ousted again in 1985. The following year, 1986, brought in Yoweri Museveni, who achieved some success in stabilizing the situation as a prelude to a return to democracy. But he faced a problem not known to his predecessors: Uganda's AIDS explosion. Some estimates suggest that by the end of 1991 more than a quarter of the children under five were infected with the HIV virus.

In 1993, Museveni restored the tradition kingdoms, including Buganda where a ne Kabaka was crowned. Museveni also he national elections in 1994, though politic parties were not permitted. Museveni's sup porters won a majority. [Map page 33] ■

> **AREA** 235,880 sq km [91,073 sq mls]
> **POPULATION** 20,621,000
> **CAPITAL (POPULATION)** Kampala (773,000)
> **GOVERNMENT** Republic in transition
> **ETHNIC GROUPS** Baganda 18%, Banyoro 14%, Teso 9%, Banyan 8%, Basoga 8%, Bagisu 7%, Bachiga 7%, Lango 6%, Acholi 5%
> **LANGUAGES** English and Swahili (both official)
> **RELIGIONS** Christianity (Roman Catholic 40%, Protestant 29%), traditional beliefs 18%, Islam 7%
> **CURRENCY** Uganda shilling = 100 cents

UKRAINE

Ukraine is the second largest country in Europe after Russia. It formed most of the south-western part of the former USSR which broke up in 1991. The country is mostly flat, with higher land in the west, south and south-east. The southern border is formed by the Black Sea.

The western Ukraine comprises the fertile uplands of Volhynia, with the Carpathians cutting across the far western corner of the country. The north is mostly lowlands, with the Dnepr River (Dnieper or Dnipro) at its heart, which include marshes and the state capital of Kiev (Kiyev or Kyyiv) in addition to arable land. This area, however, suffered most from the Chernobyl nuclear disaster of 1986, with huge tracts of land contaminated by radioactivity.

In the centre of the republic, south of Kiev and west of Kirovograd (Kirovohrad), are the rich lands with fertile chernozem soils. In the south are dry lowlands bordering the Black Sea and the Sea of Azov, with Odessa (Odesa) the main port. Still further south is the

Crimean peninsula, a favourite tourist area for Russians as well as Ukrainians.

Woodland with such trees as ash, oak and pine grows in the north, while pine forests swathe the slopes of the Carpathians and Crimean mountains. Grassy steppe once covered central Ukraine, but much of it has now been ploughed up for farmland.

ECONOMY AND RESOURCES

The main industrial cities are in the east, clustered round the coalfields and iron-ore mines of the vital Donets Basin. Ukraine's main industries are coal mining, iron and steel, agricultural machinery, petrochemicals and plastics, but there are also numerous food-processing plants based on agricultural output that includes wheat, rye, oats, maize, barley, flax, sugar beet, hops, soya, sunflower seeds, potatoes and other vegetables, meat, dairy produce and cotton. In 1993 Ukraine was the world's leading producer of sugar beet (12% of the world total) and second largest producer of barley (8%), behind Russia. Though traditionally 'the granary of the Soviet Union', Ukraine is neither the largest nor the most efficient overall producer of grain; Russia producers twice as much, and the agricultural output per capita of Belarus is some 65% higher than that of its southern neighbour.

Minerals are important to the economy; Ukraine dominated world manganese production in 1993 (with 32% of the total) and was in the top ten for iron, iron-ore and steel. In 1991 it produced nearly a quarter of the total USSR coal output. Not blessed with huge reserves of oil, the Kiev government signed an agreement in February 1992 to secure future supplies from Iran.

HISTORY AND POLITICS

In the 9th century AD, the East Slavs founded a civilization called Kievan Rus, with its capital at Kiev. Russians took over the area in 980 and the region became prosperous, but in the 13th century, Mongol armies ravaged the area. Later, the region was split into small kingdoms and large areas fell under foreign rule. In the 17th and 18th centuries, parts of Ukraine came under Polish and Russian rule, but Russia gained most of Ukraine in the late 18th century. In 1918, Ukraine gained its independence, but in 1922 it was incorporated into the Soviet Union.

Millions of people died in the 1930s as the result of Soviet policies. Millions more died during the Nazi occupation between 1941 and 1944. In 1945, the Soviet Union took control of parts of Ukraine that had been in Czechoslovakia, Poland and Romania. In the 1980s, however, Ukrainian people demanded more say over their affairs.

Following the break-up of the Soviet Union in 1991, Ukraine's declaration of independence from Moscow was ratified by referendum on 1 December 1991, when Leonid Kravchuk, the former Communist Party ideological secretary, was voted president by direct poll over five rivals. A week later, in Minsk, Kravchuk helped Boris Yeltsin create the basis for the Commonwealth of Independent States, and in the early months of 1992 Ukraine and Russia reached agreement on a number of potentially explosive issues, not least in the military field, with resolutions on nuclear weapons, the Red Army and the distribution of the Black Sea fleet.

The country, however, will not be seen as Russia's sidekick. While it suffered many of the economic agonies endured by its massive neighbour – notably chronic food shortages and the hyperinflation that followed the abolition of price controls – Ukraine set out from the beginning to be a fully-fledged and large independent nation. While Russia assumed the diplomatic powers of the Soviet Union, Ukraine already had a seat at the UN – a reward granted in 1945 for the appalling devastation caused by the German invasion in 1941 and its aftermath – and would seek separate representation on bodies such as the CSCE and OECD. [*Map page 5*] ■

AREA 603,700 sq km [233,100 sq mls]
POPULATION 51,465,000
CAPITAL (POPULATION) Kiev (2,643,000)
GOVERNMENT Multiparty republic
ETHNIC GROUPS Ukrainian 73%, Russian 22%, Jewish 1%, Belarussian 1%, Moldovan
LANGUAGES Ukrainian 73% (official), Russian
RELIGIONS Christianity (mostly Ukrainian Orthodox)
CURRENCY Karbovanet

UNITED ARAB EMIRATES

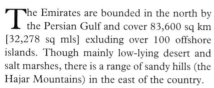

UNITED KINGDOM

The Emirates are bounded in the north by the Persian Gulf and cover 83,600 sq km [32,278 sq mls] exluding over 100 offshore islands. Though mainly low-lying desert and salt marshes, there is a range of sandy hills (the Hajar Mountains) in the east of the country.

When British forces withdrew from the Persian Gulf in 1971, six of the seven British-run Trucial States – Abu Dhabi, Ajman, Dubai, Fujairah, Sharjah and Umm al-Qaiwain – opted to form the United Arab Emirates (UAE), with Ras al-Khaimah joining in 1972. It could have been a federation of nine, but Bahrain and Qatar chose independence. Traditional values, sustained by the control of the emirs, remain strong in the UAE, inspite of a large expatriate workforce.

The UAE is the Gulf's third largest oil producer after Saudi Arabia and Iran, producing an average of 3 million barrels per day in 1993. The revenue from its oil and gas (50% of GDP) has enabled the government to invest in health, education and social services: the UAE has the highest GNP per capita figure in Asia, after Japan. Abu Dhabi has by far the largest population of the Emirates and is easily the biggest oil producer.

As well as oil and gas, manufacturing and finance play an important part in the economy. In addition, the UAE is becoming a more attractive place for tourists – in 1991 there were 189 hotels and 348,000 visitors. [*Map page 22*] ■

AREA 83,600 sq km [32,278 sq mls]
POPULATION 1,861,000
CAPITAL (POPULATION) Abu Dhabi (or Abu Zaby, 243,000)
GOVERNMENT Federation
ETHNIC GROUPS Arab 87%, Indo-Pakistani 9%, Iranian 2%
LANGUAGES Arabic, English
RELIGIONS Islam
CURRENCY UAE dirham = 100 fils

The British Isles stand on the westernmo edge of the continental shelf – two larg and several hundred small islands for the mo part cool, rainy and windswept. Despit physical closeness to the rest of Europe (32 kr [20 mls] at the nearest point – little more tha the distance across London), Britain is cur ously isolated, with a long history of politic independence and social separation from it neighbours. In the past the narrow seas serve the islanders well, protecting them agains casual invasion, while Britons in turn sailed t explore and exploit the rest of the world. Nov with increasing co-operation within the EU this insularity is rapidly breaking down.

The islands are confusingly named. 'Grea Britain', the largest in Europe and eighth largest in the world – so named to distinguish it from 'Little Britain' (Brittany, in France) – includes the kingdoms of England and Scotland and the principality of Wales; Ireland was once a kingdom, but is currently divided into the Province of Northern Ireland, under the British Crown, and the politically separate Republic of Ireland. Great Britain, Northern Ireland, and many off-lying island groups from the Scillies to the Shetlands, together make up the United Kingdom of Great Britain and Northern Ireland, commonly known as the UK. Even isolated Rockall, far out in the Atlantic Ocean, is part of the UK, but the Isle of Man and the Channel Islands are separate but direct dependencies of the Crown, with a degree of political autonomy and their own taxation systems.

Climate
Despite a subarctic position Britain is favoured climatically. Most other maritime lands between 50°N and 60°N – eastern Siberia, Kamchatka, the Aleutian Islands, southern Alaska, Hudson Bay and Labrador – are cold throughout the year, with long winters, ice-bound coasts and a short growing season. Britain's salvation is the North Atlantic Drift

Gulf Stream, a current of surface water that ~~b~~ings subtropical warmth from the southern ~~A~~tlantic Ocean, spreading it across the conti~~ne~~ntal shelf of Western Europe and warming ~~th~~e prevailing westerly winds.

The growing season, indicated roughly by ~~th~~e number of months in which mean air tem~~pe~~rature exceeds 6°C [42°F], ranges from less ~~th~~an four months in the Scottish Highlands to ~~ni~~ne months or more on the south-west coast. ~~M~~ost of lowland Britain has a growing season ~~of~~ seven to eight months, enough to ensure the ~~p~~rosperity of arable farmers in most years.

Britain's reputation for cloudiness is well ~~m~~erited. Mean duration of sunshine through~~o~~ut the year is about 5 hours daily in the south, ~~a~~nd only 3.5 hours daily in Scotland. At the ~~h~~eight of summer only the south-west receives ~~m~~ore than 7.5 hours of sunshine per day. In ~~w~~inter only the south coast, the Severn ~~e~~stuary, Oxfordshire and a sliver of south~~e~~astern Essex receive more than 1.5 hours per ~~d~~ay, while many northern areas receive less ~~th~~an half an hour daily.

Despite a reputation for rain Britain is fairly ~~d~~ry. More than half of the country receives less ~~th~~an 750 mm [30 in] annually, and parts of ~~E~~ssex have less than 500 mm [20 in] per year. ~~T~~he wettest areas are Snowdonia with about ~~5~~,000 mm [200 in], Ben Nevis and the north~~w~~estern highlands with 4,300 mm [172 in], ~~a~~nd the Lake District with 3,300 mm [132 in].

The British climate is far from static. It was ~~w~~armer at the time of the Domesday Survey ~~(~~1086) when vineyards flourished as far north ~~a~~s York, and it cooled throughout the Middle Ages, when Arctic pack-ice was reported off Shetland and Eskimos are said to have visited northern Scotland in their kayaks. Cooling continued into the mid-19th century, followed by a long period of warming up to World War II and a succession of warm summers in the 1980s and 1990s.

Population and immigration

Despite insularity the British people are of mixed stock. The earliest immigrants – land-hungry farmers from the Continent – were often refugees from tribal warfare and unrest. The Belgic tribesmen escaping from Imperial Rome, the Romans themselves (whose troops included Spanish, Macedonian and probably

Lying 16 km to 48 km [10 mls to 30 mls] from the French coast, the Channel Islands are a British dependency covering an area of only 200 sq km [78 sq mls]. The largest are Jersey with 115 sq km [45 sq mls] and 84,000 inhabitants, and Guernsey, with 78 sq km [30 sq mls] and 59,000 people. The other islands – Alderney, Sark and others – are small, with fewer than 3,000 residents.

The only part of the Duchy of Normandy retained by the English Crown after 1204, and the only part of Britain occupied by the Germans in World War II, the islands have their own legal system and government, with lower taxation than that of Britain. This, combined with a favourable climate and fine coastal scenery, has attracted a considerable number of wealthy residents, notably retired people, and established Jersey and Guernsey as offshore financial centres.

The main produce is agricultural, especially early potatoes, tomatoes and flowers for Britain, and the countryside has a vast number of glasshouses. The soil is now fertile, having been made so by the farmers' skilful use of seaweed and other fertilizers. Jersey and Guernsey cattle are famous breeds, introduced to many countries. Holiday-makers visit the islands in large numbers during the summer months, travelling by air or by the various passenger boats, especially from Weymouth. English is the official language but French is widely spoken.

North African mercenaries), the Angles, Saxons, Jutes, Danes and Normans, all in turn brought genetic variety; so too did the Huguenots, Sephardic and Ashkenazim Jews, and Dutch, French and German businessmen who followed them. Latterly the waves of immigrants have included Belarussians, Poles, Italians, Ukrainians and Czechs – most, like their predecessors, fugitives from European wars, overcrowding, intolerance and unrest.

During the 19th century Britain often took in skilled European immigrants through the front door while steadily losing her own sons and daughters – Scots and Irish peasants in

THE ISLE OF MAN

Covering 590 sq km [227 sq mls], the Isle of Man sits in the Irish Sea almost equidistant from County Down and Cumbria, but actually nearer Galloway in Scotland. The uplands, pierced by the corridor valley from Douglas to Peel, extend from Ramsey to Port Erin. Mainly agricultural, with some fishing and a few light industries, the island is now largely dependent on tourism, with the annual Tourist Trophy (motorcycle) races attracting many visitors. Douglas, the capital, has over a third of the island's total population of 70,000. Like the Channel Islands, the Isle of Man is a dependency of the British Crown with its own legislative assembly, legal system and tax controls – leading to a position as a financial centre and tax shelter.

particular – through the back. Most recent arrivals in Britain are immigrants from crowded and impoverished lands once part of the British Empire, notably the West Indies, West Africa, India and Pakistan. These and their descendants now make up about 4% of the population of Britain.

Under Roman rule the population of the British island numbered half to three-quarters of a million. By the time of the Domesday Survey it had doubled, and it doubled again by the end of the 14th century. The Black Death of the late 15th century killed one in every three or four, but numbers climbed slowly; at the Union of 1707 some 6 million English and Welsh joined about 1 million Scots under a single parliament. By 1801 the first national census revealed 8.9 million in England and Wales, 1.6 million in Scotland; Ireland missed the first two ten-year counts, but probably numbered about 5 million. In 1821 the total British population was 21 million, in 1851 31 million, and in 1921 47 million. Fortunately the rate of increase has now declined, but some parts of Britain, notably the south-east and the conurbations, are among the most heavily populated areas of the world.

ENGLAND

Visitors to England are often amazed at the variety of the landscape. Complex folding volcanic activity, glaciation and changes in sea level have all left their mark. From Northumberland to the Trent, the Pennines extend southwards as an upland with rolling hill plateaux and fine valleys, many known as 'dales'. The range includes two western outliers – the Forest of Rossendale north of Manchester, and the Forest of Bowland in north Lancashire. To either side lie the lowlands of Lancashire and Yorkshire.

The Eden Valley separates the northern Pennines from Cumbria, which includes the Lake District. This is England's most striking mountain mass, a circular area of peaks, deep valleys, splendid lakes and crags. The loftiest peak is Scafell, 978 m [3,210 ft]. In the south-west Exmoor is a fine sandstone upland, and Dartmoor a predominantly granite area with many prominent tors. Elsewhere are isolated hills, small by world standards but dramatic against the small-scale background of Britain.

Much of the English lowland consists of chalk downlands, familiar to continental visitors who enter England through Folkestone or Dover as the famous chalk cliffs. These are the exposed coastal edge of the North Downs, whose scarped northern slope forms a striking feature in the Croydon area of Greater London. The North Downs continue westwards through Surrey to the Hampshire Downs, then south and east as the South Downs, emerging at another coastal landmark – Beachy Head.

There is a northwards extension of downland through the Berkshire and Marlborough Downs to the Chilterns then north again into East Anglia to disappear under the edge of the fens near Cambridge. Formerly forested, the downlands were cleared early for pasture and agriculture, and now provide a rich and varied mixture of woodlands, parklands, fields and mostly small settlements.

Older rocks, predominantly limestones, form the ridge of the Cotswold Hills, and the rolling, hilly farmlands of Leicestershire, the Lincoln Edge (cut by the River Witham at Lincoln), and finally the North York Moors. In these older rocks are rich iron deposits, mined in Cleveland to supply ores for the steel towns of the Tees Estuary until 1964, and still mined in the Midlands.

England is drained by many fine rivers, of which the greatest are the Thames, the Severn, the fenland Ouse, the Trent, and the great Yorkshire Ouse that receives its tributaries from the many picturesque valleys – the Dales of the Pennine flank. There are many small-rivers, and a large number of the old towns that dot England were built at their crossing points – generally where dry ground existed above marshes and gave firm sites for building. Chester, for example, was founded on a patch of sandstone beside the Dee; one of the four gates of the Roman town is still called the Watergate. York, too, was built on firm ground by a river crossing, as was Manchester. London arose on the site chosen by the Romans for the first convenient crossing place of the Thames, formerly a much broader and shallower river.

WALES

United with England in 1535, Wales still preserves a sense of individuality – a separateness resting on history and sentiment rather than any clear boundary in the countryside. Although only 20% of the population speak Welsh, 75% of the inhabitants do so in the western counties of Gwynedd and Dyfed. The national sentiment is not only expressed through language, but also through literature, the arts (especially music), sport and political life. Cardiff, the capital, grew rapidly during the 19th century with the iron and steel industry and coal mining, but no Welsh town is centrally placed for the whole country; meetings of the boards representing the colleges of the University of Wales – Cardiff, Swansea, Lampeter, Aberystwyth and Bangor – take place at Shrewsbury, an English border town.

Wales is predominantly hilly and mountainous, although two-thirds of the rural area is farmland and one-third moorland. The most famous of the highland areas is Snowdonia, now a National Park covering 2,138 sq km [825 sq mls] from Snowdon to Cader Idris. But there are fine upland areas in central Wales, on both sides of the upper Severn Valley which cuts through them to the Dovey Valley and the coastal lowlands facing Cardigan Bay. South of the Severn, in the counties of Powys and Dyfed, the uplands dominate the landscape, and in the Brecon Beacons, south of the Usk Valley on which the old town of Brecon is situated, they provide another National Park, of 1,303 sq km [500 sq mls]. Many of the uplands and high lakes are sources of water for English towns, including Liverpool and Birmingham.

SCOTLAND

Scotland is a generally cool, hilly and, in the west, wet country occupying about a third of Great Britain. Physically, it can be divided into three parts: the Highlands and Islands, bounded by the edge of the mountains from Stonehaven to the mouth of the Clyde; Central Scotland – sometimes called the Central Lowlands, though it is interspersed by a number of hill ranges; and the Southern Uplands, defined in the north by a geological fault extending from Dunbar to Girvan, and in the south by the border with England.

The Highlands and Islands: More than half of Scotland's area is in the Highlands and Islands. These are divided by the Great Glen, from Fort William to Inverness, with its three lochs – Lochy, Oich and Ness (where the monster is prone to appear in the tourist season) – linked by the Caledonian Canal. Much of the whisky for which Scotland is famous is produced in the Highlands, notably near the River Spey. The north-western part of the Highlands has splendid scenery – deep, glaciated valleys dominated by mountains, and only limited areas of farmland, much of it now abandoned.

Ben Nevis, at 1,343 m [4,406 ft] dominating the town of Fort William, is the highest summit in the British Isles, and a number of peaks in the Cairngorms, including Ben Macdhui (1,311 m [4,300 ft]), are of almost equal height.

The Central Lowlands: This area includes several ranges of rolling uplands – the Sidlaw Hills north of Dundee, the Ochils south of Perth, and the Pentlands extending in a south-westerly direction from the suburbs of Edinburgh.

The Southern Uplands: Though less spectacular than the Highlands, these include many fine hills, rolling moorlands and rich valleys. From the summit of Merrick (843 m [2,764 ft]) in Galloway the Highlands can be seen to the north, the plateau of Northern

Ireland to the west, and the Lake District, the Pennines and the Isle of Man to the south.

ECONOMY AND RESOURCES

ENGLAND

Agriculture: England has a rich variety of soils, derived both locally from parent rocks and also from glacial debris or 'drift'. During the 12,000 and more years since the ice retreated, soils have been enriched, firstly by such natural processes such as flooding and the growth of forests, latterly by the good husbandry of many generations of farmers. Husbandry improved particularly from the 18th century onwards; the Industrial Revolution was accompanied by an agricultural revolution that resulted in massive increases in crop yields and in the quality of livestock.

Through the 18th and 19th centuries farming became more scientific and more specialized; as the demands from the towns grew, so did the ability of English farmers to meet increasing markets for food. The eastern counties, particularly East Anglia and Holderness (now part of Humberside), became the granaries of England, while the rich, wet grasslands of the west and the Midlands turned pastoral – Cheshire cheese is a famous product of this specialization. There were other local products – the hops of Kent and Hereford, the apples of Worcester, and the fine wools that continued to be the main product of the chalk downlands. In south Lancashire potatoes and vegetables became major crops for sale in the markets of the growing northern industrial towns; market gardening and dairying on a small scale developed near every major settlement, taking advantage of the ready market close at hand.

Scenically, England still gives the impression of being an agricultural country. Less than 10% of the area is rough moorland, about 5% is forest, and about another 10% is urban or suburban, leaving roughly three-quarters under cultivation of one kind or another. Yet only 3% of the working population is currently employed in agriculture, a figure that has declined drastically in recent years. Loss of rural populations has been an inevitable result of agricultural rationalization and improvements in farming methods, although many of

NORTH SEA OIL

The discovery of gas and oil in the North Sea in the 1960s – exploitation began a few years later – transformed Britain from an oil importer into the world's fifth largest exporter within a decade. Natural gas from the new fields rapidly replaced coal gas in the British energy system, and by 1981 the country was self-sufficient in oil. In the peak production year of 1986, the British sector of the North Sea produced 128.6 million tonnes of crude oil, accounting for over 20% of UK export earnings; in 1989, North Sea output amounted to 3% of total world production. In 1991, remaining reserves were estimated at 4 billion barrels – little more than four years' production at 1986 levels.

In taxes and royalties, North Sea oil gave an immense fillip to British government revenue, contributing more than £76 billion since 1979, and protecting the balance of payments despite severe industrial decline. There was much discussion as to the best use for this windfall money, which would taper away during the 1990s and vanish altogether in the next century; but it certainly helped finance substantial tax cuts during the controversial years of Mrs Thatcher's government. The sight of North Sea oil wealth flowing south to the Westminster treasury also provoked nationalist resentment in Scotland, off whose coast most of the oil rigs (and much of the gas) are located.

those who lost their jobs were being supported at little more than subsistence level.

Industry and urbanization: England had important reserves of coal, the major fields being on either side of the Pennines (Yorkshire, Lancashire, Northumberland and Durham), and in the Midlands (Derbyshire and Nottinghamshire). These coalfields and extensive reserves of iron ore – now largely defunct – were the basis of the Industrial Revolution of the 18th century, and the associated industrial growth of the 19th century, which together resulted in major changes in the English landscape.

Areas which previously had only small popations rose to industrial greatness. Perhaps the most striking example was Teesside where, following the exploitation of the Cleveland iron ores, the town of Middlesbrough grew from a small port (7,000 population in 1851) to a large manufacturing centre. Today Middlesbrough and its neighbouring settlements have almost 400,000 inhabitants. Similarly, small mill villages in Lancashire and Yorkshire grew into large towns while the West Midlands pottery towns and villages coalesced into the urban areas of Stoke-on-Trent.

Although the coalfields of the north saw the greatest local expansion of population, London and England's other major ports, such as Liverpool and Bristol, also developed as export markets flourished. These developments were accompanied by significant improvements in communications. From the 1840s town growth was rapid, and by the end of the 19th century 80% of the population was urban. While the working-class population was mainly housed in slums, the prosperity of the commercial and professional classes was reflected in the Victorian 'villas' that, in varying degrees of splendour, appeared in select areas of the towns.

This phase of expansion continued until World War I. By the 1930s, however, there were signs that the prosperity of many older and industrial mining areas was threatened and efforts were made to bring new industries to areas of particularly high unemployment, such as the Northumberland and Durham coalfield, West Cumberland, and the South Wales coalfield. In all of these, whole areas had become virtually derelict because their coal was exhausted, or no longer in demand.

The main areas of industrial growth since World War I have been around London and also in the West Midlands. A number of towns, for example Coventry, experienced extremely rapid growth. The introduction of conscious planning had the aim of controlling industrial expansion and preventing the indiscriminate growth of some towns, for example Oxford and Cambridge.

Today, England is a significant steel producer and most of the steel produced is used in other British industries such as shipbuilding and vehicle manufacture – although, as elsewhere in Western Europe, all three industries are currently facing considerable difficulties. Highly-skilled engineering industries are also important and centres include Birmingham, Wolverhampton and Manchester. Textiles are still a major industry, with cotton goods being produced mainly in Lancashire and woollens and worsteds in Yorkshire. Similarly, pottery is still important in the Midlands – though, like most manufacturing in Britain, it is losing out to service industries.

Planning: After World War II the need for replanning England to take account of the industrial areas was generally accepted. The existence of conurbations where towns had grown into one another was recognized by their listing in the 1951 census, which included Greater London, the West Midlands (Birmingham and the Black Country), Southeast Lancashire with North-east Cheshire (Greater Manchester), Merseyside and Tyneside. Prolonged discussion followed on the best form of new administrative structure needed in England, and ultimately, in 1974, the new scheme of local government emerged. Many county boundaries were changed but one alteration of particular significance was the definition of some new counties based on the major industrial areas.

In creating the new administrative units of Tyne and Wear, Cleveland, West Yorkshire, South Yorkshire, Greater Manchester and West Midlands, and in redefining Greater London on more generous lines, the planners at last recognized the realities of population distribution in England. Many towns are developing new industrial areas – the 'industrial estates', housing light industries on their outskirts – and since 1945 government-sponsored 'new towns' have arisen in many parts of the country, in an attempt to stem the further growth of London and existing conurbations.

London has several satellite new towns – Basildon, Harlow, Stevenage and Milton Keynes, for example, most of them founded on small existing settlements. In the north are Washington, Peterlee and Aycliffe, built around old mining villages, with new industries invited in on favourable terms. Powers to develop new towns fortunately go hand-in-hand with powers to protect the remaining countryside against casual despoilment. Agricultural land, particularly at hazard, may be protected by local planning authorities, and new building kept within bounds.

Conservation: In an age when increased prosperity has spread leisure and the means of travel to millions of people, new emphasis has been placed on recreation. One result is the National Parks, another the many scenic areas under the control of the Countryside Commission and other national bodies. In these areas there are special provisions for conserving the beauty of the English countryside, and creating amenities that help people enjoy them. Though it is never the intention that National Parks be kept as rural museums, with all development stifled, the siting of new buildings, roads and electricity cables is carefully controlled, and national need must be shown before mining and other disruptive activities can be justified.

The Forestry Commission, too, has a mandate to provide amenity sites in its forests, and to landscape new plantings in ways that provide timber, but also maintain the natural beauty of the area concerned.

WALES

Mining and industry: Some writers on Wales regard the uplands as the country's real heartland, with their sheep pastures and forested valleys, interspersed by farming villages and small towns. But over half the population live in the industrialized area of South Wales, which includes the mining valleys of Gwent, Mid Glamorgan and West Glamorgan – all of which ceased to extract coal by the 1990s – and the towns of Newport, Cardiff and Swansea with their traditional heavy-metal industries and newer factories for light industry. All are ports, and Cardiff now has many central buildings for the whole of Wales, including the National Museum and the Welsh Office.

No other area of Wales is so heavily dominated by mining and industry as Deeside. Flint and the Wrexham areas are also industrialized, with coalfields now in decline and modern light industries taking their place.

Tourism: Just as the railways stimulated economic growth in South Wales from the 1840s, so on the North Wales coast they stimulated the growth of holiday and residential towns, notably Rhyl, Colwyn Bay and Llandudno.

These attracted English residents, many them retired people from Lancashire, and t holiday industry boomed. In the motoring a it developed further, so that almost eve beach and coastal village had its guest house holiday cottages, caravan parks and campi sites. Now tourism has spread to virtually t whole of Wales. In Anglesey, many sm places have devoted visitors who favour saili as well as walking and sea bathing, while this true also of many ports of the Welsh mainlar coast. The south-west, formerly Pembrok shire but now part of Dyfed, has fine scener forming the Pembrokeshire National Pa with a coast path 268 km [167 mls] long.

Wales is rich in scenic attractions. The lanc scape is dominantly agricultural, with mixe farming, notably for dairying, cattle and shee Many upland farmers combine agricultur with the tourist trade, providing guest house or camping centres. Forestry plantations exi in many upland valleys but the main charac teristic of the countryside is farmland.

SCOTLAND

The Highlands and Islands: The financia returns from crofting (small-scale tenant farm ing) were meagre, and many old croft cottage have become holiday homes. Forests no cover many of the valleys; some of the moun tains are deer parks, owned by landlords an let to visitors for seasonal shooting. Railway reach the western coast at Mallaig and Kyle o Lochalsh, from which there are boat service to Skye – to be augmented by a controversia bridge – and the Outer Hebrides. Roads are i part single track with passing places, althougl they are gradually being improved. At the various villages there are hotels, guest house and other accommodation for visitors, and the main commercial occupations are fishing anc home weaving. The traditional weaving o Harris tweeds in the Hebrides is now industri ally organized, with much of the work done ir workshops. Skye has splendid climbing in the Cuillin Hills, and the numerous rivers and lakes are favoured by fishermen. Here, as in the rest of the Highlands, efforts to improve local industries have had some success.

The highland area east of the Great Glen is a richer country, flanked on the east by the lowlands around Aberdeen, which extend into

uchan and then westwards to Moray Firth
ound Inverness. This is sound farming
untry, famous for pedigree cattle, and from
aese lowlands tongues of farmland extend
to the valleys of the Dee, Don, Spey and
thers. Aberdeen and Fraserburgh are major
shing centres. Aberdeen has become increas-
ugly prosperous with the oil extraction from
ae North Sea.

Little known in the past, the Cairngorms
ave now been developed for winter skiing and
ammer climbing and fishing. There are still
eer forests in the uplands but much of the
ountry is used for sheep farming and tourism.
'ort William and a few other centres have
adustry based on local hydroelectricity –
luminium smelting, for example – but Oban
s the main holiday centre on the west coast.

In the north, the Orkney Islands are
onnected to Thurso (Scrabster) by boat and
lso to Aberdeen. Fishing and farming are the
mainstays of the economy, with a successful
specialization in egg production. The Shet-
ands have a far harsher environment, with
craggy hills and limited areas suited to
arming, though fishing is prominent, notably
at Lerwick. The oil industry has brought great,
f temporary, prosperity to some places in
these islands.

The Central Lowlands: Most of Scotland's
population and industrial activity occurs in
this central area, and here too are its two
largest cities – Glasgow on innumerable small
glacial hills (drumlins) in the Clyde Valley,
and the capital Edinburgh on splendid volcanic ridges, dominated by Arthur's Seat.

Clydeside is still the greatest industrial area
of Scotland. Textile industries, engineering
and shipbuilding were the basis of the prosperity of Glasgow and its neighbouring towns,
which in time grew into one another and held
more than a third of Scotland's total population. There is now a wide range of industries
in Central Scotland including electronics,
printing, brewing and carpet-making.

Edinburgh, with its port of Leith, remained
much smaller than Glasgow, with only half its
population, but is still the administrative
centre, and the seat of the main law courts and
the National Museum and Library, as well as
of many cultural organizations. A favoured
centre for retirement in Scotland, it has an

increasing tourist trade, particularly during the
Edinburgh Festival in the summer. Much of
the central area is rich farmland, especially to
the east of Edinburgh.

The Southern Uplands: The Tweed with its
numerous tributaries and – further west – the
Esk, Annan, Nith, Ken and Cree provide sheltered valleys for farming, and there is splendid
agricultural country in Galloway, where dairying has been particularly successful. Cattle
rearing with crop production is more general
in the drier east, where many farms specialize
in meat production. The hills are used for
sheep rearing. Some of the towns, notably
Hawick and Galashiels, are prominent in the
textile industry and have a large export trade.

Although tourism is relatively less important
than in the Highlands, many people come to
see the historic centres, such as Melrose and
Dryburgh Abbey. To the west, in Galloway,
there has been a policy of afforestation on the
poorer soils, and several centres have been
opened as small museums and educational
sites. The coast attracts tourists and Forest
Parks, such as that at Glen Trool close to
Merrick, have been well laid out for visitors. In
the west the towns are small, but there is heavy
traffic to Stranraer, the port for the shortest
sea crossing to Larne in Northern Ireland.

[*For the geography of Northern Ireland, see pages 173–4.*]

HISTORY AND POLITICS

Whilst Caesar made brief forays into England
in 55 and 54 BC, the country was only made
part of the Roman Empire in AD 43. Roman
rule lasted until the beginning of the 5th
century, after which the country experienced
invasions by various Germanic tribes, in
particular the Angles and Saxons. The
subsequent history of Anglo-Saxon England
from the 8th to the 11th centuries was marked
by resistance to Vikings from Scandinavia.
The last successful invasion was that of the
Normans, culminating in their victory at the
Battle of Hastings (1066) and the crowning of
William the Conqueror as king of England. In
1215, King John was forced by his barons to
accept limits on his authority when he signed
the Magna Carta, a declaration which included a guarantee to a fair trial. The following

period saw the emergence of something approaching a parliamentary system. The Hundred Years War with France ended in 1453 with England's defeat and was followed by a long civil war (War of the Roses, 1455–85).

The coming to power of the Tudors ushered in an age of prosperity and modernization. Under Elizabeth I, England became a major naval power and established colonies in America. Literature and the arts flourished. The 'Glorious Revolution' of 1688 established the sovereignty of parliament, which continued to be strengthened during the 18th century. The Industrial Revolution made Britain one of the wealthiest nations in the world and was followed by a great expansion of the Empire under the reign of Queen Victoria (1837–1901).

Britain suffered huge losses, both human and economic, during World War I. The Irish Easter Rising of 1916 led to the partition of Ireland in 1921. In World War II, Britain played a major part in the defeat of Germany. The post-war Labour government of Clement Attlee brought in measures which laid the foundation for the 'welfare state'. During the 1950s and 1960s, most remaining British colonies became independent and joined the Commonwealth. After much internal debate, Britain joined the EEC in 1973. From 1979 onwards, Conservative governments, first led by Margaret Thatcher and from 1990 by John Major, broke from the 'consensus politics' that had dominated post-war Britain and set about privatizing most public sector industries and drastically reducing the scope of the 'welfare state'. [*Map pages 6–9*] ■

AREA 243,368 sq km [94,202 sq mls]
POPULATION 58,091,000
CAPITAL (POPULATION) London (6,933,000)
GOVERNMENT Constitutional monarchy
ETHNIC GROUPS White 94%, Asian Indian 1%, Pakistani 1%, West Indian 1%
LANGUAGES English (official)
RELIGIONS Christianity (Anglican 57%, Roman Catholic 13%, Presbyterian 7%, Methodist 4%, Baptist 1%), Islam 1%, Judaism, Hinduism, Sikhism
CURRENCY Pound sterling = 100 pence

UNITED STATE OF AMERICA

The world's fourth largest country – an third most populous – the United State of America fills the North American continen between Canada and Mexico and als includes Alaska and the archipelago of Hawai. Geographically, the main part (of 48 states falls readily into an eastern section, includin the Appalachian Mountains and easter coastal plain; a central section, including th Mississippi basin and the broad prairie plain from the Dakotas to Texas; and a wester section, including the Rocky Mountains an Pacific coastlands.

The East

Eastern North America is crossed by a band o low, folded mountains: though nowhere much above 2,000 m [6,500 ft], they long formed a barrier to settlers. In the north are the Adirondacks, a southern extension of the ancient granite shield of Canada, rising to 1,629 m [5,344 ft]. From Maine to Alabama runs a broad range of sedimentary mountains, the Appalachians. Younger than the Adirondacks (though much older than the Rockies), the Appalachians separate the Atlantic coastlands of the east from the Great Lakes and low plateaux of Ohio, Kentucky and Tennessee.

North-east of New York City lie the six New England states – the fertile wooded country that, at least in summer, made the early settlers feel at home. To the south the coastal plain widens, to be split by the drowned estuaries of the Susquehanna and Potomac rivers, draining into Chesapeake Bay. From Virginia south to Florida smaller rivers drain eastwards, across a much broader plain, many of them entering coastal sounds with offshore sand bars and islands.

In New York State a major spillway cuts through the mountains between the Adirondacks and Appalachians, linking the Great Lakes with the Hudson Valley and the Atlantic Ocean. This is the line of the famous Erie Canal route, the most used of several that gave

.e early settlers access to the Ohio country ▸yond the mountains. Other routes led to ▸ttsburgh and, through the southern part of ▸e Appalachians, into Tennessee. Central ▸hio, Indiana and Illinois, which once formed ▸merica's Northwest Territory, are rolling ▸lands and plains, smoothed by glaciation in ▸e north but more rugged in the south, and ▸rained by the rambling Ohio River.

egetation: The original vegetation of east-▸rn America, on either flank of the mountains, ▸as broadleaf deciduous forest of oak, ash, ▸eech and maple, merging northwards into ▸ellow birch, hemlock and pine. In the drier ▸Aid-west these immense woodlands turned to ▸pen country. Patchy grasslands covered ▸orthern Indiana and southern Illinois; central ▸llinois was forested along most watercourses, ▸ith prairie blue-stem grasses on the drier ▸aterfluves. Around the southern Appalachians ▸aixed oak, pine and tulip-tree dominated; ▸ines covered the coastal plains to the south ▸nd east with bald cypress in northern Florida. ▸pruce blanketed the highlands from northern ▸Maine to the Adirondacks; spruce, tamarack ▸nd balsam fir covered the high Appalachians.

Most of this original forest is now gone, but ▸here is still enough left – and some regen-▸rating on abandoned farmland – to leave the ▸nountains a blaze of colour each autumn. ▸Despite more than 300 years of European ▸settlement, the overall impression of eastern ▸America, seen from the air, is still one of dense ▸semi-continuous forests, except in the exten-▸sive farmlands north of the Ohio.

The Central States

▸Within the 1,400 km [875 mls] from the Mississippi to the foothills of the Rockies, the land rises almost 3,000 m [9,850 ft], though the slope is often imperceptible to the trav-eller. From the Gulf of Mexico northwards to Minnesota and the Dakotas the rise is even less noticeable, though the flatness is occa-sionally relieved by the outcrops of uplands – the Ozarks of northern Arkansas, for example. In summer nothing bars the northwards move-ment of hot moist air from the Gulf of Mexico, nor in winter the southwards movement of dry, cold air from the Arctic. These air masses produce great seasonal contrasts of climate, exacerbated by storms, blizzards and torna-

does. Westwards from the Mississippi the climate grows progressively drier.

The plains are crossed by a series of long, wide rivers, often of irregular flow, that drain off the Rockies: the Missouri, the Platte, the Arkansas, the Canadian and the Red. In con-trast to the Ohio, which enabled travellers to pass downstream and so westwards to the Mississippi, these rivers of the plains provided little help to settlers moving westwards, due to their seasonal variations in flow and the effort which was needed to move upstream when floods gave them depth.

Vegetation: West of the margins of the Mississippi tall blue-stem prairie grasses once extended from the Canadian border to southern Texas. Only along the watercourses were there trees – cottonwood and willow in the north, merging into oak and hickory further south. Westwards the prairie grass-lands thinned to the bunch grass and needle grass of the Great Plains in a belt from central North Dakota to western Oklahoma; locally favoured areas such as western Nebraska had patches of broadleaf evergreens amidst shrubs and a variety of grasses.

West of about meridian 100°W a variety of short grasses stretched from Montana and the Dakotas southwards to north-west Texas: in the far south, on the Mexican border, low xerophytic shrubs were an indicatation of increasing aridity. Higher ground, for example the Black Hills of south-western South Dakota, supported stands of pine.

The West

The western USA is a complex mountain and plateau system, rich in scenic beauty and nat-ural history, bordered by a rugged coast that starts in the semi-deserts of the south and ends in the rain-soaked forests of the north. Americans appreciate their far west; for long the final frontier of a youthful, expanding nation, it is still the goal of tens of thousands of immigrants each year and the vacation dream of many more: tourism is the most widespread industry.

Landscape and vegetation: Topographically the west is a land of high mountain ranges divided by high plateaux and deep valleys. The grain of the country runs north-west to south-east, at a right-angle to the crustal pressures that produced it, and the highest mountains – the Rocky Mountains of a thousand legends – form a spectacular eastern flank. The southern Rockies of Colorado and New Mexico, remnants of an ancient granite plateau, are carved by weathering into ranges of spectacular peaks; Colorado alone has over 1,000 mountains of 3,000 m [10,000 ft] or more. Rising from dry, sandy, cactus-and-sagebrush desert, their lower slopes carry grey piñon pines and juniper scrub, with darker spruce, firs and pines above. At the timber line grow gnarled bristlecone pines, some 3,000 and more years old. Between the ranges, 'parks' of mixed forest and grassland support deer and other game in summer grazing. To the southwest are the dry, colourful sandstones of the Colorado Plateau, dotted with cactus and deeply gouged by the Colorado River; to the north lies the Wyoming Basin, a rangeland of rich volcanic soil that once grazed herds of bison, and now supports sheep and cattle.

The central Rocky Mountains, towering over western Wyoming, Idaho and Montana, include a number of snow-capped peaks of more than 4,000 m [13,000 ft]; their eastern outliers, the Bighorn Mountains, rise 3,000 m [10,000 ft] almost sheer above the surrounding grasslands. These are the Rockies of the tourists; each year thousands of people visit the many national parks and reserves in the splendid heartland of the Cordilleras. The scenery is matchless, the forests, grasslands, alpine tundras and marshes are ecologically fascinating, and the wild animals are reasonably accessible. There is every chance for tourists to see bison, wapiti, mule deer, moose, black and brown bears, beavers and a host of smaller mammals and birds.

West of the Rockies, beyond the dry plateau scrublands of Arizona, Utah and Nevada, a double chain of mountains runs parallel to the coast from Mexico to Canada. In the arid, sun-baked south they form the desert landscape on either side of the Gulf of California. At Los Angeles they merge, parting again to form the Sierra Nevada and the Coastal Ranges that face each other across the Great Valley of central California. They rejoin in the Klamath Mountains, then continue north on either side of a broad valley – to the west as a lowly coastal chain, to the east as the magnifi-

cently forested Cascade Range. By keeping rain away from the interior, these mountains create the arid landscapes of the central Cordilleras.

Climate and agriculture: In the damp winters and dry summers of southern California the coastal mountains support semi-desert scrub; the Sierra Nevada, rising far above them, is relatively well-watered and forested. In the early days of settlement the long, bone dry summers made farming – even ranching difficult in the central valley of California. But the peaks of Sierra Nevada, accumulating thick snow in winter, now provide a reservoir for summer irrigation. Damming and water channelling have made the semi-deserts and dry rangelands bloom all over southern and central California, which now grows temperate and tropical fruits, vegetables, cotton and other thirsty crops in abundance – despite severe drought from the late 1980s.

Through northern California and Oregon, where annual rainfall is higher and summer heat less intense, the coastal mountains are clothed in forests of tall cedars and firs; notable among them are stands of giant redwood cedars, towering well over 100 m [330 ft]. In coastal Washington Douglas firs, grand firs, Sitka spruce and giant arborvitae are the spectacular trees, rivalling the giant redwoods. Forests of giant conifers cover the Cascade Range too, providing the enormous stocks of timber on which the wealth of the American north-west was originally based.

ECONOMY AND RESOURCES

The East
Settlement and development: The eastern USA is the heartland of many of America's rural and urban traditions. In the 19th century European immigrants poured through the ports of Boston, New York, Philadelphia and Baltimore. Many stayed to swell the cities, which grew enormously. Others moved across the mountains to populate the interior and start the farms that fed the city masses. As raw materials of industry – coal and iron ore especially – were discovered and exploited, new cities grew up in the interior. Some were based on old frontier forts: for example, Fort Duquesne became Pittsburgh

ALASKA

In 1867 the USA bought Alaska from the Tsarist government of Russia for a mere $7 million. More extensive than the south-western lands acquired from Mexico, Alaska remained a territory for over 90 years, becoming America's largest state in 1959. Geographically it forms the north-western end of the Western Cordilleras; peaks in the main Alaska Range rise to over 6,000 m [20,000 ft], and the southern 'panhandle' region is a drowned fjordland backed by ice-capped mountains. A gold rush in the 1880s stimulated the subsequent development of other mineral resources – most notably copper and, especially, oil. Alaska is the first real test of the USA's resolve to balance economic development and conservation; the six largest US national parks are in Alaska. Some farming is possible on the southern coastal lowlands; the interior tablelands are tundra-covered and rich in migrant birds and mammals.

and Fort Dearborn became the city of Chicago.

Railways spread over the booming farm-lands, linking producer and consumer. Huge manufacturing cities, vast markets in their own right, developed along the Great Lakes as people continued to arrive – firstly from abroad, but latterly from the countryside, where mechanization threw people off the land into the cities and factories. In less than a hundred years between the late 18th and 19th centuries the Ohio country passed from Indian-occupied forests and plains to mecha-nized farmlands of unparalleled efficiency, virtually becoming the granary of the Western world, and spawning some of its greatest and wealthiest industrial centres.

While the north boomed, the warmer southern states slipped into rural lethargy; becoming overdependent on cotton cultiva-tion, they remained backward and outside the mainstream of American prosperity. Though fortunes were made on the rich cotton estates of the south-east, Tennessee and the southern Appalachians spelled rural poverty for many generations of settlers.

Today the pattern is much the same, though prosperity has increased throughout the east. The densest concentrations of indus-try and population lie in the north-east, especially in central New England. New York remains an important financial hub, while Washington, DC, now part of a vast, sprawl-ing megalopolis, loses none of its significance as the centre of federal government. The south-eastern states remain relatively rural and thinly populated, though they are increasingly popular with the retired, notably Florida.

The Central States
Settlement and development: Over 30 major tribes of native Indians used these vast and varied plains. Some – the Mandan, the Omaha and the Kansa along the Missouri River, for example – were settled farmers, while on the drier western plains the Blackfoot, Crow, Arapaho, Kiowa and Com-anche were nomadic, following the buffalo, the game and the pasture.

European influences revolutionized their lives. By 1800 the horse, introduced from the south by the Spanish, made the Indian population of about 100,000 mobile as never before. Then English- and French-speaking trappers and traders from the east brought firearms: the mounted Indian with a gun became too efficient a hunter, and rapidly depleted his food supply. Behind the traders came white settlers, killing off the buffalo and crowding in other native peoples that they had driven from homelands in the south-east. As railways, cattle trails and the fences of the ranchers crossed the old hunting grounds, Indian farmers and hunters alike lost their traditional lands and livelihoods to the European intruders, and the plains settlement was virtually completed by the late 19th century.

The coming of the railways after the Civil War of the 1860s not only doomed the rem-nant Indian societies, but also introduced long and often bitter competition between different types of European farming. The dry grasslands that once supported the buffalo could just as well support herds of cattle on the open range, raised to feed the eastern cities. So the range lands often became crop farms. In the dry years that followed soil deterioration and erosion began, becoming a major problem in the early decades of the present century.

With their markets in the cities of the east and in Europe, the plains farmers were caught in a vice between the desiccation of their farms and the boom and slump of their markets. By the 1930s agricultural depression led to massive foreclosing on mortgaged lands, and when the dust storms of eroded topsoil came the people were driven away – the 'Okies' of Woody Guthrie and John Steinbeck who fled to California. Much farmed land subsequently reverted to ranching.

Farming prospects improved during the later 1930s, when the New Deal brought better price structures. New approaches to farming practice, including dry farming (cropping only one year out of several), contour ploughing, diversification beyond basic grains, and widespread irrigation that was linked to the creation of a vast network of dams and reservoirs, all transformed the plains. Nevertheless, these areas are marginal to semi-desert, remaining highly susceptible to periodic changes in precipitation over a wide area: thus a poor snowfall on the Rockies may mean insufficient water for irrigation the following summer. Coupled with worldwide fluctuations in the cereals market (on which Mid-West farmers still depend heavily), farming on the plains remains very risky.

The growth of industry: In the Gulf Coast states, petroleum provides a radically different basis for prosperity. Since the exploitation of oil reserves in the early years of the century Oklahoma, Texas and Louisiana have shifted from a dependence on agriculture (notably wheat, cattle, rice and sugar production) to the refining and petrochemical industries. Oil has transformed Dallas-Fort Worth into a major US conurbation, now larger than the twin cities of Minneapolis-St Paul, which were once the chief urban focus of the agricultural economy of the upper Mississippi. At the meeting of the High Plains and the Rocky Mountains, Denver changed from a small elevated railhead town to a wealthy state capital (and further to a smog-ridden metropolis) in response to mineral wealth and the growth of aerospace industries.

Further north the cities of the central USA are great trading centres, dependent on local

HAWAII

Most recent and most southerly of the United States, Hawaii is an archipelago of eight large and over 100 smaller volcanic islands in the mid-Pacific, 3,850 km [2,400 mls] south-west of California. Only on the main island are there currently active volcanoes. High rainfall, warmth and rich soils combine to provide a wealth of year-round vegetation; originally forested, the islands are still well covered with trees and shrubs, but now provide commercial crops of sugar cane, cereals, forage for cattle, and a wide range of fruit and vegetables.

Originally settled by Polynesians and visited by James Cook in 1778, Hawaii became a port-of-call for trans-Pacific shipping and a wintering station for New England whalers, but retained its independent status until annexed by the USA in 1898. Only about 2% of its people are full-blooded Polynesians; the rest are of Chinese, Japanese, Korean, Philippine and Caucasian origins, including many immigrants from mainland USA.

About 80% live on the islands of Oahu, over half of them in the capital city of Honolulu. Agriculture, fishing and food processing are the main industries, though defence and tourism are also important to the state's economy.

agriculture for their prosperity. Wholesaling and the trans-shipping of produce have been crucial since the days of the railheads, but cities like St Louis, Kansas City and Chicago have been able to diversify far beyond their original role to become major manufacturing centres. Chicago, for example, is the main mid-western focus of the steel industries. Nowadays the interstate freeway system supplements and has partly replaced the railway networks, and air passenger traffic has increased rapidly.

From the air the landscape between the Mississippi and the Rockies is one of quilted farmlands and vast reservoirs, blending into wheatlands with extensive grasslands. Almost all the original vegetation is long gone, and most people now live in the cities, but the

ndscape still reflects the critical importance
agriculture past and present.

he West

ettlement and development: The Indian
ultures of western America included hunting,
shing, seed-gathering and primitive irrigation
rming. Some were semi-nomadic, others
ttled, living mostly in small, scattered
ommunities. The first European colonists,
preading northwards from New Spain
Mexico) in the 1760s, made little impact on
e Indians. But their forts and missions
which included San Diego, Los Angeles and
an Francisco) attracted later settlers who
roved more exploitative. From the 1840s
ressures increased with the arrival of land-
ungry Americans, both by sea and along
vagon trails from the east. After a brief
truggle, the south-west was sold to the USA;
lmost immediately the gold rushes brought
ew waves of adventurers and immigrants.

The Oregon coast, though visited by
panish, British and Russian mariners in
earch of furs from the 16th century onwards,
was first settled by American fur traders in
1811. Immigration began during the 1830s,
he famous Oregon Trail across Wyoming and
idaho from the Mississippi coming into full
use during the 1840s. After the establishment
of the 49th parallel as the boundary between
Canada and the USA, Oregon Territory
(including Washington, Idaho and part of
Montana) became part of the USA. Here in
the north-west the forests and rangelands were
equally vital to Indians and to settlers, and
many battles were fought before the Indians
were subdued and confined in tribal reserves.

Now the wagon trails are major highways,
the staging posts, mission stations and isolated
forts transformed into cities. Gold mining,
once the only kind of mining that mattered,
has given way to the delving and processing of
a dozen lesser metals, from copper to molybdenum. Fish canning, food processing, electronics and aerospace are major sources of
employment. The movie industry is based in
Los Angeles, but the city now has a broad
economy based on high-technology industries.
The mountain states – once far behind in
economic development – have caught up with
the rest of the USA.

ECONOMY

The years following the Civil War (1861–5)
saw the firm establishment of the USA as the
world's leading industrial society. Still attracting enormous numbers of emigrants from
Europe, its agricultural and industrial output
grew at unprecedented rates to the end of the
century and beyond.

Agriculture: Stimulated by education, research and new, sophisticated machinery, agriculture developed into a highly mechanized
industry for food production and processing.
Chicago's agricultural machinery industries
transformed the farmers' lives with mass-
produced ploughs, tractors, seed drills, reapers
and binders. Only a generation after the
pioneering days, farmers found themselves
tightly integrated into an economic system
with such factors as mortgages, availability of
spare parts, freight prices and world markets at
least as crucial to the success of their efforts as
climate and soil.

To the east of the western mountains farming was established in a zonal pattern which
remains intact – though much modified –
today, a pattern reflecting both the possibilities
offered by climate and soils, and the inclina-
tions and national origins of the settlers who
first farmed the lands. In the north, from
Minnesota to New England, lies a broad belt
where dairy farming predominates, providing
milk, butter and cheese for the industrial
cities. Spring wheat is grown further west,
where the climate is drier. The eastern and
central states from Nebraska to Ohio form the
famous Corn Belt – immensely productive
land, formerly prairie and forest, where corn
(maize) is the main crop.

Now much extended by the development of
new, more tolerant strains, corn production
has spread into neighbouring belts on either
side. No longer principally human food,
except in the poorer areas of the south, corn is
grown mainly for feeding to cattle and pigs,
and other livestock, which in turn supply the
meat-packing industries.

Southwards again, from Oklahoma and
Kansas to Virginia, stretches a broad belt of
mixed farming where winter wheat and corn
alternate as the dominant cereals. In the
warmer southern states lies the former Cotton
Belt, where cotton and tobacco were once the

most widespread crops; both are now concentrated into small, highly-productive areas where mechanical handling is possible, and the bulk of the land is used for a wide variety of other crops ranging from vegetables to fruit and peanuts.

Throughout American farming there has been a tendency to shift from small-scale operations to large, from labour-intensive to mechanized, and from low-capital to high-capital investment. The main centres of production are now concentrated in the western plains: much of the land originally farmed by the Pilgrim Fathers and other early settlers is now built over, or has reverted to attractive second-growth forest. By concentrating effort in this way, America has become a leading producer of meat, dairy foods, soya beans, corn, oats, wheat, barley, cotton, sugar and many other crops, both for home consumption and export.

Resources and industry: The spread of prosperity throughout a very broad spectrum of the community generated new consumer industries, to satisfy the demands of a large middle class for ever-increasing standards of comfort and material welfare. America became the pioneer of massive-scale industrial production of everything from thumbtacks to automobiles. With almost every raw material needed for production available within its own boundaries, or readily gained through trading with close neighbours, its mining and extractive industries have been heavily exploited from the start.

For several generations coal formed the main source of power and the basis of industrial prosperity. Anthracite from eastern Pennsylvania, good bituminous and coking coals from the Appalachians, Indiana, Illinois, Colorado and Utah are still in demand, and enormous reserves remain. Oil, first drilled in Pennsylvania in 1859, was subsequently found in several major fields underlying the Mid-West, the eastern and central mountain states, the Gulf of Mexico, California and Alaska. Home consumption of petroleum products has grown steadily: though the US remains a major producer, it is also by far the world's greatest consumer, and has for a long while been a net importer of oil. Natural gas too is found in abundance, usually in association with oil, and is moved to the main consumer areas through an elaborate, transcontinental network of pipes.

Today the USA is a major producer of iron and steel, mica, molybdenum, uranium and many other primary materials, and a major consumer and exporter of a wide range of manufactured goods, from chemicals and industrial machinery, to paper and electronic equipment. But though the USA remains the world's greatest economic power, its position as leading industrial nation was being threatened by Japan into the 1990s.

Population: The USA has one of the most diverse populations of any nation in the world. Until about 1860, with the exception of the native Indians and the southern blacks, the population was largely made up by immigrants of British (and Irish) origin, with small numbers of Spanish and French. After the Civil War, however, there was increasing immigration from the countries of central and south-eastern Europe – Italy, the Balkans, Poland, Scandinavia and Russia. This vast influx of Europeans, numbering about 30 million between 1860 and 1920, was markedly different in culture and language from the established population. More recently there have been lesser influxes of Japanese, Chinese, Filipinos, Cubans and Puerto Ricans, with large numbers of Mexicans (many of them illegal) from across the southern border. Although there are strong influences and pressures towards Americanization, these minority groups have tended to establish distinct social and cultural enclaves within US society as a whole.

The major westwards movement of population through the last century was replaced after 1900 by more subtle but no less important shifts of population away from rural areas and into the cities. Today there is further movement from the old, industrial centres and the tired, outmoded cities that flourished early in the century, away from the ageing buildings and urban dereliction, especially in the north and east, to new centres elsewhere.

The cities that gain population are mostly peripheral, on the Great Lakes and the coasts. The south is especially favoured for its warmth (particularly by retired people) and its closeness to the major source of energy in the USA – petroleum. Development of southern petroemical and electronic industries has helped relieve rural poverty and given new economic life, though partly at the expense of the north. However, Chicago and the eastern conurbations – New York, Boston, Philadelphia, Baltimore and Washington – still remain pre-eminent as centres of US commercial, as well as political, life.

Since its earliest inception from the 13 colonies, the USA has led the world in industrial, economic and social innovation, creating problems through sheer ebullience and solving them – more or less – through inventiveness and enterprise, and with massive, wealth-bringing resources of energy and materials. The United States today continues to enjoy one of the highest material standards of living ever known, and continues to produce what may well be its greatest asset of all – a highly skilled, literate and imaginative population.

HISTORY AND POLITICS

Leif Ericson was the first European to visit North America, around AD 1000, but the Vikings left no permanent settlements. However, about 1 million Native Americans lived in North America when Christopher Columbus reached the New World in 1492.

The first permanent European settlement in the present-day United States was founded by Spain in 1565 at Saint Augustine, Florida. Jamestown, Virginia became the first permanent English settlement in 1607. African slaves were brought to Virginia in 1619.

During the 18th century, England, France and Spain became dominant colonial powers in North America. Great Britain gained much French territory during the French and Indian War (1756–63), but policies introduced after the war led to increasing colonial resentment of British rule. The American Revolution began in 1775, and the Continental Congress issued the Declaration of Independence on 4 July 1776. American forces, aided by France, defeated the British at the Battle of Yorktown in 1781, and in 1783 the Treaty of Paris recognized American independence.

The Constitution of the United States was approved in 1787, and ratified by all thirteen original states by 1790. The Louisiana Purchase in 1803 nearly doubled the size of the US. The War of 1812, waged against

Britain, increased the nation's confidence in foreign affairs, culminating in the Monroe doctrine of 1823. Rapid westward expansion led to the acquisition of Texas in 1845 and the Oregon Territory in 1846. A huge expanse of western territory, including California was won in the Mexican-American War of 1846–8.

Conflict over slavery between the industrialized North and the agricultural South led to the American Civil War (1861–5). Slavery was abolished after the North won, while the South entered Reconstruction.

The late 19th century was marked by a huge influx of European immigrants and rapid industrial and economic development. The last Native American tribes were defeated and forced into reservations as territorial expansion continued. The US bought Alaska from Russia in 1867. Guam, the Philippines and Puerto Rico were won in the Spanish-American War of 1898, and Hawaii was annexed the same year. The Panama Canal Zone was seized in 1903.

US isolationism ended in 1917 with entry into World War I, confirming America's status as a world power. The economic boom of the 1920s was followed by the crash of 1929 and the Great Depression. The New Deal offered slight improvement during the years of the Depression, but the Japanese bombing of Pearl Harbor on 7 December 1941 led to the US entry into World War II, which fuelled economic recovery. The US ended the war in August 1945 by dropping atomic bombs on Hiroshima and Nagasaki.

Post-war tensions between the US and the USSR led to the Cold War. US forces fought in Korea (1950–3) and Vietnam (1965–73) to stop the spread of Communism. Domestic anti-Communist hysteria peaked during the 1950s. Civil rights campaigns and growing dissatisfaction with US involvement in Vietnam marked the 1960s. Riots erupted in several cities as a result of protests against social conditions and race relations. Then, at the end of the 1960s, in July 1969, US astronauts landed on the Moon.

The Watergate scandal (1973–4) altered many Americans' perception of the federal government. The economy suffered during the late 1970s, culminating in the recession of 1981–2, but a sustained recovery beginning in 1983 lasted the rest of the decade.

The fall of Communism and the division of the Soviet Union left the US as the world's sole remaining superpower, as evidenced by its leadership during the Gulf War. However, lingering domestic problems remained, including simmering race relations and increasing urban violence. Long-term economic prospects were buoyed by the conclusion of the North American Free Trade Agreement with Canada and Mexico, which went into effect in 1994. [*Map pages 28–9*] ■

AREA 9,372,610 sq km [3,618,765 sq mls]
POPULATION 260,631,000
CAPITAL (POPULATION) Washington, DC (3,924,000)
GOVERNMENT Federal republic
ETHNIC GROUPS White 80%, African American 12%, other races 8%
LANGUAGES English (official), Spanish, more than 30 others
RELIGIONS Christianity (Protestant 53%, Roman Catholic 26%, other Christian 8%), Islam 2%, Judaism 2%
CURRENCY US dollar = 100 cents

URUGUAY

After Surinam, the Eastern Republic of Uruguay, as Uruguay is officially known, is the smallest South American state. It is a low-lying rolling country of tall prairie grasses and riparian woodlands – the highest point, Mirador Nacional, which lies south of Minas, is only 501 m [1,644 ft] above sea level. The Atlantic coast and River Plate estuary are fringed with lagoons and sand dunes; the centre of the country is a low plateau, rising in the north towards the Brazilian border. The River Uruguay forms the western boundary, and is navigable as far as the falls at Salto, 300 km [186 mls] from the Plate. The climate is temperate with warm summers and mild winters, moderated by the prevailing easterly winds which blow in from the sea.

ECONOMY AND RESOURCES

Meat processing, pioneered at Fray Bentos i the 1860s, was the start of a meat-and-hid export industry that, boosted by railways t Montevideo and later by refrigerated carg ships, established the nation's fortunes. Toda a modern and moderately prosperous countr Uruguay still depends largely on exports c animal products – mostly meat, wool and dair produce – for her livelihood.

Farming is thus the main industry, thoug four out of five Uruguayans are urban-livin and almost half live in the capital. Moreover although more than 90% of Uruguay's lan could be used for agriculture, only 10% of it i currently under cultivation. The manufac turing industry today is largely centred on foo processing and packing, though with a smal domestic market the economy has diversifie into cement, chemicals, leather, textiles an steel. Uruguay's trading patterns are changing too, in an attempt to avoid reliance on Brazi and Argentina, and in 1988 trade agreement with China and the USSR were signed. Wit inadequate supplies of coal, gas and oil, the nation depends on HEP (90%) for its energy and exports electricity to Argentina.

HISTORY AND POLITICS

Originally little more than the hinterland to the Spanish base at Montevideo, Uruguay formed a buffer area between northern Portuguese and western Spanish territories. Though independent in 1828, internal struggles and civil war intervened before the country developed a basis for prosperity. European immigrants settled the coast and the valley of the River Uruguay, farming the lowlands and leaving the highlands for stock rearing.

Since 1828 Uruguay has been dominated by two political parties – Colorados (Liberals) and Blancos (Conservatives) – and from 1904 has been unique in constitutional innovations aimed at avoiding a dictatorship. The early part of the 20th century saw the development of a pioneering welfare state which in turn encouraged extensive immigration. From 1973 until 1985, however, the country was under a strict military regime accused of appalling human rights abuses. In 1989 the country had its first fully free presidential and legislative elections for eighteen years, which ere won by the Blancos. President Lacalle's rst task was to try and reduce the dependency n events in Brazil and Argentina, Uruguay's uge neighbours. [*Map page 31*] ■

AREA 177,410 sq km [68,498 sq mls]
POPULATION 3,167,000
CAPITAL (POPULATION) Montevideo (1,384,000)
GOVERNMENT Multiparty republic
ETHNIC GROUPS White 86%, Mestizo 8%, Mulatto or Black 6%
LANGUAGES Spanish (official)
RELIGIONS Christianity (Roman Catholic 66%, Protestant 2%), Judaism 1%
CURRENCY Uruguay peso = 100 centésimos

UZBEKISTAN

The Republic of Uzbekistan is one of the five republics in Central Asia which were once part of the Soviet Union. Plains cover most of western Uzbekistan, with highlands in the east, and there is a populous eastern spur cutting into Kyrgyzstan. The main rivers, the Amu Darya and Syr Darya, drain into the Aral Sea. So much water has been taken from these rivers to irrigate the land that the Aral Sea has shrunk from 66,900 sq km [25,830 sq mls] in 1960 to 33,642 sq km [12,989 sq mls] in 1993. The dried-up lake area has become desert, like much of the rest of the country.

Uzbekistan has a continental climate. The winters are cold, but temperatures soar in the summer months. The west is extremely arid, with an average annual rainfall of about 200 mm [8 in], but parts of the highlands in the east have three times as much rain.

ECONOMY AND RESOURCES
The World Bank classifies Uzbekistan as a 'lower-middle-income' developing country, and the government still controls most of the economic activity. The country produces coal, copper, gold, oil and natural gas, and in 1993 was the world's third largest producer of

uranium. Manufactures include agricultural machinery, chemicals, processed food and textiles. Agriculture is important and cotton is the main crop, though various fruits and rice are also grown. Cattle, sheep and goats are raised. Uzbekistan's exports include cotton, gold, textiles, chemicals and fertilizers.

HISTORY AND POLITICS
Turkic people first settled in the area that is now Uzbekistan about 1,500 years ago, and Islam was introduced in the 7th century AD. Mongols invaded the land in the 13th century and, in the late 14th century, the Mongol Turk Tamerlane ruled a great empire from Samarkand (Samarqand). Turkic Uzbek people invaded in the 16th century and gradually the area was divided into states known as *khanates*. A large part of eastern Uzbekistan is taken up by the Kara-Kalpak Autonomous Region, annexed to the Uzbek Soviet Socialist Republic (as it was then known) in 1936.

Russia conquered the area in the 19th century. After the Russian Revolution of 1917, the Communists took over and, in 1924, set up the Uzbek SSR. Under Communism, all aspects of Uzbek life were controlled and religious worship was discouraged, but education, health, housing and transport were improved. The Communists also increased cotton production, but caused great environmental damage in doing so.

In the 1980s, when reforms were being introduced in the Soviet Union, the people demanded more freedom. In 1990, the government stated that its laws overruled those of the Soviet Union. On 1 September 1991, Uzbekistan declared its independence after the break-up of the Soviet Union and this was confirmed in a referendum in December. Uzbekistan has kept its links with Russia through the Commonwealth of Independent States and has established new cultural and political ties with Turkey.

On 29 December 1991, Islam Karimov, leader of the People's Democratic Party (formerly the Communist Party), was elected president. Many opposition leaders have since been arrested. Karimov has asserted that economic reform will be slow in order to avoid internal disruption. In 1994 the government approved a six-year plan for the transfer of the

Uzbek language from its present Turkik form to a Latin script. [*Map page 20*] ■

AREA 447,400 sq km [172,740 sq mls]
POPULATION 22,349,000
CAPITAL (POPULATION) Tashkent (2,094,000)
GOVERNMENT Socialist republic
ETHNIC GROUPS Uzbek 71%, Russian 8%, Tajik 5%, Kazakh 4%, Tatar 2%, Kara-Kalpak 2%, Crimean Tatar, Korean, Kyrgyz, Ukrainian, Turkmen
LANGUAGES Uzbek (official)
RELIGIONS Islam
CURRENCY Som = 100 tiyin

VANUATU

An archipelago of 13 large islands and 70 islets largely of volcanic origin, the majority of the islands are mountainous with coral beaches, reefs and very limited coastal cultivation. Nearly two-thirds of the population live on four islands, 19,000 of them in the capital of Port-Vila, on the island of Efate. The Melanesian people live largely by subsistence farming and fishing, with copra, beef and veal the main exports.

Formerly the New Hebrides and governed jointly by France and Britain from 1906, the islands became an independent republic within the Commonwealth in 1980. The francophone island of Espíritu Santó attempted separation from the anglophone government, and politics have since remained unstable. [*Map page 3*] ■

AREA 12,190 sq km [4,707 sq mls]
POPULATION 165,000
CAPITAL (POPULATION) Port-Vila (19,310)
GOVERNMENT Multiparty republic
ETHNIC GROUPS Melanesian 94%, French 4%
LANGUAGES Bislama, English, French
RELIGIONS Christianity
CURRENCY Vatu = 100 centimes

VATICAN CITY

The world's smallest nation – a walle enclave on the west bank of the Rive Tiber in the city of Rome – the Vatican Cit State exists to provide an independent base fc the Holy See, governing body of the Roma Catholic Church and its 950 million adheren round the world. It consists of 44 hectare [109 acres], including St Peter's Square, wit a resident population of about 1,000 – includ ing the country's only armed force of 10 Swiss Guards. The population is made u entirely of unmarried males – and the birt rate is zero.

The Vatican is sustained by investmen income and voluntary contributions. Th popes have been prominent patrons of th arts, and the treasures of the Vatican, includ ing Michelangelo's frescoes in the Sistine Chapel, attract tourists from all over the world. Similarly, the Vatican library contains a priceless collection of manuscripts from both pre-Christian and Christian eras.

The Vatican City State is all that remains of the extensive Papal States which, until 1870, occupied most of central Italy. In 1929 Benito Mussolini recognized the independence of the Vatican City in return for papal recognition of the kingdom of Italy.

The Vatican City has its own newspaper, police and railway station, and issues its own stamps and coins. It's radio station, *Radio Vaticana*, broadcasts in 34 languages.

The popes have lived in the Vatican since the 5th century, apart from a brief period at Avignon in the 14th century ■

AREA 0.44 sq km [0.17 sq mls]
POPULATION 1,000
CAPITAL (POPULATION) Vatican City (1,000)
GOVERNMENT Papal Commission
ETHNIC GROUPS Italian, Swiss
LANGUAGES Latin (official), Italian
RELIGIONS Roman Catholic
CURRENCY Italian currency

VENEZUELA

n the north and north-west of Venezuela, where 90% of the population lives, the Andes split to form two ranges separated by the Maracaibo basin (which surounds the freshwater lake of Maracaibo). At 5,007 m [16,427 ft], snow-capped Merida is the highest of several tall peaks in the area. Above 3,000 m [10,000 ft] are the *paramos* – regions of grassland vegetation where Indian villagers live; temperatures are mild and the land is fertile. By contrast, Maracaibo swelters in tropical heat alongside the oilfields that for half a century have produced Venezuela's wealth.

The mountains running west to east behind the coast from Valencia to Trinidad have a separate geological history and gentler topography. Between the ranges are fertile alluvial basins, with many long-established market towns. Caracas, the teeming capital, was one such town before being expanded and modernized on the back of the 1970s oil boom. It now has to accommodate a rapidly swelling population and is fringed with the shanties of hopeful immigrants from poor rural areas.

South of the mountains are the *llanos* of the Orinoco – mostly a vast savanna of trees and grasslands that floods, especially in the west, during the April-to-October rains. This is now cattle-raising country. The Orinoco itself rises on the western rim in the Guiana Highlands, a region of high dissected plateaus made famous as the site of Arthur Conan Doyle's *Lost World*, and dense tropical forest makes this still a little-known area. Mount Roraima, the highest peak, rises to 2,810 m [9,217 ft] at the conjunction of the border with Guyana (with whom Venezuela has a grumbling territorial dispute – as it does with Colombia) and Brazil.

ECONOMY AND RESOURCES

Cerro Bolívar, where iron ore is mined and fed to the steel mills of Ciudad Guayana, is a new industrial city built on the Orinoco since 1960. The smelting is powered by hydroelectricity from the nearby Caroni River, and a new deep-water port allows 60,000-tonne carriers to take surplus ore to world markets. Modern developments in a primeval setting typify the changes that Venezuela is undergoing.

Oil made Venezuela a rich country, but the wealth was always distributed very unevenly and concentrated in the cities – hence the rapid urbanization that made 17 out of every 20 Venezuelans a city dweller and left enormous areas of the country unpopulated. Before the coming of oil, Venezuela was predominantly agricultural. ·

Commercially-viable reserves of oil were found in Venezuela in 1914, and by the 1930s the country had become the world's first major oil exporter – the largest producer after the USA. The industry was nationalized in 1976 but by 1990 there were signs of dangerous dependence on a single commodity controlled by OPEC and in plentiful supply, while the large foreign debt saw austerity measures that triggered a violent reaction from many Venezuelans.

The oil-producing region around Maracaibo covers an area of 77,700 sq km [30,000 sq mls] and produces three-quarters of the nation's total. Exploration for oil is also being carried out offshore in the Caribbean. Before the development of the oil industry Venezuela was predominantly an agricultural country, but 85% of export earnings are now from oil and some of the profits from the industry help to fund developments in agriculture and other industries, including the exploitation of natural gas. Gold, nickel, iron ore, copper and manganese are also found and aluminium production has increased following further discoveries of bauxite; aluminium has now replaced iron ore as the second most important export earner. Manufactures include cement, steel, chemicals, food processing, shipbuilding and vehicles.

Agriculture can supply only 70% of the country's needs. Only 5% of the arable land is cultivated and much of that is pasture. The chief crops are sugar cane, coffee, bananas, maize and oranges; there is also substantial dairy and beef production. It is thought that more than 10,000 head of cattle are smuggled into Colombia each month. The reverse is almost certainly the case for cocaine, where Venezuela acts as a

ANGEL FALLS

Called Cherun-Meru by the local Indians, and first known to Europeans in 1910, the world's highest waterfall was 'rediscovered' in 1937 when an American airman called Jimmy Angel flew his small plane into the Guiana Highlands in eastern Venezuela in search of gold – but found instead a natural wonder nearly 20 times the height of Niagara, plunging down from the plateau of Auyán Tepuí, the 'Devil's Mountain'.

In 1949 an expedition confirmed Angel's report and today light aircraft follow his route to take tourists to falls that tumble a total of 979 m [3,212 ft] on the Rio Carrao, a tributary of the Caroni. The cataract is broken only by a single ledge, the main drop measuring 807 m [2,648 ft].

conduit to the US for its Andean neighbours.

Venezuela is still the richest country in South America but now plans to diversify away from the petroleum industry, and foreign investment is being actively encouraged.

HISTORY AND POLITICS

Sighted by Columbus in 1498, the country was visited by Alonzo de Ojeda and Amerigo Vespucci in 1499, when they named it Venezuela ('Little Venice'). It was part of the Spanish colony of New Granada until 1821 when it became independent, first in federation with Colombia and Ecuador and then, from 1830, as a separate independent republic under the leadership of Simón Bolívar. Between 1830 and 1945 the country was governed mainly by dictators; after frequent changes of president, a new constitution came into force in 1961 and since then a fragile civilian-rule democracy has been enjoyed, resting on widespread repression and corruption – almost endemic in South America. Two military coup attempts were defeated by President Pérez who then resigned in May 1993 after charges of corruption. The new president is Rafael Caldera.

Demographically stable, with a growing middle class and a proven record in economic planning, Venezuela has every chance of increasing its prosperity further in a wor economic upturn – but to avoid politic problems the government must learn to di tribute the benefits more widely to its citizen [Map page 31] ■

AREA 912,050 sq km [352,143 sq mls]
POPULATION 21,378,000
CAPITAL (POPULATION) Caracas (2,784,000)
GOVERNMENT Federal republic
ETHNIC GROUPS Mestizo 67%, White 21%, Black 10%, Amerindian 2%
LANGUAGES Spanish (official)
RELIGIONS Christianity (Roman Catholic 94%)
CURRENCY Bolívar = 100 céntimos

VIETNAM

A land of mountains, coastal plains and deltas, Vietnam is perhaps Asia's most strangely shaped country. In the north the coastal lands widen into the valley and delta of the Hongha (Red) River and the valley of the Da. This region has long been the main cultural focus of the country, and it was the original core of the Annamite empire which came into being with the revolt against Chinese rule in AD 939.

In the south of the country, the coastal plains open out into the great delta of the Mekong, the world's ninth longest river at 4,500 km [2,795 mls]. For most of their length the coastal lowlands are backed in the west by the steep and deeply dissected mountains of the Annamite Chain, and to the north the country is dominated by the plateaux of Laos and Tongking, often characterized by an intensely craggy, inhospitable karstic (limestone) landscape. The mountain areas are the home of many different hill peoples.

ECONOMY AND RESOURCES

Vietnam's huge standing army of 1.2 million (plus reserves of 3 million) remains a great drain on a desperately poor nation subsisting on agriculture: rice, cassava, maize, sweet

CONFLICT IN INDO-CHINA

Vietnamese conflict dates back at least to 1939, when the Viet Minh coalition of nationalists, including Communists, began agitating for independence from France; by 1945, with experience in anti-Japanese resistance behind them, they would not accept a quiet return to colonial administration after the Japanese collapse. Proclaiming the Democratic Republic of Vietnam, within months they were fighting French troops sent from Europe. Gradually, the Viet Minh, increasingly dominated by a well-organized Communist leadership under Ho Chi Minh, began to overwhelm the French. The US, alarmed by the Viet Minh's Communism, provided weaponry and logistical support, but Presidents Truman and Eisenhower both refused to allow American military aid. The climax came in May 1954, when a besieged French army surrendered at Dien Bien Phu. At a subsequent peace conference at Geneva, the French abandoned their colony. The country was partitioned between a Communist north, its capital in Hanoi, and a non-Communist south, administered from Saigon. The Geneva accord assumed Vietnamese elections would follow, and included an explicit proviso: the division was 'provisional, and should not in any way be interpreted as constituting a political or territorial boundary'.

Still anxious to avoid military engagement, the US poured aid into the South, the supposedly Democratic Republic of Vietnam. In fact, as US intelligence reports repeatedly explained to the White House, the republic was far from democratic, and its ruling élite was quite incapable of running the country, far less inspiring its people's loyalty; most of them would vote Communist if the elections were ever held. The elections were postponed, on the grounds that Communist violence would prevent a fair outcome – probably true, but giving Hanoi justification for a guerrilla campaign in the South, spearheaded by the Viet Cong, heirs to the Viet Minh tradition.

The newly elected President Kennedy decided to make a stand against Communism in Vietnam, despite the cautious counsel of his most experienced diplomats. American aid was backed up by military advisers, then combat units. The Viet Cong continued to make headway. After Kennedy's assassination in 1963, President Johnson increased the military commitment. US aircraft blasted Vietnam with more explosives than had been used in all of World War II; American casualties began to rise – more than 50,000 would die – and with them the tide of anti-war sentiment back home. By 1968, Johnson was convinced that the war could not be won; he stood down from power. Under his successor, Richard Nixon, the war continued, drawing neighbouring Cambodia into the cauldron. Yet real military progress remained as elusive as ever.

Finally, in 1972, a peace treaty was signed. The Americans withdrew; in 1975 North Vietnamese troops rolled across the 'provisional' border, and the country was reunited. To delay a Communist victory by less than 20 years, the Americans had paid a high price in prestige abroad and political discord at home. The Vietnamese had paid vastly higher in lives. And although Vietnam triumphed in a subsequent 1979 war against its former Chinese allies, political repression and economic disaster caused its people to risk their lives by the thousand in seaborne escapes – the refugee 'Boat People' – during the 1980s.

potatoes and the world's largest population of ducks. Despite the industries of the north, based on natural resources, the economy needs to diversify along the pattern of the 'sunrise' countries of eastern Asia.

HISTORY AND POLITICS

Vietnam already had a long and turbulent history before the French, following decades of missionary involvement and a military campaign lasting 25 years, made it a French protectorate in 1883, later joined by Laos and Cambodia in the French Indo-Chinese Union. Freedom movements starting early in the 20th century made little headway until the end of World War II, when Communist-led guerrillas under Ho Chi Minh, having fought the Japanese occupation, declared Vietnam once again united and free. There followed a long war against the French (1946–54), which resulted in a Communist-dominated north centred on Hanoi and non-Communist south, divided at the 17th parallel of latitude. A second and more ferocious conflict between the north and south, involving heavy deployment of US troops – the 'Vietnam War' – began in the early 1960s and engulfed the whole region before the ceasefire in 1973. In 1975, after a relatively brief campaign between north and south, Vietnam was united under a Communist government. Vietnamese forces then invaded Cambodia in 1978 and were involved in a border war with China in 1979.

Such a recent history left Vietnam exhausted, 2 million of its people died in the American war alone and the countryside was devastated; the problems facing the reunified nation's Communist government in 1976 were enormous. Doctrinaire policies and further aggravation of the Western powers in Cambodia did not help its economic and political isolation, and in 1978 there started the sad saga of the 'Boat People' – peasants fleeing hardship and perhaps persecution in Vietnam to find a new life in Hong Kong and elsewhere; after being put into camps, many were forcibly repatriated years later.

The Hanoi regime softened its position in many ways from the late 1980s, efforts being made to establish diplomatic and trading ties with important international clients and aid donors, Soviet assistance having dwindled following the break-up of the USSR. In the 1990s Vietnam began to introduce reforms; to this end, a new constitution was adopted in June 1992 which reaffirmed Communist Party rule but also formalized free market reforms, including encouragement for foreign investment and some form of private enterprise. [*Map page 26*] ■

AREA 331,689 sq km [128,065 sq mls]
POPULATION 72,931,000
CAPITAL (POPULATION) Hanoi (3,056,000)
GOVERNMENT Socialist republic
ETHNIC GROUPS Vietnamese 87%, Tho (Tay), Chinese (Hoa), Tai, Khmer, Muong, Nung
LANGUAGES Vietnamese (official)
RELIGIONS Buddhism 55%, Christianity (Roman Catholic 7%)
CURRENCY Dong = 10 hao or 100 xu

VIRGIN IS, BRITISH

Most northerly of the Lesser Antilles, th[ey] comprise four notable low-lying islan[ds] and 36 islets and cays. The largest islar[d] Tortola, contains over three-quarters of t[he] total population of 18,000, a third of who[m] live in the capital Road Town.

Though an increasing rival to the Cayma[n] and the Turks and Caicos in terms of offsho[re] banking, tourism remains the main source [of] income, the 320,000 visitors produce 75% [of] the economic activity. Agriculture is limited [by] the low rainfall and poor soils and most foo[d] has to be imported. Rum is the chief export.

Like their larger American neighbours, t[he] British Virgin Islands were 'discovered' [by] Columbus in 1493. Dutch from 1648 b[ut] British since 1666, they are now a Briti[sh] dependency enjoying (since 1977) a stro[ng] measure of self-government. [*Map page 30*] ■

AREA 153 sq km [59 sq mls]
POPULATION 18,000
CAPITAL (POPULATION) Road Town (6,330)
GOVERNMENT British dependent territory
ETHNIC GROUPS African American 90%
LANGUAGES English
RELIGIONS Christianity (Protestant 86%)
CURRENCY US currency

VIRGIN IS, US

The US Virgin Islands were first Spanish then Danish and then, for a sum o[f] US$25 million, American from 1917 – Washington wishing to protect the approaches t[o] the Panama Canal. As an 'unicorporated territory', the residents have been US citizens since 1927. The 68 islands (dominated by the three largest – St Thomas, St Croix and St John) ost a population of 104,000, most of them split between St Croix and St Thomas, home f the capital Charlotte Amalie. Tourism is the main industry, notably cruise ships and day-ippers from the US. The islands have the highest density of hotels and 'condominiums' in the Caribbean. [*Map page 30*] ■

AREA 340 sq km [130 sq mls]
POPULATION 104,000
CAPITAL (POPULATION) Charlotte Amalie (12,330)
GOVERNMENT US territory
ETHNIC GROUPS Black 80%, White 15%
LANGUAGES English, Spanish, Creole
RELIGIONS Christianity (Baptist 42%)
CURRENCY US currency

WALLIS & FUTUNA IS

The smallest and poorest of France's three Pacific overseas territories, the Wallis and Futuna Islands comprise three main islands and numerous islets. Futuna and uninhabited Alofi, main constituents of the Hoorn group, are mountainous; the much larger Uvea, the chief island of the Wallis group, is hilly with coral reefs. Uvea contains 60% of the population, 850 of them in the capital of Mata-Utu.

French aid remains crucial to an economy based mainly on tropical subsistence agriculture; the main crops being cassava, copra, yams and bananas.

In a 1959 referendum the Polynesian islanders voted overwhelmingly in favour of change from a dependency to an overseas territory ■

AREA 200 sq km [77 sq mls]
POPULATION 19,000
CAPITAL (POPULATION) Mata-Utu (850)
GOVERNMENT French overseas territory
ETHNIC GROUPS Polynesian
LANGUAGES French, Wallisian, Futunian
RELIGIONS Christianity
CURRENCY CFP franc =100 centimes

WESTERN SAMOA

Western Samoa comprises two large islands, seven small islands (two of which, Apolima and Manono, are inhabited) and a number of islets. The main islands of Upolu and Savai'i both have a central mountainous region, heavily forested and divided by fast-flowing rivers, surrounded by narrow coastal lowlands and coral reefs. Upolu, the most fertile island, contains two-thirds of the population. The climate is tropical and hurricanes are liable to occur from time to time.

ECONOMY AND RESOURCES
The traditional lifestyle still thrives, with over 60% of the workforce engaged in agriculture, chiefly tropical fruits and vegetables, and in fishing. The main exports are coconut oil, taro and cocoa, with New Zealand the main trading partner. Many of the 38,000 tourists a year visit the home of Robert Louis Stevenson – now the official residence of King Malietoa Tanumafili II.

HISTORY AND POLITICS
The cradle of Polynesian civilization, Western Samoa first gained independence in 1889, but ten years later became a German protectorate. Administered by New Zealand from 1920, the island achieved independence as a parliamentary monarchy in 1962, following a plebiscite. New Zealand handles relations with governments and organizations outside the Pacific islands zone. The first elections using universal suffrage were held in 1991. [*Map page 2*] ■

AREA 2,840 sq km [1,097 sq mls]
POPULATION 169,000
CAPITAL (POPULATION) Apia (32,860)
GOVERNMENT Constitutional monarchy
ETHNIC GROUPS Samoan, mixed European and Polynesian
LANGUAGES Polynesian, English
RELIGIONS Christianity
CURRENCY Tala = 100 sene

YEMEN

T he Republic of Yemen faces the Red Sea and the Gulf of Aden in the south-western corner of the Arabian peninsula. Behind the narrow coastal plain along the Red Sea, the land rises to a mountain region called High Yemen. Beyond the mountains, is the Rub 'al Khali Desert. There are other mountains along the Gulf of Aden, while to the east lies a fertile valley called the Hadramawt.

The climate in Sana is moderated by the altitude of more than 2,000 m [6,000 ft] – temperatures are much lower than in Aden, which is at sea level. In August, south-west monsoon winds bring thunderstorms, but most of Yemen has a desert climate.

ECONOMY AND RESOURCES
The production of oil, first discovered in 1984, was little affected by either the Gulf War or the civil war of 1994, yet in spite of this income Yemen remains one of the poorest countries in the world. Subsistence agriculture is the chief occupation with sorghum, millet and sesame being the main crops. Exports include cotton, coffee and animal hides.

HISTORY AND POLITICS
The optimism that greeted unification of the two Yemeni countries – the Yemen Arab Republic (or North Yemen) and the People's Democratic Republic of Yemen (or South Yemen) – in May 1990 proved short-lived; support for Iraq in the Gulf War, publicized by a vote on the UN Security Council, wrought swift revenge from Iraq's Arab enemies on the ending of hostilities, with Kuwait and Saudi Arabia expelling vast numbers of Yemeni workers. This not only removed the main source of earnings for a homeland already struggling with a weak economy, but it also jeopardized hopes of much-needed foreign aid from rich Gulf nations and the West. Saudi Arabia alone forced the repatriation of some 800,000 immigrants.

The process of marrying the disparate needs

of a traditional state (an independent kingdo since 1918) and the failed Marxist regim based in the South Yemen capital of Ade (formerly a vital British staging post) h proved difficult. Though a good deal small than the South, the North provided over 65 of the population. In May 1994 civil w erupted between the north and south, wit President Saleh (a northerner) attempting t remove the vice-president (a southerner). Th war ended in July 1994 following the captur of Aden by Northern forces. [*Map page 32*]

AREA 527,970 sq km [203,849 sq mls]
POPULATION 13,873,000
CAPITAL (POPULATION) Sana (427,000)
GOVERNMENT Multiparty republic
ETHNIC GROUPS Arabs 96%, Somali 1%
LANGUAGES Arabic (official)
RELIGIONS Islam
CURRENCY North–Yemeni riyal = 100 fils; South–Yemeni dinar = 1,000 fils (in use during transition period)

YUGOSLAVIA

T he Federal Republic of Yugoslavia con- sists of Serbia and Montenegro, two of the six republics which made up the country of Yugoslavia until it broke up in 1991 and 1992. Behind the short coast along the Adriatic Sea lies a mountainous region, including the Dinaric Alps and part of the Balkan Mountains. The Pannonian Plains make up northern Yugoslavia. This fertile region is drained by the River Danube and its tribu-taries; the river enters neighbouring Romania through a scenic gorge called the 'Iron Gate'.

The coastal regions experience a Medi-terranean climate, but the interior highlands have bitterly cold winters and cool summers. Belgrade, in the north, has hot summers and cold winters. Summer is the wettest season, but there is also plenty of sunshine.

Forests of beech, hornbeam and oak, together with firs and pines at higher levels,

ver about a quarter of the country and farm-
nd and pasture cover more than half.

ECONOMY AND RESOURCES

he main industries are steel, textiles, food
rocessing and wood products. They are
ostly located around Belgrade, the capital.
griculture remains an important activity,
ajor crops include maize, wheat, tobacco
nd sugar beet, while many farmers rear cattle,
gs and sheep. Since 1991 the economy has
een very badly affected by civil wars and UN-
mposed trade sanctions.

HISTORY AND POLITICS

y 1992 Yugoslavia was an almost figmentary
tate, the discredited and politically impotent
ump of the southern Slav union created
nder Allied pressure after World War I.
Known from 1918 as the State of the Serbs,
Croats and Slovenes, and from 1929 as
Yugoslavia ('land of the south Slavs'), the
nity of the state was always under constant
hreat from nationalist and ethnic tensions.
The most serious friction was between the
Serbs, with around 35% of the population the
argest single group, and the neighbouring
Croats with 20%; but Muslims, Slovenes,
Macedonians, Montenegrins, Albanians and
Hungarians also chafed against each other.
Potential flashpoints existed not only where
sections of the Yugoslav patchwork met, but
within each patch itself.

In the interwar period the country was
virtually a 'Greater Serbia', and after Hitler
nvaded in 1941 Yugoslavs fought both the
Germans and each other. The Communist-led
Partisans of 'Tito' (Josip Broz, a Croat)
emerged victorious in 1945, re-forming Yugoslavia as a republic on the Soviet model. The
postwar Tito dictatorship kept antagonisms
out of sight, but in 1990, a decade after his
death, the first free elections since the war saw
nationalist victories in four out of the six
republics that made up the federation.

The formal secession of Slovenia and
Croatia in June 1991 began an irreversible
process of disintegration. Slovenia, the most
ethnically homogeneous of Yugoslavia's com-
ponent republics, made the transition almost
bloodlessly; but the Serbian-dominated federal army launched a brutal campaign against
the Croats, whose territory included a large
and vociferous Serbian minority. The most
destructive conflict in Europe since 1945 continued until January 1992, when the cease-fire
finally held. The fighting then moved to
Bosnia-Herzegovina, declared independent in
1992 and at once the theatre of a multilateral
civil war involving Serbs, Croats and ethnic
Bosnian Muslims.

Expelled from the United Nations in 1992,
'Yugoslavia' thereafter included only Montenegro and Serbia, Serbia's President Slobodan
Milosevic, bolstered by his people's military
successes in Croatia and Bosnia, controlled
most remaining federal resources and was
frequently at loggerheads with an impotent
federal premier.

However, Serbia had problems of its own:
international sanctions struck at an already
war-ravaged economy, while in its supposedly
autonomous Kosovo region in the south-east,
many Albanian-speaking people favour self-
government or even unification with Albania.
[*Map page 17*] ■

AREA 102,173 sq km [39,449 sq mls]
POPULATION 10,763,000
CAPITAL (POPULATION) Belgrade (1,137,000)
GOVERNMENT Federal republic
ETHNIC GROUPS Serb 62%, Albanian 17%,
Montenegrin 5%, Hungarian, Muslim, Croat
LANGUAGES Serbo-Croatian (official)
RELIGIONS Christianity (mainly Serbian
Orthodox, with Roman Catholic and
Protestant minorities), Islam
CURRENCY Yugoslav new dinar = 100 paras

ZAÏRE

The Republic of Zaïre is the world's 12th
largest country. Much of the country lies
within the drainage basin of the huge River
Zaïre, which was formerly called the River
Congo. Mountains rise in the south and east
where Zaïre's borders run through lakes
Tanganyika, Kivu, Edward and Mobutu Sese

Seko (recently renamed Lake Albert). These lakes all lie on the floor of an arm of the Great African Rift Valley.

The Equator passes through northern Zaïre. The equatorial region has high temperatures and high rainfall throughout the year, though in the subtropical south, where Lubumbashi is situated, there is a marked wet and dry season. Dense rainforests grow in northern Zaïre, but, to the south, the forests merge into savanna.

ECONOMY AND RESOURCES

In colonial days, palm and rubber plantations were developed in the equatorial Congo Basin (the world's second largest river drainage system), with mining on the Congo-Zambezi watershed and coffee-growing on the Congo-Nile watershed in the north-east. The Congo (Zaïre) River was developed as a major artery, its rapids and falls by-passed by railways – including the Boyoma (Stanley) railway, the world's most voluminous, and an important railway built from the river port of Kinshasa to the coastal port of Matadi.

Minerals from the 'Copperbelt' in the far south-eastern province of Shaba (formerly Katanga), and refined on the spot, provide much of Zaïre's export income, though shortages of skilled workers and spare parts, gross misgovernment, illegal trade, and dislocation of railway links through Angola, Zimbabwe and Mozambique because of war have all affected revenues.

Most outstanding of many minerals are copper and cobalt, with copper accounting for more than half the country's export earnings, but manganese, tin, gold and diamonds are also important. 'Strategic minerals', including cadmium, also emanate from Shaba. Industry was already substantial at independence, and the massive hydroelectric developments at Inga, below Kinshasa, which supplies power to the mining town of Kolwezi in Shaba, some 1,725 km [1,800 mls] to the south-east, should provide for further expansion under new government policies.

With its massive mineral reserves Zaïre should be among the wealthiest of African nations, but it remains a low-income nation and well inside the world's bottom 20 according to World Bank figures. While transport and communications are difficult in a huge country still dominated by dense rainforest the reasons for Zaïre's plight are almost wholly man-made.

HISTORY AND POLITICS

Formerly made up of several African kingdoms, more recently a Belgian colony, Zaïre and her peoples suffered successively from the slave trade and then the brutal methods and corruption of the Congo Free State (1884–1908), the personal possession of King Leopold II, before Belgium assumed administration until independence was granted in 1960. The country's huge size and small population stretched Belgium's modest resources.

Belgium left the country politically unprepared for its sudden withdrawal, and within days of independence the army mutinied and the richest province, Shaba (Katanga), tried to secede. Then called the Congo, the country invited the UN to intervene, but the appallingly violent civil war lasted three years. In 1965 General Mobutu seized control in a period of sustained confusion and remained in power into the 1990s, declaring a one-party state in 1967 and renaming the nation Zaïre in 1971 as part of a wide-ranging Africanization policy that also brought conflict with the Christian churches.

Mobutu's long dictatorship was a catalogue of repression, inefficiency and corruption in government and unrest, rebellion and poverty among the people, with impenetrably inconsistent policies wreaking havoc in the economy even during the various mineral booms of the 1970s and 1980s, and confused by alternating periods of nationalization and privatization. His reign was one of orchestrated chaos.

On the whole, he was supported by the West, notably France, Belgium and the USA, who valued his strategic minerals and his support to the UNITA rebels in Angola and wanted Zaïre outside the Soviet sphere of influence. But with the end of the Cold War that support evaporated: indeed, the US soon pushed hard for reform. This, combined with increasing protests, finally forced Mobutu in 1990 to concede limited multiparty elections for the summer of 1991. But the new elected leaders faced complete chaos in Kinshasa as thousands rioted against inflation spiralling towards 2,000% a year. French and Belgian

oops were sent in to restore order and evac-
ate European nationals (many of whom had
one very well from the regime), while
Mobutu – who, according to the US State
Department, enjoyed a personal wealth of
about $5 billion, around the same figure as the
ation's debts – tried desperately to cling to
ower. The signs were that Zaïre would soon
become one of the alarming flashpoints of
Africa again. [*Map page 33*] ■

AREA 2,344,885 sq km [905,365 sq mls]
POPULATION 42,552,000
CAPITAL (POPULATION) Kinshasa (3,804,000)
GOVERNMENT Single-party republic
ETHNIC GROUPS Luba 18%, Kongo 16%,
Mongo 14%, Rwanda 10%, Azandi 6%, Bangi
and Ngale 6%, Rundi 4%, Teke, Boa,
Chokwe, Lugbara, Banda
LANGUAGES French (official)
RELIGIONS Christianity (Roman Catholic 48%,
Protestant 29%, indigenous Christian churches
17%), traditional beliefs 3%, Islam 1%
CURRENCY Zaïre = 100 makuta

ZAMBIA

A vast expanse of high plateaux in the
interior of south-central Africa, most
of Zambia (formerly Northern Rhodesia) is
drained by the Zambezi and two of its major
tributaries, the Kafue and the Luangwa. The
latter and the central section of the Zambezi
occupy a low-lying rift valley bounded by
rugged escarpments. Lake Kariba, formed by
damming in 1961 and the second largest
artificial lake in Africa, occupies part of the
floor of this valley. Like the hydroelectric
power it generates, the lake is shared with
Zimbabwe, though power from the Kafue
River now supplements supplies from Kariba.
The magnificent Victoria Falls are similarly
shared between the two countries. Much of
northern Zambia is drained to the Atlantic
Ocean by headwaters of the River Zaïre,
including the Chambeshi, which loses itself

within the vast swamps of the Bangweulu
Depression.

ECONOMY AND RESOURCES

Zambia is one of the world's largest producers
of copper, but despite efforts to diversify, the
economy remains stubbornly dependent (95%
of export earnings in 1989) on this one mineral. The Copperbelt, centred on Kitwe, is the
dominant urban region while the capital,
Lusaka, provides the other major growth pole.
Rural-urban migration has increased markedly
since independence in 1964 – Zambia has
'black' southern Africa's highest proportion of
town-dwellers – but work is scarce.

Commercial farming, concentrated in central regions astride the railway, and mostly
maize, frequently fails to meet the needs of the
growing urban population, but as a landlocked
country heavily dependent on international
trade, Zambia relies on its neighbours for
access to ports via Zimbabwe, Mozambique
and South Africa. Alternatives, notably a railway, highway and oil pipeline to Dar es
Salaam, have been developed, but Zambia
continues to have serious transport problems
compounded by lack of finances.

HISTORY AND POLITICS

European contact with Zambia began in the
19th century, when the explorer David
Livingstone crossed the River Zambezi. In the
1890s, the British South Africa Company, set
up by Cecil Rhodes (1853–1902), the British
financier and statesman, made treaties with
local chiefs and gradually took over the area.
In 1911, the Company named the area
Northern Rhodesia. In 1924, Britain took over
the government of the country.

In 1953, Britain formed a federation of
Northern Rhodesia, Southern Rhodesia (now
Zimbabwe) and Nyasaland (now Malawi). But
local Africans opposed this step, because they
believed that it concentrated power in the
hands of the European minority. The federation was dissolved just ten years later in 1963
and Northern Rhodesia became independent
as Zambia in 1964.

The leading opponent of British rule,
Kenneth Kaunda, became president in 1964.
His government enjoyed reasonable income
until the copper crash of the mid-1970s, but

his collectivist policies failed to diversify the economy (before or after) and neglected agriculture. In 1972, he declared the United Nationalist Independence Party (UNIP) the only legal party, and it was nearly 20 years before democracy returned. In the 1991 elections (conceded by Kaunda after intense pressure in 1990), he was trounced by union leader Frederick Chiluba of the Movement for Multiparty Democracy (MMD) – Kaunda's first challenger in 27 years of post-colonial rule. Chiluba inherited a foreign debt of $4.6 billion – one of the world's biggest per capita figures. [*Map page 33*] ■

AREA 752,614 sq km [290,586 sq mls]
POPULATION 9,196.000
CAPITAL (POPULATION) Lusaka (982,000)
GOVERNMENT Multiparty republic
ETHNIC GROUPS Bemba 34%, Tonga 16%, Malawi 14%, Lozi 9%
LANGUAGES English (official)
RELIGIONS Christianity (Protestant 34%, Roman Catholic 26%, African Christians 8%), traditional beliefs 27%
CURRENCY Kwacha = 100 ngwee

ZIMBABWE

The Republic of Zimbabwe is a landlocked country in southern Africa. Most of the country lies on a high plateau between the Zambezi and Limpopo rivers between 900 m and 1,500 m [2,950 ft to 4,920 ft) above sea level. The main land feature is the High Veld, a ridge crossing Zimbabwe from north-east to south-west. Bordering the High Veld is the Middle Veld, the country's largest region. Below 900 m [2,950 ft] is the Low Veld. The highest land is in the east near the Mozambique border.

In summer, between October and March, the weather is hot and wet, but in winter the daily temperatures vary greatly. Frosts have been recorded between June and August. The climate also varies according to the

altitude – the Low Veld is much warmer an drier than the High Veld.

ECONOMY AND RESOURCES
Zimbabwe's relatively strong economy founded on gold and tobacco but now fa more diverse – evolved its virtual self-suffi ciency during the days of international sanc tions against Smith's white minority regime After 1980 there was a surge in most sectors with successful agrarian policies enabling the nation to supply less endowed well-off neigh bours with food in good years and the exploitation of the country's rich and varie mineral resources. However, a fast-growing population will exert pressure on both land and resources of all kinds in the 1990s. In 1992, the country suffered a terrible drought and had to appeal for foreign aid.

HISTORY AND POLITICS
Formerly Rhodesia (and Southern Rhodesia before 1965), Zimbabwe was nurtured by Britain as a 'white man's country'. When Ian Smith declared UDI in 1965, there were some 280,000 Europeans there. Guerrilla action against the Smith regime soon escalated into a full-scale civil war, eventually forcing a move to black majority rule in 1980. The rift that followed independence, between Robert Mugabe's ruling ZANU and Joshua Nkomo's ZAPU, was healed in 1989 when they finally merged after nearly three decades and Mugabe renounced his shallow Marxist-Leninist ideology. In 1990 the state of emergency that had lasted since 1965 was finally allowed to lapse – three months after Mugabe had secured a landslide election victory. [*Map page 33*] ■

AREA 390,579 sq km [150,873 sq mls]
POPULATION 11,002,000
CAPITAL (POPULATION) Harare (1,189,000)
GOVERNMENT Multiparty republic
ETHNIC GROUPS Shona 71%, Ndebele 16%, other Bantu-speaking Africans 11%, Europeans 2%
LANGUAGES English (official)
RELIGIONS Christianity 45%, traditional beliefs 40%
CURRENCY Zimbabwe dollar = 100 cents

WORLD TOWNS & CITIES

Aachen (Aix-la-Chapelle) Town in western Germany, in North Rhine-Westphalia. Ancient regional centre near border with Netherlands and Belgium, with noted cathedral; place of coronation for Holy Roman Emperors until 1531. In coal mining area; textiles, electronic engineering and food industries. [50° 47'N 6° 4'E]

Abéché Town in east-central Chad; capital of Ouaddaï Prefecture. On main road to Sudan. Old market centre for desert nomad caravans. Groundnuts important. [13° 50'N 20° 35'E]

Aberdeen Capital of Grampian region, north-east Scotland, between mouths of rivers Don and Dee. Important commercial centre, especially for North Sea oil industry. Centre of Scottish fishing industry. Textiles, paper manufacture. University. Resort. [57° 9N 2° 6'W]

Abidjan Former capital and chief port of Ivory Coast, on lowland side of lagoon. Vridi Canal cuts through sand bar; deep-water harbour built 1951. Exports cocoa, coffee, bananas, pineapples. Processes agricultural and forest products; textiles, car assembly; fish canneries. [5° 26'N 3° 58'W]

Abu Dhabi Capital of Abu Dhabi and federal capital of the United Arab Emirates. Sited on island in Arabian Gulf, linked to mainland by Maqta Bridge. Modern city, large port; oil related industries. [24° 28'N 54° 22'E]

Abuja Official capital of Nigeria, south of original town of this name which is now called Sulaija. Replaced Lagos as the federal capital and seat of government in December 1991. [9° 16'N 7° 2'E]

Accra City and port, capital of Ghana, on Gulf of Guinea. Commercial and route centre near narrowest part of coastal plain. Light industry. Focus of air routes. Exports cocoa, manganese, gold. [5° 35'N 0° 6'W]

Ad Dammam Main oil port of Saudi Arabia, on the Arabian Gulf. End of railway from Riyadh. Cement plant. [26° 25'N 50° 6'E]

Adapazari Town in north-west Turkey, on the River Sakarya. Railway junction; agricultural and trade centre. Important silk and linen industries. [40° 48'N 30° 25'E.]

Addis Ababa City and capital of Ethiopia. Rich agricultural area. Terminus of railway line from Djibouti. Large market. Altitude *c.* 2,400 m [8,000 ft]. [9° 2'N 38° 42'E]

Adelaide Seaport, capital of South Australia. The site was selected by Colonel William Light, the first Surveyor-General of South Australia. The vineyards of the Barossa Valley are nearby. [34° 52'N 138° 30'E]

Aden Seaport in southern Yemen, on Gulf of Aden. Formerly the national legislative capital of the People's Democratic Republic of Yemen (South Yemen), prior to unification with the Yemen Arab Republic (North Yemen) in 1990. Linked to Mediterranean by Red Sea and Suez Canal. Imports crude oil, foodstuffs; exports petroleum products, fuel oils, fish. Distribution trade for neighbouring territories: cotton, grain, coffee, hides, consumer goods. [12° 45'N 45° 0'E]

Agadez Town in central Niger, south of Aïr Massif, on the route from Algiers to Kano. Old caravan centre. Market for nomads; leather and wool goods. Uranium deposits to north at Anlit. [16° 58'N 7° 59'E]

Agadir Town on north-west (Atlantic) coast of Morocco. Resort, with fine beaches, rebuilt south of the older city destroyed by an earthquake in 1960. [30° 28'N 9° 55'W]

Agra City in south-west Uttar Pradesh state, northern India, on the River Yamuna. Former seat of the Moghul empire, in the 16th–17th centuries. Site of the Taj Mahal. Important wheat market. Famous for carpets, also gold and silver embroidery. [27° 17'N 77° 58'E]

Ahmadabad City in Gujarat state, western India, on the River Sabarmati. Founded in 1411 by Ahmed Shah. Judicial capital of state; state capital Gandhinagar to north-east. Textiles, especially fine cotton; handicrafts, especially gold and silver ware. Oilfields nearby. Fine mosque. [23° 0'N 72° 40'E]

Ahvaz Commercial town, railway junction and port of western Iran, 129 km [80 mls] north-east of Abadan. The modern town is built over an ancient city. Oil-based industries predominate. [31° 20'N 48° 40'E]

Ajaccio Capital of the island of Corsica, to south-east of France. Resort, fishing port

and commercial centre. The birthplace Napoleon. [41° 55'N 8° 40'E]

Ajmer Ancient walled town in Rajastha state, north-west India, on main road and rai way to Delhi. Place of Muslim pilgrimag 12th-century artificial lake. Railway wor shops. [26° 28'N 74° 37'E]

Aksum Town in north-west Ethiopia, o low-lying hills overlooking the plain. End desert caravan route. Capital of ancier Axumite empire and legendary site of Ark Covenant. [14° 5'N 38° 40'E]

Aktyubinsk (Aqtöbe) Capital of Aktyubins Oblast in north-west Kazakhstan. Chemica food and metallurgical industries, especial nickel. [50° 17'N 57° 10'E]

Akureyri Town in north Iceland at head o Eyjafjördhur, longest fjord in Iceland. Fishin and shipping industries. Tourist centre, es pecially for winter sports. [65° 40'N 18° 6'W

Al Dhahran Major port on The Gulf ir east Saudi Arabia. Business centre adjacent t Dammam in extensive oil region; University o Petroleum and Minerals. [26° 10'N 50° 7'E

Al Hufuf Oasis in the Najd, Saudi Arabia Caravan route from Riyadh to the United Arab Emirates; great mosque and active market. [25° 20'N 49° 34'E]

Al Manamah Port and capital of Bahrain, at northern end of Bahrain Island. Centre for oil industry; boatbuilding, fishing. Modern city. [26° 12'N 50° 38'E]

Albany Port and capital of New York state, north-east USA, at junction of Hudson and Mohawk rivers. Centre of large manufacturing region; textiles, paper and printing, electrical engineering. [42° 39'N 73° 45'W]

Albany Port and regional centre in Western Australia. Site of first settlement in state in 1826. [35° 1'S 117° 58'E]

Albi Town in southern France. Capital of Tarn *département*. Focus of 12th–13th century lbigensian heresy. Noted 13th–14th century rick cathedral. Traditional textile industry; ass and chemicals. [43° 56'N 2° 9'E]

Ìesund Seaport in Norway on west coast. Ìas largest fishing harbour in Norway. Centre f cod and herring fisheries; base for Arctic ealers. [62° 28'N 6° 12'E]

Ìexandria City and major Mediterranean eaport of Egypt to west of Nile Delta. ´ounded 332 BC. Ancient seat of learning. 7th-century mosque. Resort with sandy eaches. [31° 0'N 30° 0'E]

Ìlgiers Capital of Algeria, on the Mediterranean coast. Major port of Barbary States until early l9th century. Fine harbour. Modern ity built on hills with many suburbs. Tourist rade. [36° 42'N 3° 8'E]

Ìlicante Town in south-east Spain. Capital of Alicante province. Commercial centre and port in rich agricultural area (vines, almonds, olives); aluminium, cement and salt industry. Resort. [38° 23'N 0° 30'W]

Alice Springs Town in southern part of Northern Territory, Australia. Transport centre for cattle and minerals. On Stuart Highway north-south link, Darwin to Port Augusta; airport. Tourist centre. [23° 40'S 133° 50'E]

Allahabad Town in southern Uttar Pradesh state, northern India, near confluence of Yamuna and Ganges rivers. Holy city for Hindus, on main routes from Delhi to Calcutta. [25° 25'N 81° 58'E]

Alma-Ata (Almaty) Capital of Kazakhstan. Spacious modern town in scenic surroundings; miscellaneous industries. Academic and scientific centre. Famous for its apple orchards. [43° 15'N 76° 57'E]

Almadén Town in south-central Spain, in Ciudad Real. Ancient centre of mercury mining area in Sierra Morena, with leading world production. [38° 49'N 4° 52'W]

Altdorf Town in central Switzerland between the St Gotthard Pass and Lake Lucerne. Capital of Uri Canton. Known for statue of William Tell. [46° 2'N 8° 6'E]

Amiens Town in northern France, on River Somme. Capital of Somme *département*. Has a magnificent cathedral begun in 1220. Large textile, footwear and food processing industries. [49° 54'N 2° 16'E]

Amman Capital of Jordan, 40 km [25 mls] north-east of the Dead Sea. Historic city. Exports building stone, phosphates and vegetables. [31° 57'N 35° 52'E]

Amritsar Town in west Punjab state, in northern India. Founded in 1577. Centre of the Sikh religion. Golden Temple is covered in gilded copper. Woollen and silk industries and carpet manufacturing. [31° 35'N 74° 57'E]

Amsterdam Port in north-west Netherlands, in Noord Holland. Historic, commercial and cultural centre, known for its concentric canals and diamond industries. Shipbuilding, marine engineering industries; also aircraft, food and printing. [52° 23'N 4° 54'E]

Anchorage Port in Alaska, north-west USA, at head of Cook Inlet. Commercial centre and Alaska's largest town, virtually ice-free. Destroyed by an earthquake in 1964. Base for oil development. Offshore oil production. Salmon processing. [61° 13'N 149° 54'W]

Ancona Seaport in eastern Italy, on a peninsula of the Adriatic Sea. Capital of The Marches. Commercial centre and fishing port; shipbuilding, textile industry, musical instruments manufactured. [43° 37'N 13° 30'E]

Andijon Capital of Andijon Wiloyat, a region in eastern Uzbekistan. Engineering and food industries; cotton produced; oil and gas reserves to the east. [41° 10'N 72° 15'E]

Angarsk Major new town in Siberia, Russia, east of Lake Baykal. Rapidly expanding town, with spacious, planned layout. Oil refining industry. [52° 30'N 104° 0'E]

Angmagssalik Trading post and settlement on east coast of Greenland, 95 km [60 mls] south of the Arctic Circle, on Denmark Strait. US air base; important meteorological and radio station. [65° 40'N 37° 20'W]

Angoulême Town in west France. Capital of Charente *département*. Historic defensive centre. Large paper industry; brewing, agricultural engineering. [45° 39'N 0° 10'E]

Ankara Capital of Turkey, in central Turkey. Republic proclaimed here in 1923. Cultural and administrative centre. Mausoleum of Kemal Ataturk; also notable archaeological remains and museum. [39° 57'N 32° 54'E]

Annapolis Capital of Maryland, eastern USA. Centre of agricultural area on Chesapeake Bay. Oldest US State House (1772); site of Naval Academy. Vegetables, fish processing. [38° 59'N 76° 30'W]

Annecy Town in south-east France. Capital of Haute-Savoie *département*. Picturesque regional and tourist lakeside centre. Metal industries, especially ball bearings; traditional bell-founding. [45° 55'N 6° 8'E]

Antalya Seaport in southern Asiatic Turkey, on Mediterrranean. Founded 2nd century BC. St Paul sailed from here to Antioch on his first missionary journey. [36° 52'N 30° 45'E]

Antananarivo Capital of Madagascar in centre of highland area. Location of Queen's Palace, an ancient monument of the Merina kingdom. Cotton and paper mills, vehicle assembly, fertilizer plant. [18° 55'S 47° 31'E]

Antigua Town in south-central Guatemala. Site of former capital, destroyed by an earthquake in 1773. Coffee and sugar industries. [14° 34'N 90° 41'W]

Antrim Capital of Antrim District, eastern Northern Ireland. Market and linen manufacturing centre on north-east shore of Lough Neagh. [54° 43'N 6° 13'W]

Antwerp (Antwerpen) City and port in northern Belgium at head of Scheldt estuary. Capital of Antwerp province. Historic, commercial and cultural centre with noted

cathedral. Manufacturing industries; as we as non-ferrous metals, diamond processing petrochemical, car assembly and shipbuildin industries. [51° 13'N 4° 25'E]

Anuradhapura Town in north-central S Lanka. On site of capital of ancient kingdom (founded *c.* 437 BC). Many ancient ruins Pilgrimage centre to sacred Buddhist Bo Tree Rice-growing area. [8° 22'N 80° 28'E]

Anzio Fishing port and resort in west-centra Italy, in Lazio, on Mediterranean. Ancien city. Birthplace of Nero. Allied landing i 1944. [41° 28'N 12° 37'E]

Aosta Town in north-west Italy. Capital o Valle d'Aosta. Ancient regional and ecclesiastical centre with many Roman remains Important steel industry and tourist centre. [45° 43'N 7° 20'E]

Apia Capital of Western Samoa, an island group in the Pacific Ocean. Chief port on the northern coast of the volcanic island of Upolu. [13° 50'S 171° 50'W]

Appenzell Town in north-east Switzerland. Capital of Inner Rhoden, half canton of Appenzell. Centre of dairying, with characteristic wooden houses. [47° 20'N 9° 25'E]

Aracaju Port and capital of Sergipe state, on the coast of Brazil between Recife and Salvador. Industry: sugar refining, cotton mills; exports sugar, cotton, hides, rice and coffee. [10° 55'S 37° 4'W.]

Arad Town in western Romania on River Mures. Industrial and commercial centre in agricultural area; products include spirits, machinery, tiles. [46° 10'N 21° 20'E]

Arequipa City of southern Peru. Built on site of ancient Inca city. Important commercial centre. Steel, nylon, plastics, soap. Tourist centre. [16° 20'S 71° 30'W]

Arica Seaport in desert region of north-central Chile. The port for La Serena. Market town; copper; winter station of Chilean army. [18° 32'S 70° 20'W]

rlon Town in south-east Belgium, in the dennes. Capital of Arlon district, Luxemurg province. Roman town, with many mains. Food industries. [49° 42'N 5° 49'E]

rmagh Capital of County Armagh and rmagh District, in the south of Northern eland. Important ancient ecclesiastical cene and the site of the first church of St Patrick. 4° 22'N 6° 40'W]

rnhem Town in eastern Netherlands at lge of Veluwe. Capital of Gelderland. Comercial and route centre, known for battle of 944. Chemical, textile, tin-smelting and shipuilding industries. [51° 58'N 5° 55'E]

rras Town in northern France. Capital of as-de-Calais *département*. Market and manucturing centre, famous for its tapestry. ndustries include agricultural equipment and ugar processing. [50° 17'N 2° 46'E]

rusha Town in north-east Tanzania. ailway terminus; on international road from airo to Cape Town. Agricultural products: offee, wheat, sisal and sugar. Important extile industry. Starting point for safaris into National Parks. [3° 20'S 36° 40'E]

Aschaffenburg Town in central Germany on River Main in Bavaria. Regional centre with alace at foot of Spessart. Precision instruments industry. [49° 58'N 9° 8'E]

Ashdod Port and commercial centre in southern Israel with deep-water harbour. Ancient Philistine city. [31° 49'N 34° 35'E]

Ashkhabad (Ashgabat) Capital of Turkmenistan, near border with Iran. Rebuilt to withstand earthquakes since 1948 disaster. Silk, cotton and carpets.[38° 0'N 57° 50'E]

Asmara (Asmera) Capital of Eritrea. Ancient ruins. Textiles. Altitude 2,300 m [7,600 ft] above sea level. [15° 19'N 38° 55'E]

Assisi Town in north-central Italy, in Umbria. Walled town and place of pilgrimage associated with St Francis and St Clare. Tourist centre. [43° 4'N 12° 36'E]

Astrakhan Town in Russia, on Volga delta, inland from Caspian Sea. Major fishing port. [46° 25'N 48° 5'E]

Asunción Capital of Paraguay, situated on the east bank of the Paraguay River. Important transport centre; textiles, food products, footwear. [25° 0'S 57° 30'N]

Aswân Town in upper valley of River Nile in Egypt, near first cataract. Aga Khan mausoleum. Nearby Aswân Dam and the Aswân High Dam, opened in 1971, and forming Lake Nasser to south. [24° 4'N 32° 57'E]

Ath Thawrah New town in northern Syria, on the Euphrates River. Associated with Lake Assad, reservoir completed in 1970s for agricultural irrigation and hydroelectric power. [35° 50'N 38° 30'E]

Athens (Athínai) Capital of Greece and of department of Attica on Attica peninsula. Ancient centre of Greek civilization, with many antiquities, including the Acropolis (Parthenon, Propylaea, Erechtheion), the Olympieion, Hadrian's Arch, and many important museums. [37° 58'N 23° 46'E]

Atlanta Capital of the state of Georgia and largest city of south-east USA. Commercial, manufacturing and route centre, especially for air traffic. Important car- and aircraft-assembly industry; food production; printing and publishing. [33° 45'N 84° 23'W]

Auckland Town on Tamaki Isthmus, North Island, New Zealand. Original capital 1840–52. Many extinct volcanoes in vicinity. Main industrial and commercial area of New Zealand. Extensive suburbs. Intensive dairy and farming hinterland. [36° 52'S 174° 46'E]

Augsburg Town in southern Germany, in Bavaria. Ancient trading centre, formerly important for banking. Known for the Fuggerei, an old city quarter, established in 1519. Large textile industry; also electrical engineering. [48° 21'N 10° 54'E]

Aurangabad Town in Maharashtra state, west-central India, on Deccan plateau.

Administrative centre. Caves nearby with sculptures. Centre for visiting Ellora and Ajanta cave temples; wall paintings at Ajanta. [19° 50'N 75° 23'E]

Avignon Town in south-east France on Rhône River. Capital of Vaucluse *département*. Papal residence in 14th century; famous for its bridge. Centre of wine producing area; canning; textile industry. [43° 57'N 4° 50'E]

Ávila Town in central Spain. Capital of Ávila province. Highest Spanish provincial capital at 1,128 m [3,700 ft]. Famous for 11th-century walls. Birthplace of St Teresa. Textile and food industries. [40° 39'N 4° 43'W]

Ayacucho Tourist centre in Andes, south-central Peru. Silver and lead mines nearby. Capital of Ayacucho province. Site of last great battle in the war of independence (1824) nearby. [13° 0'S 74° 0'W]

Az Zarqa (Zarca) Second largest town in Jordan, north-east of Amman. Refining, tanning. Route centre. [32° 10'N 35° 37'E]

Baalbek Town in central Lebanon. It is near the site of the vast ruins of the ancient city of Heliopolis. Unique Phoenician, Roman, Greek and Arab remains. [34° 0'N 36° 12'E]

Babylon Extensive remains of ancient city in central Iraq, near Euphrates River, and the modern town of Al Hillah. Hanging Gardens of Babylon were an ancient wonder of the world. [32° 40'N 44° 30'E]

Badajoz Town in south-east Spain near Portuguese border. Capital of Badajoz province. Site of many battles. Fertilizer and textile industries. [38° 50'N 6° 59'W]

Baden Baden Town in south-western Germany, in Baden-Württemberg. International resort, spa and conference centre in wine producing area. [48° 45'N 8° 15'E]

Baden Town in north-central Switzerland in Aargau canton on Limmat River. Historic defensive centre and spa. Engineering, especially railway industry. [47° 28'N 8° 18'E]

Badulla Town in south-central Sri Lanka, highland area. Important tea-growing regio? Approached by railway through spectacul? scenery. [7° 1'N 81° 7'E]

Baghdad Capital of Iraq, at the head ? shallow-draft navigation on the Tigris Rive? Important transport centre with railway an? airline systems; also textile industry an? tobacco products. [33° 20'N 44° 30'E]

Bahawalpur Town in eastern Pakistan, o? Sutlej River, crossed by fine railway bridg? Commercial and light industrial centr? Textiles manufactured. [29° 24'N 71° 40'E]

Bahía Blanca Naval port on the coast ? central Argentina. Industries include o? refining, meat-packing, tanning and flo? milling. Exports include hides, grain an? wool. [38° 35'S 62° 13'W]

Baku Capital of Azerbaijan. Major port o? Caspian Sea, notable for extensive oil indus? try. Founded in 8th century and rich i? historic monuments. [40° 25'N 49° 45'E]

Baltimore Seaport in Maryland, easter? USA. Major commercial, industry and educa? tional centre. Large steel, shipbuilding an? food industries; aircraft parts, car assembly? chemicals. [39° 17'N 76° 37'W]

Bamako Capital of Mali, on River Niger i? south-west near Guinea border. Founded b? French in 1883. River port and administrativ? centre. Niger navigable south to Kouroussa? Dam for irrigation. [12° 34'N 7° 55'W]

Bamian Ancient city in north-east Afghani? stan, in valley north of Koh-i-Baba mountain? range. Ruins of great towers and cave? dwellings. Two Buddhist figures (AD 630)? nearby. [35° 0'N 67° 0'E]

Bandar Seri Begawan Capital of Brunei in north-west of Borneo, 20 km [12 mls] from mouth of Brunei River. Formerly Brunei Town. [4° 52'N 115° 0'E]

Bandung Indonesian city in west-central Java. Headquarters of several government departments. Produces aircraft, ammunition, quinine. Tourist centre. [6° 54'S 107° 36'E]

Banff Town in south-west Canada, in Alberta. Tourist centre for the Rocky Mountains and the large national and forest parks nearby. [51° 10'N 115° 34'W]

Bangalore Capital of Karnataka state, in southern India, on the Deccan plateau. Railway junction. Industry centre; machine tools; aircraft industry; electronics; porcelain; textiles. Tata Institute of Science. Kular goldfields to east. [12° 59'N 77° 40'E]

Bangkok Port and capital of Thailand, on the Chao Phraya River about 32 km [20 mls] above its mouth on Gulf of Thailand. Also serves Laos. Industries include textiles, building materials, motor and radio assembly. Exports include teak, rice. Famous floating market. [13° 45'N 100° 35'E]

Bangui Capital of the Central African Republic, on the River Ubangi at the head of navigation from Brazzaville. On a main north-south African route. Sawmills and textile mills; produces cotton. [4° 23'N 18° 35'E]

Banjul Port and capital of the Gambia. Situated on eastern tip of St Mary's Island on estuary of Gambia River. Founded in 1819 as military post to help stamp out slave trade. Exports groundnuts. [13° 28'N 16° 40'W]

Barcelona City in north-east Spain. Capital of Barcelona province and Catalonia region. Focus of Catalan separatism and culture. Seat of governemnt in Civil War 1936–9. Famous for its wide avenues, cathedral, palaces, 15th-century university. Leading Spanish seaport and commercial and manufacturing centre. Textile, transport equipment, paper and chemical industries. [41° 21'N 2° 10'E]

Barisal Town in Bangladesh, south of Dacca on the delta of the Ganges and Brahmaputra Rivers. Suffers from cyclones and tidal waves. Industries include boat-building and wood working; as well as the manufacture of bricks and soap. Exports rice, jute, oilseed and grain products. [22° 5'N 90° 20'E]

Barranquilla Port in northern Colombia, on Magdalena River. Accessible to ocean-going vessels. Industries include chemicals and pharmaceuticals; products include flour, rubber goods and footwear. [11° 0'N 74° 50'W]

Basel Town in north-west Switzerland on the border with France and Germany, comprising the half-canton of Basel Stadt. Historic commercial centre, noted for banking, and a port at the head of navigation on the Rhine. Large pharmaceutical industry; machinery; and food processing. [47° 35'N 7° 35'E]

Basra Port in south-west Iraq, 110 km [70 mls] from the Arabian Gulf on the Shatt al Arab Waterway. Exports dates, cereal, wool and oil. [30° 30'N 47° 50'E]

Basse-Terre Town and port, administrative capital of the French Overseas Department of Guadeloupe, Lesser Antilles in the West Indies. [16° 0'N 61° 44'W]

Bassein Port in lower Burma, 113 km [70 mls] from mouth of Bassein River, 151 km [94 mls] east of Rangoon. Exports rice and manufactures pottery. [16° 45'N 94° 30'E]

Bastia Largest town and port of Corsica, on east coast. Fishing, food and tobacco processing. Resort. [42° 40'N 9° 30'E]

Bata Main town and port of Mbini, mainland Equatorial Guinea, on Gulf of Guinea. Timber exports. [1° 57'N 9° 50'E]

Bath City in Avon, south-west England. Ancient spa with famous Roman baths and Pump Room (1795). Planned Georgian centre. Annual Festival. University (1966). Electrical engineering. [51° 22'N 2° 22'W]

Baton Rouge Capital of Louisiana, southern USA, on Mississippi River. Important river port. Commercial, industrial and route centre at northern end of 161 km [100 mls] petro-chemical complex. Food processing; aluminium smelter. [30° 27'N 91° 1'W]

Bayeux Town in northern France, in Calvados *département*. Historic and regional centre, famous for tapestry depicting Norman conquest of England. [49° 17'N 0° 42'W]

Béchar Settlement in western Algeria, near the frontier with Morocco. The town is at the start of the important trans-Saharan route to the south. [31° 38'N 2° 18'W]

Beijing (Peking) Capital and municipality of north China. Contains historic walled city dating from Kublai Khan, and old imperial palace of Mings and Manchus, formerly 'Forbidden City', now museum and major tourist attraction. Red Square, scene of political meetings and demonstrations. Residential and educational development to west. Industry concentrated to east. [39° 55'N 116° 20'E]

Beira (Bayrut) Important river port in Mozambique. Terminus of rail links to Zimbabwe, Zambia and Malawi; handles trade for interior. Timber, rice, sugar and bananas. [19° 50'S 34° 52'E]

Beirut Port and capital of Lebanon, situated on a promontory. Engineering, food processing and textiles; several universities and colleges. Economy disrupted by sectarian war (1975–91). [33° 53'N 35° 31'E]

Belém Chief port of the River Amazon basin, on the River Para. Located south of the mouths of the Amazon, in northern Brazil. Exports include timber, nuts, rubber, rice and jute. [1° 20'S 48° 30'W]

Belfast Capital of Northern Ireland, on Belfast Lough at mouth of River Lagan. Major commercial and industrial centre in area of 16th- and 17th-century English and Scottish settlement. Shipbuilding, aircraft machinery, textile industries. [54° 35'N 5° 56'W]

Belfort Historic fortress town in eastern France. Capital of Belfort *département*. Important route centre between the Vosges and Jura mountains. Large engineering industries; textiles. [47° 38'N 6° 50'E]

Belgrade Capital of the former Yugoslavia (inside Serbia) and now the capital of what remains of Yugoslavia (namely Serbia and

Montenegro). River port at the confluenc of the Danube and Sava rivers. Strateg site occupied by Romans, Huns, Byzantine Turks, Hungarians and Serbians. Industria cultural and communications centre. Variou industries. [44° 50'N 20° 37'E]

Belize City Town and port, former capita of Belize, on Caribbean coast. Exports sugar bananas, citrus fruits, fish, forestry products [17° 25'N 88° 0'W]

Belmopan Town, since 1970 the capital o Belize, in Central America, 80 km [50 mls inland to west of Belize City, the former capital. [17° 13'N 88° 48'W]

Belo Horizonte City in east Brazil, 354 km [220 mls] north of Rio de Janeiro. Capita of Minas Gerais state. Centre of agricultura and mining area producing iron, manganese, cotton and cattle and iron and steel. Also diamond-cutting and chemical industries. [19° 55'S 43° 56'W]

Benghazi (Banghazi) Town in Cyrenaica province, on eastern part of Mediterranean coast of Libya. First settled by Greeks. Rapid population growth since Saharan oil discoveries. [32° 11'N 20° 3'E]

Benin City Town and administrative centre in southern Nigeria to west of Niger delta. Site of ancient city dating back to 10th century. River port of Sapele to south. Rubber and palm oil production. [6° 20'N 5° 31'E]

Bergen Seaport in south-west Norway. Former Hanseatic port. Birthplace of Grieg. Fishing, shipbuilding industry. Area of highest rainfall in Norway. [60° 23'N 5° 20'E]

Berlin City in and joint capital of Germany, formerly enclave in East Germany since 1945 with wall dividing East and West Berlin, until reunification between East and West Germany in 1990. Due to take over as capital in 2000. Major commercial and cultural centre. Large electrical and precision engineering industry; printing and publishing. [52° 32'N 13° 24'E]

Bern Capital of Switzerland and of Bern

nton. Picturesque and historic defensive
ntre in loop of Aare River. Known for its
ck tower, bear pit and many museums.
extiles; chocolate; printing and publishing
dustry. Tourist centre. [46° 57'N 7° 28'E]

esançon Town in eastern France at the foot
the Jura Mountains. Capital of Doubs
partement. Historic fortress. Centre of the
ench watch and clock industries. Also
xtiles and brewing. [47° 15'N 6° 2'E]

ethlehem (Bayt Lahm) Town in the West
ank, formerly part of Jordan, under Israeli
dministration since 1967. Located 8 km
i mls] south-south-west of Jerusalem. Reput-
d birthplace of Christ. [31° 43'N 35° 12'E]

hadgaon (Bhaktapur) Hindu religious town
3 km [8 mls] east of Kathmandu in Nepal.
1any temples. [27° 41'N 85° 26'E]

hopal   Town and capital of Madhya
radesh state, central India. Situated on a
mall lake and enclosed by a wall. Site of the
alace of the Nawab. Large mosque. Location
f major industrial disaster in 1984 in which
:. 2,500 people died. [23° 20'N 77° 30'E]

ialystok   Town in north-eastern Poland.
ndustrial centre specializing in textiles; rail-
vay. Baroque town hall. [53° 10'N 23° 10'E]

Birmingham City, capital of West Midlands,
vest-central England. Important commercial,
manufacturing and route centre with many
:anals. Major metal-working industry, arms,
cars; chocolate (Bournville 'model' estate
established 1879); traditional jewellery manufacturing. [52° 30'N 1° 55'W]

Bishkek Capital of Kyrgyzstan. Formerly
known as Frunze. Long history; academic
centre. Rapidly expanding, largely on planned
20th-century layout. [42° 54'N 74° 46'E]

Bissau Capital and port of Guinea-Bissau,
on northern shore of River Geba. Once centre
of slave trade. [11° 45'N 15° 45'W]

Bizerta Town and port on northern coast of
Tunisia. Originally fortified Phoenician port,

former French naval base. Orchard area.
Exports minerals and agricultural products.
[37° 15'N 9° 50'E]

Blackpool Town in Lancashire, north-west
England. Major seaside resort on western
Fylde coast. Famed for tower and illumina-
tions. [53° 48'N 3° 3'W]

Bloemfontein Capital of Orange Free State,
South Africa. Seat of Appeal Court and
administrative centre of South Africa. To the
north-west are the rich gold-fields centred on
Welkom. Centre of major maize producing
area. [29° 6'S 26° 7'E]

Blois Town in central France on Loire River.
Capital of Loir-et-Cher *département*. Has
noted château. Centre of wine- and vegetable
producing area. [47° 35'N 1° 20'E.]

Bobo Dioulasso   Town in south-west
Burkina Faso. Former capital (of Upper
Volta), on railway from Ouagadougou to
Abidjan, Ivory Coast. Road junction. Market
centre for groundnuts, cotton and cattle.
Some industry. [11° 8'N 4° 13'W.]

Bogor Town in west-central Java, Indonesia.
Palace, former residence of the Governor-
General. Rubber factory; textiles, footwear. In
area producing tea, coffee, rice, sugar and rubber. Botanical gardens. [6° 34'S 106° 45'E]

Bogotá Capital of Colombia. Situated in
basin of the Cordillera Oriental over 2,700 m
[8,860 ft] above sea level. Tobacco, chemicals,
food processing. [4° 34'N 74° 0'W]

Bologna   Town in northern Italy. Commercial and route centre with oldest European
university (established AD 425); trade fair.
Railway engineering, agricultural machinery,
food industries. [44° 30'N 11° 20'E]

Bombay   Port and capital of Maharashtra
state, western India. Portuguese colony founded on islands off coast of Arabian Sea. Ceded
to British in 1661. Fine harbour; navy headquarters. Industrial centre, especially cotton
mills, motor vehicles. Exports cotton. Famous
for jewellery, wood-carving and lacquer work.

In May 1995, Hindu nationalists changed the name to Mumbai, but this has not been widely adopted. [18° 55'N 72° 50'E]

Bonn Joint capital of Germany (with Berlin until the year 2000, when Berlin will take over as the capital), in North Rhine-Westphalia, on west bank of River Rhine. Birthplace of Beethoven. Printing and publishing; furniture industry. [50° 43'N 7° 6'E]

Bordeaux Seaport in south-west France at head of Gironde estuary. Capital of Gironde *département*. Commercial centre of famous wine producing region, with large traditional wine trade. Industries include food processing, chemicals and aircraft engineering. Tourist centre. [44° 50'N 0° 36'W]

Boston Seaport and capital of Massachusetts, in north-eastern USA. Commercial and educational centre of New England. American Revolution began here. Important electrical engineering industries, especially electronics and transport equipment. Printing and publishing; important wool market; textiles; fishing. [42° 22'N 71° 4'W]

Bouaké City in central Ivory Coast. Market centre on plateau; forest to south, savanna to north. On railway from Abidjan to Burkina Faso. Light industry. [7° 40'N 5° 2'W]

Boulogne-sur-Mer Seaport in northern France, in Pas-de-Calais *département*. Leading French fishing port and cross-channel ferry port. [50° 42'N 1° 36'E]

Brasília Capital of Brazil, built for this purpose in 1960 on a tributary of the Tocantins River, in east-central Brazil. Modern architecture; main employment is in government service. [15° 47'S 47° 55'W]

Bratislava Town in Slovak Republic near Austrian and Hungarian borders. Dates back to 9th century, capital of Hungary 1541–1784. 13th-century Gothic cathedral, Church of the Franciscans, Parliament House; Slovak University. Significant as river port and railway centre, with trade in wine and grain and extensive industry. [48° 10'N 17° 17'E]

Brazzaville Capital of Congo, on north shore of Pool Malebo on Congo (Zaïre) River opposite the city of Kinshasa. Former capital of French Equatorial Africa. Rail/river transport port. Light industry. [4° 09'S 15° 12'E]

Bremen Port in north-west Germany at head of Weser estuary. Capital of Bremen Land and oldest German maritime city. Important raw materials trade. Important industries include steel, shipbuilding, food processing and aircraft engineering. [53° 4'N 8° 47'E]

Brest Capital of Brest Oblast in Belarus. As Brest-Litovsk, was famous for 1918 treaty between the former USSR and Germany. [52° 10'N 23° 40'E]

Bridgetown Town and port, capital of Barbados, West Indies, on west coast. Exports sugar, rum and molasses. Tourist centre. [13° 5'N 59° 30'W]

Brisbane Seaport, capital of Queensland, Australia. Founded as penal settlement in 1824. Fine setting between edge of uplands and coast. Warm, temperate climate. Port and heavy industry lie along Brisbane River below city centre. Oil refining. [27° 25'S 153° 2'E]

Bristol Capital of Avon, south-west England. Historic commercial centre and former important city-port on River Avon. John and Sebastian Cabot sailed to Newfoundland from here in 1497. Aircraft and confectionery industries. [51° 26'N 2° 35'W]

Brno Town in south-eastern Czech Republic. Has 16th-century town hall and 15th-century cathedral. Centre of textile industry, also manufacturing hardware, chemicals, beer, leather. [49° 10'N 16° 35'E]

Bruges (Brugge) Capital of West Flanders, in north-west Belgium. Historic textile trade centre, associated with Hanseatic League. Known for canals and traditional lace-making. Electrical engineering industry. Tourist centre. [51° 13'N 3° 13'E]

Brussels (Brussel, Bruxelles) Capital of Belgium on Senne River. Commercial and cul-ral centre. Headquarters of many international bodies, including European Union executive and NATO. Steel, car assembly, pharmaceuticals and publishing industries. Famed for its lace. [50° 51'N 4° 21'E]

Bucharest Capital of Romania on Dimbovita River near Bulgarian border. Residence of rulers of Wallachia from 14th century and capital of Romania since 1861. Major industrial and commercial centre, also focus of ecclesiastical and cultural life. Flour milling, oil refining, tanning; metal goods, textiles and chemicals. [44° 27'N 26° 10'E]

Budapest Capital of Hungary, comprising the towns of Buda and Pest, united in 1872. Has 19th-century Basilica of St Stephen and 13–15th century Coronation Church of St Matthias. Commercial, industrial, political and financial centre. Trades in grain, wine, cattle and hides. Also flour milling, brewing, iron and steel, engineering, telecommunications, precision instruments and clocks; large oil refineries. [47° 29'N 19° 5'E]

Buenos Aires Capital and chief seaport of Argentina on the Rio de la Plata. Industries include meat processing, flour milling and brewing; also local natural gas and petroleum products. Main exports grain, beef and wool. [34° 40'S 58° 20'W]

Bujumbura Capital of Burundi and lake port at northern end of Lake Tanganyika. Capital of former Ruandi-Urundi. Near River Ruzizi hydroelectric scheme. Industry centre; railway to Tanzania and Zaïre. Airport. Exports coffee, cotton and tea. [3° 16'S 29° 18'E]

Bukhara (Bukhoro) Capital of Bukhara Oblast in southern Uzbekistan. Ancient cultural centre of central Asia with many historic buildings. [39° 48'N 64° 25'E]

Bulawayo Town in south-west Zimbabwe. On main railway to South Africa through Botswana and route centre for agricultural area. Centre for sugar refining. Asbestos mining to the east. [20° 7'S 28° 32'E]

Burgos Town in northern Spain. Capital of Burgos province and first capital of Old Castile. Famous cathedral. Iron founding, ceramics and photographic equipment industries. [42° 21'N 3° 41'W]

Bursa Town in north-western Turkey and capital of ancient Bithynia. Greek and Armenian archbishopric. Famous for silk, gold and silver work, carpets, tapestry and wood products. [40° 15'N 29° 5'E]

Caernarfon Market town in Gwynedd, north-west Wales. Ancient defensive centre with large, well-preserved castle (built 1285–1322) at south-west end of Menai Straits. [53° 8'N 4° 17'W]

Caerphilly Market town in Mid Glamorgan, south Wales. Regional centre north of Cardiff. Former major cheese producer. Site of an unusual large 13th-century 'concentric' castle. [51° 34'N 3° 13'W]

Cagliari Seaport in Italy, capital of Sardinia, on south coast. Ferry and fishing port; university. Food, chemicals and cement industries. Tourist centre. [39° 15'N 9° 06'E]

Cairns Port in Queensland, Australia. Bulk sugar port and tourist centre for Great Barrier Reef. [16° 57'S 145° 45'E]

Cairo City, capital of Egypt to south of Nile delta. Largest city in Africa. Founded AD 640; university (AD 972). Many fine mosques and historic buildings. Modern 'Tower of Cairo'. [30° 1 N 31° 14'E]

Calais Seaport in northern France, in Pas-de-Calais *département*. Historic defensive centre; leading French cross-channel ferry port. Textile industry. [50° 57'N 1° 56'E]

Calcutta Port, capital of West Bengal state and second largest city in India, on Hooghly river. West of Ganges Delta, near Bangladesh border on east. Warren Hastings was first Governor of British India here in 1772. Commercial centre. Industries include textiles, especially jute; sugar refining, paper. Exports: jute, tea, coal. Massive overcrowding problem. [22° 36'N 88° 24'E]

Calgary Town in south-west central Canada in Alberta. Important commercial centre for oil and natural gas industry. Meat-packing, grain milling, manufacture industries. Famous for ranching. [51° 5'N 114° 10'W]

Callao Seaport in western Peru. Handles most of Peru's imports and a quarter of the country's exports. Fishing, meat-packing, flour milling, brewing, sugar refining, metal goods. [12° 0'S 77° 0'W]

Cambridge Capital of Cambridgeshire, eastern England; market and ancient university town on River Cam, south of Fens. First college founded 1284; many beautiful buildings, including King's College Chapel. Electronics and engineering industries. [52° 13'N 0° 8'E]

Canberra Capital of Australia, in the north-east of the Australian Capital Territory in the Great Dividing Range. Seat of government. [35° 15'S 149° 8'E]

Canea Seaport in Greece, on north-west coast of Crete. Capital of Canea department and (since 1841) of Crete. Flourishing city under Venetians. [35° 30'N 24° 4'E]

Cannes Seaport in south-east France on the Côte d'Azur in Alpes-Maritimes *département*. Fashionable resort established in the mid-l9th century. Annual international film festival in April–May. [43° 32'N 7° 1'E]

Canterbury Cathedral city in Kent, south-east England. Ancient regional centre; metropolitan city of Christian Church since AD 597, with magnificent cathedral associated with St Thomas à Becket. University of Kent. Major tourist centre. [51° 17'N 1° 5'E]

Canton City in south-east China and capital of Guangdong province. Foreign trade with Europe since 1516. Centre of river trade up Xi Jiang River; trunk rail from north and to Hong Kong. Sugar refining, newsprint, cement, shipbuilding and chemical industries. [23° 5'N 113° 10'E]

Cap Haïtien Town in Haiti. West Indies, on north coast. Centre of region of first settle-

ment and former capital. Sugar and sisal lowland area, coffee and cocoa on hill slope [19° 40'N 72° 20'W]

Cape Coast Town on coast of Ghana, we of Accra. Former capital of British colon Administrative and educational centr Historic buildings. [5° 5'N 1° 15'W]

Cape Town Seaport, capital of Wester Cape province and joint capital, with Pretor and Bloemfontein, of South Africa. Situate on fine site on bay of south-west coast c South Africa, with Table Mountain in back ground. Founded in 1652. Legislative an commercial centre and seat of government with many resorts around Cape Peninsula [33° 55'S 18° 22'E]

Caracas Capital of Venezuela, in the north Lies in basin at 900 m [3,000 ft]; its port is L Guaira. Commercial centre for oil. Textiles glassware, pharmaceuticals, chemicals, foo processing; universities. [10° 30'N 66° 55'W

Carcassonne Town in southern France Capital of Aude *département*. 11th–13th century castle and walled town. Market centre in wine producing area. [43° 13'N 2° 20'E]

Cardiff Capital of South Glamorgan, south Wales, and of Wales since 1955. Port at mouth of River Taff; commercial and educational centre with many parks. Includes cathedral city of Llandaff. Once major steam coal exporter; now iron and grain imports, with large flour industry. [51° 28'N 3° 11'W]

Carlisle Capital of Cumbria, north-west England. Commercial and manufacturing centre on Eden River, at western end of Hadrian's Wall. At forefront, in the past, of Anglo-Scottish border disputes. Industries: agricultural equipment; textiles and food, especially dairy products. [54° 54'N 2° 55'W]

Cartago Town in central Costa Rica, at the base of the Irazu volcanic peak. Capital of Costa Rica until 1823. Route centre. Coffee and cattle area. [9° 50'N 83° 55'W]

Casablanca Major port and commercial city

n north-west coast of Morocco. Serves wide nterland. Fish processing, textiles. Export of hosphates important. [33° 36'N 7° 36'W]

assino Town in central Italy, in Lazio. ncient cultural and defensive centre with bbey established by St Benedict AD 529. 'own and abbey rebuilt after destruction in 944. [41° 30'N 13° 50'E]

Castellón de la Plana Town in eastern pain and capital of Castellón province. Centre of citrus and wine producing area. Also ugar and olive processing; rope and tile ndustries. [39° 58'N 0° 3'W]

Cayenne Capital of French Guiana, on an sland off the Atlantic coast of South America. Penal colonies from 1854 to 1938. Exports hrimps and gold. [5° 5'N 52° 18'W]

Ceanannus Mór (Kells) Town in County Meath, Leinster province, in east of Republic of Ireland. Regional centre at site of monastery established by St Columba in 6th century; known for 8th–9th century illuminated Book of Kells. [53° 42'N 6° 53'W]

Cebu Second largest city in the Philippines, and capital of Cebu Island, on its east coast. One of the most important ports in Far East and Pacific area. Industry includes manufacturing cement and pottery; exports hemp, copra, cement. [10° 18'N 123° 54'E]

Cekhira Oil port on Gulf of Gabès, eastern Tunisia linked by pipeline from oilfields near Edjeleh, in the Sahara. [34° 20'N 10° 5'E]

Ceuta Town Spanish possession on northern peninsula of Morocco, separated from Gibraltar by narrow strait. [35° 52'N 5° 18'W]

Chandigarh City in India below Siwalik Hills and capital of both Punjab and Haryana states. Modern planned city, built in the 1950s; planned by Le Corbusier after partition in 1947, when the old capital of Punjab came within Pakistan. [30° 43'N 76° 47'E]

Chardzhou Town in eastern Turkmenistan. Transport centre with rail link, on Amudarya

River. Textile industry. [39° 06'N 63° 34'E]

Charleston Seaport in South Carolina, in south-eastern USA. Commercial centre, naval and air base. Preserved colonial city. Wood processing, fertilizer and shipbuilding industries. [32° 46'N 79° 56'W]

Chartres Town in northern France. Capital of Eure-et-Loire *département*. Famous for its 12th-century cathedral with stained glass. [48° 29'N 1° 30'E]

Chelyabinsk City in southern Urals, Russia. Route centre, with many light and heavy industry, notably iron and steel, mostly based on local raw materials, including lignite and a rich variety of metals. Rapid recent expansion. [55° 10'N 61° 24'E]

Chengdu Capital of Sichuan province in central south-west China. Major industrial centre on the north-west edge of the Sichuan (Red) Basin. Electronic industry and instrument making. [30° 38'N 104° 2'E]

Cherbourg Port in north-west France on north coast of Cotentin Peninsula. Transatlantic and cross-channel ferry port. Shipbuilding industry. [49° 38'N 1° 37'W]

Chernovtsy (Chernivtsi) Town in Ukraine, capital of Chernovtsy (Chernivtsi) Oblast. Attractively planned in 19th century; agricultural industries. [48° 15'N 25° 52'E]

Cheyenne Capital of Wyoming, in western USA. Commercial and route centre; livestock market and large rodeo. [41° 8'N 104° 49'W]

Chiang Mai Town in north-east Thailand, in fertile valley of Ping River, surrounded by mountains. Railway terminus. Centre of peak trade. Famous temple. [18° 48'N 98° 59'E]

Chiba City and capital of Chiba prefecture in Honshu, Japan. Industrial centre on east Tokyo Bay. Giant shipyard, oil refining, aluminium, iron and steel. [35° 30'N 140° 7'E]

Chicago City in Illinois, in north-central USA, at south-western end of Lake Michigan.

Major commercial, industrial, cultural and route centre. Grew as a processing centre for meat and grain; now steel products are as important. Locomotives, rolling stock, aircraft parts, machinery; oil refining, chemicals, printing and publishing. [41° 53'N 87° 38'W]

Chihuahua Town in northern Mexico and capital of Chihuahua state. Administrative and mining centre; silver and zinc mines in area. Timber, cattle and meat-packing industries are important. [28° 40'N 106° 03'W]

Chimkent (Shymkent) Capital of Kazakhstan, in the south, in the Syrdarya basin. Founded in 12th century. Now has varied heavy and light industry. [42° 8'N 69° 36'E]

Chittagong Seaport in Bangladesh, 16 km [10 mls] from the Bay of Bengal on the Karnafuli River, 217 km [135 mls] south-east of Dacca. Industries include engineering, chemicals, flour, rice, oil and timber milling. Soap, candles and bricks are manufactured. Exports include tin, rice, jute, sugar and oilseed. [22° 19'N 91° 48'E]

Chongjin Capital of province of North Hamgyong in North Korea, on the east coast, about 220 km (140 mls) south-west of Vladivostok, Russia. Chief port and industrial centre. Manufacture of steel, pig-iron and matches. Fish processing industry. Exports include timber, iron, fish and cotton textiles. [41° 47'N 129° 50'E]

Christchurch Town in South Island, New Zealand, on River Avon on east coast. Major commercial and manufacturing centre. Important for wheat, grain, wool and lamb. [43° 33'S 172° 47'E]

Cirebon Port on the northern coast of Java in Indonesia. Handicrafts centre. The Chinese temple is one of the oldest in Indonesia. [6° 45'S 108° 32'E]

Cochin Port on Arabian Sea coast, Kerala state, southern India. Earliest European settlement in India (by Portuguese in 1502). Coir industry and fishing industry are important. [9° 59'N 76° 22'E]

Coimbra Town in central Portugal. Ancient regional and cultural centre with university established 1308; first capital of Portugal. Textile, tanning industry. [40° 15'N 8° 27'W]

Coleraine Port in County Londonderry, in the north of Northern Ireland. Manufacturing and university centre near mouth of River Bann. Clothing, especially shirts, engineering and food industries. [55° 8'N 6° 40'W]

Cologne Town in western Germany, in North Rhine-Westphalia on west bank of River Rhine. Historic regional centre of the Rhineland, with famous cathedral and reconstructed old town. In major lignite-mining area. Large engineering industry especially cars; rolling stock; petrochemicals. Known for Eau de Cologne. [50° 56'N 6° 58'E]

Colombo Capital of Sri Lanka, on west coast. Portuguese settlers in 16th century. Dutch 1656; succeeded by British 1796. Artificial harbour. International port and commercial centre. Exports tea, rubber, coconut products. Tourist trade along coastal area, especially to south. [6° 56'N 79° 58'E]

Colón Town in Panama at Caribbean end of Panama Canal, Central America. Commercial centre. Cristóbal, twin town nearby, is port of entry for Canal. Railway to Panama City. [9° 20'N 79° 54'W]

Compiègne Town in northern France, in Oise *département*. Site of imprisonment of Joan of Arc and of signing of armistice of 1918 and French surrender in 1940. [49° 24'N 2° 50'E]

Conakry Port, capital of Guinea, situated on south coast. Founded 1889 on island at end of rocky peninsula. Still centre for administration and commerce. Textiles. Exports iron ore and bauxite. [9° 29'N 13° 49'W]

Constantine City in northern Algeria, east of Algiers. Ancient fortified Arab city built above gorge; on main routes. [36° 25'N 6° 42'E]

Conwy Walled town at the mouth of River Conwy in Gwynedd, north-west Wales. Well-preserved 13th-century castle. Market centre

...d yachting resort. [53° 17'N 3° 50'W]

Copenhagen Capital of Denmark on east coast of Zealand. Industrial, commercial and educational centre. Largest shipbuilding yards in Scandinavia, with extensive harbour. Major industries are electrical equipment, textiles, chemicals, porcelain and glassware. Tourist attractions include Tivoli Gardens and Amalienborg Palace. [55° 41'N 12° 34'E]

Córdoba City in central Argentina in agricultural area. Commercial centre. Hydroelectric power for manufacturing glass and cement. Also engineering and textiles. Astronomical observatory. [31° 20'S 64° 10'W]

Córdoba Town in southern Spain. Capital of Córdoba province. Ancient provincial capital of Romans and Moors, and noted cultural centre with magnificent mosque. Traditional silver and leather industry; copper smelting, electrical equipment, cement. Tourist centre. [37° 50'N 4° 50'W]

Corinth Town in southern Greece. Rebuilt after a destructive earthquake in 1928. Nearby to the south-west lie the important ruins of ancient Corinth, at the acropolis of the Acrocorinth. Nearby Corinth Canal built in 1893. [37° 56'N 22° 55'E]

Corinto Main port of Nicaragua, on Pacific coast. Railway connections to León, Managua and Granada. Exports coffee, cotton, sugar, timber, hides. [12° 30'N 87° 10'W]

Cork Capital of County Cork in Munster province, Republic of Ireland. Important commercial, manufacturing and route centre; port at mouth of River Lee with large meat-exporting trade. Car assembly, textiles, oil refining industry. University; cathedrals. [51° 54'N 8° 30'W]

Cotonou Port and commercial centre on the coast of Benin. Deepwater harbour built in 1964. Exports include oil palm products, groundnuts, coffee, as well as products from Niger. [6° 20'N 2° 25'E]

Coventry City in the West Midlands, west-central England. Commercial, industrial and route centre, south-east of Birmingham. First English car built here, 1898. Large car and aero-engine industry. Known for new cathedral, built 1951. [52° 25'N 1° 31'W]

Cremona Town in northern Italy, in Lombardy. Strong musical traditions; famous for violin-making (especially Stradivarius), with international school. Noted cheese industry; petrochemicals. [45° 8'N 10° 2'E]

Cumaná Port in northern Venezuela and the oldest European settlement in South America. Major fishing port. Exports include tobacco, coffee and cocoa. [10° 30'N 64° 5'W]

Curitiba City in southern Brazil, about 113 km [70 mls] from the coast. Capital of Paraná state. Trading centre for coffee, timber and maté. Paper making and furniture industries. [25° 20'S 49° 10'W]

Cuzco Town in central Peru, in a valley of the Andes. Former capital of Inca Empire; many ruined Inca sites. [13° 32'S 72° 0'W]

Czestochowa Town in south-central Poland. Place of pilgrimage to the 'Weeping Virgin' image. Textiles, iron and steel industries. [50° 49'N 19° 7'E]

Dakar Port, capital of Senegal, on Cape Verde peninsula. Founded in 1857, formerly capital of French West Africa and naval base. Phosphates, fish canning and textiles. Exports groundnuts. [14° 34'N 17° 29'W]

Dalian Port in Liaoning province, north-east China. Strategic port formerly under Russian and Japanese control, on a peninsula into the Yellow Sea. Industries include soyabean processing, shipbuilding. [38° 53'N 121° 37'E]

Dallas City in Texas, southern USA. Commercial centre, especially for cotton, banking and insurance. Textile and textile machinery industries; also petrochemicals, aircraft parts and assembly, and car industries. Major airport. [32° 47'N 96° 49'W]

Damascus Capital of Syria, situated on the

edge of an oasis. Commercial and craft centre; metal-working, silk weaving, sugar refineries. Said to be the oldest continuously inhabited city in the world. [33° 30'N 36° 18'E]

Dar es Salaam Seaport and former capital of Tanzania, on central part of coast. Oil refinery; textiles, cement and meat-canning industries. [6° 50'S 39° 12'E]

Darjeeling Town and hill station in West Bengal state, northern India. Spectacular views of snowcapped Mt Kangchenjunga; Mt Everest in distance. Famous for tea production. [27° 03'N 88° 18'E]

Darkhan Town in north central Mongolia. New industrial centre, established 1961 on main north-south railway line. One of three centres designated administratively as cities; the others are Ulan Bator and Erdenet. [49° 30'N 105° 58'E]

Darwin Capital of Northern Territory, Australia. Port and administrative centre on peninsula in north-west. Originally named Palmerston. Export of minerals from hinterland, especially uranium from Rum Jungle area. Suffered badly in typhoon in 1974. [12° 25'S 130° 51'E]

Dawson Town in north-west Canada in Yukon Territory. Declining goldmining centre of Klondike region and site of 1896–9 Gold Rush. Tourist centre. [64° 10'N 139° 30'W]

Dehra Dun Town in Uttar Pradesh state, north India, in foothills of the Himalayas. Railway terminus and transport centre. Agricultural research and administrative centre. Military academy. [30° 20'N 78° 4'E]

Delft Town in the western Netherlands, in Zuid Holland. Picturesque, historic market centre. Traditional porcelain manufacturing; cable and textile industries. [52° 1'N 4° 22'E]

Delhi City in Delhi Union Territory, northern India, and gateway to Ganges plain on Yamuna river. Major route centre. Old city with Great Temple, an immense mosque and Moghul Imperial Palace; ancient capital for various Hindu and Muslim dynasties and Moghuls before British rule. New Delhi incorporated as capital of British India 1931–47 and now capital of Republic of India. [28° 38'N 77° 17'E]

Derby Capital of Derbyshire, north-central England. Ancient commercial, industrial and route centre. Known for Crown Derby pottery. Important engineering industries especially car and aero-engines, rolling stock, synthetic textiles. [52° 55'N 1° 28'W]

Detroit Port in Michigan, northern USA across Detroit River from Windsor in Canada. Major commercial and manufacturing centre and port for car industry. Manufactures 25% of all US vehicles. Large River Rouge integrated complex: raw materials from docks to finished cars. Also aircraft, rolling stock, chemical industries. [42° 20'N 83° 3'W]

Dhaka (Dacca) Capital of Bangladesh, on Burhi Ganga River. Former Moghul capital in early 17th century; centre of Muslim rule in 18th century. International airport. Industry includes chemicals, jute and cotton milling. Fertilizers, glass and electrical goods. Exports jute, hides, tea. [23° 43'N 90° 26'E]

Dijon Town in eastern France. Capital of Côte-d'Or *département*. Ancient regional centre of Burgundy. Annual food fair and large wine trade. Famed for its mustard. Cycle and chemical industries. [47° 20'N 5° 3'E]

Djibouti Capital of the Republic of Djibouti. Port and terminus of the railway from Ethiopia. Exports hides and skins, also coffee and oilseed. [11° 30'N 43° 05'E]

Dodoma Capital of Tanzania, replaced Dar es Salaam in 1974. Route centre. Noted for cattle rearing. [6° 8'S 35° 45'E]

Doha Capital of Qatar, on Arabian Gulf. Commercial centre and seaport; modern city. Herb and camel market. [25° 15'N 51° 35'E]

Donetsk Capital of Donetsk Oblast in the Ukraine. Main industrial centre of the Donbas region (Donets Basin). Formerly named uzovka after an industrialist, Hughes, then called Stalino. [48° 0'N 37° 45'E]

Douala City and main port of Cameroon, 2 km [20 mls] up Wouri river. Market centre. Railway north to N'kongsamba and south-east to Yaoundé. Light industry. [4° 0'N 9° 45'E]

Douglas Capital of Isle of Man, England. Commercial centre and biggest resort, on east coast of island. Craft, fishing industry; aero-engineering. [54° 9'N 4° 29'W]

Dover Historic Channel port in Kent, south-east England. Large castle, started 11th century. Busiest UK passenger port. Famed for white cliffs. [51° 7'N 1° 19'E]

Dresden Town in eastern Germany. Noted for Baroque architecture. Allied bombing in World War II destroyed many fine buildings and art collections. Manufactures electrical equipment, precision tools, optical and musical instruments. Dresden china is made at Meissen. [51° 2'N 13° 45'E]

Dubai Capital of Dubai, United Arab Emirates. Port with largest harbour in Middle East; major dry dock. Economy based on oil and important distributary trade. Fishing. [25° 18'N 55° 20'E]

Dublin (Baile Atha Cliath) Capital of Irish Republic and of County Dublin in Leinster province on east coast. Commercial city, cultural and route centre and port on Dublin Bay at mouth of River Liffey. Many Georgian squares. Large brewing industry; food, tobacco processing, textiles, transport equipment. Tourist centre. Two universities (Trinity College founded 1591). [53° 20'N 6° 18'W]

Dun Laoghaire Ferry port in County Dublin, Leinster province in the east of the Republic of Ireland. Seaside resort and residential centre on the south side of Dublin Bay. Headquarters of Irish yachting association. [53° 17'N 6° 9'W]

Dundee Port and capital of Tayside region, eastern Scotland, north of Firth of Tay. Commercial, manufacturing and route centre.

Traditional jute industry; engineering; wood and food processing, especially jam. Ship-building is important, especially for the North Sea oil industry. [56° 29'N 3° 0'W]

Dunedin Town on Otago Harbour, south-east coast of South Island, New Zealand. First Scottish settlers in 1848. Sea-borne trade now from Port Chalmers. Exports wool, meat and dairy produce from farming hinterland. [45° 50'S 170° 33'E]

Dunkirk Port in northern France near Belgian border, in Nord *département*. Scene of Allied evacuation 1940. Shipbuilding and oil refining industries. [51° 2'N 2° 20'E]

Durango Town in Mexico, on a plateau east of the Sierra Madre Occidental, and capital of Durango state. Important iron reserves nearby; also silver and lead. Administrative centre and route focus. Western films made in area. [24° 3'N 104° 39'W]

Durban City and major port in Natal province, South Africa, on the east coast. Industrial centre with soap, textiles, paper and oil refining industries. Exports include agricultural products, especially maize, and coal. [29° 49'S 31° 1'E]

Durham Capital of County Durham, north-east England. Ancient and picturesque city on the River Wear, with university (1832), Norman cathedral (1093–1133) and castle (1069). Centre of former coal-mining region; Miners Gala in July. Carpets and organ manufacturing. [54° 47'N 1° 34'W]

Durrës Seaport in western Albania on Adriatic coast. Outlet for Tiranë. Trade in grain, olive oil, and tobacco. Petroleum storage and shipbuilding facilities; railway terminus. [41° 19'N 19° 28'E]

Dushanbe Capital of Tajikistan. Formerly called Stalinabad. Many educational establishments. Cotton and silk industries are important. [38° 33'N 68° 48'E]

Düsseldorf Town in western Germany and river port on Rhine. Capital of North Rhine-

Westphalia. Financial and fashion centre of Ruhr industrial area. Large chemical and metal industry, especially non-ferrous metal smelting; engineering. [51° 15'N 6° 46'E]

Dzhambul (Zhambyl) Capital of Dzhambul Oblast in Kazakhstan. Long historic associations with Islam. Notable for chemicals, such as superphosphates. [42° 54'N 71° 22'E]

Dzhezkazgan (Zhezqazghan) Capital of Dzhezkazgan Oblast in central Kazakhstan, and local industrial centre. Notable for its huge copper reserves. [47° 44'N 67° 40'E]

Edinburgh Cathedral city, capital of Scotland and of Lothian region. Important commercial, cultural, educational, manufacturing and route centre; port (Leith) on Firth of Forth. Built on hills with historic Old Town sloping east from Castle Rock and Georgian New Town sloping towards the Forth. Noted International Festival of the Arts. Engineering, food processing, brewing, paper, printing and publishing industries. Important tourist centre. [55° 57'N 3° 12'W]

Edmonton Town in south-west Canada. Capital of Alberta. Centre of Canadian oil industry and extensive pipeline system. Major commercial and route centre. Meat-packing, grain milling; chemicals; manufacturing industry. [53° 30'N 113° 30'W]

Eindhoven Town in south-east Netherlands in the region of Noord Brabant. Important manufacturing centre; site of leading light bulb industry; electronics, car assembly and milk products. [51° 26'N 5° 28'E]

El Aaiún Capital of Western Sahara (a former Spanish province), under occupation by Morocco since 1976. [27° 9'N 13° 12'W]

El Escorial Town in central Spain near Madrid. Magnificent palace and monastery built for Philip II. [40° 35'N 4° 7'W]

El Ferrol Seaport in eastern Spain, in La Coruña province. Birthplace of Franco. Shipbuilding industry. Naval base; 18th-century planned centre. [43° 29'N 8° 15'W]

El Paso City in Texas, southern USA, o the Rio Grande opposite Ciudad Juárez ▸ Mexico. Important commercial, manufactu ing and route centre. Oil refining, copp smelting, clothing, meat-packing and leath industries. [31° 45'N 106° 29'W]

Elat Seaport in southern Israel at the head c the Gulf of Aqaba (Red Sea). Israel's leadin oil port. Fishing resort and developing touri resort. [29° 30'N 34° 56'E]

Elvas Town in south-east Portugal, near th border with Spain. Historic defensive centre famous for its ramparts, aqueduct and plun orchards. [38° 50'N 7° 10'W]

Ely Cathedral city in Cambridgeshire, easter England. Regional centre on an island site i the Great Ouse River until the Fens wer drained. Magnificent cathedral established i AD 673. [52° 24'N 0° 16'E]

Encarnación Port on the Paraná River, ir the extreme south-east of Paraguay. Railwa terminus; sawmilling and tanning. Exports include timber, cattle, rice, cotton, tobacco and maté. [27° 15'S 55° 50'W]

Entebbe Town on northern shore of Lake Victoria, Uganda. Former administrative centre. Major airport. [0° 4'N 32° 28'E]

Épernay Town in north-east France, in Marne *département*. It is the centre, with Rheims, of the champagne wine industry. Famous for its extensive cellars in chalk hills. [49° 3'N 3° 56'E]

Epidauros Spa town in southern Greece, in Argolis. Site of the Sanctuary of Asclepius, god of medicine. Renowned also for its ancient theatre. [36° 46'N 23° 0'E]

Erdenet New town in north-central Mongolia, 320 km [200 mls] north-west of Ulan Bator. Large mining centre on copper and molybdenum deposits. Connected to Russian rail network. [44° 13'N 111° 10'E]

Eskisehir Town in central western Turkey. A spa town with sulphur springs. Centre of urkish meerschaum industry, based on local eposits. [39° 50'N 30° 5'E]

vora Town in southern Portugal. Ancient market centre of Alentejo region; walled town with many preserved buildings. Cork, leather and craft industries [38° 33'N 7° 57'W]

airbanks Town in Alaska, north-western USA. Transport centre: railhead, terminus of Alaska Highway and air base. Commercial entre for central Alaska; coal mining. 54° 51'N 147° 43'W]

aro Seaport in southern Portugal. Commercial centre of the Algarve region; resort and fishing port with canning, cork and salt industries. [37° 2'N 7° 55'W]

ergana (Farghona) Capital of Fergana Oblast in Uzbekistan. Centre of the large Fergana Valley oasis, known principally for cotton and silk. [40° 23'N 71° 19'E]

ez City in northern Morocco. Cultural and religious centre; sacred city of Islam, with many ancient buildings. University reputed to be oldest in the world. Famous mosque. [34° 0'N 5° 0'W]

Florence Town in north-central Italy and capital of Tuscany. Important historical, commercial and cultural centre known for its beauty; associated with Medicis, Dante and many painters including Giotto and Botticelli; site of Uffizi Museum. Important tourist centre. Engineering, leather and jewellery industries. [43° 47'N 11° 15'E]

Florianópolis Port in southern Brazil, on Santa Catarina Island, joined to the mainland by very long steel suspension bridge. Capital of Santa Catarina state. Excellent harbour. Exports sugar, fruit and tobacco; considerable coastal trade. [27° 30'S 48° 30'W]

Fontainebleau Town south of Paris, France, in Seine-et-Marne *département*. Resort with famous palace. [48° 24'N 2° 40'E]

Fort Portal Town in western Uganda. Base for exploring Ruwenzori Mountains and Ituri

equatorial forest, home of the pygmy people. Located on the main road from Kampala. Tea area. [0° 40'N 30° 20'E]

Fort-de-France Town and port, and capital of Martinique, in the West Indies. Formerly Fort Royal. The main exports include sugar and rum. [14° 36'N 61° 2'W]

Fortaleza Port, capital of Ceará state in north-east Brazil. Industry, sugar refining, flour milling; exports sugar, coffee, cotton, hides. [3° 45'S 38° 35'W]

Frankfurt-am-Main Town in central Germany, in Hesse. Birthplace of Goethe. Leading financial and air transport centre, with important trade fairs. Electrical instruments, machinery, printing and publishing and chemicals industries. [50° 7'N 8° 40'E]

Freetown Port and capital of Sierra Leone. Situated on tip of hilly peninsula, with natural harbour on Rokel River estuary. First settlement for freed slaves from US, 1787. Famous Fourah Bay College, founded 1827. Main exports: diamonds, palm kernels and iron ore. [8° 30'N 13° 17'W]

Fribourg Town in west Switzerland. Capital of Fribourg canton and centre of Swiss Catholicism; university and noted cathedral. Electrical and agricultural equipment, cheese and chocolate industries. [46° 49'N 7° 9'E]

Funchal Seaport in and capital of Madeira (Portugal) on south-east coast. Commercial centre; wine trade; sugar and fish processing industries. Resort. [32° 38'N 16° 54'W]

Fuxin City of Liaoning province, eastern China. Rapidly developing coal-mining and power producing centre. Largest strip mine in China nearby. [42° 5'N 121° 48'E]

Gaborone Capital of Botswana. Built in 1965, at altitude 1,006 m [3,300 ft]. On railway between Zimbabwe and South Africa. Light industry. [24° 45'S 25° 57'E]

Galway Capital of County Galway, Connacht province, in the west of the Republic of

Ireland, between Lough Corrib and Galway Bay. University and cathedral centre with clothing, grain and agricultural equipment industries. Tourist centre. [53° 16'N 9° 4'W]

Gao Historic market town in eastern Mali, on the River Niger. Road and river route centre and southern terminus of a trans-Saharan route. [18° 0'N 1° 10'W]

Gaya Town in Bihar state, east India, above the southern edge of the Ganges Plain. Important railway centre. Place of pilgrimage for Hindus to the Vishnupad Temple. Export and trade of rice. [24° 47'N 85° 4'E]

Gaza Coastal town in the Gaza Strip, administered by Israel since 1967. Reputed to be the ancient Philistine city whose temple was destroyed by Samson. [31° 29'N 34° 28'E]

Gdansk Seaport in northern Poland on Baltic Sea. Founded in Middle Ages; Free City between the World Wars. Shipbuilding, food processing. [54° 22'N 18° 40'E]

Geneva Town in western Switzerland comprising large part of Geneva canton. Commercial centre and headquarters of many international organizations including Red Cross, UN agencies. Traditional haven from persecution; at centre of Reformation, associated especially with Calvin. Watch, clock and jewellery industries. [46° 12'N 6° 9'E]

Genoa Seaport in north-west Italy. Capital of Liguria. Historic commercial centre with long seafaring tradition (birthplace of Columbus). Leading Italian port and oil terminal, with large shipbuilding industry; steel, machinery and textiles. [44° 24'N 8° 56'E]

Georgetown Capital of Guyana and chief port at the mouth of the Demerara River. Exports include bauxite, sugar, rice and diamonds. [6° 50'N 58° 12'W]

Ghent Town and river port in west Belgium. Capital of East Flanders. Historic, commercial, cultural and manufacturing centre of horticultural area. Cathedral. Textile industry, petrochemicals, steel. [51° 2'N 3° 42'E]

Gifu Capital of Gifu prefecture in centr Honshu, Japan. Manufacturing centre, si and paper goods. Centre of cormorant fishir on the Nagara. [35° 30'N 136° 45'E]

Giza Suburb of Cairo on west bank of Riv Nile in Egypt. Famous for the pyramids an the Sphinx in the area. [30° 0'N 31°.10']

Glasgow Port on River Clyde and capital c Strathclyde region, western Scotland. Majc Scottish commercial and industrial centr Shipbuilding, aircraft engines, textiles, foo processing, distilling, textiles, printing an publishing. [55° 52'N 4° 14'W]

Godthåb Small seaport and capital c Greenland at the entrance to Davis Strait ir the south-west. First Danish colony ir Greenland, established 1728. Fish processing [64° 10'N 51° 35'W]

Gonder Town and regional centre to the north of Lake Tana in north-west Ethiopia Ancient walled imperial city with Italian influences, formerly the capital. Several old palaces. [12° 39'N 37° 30'E]

Göteborg Seaport and second largest town o Sweden on the south-west coast. Iron and steel, shipbuilding, oil refining, timber, textiles and fishing industries. Many museums and parks. [57° 43'N 11° 59'E]

Gouda Town in western Netherlands, in Zuid Holland. Market centre of dairying area, famous for its cheese. [52° 1'N 4° 42'E]

Granada Town in southern Spain. Was the last stronghold of Moors. Cultural centre, known for its palaces. Centre of rich agricultural area. Textiles and footwear industry. [37° 10'N 3° 35'W]

Grasse Town in south-east France, in Alpes-Maritimes *département*. Centre of renowned area growing flowers and herbs for the perfume industry. [43° 38'N 6° 56'E]

Graz Town in south-east Austria. Capital of Styria. Historic regional and defensive centre, with noted university and cathedral. Industries clude transport equipment, textiles and food ocessing. [47° 4'N 15° 27'E]

renoble Town in south-east France. Capital Isère *département*. Historic, regional, route ad university centre of Isère Valley. Traitional glove industry; textiles, electrical ingineering, cement and petrochemicals. Iajor tourist centre. [45° 12'N 5° 42'E]

roningen Town in north-east Netherlands. apital of Groningen province. Market town; entre of natural gas production region. Food, bacco and light engineering industries. 53° 15'N 6° 35'E]

roznyy Capital of the Republic of Chechenia in southern Russia, since 1994 the cation of a civil war between Russian and Chechen forces. Oilfields and related industies disrupted by war. [43° 20'N 45° 45'E]

uadalajara City in western Mexico, north of Lake Chapola, Mexico's largest lake. apital of Jalisco state. Route centre with an important market. Various light industries. 20° 40'N 103° 20'W]

Guatemala City Capital of Guatemala, on plateau in south-central area. Damaged by 1976 earthquake. Light industry. Volcanic peaks to south. [14° 40'N 90° 20'W]

Guayaquil Chief port of Ecuador. Sugar refining, tanning and iron-working industries. Major exports include bananas, cocoa and coffee. [2° 15'S 79° 52'W]

Guernica Town in northern Spain, in Vizcaya province. Destroyed by German bombers in 1937, during Civil War. Regional centre with former Basque parliament and 1,000-year-old oak. [43° 19'N 2° 40'W]

Gujranwala Town in north-east Pakistan. Centre of Sikh power until second Sikh war with British (1848–9). On main road and rail route from Lahore to Rawalpindi. Textile industry. [32° 10'N 74° 12'E]

Gujrat Town in north-east Pakistan, near Chenab River. Site of battle which ended

second Sikh war (1849). Renowned gold and silver inlay work. [32° 40'N 74° 2'E]

Guryev (Atyrau) Capital of Guryev Oblast in Kazakhstan. Old Caspian fishing port, now centre of the oil industry. [47° 8'N 51° 59'E]

Gwalior Town in Madhya Pradesh state, north-central India, on southern edge of the River Ganges plain. Ancient fort and 15th-century palace of Tomar dynasty. Manufactures cotton textiles. [26° 12'N 79° 10'E]

Gyandzha (Gäncä) Second largest town of Azerbaijan, formerly known as Kirovabad. Much historic architecture. Industry based on local agricuture: silk and agricultural machinery. [40° 39'N 46° 20'E]

Györ Town and river port in north-west Hungary. Has 12th-century cathedral. Commercial and industrial centre; manufactures railway carriages and diesel machinery. [47° 41'N 17° 40'E]

Haarlem Town in north-west Netherlands. Capital of Noord Holland. Historic commercial and cultural centre at northern end of intensive bulb-growing area. Traditional textile industry. [52° 23'N 4° 39'E]

Hague, The Capital of the Netherlands and of Zuid Holland. Commercial and residential centre with resort, Scheveningen, at North Sea coast. Site of International Court of Justice. [52° 7'N 4° 17'E]

Haifa Chief seaport of Israel, at the foot of Mount Carmel. Oil refining; manufacturing; naval base. [32° 46'N 35° 0'E]

Haiphong City in Vietnam, on the Red River delta, south-east of Hanoi and 8 km [5 mls] from the Gulf of Tongking. Manufactures cement, textiles, phosphates, plastics. Exports minerals and rice. [20° 47'N 106° 41'E]

Halifax Seaport and capital of Nova Scotia on the south-east coast of Canada. Ice-free port and naval base (established 1749). Fishing industry. Commercial centre of Atlantic provinces. [44° 38'N 63° 35'W]

Hamburg Second largest city, leading port and Land of Germany. Historic trading centre at confluence of Alster and Elbe Rivers. Important shipbuilding, engineering, oil refining, food, brewing, printing and publishing industries. [53° 33'N 10° 0'E]

Hameenlinna Town in southern Finland, on Lake Vanajavesi. Terminus of motorboat service to Tampere. Birthplace of Sibelius. Swedish castle dates from 12th–13th centuries. [61° 0'N 24° 28'E]

Hamhung Capital of southern Hamgyong province in North Korea. Important industrial town, centre of pre-war aluminium industry; oil refineries and chemical plants; fertilizers and textiles. [39° 54'N 127° 30'E]

Hamilton Town on Waikato River in central area of North Island, New Zealand. Important road and rail junction. Regional centre for dairy and fat lamb farming. Agricultural research centre. [37° 47'S 175° 19'E]

Hammerfest Town on the northern coast of Norway, most northerly in Europe. Tourist centre for observation of midnight sun. Fish producs, furs exported. [70° 39'N 23° 41'E]

Hangzhou Capital of Zhejiang province, eastern China. River port on Fuchan Jiang River and southern terminus of Grand Canal. [30° 18'N 120° 11'E]

Hanoi River port and capital of the Republic of Vietnam, on the Red River 100 km [60 mls] from the Gulf of Tongking. Rail and industrial centre; international airport. Engineering, rice milling, tanning and brewing; textiles, leather goods and matches manufactured. [21° 5'N 105° 55'E]

Harare Capital of Zimbabwe, in the east-central region. Formerly Salisbury. Altitude 1,524 m [5,000 ft]. Important route centre. Bacon, flour, tobacco and leather goods. Citrus fruits in Magoe area to north. Sugar refining. [17° 43'S 31° 2'E]

Hartford Capital of Connecticut, north-east USA. Commercial centre, most notably for insurance. Large aircraft industry, especial jet engines; metal goods, especially gun [41° 45'N 72° 42'W]

Hassi Messaoud Settlement at oil well ar on margins of Great Eastern Erg in nort east Algeria. Oil and gas pipelines to Med terranean coast. [31° 43'N 6° 8'E]

Havana City and port, capital of Cuba, We Indies, on Gulf of Mexico. Founded in 151 Manufactures cigars from fine tobacco grow in west. Other light industries. Exports tob acco, sugar, rum, coffee. [23° 7'N 82° 25'W

Hebron Town in the West Bank (former part of Jordan administered by Israel sinc 1967) to south-west of Jerusalem. Rich agr cultural valley; industry includes glass makin and tanning. Believed to have been the hom of Abraham. [31° 32'N 35° 6'E]

Heidelberg Town in south-west German in Baden-Württemberg. Cultural centre with oldest German university (1386) and famou castle. Printing and publishing, car part industry. [49° 23'N 8° 41'E]

Helsingør Seaport in Denmark at narrowes point of Øresund on Jutland peninsula Dominated by Kronborg Castle. Old marke and garrison town, with ferry links to Helsingborg in Sweden. [56° 2'N 12° 35'E]

Helsinki Capital of Finland on southern coast. Main industrial, commercial and cultural centre. University, also scientific and cultural institutes. Important for manufacture of timber products, machinery and textiles. [60° 15'N 25° 3'E]

Herat Old town in north-west Afghanistan. Route centre with roads into Iran and the former USSR; ancient trade route to India and Iran. Earthworks, palaces, mosques and tombs. Many times destroyed by invaders and rebuilt. [34° 20'N 62° 7'E]

Hiroshima City and capital of Hiroshima prefecture in south Honshu, Japan. Important industrial centre; motor vehicles, shipbuilding. Largely destroyed by explosion of first atomic

...mb, 6 August 1945. [34° 24'N 132° 30'E]

Ho Chi Minh City (Saigon) Important river port and the largest city in Vietnam, on the Saigon River, 55 km [34 mls] from the South China Sea. Centre of light industry, including rice milling, brewing, distilling and textile manufacturing. [10° 58'N 106° 40'E]

Hobart Port and capital of Tasmania, Australia, on the River Derwent estuary in the south-east. Fine natural harbour, surrounded by hills. Hydroelectric power important for diversified industry in surrounding area. Exports apples. [42° 50'S 147° 21'E]

Hohhot Capital of Inner Mongolian Autonomous Region of China. Rail link with Beijing. Commercial centre of Mongol herding lands. [40° 52'N 111° 40'E]

Honiara Capital of Solomon Islands, west Pacific Ocean, on north coast of island of Guadalcanal. Administrative centre, situated in driest part of island. [9° 27'S 159° 57'E]

Honolulu Capital of Hawaii, USA, on Oahu Island in mid-Pacific Ocean. Commercial and transport centre of islands, with large airport and port. Important tourist and defence industry; also sugar cane and pineapple processing. [21° 19'N 157° 52'W]

Houston Port in Texas, southern USA, at head of Houston Ship Canal on Gulf of Mexico. Commercial, cultural and manufacturing centre of oil and gas region. Major petrochemical industry and equipment manufacturer, especially pipes and drilling gear. Site of NASA Space Center. [29° 46'N 95° 22'W]

Hradec Králové Town in northern Czech Republic at confluence of Adler and Elbe rivers. University and Gothic cathedral (1312). Textiles, musical instruments, furniture and metal-work. [50° 15'N 15° 50'E]

Huancayo Town in central Peru, in the Andes. Trading centre for maize, wheat, alfalfa famous Indian market. [12° 5'S 75° 12'W]

Hyderabad City in south-east Pakistan, on

Indus River at lowest bridging point. Railway centre. Textiles, glass, leather. Famous for embroideries. [25° 23'N 68° 24'E]

Iasi Town in north-east Romania. Commercial and cultural centre. Archbishopric, university and national theatre; home of many churches and palaces. [47° 10'N 27° 40'E]

Ibadan Administrative centre in south-west of Nigeria. On main road and rail routes linking interior with port of Lagos. Cocoa and palm kemels are main products of area. Light industry; textiles. [7° 22'N 3° 58'E]

Iloilo Town and port beside Iloilo Strait in south-east of island of Panay in the Philippines. Commercial, manufacturing and cultural centre. Exports include rice, sugar and copra. [10° 45'N 122° 33'E]

Inch'on City on the Yellow Sea coast of South Korea. Capital of Kyonggi province and the port for Seoul, restricted by wide tidal variation. Exports rice, dried fish, soyabeans. Manufactures steel, glass, textiles and chemicals. [37° 27'N 126° 40'E]

Indianapolis Capital of Indiana, north-central USA. Important commercial and route centre. Large aircraft, car engine and parts industries; electronics and pharmaceuticals. Food processing, especially meat-packing and grain milling. [39° 46'N 86° 09'W]

Innsbruck Town in western Austria at the foot of the Karwendel Mountains. Capital of Tirol. Noted tourist and route centre. University and cathedral town with many historic buildings. [47° 16'N 11° 23'E]

Invercargill Town on southern coast of South Island, New Zealand. Chief commercial centre for Southland Plain. Harbour at Bluff. Meat-freezing, grain and wool industries. [46° 24'S 168° 24'E]

Inverness Capital of Highland region, northern Scotland. Commercial centre in agricultural area at head of Moray Firth. Sea and canal port. Distilling, textiles; service centre for North Sea oil. [57° 29'N 4° 12'W]

Inyanga Regional centre in eastern Zimbabwe, serving farming area. Tea production. Centre for east highlands holiday area, including national park. [18° 12'S 32° 40'E]

Ioannina Town in north-west Greece on the shore of Lake Ioanninon. Notable 11th-century citadel. Famous for fine jewellery and crafts. [39° 40'N 20° 51'E]

Ipoh Capital of Perak in Malaysia. Commercial centre of Kinta Valley tin-mining area; also extensive rubber plantations. Chinese rock temples. [4° 35'N 101° 5'E]

Iquitos Port on Amazon River, north Peru. Commercial centre for vast area; head of navigation for ocean-going steamers. Exports nuts, timber, rubber. [3° 45'S 73° 0'W]

Iráklion Seaport in Greece, largest city in Crete, on north-central coast. Manufactures soap and leather goods. [35° 20'N 25° 12'E]

Irkutsk Town in eastern Siberia, Russia. Major industrial and transport centre of the region. Long history; some old buildings. [52° 18'N 104° 20'E]

Islamabad Capital of Pakistan. Modern planned city in north-east, just north-west of Rawalpindi. Rawal Dam and reservoir within capital for water supply. [33° 40'N 73° 10'E]

Istanbul City in Turkey on both sides of Bosporus. Largest town and former capital of Turkey. Founded as Byzantium by Greeks *c.* 660 BC, changed to Constantinople AD 330 and Istanbul in 1930. Capital of Byzantine Empire until 1453. Seat of Ottoman Empire until 1922. Industrial, commercial, cultural and tourist centre. Many churches and mosques, and fine examples of Byzantine art and architecture. [42° 0'N 21° 0'E]

Izmir Seaport in western Turkey. Settlements date back to 3rd millennium BC. Site of ancient Smyrna. Largest port in Asian Turkey. Exports grapes, figs, opium, raisins, carpets and silk. [38° 25'N 27° 8'E]

Jaffna Town in northern Sri Lanka, on south lagoon coast of Jaffna peninsula. Portugue occupation 1617; Dutch 1658; remains forts. Salt produced in area; caustic soda mar ufactured. [9° 45'N 80° 2'E]

Jaipur Walled city, capital of Rajasthan stat north-west India. Founded 1727. Commerci and route centre. Maharajah's Palace of for mer Jaipur state. Textiles. [27° 0'N 75° 50'I

Jakarta Seaport in north-west Java, capital and largest city in Indonesia. Communica ions, trade and industrial centre. University Indonesia. [6° 9'S 106° 49'E]

Jammu Town in southern Jammu an Kashmir state in north Indian subcontinen on Tawi river, tributary of Chenab rive Winter capital of state. [32° 43'N 74° 54'E]

Jebel Dhanna Major new port, oil termina and industrial centre on southern Arabian Gulf in western Abu Dhabi, United Aral Emirates. [24° 11'N 52° 35'E]

Jerez de la Frontera Town in south-wes Spain. Capital of Cádiz province. Centre o sherry producing area; noted for horsebreeding; distilling industry. [36° 41'N 6° 7'W]

Jericho Town in Jordan, in the valley of the River Jordan, 22 km [14 mls] east-north-east of Jerusalem. Site of important ancient city below sea level. [31° 25'N 35° 27'E]

Jerusalem Town partly in Israel and partly in Jordanian territory administered by Israel since 1967. Sited on two rocky hills 56 km [35 mls] from the Mediterranean coast. Holy city of Jews, Muslims and Christians; site of many holy places; churches, synagogues and mosques. Tourist area. [3° 47'N 35° 10'E]

Jidda Major seaport of Hijaz in western Saudi Arabia. Originally founded AD 647, on Red Sea. Financial and commercial centre; chief port for Mecca. [21° 29'N 39° 10'E]

Jinja Town in Uganda, north of Lake Victoria, 80 km [50 mls] east of Kampala. Route centre and industrial area. Owen Falls hydroelectric power station nearby. Textiles, rewing, tobacco and copper smelting (ore om Kilembe). [0° 25'N 33° 12'E]

nzhou Old Manchurian city of Liaoning rovince, north-eastern China. Now centre of ndustrial district, with chemicals and electronics industry. Originally developed by the apanese in the 1930s. [41° 7'N 121° 6'E]

odhpur Walled town in Rajasthan state, orth-west India, on edge of Thar Desert. Old rading centre. Once capital of Manwar state. Textiles. [26° 23'N 73° 8'E]

ohannesburg City in the province of Pretoria, Witwatersrand and Vereeniging (PWV), South Africa, lying 1,829 m [6,000 ft] above sea level. Centre of gold-mining area of Witwatersrand. Important industrial area to south, which produces coal; huge iron-and-steel works nearby. [26° 10'S 28° 2'E]

Johor Baharu City, capital of Johor in Malaysia, southern end of Malay Peninsula. Area produces rubber, rice and pineapples. Fine Sultan's Palace. [1° 29'N 103° 46'E]

Jönköping Town in southern Sweden at southern end of Lake Vättern. Centre of Sweden's match-making industry; paper and textile industries. [57° 45'N 14° 10'E]

Jos Town on Jos Plateau in central Nigeria. Assob Waterfalls nearby to south. Commercial centre for tin-mining area. [9° 53'N 8° 51'E]

Juneau Ice-free port and capital of Alaska, north-western USA. Commercial centre in gold-mining area. Sawmilling and salmon-processing industries. [58° 18'N 134° 25'W]

Kabul Capital of Afghanistan, at 2,100 m [6,900 ft], on Kabul River. Commands passes through mountains into Pakistan. Manufactures marble-ware, glass. [34° 28'N 69° 11'E]

Kabwe Town in central Zambia. Important lead and zinc mining centre for the surrounding region. [14° 30'S 28° 29'E]

Kaduna Town in north-central Nigeria, on Kaduna River. Formerly capital of northern Nigeria. Shiroro HEP Dam on Kaduna River to south. Administrative centre; railway junction. Cotton and textiles. [10° 30'N 7° 21'E]

Kaesong Ancient city in North Korea, near the border with South Korea, north-west of Seoul. Famous for its porcelain. Trade in ginseng for medicinal use. [31° 58'N 126° 35'E]

Kainji New town in western Nigeria on Niger River, south of important Kainji Dam and Reservoir. Main road connections to south and east. [9° 42'N 4° 37'E]

Kalgoorlie Town (with Boulder) in southern Western Australia state on the Trans-Australian Railway. Developed in 1893. Gold and nickel mining in the 'Golden Mile' area to the south. [30° 40'S 121° 22'E]

Kaliningrad Capital of Kaliningrad Oblast, a detached enclave of Russia on the Baltic coast. Former German name Konigsberg; a Baltic shipbuilding port. Population largely composed of army personnel. [54° 42'N 20° 32'E]

Kampala Capital of Uganda, north of Lake Victoria. Fine site, built on several low hills. Route centre. Light industry. Makerere University oldest in east Africa. Small port, Port Bell, on lake. [0° 20'N 32° 30'E]

Kandy Town in central Sri Lanka, on small lake. Former capital of old kingdom of Kandy (1592–1815). Ceded to British 1815. Centre of tea trade. Buddhist Temple of the Tooth. Old palace. [7° 18'N 80° 43'E]

Kano City in northern Nigeria, in highly populated area. Commercial centre grown up around old walled town of Hausa people. Road and rail centre. Important groundnuts trade. [12° 2'N 12° 30'E]

Kanpur City in central Uttar Pradesh state, northern India, on the River Ganges. Formerly known as Cawnpore; scene of massacre during Indian Mutiny (1857). Important industrial centre. [26° 28'N 80° 20'E]

Kaohsiung Port in south-west Taiwan. Southern terminus of main railway. Chief market centre for south. Duty-free export-processing zone. Textiles, cement, aluminium, oil refineries. [22° 38'N 120° 18'E]

Karachi City and seaport in Pakistan, west of River Indus delta on edge of desert area. Former capital (1947–59). Commercial and route centre; shipbuilding and repairing. Important airport. [24° 53'N 67° 0'E]

Karaganda (Qaraghandy) Capital of Karaganda Oblast and chief industrial centre of Kazakhstan. Coal mining, steel works. Large urban agglomeration. [49° 50'N 79° 10'E]

Karlskrona Seaport and chief naval base of Sweden on south-eastern coast. Important fishing and china industries. Ice-free harbour. [56° 10'N 15° 35'E]

Kathmandu (Katmandu) Capital of Nepal, in valley of Himalayas. Communications and transport centre. Many temples and palaces. [27° 45'N 85° 20'E]

Katowice Town in south-central Poland, part of a heavy industrial area which, as Upper Silesia, was part of Germany until 1921. [50° 17'N 19° 5'E]

Kawasaki City in east-central Honshu, Japan. Industrial suburb between Tokyo and Yokohama, important for heavy industry. 12th-century temple. [35° 35'N 139° 42'E]

Kazan Capital of the Tatarstan Republic, Russian, west of the Urals. Major transport centre with a wide variety of heavy industry. [55° 48'N 49° 3'E]

Kecskemét Town in south-east Hungary. Trade centre for fruit-growing area, with associated industry of distilling, preserving fruit and eggs and the manufacture of agricultural implements. [46° 57'N 19° 42'E]

Kemerovo City in southern Siberia, Russia. Centre of the Kuzbas industrial zone; coal and associated industries. [55° 20'N 86° 5'E]

Kemi Seaport in west Finland at head of Gulf of Bothnia. Large harbour. Centre of the

Finnish timber industry with many sawmill Industries include the manufacture of cell lose and fishing. [65° 44'N 24° 34'E]

Kenema Town in eastern Sierra Leon Administrative centre and focus of diamon and forest trade. Alluvial diamonds main from Sewa River; cocoa. [7° 50'N 11° 14'W

Kermanshah City in western Iran. Centre of fertile grain producing area on caravan route Sugar and oil refineries. [34° 19'N 47° 4'E]

Kharkov (Kharkiv) Capital of Kharkov Oblas in the Ukraine. Long-established route focu and centre of vehicle and aircraft industry Attractive centre despite wartime destruction [49° 58'N 36° 20'E]

Khartoum Capital of Sudan, between Whit and Blue Nile. Communications centre. Cot ton industry. [15° 31'N 32° 35'E]

Kherson Capital of Kherson Oblast in the Ukraine. A Black Sea port on the Rive Dnieper (Dnipro, Dnepr), now a popula resort. [46° 35'N 32° 35'E]

Khmelnitskiy (Khmelnytskyy) Capital of Khmelnitskiy Oblast in Ukraine. Named after a 17th-century revolutionary. Agricultural and food-processing centre. [49° 23'N 27° 0'E]

Khorramshahr Port in western Iran. Situated at the confluence of the Shatt-al-Arab river and the Karun river near the frontier with Iraq. Oil-refining centre and major trading port, exporting cotton, dates, hides and skins. [30° 29'N 48° 15'E]

Khudzhand Formerly Leninabad, capital of Khudzhand Oblast in Tajikistan. Town with a long, violent history. Cotton, silk and food processing. [40° 14'N 69° 40'E]

Khulna City in Bangladesh, on the Ganges delta 129 km [80 mls] south-west of Dacca. Rice, flour and cotton milling. Jute, newsprint, hardboard; boatbuilding. [22° 45'N 89° 34'E]

Kielce Town in south-east Poland, with a wide variety of industry including marble and

...ssworks; as well as iron, lead and zinc ...ning industries. [50° 52'N 20° 42'E]

...ev (Kiyev, Kyyiv) Capital of Ukraine and Kiev Oblast, on the River Dnieper (Dnipro, ...nepr). Major industrial and transport centre. ...unded 1,500 years ago; notable for its many ...chitectural features, especially churches and ...onasteries. [50° 30'N 30° 28'E]

...igali Capital of Rwanda. Commercial cen-...e, with airport. Trade in cattle and hides. ...entre of resurgence of ethnic violence in the ...990s between the Hutu and Tutsi ethnic ...oups. [1° 59'S 30° 4'E]

...ilindini Modern port on western side of ...lombasa Island, Kenya. Exports: coffee, cot-...on, sisal, tea, soda ash. Also handles traffic ...om Uganda and north-eastern Tanzania. ...° 4'S 39° 40'E]

...imberley Market and industrial centre in ...range Free State, South Africa. Centre of ...iamond-mining industry since diamond rush ...f 1870s. [28° 43'S 24° 46'E]

...ingston Capital of Jamaica, in the West ...ndies, on the south coast. Modern port facil-...ies with deep water harbour. Commercial ...entre. Light industries including textiles. ...ailway to Montego Bay in the north-west and ...o Port Antonio, chief banana port, in the ...orth-east. [18° 0'N 76° 50'W]

...inshasa Capital of Zaïre on River Zaïre at ...ool Malebo (Stanley Pool). River port, linked ...y railway to Matadi at river mouth. Hydro-...lectricity from Inga Dam downstream. River ...avigable up to Kisangani. Commercial cen-...re; textiles, brewing and various industries. ...4° 20'S 15° 15'E].

...irkuk Town in north-central Iraq. Agric-...ultural and market centre. Sheep-raising area; crops include grain and fruit. Centre of im-portant oilfield with pipelines to Syria and Lebanon. [35° 30'N 44° 21'E]

Kirkwall Capital of Orkney, Scotland, on Mainland, the largest island. Noted for 12th-century cathedral built during Norse rule.

Port, commercial and service centre, espe-cially for oil industry. [58° 59'N 2° 59'W]

Kirovograd (Kirovohrad) Capital of Kirovo-grad Oblast in the Ukraine. Industry based on local agriculture, sugar, meat, and agricultural machinery. [48° 35'N 32° 20'E]

Kiruna Most northerly town in Sweden. Centre of Swedish iron-ore industry; on the Lappland railway. [67° 52'N 20° 15'E]

Kisangani Town on River Zaïre in central Zaïre. River navigation west to Kinshasa. Up-stream are famous Boyoma Falls. Railway link south to Ubundi. [0° 35'N 25° 14'E]

Kishinev (Chişinau) Capital of Moldova in eastern Europe. Belonged to Romania for part of 20th century. Large food, tobacco and wine industries. [47° 0'N 28° 50'E]

Kitakyushu Seaport in northern Kyushu, Japan. Formed in 1963 by merging of Kokura, Moji, Tobata, Wakamatsu and Yawata on Shimonoseki Strait. [33° 56'N 130° 50'E]

Kitwe A modern, expanding town in the Copper Belt area of central Zambia. Third largest town in Zambia. [12° 54'S 28° 13'E]

Klagenfurt Town in southern Austria. Capital of Carinthia. Historic defensive, route and tourist centre. Leather, wood processing industries. [46° 38'N 14° 20'E]

Klaipeda Historically notable Baltic seaport in western Lithuania. Fishing and timber industries; oil exporting. [55° 43'N 21° 10'E]

Knossos Ancient city of Greece in northern Crete, south-east of Iráklion. Centre of Cretan Bronze Age culture and Minoan civilization. [35° 16'N 25° 10'E]

Kobe Seaport city, capital of Hyogo prefec-ture in southern Honshu, Japan. Industrial centre; port facilities second only to Yokohama in importance. Iron and steel, ship-building, rubber, aircraft. Exports oil, tea, camphor, cotton. Devastating earthquake killed 5,000 in 1995. [34° 45'N 135° 10'E]

Kofu Capital of Yamanashi prefecture in central Honshu, Japan. Agricultural centre for vegetables and fruit, especially grapes. Important market for silk fabrics, raw silk and cocoons. [35° 40'N 138° 30'E]

Kolwezi Town in Shaba province in southern Zaïre, 1,443 m [4733 ft] above sea level. Important cobalt and copper mines, and mineral processing. [10° 40'S 25° 25'E]

Kosice Town in eastern Slovak Republic. Episcopal city; 14th-century Gothic cathedral. Manufactures include tobacco, textiles and wine. [48° 42'N 21° 15'E]

Kowloon Town on Kowloon peninsula on mainland of south-east China, part of the British Crown Colony (until 1999) of Hong Kong and separated from the island by Hong Kong harbour. Major trading and industrial centre. [22° 20'N 114° 15'E]

Kozhikode (Calicut) Town and ancient port in Kerala state, south-west India, on Malabar Coast of Arabian Sea. Noted for cotton cloth – hence 'calico'. [11° 15'N 75° 43'E]

Kraków Town in south Poland. Historic architecture: castle, cathedral and university. Heavy industrial centre (iron and steel, engineering); salt mines. [50° 4'N 19° 57'E]

Krasnovodsk (Krasnowodsk) City in the west of Turkmenistan on the Caspian Sea. Caspian train and ferry port; oil and cotton exports. [40° 0'N 52° 52'E]

Krasnoyarsk Capital of Krasnoyarsk Kray in Siberia, Russia. Large reservoir and power station. Gold-mining centre, timber, furs, shipbuilding, heavy industry. [56° 8'N 93° 0'E]

Kremenchug (Kremenchuk) Industrial town on the River Dnieper in Ukraine. Large Kremenchug reservoir and power station nearby. Timber, textiles, iron ore. [49° 5'N 33° 25'E]

Krems Town in north-east Austria on the northern bank of the River Danube. Capital of Lower Austria. Centre of Weinviertel wine industry. [48° 25'N 15° 36'E]

Kronshtadt Historic naval base, fortress a shipbuilding port on an island in the Gulf Finland, Russia. [60° 5'N 29° 45'E]

Kuala Lumpur City and capital of Malays 40 km [25 mls] inland from the south-we coast of the Malay Peninsula. On the railw from Singapore to Bangkok. A commerc and railway centre, it grew around the tin a later rubber industry. [3° 9'N 101° 41'E]

Kuching Town and capital of Sarawak Malaysia. Port on River Sarawak with fer connections to Malay Peninsula. Rice ar sago milling. [1° 33'N 110° 25'E]

Kulyab (Kulob) Capital of the re-establishe Kulyab Oblast in Tajikistan. Textile industr notably cotton. [37° 55'N 69° 50'E]

Kumasi City in south-west Ghana. Comme cial centre serving cocoa producing are Distribution, education and route centr National Cultural Centre. [6° 41'N 1° 38'W

Kunming Capital of Yunnan province south-central China. Major transport centre i mountainous area. Copper smelter and iro and steel plant. [25° 1'N 102° 41'E]

Kursk City in western Russia, south o Moscow. Large iron-ore deposits (the 'Kurs. Magnetic Anomaly'). [51° 42'N 36° 11'E]

Kustanay (Qostanay) Capital of Kustana Oblast in northern Kazakhstan. Large iron ore deposits nearby. Artificial fibres and foo processing. [53° 10'N 63° 35'E]

Kutaisi Ancient town in western Georgia Some important old buildings survive despite unsettled history. Silk, wine and tobacc industries. [42° 19'N 42° 40'E]

Kuwait City Capital of Kuwait at head of Arabian Gulf. Good harbour and considerable trade. Traditional industry of pearling and fishing eclipsed by oil-related industries: petrochemical plants. [20° 30'N 48° 0'E]

Kyoto City, capital of Kyoto prefecture in western Honshu, Japan. Ancient capital of apan, famed for its many temples and histori-al buildings. Cultural and religious centre; mperial University (1897) and medical school. Now also important manufacturing city: electrical equipment, aircraft, chemicals. Many craft industries: pottery, bronze, porce-ain, silk, velvet. [35° 0'N 135° 45'E]

Kyrenia Seaport in northern Cyprus at foot of coastal mountain range. Town supposedly founded 10th century BC. Byzantine castle. [35° 20'N 33° 20'E]

La Chaux de Fonds Town in north-western Switzerland in Jura Mountains, in Neuchâtel canton. Centre of Swiss watch- and clock-making in Jura. [47° 7'N 6° 50'E]

La Coruña Seaport in north-west Spain. Capital of La Coruña province. Armada sailed from here 1588. Fishing industries, engineer-ing, oil refining, glass. [43° 20'N 8° 25'W]

La Paz Administrative capital of Bolivia, in valley at foot of Mt Illimani, in the Andes near the Peruvian border. The highest capital in the world at 3,657m [12,000 ft]. Principal industrial and trading centre of Bolivia; manu-factures electrical appliances, furniture, chem-icals, textiles, glass. [16° 20'S 68° 10'W]

La Paz Capital of Baja California Sur (Lower California) state, Mexico, on eastern side of the peninsula, on Gulf of California. Imp-ortant pearl industry. [24° 10'N 110° 20'W]

Lagos Former capital and main seaport of Nigeria, on natural harbour. Oldest settle-ment, founded on slave trade, on lagoon island of Lagos; spread to other islands and mainland. Industrial centre. Exports mainly oil, cocoa, groundnuts. [6° 25'N 3° 27'E]

Lahore City in northern Pakistan. Was the capital of Mogul, then Sikh, empires. Industrial route, cultural and educational centre. Badshahi Mosque is world's largest. Tomb of the Sikh ruler Ranjit Singh. Railway engineering. [31° 32'N 74° 22'E]

Lalitapur Market town 3 km [2 mls] south of Kathmandu in Nepal. An ancient city that was

the capital of the first king of Nepal; numerous temples. [27° 40'N 85° 20'E]

Larnaca Seaport in south-east Cyprus, on site of ancient city of Cilcium. Exports wine, fruit, olive oil, brandy, soap and tobacco prod-ucts. Tourist area. [34° 54'N 33° 39'E]

Las Palmas Capital of Las Palmas province on Gran Canaria Island and largest town of the Canary Islands (Spain). Commercial cen-tre and port; food processing, iron founding, machinery and textile industries. Important tourist centre. [28° 7'N 15° 26'W]

Las Vegas Resort in Nevada, western USA. Major gaming and hotel centre. Manufactures gaming equipment. Magnesium smelting. [36° 10'N 115° 9'W]

Latakia Seaport of western Syria. Centre of rich agricultural region. Traditional and still important export is tobacco; also asphalt, eggs, cereals, pottery. [35° 30'N 35° 45'E]

Lausanne Town in western Switzerland on site steeply sloping to Lake Geneva. Capital of Vaud canton. Ancient ecclesiastical and educational centre; noted cathedral and univ-ersity. Commerical centre with annual fair. Resort. [46° 32'N 6° 38'E]

Le Havre Port in northern France at mouth of Seine estuary, in Seine-Maritime *départe-ment*. Important transatlantic and cross-channel traffic. Oil-refining industry; ship-building, food processing. [49° 30'N 0° 5'E]

Leeds Capital of West Yorkshire, northern England. Important commercial, manufactur-ing and route centre; known for its large Victorian town hall. Major clothing industry, engineering, especially transport and factory equipment. [53° 48'N 1° 34'W]

Leeuwarden Town in northern Netherlands. Capital of Friesland. Centre of intensive dairy-ing region, with large cattle market. Butter and cheese industries. [53° 15'N 5° 48'E]

Leh Town in east Jammu and Kashmir state, north Indian subcontinent, on River Indus, at

3,500 m [11,500 ft]. Trade centre. Meteorological observatory. Starting point of expeditions into Himalayas. [34° 9'N 77° 35'E]

Leiden Town in north-west Netherlands, in Zuid Holland. Historic university town and former textile-trading port at southern end of bulb-growing area. Printing industry. Birth place of Rembrandt. [52° 09'N 4° 30'E]

Leipzig Town in eastern Germany. Ancient buildings, including 15th-century Church of St Thomas. Produces iron and steel, chemicals, paper, plastics, electrical and agricultural machinery. Famous for publishing and industry fairs. [51° 20'N 12° 23'E]

León Town in north-west Spain. Capital of Leon province. In coal-mining area. Walled medieval town; noted 13th–14th century cathedral. Livestock market; chemical industry. [42° 38'N 5° 34'W]

León Town in west of Nicaragua, on lowland west of Lake Managua, near Pacific coast. Former capital, cultural centre. Original town destroyed by earthquake in 1609; ruins near volcano Momotombo. [12° 20'N 86° 51'W]

Lerwick Capital of Shetland Islands, northern Scotland, on east coast of Mainland Island. Commercial centre and fishing port with large processing industries. Most northerly town in the United Kingdom with strong Norse character. Major centre for North Sea oil industry. [60° 10'N 1° 10'W]

Lhasa Capital of Tibet Autonomous Region, China, at 3,658 m [12,000 ft], on Tsangpo River, tributary of Brahmaputra. Dominated by spectacular Potala, former palace monastery of Dalai Lama. [29° 25'N 0° 58'E]

Libreville Port and capital of Gabon. On Gabon River estuary on north coast. Freed slaves put ashore here by French in 19th century. Timber exports important, also cocoa and oil. [0° 25'N 9° 26'E]

Liège Town and river port in eastern Belgium. Capital of Liège province. Commercial, manufacturing and route centre. Major steel

producer; also heavy engineering, chemicals and glass industries. [50° 38'N 5° 35'E]

Lille Town in north-east France. Capital of Nord *département*. Historic defensive centre with famous Vauban citadel. Leading textile industry. [50° 38'N 3° 3'E]

Lillehammer Town in central Norway. Tourist centre for both winter and summer sports. Winter olympics held here February 1994. [61° 8'N 10° 30'E]

Lilongwe Capital of Malawi in the centre of the country. Declared capital 1975. Modern administrative centre. Tobacco grown in the north. [14° 0'S 33° 48'E]

Lima Capital of Peru, in dry foggy coastal area. Oldest university in South America. Its port is Callao. Oil refining and manufacturing; tanning, furniture, pharmaceutical, textile and vehicle industries. [12° 0'S 77° 0'W]

Limassol Seaport in southern Cyprus. 15th-century castle. Centre for agricultural production of surrounding regions. Exports wine and asbestos. Tourist centre. [34° 2'N 33° 1'E]

Limerick Capital of County Limerick in Munster province, south-west Republic of Ireland. Historic, commercial, manufacturing and route centre; port at head of Shannon estuary. Large food-processing industry, especially bacon, grain, dairy products; clothing. Traditional lace industry. [52° 40'N 8° 38'W]

Limoges Town in west-central France. Capital of Haute-Vienne *département*. Famous for porcelain and shoes. Textiles, car and motorcycle parts. [45° 50'N 1° 15'E]

Linköping Town in south-east Sweden. Important medieval town, with fine Gothic cathedral. Industrial centre for aircraft, cars, textiles and furniture. [58° 28'N 15° 36'E]

Linz Town in northern Austria on the River Danube. Capital of Upper Austria. Commercial and manufacturing centre and river port. Large chemical and steel industries; as well as textile industry. [48° 18'N 14° 18'E]

Lisbon Capital of Portugal at mouth of River Tagus. Commercial and route centre with large naval harbour. Site of departure of many voyages of discovery in 15th-17th centuries. Destroyed by earthquake in 1755. Passenger, freight and fishing port. Cork, food, steel and shipbuilding industries. [38° 42'N 9° 10'W]

Liverpool Cathedral city and capital of Merseyside, north-west England. Important commercial centre and port with leading UK, Atlantic and export trade. Two cathedrals; Liver and Cunard buildings are famous landmarks. Large food-processing industry, especially flour and sugar; car assembly; pulp and paper manufacture. [53° 25'N 3° 0'W]

Livingstone Town on River Zambezi in southern Zambia. Railway to Shaba (in Zaïre) led to the development of mineral resources. Sawmilling. Tourist centre for Victoria Falls. [17° 46'S 25° 52'E]

Ljubljana Capital of Slovenia. Baroque cathedral, university and 15th-century castle. Main industries are iron foundries and paper mills; publishing industry. [46° 4'N 14° 33'E]

Lobito Major port in central part of Angola. Good modern harbour. Terminus of Trans-African Railway. Exports copper, zinc, uranium and cobalt from Shaba (in Zaïre). Fish drying and canning. [12° 18'S 13° 35'E]

Lod Town 17 km [10 mls] from Tel Aviv Jaffa, Israel. Reputed birthplace of St George. International airport; railway junction. Electronic equipment. [31° 57'N 34° 54'E]

Lódz Town in central Poland. Important textile industry; planned layout development in 19th century. [51° 45'N 19° 27'E]

Logroño Town in northern Spain. Capital of Logroño province. Centre of Rioja agricultural region in Ebro Valley. Wine, vegetable, chemical and textile industries. [42° 28'N 2° 27'W]

Lomé Capital and chief port of Togo, near the border with Ghana. Main exports are phosphates, cocoa, coffee, palm kernels and cotton. [6° 09'N 1° 20'E]

London Capital of United Kingdom of Great Britain and Northern Ireland. Major international financial, cultural and educational centre. Route focus, with leading international airport and largest UK importing port (especially food and raw materials). Manufacturing industries, especially electrical and precision goods, pharmaceuticals, publishing, printing. Major tourist centre: many famous buildings, such as St Pauls Cathedral, Houses of Parliament, Westminster Abbey. [51° 30'N 0° 5'W]

Londonderry Port and capital of County Londonderry, in the north of Northern Ireland. Historic walled city near mouth of River Foyle. Scene of famous siege and defeat of James II in 1689. Large clothing industry, especially shirts; as well as distilling and food industries. [55° 0'N 7° 23'W]

Los Angeles Port on Pacific coast of southern California, USA. Major agglomeration and tourist centre in oil producing area. Oil-refining and shipbuilding industries; leading centre of aerospace and film industries; clothing, car parts and assembly, paper and printing. Processing centre for local fruit especially citrus, vegetables, dairy products and tuna fish. [34° 4'N 118° 15'W]

Lourdes Town in south-west France, in Hautes-Pyrenees *département*. Major pilgrimage and tourist centre, associated with St Bernadette. [43° 6'N 0° 3'W]

Louvain Town in Brabant, central Belgium. Historic, regional and commercial centre, with textile trade. Roman Catholic university established 1425. Brewing; electrical and engineering industries [50° 52'N 4° 42'E]

Luanda Capital city and port on bay in northern Angola. Founded by Portuguese in 1575 for slave trade; rebuilt 1938. Railway east to Malanje. Cotton and important coffee exporter. [8° 50'S 13° 15'E]

Luang Prabang Town in north-central Laos, at junction of Mekong and Kahn rivers. Former royal capital. Hydroelectric power on Dong River to south. Rubber, rice and teak production in area. [19° 52'N 102° 10'E]

Lübeck Seaport in northern Germany, in Schleswig-Holstein. Former capital of the Hanseatic League. Industries include shipbuilding and metal-working. Known for its marzipan. [53° 52'N 10° 41'E]

Lublin Town in south-east Poland. Temporary capital of Poland, 1918 and 1944. Agricultural trade and food-processing centre; new copper reserves nearby. [51° 12'N 22° 38'E]

Lubumbashi City in Shaba province in southern Zaïre. On the main railway system. Important administrative and commercial centre for copper and cobalt mining area. Varied industries. [11° 40'S 27° 28'E]

Lucerne Town in north-central Switzerland, at north-western end of Lake Lucerne. Capital of Lucerne canton. Famous resort with annual music festival. Also known for its wooden bridges. [47° 3'N 8° 18'E]

Lucknow Capital of Uttar Pradesh state, northern India. Famous siege (1857) during Indian Mutiny. Route centre. Carpet and paper manufactured; and railway engineering industry. [26° 50'N 81° 10'E]

Lugansk (Luhansk) Capital of Lugansk Oblast in Ukraine. Formerly Voroshilovgrad. Many heavy industries; centre of the Donbas industrial region. [48° 38'N 39° 15'E]

Lund Town in southern Sweden. University and 11th-century cathedral. Industrial centre; printing and publishing. [55° 44'N 13° 12'E]

Lusaka Capital of Zambia, on River Kafue in the south. Altitude 1,219 m [4,000 ft]. On main railway and important road junction with Great East road to Malawi. Chemical and brewing industries. [15° 28'S 28° 16'E]

Luxembourg Capital of the Grand Duchy of Luxembourg. International commercial centre, especially for banking, with many European organization headquarters, including EC Court of Justice. [49° 37'N 6° 9'E]

Luxor Town on eastern bank of River Nile in upper Egypt. On site of ancient Thebes;

Temple of Luxor dates from 1417 BC. Karn nearby. [25° 41'N 32° 38'E]

Lvov (Lviv, Lvyv) Main city of weste Ukraine and capital of Lvov Oblast. Poli between the World Wars; many histo churches. [49° 50'N 24° 0'E]

Lyon River port in eastern France at t confluence of the Rhône and Saône river Capital of Rhône *département*. Ancient com mercial, financial and route centre. Major si industry; chemicals, machinery, and mot vehicles. [45° 46'N 4° 50'E]

Maastricht River port in south-east Nethe lands. Capital of Limburg. Historic com mercial and route centre. Ceramic, glass an cement industries. Treaty on European Unio signed December 1991 (came into force o 1 November 1993). [50° 50'N 5° 40'E]

Madras City and port of Tamil Nadu stat southern India; on Bay of Bengal, with art ficial harbour. Founded by British in 165 as Fort St George. Railway focus. Textiles Exports cotton and hides. [13° 8'N 80° 19'E

Madrid Capital of Spain and of Madri province. Commercial and route centre established as the capital in 1561. Famou Prado Museum. Luxury goods, printing transport equipment, chemicals industry Tourist centre. [40° 25'N 3° 45'W]

Mainz Town in west-central Germany, a confluence of Main and Rhine rivers. Capita of Rhineland-Palatinate. Has noted cathedra and largest German wine market. Site o Gutenberg's development of printing. Chemi cals and coffee processing. [50° 0'N 8° 17'W

Makhachkala Capital of the Dagestar Republic in southern Russia. Caspian Sea por with a wide variety of manufacturing indus tries; also oil refineries. [43° 0'N 47° 30'E]

Malabo Capital of Equatorial Guinea on northern coast of island of Bioko (Fernando Póo). Cocoa, coffee, copra. [3° 45'N 8° 50'E]

Málaga Seaport in southern Spain. Capital of

Málaga province. Commercial centre of Costa del Sol, known for its wines. Textile and food industries. Resort. [36° 43'N 4° 23'W]

Malang City in south central Java in Indonesia. Centre of a fertile agricultural basin and an important coffee producing area. [7° 59'S 112° 45'E]

Malmö Seaport in south-west Sweden. Train and ferry links with Copenhagen; naval base. Major industries include agricultural products, textiles, shipbuilding and engineering. [55° 36'N 12° 59'E]

Managua Capital of Nicaragua, on southern shore of Lake Managua. Original town destroyed by earthqucke in 1931, rebuilt on modern lines, but centre again destroyed by earthquake in 1972. Rebuilt as three satellite towns. Volcano Momotombo to north. Highway to Honduras. [12° 6'N 86° 20'W]

Manaus Port on the Rio Negro near its junction with the Amazon river, northern Brazil. Trading port for products of the Amazon basin; accessible to ocean-going ships. Thermal-electric power plant; oil refinery; notable botanic gardens. [3° 0'S 60° 0'W]

Manchester Capital of Greater Manchester Metropolitan County in north-west England. Important commercial, cultural and industrial centre at east end of Manchester Ship Canal. Traditional centre of cotton textile industry, with important markets and spinning industry. Engineering, especially for the textile, transport and food industries. [53° 30'N 2° 15'W]

Mandalay Second largest city of Burma, on the Irrawaddy River. Capital of the Mandalay Division and commercial centre of Upper Burma. Manufactures matches, silk, gold and silverware. [22° 57'N 96° 4'E]

Mangyshlak (Mangghystau) Capital of Mangyshlak Oblast in Kazakhstan, on the east coast of the Caspian Sea. Notable for its large new oilfields. [44° 30'N 52° 30'E]

Manila Capital of the Philippines, in the south-west of Luzon island in Manila Bay.

Chief port, commercial, cultural and industrial centre. Sugar refining and manufacturing of textiles; exports sugar and manila hemp. [14° 40'N 121° 30'E]

Manizales City in west-central Colombia, in the Cordillera Central. Important coffee-producing centre; textiles, leather goods, beer. [5° 5'N 75° 32'W]

Maputo Capital of Mozambique. Port with fine harbour; railway link to Zimbabwe. Fruit in area and cashew nuts to south along coast. Tourist centre. [25° 58'S 32° 32'E]

Maracaibo Deep-water port in north-west Venezuela, on north-west shore of Lake Maracaibo. Expanded after discovery of oil in 1917. Exports oil, coffee, cocoa and sugar. Manufactures chemicals, textiles, soap and rope. [10° 40'N 71° 30'W]

Maracay City in northern Venezuela, northeast of Lake Valencia. Centre of Venezuelan cattle industry; paper, textiles, chemicals, sugar refining; gas wells. [10° 15'N 67° 28'W]

Maribor Town in Slovenia. Has notable 12th-century cathedral. Market (wine and grain) and manufacturing centre: leather, boots and shoes. [46° 36'N 15° 40'E]

Marrakesh City in foothills of High Atlas Mountains in Morocco. Former capital. Famous market square; ancient mosques; notable high minaret. [31° 9'N 8° 0'W]

Marseilles Port in south-east France. Capital of Bouches-du-Rhone *département*. Important commercial centre and leading French port, with petrochemical industry. Large food-processing industry; fertilizers, ship repairing and marine engineering. [43° 18'N 5° 23'E]

Mary Capital of Mary Oblast in Turkmenistan. Ancient town now a centre of cotton, silk and carpets. [37° 40'N 61° 50'E]

Maseru Capital of Lesotho. Short railway from Maseru north to the Bloemfontein to KwaZulu-Natal line in South Africa. Building materials factory. [29° 18'S 27° 30'E]

Masvingo Town in southern Zimbabwe. Oldest European settlement. National park to south, near game reserve. [20° 10'S 30° 49'E]

Matadi Chief port of Zaïre, on River Zaïre. Railway to Kinshasa linking to inland waterways. Exports mainly palm oil, rubber, cotton, and coffee. [5° 52'S 13° 31'E]

Matrah Important deep-water port adjacent to Muscat, Oman. Warehouse facilities; terminus of caravan routes. Trades in dates and fruit. [23.37 N 58.34 E]

Mbabane Capital of Swaziland in the northwest of the country in the Dalgeni Hills. The capital was transferred here from Manzini in 1902. [26° 18'S 31° 6'E]

Mbuji-Mayi City in southern Kasai area of Zaïre. Important mining centre for industrial diamonds. [6° 10'S 23° 39'E]

Mecca Sacred Muslim city of Hijaz, western Saudi Arabia, in a valley surrounded by low hills. Birthplace of Mohammed and site of the Ka'bah Shrine. Its Red Sea port is at Jiddah to the west. [21° 30'N 39° 54'E]

Medan Largest city of Sumatra, in north-east Sumatra, Indonesia, on the Deli River. Communications centre. Centre of fertile region. Exports tobacco, coffee, tea and palm oil. University. [3° 40'N 98° 38'E]

Medellín City in west-central Colombia, in the Cordillera Central. Main textile centre of Colombia; coffee market. Chief centre for gold and silver mining. Chemicals, leather, pottery, steel, glass. [3° 15'N 75° 35'W]

Medina Inland city in Hijaz, western Saudi Arabia. Sacred Muslim city containing the tomb of Mohammed and other important mosques. Trade in agricultural produce, such as dates, cereals and fruit. [24° 35'N 39° 52'E]

Melbourne Capital of Victoria, Australia, on almost enclosed Port Philip Bay. Second largest city in Australia. Established 1835 and greatly expanded from 1850 with discovery of gold. Extensive suburban development. Important manufacturing centre; oil refineries Rich pastoral hinterland. [37° 50'S 145° 0'E

Melilla Modern commercial city on northern coast of Morocco (Spanish enclave). Administered from Málaga. Since 1863 has had free port status. [35° 21'N 2° 57'W]

Memphis River port in Tennessee, south east USA, on Mississippi River. Commercial manufacturing and route centre. Major cotton and hardwood markets. Furniture and flooring industries; cotton seed oil, farm equipment. Regarded as birthplace of blues music. Graceland, home of Elvis Presley, nearby. [35° 8'N 90° 3'W]

Mendoza City in Argentina, in foot hills of Andes on main route from Argentina to the port Valparaiso in Chile. Commercial centre of an irrigated agricultural and wine-growing region. [32° 50'S 68° 52'W]

Mérida Town in Mexico, capital of Yucatán state, in north of Yucatán Peninsula. Founded 1542 on site of Mayan city; many ruins in area. Sisal cultivation. [20° 59'N 89° 39'W]

Mashhad City in north-east Iran, near Turkmen and Afghan borders. Important trade centre, dealing in carpets and cotton goods. Tanning, flour milling and rug making industries. A holy city and place of pilgrimage for Shia Muslims. [36° 20'N 59° 35'E]

Mexico City Capital of Mexico, situated in south-central part of country on plateau over 3,000 m [7,000 ft] above sea level. Built on site of ancient Aztec capital. Volcanoes of Popocatépetl and Iztaccihuatl to south-east. Major industrial centre. One of the world's largest cities with one of the fastest growing urban populations. [19° 20'N 99° 10'W]

Miami Resort in Florida, south-east USA, on Atlantic coast at southern end of peninsula near the Everglades. Commercial centre. Important air-traffic centre; cruise port. Tourist service industry. [25° 47'N 80° 11'W]

Milan Town in north-east Italy. Capital of Lombardy. Leading Italian commercial and anufacturing centre, with famous cathedral d opera house (La Scala) and important de fair. Electrical engineering, publishing dustry. [45° 28'N 9° 10'E]

inneapolis City in Minnesota, north USA, head of navigation of Mississippi River. ajor commercial and route centre. Twin city St Paul on opposite bank. Focus for grain ade and milling industries; electronics and mputer centre, especially for aircraft indus-y. Oil refining. [44° 59'N 93° 16'W]

insk Capital of Belarus and of Minsk blast. Major industrial, transport and manu-cturing centre. [53° 52'N 27° 30'E]

iyazaki Seaport, capital of Miyazaki pre-cture in south-east Kyushu, Japan. Famous rine. [31° 56'N 131° 30'E]

oçambique Town on central part of coast f Mozambique. First Portuguese settlement uilt in 1504 on an island. [15° 3'S 40° 42'E]

ogadishu Capital and main port of omalia, on Indian Ocean. Site of ancient ettlement; Arabic influence in old quarter. xports livestock, sugar. [2° 2'N 45° 25'E]

ogilev (Mahilyow) Capital of Mogilev blast in Belarus. Founded in 13th century; ow an industrial town specializing in syn-hetic fibres. [53° 55'N 30° 18'E]

okpo Seaport on south-west coast of south-rn Cholla province in South Korea. A deep-water port on the Yellow Sea and the southern erminus of the west coast railway to Seoul. Industrial centre. Cotton ginning, rice milling and fishing. [34° 50'N 126° 25'E]

Mombasa Historic seaport of Kenya. Site of medieval town, built on island. Modern harbour of Kilindi on western side of island, now chief port. Oil refinery. Railway to interior. [4° 2'S 39° 43'E]

Monaghan Capital of County Monaghan, Ulster province, in north Republic of Ireland. Cathedral and market centre with dairy and bacon industries. [54° 15'N 6° 58'W]

Monrovia Port, capital of Liberia, on north-ern part of coast. Founded in 1822 for freed slaves from USA. Railway to north. Exports rubber and iron ore. [6° 18'N 10° 47'W]

Montego Bay Town and resort on the north-west coast of Jamaica in the West Indies. Fine beaches and tourist facilities. Important deep-sea fishing centre. [18° 30'N 78° 0'W]

Monterrey City in Mexico, east of Sierra Madre Oriental range. Capital of Nuevo León state. Important route and industry centre. Iron, steel and lead. [25° 40'N 100° 30'W]

Montevideo Seaport on the Rio de la Plata and capital of Uruguay. Industrial and cultural centre; meat-packing, tanning, flour milling, wines, soap, footwear and textiles. Exports animal products. Resort. [34° 50'S 56° 11'W]

Montpellier Town in southern France. Capital of Hérault *département*. Ancient univ-ersity. Large wine market; food, pharmceutical and perfume industry. [43° 37'N 3° 52'E]

Montreal City and port in south-east Canada, in Québec, on St Lawrence Seaway. Mostly French-speaking. Major commercial and manufacturing centre. Grain processing; oil refining; aircraft, railway equipment and clothing industries; publishing and printing. [45° 31'N 73° 34'W]

Morelia Town in Mexico, capital of the state of Michoacan. Altitude 1,900 m [6,235 ft]. Founded in 1541 as a mining settlement named Valladolid. Planetarium opened in 1975. [19° 40'N 101° 11'W]

Moscow Capital of Russia and its largest city. Founded in 12th century, burnt down 1812, though some notable buildings remain, inc-luding the Kremlin, the seat of government. Chief political, cultural and transport centre with many industries. [55° 45'N 37° 35'E]

Mosul City on west bank of the Tigris river, northern Iraq. Centre of agricultural and oil-producing area. [36° 15'N 43° 5'E]

Moulmein Seaport in Burma, on the Gulf of

Martaban. Capital of the Tenasserim Division at mouth of the Salween River. Exports rice and teak. [16° 30'N 97° 40'E]

Mount Isa Town in Selwyn Range, in western New South Wales, Australia. Important copper-mining centre. [20° 42'S 139° 26'E]

Mullingar Capital of County Westmeath, in Leinster province, central Republic of Ireland. Cathedral, route and market centre of leading cattle area. Centre of former Kingdom of Meath. [53° 31'N 7° 20'W]

Munich City in southern Germany; capital of Bavaria. Major commercial, manufacturing and cultural centre, with many famous buildings including Frauenkirche, Pinakothek and Residenz. Leading brewing industry with Oktoberfest. Electrical engineering, transport equipment, printing and publishing. Tourist centre. [48° 8'N 11° 33'E]

Murmansk Ice-free port on Barents Sea, in the extreme north-west of Russia. It is the country's largest fishing port with important shipyards. [68° 57'N 33° 10'E]

Muscat Capital of Oman, on Gulf of Oman. Former port of some importance; most trade now goes to Matrah. [23° 37'N 58° 36'E]

Mymensingh District capital in Bangladesh, on the Brahmaputra fertile flood plain to north of Dacca. Agricultural centre. Engineering and jute processing. [24° 45'N 90° 24'E]

Mysore Town in Karnataka state, south-west India, in high valley between two ridges. Was capital of former Mysore state. Notable Maharaja's Palace (1897). Commercial centre. Silk weaving. Manufacturing sandalwood oil. [13° 15'N 77° 0'E]

N'Djamena Capital of Chad, at confluence of Logone and Chari rivers in extreme west. Livestock market. [12° 10'N 14° 59'E]

Naas Capital of County Kildare, in Leinster province, east-central Republic of Ireland. Market and horse racing centre east of The Curragh. [53° 12'N 6° 40'W]

Nagasaki Seaport, capital of Nagasaki prefecture in Kyushu, Japan. Centre of Japanese Christianity. Half of city destroyed by second atomic bomb dropped in August 194.. Beautiful natural harbour. Exports coal, cotton goods, raw silk and tea. Manufactures aircraft, ships and electrical equipment. [32° 47'N 129° 50'E]

Nagoya Major port and capital of Aichi prefecture in southern Honshu, Japan. Industrial centre and centre of the Japanese pottery and porcelain industries. Also manufactures aircraft, cars, machine tools, textiles, dyes and chemicals. [35° 10'N 136° 50'E]

Nairobi City and capital of Kenya. Commercial and route centre. Light industry. Tourist trade to national park nearby. Coffee and sisal from Muranga (Fort Hall) area by railway. [1° 17'S 36° 48'E]

Nakuru Town in Rift Valley in Kenya, on Lake Nakuru. Market centre in agricultural region. Pyrethrum extracting. Lake famous for flamingos. [0° 16'S 36° 4'E]

Nancy Town in north-eastern France. Capital of Meurthe-et-Moselle *département*. Noted for 18th-century planned centre. Glass and steel industries. [48° 42'N 6° 12'E]

Nanking Capital of Kiangsu province, eastern China. Former capital of Nationalist China. Manufacturing centre, on south bank of Lower Yellow River, for traditional textiles and porcelain. [32° 2'N 118° 47'E]

Naples Seaport in southern Italy. Capital of Campania. Commercial and manufacturing centre of the south, known for its beauty and site on bay north-west of Vesuvius. Founded by Greeks, with strong cultural tradition. Port with leading Italian passenger traffic; steel, aircraft and railway engineering, textiles, paper and food industries. [40° 50'N 14° 17'E]

Narayanganj City in Bangladesh, south-east of Dhaka on the Meghna River. Growing industrial area. Power station, boatbuilding, shoe factory, cotton textiles, jute and grain milling. [23° 40'N 90° 33'E]

Narvik Seaport in north-west Norway with ice-free harbour. Rail terminus of Lappland railway. Exports iron ore from Sweden. [68° 28'N 17° 26'E]

Naryn Capital of Naryn Oblast in Kyrgyz-tan. Local administrative centre; large reser-voirs and hydroelectric power stations nearby. [41° 26'N 75° 58'E]

Nashville Capital of Tennessee, south-east USA. Commercial and manufacturing centre. Major recording industry; textiles, religious publishing and printing. [36° 10'N 86° 47'W]

Nassau Capital of the Bahamas, on north-east coast of New Providence Island, West Indies. Tourist centre. [25° 5'N 77° 20'W]

Nazareth Town in northern Israel. Junction point of highways from Haifa and Jerusalem to Lake Tiberias. Childhood home of Christ. Textiles, leather goods. [32° 42'N 35° 17'E]

Ndola Modern town in northern Zambia. Important centre for Copper Belt. Second largest town in Zambia. [13° 0'S 28° 34'E]

Negombo Town and resort on west coast of Sri Lanka, north of Colombo. At mouth of lagoon, with fine beaches. Exports coconuts and cinnamon. [7° 12'N 79° 50'E]

Neuchâtel Town in western Switzerland on western shore of Lake Neuchâtel. Capital of Neuchâtel canton. University town with major wine market. Watch and clock research centre. [47° 0'N 6° 55'E]

New Delhi Capital of India, in Delhi Union Territory, northern India. Built south of old city of Delhi as capital planned by British; was capital of British India, 1931–47. Tree-lined avenues and gardens. [28° 37'N 77° 13'E]

New Orleans Major port in Louisiana, southern USA, on Mississippi river. Important commercial and cultural centre with leading cotton market. Famed for French Quarter Dixieland jazz. Large petrochemical indus-try; sugar milling, shipbuilding and bauxite-processing industries. [29° 58'N 90° 4'W]

New Plymouth Port and regional centre on North Island, New Zealand, in intensively farmed Taranaki lowlands. [39° 4'S 174° 5'E]

New York City in New York state, north-east USA, on Manhattan and Long Island at mouth of Hudson River. Major international financial, manufacturing and cultural centre. Transport focus; largest US port, handling especially oil and oil products. Headquarters of UN; World Trade Centre. Clothing, print-ing and publishing industries; leather goods. Important tourist centre; known as 'Big Apple'. [40° 45'N 74° 0'W]

Newcastle Seaport and regional centre in New South Wales, Australia. On edge of important coalfield. Developed from coal-mining village; exports coal. Heavy industry. [33° 0'S 151° 46'E]

Newcastle upon Tyne Capital of Tyne and Wear county in north-east England; commer-cial, cultural and industrial centre of Tyneside conurbation. Route focus; port, especially for coal export; ferry terminal for Scandinavia. Shipbuilding industries; engineering, chemi-cals and glass. [54° 59'N 1° 37 W]

Niamey Capital of Niger, on River Niger near south-west border. Route centre. Agricultural market in productive area. [13° 27'N 2° 6'E]

Nice Seaport and resort in south-east France. Capital of Alpes-Maritimes *département*. Route centre and ferry port. Market for horticultural area (noted for mimosa). [43° 42'N 7° 14'E]

Nicosia Capital of Cyprus in centre of the island. Enclosed by walls built for defence in 15th century. Ancient buildings including 14th-century cathedral. Varied manufacturing industries. [35° 10'N 33° 25'E]

Nîmes Town in southern France. Capital of Gard *département*. Ancient commercial and route centre famed for its Roman amphi-theatre and aqueduct. Large textile industry and agricultural machinery. [43° 50'N 4° 23'E]

Nizhniy Novgorod Capital of Nizhniy Nov-gorod Oblast, on Volga River, east of Moscow,

Russia. Formerly called Gorkiy. Developed in mid-20th century into one of the main industrial cities. Light and heavy industries. [56° 20'N 44° 0'E]

Norilsk Northernmost town in Russia in a remote part of Krasnoyarsk Kray, near the mouth of the Yenisey River. Coal, uranium and platinum mines. [69° 20'N 88° 6'E]

Nottingham Capital of Nottinghamshire, north-central England, on River Trent, south of Sherwood Forest. Commercial and industrial centre. Traditional lace and hosiery; major bicycle manufacturing, tobacco processing, pharmaceuticals. [52° 57'N 1° 10'W]

Nouakchott Port and capital of Mauritania, near coast in semi-arid central area. On main north-south trunk road (Morocco-Senegal). Copper exported from Akjoujt area to north-east. [18° 9'N 15° 58'W]

Nouméa Capital of New Caledonia, Melanesia, in west Pacific. Large European population. Nickel and chrome exported. [22° 17'S 166° 30'E]

Novgorod Capital of Novgorod Oblast in north-west Russia. Historic town with 11th-century cathedral. [58° 30'N 31° 25'E]

Novosibirsk Largest city of Siberia, Russia and capital of Novosibirsk Oblast on River Ob. Important industrial, educational and transport centre; vast reservoir and hydroelectric station nearby. Includes Akademgorodok, a scientific research city. [55° 0'N 83° 5'E]

Nukus Capital of Karakalpakstan Republic, Uzbekistan, in the region of the Khorezm oasis. Important local administrative centre. [42° 20'N 59° 7'E]

Nuremberg Town in south-central Germany in Bavaria. Historic commercial, cultural and manufacturing centre with walled inner town. Large electrical engineering and vehicle industries; toys, confectionery. [49° 26'N 11° 5'E]

Oaxaca de Juárez Town in southern Mexico in highland valley area. Capital of Oaxaca

state. Archaeological sites nearby. Wheat oranges, coffee, tobacco. [17° 2'N 96° 40'W

Odessa (Odesa) Historic Black Sea port an resort in the Ukraine. Capital of Odess Oblast and a major educational centre. Wid range of heavy engineering, including ship building. Possesses catacombs. Associate with 1905 revolution. [46° 30'N 30° 45'E]

Oklahoma Capital of Oklahoma state, south central USA. Commercial and route centre fo oil producing, ranching and wheat area Oilfield and construction machinery, aircraf assembly; air base. Large grain-milling an meat-packing industry. [35° 30'N 97° 30'W

Olomouc Town in eastern Czech Republic Formerly capital of Moravia. University (1576). Gothic cathedral; 15th-century towr hall. Manufacturing, including malt, sugar and starch. [49° 38'N 17° 12'E]

Omdurman City in Sudan on Nile, opposite Khartoum. Commercial and industrial centre. Mahdi's tomb. [15° 40'N 32° 28'E]

Oporto Seaport in north-west Portugal near mouth of Douro River. Commercial and manufacturing centre, with long-established port wine trade. Textile industries; engineering and ceramics. [41° 8'N 8° 40'W]

Oran City and port on Mediterranean coast of Algeria. Former French naval base. Old Moorish city with many mosques. Cereals, wines, fruit and skins. [35° 45'N 0° 39'W]

Orlando City in Florida, south-eastern USA. Commercial, manufacturing and route centre of citrus belt, with many lakes to west of Cape Canaveral. Aerospace industry; large fruit-and vegetable-processing industry. Resort based on Disneyland. [28° 33'N 81° 23'W]

Osaka Seaport and capital of Osaka prefecture in southern Honshu, Japan. The third largest city of Japan. Manufacturing and heavy industry; metals, machinery. Important commercial and banking centre. Has a fine castle and temples. University dating from 1931. [34° 40'N 135° 30'E]

slo   Capital and largest port of Norway, at
rthern end of Oslo Fjord. Many fine build-
gs including Royal Palace and City Hall;
aritime Museum at Bygdøy. Administrative,
mmercial and cultural centre. Shipbuilding,
gineering, wood-pulp, fishing and dairy
oduce industries. [59° 55'N 10° 45'E]

stend   Seaport and resort in Belgium, on the
orth Sea, in West Flanders. Ferry terminal.
eading Belgian fishing port and shipbuilding
ntre. [51° 15'N 2° 54'E]

ttawa   Capital of Canada, on Ottawa River
 south-east Ontario. Administrative, comercial, cultural and tourist centre. Notable
arliament buildings. [45° 27'N 75° 42'W]

uagadougou   Capital of Burkina Faso, in
entral position. Modern town on site of
apital of Mossi Empire from 15th century.
oad centre; terminus of railway from
bidjan, Ivory Coast. [12° 25'N 1° 35'W]

xford   Capital of Oxfordshire, south-central
ngland, on River Thames. Commercial,
ducational and industrial centre with ancient
niversity, founded in 12th century; many
oted buildings, quadrangles and gardens.
5° 45'N 1° 15'W]

Padang   Seaport city in western Sumatra,
ndonesia, and one of the oldest Dutch settlements in Sumatra. The harbour is at
Telukbayur (Emmahaven), 8 km [5 mls]
way. Exports coal, copra, coffee, rubber,
tobacco, tea and palm oil. [1° 0'S 100° 20'E]

Palembang   City in south-central Sumatra in
Indonesia. Important trade and communications centre. Nearby oilfields. Also coal,
rubber and coffee. [3° 0'S 104° 52'E]

Palermo   Seaport in southern Italy, capital of
Sicily, on north coast. Ancient commercial
centre founded by Phoenicians. Rich agricultural area, Conca d'Oro, with wine, citrus
fruits and olive processing. Shipbuilding and
repairing industries. [38° 8'N 13° 20'E]

Palma de Mallorca   Seaport of Spain, capital of Majorca and of Balearic Islands. Com-

mercial centre with food and textile industries.
International resort. [39° 35'N 2° 39'E]

Palmerston North   Town and regional centre in south-west lowlands of North Island,
New Zealand. Major communications centre.
Agricultural and dairy products. Agricultural
research centre. [40° 21'S 175° 39'E]

Panama   Capital of the Republic of Panama,
near Pacific end of Panama Canal. Docks at
Balboa nearby; railway. Inter-American Highway to Costa Rica begins at Thatcher Ferry
Bridge over Canal. [9° 0'N 79° 25'W]

Papeete   Seaport and capital of French
Polynesia, on the north-west coast of Tahiti,
south Pacific. Busy harbour, built around a
coastal lagoon; exports copra, phosphates,
pearl shell and vanilla. Sugar refining and soap
manufacturing. [17° 32'S 149° 34'W]

Paramaribo   Capital of Surinam and river
port near the Atlantic. Exports coffee, bauxite,
timber and citrus fruits. [5° 50'N 55° 10'W]

Paris   Capital of France and river port on
River Seine. Outstanding French commercial,
cultural, route and manufacturing centre;
world centre of fashion. Many noted buildings, especially Eiffel Tower, Notre Dame and
Arc de Triomphe. Large engineering industry
especially cars and aircraft. Clothing, printing.
Major tourist centre. [48° 50'N 2° 20'E]

Pavlodar   Capital of Pavlodar Oblast in
northern Kazakhstan. Aluminium, gold, iron
ore. Oil refining. [52° 33'N 77° 0'E]

Pécs   Town in south-west Hungary. Old
trade centre of coal-mining region. Uranium
deposits. Leather goods, wine, porcelain,
tobacco and clothing. [46° 5'N 18° 15'E]

Pegu   Ancient 6th-century town in Burma, on
the Pegu River. Capital of the Pegu Division.
Manufactures pottery. [17° 20'N 96° 29'E]

Périgueux   Town in south-west France, capital of Dordogne *département*. Historic market
town known for its truffles and paté; distilling
industry. [45° 10'N 0° 42'E]

Pernik Town in south-west Bulgaria. Coal-mining town and centre of Bulgaria's heavy industry. Produces iron and steel, and crystal glass. [42° 35'N 23° 2'E]

Perpignan Town in southern France, capital of Pyrénées-Orientales *département*. Centre of orchard, vineyard and market gardening area. [42° 42'N 2° 53'E]

Perth Capital of Western Australia, on low-lying coastal plain in south-west of state with Darling Range to east. Spreads along both banks of the Swan River. Industrial suburban zone. [31° 57'S 115° 52'E]

Perugia Town in central Italy. Capital of Umbria. Ancient university and defensive centre, with confectionery and paper industries. [43° 6'N 12° 24'E]

Peshawar Town in north-west Pakistan, commanding the Khyber Pass, on old trade route to Afghanistan. Bazaars. Cereals, rice, sugar cane, cotton, tobacco grown with irrigation from Kabul River. [34° 2'N 71° 37'E]

Petah Tikva Industrial centre in central Israel. First modern Jewish settlement in Palestine, 1878. Chemicals, textiles and agricultural machinery. [32° 6'N 34° 53'E]

Petropavlovsk-Kamchatskiy Capital of Kamchatka Oblast in far eastern Siberia, Russia. Important fishing port on Pacific Ocean. [53° 3'N 158° 43'E]

Petrozavodsk Capital of Karelia Republic in north-west Russia, on Lake Onega. Industries include tractor manufacturing; also an important touring centre. [61° 41'N 34° 20'E]

Philadelphia Port in Pennsylvania, eastern USA, on Delaware River. Major commercial and cultural centre. Large oil refining, chemical and machinery industries. Naval base. [39° 57'N 75° 10'W]

Phnom Penh Capital of Cambodia, at head of Mekong River delta. Transport centre and river port, with shipping, dried fish, rice and textile industries. [11° 33'N 104° 55'E]

Phoenix Capital of Arizona and commerc route and manufacturing centre for the sou west USA. At northern end of major copp mining area, in irrigated agricultural regi Large electronics, aircraft and food-processi industries. [33° 27'N 112° 4'W]

Piraeus Seaport in south-eastern Gree south-west of Athens. Industrial and comm cial centre; shipbuilding, textiles and c refining industries. [37° 57'N 23° 42'E]

Pisa Town in west-central Italy, in Tuscar Former city state and port with ancie university and many fine buildings. Famo for its leaning tower. [43° 43'N 10° 24'E]

Pittsburgh City in Pennsylvania, easte USA, where Allegheny and Monongahe rivers form Ohio River. Commercial, indu trial and transport centre. Major steel pro ucer; aluminium and steel rolling; and rollir machinery. Centre of large bituminous coa natural gas and oilfields. [40° 26'N 80° 0'W

Plovdiv Town in southern Bulgaria. Ruins 13th-century fortress. Industries include chem icals, textiles, tanning and footwear product [42° 8'N 24° 44'E]

Plymouth Port in Devon, at mouth of Rive Tamar, in south-west England. Commercia centre for large part of south-west Englanc naval base (with Devonport). Drake sighte Spanish Armada from Plymouth Hoe, 1588 [50° 23'N 4° 09'W]

Plzen Town in western Czech Republic University, 14th-century cathedral, 16th century town hall. Manufactures munitions locomotives, aircraft, electrical motors, leathe and Pilsner lager. [49° 45'N 13° 22'E]

Podgorica Town in southern Yugoslavia capital of Montenegro. Agricltural processing and aluminium smelting. [42° 30'N 19° 19'E]

Pointe Noire Town and port on coast of Congo. Terminus of railway from Brazzaville. Exports timber; also manganese from Gabon; cotton from Central African Republic. Light industry and fishing. [4° 46'S 11° 53'E]

ontianak Port in western Borneo (Kalimantan), Indonesia. Large trading and distribution centre for west. Exports rubber, copra, rest products and gold. [0° 3'S 109° 15'E]

ort Elizabeth Seaport in southern Eastern ape province, South Africa. Founded by ritish settlers after the Napoleonic wars. Manufacturing centre, including car industry. ruit canning and fishing industries. Famous ake park. [33° 58'S 25° 40'E]

ort Gentil Port in Gabon, at mouth of avigable Ogooué river. Lumber floated down ver, especially valuable akoumé, and then xported. Plywood factory. [0° 40'S 8° 50'E]

ort Harcourt Town and port on Bonny River, east of Niger Delta in Nigeria. Railway erminus. Industrial centre; Important oil efining centre, with oil and gas pipelines from elta area. Exports palm products, cocoa, roundnuts. [4° 40'N 7° 10'E]

ort Laoise Capital of County Laois in Leinster province, central Republic of Ireland. Market centre in agricultural region; known or its prison. [53° 2'N 7° 20'W]

ort Moresby Seaport and capital of Papua New Guinea, on west coast of south-east peninsula of New Guinea. [9° 24'S 147° 8' E]

Port of Spain Capital of Trinidad and Tobago, West Indies, on the Gulf of Paria. Principal port and air transport centre for the Caribbean. Produces rum, plastics; oil, sugar, citrus fruits exported. [10° 40'N 61° 31'W]

Port Pirie Port in southern South Australia on Spencer Gulf. Developed as main port for lead, silver and zinc ores from Broken Hill mines. [33° 1'S 138° 0'E]

Port Said City and chief port in Egypt, at northern end of the Suez Canal. Founded in 1859. Railway to Cairo. Chief export is cotton. [31° 16'N 32° 18'E]

Port Sudan Port in Sudan, on Red Sea. Exports cotton, hides. Oil refining; salt works. Coral reefs off coast. [19° 32'N 37° 9'E]

Port-au-Prince Port and capital of Haiti, West Indies, on deep bay on west coast. Fine natural harbour. Commercial centre. Sugar industry is important. Light manufacturing development. [18° 40'N 72° 20'W]

Portalegre Town in eastern Portugal. Textile centre famous for its tapestries, with many 16th- and 17th-century buildings. Cork industry. [39° 19'N 7° 25'W]

Portland River port in Oregon, north-west USA, at confluence of rivers Willamette and Columbia. Commercial and manufacturing centre. Wood processing and lumber equipment industries; electronics, clothing, food processing, fishing. [45° 32'N 122° 37'W]

Pôrto Alegre Seaport at the end of the Lagoa dos Patos, south-east Brazil. Capital of Rio Grande do Sul state. Shipyards; meat-packing industries. Exports meat products, wool, rice, tobacco and grapes. [30° 5'S 51° 10'W]

Porto-Novo Capital of Benin, situated on a coastal lagoon. Founded by Portuguese in 17th century as slave trade centre. Now administrative centre. [6° 23'N 2° 42'E]

Portsmouth Port in Hampshire, southern England. Important naval base and dockyard on north shore of Spithead. Ferryport for Isle of Wight. Nelson's flagship Victory moored here. [50° 48'N 1° 6'W]

Potosí Town high in the Andes, south-central Bolivia. At 4,180 m [13,700 ft] is one of the highest towns in the world. Important mining centre for silver, tin, copper lead; manufactures electrical equipment, furniture, iron and steel, and footwear. [19° 38'S 65° 50'W]

Potsdam Town in east-central Germany. Has Sans Souci Palace, scene of 1945 conference; noted scientific and technical institutes. Manufactures engines, textiles, chemicals and precision instruments. [52° 23'N 13° 4'E]

Poznan Town in west-central Poland, on River Warta. Old city with many ancient buildings surviving or rebuilt. Heavy industrial centre. [52° 25'N 16° 51'E]

Prague Capital of Czech Republic on River Vltava. Ancient cultural, historical and political centre; 14th-century town hall, Hradcany Palace (16th–17th century), Charles University (founded 1348), St Vitus Cathedral (begun 1344). Communications centre, with many educational institutes and societies. Manufactures include textiles, chemicals, paper, glass, leather, machinery, and printing and publishing industries. [50° 5'N 14° 22'E]

Praia Capital of Cape Verde, on south shore of São Tiago Island, in the eastern Atlantic Ocean. Naval shipyard. [15° 0'N 24° 0'W]

Pretoria Inland city to the north of Johannesburg, South Africa, in the province of Pretoria, Witwatersrand and Vereeniging (PWV). Administrative capital of South Africa. Many historic relics, both Afrikaner and British, including President Kruger's house, now a museum. Iron ore in area. Two universities (1873, 1908). [25° 44'S 28° 12'E]

Providence Port, capital of Rhode Island, north-eastern USA, at head of Narragansett Bay. Established in 1636 as haven of religious liberty. Textiles; jewellery and silverware industries; oil refining. [41° 49'N 71° 24'W]

Puebla Town in highland area of Mexico. Capital of Puebla state. Administrative, route and agricultural centre. Textiles, especially cotton industry. Famous for tiles and onyx ware. [19° 0'N 98° 10'W]

Pune City in Maharashtra state, central India, in area west of Ghats mountains on the Mutha and Mula rivers. Railway junction. Military centre, developed by British after 1817. Cotton and paper manufacturing. Aga Khan's palace. [18° 29'N 73° 57'E]

Punta Arenas Seaport in southern Chile, on Strait of Magellan. Southern most town in Chile. Exports wool and meat. Military and naval base. [53° 10'S 71° 0'W]

Pusan City on the south-east coast of South Korea, developed into a major port under Japanese rule 1910–45. Terminus for the Korean trunk railway. Industries includes railway engineering, shipbuilding, rice milling, textiles and salt refining. Exports rice, fish and soyabeans. [35° 5'N 129° 0'E]

Pyongyang City and capital of North Korea on the right bank of the Taedong River. Hydroelectric power on Yalu River. Industrial centre in an anthracite mining area, manufactures textiles, chemicals, paper and matches. Refines sugar. Remains of ancient wall. [38° 24'S 127° 17'E]

Qom Town in north-east central Iran, south-south-west of Tehran, Holy City of Shi'it Moslems. Centre of grain and cotton region. Textiles and potteries. [34° 40'N 51° 0'E]

Quebéc Town in south-east Canada. Capital of Quebéc province. Long established (1608) administrative and cultural centre; French-speaking. Picturesque old city on two levels. Pulp and paper, food processing and textile mills; shipbuilding. [46° 52'N 71° 13'W]

Quezon City City and former capital of the Philippines, adjoining Manila to the north east. Mainly residential. [14° 38'N 121° 0'E]

Quito Capital of Ecuador. Situated on fertile plateau in Andes, 2,890 m [9,480 ft] high almost on Equator. Textiles, leather goods and carpets. [0° 15'S 78° 35'W]

Rabat Capital of Morocco, on north-west coast. Modern city on site of 10th-century *ribat* or fortified monastery. [34° 2'N 6° 48'W]

Rabaul Town in north of Gazelle Peninsula of New Britain in Bismarck Archipelago, Papua New Guinea. Administrative centre of Archipelago. Fertile area. Copra and cocoa important. [4° 24'S 152° 8'E]

Rangoon Capital of Burma (Myanmar), largest city and chief seaport, 84 km [21 mls] up Rangoon River. Exports rice, cotton and teak. Oil refining, timber working and rice milling. Major airport. [16° 45'N 96° 12'E]

Rangpur Town in north-west Bangladesh, north-north-west of Dacca. Market centre for tobacco, jute, rice and oilseed. Railway.

ctrical machinery, carpets, cutlery and cks manufactured. [24° 42'N 89° 22'E]

walpindi City in northern Pakistan. mporary capital from 1959 until comple- n of Islamabad to north-east. On Grand unk Road (west-east). Former military sta- n. Railway engineering. [33° 38'N 73° 8'E]

cife Major seaport in eastern Brazil. pital of Pernambuco state. Extensive dern port facilities. Exports sugar, cotton, nber and agricultural produce. Airport; val and military base. [8° 0'S 35° 0'W]

egina Town in south-central Canada, on oosejaw Creek. Capital of Saskatchewan. rvice and distribution centre for large neat-growing district. Grain processing, oil fining, steel mills. [50° 27'N 104° 35'W]

eykjavik Capital of Iceland, in the south- est on a peninsula extending into Faxa Bay. ounded by Vikings in AD 874. Commercial, ltural and industrial centre, with important arbour. Fish processing and shipbuilding dustries. [64° 10'N 21° 57'W]

ichmond Port, capital of Virginia, eastern JSA at head of navigation of James River. Commercial and cultural centre; was capital f Confederacy. Large tobacco industry; hemicals, wood and food-processing indus- ries; bauxite smelting. [37° 33'N 77° 27'W]

Riga Baltic seaport and capital of Latvia. ndustrial and transport centre, with many old hurches. Famous resort. [56° 53'N 24° 8'E]

Rijeka Seaport in western Croatia. Hungarian until 1918. Annexed by Italy 1924. Ceded to Yugoslavia 1947. Roman triumphal arch; athedral (1377). Manufactures ships, tor- pedoes and machinery. [45° 20'N 14° 21'E]

Rio de Janeiro Principal port of Brazil and capital until 1960. Situated on one of the argest harbours in the world, noted for its scenery. Exports coffee, sugar and iron ore. Major industry associated with large port; one of the leading tourist centres of South America with many seaside resorts. [23° 0'S 43° 12'W]

Riyadh Capital of Saudi Arabia, situated in an oasis in the Najd. Railway to Dammam. Commercial centre with oil processing indus- tries. [24° 41'N 46° 42'E]

Rome Capital of Italy and of Lazio. 'Eternal city' founded by Romulus and Remus on River Tiber; capital of ancient empire with many remains, especially Coliseum, and of Roman Catholic faith. Commercial, educa- tional and tourist centre, with printing, cloth- ing and film industries. [41° 54'N 12° 30'E]

Rosario Argentina's largest inland port on the River Paraná, upstream from the Rio de la Plata. Founded 1725. Railway junction; agri- cultural trading centre; brewing; manufactures bricks and furniture; exports wheat, meat and hides from the Pampas. [33° 0'S 60° 40'W]

Roskilde Market town in Denmark, in east Zealand. Cathedral is burial place of Danish kings. Industrial centre. [55° 50'N 12° 2'E]

Rotorua Resort in central part of North- Island, New Zealand. On volcanic plateau in famous thermal springs region with many lakes. Local Maori population. Arts and Crafts institute. Resort. [38° 9'S 176° 16'E]

Rotterdam Seaport in Zuid Holland, in south-west Netherlands. Major international port, at Europoort, at outlet of Rhine and Maas (Meuse) rivers. Petrochemicals, ship- building, food processing and paper industry. Site of Euromast tower. [51° 55'N 4° 30'E]

Rovaniemi Town in northern Finland at confluence of Kemijoki and Oumasjoki rivers. Capital of Finnish Lappland. Destroyed by fire during World War II and rebuilt to plans of Alvar Aalto. [66° 29'N 25° 41'E]

Sacramento Capital of California, western USA. Commercial manufacturing and route centre of Great Valley. Major food-processing industry, especially rice, peaches, vegetables and nuts. Aerospace industry. Canal link with Pacific. [38° 35'N 121° 29'W]

St Gallen Town in north-east Switzerland and capital of St Gallen canton. Ancient educational centre founded round 7th-century abbey. Major textile centre of Switzerland; linen, embroidery. [47° 26'N 9° 22'E]

St George's Port and capital of Grenada, Windward Islands, West Indies. Founded by French in 1705, British 1783-1974. Picturesque sheltered harbour. [12° 5'N 61° 43'W]

St John's Seaport in eastern Canada. Capital of Newfoundland, on south-east Newfoundland Island. First settled 1593. Fishing port and railhead; industry. [45° 20'N 52° 40'W]

St Louis City and river port in Missouri, central USA, on Mississippi River. Major commercial, route and cultural centre. Large transport industry, especially aerospace and car assembly; brewing; oil refining; chemicals; steel manufacture. [38° 37'N 90° 12'W]

St Louis Town in northern Senegal, at mouth of Senegal River. Founded as French headquarters on Sor island in 1659, and capital 1895-1902. Fishing centre and communications centre for trade. [16° 8'N 16° 27'W]

St Petersburg Second city of Russia. Founded 1703 by Peter the Great; originally named St Petersburg; then Petrograd, then Leningrad. Built on islands separated by River Neva and many canals. Was the capital for two centuries. Major port; industry and transport focus. [59° 55'N 30° 20'E]

Salamanca Town in west Spain, capital of Salamanca province. Grain, leather and fertilizer industries. University town (1215) with famous Roman bridge. [40° 58'N 5° 39'W]

Thessaloniki Town in north-eastern Greece at head of Gulf of Thessaloniki. Industry and communications centre, exports metallic ores, tobacco, hides. Manufactures textiles, chemicals and metal products. [40° 38' N 22° 58'E]

Salvador Seaport and capital of Bahia state, eastern Brazil. Modern port, naval base and dockyard. Tourist centre. [13° 0'S 38° 30'W]

Salzburg Town in eastern Austria, capital of Salzburg province. Commercial and cultural

centre with famous annual music festival as ciated especially with Mozart (who was b here). Notable buildings. [47° 48'N 13° 2

Samara Capital of Samara Oblast in Rus and old established centre of vast 'Volga Be industrial zone. Formerly Kuybyshev. Ra expansion; oil refining complexes; sulph Hydroelectric power from large reserv nearby. [53° 10'N 50° 10'E]

Samarkand (Samarqand) Ancient city Uzbekistan. Capital of Samarkand Oblast a an academic centre. Noted for its mosqu Important silk industry. [39° 40'N 66° 55'

San Francisco Seaport in California, we USA, on peninsula between San Francis Bay and the Pacific Ocean. Major commerc and manufacturing centre linked to north Golden Gate Bridge. Destroyed by earthqua and fire in 1906. Site of Stanford Universit Shipbuilding, electronics, fishing, oil refinin Tourist centre. [37° 47'N 122° 25'W]

San José Capital of Costa Rica, in centr highland and basin area. Founded in 173 Route centre. Coffee, cocoa and sugar pr duced. Light industry. [9° 55'N 84° 2'W]

San Juan Port, capital of Puerto Rico, c north coast. Founded 1510; notable ruin Oil refinery; ship repairing; sugar; deep-se fishing. Tourist centre. [18° 28'N 66° 7'W]

San Luis Potosí Town and state capital o central plateau of Mexico. Administration an route centre established in 16th century fc San Pedro silver mines. [22° 9'N 100° 59'W

San Salvador Capital of El Salvador, i south-central area, surrounded by mountains Destroyed by earthquake in 1854. Commer cial and cultural centre. [13° 40'N 89° 10'W

San Sebastián Seaport in northern Spain capital of Guipúzcoa province. Commercia centre and resort on Basque coast. Fishing cement, chemicals. [43° 17'N 1° 58'W]

Sana Capital of Republic of Yemen. Walle city with many mosques, in mountainous area.

Handicrafts and textiles. [15° 24'N 44° 14'E]

Santa Cruz Capital of Santa Cruz de Tenerife province, Tenerife, Canary Islands (Spain). Main manufacturing centre and port. Large exporter of bananas and tomatoes. Tourist centre. [28° 28'N 16° 15'W]

Santiago Capital of Chile, on plain at 518 m [1,700 ft]. Cultural centre and principal industrial city of Chile. Destroyed by an earthquake in 1647. [33° 24'S 70° 40'W]

Santo Domingo Port and capital of Dominican Republic, West Indies, on Caribbean coast. First capital of Spanish South America. 16th-century cathedral; university. Important agricultural area; exports mainly sugar. Some light industry. [18° 30'N 69° 59'W]

Santos Seaport for São Paulo, east Brazil. One of the chief ports of Brazil and world's largest coffee exporting port. One of Brazil's principal seaside resorts. [24° 0'S 46° 20'W]

São Paulo Largest city and principal industrial centre of Brazil. Capital of São Paulo state, west Brazil. Port at Santos. Industries include textiles, chemicals, steel and automobiles. Oil refineries. [23° 32'S 46° 37'W]

Sarajevo Capital of Bosnia-Herzegovina. Scene of assassination of Archduke Franz Ferdinand in 1914, leading to World War I. Centre of Yugoslav Muslims; many mosques. Tobacco, cigars, carpets, silk and pottery. Centre of ethnic war between Serbs, Croats and Muslims since 1991. [43° 52'N 18° 26'E]

Seattle Seaport in Washington, north-west USA, on Puget Sound. Commercial, manufacturing and route centre. Port deals mainly with Far East and Alaska. Major aircraft industry, especially commercial jets. Shipbuilding; wood, fish and grain processing industries. [47° 36'N 122° 20'W]

Segovia Town in north-central Spain. Capital of Segovia province. Ancient defensive centre on spectacular rocky site at 1,000 m [3,280 ft]; famous Roman aqueduct. Traditional wool industry. [40° 57'N 4° 10'W]

Sekondi-Takoradi Twin city on west coast of Ghana. Port (Takoradi) and business centre. Locomotive repair yards and sawmills. Produces timber, cocoa, manganese, bauxite. [4° 58'N 1° 45'W]

Semipalatinsk (Semey) Capital of Semipalatinsk Oblast in east Kazakhstan, on Irtysh (Ertis) River. Meat-packing industry. Centre of a rural steppe region. [50° 30'N 80° 10'E]

Sendai Capital of Miyagi prefecture north Honshu, Japan. Cultural centre, with Tokyo Imperial University (1907) and several technical schools. Trade in salt and fish. Metallurgy, lacquer ware. [38° 15'N 140° 53'E]

Seoul Capital of South Korea. Upstream from mouth of the Han River and its seaport Inch'on. A focal point of transport systems, in the richest and most extensive plain of the country. Industries include tanning, flour milling, railway and metallurgical engineering and textile-based industries. Olympic Games held here in 1988. [37° 31'N 126° 58'E]

Sevastopol Important Black Sea port in the Crimea, southern Ukraine. Razed in two wars; now a popular resort. [44° 35'N 33° 30'E]

Seville Town and river port in south-western Spain. Capital of Seville province and of Andalusia. Commercial and route centre since Roman times, famous for its architecture and Holy Week. Shipbuilding; textile, food-processing, distilling and transport equipment industries. Tourist centre. [37° 23'N 6° 0'W]

Sfax City and port on coastal plain in eastern Tunisia. Important olive-growing area. Olive oil, phosphates, esparto grass and dates exported. [34° 49'N 10° 48'E]

Shanghai City and municipality of east-central China on tributary of the Yangtze River just inland from coast of East China Sea. Heavy industry; iron and steel, chemicals and machine building. Textiles and food processing also important. [31° 15'N 121° 26'E]

Sheffield City in South Yorkshire, northern England. Commercial and industrial centre on hilly site, east of Pennines. Traditional steel-working industry, famed for cutlery, silver plate; engineering. [53° 23'N 1° 30'W]

Shenyang Capital of Liaoning province, north-east China. On the Hun Ho River, a for-mer Manchu capital. Produces about one quarter of China's machinery. Important metal manufuring centre; textiles, paper, glass and processed foods. [41° 48'N 123° 27'E]

Shiraz Industrial and commercial city in south-west-central Iran, on road from Tehran to Bushehr. Textiles, fertilizers, handicrafts; Tourist centre. [29° 42'N 52° 30'E]

Saïdi Town on coast of Lebanon. Important city of Ancient Phoenicians. Oil pipeline terminus for Saudi Arabia. Oil refining; glass and dye trade. [33° 35'N 35° 25'E]

Simbirsk Capital of Ulyanovsk Oblast in Russia, on River Volga. Formerly Ulyanovsk. Birthplace of Lenin (real name Ulyanov); Lenin museum. [54° 20'N 48° 25'E]

Skopje Capital of the Former Yugoslav Republic of Macedonia in the north on the River Vardar. Largely destroyed by an earth-quake in 1963. Road and rail junction. Flour milling, brewing, wine-making, cigarettes, car-pets and cement. [42° 1' N 21° 32'E]

Sligo Capital of County Sligo in Connacht province, north-west Republic of Ireland. Regional and cathedral centre; port between Lough Gill and Sligo Bay. Bacon and grain processing. Tourist area. [54° 17'N 8° 28'W]

Sofia Capital of Bulgaria. Founded by the Romans; under Turkish rule for 500 years; passed to Bulgaria in 1877. Cultural, indus-trial and transport centre. Important railway links with Istanbul. University; many interest-ing buildings including 19th-century cathedral and 6th-century church of St Sophia. Engin-eering, chemicals, textiles, metallurgy and food processing. [42° 45'N 23° 20'E]

Sparta Town in southern Greece. Capital of Lakonia. Important city state of ancient Greece. Commercial centre, products include

citrus fruits and olive oil. [37° 5'N 22° 25'E]

Split Seaport in southern Croatia on Adriati Sea. Diocletian's Palace AD 295–306. Com mercial and shipping centre. Fisheries an numerous industries. [43° 31'N 16° 26'E]

Srinagar Chief town and summer capita of Jammu and Kashmir state, north India Area renowned for beautiful scenery. T north-east is scenic Dal Lake, with floatin gardens. 8th-century Shankaracharya Temple Carpet mills, silver, leather, woodwork and cashmere goods. [34° 5'N 74° 50'E]

Stanley Capital and main port of Falklan Islands, south Atlantic Ocean. Seal oil, wool skins, tallow. Imports: food, electrical machin-ery, coal, oil and timber. [51° 40'S 59° 51'W]

Stavanger Seaport on south-west coast of Norway, with harbour sheltered by offshore islands. Centre of oil industry. Fish-curing, canning, shipbuilding. [58° 57'N 5° 40'E]

Stavropol Capital of Stavropol Kray in Russia, in the northern Caucasus. Natural gas plant; leather industry. [45° 5'N 42° 0'E]

Stirling Capital of Central region, Scotland. Commercial and route centre in the Forth River valley in rich agricultural area known as Carse of Stirling. Historic strategic centre with castle. Important cattle market. Agricultural equipment industry. [56° 7'N 3° 57'W]

Stockholm Capital and seaport of Sweden, on Baltic coast. Many fine buildings, including City Hall, churches and museums. Important commercial and educational centre. Ship-building, timber, iron, paper and textiles. Tourist attractions such as Skansen open-air park and Vasa Museum. [59° 20'N 18° 3'E]

Stornoway Capital of Western Isles region, north-west Scotland, and only town on Isle of Lewis. Centre of Harris tweed industry; fish-ing port and oilfield equipment manufacture. Tourist centre. [58° 12'N 6° 23'W]

Strasbourg Town in eastern France. Capital of Bas-Rhin *département*. Historic regional ntre; canal and river port. Famous cathe-al; site of European Parliament. Textiles, ngineering, food and printing industries. 8° 35'N 7° 42'E]

tuttgart Town in south-west Germany. apital of Baden-Württemberg. River port, mmercial and manufacturing centre. Early te of automotive engineering, with noted useum. Electrical engineering, printing, ublishing and textiles. [48° 46'N 9° 10'E]

ucre Legislative capital of Bolivia, founded 538. Altitude 2,705 m [8,900 ft]. above sea vel. Old university (1624) and 17th-century athedral. Agricultural centre; food process-ng; oil refining. [19° 0'S 65° 15'W]

uez City at southern end of Suez Canal in astern Egypt. Oil refining; fertilizers. Railway o Cairo and Port Said. [29° 58'N 32° 31'E]

urabaya City in north-east Java in Indon-sia. Major seaport and chief naval base; one f the most important trade centres of the Far East. Shipbuilding, oil refining, food process-ng. Exports: rice, sugar, tobacco, maize, coffee and cassava. [7° 17'S 112° 45'E]

Surat Ancient town and port in Gujarat state, west India, on Gulf of Khambhat. Noted for silks, gold and silver brocades and cotton textiles. [21° 12'N 72° 55'E]

Suva Capital of Fiji, on south-east coast of Viti Levu, Fiji Islands, south-west Pacific. Administrative and manufacturing centre. On major air and sea routes. [18° 6'S 178° 30'E]

Sverdlovsk Capital of Sverdlovsk Oblast and chief city of Urals industrial region, Russia. Large airport and several railways, including Trans-Siberian. Mineralogy museum. Coal, iron, gold and platinum. [56° 50'N 60° 30'E]

Swansea Port, capital of West Glamorgan, Wales. Commercial centre of area with large metals industry. Tin plating, nikel, titanium processing; oil refining. Formerly the world's major coal exporter. [51° 37'N 3° 57'W]

Sydney Seaport and capital of New South

Wales, on Jackson Bay in south-east Australia. Largest city in Australia; founded as British convict settlement in 1788. Fine natural harbour with famous bridge and notable Opera House. Administrative, commercial and financial centre, but also important manu-facturing centre. [33° 53'S 151° 10'E]

Taegu City and capital of northern Kyong-sang province in South Korea, north-north-west of Pusan. In the basin of the Nakkong River at the centre of an agricultural district, it is a commercial city with good rail and road communications. Produces grain, fruit, tobacco and textiles. [35° 50'N 128° 37'E]

Tainan Town in southern Taiwan, on west-ern coast. Former capital and important port. Dutch settled here 1623. Administrative, mar-ket and cultural centre. Rice and sugar cane in area. Textile industry. [23° 17'N 120° 18'E]

Taipei City and capital of Taiwan, in extreme north. Seat of Chinese Nationalist Govern-ment; administrative and educational centre. Rice-growing area. Food processing and tex-tiles. Tourist centre. [25° 4'N 121° 29'E]

Tallinn Capital of Estonia, on Gulf of Fin-land. Historic port with many old buildings; 13th-century citadel and the Toomkirik (cathedral) built in the 13th–15th centuries. Transport junction. [59° 22'N 24° 48'E]

Tangier (Tanger) Historic town on north peninsula of Morocco, overlooking Strait of Gibraltar. Commercial and administrative centre and resort. Site of ancient Phoenician settlement. [35° 50'N 5° 49'W]

Tarragona Seaport in north-eastern Spain. Capital of Tarragona province. Roman capital of Iberia. Wine, distilling and petrochemical industries. [41° 5'N 1° 17'E]

Tashauz (Dashhowuz) Capital of Tashauz Oblast in the Khorezm Oasis, Turkmenistan. Cotton processing town. [41° 49'N 59° 58'E]

Tbilisi (Tiflis) Capital of Georgia, in a scenic setting south of the Caucasus, on the River Kura. Founded in 4th century AD. Now a major national, industrial and cultural centre and international air transport focus. World's first funicular railway built here in 1905. Many old buildings. [41° 43'N 44° 50'E]

Tegucigalpa Capital of Honduras, Central America, in southern highlands on Choluteca River. Founded by Spanish in 1524 as a silver-mining centre. Modern town on slopes of Mt El Picacho; other high peaks nearby. Commercial and road centre. [14° 5'N 87° 14'W]

Tehran Capital of Iran, 105 km [65 mls] south of the Caspian Sea, at foot of southern slope of Elburz Mountains. Transport, industrial and cultural centre. Carpets, chemicals and cars. Tourist centre. [35° 44'N 51° 30'E]

Tel-Aviv-Jaffa City in Israel. Founded 1909 by Zionists. Main education and financial centre of the country. [32° 4'N 34° 48'E]

Thimphu Capital of Bhutan, in high valley of Himalayas, 2,600 m [8,500 ft] above sea level. Ricefields in area. Royal Palace built in 1961. [27° 31'N 89° 45'E]

Thon Buri Suburb of Bangkok, southern Thailand, on opposite bank of Chao Phraya River. Former capital. [13° 43'N 100° 29'E]

Thorshavn Capital of the Faroe Islands, on the largest island, Strømø. Ancient fortress; fishing port. Lighthouse. [62° 2'N 6° 47'W]

Thule Settlement on the coast of Hayes Peninsula, north-west Greenland. Danish trading post founded 1910. Seaport open for two to three months per year. American air base and site of ballistic missile early warning system. [77° 40'N 69° 0'W]

Tianjin City in north-east China and independent municipal district. On the Hai He River, 40 km [25 mls] inland, connected to the Yangtze River by the Grand Canal. Industrial and commercial city, with important metallurgical industries. [39° 8'N 117° 10'E]

Timbuktu Historic town to north of Niger River in central Mali. Once Islamic cultural centre and focus of caravan routes. Ancient mosques. Salt brought from old lake beds north-west. [16° 50'N 3° 0'W]

Tiranë Capital of Albania, most industrialized Albanian town, at edge of fertile coast plain. Chiefly Muslim. Founded in 17th century by Turks. Market centre for agricultural products. [41° 18'N 19° 49'E]

Tokyo Capital of Japan and of Tokyo prefecture, east-central Honshu. Founded in 145_ Site of the Imperial Palace. Practically destroyed in 1923 by earthquake, tidal wave and fire. Major industrial, commercial and educational centre with varied industries and institutes, including several universities. Has major pollution problems, and marshy site requires expensive reclamation from the sea. Together with Osaka-Kobe-Kyoto, spoken of as the Tokaido megalopolis. [35° 45'N 139° 45'E]

Toledo Town in central Spain. Capital of Toledo province. Ancient cultural and defensive centre with famous cathedral on rocky site. Traditional inlaid metal industry. Tourist centre. [39° 50'N 4° 2'W]

Toronto City and river port in south-east Canada on north-west Lake Ontario. Capital of Ontario province and Canada's largest city. Commercial and manufacturing centre of most populated area of Canada. University (1827), two airports. Food, metal and electrical industries. [43° 39'N 79° 20'W]

Toulouse Town in southern France. Capital of Haute-Garonne *département*. Has ancient university and famous Romanesque church. Aircraft industries, chemicals and food-processing. [43° 37'N 1° 27'E]

Tralee Capital of County Kerry, in Munster province, south-west Republic of Ireland. Regional centre and resort at north-east end of Dingle Peninsula. Important bacon industry. [52° 16'N 9° 42'W]

Trenton Capital of New Jersey, eastern USA, at head of navigation on Delaware River. Manufacturing centre. Large steelworks; consumer goods manufactured. Site of Princeton University. [40° 14'N 74° 46'W]

rier Town in North Rhine-Westphalia, outh-west Germany. Ancient regional and ecclesiastical centre. Site of Roman Porta Nigra. Birthplace of Karl Marx. [49° 45'N 6° 37'E]

ripoli Capital of Libya and port on western Mediterranean coast, in Tripolitania province. Established by the Phoenicians and developed by the Romans. Ancient city wall. Population growth since Saharan oil discoveries; second largest city in Lebanon. [32° 49'N 13° 7'E]

Trivandrum Capital of Kerala state, southern India, on the Malabar coast. Built on hills. Large temple to Vishnu. Textiles and coconuts; wood carving. [8° 41'N 77° 0'E]

Trondheim Seaport in western Norway at head of the ice-free Trondheim fjord. Shipbuilding. Exports timber, dairy produce and copper from Røros. [63° 36'N 10° 25'E]

Trujillo Town in western Peru. Ruins of pre-Incan city nearby. Commercial and industrial centre for sugar, rice, soap, cocaine, candles and machinery, [8° 6'S 79° 0'W]

Tselinograd (Aqmola) Capital of Tselinograd Oblast, on the River Ishim in Kazakhstan. Founded 1830. Railway focus; various heavy industries. [51° 10'N 71° 30'E]

Tunis Capital of Tunisia on Gulf of Tunis. Important north coast port; outport La Goulette. Docks linked to sea by canal through Lake of Tunis. Modern town alongside old Arab quarter; fine markets and mosques. Exports: textiles, olive oil, carpets, iron ore and phosphates. [36° 50'N 10° 11'E]

Turin Town in north-east Italy. Capital of Piedmont province. Commercial and manufacturing centre; 17th to 18th-century city with rectangular plan. Major car industry, aircraft engineering and textiles. Noted vermouth manufacture; publishing. [45° 4'N 7° 40'E]

Turku Seaport in south-west Finland at the mouth of the Aurajoki River on the Gulf of Bothnia. Capital of Finland until 1812. Industrial and agricultural centre. Shipbuilding, textiles and tobacco. [60° 30'N 22° 19'E]

Ujjain Town in Madhya Pradesh state, central India, on River Sipra. One of the seven sacred cities of Hindus. [23° 11'N 75° 50'E]

Ulan Bator City and capital of the Mongolian People's Republic, in north-central Mongolia. Focus of several trans-Mongolian roads and camel caravans, and on the main railway from Russia to China. Industries include saddle and knitwear products. Contains almost one quarter of Mongolia's total population. [47° 55'N 106° 53'E]

Uppsala Town in south-west Sweden. Ancient cultural and religious centre, with many Viking remains. Major university town with Gothic cathedral. [58° 9'N 12° 19'E]

Ushuaia Town in south of Tierra del Fuego, southern Argentina. The most southerly town in the world. Lumbering, sheep rearing and fishing all important. [54° 50'S 68° 23'W]

Ust-Kamenogorsk River port and capital of East Kazakhstan Oblast in far eastern Kazakhstan, on right bank of Irtysh River. Chemical industry; lead and zinc mining; hydroelectric and nuclear power. [50° 0'N 82° 36'E]

Utrecht Town in central Netherlands on Amsterdam-Rijnkanaal. Capital of Utrecht province. Important historic, commercial, ecclesiastical and route centre. University (1634); large annual trade fair. Rolling stock and distilling industry. [52° 5'N 5° 8'E]

Vadodara Town in Gujarat state, western India, on coastal plain. Was capital of former state of Baroda. Many fine buildings; cultural centre; Fine Arts School. Railway junction. Textiles. [22° 20'N 73° 10'E]

Vaduz Capital of Liechtenstein, in the Rhine Valley. Commercial centre. 12th-century castle rebuilt after Swabian War in 1499. Textile, and food industries. [47° 8'N 9° 31'E]

Valencia Town in south-east Spain on River Turia. Capital of Valencia province. Ancient city, founded by Greeks, with many fine buildings; Gothic-Baroque cathedral; university (1500). Centre of rich agricultural area, with port at El Grao. Shipbuilding, engineering and textile industries. [39° 27'N 0° 23'W]

Valladolid   Town in north-central Spain. Capital of Valladolid province. Former capital of Old Castile. Commercial, manufacturing and route centre, with old university (1346). Agricultural machinery; aluminium industry; grain milling. [41° 38'N 4° 43'W]

Valletta   Capital of Malta at the end of a rocky peninsula on the east coast. Many old buildings, including the cathedral and the Auberge de Castille. Commercial and cultural centre. Formerly important as naval base, now an important harbour. New light engineering and food processing industries. Tourism very important. [35° 54'N 14° 31'E]

Valparaiso   Principal port of Chile, founded in 1536. Leather goods, vegetable oils and chemicals manufactured. Sugar refining; foundries. Copper, silver nitrate and wheat exported. Naval base. [33° 2'S 71° 40'W]

Vancouver   Seaport in south-west Canada in British Columbia. Commercial centre and port at mouth of ice-free Fraser River handling especially grain and wood products. Wood and fish processing, oil refining, brewing and manufacturing industries. Large Chinatown. Tourist area. [49° 15'N 123° 10'W]

Varanasi   Ancient town in Uttar Pradesh state, northern India, on River Ganges. Flights of steps (*ghats*) down to river. Holy city of Hinduism; centre of Siva culture. Brasswork famous. [25° 22'N 83° 0'E]

Venice   Town and seaport in north-east Italy built on group of small islands; joined to mainland by bridge to Mestre. Former city state and major port, famous for its beauty, especially St Mark's Cathedral and Grand Canal; many canals and bridges. Traditional glass and textile industries. Important tourist centre. [45° 27'N 12° 20'E]

Veracruz Llave   Important port in Mexico on Bay of Campeche, Gulf of Mexico, at narrow part of coastal plain. Port for Spanish fleets in 16th and 17th centuries. Oranges,

bananas, coffee, sugar, rice, cattle, pigs, ma hogany and vanilla are important product [19° 10'N 96° 10'W]

Versailles   Town in northern France, south west of Paris. Capital of Yvelines *départemen.* Site of famous palace built for Louis XIV which served as a royal palace until 1792 Peace treaty signed 1919. [48° 48'N 2° 8'E]

Vichy   Town in central France, in Allie *département.* Spa famous for its bottled water Pharmaceutical industry. Seat of proGerman government 1940–4. [46° 9'N 3° 26'E]

Victoria   Seaport on north-west Hong Kong Island, south-east China Administrative centre of British colony of Hong Kong, built largely on reclaimed lands. University of Hong Kong. [22° 16'N 114° 13'E]

Vienna   Capital of Austria, city and river port on the Danube at edge of Wiener Wald. Major historical, cultural, comercial and manufacturing centre. Former seat of Habsburgs, known especially for music and architecture (including Hofburg, Schönbrunn, Stephansdom). Clothing industry, especially fur; also porcelain, leather and printing industries. Important tourist centre. [48° 12'N 16° 12'E]

Vientiane   Town and river port, capital of Laos, on Mekong River, here forming border with Thailand. Administrative and commercial centre. Ferry across Mekong River from Thadeau, 19 km [12 mls] to east, to Nong Khai, Thailand. 'Friendship Bridge' over Mekong opened in 1994 and links road routes from Singapore to China. Timber, cotton and silk trade. [17° 58'N 102° 36'E]

Vilnius   Capital of Lithuania. Formerly Polish. Historic town with castle, cathedral (1977–1801) and old university (1579). Various light industries. One of the largest industrial centres of the former Soviet Baltic region. [54° 38'N 25° 19'E]

Vladikavkaz   Capital of the Republic of North Ossetia, northern Caucasus Mountains in Russia. The town was formerly called Ordzhonikidze. Industry based on local non-rous metals, including silver. Mountain ort. [43° 0'N 44° 35'E]

adivostok Capital of Primorye (Maritime) ay, eastern Russia. Main centre of far east Sea of Japan. Terminus of Trans-Siberian ailway; major port. [43° 10'N 131° 53'E]

olgograd City and capital of Volgograd oblast in southern Russia, on Volga River. ormerly called Stalingrad. End of Volga-Don anal. Scene of World War II decisive battle. transport centre and river port. Major heavy dustry; oil refinery. [48° 40'N 44° 25'E]

aco Town in Texas, southern USA. A gional centre in productive mixed farming ea. Food processing, tyre manufacturing. In the headlines in April 1993 when 72 members f the Branch Davidian cult perished in a fire. 31° 33'N 97° 9'W]

Valvis Bay Port on coast of Namibia. dministered by South Africa until 1 March 994 when it was returned to Namibia. Railway connection to South Africa. Mineral xports and fishing. [23° 0'S 14° 28'E]

Warsaw Capital of Poland on Vistula River. Under Russian rule from 1815. Became capi- al of Poland in 1919. Completely rebuilt after destruction in 1944. Major industrial, com- mercial, academic and educational centre; a ocus of eatern European communications of ll sorts. Manufactures electrical equipment, chemicals, textiles. Metal-working and sugar- efining industries. [52° 13'N 21° 0'E]

Washington DC Capital of the USA on Potomac River. Established 1790 as a planned city. Government and legal services; Library of Congress; research institutes, especially medi- cal. Major tourist centre with many famous landmarks, such as the White House, home of the US President. [38° 54'N 77° 2'W]

Waterford Capital of County Waterford, in Munster province, southern Ireland. Port and historic, commercial and manufacturing cen- tre at mouth of River Suir. Noted traditional glass industry; bacon, grain processing and iron founding industries. [52° 16'N 7° 8'W]

Waterloo Town in central Belgium, in the region of Brabant. Scene of Napoleon's defeat by Wellington and Blücher in 1815. [50° 43'N 4° 25'E]

Wellington Capital of New Zealand, on southern coast of North Island. Founded 1840. Seaport and important commercial cen- tre. Built on steep slopes around harbour with mountains in background. Exports meat, wool and dairy products. [41° 19'S 174° 46'E]

Willemstad Port and capital of Netherlands Antilles (Netherlands) on the island of Curaçao, West Indies. Fine deep-water har- bour with modern facilities. Ship repairing; bunkering. Oil refinery. [12° 5'N 69° 0'W]

Willow Small town in southern Alaska, north-western USA, 110 km [70 mls] north- west of Anchorage. Chosen in 1976 as site of future state capital. [61° 42'N 150° 8'W]

Windhoek Capital of Namibia, on central plateau. Railway connection to Walvis Bay on coast and to South Africa. Cattle ranching. Diamonds mined and cut. [22° 35'S 17° 4'E]

Woomera Town in South Australia. British and Australian rocket testing station named after Aboriginal spear-throwing device, found- ed after World War II. [31° 5'S 136° 50'E]

Wuhan Metropolis of Hubei province, cen- tral China. A tri-city conurbation, consisting of Hankow, Hanyang and Wuchan, at the confluence of the Han Shui and Yangtze rivers, at railway crossing point. Important iron-and-steel plants. [30° 31'N 114° 18'E]

Xian Capital of Shanxi province, China. Im- portant route focus in central China. First capital of fuedal China. Terracotta warriors discovered in 1974. Cotton and flour mills; agricultural machinery; mining equipment. Tourist centre. [34° 15'N 109° 0'E]

Yakutsk Capital of Sakha (formerly Yakutia) Republic, Russia, on River Lena. Important regional centre for north-eastern Siberia. Timber and fur trade; coal and natural gas nearby. [62° 5'N 129° 50'E]

Yaoundé Capital of Cameroon, 270 km [170 mls] inland, in the south-west of the country. Became the capital of French Cameroon in 1921, though it was replaced by Douala between 1940–6. Road and rail centre. Sugar refining; cigarettes. [3° 50'N 11° 35'E]

Yaroslavl River port and capital of Yaroslavl Oblast in central Russia, on the River Volga. The oldest town on the Volga. Major centre of heavy industry, chemicals, textiles. Many old churches. [57° 35'N 39° 55'E]

Yerevan Capital of Armenia on the River Razdan. One of the world's most ancient cities with many historic buildings; remains of 16th-century Turkish fortress. Important industrial centre, producing diverse manufactured goods. Vodka and wine exported. Rapid post-war expansion. [40° 10'N 44° 31'E]

Yogyakarta Important city of south-central Java in Indonesia. Cultural centre in a region of intensive cultivation and dense population. [7° 49'S 110° 22'E]

Yokohama Seaport city and capital of Kanagawa prefecture in south-east Honshu, Japan. First Japanese port to be opened to foreign trade in 1858. Manufacturing centre; ranks first in Japanese shipbuilding and important in manufacture of cars and heavy electrical equipment. Oil refining; iron-and-steel industries. [35° 27'N 139° 28'E]

Ypres Town in western Belgium, in West Flanders. Historic textile trade centre and defensive site; battles of World War I. Linen and food industries. [50° 51'N 2° 53'E]

Yuzhno-Sakhalinsk Capital of Sakhalin Oblast, at southern end of Sakhalin Island in eastern Siberia, Russia. Local industrial and administrative centre. [46° 58'N 142° 45'E]

Zagorsk Town north-east of Moscow, Russia. Formerly called Sergiyev Posad. Notable for monastery, centre of the Russian Orthodox Church; also traditional wood crafts. [56° 20'N 38° 10'E]

Zagreb Capital of Croatia in the north of the country on the River Sava. Old quarter medieval architecture. Important cultural a commercial centre. University (1669). Pet chemical industry. [45° 50'N 16° 10'E]

Zaporozhye (Zaporizhzhya) River port a capital of Zaporozhye Oblast, south-easte Ukraine, on River Dnepr (Dnipro, Dnyapr Founded 1770 as a fortress. Major industr and transport centre; large early hydroelect power station (1927). [47° 50'N 35°10'E]

Zaria Town on plateau in north-cent Nigeria. Includes remains of ancient wall Hausa city. Railway and road centre; cotto growing area. Agricultural research cent nearby. [11° 0'N 7° 40'E]

Zeebrugge Seaport in Belgium, in We Flanders. Deep-water container port linked oil and natural gas terminal. Fishing port ar resort. [51° 19'N 3° 12'E]

Zhengzhou Capital of Henan province, eas central China. Main rail centre of north Chin Plain. Major cotton mill industry. Wheat ma ket; food processing. [34° 45'N 113° 34'E]

Zhitomir (Zhytomyr) Capital of Zhitom Oblast in Ukraine. Agricultural trade centr hops, wheat; woodworking and syntheti textiles. Railway focus. [50° 20'N 28° 40'E]

Zinder Town and regional centre in souther Niger. Former capital. Main market for hide and skins; leather and textile industries Groundnuts important. Route centre: trad with Kano (Nigeria). [13° 48'N 9° 0'S]

Zouerate Modern mining settlement in nor thern Mauritania, east of Fdérik. Terminu of railway to Atlantic port, serving iron-or mine of Kediet Ijill. [22° 44'N 12° 21'W]

Zürich Town in north-east Switzerland a northern end of Zürichsee, at the foot o the Alps. Capital of Zürich canton and largest city in Switzerland. International finance cen tre, famous for banking. Many old buildings including 11th-century Grossmünster and 13th-century St Peter's Church. Textile and machinery industries. [47° 22'N 8° 32'E]

WORLD
STATISTICS

POPULATION

POPULATION OF COUNTRIES

thousands

	1970	1980	1990	2000 Estimate
World	3,697,849	4,448,037	5,292,195	6,260,800
Afghanistan	13,623	16,063	16,557	26,511
Albania	2,138	2,671	3,245	3,795
Algeria	13,746	18,740	24,960	32,904
American Samoa	27	32	38	39
Andorra	20	32	47	49
Angola	5,588	7,723	10,020	13,295
Anguilla	6	7	7	8
Antigua & Barbuda	66	75	76	79
Argentina	23,962	28,237	32,322	36,238
Armenia	2,520	3,067	3,335	3,608
Aruba	61	64	60	58
Australia	12,552	14,695	16,873	18,855
Austria	7,467	7,549	7,583	7,613
Azerbaijan	5,172	6,165	7,134	7,987
Bahamas	171	210	253	295
Bahrain	220	347	516	683
Bangladesh	66,671	88,219	115,593	150,589
Barbados	239	249	255	265
Belarus	9,040	9,650	10,260	10,811
Belgium	9,656	9,852	9,845	9,832
Belize	120	145	187	230
Benin	2,693	3,459	4,630	6,369
Bermuda	55	56	58	62
Bhutan	1,045	1,245	1,516	1,906
Bolivia	4,325	5,570	7,314	9,724
Bosnia	3,703	4,107	4,347	4,601
Botswana	623	902	1,304	1,822
Brazil	95,847	121,286	150,368	179,487
Brit. Indian Oc. Terr.	2	2	2	2
British Virgin Is.	10	12	13	15
Brunei	133	228	266	333
Bulgaria	8,490	8,862	9,010	9,071
Burkina Faso	5,550	6,957	8,996	12,092
Burma	27,346	34,818	41,675	51,129
Burundi	3,522	4,132	5,472	7,358
Cambodia	6,938	6,400	8,246	10,046
Cameroon	6,610	8,653	11,833	16,071
Canada	21,324	24,043	26,521	28,488
Cape Verde Is.	267	289	370	515
Cayman Is.	11	18	25	35
Central African Rep.	1,849	2,320	3,039	4,074
Chad	3,652	4,477	5,678	7,337
Chile	9,504	11,145	13,173	15,272
China	830,675	996,134	1,139,060	1,299,180
Christmas Is.	2.6	3	3	3
Cocos Is.	0.6	0.5	1	1
Colombia	21,360	26,906	32,978	39,397
Comoros	245	334	460	789
Congo	1,263	1,669	2,271	3,167
Cook Is.	21	19	18	17
Costa Rica	1,731	2,284	3,015	3,711
Croatia	4,411	4,588	4,770	4,822
Cuba	8,520	9,679	10,608	11,504
Cyprus	615	629	701	762
Czech Republic	...	...	...	10,456
Czechoslovakia	14,334	15,311	15,667	16,180
Denmark	4,929	5,123	5,143	5,153
Djibouti	168	304	409	552
Dominica	71	73	82	87
Dominican Republic	4,423	5,697	7,170	8,621
Ecuador	6,051	8,123	10,587	13,319
Egypt	33,053	40,875	53,153	64,210
El Salvador	3,588	4,525	5,252	6,739
Equatorial Guinea	291	217	352	455
Eritrea	...	...	...	4,218
Estonia	1,365	1,481	1,583	1,669

	1970	1980	1990	2000 Estimate
Ethiopia	30,623	38,750	49,240	66,36
Ethiopia (less Eritrea)	...	...	...	64,0
Falkland Is.	1.8	2	2	
Faroe Is.	39	41	47	
Fiji	520	634	764	8
Finland	4,606	4,780	4,975	5,0
France	50,772	53,880	56,138	58,1
French Guiana	48	66	98	13
French Polynesia	109	147	206	26
Gabon	504	806	1,172	1,61
Gambia, The	464	641	861	1,1
Georgia	4,708	5,075	5,460	5,79
Germany	77,709	78,303	79,479	76,96
Ghana	8,612	10,736	15,028	20,56
Gibraltar	26	29	30	3
Greece	8,793	9,643	10,047	10,19
Greenland	47	52	56	6
Grenada	94	107	85	8
Guadeloupe	320	327	343	36
Guam	86	108	118	12
Guatemala	5,246	6,917	9,197	12,22
Guinea	3,900	4,461	5,755	7,83
Guinea-Bissau	525	795	964	1,19
Guyana	709	759	796	89
Haiti	4,535	5,370	6,513	8,00
Honduras	2,627	3,662	5,138	6,84
Hong Kong	3,942	5,039	5,851	6,33
Hungary	10,338	10,711	10,552	10,53
Iceland	204	228	253	27
India	554,911	688,856	827,057	1,041,54
Indonesia	120,280	150,958	179,300	218,66
Iran	28,429	38,900	54,607	68,75
Iraq	9,356	13,291	18,920	26,33
Ireland	2,954	3,401	3,500	4,08
Israel	2,974	3,878	4,600	5,32
Italy	53,822	56,434	57,061	57,19
Ivory Coast	5,515	8,194	11,997	17,60
Jamaica	1,869	2,133	2,456	2,73
Japan	104,331	116,807	123,460	128,47
Jordan	2,299	2,923	4,009	5,55
Kazakhstan	13,110	14,939	16,742	18,33
Kenya	11,498	16,632	24,031	35,06
Kiribati	49	58	66	7
Korea, North	14,619	18,260	21,773	26,11
Korea, South	31,923	38,124	42,793	46,40
Kuwait	744	1,375	1,500	2,63
Kyrgyzstan	2,965	3,630	4,395	5,18
Laos	2,713	3,205	4,139	5,46
Latvia	2,374	2,543	2,684	2,81
Lebanon	2,469	2,669	2,701	3,32
Lesotho	1,064	1,339	1,774	2,37
Liberia	1,385	1,876	2,575	3,57
Libya	1,986	3,043	4,545	6,50
Liechtenstein	21	26	28	2
Lithuania	3,148	3,439	3,737	4,00
Luxembourg	339	364	373	37
Macau	245	287	479	65
Macedonia	1,629	1,900	2,024	2,15
Madagascar	6,742	8,785	12,004	16,62
Malawi	4,518	6,183	8,754	12,45
Malaysia	10,853	13,763	17,891	21,98
Maldives	114	154	215	28
Mali	5,484	6,863	8,156	12,68
Malta	326	364	353	36
Martinique	326	326	341	36
Mauritania	1,221	1,551	2,024	2,70
Mauritius	826	966	1082	1,20
Mexico	52,771	70,416	86,154	107,23
Moldova	3,595	4,001	4,365	4,50
Monaco	24	26	28	3
Mongolia	1,256	1,663	2,190	2,84
Montserrat	12	14	12	1

	1970	1980	1990	2000 Estimate		1970	1980	1990	2000 Estimate
rocco	15,310	19,382	25,061	31,559	Solomon Is.	163	231	320	429
zambique	9,395	12,095	15,656	20,493	Somalia	3,668	5,345	7,497	9,736
mibia	1,016	1,306	1,500	2,437	South Africa	22,458	28,270	35,282	43,666
uru	7	8	9	10	Spain	33,779	37,542	39,187	40,667
oal	11,488	14,858	19,143	24,084	Sri Lanka	12,514	14,819	17,217	19,416
therlands	13,032	14,144	14,951	15,829	Sudan	13,859	18,681	25,203	33,625
therlands Antilles	222	247	188	203	Surinam	372	352	405	497
w Caledonia	110	142	167	195	Swaziland	419	563	788	1,121
w Zealand	2,820	3,113	3,392	3,662	Sweden	8,043	8,310	8,444	8,560
caragua	2,053	2,771	3,871	5,261	Switzerland	6,187	6,319	6,609	6,762
ger	4,165	5,586	7,731	10,752	Syria	6,258	8,800	12,530	17,826
geria	56,581	70,000	86,000	149,621	Taiwan	14,676	17,805	20,100	22,000
ue	3	4	3	2	Tajikistan	2,942	3,967	5,303	6,874
rfolk Is.	2	2	2	2	Tanzania	13,513	18,867	25,635	39,639
rway	3,877	4,086	4,212	4,331	Thailand	35,745	46,718	57,196	63,670
nan	654	984	1,502	2,176	Togo	2,020	2,615	3,531	4,861
kistan	65,706	85,299	112,050	162,409	Tokelau	1	2	2	2
lau (Belau)	103	136	142	145	Tonga	85	96	95	92
nama	1,531	1,956	2,418	2,893	Trinidad & Tobago	971	1,082	1,281	1,484
pua New Guinea	2,422	3,086	3,874	4,845	Tunisia	5,127	6,384	8,180	9,924
raguay	2,351	3,147	4,277	5,538	Turkey	35,321	44,438	58,687	66,789
ru	13,193	17,295	22,330	26,276	Turkmenistan	2,189	2,860	3,668	4,479
ilippines	37,540	48,317	62,413	77,473	Turks & Caicos	6	6	10	12
tcairn	0.09	0.06	0.06	0.06	Tuvalu	6	7	9	11
land	32,526	35,574	38,423	40,366	Uganda	9,806	13,120	18,794	26,958
rtugal	9,044	9,766	10,285	10,587	Ukraine	47,317	50,033	51,892	53,754
erto Rico	2,718	3,206	3,480	3,836	USSR (former)	242,766	265,546	288,595	308,363
atar	111	229	368	499	United Arab Em.	223	1,015	1,589	1,951
eunion	441	508	598	692	United Kingdom	55,632	56,330	57,237	58,393
mania	20,253	22,201	23,160	24,346	United States	205,051	227,757	249,224	266,096
ssia	130,392	138,936	148,292	155,240	US Virgin Is.	62	106	116	135
wanda	3,728	5,163	7,237	10,200	Uruguay	2,808	2,914	3,094	3,274
Christopher-Nevis	52	52	44	44	Uzbekistan	11,973	15,975	20,515	25,224
Helena	5	6	7	10	Vanuatu	86	118	158	206
Lucia	101	120	150	177	Vatican City	1	1	1	1
Pierre et Miquelon	6	6	6	6	Venezuela	10,604	15,024	19,735	24,715
Vincent & G.	88	99	112	128	Vietnam	42,729	53,700	66,693	82,427
an Marino	18	21	23	25	Wallis & Futuna	9	9	17	26
ão Tomé & Príncipe	74	85	121	151	Western Sahara	76	135	178	228
audi Arabia	5,745	9,372	14,134	20,697	Western Samoa	143	157	168	171
enegal	4,158	5,538	7,327	8,716	Yemen	6,332	7,675	11,282	13,219
eychelles	52	65	69	75	Yugoslavia	20,371	22,304	23,807	24,900
ierra Leone	2,656	3,263	4,151	5,437	Yugoslavia (Serbia)	8,910	9,866	10,304	11,114
ingapore	2,075	2,300	2,700	2,997	Zaïre	19,769	26,225	35,568	49,190
lovak Republic	...	...	...	5,513	Zambia	4,189	5,738	8,452	12,267
lovenia	1,718	1,886	1,968	2,012	Zimbabwe	5,260	7,126	9,709	13,123

POPULATION CHANGE

percentage change in the decade

	1950–60	1960–70	1970–80	1980–90	1990–2000
World	20	22.5	20.3	19	18.3
Afghanistan	20.3	26.4	17.9	3.1	60.1
Albania	31	32.7	24.9	21.5	16.9
Algeria	23.4	27.3	36.3	33.2	31.8
American Samoa	10.5	28.6	18.5	18.8	2.6
Andorra	53.9	150	60	46.9	4.3
Angola	16.6	16	38.2	29.7	32.7
Anguilla	20	0	16.7	0	14.3
Antigua & Barbuda	19.6	20	13.6	1.3	3.9
Argentina	20.2	16.2	17.8	14.5	12.1
Armenia	37.9	35	21.7	8.7	19
Aruba	3.5	3.4	4.9	-6.3	-3.3
Australia	25.5	21.7	17.1	14.8	11.7
Austria	1.6	5.9	1.1	0.5	0.4
Azerbaijan	34.5	32.8	19.2	15.7	16.7
Bahamas	43	51.3	22.8	20.5	16.6
Bahrain	34.5	41	57.7	48.7	32.4
Bangladesh	23.1	29.7	32.3	31	30.3
Barbados	9.5	3.5	4.2	2.4	3.9
Belarus	5.7	10.4	6.7	6.3	4.3
Belgium	5.9	5.5	2	-0.1	-0.1
Belize	35.8	31.9	20.8	29	23
Benin	9.3	20.4	28.4	33.9	37.6
Bermuda	15.4	22.2	1.8	3.6	6.9
Bhutan	18.3	20.4	19.1	21.8	25.7
Bolivia	23.9	26.2	28.8	31.3	33
Bosnia	21.7	14.3	10.9	5.8	5.8
Botswana	23.7	29.5	44.8	44.6	39.7
Brazil	35.8	32	26.5	24	19.4
Brit. Indian Oc. Terr.	0	0	0	0	0
British Virgin Is.	21.7	34.3	22.5	8.3	15.4
Brunei	95.7	47.8	71.4	16.7	25.2
Bulgaria	8.5	7.9	4.4	1.7	0.7
Burkina Faso	21.8	24.7	25.4	29.3	34.4
Burma	20.7	25.6	27.3	19.7	22.7
Burundi	20	19.5	17.3	32.4	34.5
Cambodia	25	27.7	-7.8	28.8	21.8
Cameroon	18.6	24.8	30.9	36.8	41.1
Canada	30.4	19.1	12.8	10.3	7.4
Cape Verde Is.	34.2	36.2	8.2	28	39.2
Cayman Is.	26.7	38.2	71.4	38.9	40
Central African Rep.	16.7	20.5	25.5	31	34.1
Chad	15.3	19.2	22.6	26.8	29.2
Chile	25.2	24.8	17.3	18.2	15.9
China	18.5	26.3	19.9	14.3	14.1
Christmas Is.	170	-3.7	15.4	0	0

	1950–60	1960–70	1970–80	1980–90	1990–2000
Cocos Is.	−41	1.7	−16.7	100	0
Colombia	33.4	34	26	22.6	19.5
Comoros	24.3	14	36.3	37.7	45.7
Congo	22.3	27.8	32.1	36.1	39.5
Cook Is.	20	16.7	−9.5	−5.3	−5.6
Costa Rica	43.4	40	31.9	32	23.1
Croatia	7.5	6.5	4	4	4
Cuba	19.4	22	13.6	9.6	8.4
Cyprus	16	7.3	2.3	11.4	8.7
Czechoslovakia	10.2	5	6.8	2.3	3.3
Denmark	7.3	7.6	3.9	0.4	0.2
Djibouti	33.3	110	81	34.5	35
Dominica	17.6	18.3	2.8	12.3	6.1
Dominican Republic	37.3	36.9	28.8	25.9	20.2
Ecuador	33.3	37.1	34.2	30.3	25.8
Egypt	27.5	27.5	23.7	30	20.8
El Salvador	32.5	39.6	26.1	16.1	28.3
Equatorial Guinea	11.5	15.5	−25.4	62.2	29.3
Estonia	10.4	12.3	8.5	6.9	4
Ethiopia	23.6	26.6	26.5	27.1	34.8
Falkland Is.	0	−14.3	11.1	0	0
Faroe Is.	12.9	11.4	5.1	14.6	4.3
Fiji	36.3	32	21.9	20.5	15.6
Finland	10.5	4	3.8	4.1	2.1
France	9.2	11.1	6.1	4.2	3.6
French Guiana	24	54.8	37.5	48.5	32.7
French Polynesia	32.3	32.9	34.9	40.1	30.1
Gabon	3.6	3.7	59.9	45.4	37.5
Gambia, The	19.7	31.8	38.1	34.3	30
Georgia	17.9	13.2	7.8	7.6	5.8
Germany	6.3	6.9	0.8	1.5	−3.2
Ghana	38.2	27.1	24.7	40	36.8
Gibraltar	4.3	8.3	11.5	3.4	6.7
Greece	10.1	5.6	9.7	4.2	1.5
Greenland	43.5	42.4	10.6	7.7	7.1
Grenada	18.4	4.4	13.8	−20.6	−2.4
Guadeloupe	31	16.4	2.2	4.9	6.4
Guam	13.6	28.4	25.6	9.3	8.5
Guatemala	33.5	32.3	31.9	33	32.9
Guinea	23	24.4	14.4	29	36.1
Guinea-Bissau	7.3	−3.1	51.4	21.3	24.2
Guyana	34.5	24.6	7.1	4.9	11.9
Haiti	16.7	19.1	18.4	21.3	22.9
Honduras	38.1	35.8	39.4	40.3	33.2
Hong Kong	55.8	28.2	27.8	16.1	8.3
Hungary	6.9	3.5	3.6	−1.5	−0.2
Iceland	23.1	15.9	11.8	11	8.3
India	23.7	25.4	24.1	20.1	25.9
Indonesia	20.9	25	25.5	18.8	22
Iran	27.4	31.9	36.8	40.4	25.9
Iraq	32.7	36.6	42.1	42.4	39.2
Ireland	−4.5	4.2	15.1	2.9	16.7
Israel	68	40.7	30.4	18.6	15.7
Italy	6.6	7.2	4.9	1.1	0.2
Ivory Coast	36.9	45.2	48.6	46.4	46.7
Jamaica	16.1	14.7	14.1	15.1	11.4
Japan	12.5	10.9	12	5.7	4.1
Jordan	37	35.6	27.1	37.2	38.6
Kazakhstan	49.1	31.2	14	12.1	13.5
Kenya	33	38	44.7	44.5	45.9
Kiribati	28.1	19.5	18.4	13.8	9.1
Korea, North	10.9	35.5	24.9	19.2	20
Korea, South	22.8	27.7	19.4	12.2	8.4
Kuwait	82.9	167.6	84.8	9.1	75.9
Kyrgyzstan	24.9	36.4	22.4	21.1	22.9
Laos	24	24.6	18.1	29.1	32
Latvia	15.1	11.5	7.1	5.5	3.1
Lebanon	28.7	33	8.1	1.2	23.2
Lesotho	18.5	22.3	25.8	32.5	33.6
Liberia	26.1	33.3	35.5	37.3	38.8
Libya	31.1	47.2	53.2	49.4	43
Liechtenstein	14.3	31.3	23.8	7.7	0
Lithuania	8.3	13.3	9.2	8.7	5.3
Luxembourg	6.1	8	7.4	2.5	1.1
Macau	−10.1	45	17.1	66.9	37
Macedonia	13.3	17	16.6	6.5	6.6
Madagascar	25.5	27	30.3	36.6	38.5
Malawi	22.5	28	36.9	41.6	42.3

	1950–60	1960–70	1970–80	1980–90	1990–2
Malaysia	33.2	33.3	26.8	30	2
Maldives	12.2	23.9	35.1	39.6	3
Mali	24.3	25.3	25.1	18.8	5
Malta	5.4	−0.9	11.7	−3	
Martinique	27	15.6	0	4.6	
Mauritania	20.1	23.2	27	30.5	3
Mauritius	33.9	25.2	16.9	12	
Mexico	35.7	38.8	33.4	22.4	2
Moldova	28.3	19.7	11.3	9.1	
Monaco	4.5	4.3	8.3	7.7	
Mongolia	26	31	32.4	31.7	
Montserrat	−6.9	−3.3	19.7	−14.3	
Morocco	29.9	31.7	26.6	29.3	2
Mozambique	20.4	25.9	28.7	29.4	3
Namibia	22.7	24.4	28.5	14.9	6
Nauru	28.1	70.7	14.3	12.5	1
Nepal	14.9	22.2	29.3	28.8	2
Netherlands	13.5	13.5	8.5	5.7	
Netherlands Antilles	18.5	15.6	11.3	−23.9	
New Caledonia	33.9	39.2	29.1	17.6	1
New Zealand	24.3	18.9	10.4	9	
Nicaragua	36	37.5	35	39.7	3
Niger	26.2	37.5	34.1	38.4	3
Nigeria	28.4	33.7	23.7	22.9	2
Niue	25	−32	17.7	−25	−3
Norfolk Is.	0	87.5	33.3	0	
Norway	9.7	8.3	5.4	3.1	2
Oman	22.3	29.5	50.5	52.6	44
Pakistan	26.4	31.5	29.8	31.4	44
Palau (Belau)	36.8	32.1	32	4.4	7
Panama	28.6	33.4	27.8	23.6	19
Papua New Guinea	19	26.1	27.4	25.5	25
Paraguay	31.3	32.5	33.9	35.9	29
Peru	30.1	32.8	31.1	29.1	17
Philippines	31.3	36.2	28.7	29.2	24
Pitcairn Is.	25	−40	−33.3	0	
Poland	19.1	10	9.4	8	5
Portugal	5	2.5	8	5.3	2
Puerto Rico	6.3	15.3	18	8.5	10
Qatar	80	146.7	106.3	60.7	35
Réunion	31.9	30.1	15.2	17.7	15
Romania	12.9	10	9.6	4.3	3
Russia	14.2	8.7	6.6	6.7	4
Rwanda	29.3	36	38.5	40.2	40
St Christopher-Nevis	14	−8.8	0	−15.4	
St Helena	19.1	0	20	16.7	42
St Lucia	11.4	14.8	18.8	25	1
St Pierre & Miquelon	4.4	16.7	7.1	0	
St Vincent & G.	19.4	10	12.5	13.1	14
San Marino	15.4	20	16.7	9.5	8
São Tomé & Príncipe	6.7	15.6	14.9	42.4	24
Saudi Arabia	27.3	41	63.1	50.8	46
Senegal	27.5	30.5	33.2	32.3	1
Seychelles	23.5	23.8	25	6.2	8
Sierra Leone	15.3	18.5	22.9	27.2	3
Singapore	59.9	27	10.8	17.4	11
Slovenia	7.3	8.7	9.8	4.3	4
Solomon Is.	18.3	32.5	41.7	38.5	34
Somalia	21.1	25	45.7	40.3	29
South Africa	27.1	29.1	25.9	24.8	23
Spain	8.7	10.9	11.1	4.4	3
Sri Lanka	28.8	26.5	18.4	16.2	12
Sudan	21.5	24.1	34.8	34.9	33
Surinam	34.9	28.3	−5.4	15.1	22
Swaziland	23.5	28.5	34.4	40	42
Sweden	6.6	7.5	3.3	1.6	1
Switzerland	14.2	15.4	2.1	4.6	2
Syria	30.5	37.2	40.6	42.4	42
Taiwan	41.1	36	21.3	12.9	9
Tajikistan	36	41.2	34.8	33.7	32
Tanzania	27.1	34.8	39.6	35.9	54
Thailand	31.9	35.4	30.7	22.4	11
Togo	13.9	33.4	29.5	35	37
Tokelau	66.7	−30	42.9	0	0
Tonga	30	30.8	12.9	−1	−3.2
Trinidad & Tobago	32.5	15.2	11.4	18.4	15.8
Tunisia	19.6	21.5	24.5	28.1	21.3
Turkey	32.2	28.4	25.8	32.1	13.8

	1950–60	1960–70	1970–80	1980–90	1990–2000
kmenistan	31.6	37.3	30.7	28.3	25
ks & Caicos	−5	−1.8	7.1	66.7	20
alu	0	20	23.3	21.6	22.2
anda	37.8	49.4	33.8	43.2	43.4
aine	15.9	10.6	5.7	3.7	1.3
SR (former)	19	13.3	9.4	8.7	6.8
ted Arab Emirates	28.6	147.8	355.2	56.6	22.8
ted Kingdom	3.5	6.2	1.3	1.6	2
ted States	18.7	13.5	11.1	9.4	6.8
Virgin Is.	18.2	94.4	71	9.4	16.4
uguay	13.4	10.6	3.8	6.2	5.8
bekistan	35.6	39.9	33.4	28.4	27
nuatu	25	32.3	37.2	33.9	30.4
ican City	0	0	0	0	0

	1950–60	1960–70	1970–80	1980–90	1990–2000
Venezuela	49.8	41.3	41.7	31.4	25.2
Vietnam	16	23	25.7	24.2	23.6
Wallis & Futuna	14.3	8.8	3.5	88.9	52.9
Western Sahara	128.6	137.5	77.6	31.9	28.1
Western Samoa	35.4	28.8	9.8	7	1.8
Yemen	21.6	20.7	21.2	47	17.2
Yugoslavia	12.6	10.7	9.5	6.7	4.6
Yugoslavia (Serbia)	12.9	10.7	10.7	4.4	4.4
Zaïre	25.7	29.1	32.7	35.6	38.3
Zambia	28.7	33.4	37	47.3	45.1
Zimbabwe	39.6	38	35.5	36.2	35.2

The estimates for 2000 are those of the UN. They use the medium variants of the population controls.

BIRTH AND DEATH RATES

irths/deaths per 1,000 population

	Birth Rate					Death Rate				
	1950 –55	1960 –65	1970 –75	1980 –85	1990 –95	1950 –55	1960 –65	1970 –75	1980 –85	1990 –95
orld	38	35	32	28	26	20	15	12	10	9
ghanistan	48	53	52	49	52	32	30	26	23	22
bania	38	40	32	27	22	14	10	7	6	6
geria	51	50	48	41	35	24	19	15	10	7
ndorra	...	18	...	15	13	10	6	5	...	4
ngola	50	49	48	47	47	35	30	25	22	19
nguilla	...	...	...	...	25	...	...	...	...	10
ntigua & Barbuda	35	32	20	15	15	12	9	7	6	5
rgentina	25	23	23	23	20	9	9	9	9	9
rmenia	...	...	...	...	20	...	...	...	...	6
ustralia	23	22	20	16	14	9	9	9	7	8
ustria	15	19	14	12	12	12	13	13	12	12
zerbaijan	...	...	...	...	25	...	...	...	...	6
ahamas	35	31	28	23	19	12	8	6	5	5
ahrain	45	47	36	31	25	16	14	8	5	3
angladesh	47	47	49	45	41	24	22	21	18	14
arbados	33	29	21	17	16	13	9	9	9	9
elarus	...	...	...	...	15	...	...	...	...	10
elgium	17	17	14	12	12	12	12	12	11	12
elize	41	46	40	39	37	12	8	6	5	4
enin	43	48	49	49	49	37	31	26	21	18
ermuda	28	26	20	18	16	9	7	7	7	7
hutan	44	42	41	39	38	27	24	21	18	16
olivia	47	46	45	44	41	24	22	19	16	12
osnia	...	...	...	...	14	...	...	...	...	6
otswana	49	53	52	49	44	23	20	17	14	10
razil	45	42	34	31	26	15	12	10	8	8
ritish Virgin Is.	40	33	26	22	20	11	9	7	6	6
runei	54	43	35	32	29	15	8	5	4	3
ulgaria	21	17	16	14	12	10	8	9	11	12
urkina Faso	51	51	50	47	47	32	27	24	20	17
urma	42	41	38	34	30	24	20	14	11	9
urundi	49	45	44	47	47	25	22	21	19	16
ambodia	45	45	40	46	37	24	20	23	20	15
ameroon	44	45	46	47	47	27	24	20	17	13
anada	28	25	16	15	13	9	8	7	7	8
ape Verde Is.	51	49	39	39	41	19	15	12	10	7
ayman Is.	31	32	28	20	15	7	7	6	6	4
entral African Republic	44	43	43	46	45	29	25	22	19	16
had	45	46	45	44	43	32	29	25	21	18
hile	37	37	28	24	23	14	12	9	6	6
hina	38	38	31	19	21	25	17	9	7	7
hristmas Is.	49	26	...	...	16	6	5	5	...	...
ocos Is.	...	30	21	...	20	...	9	7	...	...
olombia	47	44	35	29	26	17	12	9	6	6
omoros	47	52	49	48	47	24	21	18	14	12
ongo	44	45	46	46	46	25	22	19	16	13
ook Is.	41	47	32	28	24	19	9	5	5	5
osta Rica	47	45	32	30	26	13	9	6	4	4

	Birth Rate					Death Rate				
	1950 –55	1960 –65	1970 –75	1980 –85	1990 –95	1950 –55	1960 –65	1970 –75	1980 –85	1990 –95
Croatia	...	...	...	...	12	...	...	...	...	11
Cuba	30	35	27	16	17	11	9	7	6	7
Cyprus	27	25	18	20	17	11	11	10	8	8
Czechoslovakia	22	16	18	15	14	11	10	11	12	11
Denmark	18	17	15	10	11	9	10	10	11	11
Djibouti	50	50	50	48	46	31	27	23	19	16
Dominica	39	43	...	21	21	17	12	...	6	5
Dominican Rep.	51	49	39	34	28	20	15	10	8	6
Ecuador	47	46	41	35	31	19	14	11	8	7
Egypt	49	45	38	39	31	24	20	16	13	9
El Salvador	48	48	43	38	36	20	15	11	11	7
Equatorial Guinea	42	41	42	43	44	32	28	24	21	18
Estonia	...	...	...	...	15	...	...	...	...	12
Ethiopia	52	50	48	45	48	32	27	23	24	18
Falkland Is.	23	22	19	15	9	12	11	12	8	6
Faroe Is.	25	23	20	16	18	8	7	7	7	8
Fiji	44	39	32	31	24	14	11	9	8	6
Finland	23	18	13	14	12	10	9	10	9	10
France	20	18	16	15	13	13	11	11	11	10
French Guiana	28	30	29	28	28	16	13	8	7	6
French Polynesia	43	45	37	30	28	12	10	9	8	5
Gabon	33	34	33	34	43	27	23	20	18	16
Gambia, The	47	51	49	48	45	34	31	27	23	20
Georgia	...	...	...	...	16	...	...	...	...	9
Germany	16	18	11	11	11	11	12	13	13	12
Ghana	48	48	46	45	44	22	19	16	14	12
Gibraltar	23	25	20	18	17	10	9	8	7	7
Greece	19	18	16	14	12	7	8	9	9	10
Greenland	44	47	43	28	22	19	9	6	7	8
Grenada	40	39	26	25	25	14	10	8	7	7
Guadeloupe	39	37	29	21	20	13	8	8	7	7
Guam	29	26	34	30	27	5	5	4	4	4
Guatemala	51	48	45	43	39	22	18	13	11	8
Guinea	55	52	52	51	51	34	30	27	24	20
Guinea-Bissau	41	40	41	43	43	30	28	27	25	21
Guyana	43	41	35	29	24	18	14	10	9	7
Haiti	44	42	39	37	35	28	22	18	15	12
Honduras	51	51	49	42	37	22	18	14	9	7
Hong Kong	38	33	20	17	12	9	6	5	5	6
Hungary	21	14	16	13	12	11	10	12	14	13
Iceland	28	26	21	18	15	8	7	7	7	7
India	44	42	38	35	31	25	19	16	13	10
Indonesia	43	43	38	32	27	26	22	17	11	9
Iran	48	47	44	42	33	25	20	15	10	7
Iraq	49	49	47	44	41	22	19	15	9	7
Ireland	21	22	22	20	18	13	12	11	9	9
Israel	33	26	27	24	21	7	6	7	7	7
Italy	18	19	16	11	11	10	10	10	10	11
Ivory Coast	53	53	51	50	50	28	24	19	16	13
Jamaica	35	40	33	27	22	12	9	8	6	6
Japan	24	17	19	13	12	9	7	7	6	8
Jordan	47	53	50	38	39	26	22	14	8	5
Kazakhstan	...	...	...	...	22	...	...	...	...	8
Kenya	53	53	53	51	47	25	21	17	13	10
Korea, North	37	41	36	22	5	32	13	8	6	5

	Birth Rate					Death Rate				
	1950–55	1960–65	1970–75	1980–85	1990–95	1950–55	1960–65	1970–75	1980–85	1990–95
Korea, South	32	13	9	6	15	32	13	9	6	6
Kuwait	45	45	44	35	26	11	9	5	3	2
Kyrgyzstan	...	...	...	...	29	...	...	...	...	7
Laos	46	45	44	45	44	25	23	23	19	15
Latvia	...	...	...	...	14	...	...	...	...	12
Lebanon	41	43	32	29	30	19	13	9	9	8
Lesotho	42	43	42	42	40	27	23	19	14	11
Liberia	48	50	48	47	47	27	24	20	17	14
Libya	48	49	49	46	43	23	18	15	11	8
Liechtenstein	22	22	16	14	13	9	8	8	7	6
Lithuania	...	...	...	...	15	...	...	...	...	10
Luxembourg	15	16	12	12	12	12	12	12	11	11
Macau	...	21	11	...	17	13	8	6	5	3
Macedonia	...	...	...	...	17	...	...	...	...	7
Madagascar	48	48	46	46	45	27	23	19	15	13
Malawi	52	55	57	57	55	31	28	24	22	19
Malaysia	45	43	35	32	28	20	13	9	6	5
Maldives	34	37	40	41	41	29	27	20	10	8
Mali	53	52	51	51	51	32	29	25	22	19
Malta	29	23	18	17	13	10	9	9	9	9
Martinique	40	36	26	18	18	13	9	7	7	7
Mauritania	48	48	47	47	46	31	28	24	21	18
Mauritius	47	43	26	22	17	16	9	7	6	6
Mexico	47	46	43	32	27	16	11	9	6	5
Moldova	...	...	...	...	18	...	...	...	...	9
Monaco	14	19	8	...	20	14	16	12	15	17
Mongolia	44	43	42	38	34	22	17	13	10	8
Montserrat	32	27	24	20	17	14	10	10	10	10
Morocco	50	50	46	37	33	26	20	16	11	8
Mozambique	46	47	46	46	44	30	25	22	20	17
Namibia	45	46	45	44	42	25	23	18	14	11
Nauru	27	32	...	...	23	7	7	4	5	5
Nepal	46	46	47	43	36	27	25	21	17	13
Netherlands	22	21	15	12	13	8	8	8	8	9
Neths. Antilles	35	32	21	19	18	5	5	5	5	6
New Caledonia	27	33	33	29	25	10	9	9	7	6
New Zealand	26	26	21	16	16	9	9	8	8	8
Nicaragua	54	50	47	44	39	23	17	13	10	7
Niger	54	53	52	52	51	32	28	25	22	19
Nigeria	51	52	49	49	47	27	24	20	17	14
Niue	37	42	29	26	21	15	9	10	7	5
Norfolk Is.	15	12	11	11	11	14	16	6	7	8
Norway	19	17	17	12	13	8	10	10	10	11
Oman	51	50	50	48	43	32	26	20	13	6
Pakistan	50	48	48	50	42	29	22	18	14	11
Palau (Belau)	29	34	35	33	31	6	7	5	5	4
Panama	40	41	36	28	25	13	10	7	5	5
Papua New Guinea	44	44	41	35	33	29	21	17	13	11
Paraguay	47	42	37	36	33	9	8	7	7	6
Peru	47	46	41	34	29	22	18	13	11	8
Philippines	49	44	37	36	30	20	13	11	9	7
Pitcairn Is.	45	8	15	...		16	10	...	...	
Poland	30	20	18	19	15	11	8	8	10	10
Portugal	24	24	20	15	13	12	11	11	10	10
Puerto Rico	37	31	24	21	18	9	7	7	7	8
Qatar	46	41	31	35	28	22	17	12	5	4
Réunion	39	40	31	24	21	13	10	7	6	6
Romania	25	17	19	16	15	12	9	9	10	11
Russia	...	...	...	...	15	...	...	...	...	10
Rwanda	47	51	53	52	50	23	21	21	19	16

	Birth Rate					Death Rate			
	1950–55	1960–65	1970–75	1980–85	1990–95	1950–55	1960–65	1970–75	1980–85
St Christopher-Nevis	37	36	18	24	21	14	11	8	10
St Helena	28	28	25	...	9	9	10	10	8
St Lucia	36	42	39	29	21	15	12	8	6
St Vincent & G.	42	46	30	26	23	16	12	9	7
Samoa	37	33	29	30	31	7	5	4	6
San Marino	18	18	16	14	10	8	8	8	8
São Tomé & Príncipe	41	50	45	40	35	26	19	11	11
Saudi Arabia	49	49	48	43	42	26	21	17	9
Senegal	49	50	49	47	44	28	27	24	19
Seychelles	31	41	32	28	24	12	12	9	9
Sierra Leone	48	48	49	48	48	34	32	29	25
Singapore	44	34	21	17	16	11	7	5	5
Slovenia	...	...	...	...	13	...	...	...	...
Solomon Is.	...	...	...	...	42	15	15	14	12
Somalia	49	48	48	53	47	31	27	23	22
South Africa	43	42	36	33	31	20	17	13	11
Spain	20	22	20	13	13	10	9	8	8
Sri Lanka	39	35	29	27	21	12	9	8	6
Sudan	47	47	47	46	43	27	25	21	17
Surinam	44	44	35	29	25	13	10	8	7
Swaziland	50	49	48	47	47	28	23	18	14
Sweden	16	15	14	11	13	10	10	10	11
Switzerland	17	19	14	12	12	10	10	9	9
Syria	47	47	47	46	43	21	17	12	9
Taiwan	45	36	24	21	17	10	6	5	5
Tajikistan	...	...	...	...	37	...	...	...	...
Tanzania	49	52	51	51	50	27	23	19	15
Thailand	47	44	35	28	20	19	13	9	8
Togo	47	48	46	45	45	29	24	19	16
Tokelau	...	...	...	...	22	14	12	9	8
Tonga	37	33	32	31	29	9	4	3	3
Trinidad & Tobago	38	38	26	28	23	11	8	7	7
Tunisia	46	47	37	34	27	23	18	12	8
Turkey	48	43	35	31	27	24	16	12	9
Turkmenistan	...	...	...	...	33	...	...	...	...
Turks & Caicos	39	39	30	26	26	13	11	8	6
Tuvalu	34	28	23	...	29	19	9	7	...
Uganda	51	49	50	53	52	25	20	19	17
Ukraine	...	...	...	...	13	...	...	...	...
USSR (former)	26	22	18	19	17	9	7	9	11
United Ar. Em.	48	44	33	27	20	23	17	10	4
United Kingdom	16	18	15	13	14	12	12	12	12
United States	24	22	16	16	14	10	9	9	9
Uruguay	21	22	21	18	17	11	10	10	10
Uzbekistan	...	...	...	...	32	...	...	...	...
Venezuela	47	44	36	33	28	12	9	7	6
Vietnam	42	41	38	35	30	29	21	14	11
Yemen	53	54	55	54	51	32	27	22	18
Yugoslavia (former)	29	22	18	17	14	12	9	9	9
Yugoslavia (Serbia)	...	...	...	...	15	...	...	...	...
Zaïre	47	47	47	45	45	26	22	19	16
Zambia	50	49	49	51	50	26	21	18	15
Zimbabwe	52	52	49	43	40	23	19	15	12

The figures are yearly averages for the period shown.
The figures for 1990–95 are estimates of the UN.

INFANT MORTALITY

deaths under one year per 1,000 live births

	1950–55	1970–75	1990–95
Afghanistan	227	194	162
Albania	145	58	32
Algeria	185	132	61
Angola	231	173	127

	1950–55	1970–75	1990–95
Argentina	64	49	29
Armenia	...	...	20
Australia	24	17	7
Austria	53	24	9
Azerbaijan	...	...	25
Bahamas	82	...	21
Bahrain	175	55	12
Bangladesh	180	140	108
Barbados	132	33	10
Belarus	...	...	12
Belgium	45	19	8

	1950–55	1970–75	1990–95		1950–55	1970–75	1990–95
nin	210	136	85	Madagascar	245	172	110
utan	197	153	118	Malawi	212	191	138
livia	176	151	93	Malaysia	99	42	20
snia	...	...	15	Maldives	...	...	73
tswana	130	95	58	Mali	213	203	159
azil	135	91	57	Malta	75	22	9
unei	112	20	7	Martinique	65	35	10
lgaria	92	26	14	Mauritania	207	160	117
rkina Faso	226	173	127	Mauritius	99	55	20
rma	183	100	59	Mexico	114	71	36
rundi	166	143	110	Moldova	...	...	20
mbodia	165	181	116	Mongolia	148	98	60
ameroon	190	119	86	Morocco	180	122	68
anada	36	16	7	Mozambique	205	168	130
ape Verde Is.	129	82	37	Namibia	168	134	97
entral African Republic	198	132	95	Nepal	197	153	118
had	211	166	122	Netherlands	24	12	7
hile	126	70	19	New Caledonia	40	38	34
hina	195	61	27	New Zealand	26	16	9
olombia	123	73	37	Nicaragua	167	100	50
omoros	180	135	89	Niger	207	166	124
ongo	170	90	65	Nigeria	207	135	96
osta Rica	94	51	17	Norway	23	12	6
roatia	...	...	10	Oman	231	145	34
uba	82	36	13	Pakistan	190	140	98
yprus	53	29	10	Panama	93	43	21
zechoslovakia	54	21	13	Papua New Guinea	190	105	53
enmark	28	12	6	Paraguay	106	53	39
jibouti	207	154	112	Peru	159	110	76
ominica	130	20	17	Philippines	100	64	40
ominican Republic	149	94	57	Poland	95	27	17
cuador	150	95	57	Portugal	91	45	13
gypt	200	150	57	Puerto Rico	63	25	13
l Salvador	175	110	53	Qatar	180	57	26
quatorial Guinea	204	157	117	Réunion	141	41	12
stonia	...	...	14	Romania	101	40	19
thiopia	190	155	122	Russia	...	...	17
iji	88	45	24	Rwanda	160	140	112
inland	34	12	5	St Christopher-Nevis	86	...	24
rance	45	16	7	St Lucia	116	...	18
abon	194	132	94	St Vincent & Grenadines	115	...	22
ambia, The	231	179	132	São Tomé & Príncipe	...	60	45
eorgia	...	...	19	Saudi Arabia	200	120	58
ermany	53	20	8	Senegal	184	122	80
hana	149	107	81	Seychelles	...	...	18
reece	60	34	13	Sierra Leone	231	193	143
reenland	120	...	27	Singapore	66	19	7
renada	80	40	15	Slovenia	...	...	9
uadeloupe	68	42	12	Solomon Is.	...	...	50
uatemala	141	95	48	Somalia	190	155	122
uinea	222	177	134	South Africa	152	110	62
uinea-Bissau	211	183	140	Spain	62	21	9
uyana	119	79	48	Sri Lanka	91	56	24
aiti	220	135	86	Sudan	185	145	99
onduras	169	110	57	Surinam	89	49	28
ong Kong	79	17	6	Swaziland	160	144	107
ungary	71	34	17	Sweden	20	10	6
celand	21	12	5	Switzerland	29	13	7
ndia	190	135	88	Syria	160	88	39
ndonesia	160	114	65	Taiwan	34	...	6
ran	190	122	40	Tajikistan	...	...	43
raq	165	96	56	Tanzania	160	130	97
reland	41	18	8	Thailand	132	65	24
srael	41	23	10	Togo	204	129	85
taly	60	26	9	Tonga	57	59	23
vory Coast	186	129	87	Trinidad & Tobago	79	30	14
amaica	85	42	14	Tunisia	175	120	44
apan	51	12	5	Turkey	233	138	62
ordan	160	82	36	Turkmenistan	...	...	53
azakhstan	...	...	25	Turks & Caicos	125	...	13
enya	150	98	64	Tuvalu	123	...	34
iribati	121	89	59	Uganda	160	116	94
orea, North	115	47	24	Ukraine	...	...	13
orea, South	115	47	21	USSR (former)	73	26	20
uwait	125	43	15	United Arab Emirates	180	57	22
yrgyzstan	...	...	31	United Kingdom	28	17	8
aos	180	145	97	United States	28	18	8
atvia	...	...	11	Uruguay	57	46	20
ebanon	87	48	40	Uzbekistan	...	...	36
esotho	160	130	89	Vanuatu	...	...	85
iberia	194	181	126	Venezuela	106	49	33
ibya	185	117	68	Vietnam	180	120	54
ithuania	...	...	10	Western Samoa	41	...	47
uxembourg	43	16	9	Yemen	231	168	107
acedonia	...	...	35	Yugoslavia	128	45	21

Yugoslavia (Serbia)	...	...	24
Zaire	182	117	75
Zambia	150	100	72
Zimbabwe	120	93	55

Infant mortality is the number of deaths per year of children under one year per 1,000 births. The figures are yearly averages for the period shown.

AGE

percentage

	1950					1990				
	0-4	5-14	15-24	25-59	60+	0-4	5-14	15-24	25-59	60+
World	14	21	18	39	8	12	20	19	40	9
Afghanistan	20	27	19	31	3	18	24	20	34	5
Albania	14	25	19	32	10	11	22	19	40	8
Algeria	16	24	19	35	7	15	28	21	30	5
Angola	17	24	19	35	5	18	27	19	32	5
Argentina	11	19	18	44	7	10	20	16	41	13
Armenia	...	...	...	...	...	10	20	16	43	11
Australia	11	16	15	46	13	7	15	16	46	15
Austria	7	15	14	48	15	6	12	15	48	20
Azerbaijan	...	...	...	...	...	12	21	18	40	9
Bahrain	18	25	19	34	5	13	20	15	49	3
Bangladesh	15	23	18	38	6	17	27	21	31	5
Barbados	12	21	18	41	9	8	17	19	41	15
Belarus	...	...	...	...	...	8	15	14	46	17
Belgium	8	13	15	48	16	6	12	14	48	21
Benin	15	21	16	34	14	19	27	19	30	5
Bhutan	16	24	19	36	6	15	24	19	36	6
Bolivia	17	25	19	34	5	17	27	19	32	5
Botswana	18	28	20	28	6	20	29	18	27	5
Brazil	17	25	20	34	4	13	23	19	39	7
Bulgaria	10	17	19	44	10	6	14	14	47	19
Burkina Faso	18	26	19	33	5	18	26	19	32	5
Burma	16	22	18	39	6	13	24	21	36	6
Burundi	16	25	19	35	5	19	27	19	31	5
Cambodia	17	26	19	34	5	17	18	20	40	5
Cameroon	16	24	19	36	6	19	27	19	30	5
Canada	12	18	16	43	11	7	14	14	49	16
Cape Verde Is.	11	24	24	36	7	18	27	22	27	6
Central African Republic	14	22	18	38	8	18	27	18	32	6
Chad	15	23	18	37	7	17	25	19	33	6
Chile	14	23	18	38	7	11	19	19	42	9
China	14	20	18	41	8	10	17	22	42	9
Colombia	18	25	19	33	6	13	24	21	37	6
Comoros	18	26	19	32	5	19	28	20	29	4
Congo	16	24	19	36	6	19	27	19	30	5
Costa Rica	18	25	19	32	6	13	23	19	38	6
Cuba	13	22	17	40	7	8	14	21	44	12
Cyprus	14	21	18	39	9	9	17	15	45	14
Czechoslovakia	10	16	16	47	12	7	16	15	46	17
Denmark	10	17	14	47	13	5	12	15	48	20
Djibouti	17	24	18	36	5	18	27	18	32	4
Dominican Rep.	19	26	19	31	5	14	24	21	36	6
Ecuador	17	25	18	33	7	14	25	21	34	6
Egypt	16	24	19	36	5	15	25	19	36	6
El Salvador	17	26	19	33	5	16	29	21	29	6
Equatorial Guinea	13	21	18	39	9	17	25	18	33	6
Estonia	...	...	...	...	...	8	15	14	46	17
Ethiopia	18	26	19	32	5	19	27	19	31	5
Fiji	19	28	19	30	5	12	25	19	39	5
Finland	13	18	16	44	10	6	13	13	49	18
France	10	13	15	46	16	7	13	15	46	19
Gabon	12	19	17	40	12	15	18	22	37	9
Gambia, The	16	23	19	37	5	18	26	18	33	5
Georgia	...	...	...	...	...	8	16	15	45	16
Germany	7	17	14	51	11	6	10	14	45	25
Ghana	19	27	19	32	4	18	27	19	31	5
Greece	10	19	20	42	10	6	14	15	46	20
Guadeloupe	17	22	17	37	7	10	17	20	41	12

	1950					1990				
	0-4	5-14	15-24	25-59	60+	0-4	5-14	15-24	25-59	60+
Guatemala	18	26	20	31	4	18	28	20	30	
Guinea	18	25	19	34	4	19	27	19	30	
Guinea-Bissau	15	22	19	38	6	17	24	18	35	
Guyana	18	23	18	34	7	12	22	23	38	
Haiti	15	22	17	38	8	15	25	20	34	
Honduras	18	27	20	32	3	17	28	21	30	
Hong Kong	16	14	23	43	4	6	15	16	50	
Hungary	9	16	17	47	11	6	14	14	47	
Iceland	13	18	17	42	11	8	17	17	44	
India	15	24	19	36	6	13	23	19	37	
Indonesia	14	25	20	35	6	12	23	21	37	
Iran	17	22	17	35	8	15	29	20	31	
Iraq	19	27	19	31	4	18	28	19	30	
Ireland	11	18	15	41	15	9	19	18	40	
Israel	14	18	17	45	6	11	21	18	39	
Italy	9	17	17	45	12	5	12	16	47	
Ivory Coast	17	26	20	33	4	20	28	18	30	
Jamaica	14	23	19	39	6	11	22	23	35	
Japan	13	22	20	37	8	6	13	15	49	
Jordan	19	27	17	30	7	17	27	22	29	
Kazakhstan	...	...	...	...	...	11	21	17	42	
Kenya	17	22	19	35	6	20	30	19	26	
Korea, North	16	26	19	34	6	11	18	25	40	
Korea, South	16	26	19	34	5	8	18	21	46	
Kuwait	15	21	22	37	5	13	23	16	46	
Kyrgyzstan	...	...	...	...	...	15	24	18	35	
Laos	16	26	20	34	5	18	26	19	33	
Latvia	...	...	...	...	...	7	15	13	47	1
Lebanon	14	21	19	36	10	14	22	22	34	
Lesotho	16	24	18	34	7	17	26	18	33	
Liberia	17	25	19	35	5	18	27	19	31	
Libya	17	25	19	32	7	18	28	19	31	
Lithuania	...	...	...	...	...	8	15	15	47	1
Luxembourg	6	14	16	49	15	6	11	13	51	1
Madagascar	17	25	19	34	5	18	27	19	31	
Malawi	19	26	19	31	5	21	28	18	29	
Malaysia	17	24	18	34	7	15	24	20	37	
Mali	18	26	19	33	4	20	27	19	30	
Malta	15	20	17	38	9	7	16	14	48	1
Martinique	15	22	18	37	8	9	15	19	43	1
Mauritania	17	25	19	35	5	18	26	19	32	
Mauritius	18	27	19	31	5	9	21	19	44	
Mexico	17	27	19	32	5	13	24	22	35	
Moldova	...	...	...	...	...	10	22	14	41	13
Mongolia	17	25	19	34	6	16	26	20	34	
Morocco	18	27	19	32	5	15	25	20	33	
Mozambique	17	25	19	35	5	18	26	19	32	
Namibia	17	24	19	34	6	18	27	18	31	
Nepal	15	25	20	34	7	16	26	19	34	
Netherlands	12	17	16	43	12	6	12	16	49	17
New Zealand	12	17	14	44	13	8	15	17	45	15
Nicaragua	18	26	20	32	4	18	28	20	30	
Niger	18	26	19	33	4	20	28	19	30	
Nigeria	19	27	19	31	4	20	28	19	30	
Norway	10	15	13	48	14	6	13	16	44	21
Oman	17	25	19	34	5	19	27	17	33	
Pakistan	15	23	19	35	8	19	27	19	31	
Panama	17	25	18	35	6	12	23	21	37	
Papua New Guinea	15	24	19	35	6	15	25	21	34	
Paraguay	16	27	20	32	5	15	25	20	35	5
Peru	17	25	19	34	6	13	24	21	36	6
Philippines	18	26	18	33	6	15	25	20	35	5
Poland	12	18	19	43	8	8	17	14	46	15
Portugal	11	19	19	42	11	7	15	17	44	18
Puerto Rico	17	27	19	32	6	9	17	19	41	14
Qatar	17	25	19	34	6	14	21	16	46	4
Réunion	16	25	19	36	4	11	21	22	39	8
Romania	10	18	20	43	9	8	16	17	44	16
Russia	...	...	...	...	...	8	14	13	45	20
Rwanda	19	27	19	31	4	20	29	19	28	4
Saudi Arabia	17	25	18	34	6	18	27	17	33	4
Senegal	17	25	19	34	6	18	27	19	31	5
Sierra Leone	16	23	19	37	5	18	26	19	32	5
Singapore	16	24	18	38	4	9	15	17	51	9
Somalia	17	24	18	36	5	19	28	17	32	4

	1950					1990						1950					1990				
	0-4	5-14	15-24	25-59	60+	0-4	5-14	15-24	25-59	60+		0-4	5-14	15-24	25-59	60+	0-4	5-14	15-24	25-59	60+
th Africa	15	23	18	37	6	14	23	19	37	6	Turkmenistan	...	...	...	...	...	16	25	19	34	6
in	10	17	18	44	11	6	14	17	45	18	Uganda	19	25	19	32	5	21	29	19	28	4
Lanka	16	25	20	34	6	11	22	19	41	8	Ukraine	...	...	...	...	...	7	14	14	46	19
lan	18	26	19	32	5	18	27	19	31	5	USSR (former)	11	20	21	40	9	9	17	15	45	15
inam	17	23	18	34	8	13	21	22	37	7	United Ar. Em.	17	25	19	34	6	11	20	13	53	3
aziland	18	25	19	33	5	19	28	19	29	5	United Kingdom	9	14	14	49	16	7	12	15	46	21
eden	9	15	12	49	15	6	11	14	46	23	United States	11	16	15	46	12	7	14	15	47	17
tzerland	9	15	14	48	14	6	11	14	50	20	Uruguay	10	18	18	43	12	8	17	16	42	17
ia	17	25	19	33	7	19	29	19	28	4	Uzbekistan	...	...	...	...	...	16	26	19	34	5
wan	19	24	20	34	4	8	20	19	44	9	Venezuela	19	25	19	34	3	14	24	20	36	6
kistan	...	...	...	...	...	18	27	18	31	6	Vietnam	13	22	19	40	7	14	25	21	33	7
zania	20	27	19	29	5	20	29	19	28	4	Yemen	18	25	19	34	6	21	29	20	26	4
ailand	17	26	20	32	5	10	23	22	39	6	Yugoslavia	11	20	21	40	9	7	16	15	47	15
go	17	24	18	34	7	18	27	19	31	5	Zaïre	18	26	19	32	6	19	28	19	31	4
idad & obago	17	24	16	37	6	12	22	18	40	8	Zambia	19	26	19	32	4	21	28	19	28	4
isia	16	23	18	35	8	14	24	20	35	6	Zimbabwe	18	27	19	32	5	18	27	21	30	4
key	15	24	21	35	6	13	22	20	38	7											

This table shows the percentage of the total population in each of the five age-groups for 1950 and 1990.

LIFE EXPECTANCY

	1950–55		1970–75		1990–95			1950–55		1970–75		1990–95	
	male	female	male	female	male	female		male	female	male	female	male	female
ghanistan	31	32	38	38	43	44	Equatorial Guinea	33	35	39	42	46	50
bania	54	56	66	70	70	75	Estonia	...	...	...	...	66	75
geria	42	44	54	56	65	67	Ethiopia	31	34	39	43	45	49
ngola	29	32	37	40	45	48	Fiji	49	52	56	60	64	68
gentina	60	65	64	71	68	75	Finland	63	70	67	75	72	80
menia	...	...	...	...	78	73	France	64	70	69	76	73	81
ustralia	67	72	68	75	74	80	Gabon	37	40	43	47	52	55
ustria	63	68	67	74	72	79	Gambia, The	29	32	36	39	43	47
zerbaijan	...	...	...	...	67	75	Georgia	...	...	...	...	69	76
ahrain	50	53	62	65	70	74	Germany	65	70	68	74	72	78
angladesh	38	35	46	44	53	53	Ghana	40	44	48	52	54	58
arbados	55	60	67	72	73	78	Greece	64	68	71	74	74	79
elarus	...	...	...	...	64	75	Guadeloupe	55	58	65	71	71	78
elgium	65	70	68	75	72	79	Guatemala	42	42	53	56	62	67
enin	31	34	39	42	46	50	Guinea	31	32	37	38	44	45
hutan	37	36	43	42	51	49	Guinea-Bissau	31	34	35	38	42	45
olivia	39	43	45	49	54	58	Guyana	51	54	58	62	62	68
osnia	...	...	...	...	68	73	Haiti	36	39	47	50	55	58
otswana	41	44	49	53	58	64	Honduras	41	44	52	56	64	68
razil	49	53	58	62	64	69	Hong Kong	57	65	69	76	75	80
ulgaria	62	66	69	74	70	76	Hungary	62	66	67	73	68	75
urkina Faso	32	35	40	43	48	51	Iceland	70	74	71	77	75	81
urma	39	41	51	54	61	64	India	39	38	51	49	60	61
urundi	38	41	41	45	48	51	Indonesia	37	38	48	51	61	65
ambodia	38	41	39	42	50	52	Iran	46	46	56	56	67	68
ameroon	35	38	44	47	54	57	Iraq	43	45	56	58	65	67
anada	67	72	70	77	74	81	Ireland	66	68	69	74	73	78
ape Verde Is.	47	50	56	59	67	69	Israel	64	66	70	73	74	78
entral African Republic	33	38	40	46	48	53	Italy	64	68	69	75	73	80
had	31	34	38	41	46	49	Ivory Coast	35	38	44	47	53	56
hile	52	56	61	67	69	76	Jamaica	56	59	67	71	71	76
hina	39	42	63	64	69	73	Japan	62	66	71	76	76	82
olombia	49	52	60	63	66	72	Jordan	42	44	55	58	66	70
omoros	40	41	47	48	56	57	Kazakhstan	...	...	...	...	64	73
ongo	36	41	44	49	52	57	Kenya	39	43	49	53	59	63
osta Rica	56	59	66	70	73	78	Korea, North	46	49	59	64	68	74
roatia	...	...	...	...	67	74	Korea, South	46	49	59	64	68	74
uba	58	61	69	73	74	78	Kuwait	54	58	65	69	72	77
yprus	65	69	70	73	74	79	Kyrgyzstan	...	...	...	...	65	73
zechoslovakia	64	68	67	74	69	76	Laos	37	39	39	42	50	53
enmark	70	72	71	76	73	79	Latvia	...	...	...	...	64	75
jibouti	32	35	39	43	47	51	Lebanon	54	58	63	67	65	69
ominican Rep.	45	47	58	62	65	70	Lesotho	34	41	44	53	54	63
cuador	47	50	57	61	65	69	Liberia	36	39	46	49	54	57
gypt	41	44	51	53	60	63	Libya	42	44	51	55	62	65
El Salvador	44	47	57	61	64	69	Lithuania	...	...	...	...	67	76
							Luxembourg	63	69	67	74	72	79
							Macedonia	...	...	...	...	68	72
							Madagascar	36	39	45	48	54	57
							Malawi	36	37	40	42	48	50
							Malaysia	47	50	61	65	69	73

	1950–55 male	female	1970–75 male	female	1990–95 male	female		1950–55 male	female	1970–75 male	female	1990–95 male	fema
Mali	31	34	37	40	44	48	Slovenia	...	...	...	...	67	75
Malta	64	68	69	73	72	76	Somalia	32	35	39	43	45	49
Martinique	55	58	66	72	73	79	South Africa	44	46	51	57	60	66
Mauritania	32	35	39	42	46	50	Spain	62	66	70	76	74	80
Mauritius	50	52	61	65	68	73	Sri Lanka	58	56	64	66	70	74
Mexico	49	52	60	65	67	74	Sudan	36	38	41	44	51	53
Moldova	...	...	...	...	65	72	Surinam	54	58	62	67	68	73
Mongolia	41	44	53	55	62	65	Swaziland	34	37	45	50	56	60
Morocco	42	44	51	55	62	65	Sweden	70	73	72	78	75	81
Mozambique	32	35	41	44	47	50	Switzerland	67	72	71	77	75	81
Namibia	38	40	48	50	58	60	Syria	45	47	55	59	65	69
Nepal	37	36	44	43	54	53	Tajikistan	...	...	...	...	67	72
Netherlands	71	73	71	77	74	81	Thailand	45	49	58	62	65	69
New Zealand	68	72	69	75	73	79	Togo	35	38	44	47	53	57
Nicaragua	41	44	54	56	65	68	Trinidad & Tobago	56	59	64	69	70	75
Niger	32	35	38	41	45	48	Tunisia	44	45	55	56	67	69
Nigeria	35	38	43	46	51	54	Turkey	42	45	56	60	65	68
Norway	71	75	71	78	74	81	Turkmenistan	...	...	...	...	63	70
Oman	36	37	48	50	66	70	Uganda	39	42	45	49	51	55
Pakistan	40	38	50	48	59	59	Ukraine	...	...	...	...	66	75
Panama	54	56	65	68	71	75	USSR (former)	60	69	64	74	67	75
Papua New Guinea	36	35	48	48	55	57	United Arab Em.	47	49	61	64	70	74
Paraguay	61	65	64	68	65	70	United Kingdom	67	72	69	75	73	79
Peru	43	45	54	57	63	67	United States	66	72	68	75	73	80
Philippines	46	49	56	59	63	67	Uruguay	63	69	66	72	69	76
Poland	59	64	67	74	68	76	Uzbekistan	...	...	...	...	66	73
Portugal	57	62	65	71	71	78	Venezuela	54	57	64	69	67	74
Puerto Rico	63	67	69	76	73	79	Vietnam	39	42	48	53	62	66
Qatar	47	49	61	64	68	73	Yemen	33	33	43	43	52	52
Réunion	50	56	60	68	68	76	Yugoslavia	57	59	66	71	70	76
Romania	59	63	67	71	69	74	Yugoslavia (Serbia)	...	...	...	...	68	73
Russia	...	...	...	...	64	74	Zaïre	38	41	44	48	52	56
Rwanda	39	42	43	46	49	52	Zambia	36	39	46	49	54	57
Saudi Arabia	39	41	52	56	64	68	Zimbabwe	40	43	50	53	59	63
Senegal	36	38	39	41	48	50							
Sierra Leone	29	32	34	37	41	45							
Singapore	59	62	67	72	72	77							

Life expectancy is the age to which a baby can expect to live with the rate of mortality pertaining at the time of birth. The figures given are averages for the period shown.

URBAN POPULATION

percentage of total population

	1950	1970	1990	2000
Afghanistan	6	11	22	29
Albania	20	34	35	40
Algeria	22	40	45	51
Angola	8	15	28	36
Antigua & Barbuda	46	34	32	39
Argentina	65	78	86	89
Armenia	...	...	70	...
Australia	75	85	86	86
Austria	49	52	58	61
Azerbaijan	...	...	54	...
Bahamas	62	58	59	65
Bahrain	64	78	83	85
Bangladesh	4	8	14	18
Barbados	34	37	45	51
Belarus	...	...	67	...
Belgium	92	94	97	98
Belize	57	51	52	58
Benin	7	16	42	53
Bermuda	100	100	100	100
Bhutan	2	3	5	8
Bolivia	38	41	51	59
Bosnia	...	...	36	...
Botswana	0	8	24	33
Brazil	36	56	77	83
Brunei	27	62	58	59
Bulgaria	26	52	70	76
Burkina Faso	4	6	9	12
Burma	16	23	25	28

	1950	1970	1990	2000
Burundi	2	2	7	12
Cambodia	10	12	12	15
Cameroon	10	20	49	60
Canada	61	76	76	79
Cape Verde Is.	8	19	62	70
Cayman Is.	100	100	100	100
Central African Republic	16	30	47	55
Chad	4	11	33	44
Chile	58	75	86	89
China	11	20	21	25
Colombia	37	57	70	75
Comoros	3	11	28	34
Congo	31	35	42	50
Cook Is.	32	30	35	42
Costa Rica	34	40	54	61
Croatia	...	...	51	...
Cuba	49	60	75	80
Cyprus	30	41	53	60
Czechoslovakia	37	55	69	74
Denmark	68	80	86	89
Djibouti	41	62	81	84
Dominican Republic	24	40	60	68
Ecuador	28	40	57	65
Egypt	32	42	49	55
El Salvador	37	39	44	50
Equatorial Guinea	16	39	65	71
Estonia	...	...	72	...
Ethiopia	5	9	13	17
Faroe Is.	18	28	31	36
Fiji	24	35	44	51
Finland	32	50	68	74
France	56	71	74	76
French Guiana	54	67	75	79

	1950	1970	1990	2000
nch Polynesia	28	56	65	70
oon	11	26	46	54
mbia, The	11	15	23	29
orgia	...	...	56	...
rmany	72	78	84	86
ana	15	29	33	38
eece	37	53	63	68
adeloupe	42	41	49	55
atemala	31	36	42	48
inea	6	14	26	33
inea-Bissau	10	15	20	25
yana	28	29	34	42
iti	12	20	30	37
nduras	18	29	44	52
ng Kong	89	90	93	94
ungary	37	46	60	67
eland	74	83	91	92
dia	17	20	28	34
donesia	12	17	29	37
an	28	41	55	61
aq	35	56	74	79
eland	41	52	59	64
rael	65	84	92	94
aly	54	64	69	72
ory Coast	13	27	47	55
amaica	27	42	52	59
apan	50	71	77	78
ordan	35	51	68	74
azakhstan	...	...	58	...
enya	6	10	24	32
ribati	10	26	36	43
orea, North	31	50	67	73
orea, South	21	41	72	81
uwait	59	72	96	97
yrgyzstan	...	...	38	...
aos	7	10	19	25
atvia	...	...	71	...
ebanon	23	59	84	87
esotho	1	9	20	32
iberia	13	26	44	52
ibya	19	36	70	76
iechtenstein	20	21	28	33
ithuania	...	...	69	...
uxembourg	59	62	84	87
Macau	97	97	99	99
Macedonia	...	...	54	...
Madagascar	8	14	25	32
Malawi	4	6	15	21
Malaysia	20	27	42	50
Maldives	11	14	21	24
Mali	9	14	19	23
Malta	61	78	87	90
Martinique	28	54	75	79
Mauritania	3	14	42	54
Mauritius	29	42	42	46
Mexico	43	59	73	77
Moldova	...	...	48	...
Monaco	100	100	100	100
Mongolia	19	45	51	55
Montserrat	22	11	12	16
Morocco	26	35	49	56
Mozambique	2	6	27	41
Namibia	15	34	57	66
Nepal	2	4	10	14
Netherlands	83	86	89	89
Netherlands Antilles	49	50	55	61
New Caledonia	40	49	81	87
New Zealand	73	81	84	85
Nicaragua	35	47	60	66
Niger	5	9	20	27

	1950	1970	1990	2000
Nigeria	10	20	35	43
Niue	24	21	23	30
Norway	32	65	74	77
Oman	2	5	11	15
Pakistan	18	25	32	38
Palau (Belau)	22	41	60	66
Panama	36	48	55	61
Papua New Guinea	1	10	16	20
Paraguay	35	37	48	54
Peru	36	57	70	75
Philippines	27	33	42	49
Poland	39	52	63	67
Portugal	19	26	33	39
Puerto Rico	41	58	74	79
Qatar	63	80	90	91
Réunion	24	44	64	70
Romania	28	42	50	53
Russia	...	...	74	...
Rwanda	2	3	8	11
St Christopher-Nevis	22	34	49	56
St Lucia	38	40	46	53
St Vincent & Grenadines	13	15	21	27
São Tomé & Príncipe	13	23	42	51
Saudi Arabia	16	49	77	82
Senegal	31	33	38	45
Seychelles	27	26	59	69
Sierra Leone	9	18	32	40
Singapore	100	100	100	100
Slovenia	...	...	49	...
Solomon Is.	8	9	11	14
Somalia	13	23	36	44
South Africa	43	48	59	65
Spain	52	66	78	83
Sri Lanka	14	22	21	24
Sudan	6	16	22	27
Surinam	47	46	48	54
Swaziland	1	10	33	45
Sweden	66	81	84	86
Switzerland	44	55	60	62
Syria	31	43	52	57
Taiwan	...	...	75	...
Tajikistan	...	...	31	...
Tanzania	4	7	33	47
Thailand	11	13	23	29
Togo	7	13	26	33
Tonga	13	21	21	25
Trinidad & Tobago	23	39	69	75
Tunisia	31	44	54	59
Turkey	21	38	48	54
Turkmenistan	...	...	45	...
Turks & Caicos	40	41	51	58
Uganda	3	8	10	14
Ukraine	...	...	68	...
USSR (former)	39	57	68	71
United Arab Emirates	25	42	78	78
United Kingdom	84	89	93	94
United States	64	74	74	75
Uruguay	78	82	86	87
Uzbekistan	...	...	40	...
Vanuatu	5	14	22	85
Venezuela	53	72	91	94
Vietnam	12	18	22	27
Western Sahara	68	43	57	63
Western Samoa	13	20	23	27
Yemen	5	10	32	38
Yugoslavia	22	35	50	58
Yugoslavia (Serbia)	...	...	48	...
Zaïre	19	30	40	46
Zambia	9	30	56	65
Zimbabwe	11	17	28	35

CITIES

This list shows the principal cities with more than 500,000 inhabitants (for Brazil, China, India, Japan, Russia and the USA, only cities with more than 1 million inhabitants are included). The figures are taken from the most recent census or estimate available, and as far as possible are the population of the metropolitan area (for example, greater New York, Mexico or London). All the figures are in thousands. For the capital and largest cities, English conventional name forms have been used (for example, Cairo, Moscow or Rome), but local name forms have been used for the smaller cities (for example, Kraków).

Place	Population (Thousands)	Place	Population (Thousands)	Place	Population (Thousands)	Place	Population (Thousands)
Afghanistan		Montréal	3,127	Baotou	1,200	Frankfurt	6
Kabul	1,424	Vancouver	1,603	Suining	1,195	Essen	6
Algeria		Ottawa-Hull	921	Luoyang	1,190	Dortmund	6
Algiers	1,722	Edmonton	840	Macheng	1,190	Stuttgart	5'
Oran	664	Calgary	754	Xintai	1,167	Düsseldorf	5'
Angola		Winnipeg	652	Yichun	1,167	Bremen	5'
Luanda	1,544	Québec	646	Ürümqi	1,160	Duisburg	5
Argentina		Hamilton	600	Puyang	1,125	Hanover	5'
Buenos Aires	11,256	**Central African Republic**		Datong	1,110	Leipzig	5'
Córdoba	1,198	Bangui	597	Handan	1,110	**Ghana**	
Rosario	1,096	**Chad**		Shaoxing	1,091	Accra	9
Mendoza	775	Ndjaména	530	Ningbo	1,090	**Greece**	
La Plata	640	**Chile**		Zhongshan	1,073	Athens	3,0
San Miguel de Tucumán	622	Santiago	5,343	Nanning	1,070	**Guatemala**	
Mar del Plata	520	**China**		Huangshi	1,069	Guatemala	2,00
Armenia		Shanghai	12,320	Laiwu	1,054	**Guinea**	
Yerevan	1,254	Beijing (Peking)	9,750	Leshan	1,039	Conakry	70
Australia		Tianjin	7,790	Heze	1,017	**Haiti**	
Sydney	3,657	Chongqing	6,511	Linhai	1,012	Port-au-Prince	1,14
Melbourne	3,081	Wenzhou	5,948	Changshu	1,004	**Honduras**	
Brisbane	1,302	Guangzhou	5,669	**Colombia**		Tegucigalpa	6
Perth	1,193	Hangzhou	5,234	Bogotá	4,921	**Hong Kong**	
Adelaide	1,050	Shenyang	5,055	Cali	1,624	Kowloon	2,03
Austria		Dalian	4,619	Medellín	1,581	Hong Kong	1,25
Vienna	1,560	Jinzhou	4,448	Barranquilla	1,019	Tsuen Wan	69
Azerbaijan		Wuhan	4,273	Cartagena	688	**Hungary**	
Baku	1,149	Qingdao	4,205	**Congo**		Budapest	2,01
Bangladesh		Chengdu	4,025	Brazzaville	938	**India**	
Dhaka	6,105	Jilin	3,974	Pointe-Noire	576	Bombay	12,57
Chittagong	2,041	Nanjing	3,682	**Croatia**		Calcutta	10,91
Khulna	877	Jinan	3,376	Zagreb	931	Delhi	8,08
Rajshahi	517	Xi'an	2,911	**Cuba**		Madras	5,36
Belarus		Harbin	2,830	Havana	2,119	Hyderabad	4,28
Minsk	1,613	Yingkou	2,789	**Czech Republic**		Bangalore	4,08
Gomel	506	Dandong	2,574	Prague	1,216	Ahmadabad	3,29
Belgium		Anshan	2,517	**Denmark**		Pune	2,48
Brussels	954	Nanchang	2,471	Copenhagen	1,337	Kanpur	2,11
Bolivia		Zibo	2,460	**Dominican Republic**		Nagpur	1,66
La Paz	1,126	Lanzhou	2,340	Santo Domingo	1,601	Lucknow	1,642
Santa Cruz	696	Lupanshui	2,247	**Ecuador**		Surat	1,51
Bosnia-Herzegovina		Fushun	2,045	Guayaquil	1,508	Jaipur	1,01
Sarajevo	526	Taiyuan	2,177	Quito	1,101	Kochi	1,14
Brazil		Changchun	2,110	**Egypt**		Coimbatore	1,136
São Paulo	9,480	Kunming	1,976	Cairo	6,800	Vadodara	1,11
Rio de Janeiro	5,336	Tianshui	1,967	Alexandria	3,380	Indore	1,104
Salvador	2,056	Zhengzhou	1,943	El Gîza	2,144	Patna	1,09
Belo Horizonte	2,049	Fuxin	1,693	Shubra el		Madurai	1,094
Fortaleza	1,758	Zigong	1,673	Kheima	834	Bhopal	1,064
Brasília	1,596	Fuzhou	1,652	**El Salvador**		Vishakhapatnam	1,052
Curitiba	1,290	Liaoyang	1,612	San Salvador	1,522	Varanasi	1,028
Recife	1,290	Zhaozhuang	1,612	**Ethiopia**		Ludhiana	1,012
Nova Iguaçu	1,286	Botou	1,593	Addis Ababa	2,213	**Indonesia**	
Pôrto Alegre	1,263	Hepei	1,541	**Finland**		Jakarta	7,886
Belém	1,246	Guiyang	1,530	Helsinki	977	Surabaya	2,224
Manaus	1,011	Huainan	1,519	**France**		Medan	1,806
Bulgaria		Tangshan	1,500	Paris	9,319	Bandung	1,567
Sofia	1,141	Linyi	1,385	Lyons	1,262	Semarang	1,027
Burkina Faso		Qiqihar	1,380	Marseilles	1,087	Palembang	787
Ouagadougou	634	Tai'an	1,370	Lille	959	Ujung Pandang	709
Burma (Myanmar)		Changsha	1,330	Bordeaux	696	Malang	512
Rangoon	2,513	Shijiazhuang	1,320	Toulouse	650	**Iran**	
Mandalay	533	Huaibei	1,308	Nice	516	Tehran	6,476
Cambodia		Pingxiang	1,305	**Georgia**		Mashhad	1,759
Phnom Penh	800	Xintao	1,272	Tbilisi	1,279	Esfahan	1,127
Cameroon		Yangcheng	1,265	**Germany**		Tabriz	1,089
Douala	884	Yulin	1,255	Berlin	3,446	Shiraz	965
Yaoundé	750	Dongguang	1,230	Hamburg	1,669	Ahvaz	725
Canada		Chao'an	1,227	Munich	1,229	Qom	681
Toronto	3,893	Hohhot	1,206	Cologne	957	Bakhtaran	624

	Population (Thousands)
q	
ghdad	3,841
yala	961
Sulaymaniyah	952
oil	770
osul	644
dhimain	521
land	
blin	1,024
ael	
l Aviv–	
Jaffa	1,844
rusalem	544
ly	
ome	2,791
ilan	1,432
aples	1,206
urin	992
alermo	734
enoa	701
ory Coast	
oidjan	1,929
amaica	
ngston	588
apan	
okyo	11,936
okohama	3,220
saka	2,624
agoya	2,155
apporo	1,672
obe	1,477
yoto	1,461
ukuoka	1,237
awasaki	1,174
iroshima	1,086
itakyushu	1,026
ordan	
mman	1,272
Az-Zarqa	605
azakhstan	
lma-Ata	1,147
araganda	613
enya	
airobi	1,429
orea, North	
yongyang	2,639
amhung	775
hongjin	754
hinnamp'o	691
inuiju	500
orea, South	
eoul	10,628
usan	3,798
aegu	2,229
nchon	1,818
wangju	1,145
aejon	1,062
lsan	683
uch'on	668
uwon	645
ongnam	541
honju	517
yrgyzstan	
ishkek	641
atvia	
iga	917
ebanon	
eirut	1,500
ripoli	500
ibya	
ripoli	990
ithuania	
ilnius	593
acedonia	
kopje	563
adagascar	
ntananarivo	802
alaysia	
uala Lumpur	938
ali	
amako	746

	Population (Thousands)
Mexico	
Mexico City	15,048
Guadalajara	2,847
Monterrey	2,522
Puebla	1,055
León	872
Ciudad Juárez	798
Tijuana	743
Culiacán Rosales	602
Mexicali	602
Acapulco de Juárez	592
Mérida	557
Chihuahua	530
San Luis Potosí	526
Aguascalientés	506
Moldova	
Chişinau	667
Mongolia	
Ulan Bator	575
Morocco	
Casablanca	2,409
Rabat-Salé	893
Fès	562
Marrakesh	549
Mozambique	
Maputo	1,070
Netherlands	
Amsterdam	1,091
Rotterdam	1,069
The Hague	694
Utrecht	543
New Zealand	
Auckland	896
Nicaragua	
Managua	682
Nigeria	
Lagos	1,347
Ibadan	1,295
Kano	700
Ogbomosho	661
Norway	
Oslo	746
Pakistan	
Karachi	5,181
Lahore	2,953
Faisalabad	1,104
Rawalpindi	795
Hyderabad	752
Multan	722
Gujranwala	659
Peshawar	556
Paraguay	
Asunción	945
Peru	
Lima-Callao	6,415
Arequipa	635
Trujillo	532
Callao	515
Philippines	
Manila	6,720
Quezon City	1,667
Davao	868
Cebu	641
Caloocan	629
Poland	
Warsaw	1,655
Lódz	847
Kraków	751
Wroclaw	643
Poznan	590
Portugal	
Lisbon	2,561
Oporto	1,174
Romania	
Bucharest	2,064
Russia	
Moscow	8,957
St Petersburg	5,004
Novosibirsk	1,472
Nizhniy Novgorod	1,451
Yekaterinburg	1,413

	Population (Thousands)
Samara	1,271
Omsk	1,193
Chelyabinsk	1,170
Perm	1,108
Kazan	1,107
Ufa	1,100
Volgograd	1,031
Rostov	1,027
Saudi Arabia	
Riyadh	2,000
Jedda	1,400
Mecca	618
Medina	500
Senegal	
Dakar	1,730
Singapore	
Singapore	2,818
Somali Republic	
Mogadishu	1,000
South Africa	
Cape Town	1,912
Johannesburg	1,726
East Rand	1,038
Durban	982
Pretoria	823
Port Elizabeth	652
West Rand	647
Vereeniging	540
Spain	
Madrid	3,121
Barcelona	1,707
Valencia	753
Seville	659
Zaragoza	586
Málaga	512
Sri Lanka	
Colombo	1,863
Sudan	
Khartoum	561
Omdurman	526
Sweden	
Stockholm	1,503
Gothenburg	734
Switzerland	
Zürich	840
Syria	
Damascus	1,451
Aleppo	1,445
Holms	518
Taiwan	
Taipei	2,718
Kaohsiung	1,396
Taichung	774
Tainan	690
Panchiao	543
Tajikistan	
Dushanbe	602
Tanzania	
Dar es Salaam	1,361
Thailand	
Bangkok	5,876
Togo	
Lomé	500
Tunisia	
Tunis	1,395
Turkey	
Istanbul	7,309
Ankara	3,022
Izmir	2,665
Adana	1,430
Bursa	1,031
Konya	1,015
Gaziantep	760
İçel	701
Kayseri	588
Uganda	
Kampala	773
Ukraine	
Kiev	2,643
Kharkhiv	1,622
Dnipropetrovsk	1,190

	Population (Thousands)
Donetsk	1,121
Odesa	1,096
Zaporizhya	898
Lviv	807
Kryvyy Rih	729
Mariupol	523
Mykolayiv	515
Luhansk	505
United Kingdom	
London	6,933
Birmingham	1,012
Leeds	725
Glasgow	681
Sheffield	532
United States	
New York	18,087
Los Angeles	14,532
Chicago	8,066
San Francisco	6,253
Philadelphia	5,899
Detroit	4,665
Boston	4,172
Washington, DC	3,924
Dallas	3,885
Houston	3,711
Miami	3,193
Atlanta	2,834
Cleveland	2,760
Seattle	2,559
San Diego	2,498
Minneapolis-SP.	2,464
St Louis	2,444
Baltimore	2,382
Pittsburgh	2,243
Phoenix	2,122
Tampa	2,098
Denver	1,848
Cincinnati	1,744
Milwaukee	1,607
Kansas City	1,566
Sacramento	1,481
Portland	1,478
Norfolk	1,396
Columbus	1,377
San Antonio	1,303
Indianapolis	1,250
New Orleans	1,239
Buffalo	1,189
Charlotte	1,162
Hartford	1,086
Salt Lake City	1,072
Uruguay	
Montevideo	1,384
Uzbekistan	
Tashkent	2,094
Venezuela	
Caracas	2,784
Maracaibo	1,364
Valencia	1,032
Maracay	800
Barquisimeto	745
Ciudad Guayana	524
Vietnam	
Ho Chi Minh	3,924
Hanoi	3,056
Haiphong	1,448
Yugoslavia	
Belgrade	1,137
Zaïre	
Kinshasa	3,804
Lubumbashi	739
Mbuji-Mayi	613
Kolwezi	544
Zambia	
Lusaka	982
Zimbabwe	
Harare	1,189
Bulawayo	622

ENERGY

PRODUCTION, TRADE AND CONSUMPTION

million tonnes of coal-equivalent

	Production		Imports		Exports		tonnes of c-e per capita Consumption per capita		Consumptio to
	1970	1990	1970	1990	1970	1990	1970	1990	19
World	...	10,876	...	3,516	...	3,525	...	1.93	10,2
Afghanistan	3.44	4.15	0.33	0.9	3.08	1.37	0.05	0.22	3.
Albania	2.65	6.31	0.03	0.25	0.12	0.08	0.6	1.26	4.
Algeria	72.45	156.7	0.96	1.34	70.16	112.5	0.37	1.48	36
American Samoa	0	0	0.06	0.27	0	0	2.44	3.61	0.
Angola	7.49	34.04	0.39	0.02	6.38	31.62	0.16	0.09	0.8
Antigua & Barbuda	0	0	0.88	0.24	0.28	0.01	2	1.9	0.
Argentina	37.29	67.55	4.53	4.03	0.15	6.5	1.58	1.83	58.
Australia	59.65	212.21	26.8	19.16	17.2	100.05	4.83	7.53	127.
Austria	11.15	8.23	15.48	25.03	0.84	1.37	3.27	4.06	30.8
Bahamas	0	0	4.58	4.29	2.95	3.01	4.07	2.49	0.
Bahrain	6.03	10.39	12.64	14.51	14.31	13.04	2.64	15.59	0.C
Bangladesh	...	5.54	...	3.39	0	0	...	0.06	8.4
Barbados	0.01	0.13	0.47	0.51	0	0.01	0.82	1.66	0.4
Belgium	11.46	7.45	64.98	85.39	12.87	26.94	5.61	5.92	58.2
Belize	0	0	0.06	0.18	0	0	0.49	0.65	0.1
Benin	...	0.42	...	0.26	0	0.42	0.05	0.05	0.2
Bermuda	0	0	0.31	0.31	0	0	1.96	4.82	0.2
Bolivia	1.76	5.6	0.02	2.94	0.86	0	0.23	0.36	2.
Brazil	18.69	80.12	28.05	57.88	1.5	5.71	0.44	0.77	115.1
British Virgin Is.	0	0	0.01	0.02	0	0	0.9	1.77	0.C
Brunei	10.07	25.26	0.02	0.05	9.79	21.48	2.18	14.94	3.9
Bulgaria	16.15	17.81	16.58	26.99	0.4	1.2	3.77	4.3	38.7
Burkina Faso	0	0	...	0.26	0	0	...	0.03	0.2
Burma	1.3	2.93	0.49	0.05	0	0	0.06	0.06	2.5
Burundi	0	0.02	0	0.1	0	0	0.01	0.02	0.1
Cameroon	0.14	12.44	0.37	0.03	0	10.3	0.07	0.24	2.8
Canada	204.98	364.55	74.8	62.15	84.45	151.34	8.81	10.26	271.9
Cape Verde	0	0	0	0.05	0	0	0.05	0.11	0.0
Cayman Is.	0	0	0.02	0.13	0	0	2.1	4.76	0.1
Central African Rep.	0.005	0.01	0.11	0.12	0	0	0.05	0.04	0.1
Chad	0	0	0.09	0.14	0	0	0.02	0.02	0.
Chile	6.11	7.51	4.48	9.95	0.02	0.3	1.15	1.25	16.4
China	304	1,002	0.62	7.69	2.15	61.04	0.35	0.81	922.18
Colombia	21.79	58.45	0	1.91	7.99	31.99	0.61	0.77	25.42
Comoros	0	0	0.01	0.03	0	0	0.04	0.06	0.03
Congo	0.05	11.59	0.17	0.02	0.03	10.64	0.15	0.37	0.85
Costa Rica	0.12	0.43	0.64	1.46	0.07	0.05	0.37	0.59	1.77
Cuba	0.24	1.27	8.74	18.58	0	2.91	0.99	1.45	15.33
Cyprus	0	0	0.81	2.31	0	0	1.21	2.52	1.77
Czechoslovakia	63.75	59.33	22.21	41.05	6.69	5.91	5.39	5.59	87.65
Denmark	0.05	12.97	33.61	21.83	3.22	9.47	5.44	4.66	23.98
Djibouti	0	0	1.07	0.75	0	0	0.3	0.44	0.18
Dominica	0	0	0.01	0.03	0	0	0.18	0.37	0.03
Dominican Republic	0.1	0.1	1.35	2.68	0		0.32	0.37	2.62
Ecuador	0.38	22.29	1.45	0.38	0.06	14.74	0.28	0.73	7.69
Egypt	24.55	79.52	5.89	1.23	21.36	37.02	0.26	0.74	38.57
El Salvador	0.06	0.26	0.64	1.15	0	0.08	0.19	0.25	1.3
Equatorial Guinea	0	0	0.02	0.06	0	0	0.06	0.15	0.05
Ethiopia	0.03	0.1	0.02	1.61	0	0.2	0.06	0.03	1.27
Faroe Is.	0	0	0.12	0.29	0	0	3.28	6.4	0.3
Fiji	0	0.04	0.45	0.6	0.02	0.12	0.45	0.56	0.01
Finland	1.18	5.63	22.46	27.22	0.3	2.12	4.07	5.93	29.51
France	60.8	66.85	175	191.79	14.42	25.41	3.84	3.97	222.74
French Guiana	0	0	0.05	0.28	0	0	0.96	2.59	0.25
French Polynesia	0	0	0.21	0.39	0	0	0.82	1.47	0.3
Gabon	7.91	19.5	0.01	0.05	7.33	17.93	0.46	0.72	0.84
Gambia	0	0	0.02	0.09	0	0	0.05	0.11	0.09
Germany	254.96	233.36	228.64	677.66	40.2	37.23	5.4	5.75	457.3
Ghana	0.35	0.66	1.32	1.78	0.13	0.13	0.17	0.1	1.52
Gibraltar	0	0	0.24	0.72	0	0	0.77	0.93	0.03
Greece	2.03	11.22	10.03	30.65	0.23	9.16	1.11	3.04	30.57
Greenland	0.02	0	0.16	0.27	0	0.01	3.68	4.66	0.26
Grenada	0	0	0.02	0.07	0	0	0.22	0.68	0.06
Guadeloupe	0	0	0.15	0.63	0	0	0.45	1.43	0.49

	Production		Imports		Exports		Consumption per capita		Consumption total
	1970	1990	1970	1990	1970	1990	1970	1990	1990
⌐uam	0	0	1.09	0.86	0.13	0	6.49	5.98	0.71
⌐uatemala	0.04	0.51	1.14	1.57	0	0.09	0.19	0.19	1.73
⌐uinea	0	0.02	0.36	0.49	0	0	0.09	0.09	0.49
⌐uinea-Bissau	0	0	0.03	0.11	0	0	0.05	0.1	0.1
⌐uyana	0	0	0.74	0.31	0	0	1.04	0.38	0.3
⌐aiti	...	0.04	0.17	0.32	0	0	0.04	0.05	0.34
⌐onduras	0.02	0.11	1.11	0.79	0.5	0	0.23	0.19	1.73
⌐ong Kong	0	0	5.49	17.71	0.07	3.17	0.96	1.77	10.36
⌐ungary	20.66	17.2	11.72	22.41	1.53	4.7	2.81	3.28	34.66
⌐eland	0.18	0.57	0.75	1.02	0	0	4.11	6.23	1.58
⌐dia	67.76	240.17	17.95	44.52	0.42	0.62	0.14	0.31	264.92
⌐donesia	63.91	162.88	0.5	13.52	44.78	112.44	0.12	0.3	55.42
⌐an	295	261.61	0	10.59	257	172.96	0.96	1.65	90.34
⌐aq	112	150.28	0.05	0	107	124.58	0.61	0.87	16.55
⌐eland	1.76	4.88	7.86	10.64	1.02	0.93	2.58	3.66	13.63
⌐rael	7.46	0.06	1.55	16.31	0.29	1.46	2.14	3.19	14.68
⌐aly	25.8	32.21	182	207.66	34.89	26.84	2.65	3.68	209.85
⌐ory Coast	0.03	0.65	1.23	3.93	0.12	0.35	0.2	0.19	2.27
⌐amaica	0.02	0.02	3.04	2.25	0.22	0.09	1.21	0.83	2.04
⌐apan	...	47.65	...	507.06	...	11.49	...	4.15	512.11
⌐ordan	...	0.03	0.77	4.95	0	0	0.27	1.82	4.34
⌐enya	0.04	0.35	3.59	3.48	1.38	0.77	0.1	0.11	2.67
⌐iribati	0	0	...	0.01	0	0	...	0.15	0.01
⌐orea, North	26.63	52.4	1.92	7.67	0.09	0.05	2.05	2.76	60.07
⌐orea, South	9.53	18.35	13.05	102.47	0.63	4.86	0.67	2.47	105.85
⌐uwait	224	96.67	0	2.73	208	79.93	4.77	7.01	14.29
⌐aos	0	0.1	0.27	0.1	0	0.06	0.09	0.04	0.15
⌐ebanon	0.11	0.07	3.18	4.23	0.58	0	0.68	1.52	4.11
⌐iberia	0.03	0.03	0.76	0.25	0	0	0.48	0.09	0.24
⌐ibya	232.37	110.52	0.7	0.01	232.03	80.06	0.67	4.72	21.46
⌐uxembourg	0.11	0.1	5.84	5.01	0	0.11	17.05	12.95	4.83
⌐acau	0	0	0.09	0.5	0	0	0.36	1.03	0.49
⌐adagascar	0.01	0.04	0.87	0.51	0.34	0.05	0.07	0.04	0.48
⌐alawi	0.02	0.07	0.2	0.25	0	0	0.04	0.04	0.3
⌐alaysia	1.5	61.45	15.09	13.53	8.53	47.26	0.56	1.51	26.95
⌐ali	0	0.02	0.11	0.22	0	0	0.02	0.01	0.22
⌐alta	0	0	0.46	0.83	0	0	0.92	2.03	0.72
⌐artinique	0	0	0.18	0.91	0	0.3	0.53	1.77	0.6
⌐auritania	0	0	0.2	1.35	0	0	0.16	0.58	1.17
⌐auritius	0.01	0.01	0.3	0.88	0	0	0.33	0.49	0.54
⌐exico	53.81	256.92	3.65	8.24	5.27	101.39	1.04	1.75	155.28
⌐ongolia	0.72	3.07	0.37	1.06	0	0.21	0.87	1.79	3.92
⌐orocco	0.73	0.77	2.21	9.95	0.08	0	0.19	0.37	9.21
⌐ozambique	0.03	0.05	1.66	0.53	0.53	0	0.14	0.03	0.49
⌐auru	0	0	0.03	0.07	0	0	4.43	6.78	0.06
⌐epal	0	0.09	0.15	0.28	0	0.04	0.01	0.02	0.38
Netherlands	45.22	92.85	104	133.52	58.32	109.74	4.59	7.21	107.79
Netherlands Antilles	0	0	71.55	17.17	57.51	11.8	33.81	9.73	1.83
New Caledonia	0.03	0.06	1.05	0.72	0	0.01	9.44	4.4	0.73
New Zealand	3.7	13.64	5.04	4.45	0.08	1.11	2.79	4.99	16.95
Nicaragua	0.04	0.07	0.66	0.97	0	0	0.32	0.26	1.01
Niger	...	0.16	0.09	0.32	0	0	0.02	0.06	0.46
Nigeria	79.19	128.93	1	4.03	74.5	110.72	0.05	0.19	20.4
Norway	7.48	171.26	16.01	6.57	3.39	144.98	4.55	6.91	29.14
Oman	24.11	52.42	0.63	0.14	24.11	46.22	0.17	3.96	5.94
Pakistan	...	22.26	...	12.69	...	0.47	...	0.28	34.04
Palau (Belau)	0	0	0.08	0.13	0	0	0.62	0.65	0.12
Panama	...	0.27	...	4.89	...	0.46	...	0.61	1.48
Papua New Guinea	0.02	0.06	0.35	1.14	0	0.02	0.14	0.29	1.13
Paraguay	0	0.29	0	0.78	0	0.07	0	0.23	0.97
Peru	6.43	11.99	2	2.29	0.34	3.06	0.61	0.49	10.57
Philippines	0.29	2.56	13.3	19.63	1.12	0.59	0.26	0.3	18.76
Poland	131	140.47	15.42	35.03	28.03	27.53	3.56	3.72	142.87
Portugal	0.99	1.31	7.85	24.05	0.69	3.36	0.74	1.87	19.21
Puerto Rico	0.03	0.03	14.35	13.71	5.05	1.47	3.46	3.01	10.46
Qatar	26.6	36.74	0.08	0	25.29	28.56	13.26	23.69	8.72
Reunion	0.01	0.06	0.13	0.46	0	0	0.31	0.84	0.5
Romania	64.85	63.54	6.18	39.68	7.65	12.94	2.99	3.73	86.83
Rwanda	0.01	0.02	0.03	0.2	0	0	0.01	0.03	0.21
São Tomé & Príncipe	0	0	...	0.03	0	0	...	0.27	0.03
Saudi Arabia	277	521.8	0.73	0.59	251	391.48	0.47	6.39	90.36
Senegal	0	0	2.36	1.52	0.05	0.05	0.12	0.14	1.03
Seychelles	0	0	0.03	0.21	0	0	0.29	1.15	0.08
Sierra Leone	0	0	0.61	0.45	0	0	0.12	0.07	0.31
Singapore	0	0	29.42	85.78	17.38	47.1	2.01	5.54	15.08

	Production		Imports		Exports		Consumption per capita		Consumpt. to
	1970	1990	1970	1990	1970	1990	1970	1990	19
Solomon Is.	0	0	0.02	0.08	0	0	0.11	0.24	0.
Somalia	0	0	0.11	0.04	0	0	0.04	0.37	0.
South Africa	48.52	133.71	16.61	22.47	1.84	42.98	2.19	2.6	106.
Spain	14.12	28.94	49.75	97.83	17.94	14.41	1.47	2.53	98.
Sri Lanka	0.09	0.39	2.97	2.71	0.14	0.14	0.14	0.13	2.
St Christopher-Nevis	0	0	0	0.03	0	0	...	0.71	0.
St Lucia	0	0	0	0.08	0	0	0.32	0.52	0.
St Pierre & Miquelon	0	0	0	0.12	0	0	3.2	7.33	0.
St Vincent & G.	0	0	0	0.04	0	0	0.17	0.37	0.
Sudan	0.01	0.12	2.35	1.86	0	0.05	0.15	0.06	0.
Surinam	0.12	0.54	0.74	0.63	0	0.11	2.32	1.81	0.
Sweden	5.14	17.36	49.06	38.48	2.78	13.27	5.77	4.74	39.9
Switzerland	3.91	6.72	20.04	23.84	1.57	3.06	3.21	3.91	25.
Syria	6.18	33.74	1.86	1.08	5.15	19.38	0.38	1.06	13.
Tanzania	0.04	0.08	1.68	1.04	0.83	0.05	0.06	0.04	0.
Thailand	0.37	16.26	7.34	26.88	0.05	1.06	0.18	0.74	41.0
Togo	0	0	0.13	0.23	0	0	0.06	0.06	0.2
Tonga	0	0	0.01	0.04	0	0	0.14	0.37	0.0
Trindad & Tobago	13.01	18.6	23.14	1.51	27.99	10.82	4.4	6.86	8.7
Tunisia	6.05	7.14	0.86	5.11	4.7	5.68	0.29	0.81	6.6
Turkey	11.96	24.29	6.01	40.98	0.3	3.19	0.48	1.04	58.0
Uganda	0.09	0.07	0.64	0.4	0.04	0.02	0.07	0.02	0.
USSR (former)	1,216	2,357	17.04	23.93	163	380.29	4.13	6.69	1,93
United Arab Em.	55.12	180.26	0.28	_	54.8	146.57	2.52	20.18	32.0
United Kingdom	145	278.68	173	115.48	28.67	103.23	4.87	4.99	286.5
United States	2,102	2,102	276	588.08	74	131.05	10.82	9.96	2,48
US Virgin Is.	0	0	21.28	24.31	13.06	15.36	42.42	11.71	1.3
Uruguay	0.15	0.78	2.85	1.96	0	0.16	0.89	0.75	2.3
Vanuatu	0	0	0.04	0.06	0	0	0.22	0.2	0.0
Venezuela	298	198.41	0.31	0.13	258	135.71	2.24	2.84	56.0
Vietnam	3.07	9.51	9.76	4.33	0.24	4.54	0.3	0.14	9.3
Wake Is.	0	0	0.52	0.58	0	0	38	19	0.0
Western Sahara	0	0	...	0.1	0	0	...	0.52	0.0
Western Samoa	0	0	0.02	0.06	0	0	0.11	0.38	0.0
Yemen	0	12.09	10.05	1.11	8.19	11.51	0.18	0.17	1.5
Yugoslavia	21.44	35.38	9.68	27.27	1.04	1.22	1.41	2.41	57.3
Zaïre	0.49	2.88	1.48	1.52	0.19	1.69	0.07	0.07	2.3
Zambia	0.61	1.27	1.01	0.79	0	0.25	0.39	0.2	1.
Zimbabwe	3.61	5.39	0.7	1.17	0.54	0.16	0.71	0.65	6.3

South Africa includes Botswana, Lesotho, Namibia and Swaziland.

GROSS NATIONAL PRODUCT

	GNP 1991	GNP per capita 1991	GDP share agriculture 1991	GDP share industry 1991	GDP share manufacture 1991	GDP share services 1991	Average annual rate of change 1980–91	Consumer price index Jan 1993	
	million $US	$US	%	%	%	%	%	1980=100	
¬hanistan	...	450	52	33	25	15	–6	...	
¬ania	...	1,000	33	51	45	16	4.5	...	
¬eria	52,239	2,020	14	50	10	36	–0.8	374	92
¬erican Samoa	...	6,000	...	...	...	...	...	...	
¬ola	...	620	13	42	4	45	4	...	
¬gua & Barbuda	355	4,770	6	24	3	70	3.8	...	
¬entina	91,211	2,780	15	40	35	45	–1.5	284,555	
¬enia	7,233	2,150	14	71	50	15	2.1	...	
¬ba	...	6,000	...	...	...	...	...	...	
¬stralia	287,765	16,590	3	31	15	66	1.2	228	
¬stria	157,528	20,380	3	36	25	61	2.1	153	
¬rbaijan	12,065	1,670	31	55	43	14	0.4	...	
¬amas	3,044	11,720	4	13	10	83	1.3	196	
¬rain	3,679	6,910	1	25	18	74	–3.8	...	
¬gladesh	23,449	220	36	16	9	48	1.9	311	
¬bados	1,711	6,630	7	14	7	79	1.3	200	
¬arus	32,131	3,110	26	56	45	18	3.3	...	
¬gium	192,370	19,300	2	30	22	68	2.1	166	
¬ize	389	2,050	19		25	...	2.5	163	
¬nin	1,848	380	37	14	9	49	–1.1	...	
¬rmuda	...	25,000	...	...	...	...	2.1	...	
¬utan	260	180	43	27	10	30	6.8	...	
¬livia	4,799	650	24	30	14	46	–2	1,468,493	91
¬snia	...	...	15	61	54	24	1.8	...	
¬tswana	3,335	2,590	5	54	4	41	5.8	329	
¬azil	447,324	2,920	10	39	26	51	0.4	5,212,188	
¬unei	...	6,000	2	45	9	53	1.6	...	
¬lgaria	16,316	1,840	13	63	57	24	1.7	...	
¬rkina Faso	3,213	350	44	20	12	36	1.3	108	
¬rma	...	500	51	12	9	37	1.9	502	
¬rundi	1,210	210	55	16	12	29	1.4	240	
¬mbodia	1,725	200	...	...	...	...	...	...	
¬meroon	11,320	940	27	22	12	51	–0.9	...	
¬nada	568,765	21,260	3	21	23	76	2.1	192	
¬pe Verde Is.	285	750	14	25	5	61	2.2	132	
¬ntral African Republic	1,218	390	41	16	8	43	–1.5	129	
¬ad	1,212	220	43	18	16	39	3.8	...	
¬ile	28,897	2,160	8	30	30	62	1.7	950	
¬ina	424,012	370	27	42	38	31	7.8	...	
¬lombia	41,922	1,280	17	35	20	48	1.2	1,519	
¬moros	245	500	41	10	5	49	–1	...	
¬ngo	2,623	1,120	12	37	8	51	–0.2	204	
¬sta Rica	6,156	1,930	18	25	19	57	1	1,604	
¬oatia	...	...	14	50	43	36	1.4	...	
¬ba	...	1,000	12	52	39	36	2.1	...	
¬prus	6,135	8,640	7	27	15	66	4.9	188	
¬zechoslovakia	38,427	2,450	8	56	...	36	0.4	230	
¬enmark	121,695	23,660	5	28	19	67	2.1	186	
¬jibouti	...	1,000	5	15	7	80	2.1	...	
¬ominica	175	2,440	27	16	7	57	4.7	176	
¬ominican Republic	6,807	950	18	25	13	57	–0.2	...	
¬cuador	10,772	1,020	15	35	21	50	–0.3	5,370	
¬gypt	33,068	620	18	30	13	52	2	681	
¬l Salvador	5,697	1,070	10	24	19	66	–0.3	804	
¬quatorial Guinea	142	330	54	7	...	39	3.4	...	
¬stonia	6,088	3,830	26	56	44	18	2.1	...	
¬thiopia	6,144	120	47	13	9	40	–1.6	220	
¬iji	1,377	1,830	24	21	10	55	0	158	
¬inland	121,982	24,400	6	34	22	60	2.5	206	
¬rance	1,167,749	20,600	3	29	21	68	1.8	196	
¬rench Guiana	...	4,000	35	...	...	...	...	211	
¬rench Polynesia	...	6,000	5	15	7	80	5.2	199	
¬abon	4,419	3,780	9	45	6	46	–4.2	157	
¬ambia, The	322	360	34	12	10	54	–0.1	595	
¬eorgia	9,000	1,640	28	54	40	18	2.2	...	
¬ermany	1,516,785	23,650	2	39	23	59	2.2	141	
¬hana	6,176	400	53	17	10	30	–0.3	4,853	
¬ibraltar	...	4,000	...	...	...	...	...	188	
¬reece	65,504	6,230	17	27	14	56	1.2	850	
¬reenland	...	6,000	30	...	...	...	...	...	

	GNP 1991	GNP per capita 1991	GDP share agriculture 1991	GDP share industry 1991	GDP share manufacture 1991	GDP share services 1991	Average annual rate of change 1980–91	Consumer price index Jan 1993
	million $US	$US	%	%	%	%	%	1980=
Grenada	198	2,180	21	19	5	60	5.3	121
Guadeloupe	...	7,000	...	...	...	...	2.3	194
Guatemala	8,816	930	26	20	...	54	-1.8	485
Guinea	2,669	450	29	35	5	36	3.6	...
Guinea-Bissau	194	190	46	12	8	42	1.3	...
Guyana	233	290	25	31	10	44	-4.2	...
Haiti	2,471	370	31	38	15	31	-2.4	270
Honduras	3,010	570	22	27	16	51	-0.7	318
Hong Kong	77,302	13,200	0	25	17	75	5.4	275
Hungary	28,244	2,690	10	34	29	56	0.7	481
Iceland	5,814	22,580	10	15	18	75	1.3	2,003
India	284,668	330	31	27	18	42	3.3	307
Indonesia	111,409	610	19	41	21	40	3.9	133
Iran	127,366	2,320	21	21	9	58	-1.1	328
Iraq	...	2,000	25	41	12	34	4.4	605
Ireland	37,738	10,780	11	9	3	80	2.2	224
Israel	59,128	11,330	5	24	19	71	1.8	90,898
Italy	1,072,198	18,580	3	33	21	64	2.1	284
Ivory Coast	8,523	690	38	22	21	40	-3.4	...
Jamaica	3,365	1,380	5	40	17	55	-0.3	420
Japan	3,337,191	26,920	3	42	25	55	3.7	129
Jordan	3,881	1,120	7	26	13	67	-3.3	226
Kazakhstan	41,691	2,470	34	49	30	17	0.9	...
Kenya	8,505	340	27	22	12	51	0.3	173
Kiribati	53	750	30	8	1	62	0.5	...
Korea, North	22,000	1,000	...	...	...	...	...	...
Korea, South	274,464	6,340	8	45	28	47	8.8	189
Kuwait	...	16,000	1	56	9	43	0.5	...
Kyrgyzstan	6,900	1,550	42	45	33	15	2.1	...
Laos	965	230	59	17	7	24	1.2	...
Latvia	9,193	3,410	24	55	45	21	2.8	...
Lebanon	...	2,000	8	21	13	71	-16	...
Lesotho	1,053	580	14	38	13	48	0	114
Liberia	...	600	37	28	5	35	0.5	...
Libya	...	5,500	5	50	7	45	-2	...
Liechtenstein	...	33,000	...	...	...	...	...	...
Lithuania	10,220	2,710	32	49	36	19	2.5	...
Luxembourg	11,761	31,080	3	41	31	56	3.8	108
Macau	...	6,000	1	34	28	65	6	164
Macedonia	...	...	17	60	...	23	2	...
Madagascar	2,560	210	33	14	12	53	-2.4	684
Malawi	1,996	230	35	20	13	45	0.1	683
Malaysia	45,787	2,490	23	42	16	35	2.9	112
Maldives	101	460	14	53	...	33	6.7	...
Mali	2,412	280	44	12	11	44	-0.1	103
Malta	2,598	6,850	4	41	27	55	3.8	101
Martinique	...	4,000	...	...	...	...	4	212
Mauritania	1,026	510	22	31	6	47	-1.8	...
Mauritius	2,623	2,420	11	33	23	56	6.1	108
Mexico	252,381	2,870	9	30	22	61	-0.5	22,367
Moldova	9,529	2,170	40	44	34	16	1.8	...
Mongolia	...	600	16	33	27	51	...	...
Montserrat	...	4,000	4	6	...	90	...	...
Morocco	26,451	1,030	19	31	18	50	1.6	229
Mozambique	1,163	70	37	46	23	17	-3.6	...
Namibia	2,051	1,120	10	28	4	62	-1.5	...
Nepal	3,453	180	59	14	5	27	2.1	339
Netherlands	278,839	18,560	4	32	20	64	1.5	138
Netherlands Antilles	...	6,000	1	10	...	89	2	154
New Caledonia	...	4,000	25	7	5	68	...	203
New Zealand	41,626	12,140	9	27	18	64	0.2	287
Nicaragua	1,897	340	30	23	19	47	-4.6	...
Niger	2,361	300	38	19	8	43	-4.1	93
Nigeria	34,057	290	37	38	10	25	-1.7	230
Norway	102,885	24,160	3	36	14	61	2.2	222
Oman	8,787	5,500	4	52	4	44	4.5	...
Pakistan	46,725	400	26	26	17	48	3.2	210
Panama	5,254	2,180	10	11	14	79	-1.8	124
Papua New Guinea	3,307	820	26	35	10	39	-0.7	199
Paraguay	5,374	1,210	22	24	18	54	-0.8	1,087
Peru	38,295	1,020	8	30	22	62	-2.6	1,062
Philippines	46,138	740	21	34	26	45	-1.2	171
Poland	70,640	1,830	7	59	50	34	0.5	274

	GNP 1991	GNP per capita 1991	GDP share agriculture 1991	GDP share industry 1991	GDP share manufacture 1991	GDP share services 1991	Average annual rate of change 1980–91	Consumer price index Jan 1993
	million $US	$US	%	%	%	%	%	1980=100
tugal	58,451	5,620	9	37	29	54	2.7	112
erto Rico	22,498	6,330	1	41	39	58	0.9	145
tar	6,968	16,000	2	39	13	59	–10.9	...
union	...	6,000	6	17	9	77	...	197
mania	31,079	1,340	19	49	...	32	–0.1	...
ssia	479,546	3,220	19	58	45	23	1.3	...
vanda	1,930	260	38	22	20	40	–2.6	203
Christopher-Nevis	156	3,960	10	25	27	65	5.8	...
Lucia	380	2,500	16	22	17	62	2.9	135
Vincent & Grenadines	187	1,730	17	25	9	58	5.2	126
o Tomé & Principe	42	350	31	11	...	58	–3.5	...
udi Arabia	105,133	7,500	7	52	7	41	–4.2	99
negal	5,500	720	20	19	13	61	0	172
ychelles	350	5,110	7	21	9	72	2.5	140
erra Leone	904	210	43	14	3	43	–1.3	64,969
ngapore	39,249	12,890	0	38	29	62	4.9	133
ovenia	...	...	8	62	53	30	1.2	...
lomon Is.	184	560	35	7	3	58	3.5	416
malia	...	150	65	10	5	25	2.3	...
outh Africa	90,953	2,600	5	44	25	51	0.9	532
ain	486,614	12,460	6	39	30	55	2.9	278
i Lanka	8,665	500	27	25	14	48	2.5	427
dan	10,107	450	36	15	9	49	–2.4	...
rinam	1,649	3,610	11	26	10	63	–4.5	741
waziland	874	1,060	23	40	37	37	3.1	125
weden	218,934	25,490	3	34	22	63	1.7	235
witzerland	225,890	33,510	4	42	...	54	1.6	156
yria	14,234	1,110	30	23	...	47	–2.1	820
aiwan	161,000	8,000	4	43	34	53	8	...
ajikistan	5,669	1,050	37	42	27	21	–0.1	...
anzania	2,424	100	61	5	4	34	–1.1	2,031
hailand	89,548	1,580	12	39	27	49	5.9	173
ogo	1,530	410	33	23	10	44	–1.7	148 91
onga	110	1,100	41	19	12	40	1.5	220
rinidad & Tobago	4,525	3,620	3	39	9	58	–5.2	330
unisia	12,417	1,510	13	33	17	54	1.2	255
urkey	103,888	1,820	18	34	24	48	2.9	1,588
urkmenistan	6,387	1,700	43	41	23	16	0.7	...
ganda	2,762	160	51	12	4	37	3.3	...
kraine	121,458	2,340	28	53	43	19	2.3	...
JSSR (former)	2,700,000	9,200	23	56	43	21	3.3	...
nited Arab Emirates	32,813	19,500	2	55	9	43	–5.8	...
nited Kingdom	963,696	16,750	2	37	30	61	2.6	208
nited States	5,686,038	22,560	2	29	25	69	2.1	172
ruguay	8,895	2,860	10	32	25	58	–0.4	46,750
zbekistan	28,255	1,350	42	40	26	18	0.8	...
anuatu	175	1,120	34	11	6	55	–0.2	113
enezuela	52,775	2,610	5	47	16	48	–1.5	1,072
ietnam	...	300	42	35	33	23	2	...
Western Samoa	156	930	51	12	...	37	5.1	320
emen	6,746	540	22	26	9	52	6.7	...
ugoslavia	70,038	2,900	12	48	...	40	–1.4	36,886
Yugoslavia (Serbia)	...	...	18	52	46	30	1.8	...
Zaire	8,123	220	30	32	9	38	–1.6	...
Zambia	3,394	420	16	47	36	37	–2.9	11,092
Zimbabwe	6,220	620	20	32	26	48	0.2	...

The Gross National Product (GNP) is a measure of a country's total production of goods and services including the net income from overseas. Owing to difficulties in the use of exchange rates and individual nation's methods of calculating the GNP, the figures must be used cautiously. Gross Domestic Product (GDP) is the value of domestic production and excludes net overseas income. Note that manufacturing is also included within the industry total. Services also includes items which cannot be included in the other groups.

The consumer price index is for early 1993 unless stated otherwise in the last column.

PRODUCTION STATISTICS

AGRICULTURAL, FOREST AND FISHING PRODUCTS

BARLEY

thousand tonnes

	1950	1970	1980	1990	1991	Rank	%
World	59,267	129,036	156,649	181,946	169,385		
Afghanistan	269	363	313	216	217		
Algeria	808	470	592	833	1,751		
Argentina	656	497	229	330	320		
Australia	531	2,372	3,278	4,055	4,025		
Austria	210	954	1,288	1,521	1,360		
Belgium	254	608	844	625	660		
Brazil	15	26	94	157	188		
Bulgaria	332	1,108	1,439	1,387	1,495		
Canada	4,245	10,024	11,199	13,925	12,463	3	7.4
Chile	79	97	103	92	109		
China	12,360	6,434	3,133	3,000	3,000		
Colombia	50	92	101	100	102		
Czechoslovakia	1,046	2,543	3,524	4,071	3,793		
Denmark	1,708	5,175	6,250	4,987	4,978	9	2.9
Egypt	123	93	111	129	110		
Ethiopia	720	727	1,021	899	965		
Finland	201	943	1,421	1,720	1,749		
France	1,534	8,865	10,997	10,020	10,651	4	6.3
Germany	1,995	7,312	13,385	13,992	14,449	2	8.5
Greece	211	655	838	341	500		
Hungary	654	749	848	1,369	1,552		
India	2,384	2,642	2,020	1,486	1,642		
Iran	767	1,042	1,548	3,360	3,600		
Iraq	722	692	726	1,854	520		
Ireland	163	854	1,643	1,380	1,281		
Italy	258	326	914	1,703	1,774		
Japan	2,020	629	392	346	269		
Korea, North	155	353	155	150	145		
Korea, South	846	1,589	1,059	416	340		
Libya	84	70	97	141	145		
Mexico	160	240	486	492	584		
Morocco	1,483	2,190	1,712	2,138	3,252		
Netherlands	201	366	265	219	230		
New Zealand	49	222	254	435	440		
Norway	109	545	636	740	680		
Pakistan	120	97	141	131	140		
Peru	208	164	115	80	100		
Poland	1,061	2,162	3,563	4,217	4,257	10	2.5
Portugal	96	64	45	79	82		
Romania	412	615	2,360	2,680	2,951		
Saudi Arabia	13	13	8	350	375		
South Africa	41	27	102	262	183		
Spain	1,909	3,922	6,571	9,415	9,141	6	5.4
Sweden	231	1,836	2,323	2,123	1,869		
Switzerland	55	147	220	343	357		
Syria	321	375	1,129	846	950		
Tunisia	218	126	279	477	721		
Turkey	2,270	3,720	5,480	7,300	7,800	7	4.6
USSR (former)	6,354	35,132	42,502	56,600	42,000	1	24.8
United Kingdom	2,061	8,257	10,058	7,900	7,700	8	4.5
United States	5,843	9,476	8,838	9,192	10,113	5	5.9
Uruguay	23	38	71	133	156		
Yemen	5	157	49	55	22		
Yugoslavia	323	442	726	692	742		

BEEF AND VEAL

thousand tonnes

	1950	1970	1980	1990	1991	Rank	%
World	20,621	38,871	44,110	51,632	51,452		
Afghanistan	25	66	69	65	65		
Algeria	13	24	44	60	60		
Angola	4	40	50	56	57		
Argentina	1,972	2,503	2,933	2,610	2,640	4	5.1
Australia	628	997	1,683	1,677	1,760	7	3.4
Austria	85	155	199	224	220		
Bangladesh	...	141	140	140	142		
Belgium	129	264	306	323	329		
Bolivia	31	51	88	146	152		
Brazil	1,092	1,822	2,104	2,775	2,800	3	
Bulgaria	38	78	117	120	112		
Burma	1	67	76	85	86		
Cameroon	21	35	50	70	70		
Canada	503	864	977	924	879		
Chad	39	31	30	63	65		
Chile	132	165	171	242	240		
China	1,330	1,433	1,680	1,102	1,302	9	
Colombia	281	422	607	795	823		
Costa Rica	15	44	80	85	91		
Cuba	179	199	145	141	140		
Czechoslovakia	181	336	380	404	294		
Denmark	149	193	245	202	212		
Dominican Republic	15	32	49	68	67		
Ecuador	23	45	79	100	110		
Egypt	130	119	119	222	229		
Ethiopia	166	243	214	245	245		
Finland	45	109	115	118	122		
France	964	1,577	1,832	1,750	1,934	6	3
Germany	662	1,633	1,890	2,112	2,183	5	4
Greece	9	86	110	82	80		
Guatemala	35	57	56	59	53		
Honduras	16	32	61	46	45		
Hungary	96	122	145	101	92		
India	173	66	771	852	857		
Indonesia	206	133	156	173	192		
Iran	50	75	168	230	250		
Iraq	21	42	46	50	39		
Ireland	193	217	384	491	550		
Italy	268	1,062	1,120	1,165	1,164	10	2
Ivory Coast	2	39	41	42	45		
Japan	61	270	430	549	573		
Kenya	10	131	183	329	326		
Korea, North	12	22	31	45	53		
Korea, South	7	37	93	130	130		
Madagascar	122	114	129	142	142		
Mali	27	38	40	71	75		
Mexico	145	450	743	1,790	1,550	8	
Mongolia	74	49	72	66	63		
Morocco	50	91	113	141	145		
Namibia	40	27	33	63	66		
Netherlands	135	337	420	540	495		
New Zealand	187	387	502	479	535		
Nicaragua	20	59	58	38	38		
Niger	33	29	37	21	21		
Nigeria	113	205	250	282	288		
Norway	41	57	73	83	84		
Pakistan	205	155	184	312	326		
Panama	13	35	41	58	60		
Paraguay	86	124	107	148	160		
Peru	65	96	87	117	112		
Philippines	42	73	89	82	78		
Poland	178	513	654	725	708		
Portugal	31	87	107	115	108		
Romania	101	214	297	176	160		
Somalia	13	45	41	57	57		
South Africa	245	398	590	661	678		
Spain	101	296	411	514	490		
Sudan	51	126	246	218	231		
Sweden	118	159	156	146	146		
Switzerland	75	133	162	164	172		
Tanzania	95	123	129	195	197		
Thailand	16	89	142	172	179		
Turkey	37	187	209	285	300		
Uganda	40	68	91	77	79		
USSR (former)	1,726	5,508	6,720	8,800	8,200	2	15.9
United Kingdom	588	921	1,063	1,001	1,019		
United States	4,785	10,062	10,092	10,465	10,531	1	20.5
Uruguay	292	338	331	333	350		
Venezuela	67	208	341	382	370		
Vietnam	11	33	41	105	110		
Yugoslavia	97	244	333	352	260		
Zimbabwe	39	90	79	78	77		

	1950	1970	1980	1990	1991	Rank	%
Nigeria	10,422	9,473	10,833	19,043	20,000	3	13
Paraguay	903	1,442	1,977	3,550	3,900	8	2.5
Peru	288	477	453	430	440		
Philippines	290	436	2,226	1,854	1,900		
Rwanda	300	333	578	550	560		
Senegal	61	159	28	69	69		
Sri Lanka	220	376	520	384	410		
Sudan	87	133	125	6	8		
Tanzania	900	3,373	5,547	6,922	6,266	6	4.1
Thailand	269	3,208	15,128	20,701	20,300	2	13.2
Togo	233	562	404	593	500		
Uganda	2,024	1,058	2,122	3,339	3,350		
Venezuela	152	317	322	302	310		
Vietnam	282	960	3,238	2,525	3,000		
Zaire	6,000	10,232	12,942	17,600	18,227	4	11.9
Zambia	135	159	183	260	2700		

CAMELS

ousand head

	1950	1970	1980	1990	1991	Rank	%
rld	10,819	15,965	17,122	19,509	19,627		
hanistan	350	300	267	265	266		
eria	144	173	150	125	130		
~rain	...	1	1	1	1		
~kina Faso	...	5	6	5	5		
~ad	266	397	432	549	565	8	2.9
~na	...	693	597	475	463	10	2.4
~bouti	15	22	51	59	60		
~ypt	165	120	91	197	200		
~iopia	855	981	980	1,050	1,050	4	5.4
~ia	638	1,110	1,050	1,450	1,490	3	7.6
~n	450	135	111	130	130		
~q	181	262	72	59	40		
~ael	...	10	11	10	10		
~rdan	...	13	13	18	18		
~nya	152	507	608	810	820	7	4.2
~uwait	...	10	5	6	6		
~ya	324	163	134	140	150		
~li	79	217	230	241	241		
~auritania	160	707	734	915	920	6	4.7
~ongolia	741	636	601	558	562	9	2.9
~orocco	195	205	157	43	43		
~ger	224	340	404	360	360		
~geria	...	19	17	18	18		
~man	...	11	41	87	90		
~akistan	466	700	844	990	1,005	5	5.1
~atar	...	8	10	22	23		
~audi Arabia	265	107	277	389	390		
~enegal	...	7	7	15	15		
~omalia	2,730	4,700	5,883	6,855	6,860	1	35.5
~udan	1,550	2,495	2,611	2,742	2,757	2	14.1
~yria	...	10	7	5	5		
~unisia	186	233	173	230	230		
~urkey	...	37	12	2	2		
~nited Arab Em.	...	100	57	115	118		
~SSR (former)	306	248	235	300	300		
~emen	123	224	158	175	180		

CASSAVA

thousand tonnes

	1950	1970	1980	1990	1991	Rank	%
World	55,200	96,760	121,472	150,768	153,689		
Angola	1,006	1,597	1,850	1,900	1,850		
Argentina	344	296	202	140	150		
Benin	700	533	631	957	889		
Bolivia	77	223	204	487	499		
Brazil	12,466	29,922	24,315	24,285	24,632	1	16
Burundi	700	843	412	569	580		
Cameroon	1,000	637	1,273	1,200	1,230		
Central Afr. Rep.	616	767	920	520	520		
Chad	19	140	205	330	342		
China	...	1,938	3,390	3,216	3,320		
Colombia	825	1,380	2,070	1,939	2,081		
Congo	500	461	631	770	780		
Cuba	179	217	287	300	300		
Dominican Rep.	148	173	98	127	134		
Ecuador	18	382	216	134	130		
Gabon	100	155	242	250	250		
Ghana	512	1,533	1,894	2,717	3,600	10	2.3
Guinea	218	482	480	450	450		
Haiti	104	205	252	300	290		
India	1,255	4,993	5,921	5,674	5,600	7	3.6
Indonesia	6,817	10,695	13,500	15,830	16,330	5	10.6
Ivory Coast	623	546	1,067	1,393	1,435		
Kenya	350	510	588	650	650		
Liberia	397	264	300	300	300		
Madagascar	866	1,227	1,641	2,292	2,290		
Malawi	545	150	135	145	168		
Malaysia	350	271	347	410	414		
Mali	142	36	59	73	73		
Mozambique	1,860	2,549	3,100	4,056	3,690	9	2.4
Niger	21	182	191	213	216		

CATTLE

thousand head

	1950	1970	1980	1990	1991	Rank	%
World	798,153	1,094,915	1,219,756	1,293,641	1,294,604		
Afghanistan	2,500	3,660	3,723	1,650	1,650		
Algeria	784	872	1,356	1,427	1,443		
Angola	1,263	2,514	3,117	3,100	3,100		
Argentina	42,320	48,841	55,620	50,582	50,080	7	4
Australia	14,534	22,382	26,161	23,191	23,430		
Austria	2,207	2,440	2,553	2,562	2,584		
Azerbaijan	...	...	1,800	...	1,800		
Bangladesh	19,000	25,395	25,053	23,244	23,500		
Belarus	...	...	6,800	...	7,000		
Belgium	2,150	2,882	3,104	3,069	3,000		
Bolivia	2,227	2,298	4,570	5,538	5,600		
Botswana	1,019	1,660	2,906	2,696	2,500		
Brazil	51,305	75,658	116,645	148,000	152,000	2	12
Bulgaria	1,688	1,277	1,782	1,575	1,457		
Burkina Faso	1,120	2,556	2,760	2,900	2,900		
Burma	4,494	6,949	8,565	9,298	9,310		
Burundi	1,019	676	614	432	435		
Cambodia	842	2,233	831	2,100	2,150		
Cameroon	1,540	2,308	3,521	4,697	4,700		
Canada	7,945	11,678	13,328	12,249	12,369		
Central Afr. Rep.	306	677	1,662	2,595	2,677		
Chad	3,260	4,500	4,360	4,297	4,400		
Chile	2,293	2,923	3,650	3,404	3,300		
China	46,404	63,168	52,567	79,493	81,407	5	6
Colombia	14,910	20,233	24,110	24,550	24,875	10	2
Costa Rica	601	1,498	2,183	1,762	1,741		
Cuba	4,333	6,146	5,166	4,920	4,920		
Czechoslovakia	3,966	4,253	4,935	5,129	4,923		
Denmark	2,998	2,855	2,970	2,241	2,220		
Dominican Rep.	711	1,176	1,918	2,240	2,250		
Ecuador	1,467	2,391	2,987	4,359	4,200		
Egypt	1,356	2,108	1,906	3,463	3,500		
El Salvador	795	1,164	1,234	1,220	1,243		
Ethiopia	18,901	26,310	26,000	30,000	30,000	8	2
Finland	1,700	1,907	1,747	1,363	1,315		
France	15,606	21,669	23,825	21,419	21,446		
Georgia	...	...	1,600	...	1,300		
Germany	14,151	19,281	20,672	20,287	19,488		
Ghana	374	902	804	1,145	1,300		
Guatemala	977	1,474	1,886	1,900	1,695		
Guinea	1,060	1,300	1,753	1,800	1,800		
Haiti	582	800	1,000	1,450	1,400		
Honduras	884	1,578	1,980	2,424	2,388		
Hungary	2,052	1,952	1,936	1,598	1,571		
India	155,239	177,447	186,500	197,300	198,400	1	15
Indonesia	4,112	6,273	6,505	10,550	10,350		
Iran	3,388	5,239	5,450	6,650	6,800		
Iraq	1,510	2,633	1,630	1,675	1,400		
Ireland	4,211	5,940	6,043	5,899	6,029		
Italy	8,281	9,436	8,697	8,746	8,647		
Japan	2,397	3,582	4,261	4,760	4,863		
Kazakhstan	...	...	8,700	...	9,800		
Kenya	5,859	8,433	10,418	13,793	13,700		
Korea, North	538	733	945	1,300	1,350		
Korea, South	598	1,244	1,728	2,051	2,126		
Latvia	...	...	1,400	...	1,400		
Lithuania	...	...	2,200	...	2,300		

	1950	1970	1980	1990	1991	Rank	%
Madagascar	5,709	8,519	10,147	10,254	10,265		
Mali	3,000	5,400	5,670	5,000	5,000		
Mauritania	514	2,250	1,262	1,350	1,360		
Mexico	14,489	24,668	27,706	32,054	29,847	9	2
Mongolia	1,988	2,026	2,452	2,693	2,849		
Morocco	2,188	3,617	3,362	3,400	3,500		
Mozambique	699	1,274	1,400	1,380	1,370		
Namibia	1,492	2,500	2,403	2,087	2,131		
Nepal	5,507	6,292	6,893	6,281	6,350		
Netherlands	2,659	4,281	5,071	4,731	4,830		
New Zealand	4,932	8,734	8,063	8,065	8,200		
Nicaragua	1,068	2,275	2,373	1,680	1,680		
Niger	2,818	4,077	3,343	2,200	2,200		
Nigeria	9,546	11,883	12,267	13,947	14,500		
Norway	1,204	949	989	953	953		
Pakistan	11,500	14,584	15,268	17,573	17,785		
Panama	567	1,201	1,425	1,388	1,399		
Paraguay	4,600	4,433	5,966	8,254	8,260		
Peru	2,830	3,999	3,958	4,102	3,630		
Philippines	710	1,653	1,885	1,629	1,677		
Poland	6,895	10,990	12,494	10,049	8,844		
Portugal	878	1,252	1,332	1,335	1,375		
Romania	4,387	4,947	6,351	6,291	5,381		
Russia	...		58,100		57,000	6	4
Senegal	720	2,557	2,424	2,740	2,813		
Somalia	1,430	3,750	4,437	5,100	4,900		
South Africa	11,912	11,114	13,647	13,398	13,512		
Spain	4,356	4,236	4,608	5,126	5,126		
Sri Lanka	1,131	1,601	1,662	1,800	1,814		
Sudan	3,957	12,300	18,376	20,583	21,028		
Sweden	2,595	1,934	1,928	1,718	1,675		
Switzerland	1,544	1,866	2,008	1,855	1,829		
Tajikistan	...		1,200		1,400		
Tanzania	6,356	10,141	12,616	13,047	13,138		
Thailand	4,608	4,470	4,228	5,669	6,052		
Turkey	10,121	13,235	15,467	12,173	11,377		
Turkmenistan	...				800		
Uganda	2,547	3,987	5,063	4,913	5,000		
Ukraine	...		25,400		24,600		
USSR (former)	55,778	96,707	114,748	118,400	115,600	3	9
United Kingdom	10,277	12,632	13,321	11,922	11,846		
United States	80,569	112,321	112,152	98,162	98,896	4	8
Uruguay	8,154	8,730	10,965	8,723	8,889		
Uzbekistan	...		3,500		4,600		
Venezuela	5,769	8,292	10,527	13,272	13,368		
Vietnam	1,541	1,750	1,646	3,199	3,282		
Yemen	1,030	842	973	1,175	1,180		
Yugoslavia	4,866	5,143	5,467	4,705	4,527		
Yugoslavia (Serbia)	...				2,097		
Zaire	640	968	5,063	1,550	1,600		
Zambia	881	1,580	2,238	2,920	3,045		
Zimbabwe	2,956	5,178	5,378	5,900	5,950		

	1950	1970	1980	1990	1991	Rank
Greece	41	142	195	199	207	
Guatemala	1	11	10	11	11	
Honduras	8	7	8	8	8	
Hungary	5	42	68	80	81	
Iran	15	74	107	183	184	
Iraq	13	25	35	34	27	
Ireland	3	30	58	72	75	
Israel	7	32	55	76	76	
Italy	265	470	608	700	692	5
Japan	...	40	68	81	85	
Jordan	...	2.8	2	29	29	
Lebanon	5	7	10	7	7	
Mexico	7	77	97	115	115	
Netherlands	130	284	458	584	614	6
New Zealand	101	102	93	125	129	
Niger	...	7.4	16	11	11	
Norway	24	53	71	84	82	
Peru	8	36	34	169	169	
Poland	13	249	379	333	293	9
Portugal	8	23	38	55	54	
Romania	13	83	129	99	102	
South Africa	9	29	31	42	40	
Spain	41	80	145	156	155	
Sudan	...	38	55	65	69	
Sweden	57	64	101	116	113	
Switzerland	53	87	123	132	132	
Syria	11	27	52	65	67	
Turkey	44	94	128	139	141	
USSR (former)	229	1,006	1,520	2,064	1,845	2
United Kingdom	44	139	238	312	310	8
United States	673	1,319	2,262	3,127	3,090	1	21
Uruguay	5	8.4	12	16	17	
Venezuela	16	28	62	96	92	
Yemen	...	13	20	23	23	
Yugoslavia	54	99	145	135	135	

COCOA BEANS

thousand tonnes

	1950	1970	1980	1990	1991	Rank
World	763	1491	1,636	2,528	2,455	
Bolivia	2	1	2	4	4	
Brazil	130	183	330	355	345	2 14.
Cameroon	52	115	120	99	95	8 3.
Colombia	11	20	35	56	59	9 2.
Congo	1	2	2	2	2	
Costa Rica	5	5	7	5	5	
Cuba	3	1	1	2	2	
Dominican Rep.	30	32	32	59	50	10
Ecuador	27	57	83	147	136	6 5.5
Equatorial Guinea	16	25	8	7	7	
Gabon	3	5	4	2	2	
Ghana	253	430	268	295	295	3 12
Grenada	3	3	2	2	2	
Guatemala	1	1	2	1	1	
Guinea	...	...	4	2	2	
Haiti	2	3	3	5	5	
Honduras	0.1	1	1	3	3	
India	1	1	2	6	6	
Indonesia	1	2	11	154	214	5 8.7
Ivory Coast	53	195	427	750	710	1 28.9
Jamaica	2	2	2	2	2	
Liberia	1	2	5	4	2	
Madagascar	0.3	1	2	3	3	
Malaysia	...	4	38	235	225	4 9.2
Mexico	8	27	35	46	39	
Nigeria	105	261	169	150	115	7 4.7
Panama	2	1	2	1	1	
Papua New Guinea	...	27	30	40	33	
Peru	4	2	5	11	11	
Philippines	1	4	4	10	9	
Samoa	3	3	2	1	1	
São Tomé & P.	8	10	7	3	3	
Sierra Leone	2	5	9	24	24	
Solomon Is.	...	1	1	3	3	
Sri Lanka	3	2	2	4	4	
Tanzania	1	2	1	3	3	
Togo	4	27	14	9	8	
Trinidad & Tobago	8	4	3	2	2	

CHEESE

thousand tonnes

	1950	1970	1980	1990	1991	Rank	%
World	...	7,732	11,363	14,539	14,163		
Afghanistan	...	9	19	18	18		
Albania	1	6	11	12	11		
Argentina	95	178	247	270	280		
Australia	45	76	144	175	176		
Austria	16	59	93	113	113		
Belgium	13	39	47	69	72		
Brazil	24	49	58	60	60		
Bulgaria	38	127	163	192	181		
Burma	4	12	18	28	29		
Canada	48	121	206	286	291	10	2.1
Chile	10	18	20	32	31		
China	...	171	75	145	143		
Colombia	...	39	44	51	51		
Cuba	3	1	11	16	16		
Czechoslovakia	13	111	173	205	181		
Denmark	69	113	218	295	290		
Ecuador	...	10	12	13	13		
Egypt	129	204	240	311	319	7	2.3
Finland	14	40	72	93	85		
France	252	780	1,137	1,363	1,425	3	10.1
Germany	193	660	986	1,342	1,193	4	8.4

	1950	1970	1980	1990	1991	Rank	%
nuatu	...	1	1	2	2		
nezuela	18	19	16	16	15		
ire	1.9	6	5	4	4		

COCONUTS

housand tonnes

	1950	1970	1980	1990	1991	Rank	%
orld	18,078	27,614	35,270	42,180	42,385		
angladesh	53	66	75	82	80		
enin	38	20	20	20	20		
razil	241	331	507	709	792	10	1.9
urma	17	67	95	183	182		
ambodia	10	44	28	48	48		
hina	...	53	59	65	67		
olombia	36	35	64	119	117		
omoros	60	69	53	50	50		
ominican Rep.	29	57	69	140	150		
cuador	13	25	73	42	43		
l Salvador	...	30	55	78	78		
iji	215	260	217	239	239		
rench Polynesia	169	178	130	110	110		
hana	73	257	225	220	225		
uam	...	22	30	39	40		
uyana	44	56	30	48	48		
aiti	27	24	34	35	35		
ndia	3,656	4,472	4,192	7,207	6,550	3	15.5
ndonesia	3,614	5,892	11,200	12,550	14,000	1	33
vory Coast	10	49	156	480	515		
amaica	74	150	176	200	200		
enya	65	77	85	75	76		
iribati	45	62	73	42	63		
adagascar	9	19	67	84	84		
alaysia	1,006	1,039	1,211	1,157	1,155	6	2.7
artinique	18	2	1	1	1		
exico	204	998	851	1,091	1,101	7	2.6
ozambique	338	400	453	420	420		
ew Caledonia	20	21	14	10	10		
igeria	150	86	90	105	105		
alau (Belau)	75	101	203	140	140		
anama	50	28	23	19	20		
apua N. Guinea	383	741	835	798	900	9	2.1
hilippines	4,453	7,601	9,142	9,552	8,923	2	21.1
uerto Rico	23	9	9	6	5		
t Lucia	21	35	34	33	33		
amoa	122	193	162	138	160		
ão Tomé & P.	41	42	36	42	42		
eychelles	53	42	22	10	9		
olomon Is.	77	184	201	180	210		
ri Lanka	1,975	1,963	1,692	1,924	1,800	4	4.2
anzania	246	310	310	365	370		
hailand	413	713	781	1,483	1,328	5	3.1
ogo	45	17	14	14	14		
onga	100	88	91	25	25		
rinidad & Tobago	129	105	49	40	40		
anuatu	135	247	326	357	293		
enezuela	74	147	160	177	175		
ietnam	80	100	290	940	1,000	8	2.4

COFFEE

thousand tonnes

	1950	1970	1980	1990	1991	Rank	%
World	2,222	4,266	5,173	6,282	6,088		
Angola	50	216	27	5	6		
Bolivia	2	11	19	29	30		
Brazil	1,077	1,197	1,475	1,463	1,497	1	24.6
Burundi	7	21	30	34	38		
Cameroon	9	90	108	102	58		
Central Afr. Rep.	4	10	17	16	17		
China	...	4	10	33	35		
Colombia	352	483	740	845	870	2	14.3
Costa Rica	23	82	106	151	158		
Cuba	31	29	21	27	26		

	1950	1970	1980	1990	1991	Rank	%
Dominican Rep.	28	44	58	59	46		
Ecuador	21	60	82	135	114		
El Salvador	75	139	183	156	149		
Equat. Guinea	6	7	6	7	7		
Ethiopia	27	172	192	206	168	10	2.8
Ghana	1	6	2	1	1		
Guatemala	58	125	167	202	195	7	3.2
Guinea	5	9	14	8	8		
Haiti	35	31	39	37	37		
Honduras	13	39	71	118	122		
India	20	82	126	118	173	9	2.8
Indonesia	39	186	295	411	408	3	6.7
Ivory Coast	50	243	298	284	240	6	3.9
Jamaica	3	2	2	1	2		
Kenya	11	57	89	105	90		
Liberia	2	5	10	2	2		
Madagascar	33	63	82	80	80		
Malawi	1	1	1	6	8		
Malaysia	2	6	6	5	5		
Mexico	63	182	228	440	299	4	4.9
Nicaragua	20	38	59	43	28		
Nigeria	1	4	4	1	1		
Panama	3	5	7	10	11		
Papua New Guinea	...	26	51	67	62		
Paraguay	1	5	9	18	19		
Peru	6	68	90	81	82		
Philippines	4	48	129	134	113		
Puerto Rico	10	12	12	13	13		
Rwanda	5	14	23	45	43		
Sierra Leone	1	6	11	26	26		
Sri Lanka	1	9	11	8	7		
Tanzania	14	49	54	52	56		
Thailand	1	1	10	61	55		
Togo	3	11	8	9	12		
Uganda	35	215	112	129	180	8	3
United States	3	1	1	1	1		
Venezuela	44	60	57	76	66		
Vietnam	2	5	28	260	285	5	4.7
Yemen	5	4	4	7	8		
Zaire	21	69	90	120	102		
Zimbabwe	2	2	5	15	14		

COTTON LINT

thousand tonnes

	1950	1970	1980	1990	1991	Rank	%
World	7,581	12,010	14,402	18,447	20,641		
Afghanistan	7	25	29	9	12		
Angola	6	28	11	11	11		
Argentina	112	114	134	270	290	10	1.4
Australia	4	27	78	305	433	8	2.1
Benin	2	9	7	59	67		
Brazil	350	631	555	660	700	6	3.4
Bulgaria	11	13	5	3	5		
Burkina Faso	3	10	25	77	77		
Burma	19	14	20	21	21		
Cameroon	10	21	32	44	35		
Central Afr. Rep.	12	20	9	13	11		
Chad	18	40	30	60	60		
China	786	1,988	2,627	4,508	5,663	1	27.4
Colombia	8	122	94	140	142		
Egypt	396	520	504	303	294	9	1.4
El Salvador	8	49	57	6	4		
Ethiopia	2	13	26	19	19		
Greece	21	115	115	209	190		
Guatemala	2	71	142	41	38		
India	575	1,088	1,280	1,659	1,700	5	8.2
Iran	25	155	82	138	146		
Israel	...	37	83	51	22		
Ivory Coast	1	14	54	116	133		
Korea, North	10	3	3	9	10		
Korea, South	22	4	2	...	...		
Mali	1	22	48	99	115		
Mexico	222	354	352	201	202		
Mozambique	24	42	17	28	25		
Nicaragua	8	80	70	23	30		
Nigeria	13	62	31	36	45		
Pakistan	261	595	730	1,637	2,112	4	10.2
Paraguay	13	10	85	215	259		

	1950	1970	1980	1990	1991	Rank	%
Peru	76	89	86	73	65		
South Africa	3	19	54	53	61		
Spain	8	52	58	75	83		
Sri Lanka	1	1	2	...	...		
Sudan	67	235	116	83	91		
Syria	30	150	126	159	200		
Tanzania	10	70	53	47	64		
Thailand	7	31	57	32	35		
Togo	1	2	7	34	42		
Turkey	119	441	488	611	565	7	2.7
Uganda	66	79	5	4	8		
USSR (former)	971	2,132	2,733	2,634	2,420	3	11.7
United States	3,105	2,225	3,004	3,375	3,819	2	18.5
Venezuela	4	15	14	31	23		
Zaire	46	21	8	26	26		
Zambia	1	3	6	10	25		
Zimbabwe	1	43	54	67	73		

	1950	1970	1980	1990	1991	Rank	
Poland	185	387	489	422	380		
Portugal	23	37	62	80	96		
Romania	50	165	328	380	370		
Russia	...	...	2,021	2,220	2,229	5	6
Saudi Arabia	2	7	42	160	164		
South Africa	33	115	160	205	191		
Spain	138	460	666	621	657		
Sri Lanka	8	20	29	46	48		
Sudan	6	17	32	33	34		
Sweden	84	102	114	117	106		
Switzerland	27	39	43	35	36		
Syria	6	16	69	61	65		
Taiwan	5	31.7	108	216	208		
Tanzania	8	15	36	38	40		
Thailand	66	117	105	127	128		
Turkey	45	96	217	398	375		
Ukraine	...	...	751	760	765		
USSR (former)	684	2,250	3,759	4,540	4,400	2	12
United Kingdom	426	878	834	624	646		
United States	3,717	4,057	4,124	4,022	4,005	3	11.
Uzbekistan	...	...	83.2	110	115		
Venezuela	4	76	129	107	107		
Vietnam	17	84	55	96	100		
Yugoslavia	43	137	218	228	237		
Yugoslavia (Serbia)	...	...	...	...	92		
Zambia	2	8	28	34	35trf		

EGGS – HEN'S

thousand tonnes

	1950	1970	1980	1990	1991	Rank	%
World	9,364	20,922	28,316	34,859	35,375		
Argentina	130	182	254	322	324		
Australia	116	185	198	188	187		
Austria	24	86	97	96	93		
Azerbaijan	...	...	40.9	46	46.2		
Bangladesh	12	34	39	49	40		
Belarus	...	...	154	170	172		
Belgium	107	229	201	180	185		
Brazil	177	337	765	1,300	1,400	6	4
Bulgaria	36	89	132	135	111		
Burma	6	17	31	34	35		
Canada	216	328	331	321	320		
Chile	13	58	66	91	91		
China	566	3,309	2,882	6,559	6,845	1	19.3
Colombia	43	95	177	255	267		
Croatia	...	...	...	...	47.9		
Cuba	14	64	99	110	110		
Czechoslovakia	76	186	243	283	266		
Denmark	117	84	77	82	84		
Ecuador	5	13	43	56	57		
Egypt	18	55	78	141	128		
El Salvador	3	23	37	39	39		
Ethiopia	39	66	73	79	79		
Finland	21	64	78	76	67		
France	411	644	850	902	942	9	2.7
Georgia	...	...	35.1	36	36.1		
Germany	280	1,125	1,123	1,043	912	10	2.6
Greece	21	100	123	121	138		
Guatemala	13	29	40	64	64		
Hungary	51	176	250	260	230		
India	53	262	682	1,283	1,357	7	3.8
Indonesia	94	32	178	380	400		
Iran	34	56	155	270	278		
Iraq	6	10	48	50	35		
Ireland	56	40	35	29	30		
Israel	17	74	92	98	106		
Italy	274	549	659	702	707		
Japan	120	1,735	1,998	2,397	2,466	4	7
Kazakhstan	...	...	170	190	197		
Kenya	8	12	20	42	42		
Korea, North	21	55	104	145	148		
Korea, South	3	131	256	393	489		
Latvia	...	...	38	38	38.5		
Lebanon	2	27	41	52	53		
Libya	2	2	16	34	35		
Lithuania	...	...	49.5	58	59.5		
Malaysia	11	63	122	202	212		
Mexico	77	334	636	1,010	1,141	8	3.2
Moldova	...	...	46	51	53		
Morocco	37	44	73	88	93		
Netherlands	145	268	540	648	646		
New Zealand	30	52	57	46	46		
Nigeria	29	102	180	225	225		
Norway	23	38	45	51	53		
Pakistan	6	15	96	220	238		
Peru	11	28	60	99	117		
Philippines	38	117	201	286	267		

FISH BY AREA

thousand tonnes

		1970	1980	1989	1990	Rank	%
World		70,000	72,042	100,332	97,246		
Marine areas		60,930	64,383	86,451	82,801		
18	Arctic Sea	0	0	0	0		
21	Atlantic, NW	4,239	2,867	3,086	3,221	8	3.9
27	Atlantic, NE	10,666	11,799	9,947	9,183	3	11.1
31	Atlantic, WC	1,440	1,795	1,805	1,697		
34	Atlantic, EC	2,830	3,432	3,956	4,098	5	4.9
37	Mediterranean & Black Sea	1,120	1,649	1,716	1,489		
41	Atlantic, SW	1,081	1,274	2,255	2,029	10	2.5
47	Atlantic, SE	2,460	2,170	2,096	1,530		
48	Atlantic, Antarctic	0	453	467	393		
51	Indian, W	1,620	2,098	3,378	3,376	7	4.1
57	Indian, E	789	1,458	2,732	2,828	9	3.4
58	Indian, Antarctic	0	138	31.4	35		
61	Pacific, NW	12,997	18,759	26,295	25,688	1	31
67	Pacific, NE	2,652	1,975	3,280	3,428	6	4.1
71	Pacific, WC	4,176	5,487	7,248	7,311	4	8.8
77	Pacific, EC	902	2,417	1,758	1,519		
81	Pacific, SW	221	382	1,063	1,031		
87	Pacific, SE	13,732	6,228	15,338	13,945	2	16.8
88	Pacific, Antarctic	0	3.2	1.1	0.7		
Inland waters		9,020	7,625	13,882	14,444		
1	Africa	1,308	1,404	1,866	1,905		
2	N. America	136	146	537	537		
3	S. America	249	280	340	333		
4	Asia	6,251	4,673	9,618	10,197		
5	Europe	225	373	479	473		
6	Oceania	2	2	23	24		
7	USSR (former)	853	747	1,020	975		

The figures include the produce from both inland and marine fishing. In 1990 fish from inland waters accounted for 15% of the world total catch. The figures in both of the tables refer to fish caught in the inland waters or the craft of the country. The flag of the vessel rather than the port of landing is the criteria for assigning the catch to a country. All the figures refer to the live weight of the catch. Whales are not included and are shown in the table entitled Whaling.

FISH BY NATION

...ousand tonnes

	1948	1970	1980	1989	1990	Rank	%
...ld	19,600	70,000	72,042	100,332	97,246		
...ola	113	368	86	111	107		
...entina	71	215	385	487	556		
...stralia	39	103	132	176	210		
...gladesh	...	247	650	844	848		
...gium	71	53	46	40	42		
...zil	145	517	818	850	800		
...garia	64	92	126	102	56		
...ma	...	432	580	734	744		
...mbodia	...	52	52	77	105		
...nada	1,053	1,389	1,347	1,573	1,624		
...ad	...	120	115	110	115		
...le	65	1,181	2,817	6,454	5,195	6	5.3
...na	2,500	6,868	4,235	11,220	12,095	1	12.4
...ombia	15	76	76	98	101		
...ba	8	106	187	192	188		
...nmark	226	1,227	2,029	1,928	1,517		
...uador	3	92	644	740	391		
...ypt	43	72	140	294	313		
...oe Is.	92	208	275	300	283		
...land	46	81	143	111	97		
...ance	513	764	789	914	897		
...orgia	...	...	...	...	104		
...rmany	414	945	542	411	391		
...ana	24	172	232	362	392		
...eece	34	78	104	139	140		
...eenland	21	40	104	163	138		
...ong Kong	34	124	195	243	235		
...eland	478	734	1,515	1,505	1,508		
...dia	1,000	1,756	2,442	3,641	3,791	7	3.9
...donesia	500	1,229	1,842	2,948	3,081	8	3.2
...an	...	...	44	261	250		
...eland	25	79	149	200	231		
...aly	183	387	448	551	525		
...ory Coast	20	58	86	101	109		
...apan	2,526	9,366	10,434	11,173	10,354	3	10.6
...enya	30	34	48	146	142		
...orea, North	...	...	1,400	1,700	1,750		
...orea, South	294	934	2,091	2,833	2,750	9	2.8
...atvia	...	...	...	...	130		
...thuania	...	...	...	...	317		
...adagascar	...	48	50	100	107		
...alaysia	145	368	737	607	603		
...ali	...	90	80	72	65		
...exico	68	387	1,223	1,470	1,401		
...orocco	69	256	330	520	566		
...etherlands	294	301	340	451	438		
...ew Zealand	36	59	191	565	565		
...igeria	...	227	480	300	316		
...orway	1,422	2,980	2,409	1,909	1,747		
...man	...	100	79	118	120		
...akistan	...	158	279	446	479		
...anama	1	42	216	189	162		
...eru	84	12,613	3,735	6,854	6,875	4	7.1
...hilippines	195	992	1,557	2,099	2,209		
...oland	47	469	641	565	473		
...ortugal	292	498	279	332	322		
...omania	...	59	174	225	128		
...enegal	70	189	233	288	300		
...outh Africa	118	1,583	615	879	536		
...pain	547	1,539	1,265	1,560	1,458		
...ri Lanka	24	98	186	205	165		
...weden	194	295	241	258	260		
Taiwan	122	613	936	1,456	1,317		
Tanzania	30	185	228	377	377		
Thailand	161	1,448	1,798	2,782	2,650	10	2.7
Turkey	80	184	427	457	382		
Uganda	11	129	166	212	245		
Ukraine					1,100		
USSR (former)	1,485	7,252	9,476	11,310	10,389	2	10.7
United Kingdom	1,206	1,099	919	832	811		
United States	2,417	2,777	3,635	5,763	5,856	5	6
Uruguay	4	13	120	122	91		
Venezuela	92	126	185	329	332		
Vietnam	200	817	613	868	850		
Yemen	...	128	94	73	89		
Zaire	18	137	102	166	162		

GRAPES

thousand tonnes

	1950	1970	1980	1990	1991	Rank	%
World	34,381	54,583	65,991	59,873	57,188		
Afghanistan	138	377	468	365	365		
Albania	21	62	68	66	52		
Algeria	1,738	1,263	398	263	260		
Argentina	1,586	2,636	3,230	2,600	2,000	7	3.5
Australia	450	620	775	844	915		
Austria	132	337	377	427	420		
Brazil	247	528	604	786	619		
Bulgaria	504	1,128	1,029	731	741		
Canada	36	69	74	58	68		
Chile	473	762	1,067	1,171	1,130		
China	48	155	182	962	1,105		
Cyprus	59	190	208	160	200		
Czechoslovakia	60	128	189	221	198		
Egypt	79	115	280	585	610		
France	7,995	9,706	10,470	8,200	7,020	2	12.3
Germany	324	1,049	888	1,149	1,160		
Greece	1,124	1,569	1,504	1,192	1,300		
Hungary	527	809	788	863	863		
India	...	219	195	303	314		
Iran	254	628	1,073	1,402	1,450	9	2.5
Iraq	30	75	220	420	360		
Israel	15	69	77	99	96		
Italy	7,076	10,638	12,396	8,438	9,230	1	16.1
Japan	38	240	328	300	300		
Korea, South	2	35	61	131	148		
Lebanon	81	98	142	183	200		
Mexico	40	160	485	463	435		
Morocco	92	213	210	197	200		
New Zealand	4	14	39	60	62		
Peru	54	62	54	45	47		
Portugal	1,113	1,403	1,570	1,600	1,450	10	2.5
Romania	623	1,020	1,518	935	849		
Saudi Arabia	...	24	60	103	103		
South Africa	412	820	1,202	1,463	1,470	8	2.6
Spain	2,541	4,048	6,587	6,474	5,087	4	8.9
Switzerland	102	129	122	174	178		
Syria	172	221	351	423	475		
Tunisia	105	125	123	89	90		
Turkey	1,500	3,779	3,600	3,500	3,600	6	6.3
USSR (former)	753	4,220	6,648	5,600	5,400	3	9.4
United States	2,670	3,325	4,549	5,135	4,944	5	8.6
Uruguay	114	129	108	123	113		
Yemen	...	21	56	142	145		
Yugoslavia	867	1,232	1,400	1,109	1,100		

GROUNDNUTS

thousand tonnes

	1950	1970	1980	1990	1991	Rank	%
World	9,572	18,347	18,277	23,410	23,366		
Angola	10	20	20	20	20		
Argentina	100	280	451	333	429	9	1.8
Australia	9	30	48	21	34		
Bangladesh	...	45	28	42	52		
Benin	10	47	60	79	69		
Brazil	138	876	433	137	140		
Burkina Faso	51	68	70	140	152		
Burma	154	492	390	459	505	7	2.2
Burundi	2	21	56	97	98		
Cambodia	4	21	4	3	3		
Cameroon	92	206	137	100	110		
Central Afr. Rep.	10	68	123	105	106		
Chad	64	95	93	108	115		
China	2,114	2,634	3,501	6,433	6,060	2	25.9
Congo	10	17	14	26	27		
Cuba	14	15	15	15	15		
Dominican Rep.	14	76	40	34	35		
Ecuador	2	7	14	18	30		
Egypt	18	40	26	31	35		
Ethiopia	21	24	27	54	55		
Gambia, The	62	129	79	75	85		
Ghana	43	88	125	193	200		

	1950	1970	1980	1990	1991	Rank	%		1950	1970	1980	1990	1991	Ran
Guinea	18	25	83	52	52			Indonesia	560	666	616	740	750	
Guinea-Bissau	50	36	32	18	20			Iran	358	400	274	270	270	
Haiti	2	2	35	46	45			Iraq	290	98	54	60	48	
India	3,197	5,807	5,999	7,622	7,000	1	30	Ireland	384	122	69	54	53	
Indonesia	283	462	723	930	920	5	3.9	Italy	779	292	271	269	280	
Israel	2	17	22	21	20			Japan	1,083	159	23	23	24	
Ivory Coast	15	42	73	134	140			Lesotho	101	103	102	121	122	
Japan	21	120	61	40	35			Mali	60	170	144	62	62	
Korea, South	1	8	13	29	30			Mexico	3,181	5,579	6,195	6,170	6,175	3
Madagascar	12	42	37	30	30			Mongolia	2,085	2,262	2,047	2,200	2,255	8
Malawi	...	182	176	39	64			Morocco	350	380	278	190	190	
Mali	88	144	136	180	160			Netherlands	273	95	66	65	65	
Mexico	55	81	73	133	110			New Zealand	204	75	71	99	100	
Morocco	...	3	34	40	40			Nicaragua	150	212	275	250	250	
Mozambique	22	140	83	113	115			Niger	75	197	253	302	305	
Nicaragua	...	1	21	12	11			Nigeria	260	325	250	208	206	
Niger	61	223	105	60	60			Norway	191	36	18	19	19	
Nigeria	690	1,660	466	1,166	1,219	4	5.2	Pakistan	420	385	473	460	461	
Pakistan	2	55	60	89	76			Panama	138	160	165	156	156	
Paraguay	11	17	34	41	39			Paraguay	302	334	316	335	335	
Philippines	19	17	43	35	34			Peru	496	669	650	660	660	
Senegal	558	794	690	703	700	6	3	Philippines	210	300	302	200	200	
Sierra Leone	7	19	12	20	21			Poland	2,673	2,573	1,787	941	939	
South Africa	93	364	297	111	110			Portugal	87	36	29	26	26	
Spain	12	7	5	4	5			Romania	979	686	564	663	670	
Sudan	19	370	760	123	193			Senegal	25	196	222	400	400	
Syria	1	18	18	22	23			South Africa	682	258	225	230	230	
Taiwan	60	122	86	85	85			Spain	686	287	243	241	241	
Tanzania	20	32	54	60	65			Sweden	439	60	55	58	58	
Thailand	60	128	128	162	164			Switzerland	135	53	45	45	49	
Togo	13	20	25	26	33			Syria	101	70	52	41	45	
Turkey	7	40	52	63	53			Thailand	219	172	28	18	18	
Uganda	153	207	80	172	173			Tunisia	73	96	51	55	56	
United States	839	1,289	1,550	1,634	2,242	3	9.6	Turkey	1,136	1,103	804	545	513	
Vietnam	8	78	94	218	212	10	0.9	USSR (former)	12,800	7,641	5,623	5,920	5,900	4	9
Zaire	155	258	334	425	435	8	1.9	United Kingdom	552	143	147	169	170	
Zambia	2	24	18	25	45			United States	7,757	7,667	5,053	5,400	5,650	5	9
Zimbabwe	21	111	101	119	107			Uruguay	667	427	493	465	470	
								Venezuela	344	423	478	495	495	
								Vietnam	40	105	123	143	145	
								Yugoslavia	1,063	1,078	630	314	300	

HORSES

thousand head

	1950	1970	1980	1990	1991	Rank	%
World	79,740	62,642	59,692	61,164	61,620		
Afghanistan	195	400	403	400	400		
Albania	50	43	45	102	100		
Algeria	209	142	173	195	202		
Argentina	7,265	3,623	3,024	3,400	3,400	6	5.5
Australia	1,055	454	486	310	310		
Austria	282	53	43	48	49		
Belgium	257	76	38	21	20		
Bolivia	158	291	330	320	320		
Brazil	6,942	4,861	5,070	6,000	6,200	2	10.1
Bulgaria	511	183	121	115	113		
Burkina Faso	55	88	70	70	70		
Burma	12	71	112	120	121		
Canada	1,580	362	363	415	415		
Chad	120	153	166	195	182		
Chile	523	478	450	520	520		
China	5,503	7,300	11,144	10,294	10,174	1	16.5
Colombia	1,208	1,114	1,683	1,975	1,980	9	3.2
Costa Rica	76	109	113	114	114		
Cuba	410	683	810	629	629		
Czechoslovakia	613	144	47	42	39		
Denmark	495	45	50	38	38		
Dominican Rep.	137	184	204	315	320		
Ecuador	111	242	314	492	512		
El Salvador	130	79	88	93	93		
Ethiopia	1,021	1,393	1,602	2,650	2,700	7	4.4
Finland	389	88	33	44	45		
France	2,403	691	352	319	322		
Germany	2,266	411	447	424	491		
Greece	259	251	115	50	50		
Guatemala	166	149	100	113	114		
Haiti	253	335	411	435	435		
Honduras	178	173	165	170	170		
Hungary	665	233	127	77	79		
Iceland	43	34	51	70	69		
India	1,514	1,010	900	960	965	10	1.6

MAIZE

thousand tonnes

	1950	1970	1980	1990	1991	Rank	%
World	134,763	278,615	423,724	479,340	478,775		
Afghanistan	350	707	785	430	420		
Angola	285	467	303	180	299		
Argentina	2,839	8,717	9,333	5,049	7,768	10	1.6
Austria	120	677	1,338	1,620	1,524		
Benin	181	201	289	418	390		
Bolivia	163	291	422	407	510		
Bosnia	...	...	...	...	620		
Brazil	5,841	13,680	19,265	21,339	22,604	3	4.7
Bulgaria	720	2,436	2,626	1,221	2,718		
Cameroon	212	283	418	380	450		
Canada	388	2,487	5,901	7,157	7,319		
Chile	68	217	471	823	836		
China	14,082	27,820	60,720	97,158	93,350	2	19.5
Colombia	733	856	868	1,213	1,274		
Croatia	...	...	...	...	2,100		
Cuba	243	85	95	95	95		
Czechoslovakia	316	511	800	468	862		
Ecuador	79	239	247	501	665		
Egypt	1,378	2,370	3,159	4,799	5,270		
El Salvador	191	340	517	603	504		
Ethiopia	160	909	1,224	1,636	1,590		
France	452	7,394	9,641	9,291	12,787	5	2.7
Germany	20	500	752	1,552	1,928		
Ghana	168	417	380	553	932		
Greece	225	498	1,165	1,992	1,700		
Guatemala	437	751	947	1,293	1,150		
Haiti	203	245	179	163	145		
Honduras	211	339	407	559	584		
Hungary	2,081	4,542	7,022	4,500	7,509		
India	2,165	6,087	6,486	9,073	8,200	8	1.7
Indonesia	1,535	2,575	4,035	6,734	6,409		
Italy	2,306	4,601	6,590	5,864	6,208		

	1950	1970	1980	1990	1991	Rank	%
y Coast	...	257	352	484	510		
aya	591	2,292	1,714	2,630	2,250		
ea, North	375	1,493	3,833	4,400	4,500		
uania	...	...	...	...	1,400		
awi	307	1,066	1,275	1,343	1,590		
xico	3,090	9,025	11,866	14,635	13,527	4	2.8
rocco	302	380	245	436	335		
zambique	122	364	383	453	327		
pal	829	796	690	1,231	1,235		
eria	644	1,215	599	1,832	1,900		
kistan	384	697	925	1,185	1,190		
aguay	112	197	535	1,139	980		
u	275	605	569	632	669		
lippines	695	2,009	3,174	4,854	4,655		
rtugal	421	599	486	666	677		
mania	2,495	7,354	11,823	6,810	10,493	6	2.2
uth Africa	2,629	6,691	11,322	8,900	8,200	9	1.7
ain	520	1,804	2,227	3,086	3,151		
nzania	347	817	1,762	2,445	2,332		
ailand	31	1,979	3,103	3,722	3,990		
rkey	747	1,058	1,263	2,100	2,100		
ganda	121	420	360	584	600		
SSR (former)	5,751	9,993	9,076	9,900	8,500	7	1.8
nited States	74,308	122,649	192,084	201,508	189,867	1	39.7
enezuela	303	698	547	1,002	1,100		
etnam	180	272	410	671	652		
goslavia (Serbia)	...	...	...	...	6,000		
aire	324	426	604	870	906		
ambia	45	786	941	1,093	1,448		
mbabwe	167	966	1,829	1,994	1,586		

	1950	1970	1980	1990	1991	Rank	%
Mexico	1,539	3,912	6,949	6,332	6,925		
Morocco	271	450	753	980	990		
Netherlands	5,437	8,182	11,832	11,226	11,220		
New Zealand	4,720	6,112	6,586	7,700	7,973		
Nigeria	334	313	354	354	360		
Norway	1,532	1,726	1,926	1,959	1,928		
Pakistan	2,800	2,070	2,189	3,320	3,449		
Peru	237	828	796	777	786		
Poland	9,091	14,951	16,250	15,832	15,050	9	3.2
Portugal	219	607	750	1,513	1,550		
Puerto Rico	151	372	420	402	388		
Romania	1,900	2,774	3,987	3,242	3,150		
Russia	...	...	...	...	55,700	3	12
Somalia	65	139	319	530	497		
South Africa	1,740	2,816	2,553	2,509	2,515		
Spain	2,191	4,427	5,984	5,825	6,200		
Sudan	667	753	1,352	2,251	2,299		
Sweden	4,609	2,996	3,452	3,432	3,242		
Switzerland	2,483	3,172	3,653	3,866	3,850		
Syria	80	197	504	771	779		
Tajikistan	...	...	...	...	575		
Tanzania	356	692	372	459	463		
Turkey	1,315	2,565	3,449	2,860	2,865		
Ukraine	...	...	...	...	24,508	7	5.3
USSR (former)	33,228	81,967	90,557	108,700	100,000	1	21.5
United Kingdom	9,967	13,007	15,917	15,203	15,022	10	3.2
United States	52,349	53,173	58,139	67,260	67,373	2	14.5
Uruguay	449	744	811	1,311	900		
Uzbekistan	...	...	...	...	3,034		
Venezuela	203	947	1,353	1,497	1,591		
Yugoslavia	1,463	2,591	4,370	4,369	4,315		

MILK - COW'S

housand tonnes

	1950	1970	1980	1990	1991	Rank	%
World	233,025	363,193	417,347	477,565	464,468		
Afghanistan	238	521	552	340	340		
Algeria	92	292	514	595	596		
Argentina	3,758	4,527	5,311	6,400	6,200		
Australia	5,538	7,468	5,590	6,435	6,578		
Austria	1,998	3,218	3,434	3,350	3,355		
Azerbaijan	...	...	...	...	970		
Bangladesh	890	678	833	742	750		
Belarus	...	...	...	...	7,457		
Belgium	3,323	3,971	4,042	4,020	3,900		
Brazil	2,581	7,317	11,378	15,000	15,300	8	3.3
Bulgaria	278	1,249	1,843	2,101	1,756		
Burma	250	400	283	446	456		
Canada	7,051	8,247	7,830	7,535	7,340		
Chile	683	1,029	1,078	1,423	1,490		
China	2,005	3,233	1,143	4,361	4,816		
Colombia	1,035	2,250	2,187	3,500	3,600		
Cuba	460	672	1,045	1,100	1,070		
Czechoslovakia	3,188	4,823	5,830	6,931	5,826		
Denmark	4,915	4,588	5,126	4,742	4,640		
Dominican Rep.	140	282	427	420	420		
Ecuador	174	705	924	1,539	1,505		
Egypt	362	575	648	1,060	1,140		
Estonia	...	...	...	...	1,208		
Ethiopia	344	516	590	748	752		
Finland	2,414	3,401	3,236	2,730	2,477		
France	14,578	27,467	26,720	26,561	26,600	6	5.7
Georgia	...	...	...	...	602		
Germany	15,997	29,904	31,724	31,307	29,300	4	6.3
Greece	147	546	666	735	690		
Hungary	1,443	1,851	2,559	2,846	2,625		
India	7,743	7,633	13,420	27,500	27,000	5	5.8
Iran	539	915	1,125	1,397	1,428		
Ireland	2,265	3,685	4,729	5,402	5,527		
Israel	97	447	702	952	965		
Italy	7,009	9,427	10,546	10,376	10,000		
Japan	369	4,703	6,526	8,190	8,180		
Kazakhstan	...	...	...	...	5,642		
Kenya	120	841	938	2,320	2,189		
Korea, South	1	51	449	1,752	1,848		
Kyrgyzstan	...	...	...	...	1,148		
Latvia	...	...	...	...	1,893		
Lithuania	...	...	...	...	3,157		
Madagascar	29	32	36	473	472		

MILLET

thousand tonnes

	1950	1970	1980	1990	1991	Rank	%
World	20,000	29,417	25,610	29,896	28,970		
Afghanistan	10	20	33	26	26		
Angola	...	78	49	63	61		
Argentina	151	168	245	91	65		
Australia	7	37	26	38	43		
Bangladesh	40	40	40	63	60		
Burkina Faso	221	352	390	449	757	7	2.6
Burma	56	65	80	126	138		
Burundi	22	26	10	13	12		
Cameroon	350	343	98	65	63		
Central Afr. Rep.	29	43	11	12	10		
Chad	600	615	182	168	302		
China	3,000	5,473	5,790	4,576	4,501	2	15.5
Egypt	1,000	847	638	215	200		
Ethiopia	190	117	203	273	260		
Gambia, The	20	40	26	47	51		
Ghana	100	120	117	75	112		
Guinea	50	50	60	60	60		
India	6,064	10,182	9,189	10,462	9,000	1	31
Ivory Coast	33	30	37	44	52		
Japan	127	12	1	2	1		
Kenya	50	31	84	62	63		
Korea, North	320	407	66	60	62		
Korea, South	60	47	4	2	2		
Mali	500	784	461	737	792	6	2.7
Mauritania	45	81	3	3	4		
Namibia	16	19	34	58	50		
Nepal	52	128	121	232	220		
Niger	400	974	1,311	1,113	1,853	5	6.4
Nigeria	1,000	2,792	2,496	5,136	4,200	3	14.5
Pakistan	300	300	255	196	200		
Russia	...	...	...	...	...		
Senegal	300	543	555	514	560	9	1.9
Sudan	181	424	436	85	308	10	1.1
Syria	65	18	16	4	4		
Tanzania	250	140	360	200	270		
Togo	80	121	44	58	70		
Turkey	78	54	21	6	6		
Uganda	510	737	473	564	600	8	2.1
USSR (former)	1,705	2,477	1,759	3,647	3,600	4	12.4
United States	100	100	107	140	150		
Yemen	70	70	96	50	20		
Zaire	20	22	24	31	31		

	1950	1970	1980	1990	1991	Rank	%
Zambia	50	79	22	32	31		
Zimbabwe	50	190	153	143	122		

OLIVES

thousand tonnes

	1950	1970	1980	1990	1991	Rank	%
World	4,943	7,650	9,193	9,203	10,617		
Albania	12	33	31	24	18		
Algeria	151	150	154	65	130	9	1.2
Argentina	19	70	92	98	98	10	0.9
Chile	15	12	10	11	11		
Cyprus	11	14	12	11	11		
Egypt	2	7	5	42	31		
France	27	16	13	8	9		
Greece	515	876	1,465	1,050	1,800	3	17
Iran	13	10	9	14	10		
Iraq	9	9	3	3	3		
Israel	9	13	29	42	20		
Italy	1,218	2,530	2,962	913	3,250	1	30.6
Jordan	28	18	23	64	40		
Lebanon	32	48	37	62	40		
Libya	27	38	139	68	70		
Mexico	10	10	26	15	15		
Morocco	88	329	269	445	440	5	4.1
Peru	3	9	11	10	10		
Portugal	490	422	271	196	296	7	2.8
Spain	1,602	1,897	2,025	3,369	2,891	2	27.2
Syria	57	110	265	461	201	8	1.9
Tunisia	277	476	521	825	330	6	3.1
Turkey	268	438	727	1,100	800	4	7.5
United States	46	54	65	119	54		
Yugoslavia	28	10	18	33	18		

OLIVE OIL

thousand tonnes

	1950	1970	1980	1990	1991	Rank	%
World	940	1,553	1,832	1,573	2,007		
Albania	1	4	4	4	3		
Algeria	18	21	19	8	16	9	0.8
Argentina	2	17	16	8	9		
Chile	2	1	1	1	1		
Cyprus	2	2	2	2	2		
France	3	2	2	2	2		
Greece	115	178	309	188	355	3	17.7
Iran	1	1	1	2	2		
Israel	1	1	2	...	...		
Italy	241	553	635	175	685	1	34.1
Jordan	14	3	4	8	11	10	0.5
Lebanon	2	11	7	5	4		
Libya	4	7	28	10	10		
Morocco	13	41	28	43	53	6	2.6
Portugal	65	70	47	27	26	8	1.3
Spain	334	419	435	679	608	2	30.3
Syria	9	23	59	91	43	7	2.1
Tunisia	60	103	101	182	75	5	3.7
Turkey	47	86	129	110	96	4	4.8
Yugoslavia	4	2	3	6	3		

ORANGES

thousand tonnes

	1950	1970	1980	1990	1991	Rank	%
World	12,203	25,453	36,387	52,079	55,308		
Algeria	215	351	269	184	190		
Argentina	362	892	693	750	740		
Australia	123	263	398	492	492		

	1950	1970	1980	1990	1991	Rank	%
Belize	...	33	37	69	70		
Bhutan	...	...	25	58	62		
Bolivia	15	53	85	81	96		
Brazil	1,316	3,084	10,243	17,506	18,942	1	
Cambodia	2	41	22	43	45		
Chile	63	42	58	102	110		
China	206	727	783	4,977	5,385	3	9
Colombia	...	91	233	350	350		
Costa Rica	13	59	75	86	86		
Cuba	46	112	251	604	600		
Cyprus	24	119	36	63	49		
Dominican Rep.	34	63	68	65	64		
Ecuador	168	160	521	77	75		
Egypt	263	760	956	1,574	1,600	8	2
El Salvador	...	38	100	107	107		
Ghana	17	107	100	50	50		
Greece	97	418	577	886	703		
Honduras	8	18	38	49	50		
India	226	900	1,170	1,840	1,890	7	3
Indonesia	...	93	322	400	435		
Iran	47	65	170	1,192	1,270	9	2
Iraq	...	28	124	180	145		
Israel	258	917	866	878	567		
Italy	548	1,403	1,659	1,761	1,942	6	3
Jamaica	54	70	36	60	60		
Japan	378	321	352	280	290		
Jordan	1	14	23	54	55		
Lebanon	47	167	215	250	270		
Libya	3	19	62	91	95		
Madagascar	10	49	59	85	84		
Mexico	480	1,377	1,811	1,064	2,175	5	3
Morocco	158	665	705	771	920		
Nicaragua	...	45	53	66	68		
Pakistan	135	312	702	1,100	1,100	10	1.9
Panama	33	51	43	25	25		
Paraguay	171	194	280	366	367		
Peru	368	246	136	165	165		
Portugal	68	100	94	101	135		
Puerto Rico	30	32	31	29	28		
South Africa	199	533	581	697	689		
Spain	975	1,884	1,657	2,561	2,504	4	4.5
Sudan	...	35	12	10	15		
Syria	3	6	35	171	202		
Thailand	...	44	54	56	57		
Tunisia	25	58	113	123	117		
Turkey	66	445	690	739	739		
USSR (former)	20	72	261	250	375		
United States	4,509	7,302	9,519	7,083	7,258	2	13
Uruguay	58	42	55	111	121		
Venezuela	60	205	350	433	432		
Vietnam	...	43	80	105	105		
Zaire	...	126	141	153	155		

Figures for 1950 include tangerines.

PALM OIL

thousand tonnes

	1950	1970	1980	1990	1991	Rank	%
World	1,008	1,971	4,979	11,163	11,873		
Angola	36	40	40	40	40		
Benin	34	28	30	40	40		
Brazil	1	7	14	66	70		
Cameroon	22	63	77	108	105		
China	...	108	165	133	140	9	1.2
Colombia	...	27	71	252	268	4	2.3
Congo	4	8	15	17	17		
Costa Rica	...	13	33	60	64		
Ecuador	...	6	37	150	157	8	1.3
Equat. Guinea	4	4	5	5	5		
Gambia, The	2	2	3	3	3		
Ghana	30	19	21	85	87		
Guinea	10	44	41	50	51		
Guinea-Bissau	8	4	5	5	5		
Honduras	1	6	10	78	80		
Indonesia	114	218	721	2,186	2,700	2	22.7
Ivory Coast	6	46	158	208	218	6	1.8
Liberia	40	14	26	30	31		
Malaysia	49	457	5,030	6,095	6,145	1	51.8

	1950	1970	1980	1990	1991	Rank	%
eria	422	528	667	820	900	3	7.6
ua New Guinea	...	0.02	41	114	114	10	1
aguay	1	7	5	4	4		
u	...	...	5	25	23		
ippines	...	2	43	45	48		
egal	...	5	6	6	6		
ra Leone	35	46	47	56	59		
omon Is.	...	...	15	23	23		
iland	...	...	20	226	234	5	2
o	3	17	20	14	14		
e	172	232	168	180	182	7	1.5

	1950	1970	1980	1990	1991	Rank	%
Canada	408	600	979	1,133	1,110		
Chile	42	44	49	123	142		
China	3,298	9,639	11,704	23,756	25,460	1	35.9
Colombia	51	69	98	112	115		
Cuba	36	34	50	89	90		
Czechoslovakia	399	566	823	913	771		
Denmark	305	722	953	1,208	1,255		
Ecuador	7	28	58	65	67		
Finland	57	109	171	187	177		
France	811	1,388	1,775	1,871	1,820	7	2.6
Germany	1,189	3,061	4,393	4,457	3,909	4	5.5
Greece	19	54	144	148	151		
Hong Kong	5	120	178	188	190		
Hungary	194	598	899	1,040	1,030		
India	24	52	327	360	364		
Indonesia	35	53	111	302	275		
Ireland	65	147	152	159	168		
Italy	233	590	1,075	1,333	1,330	10	1.9
Japan	46	735	1,434	1,555	1,490	9	2.1
Korea, North	12	54	113	164	161		
Korea, South	7	80	276	550	530		
Malaysia	31	76	133	205	195		
Mexico	58	240	467	757	812		
Netherlands	206	704	1,142	1,661	1,639	8	2.3
New Zealand	39	40	34	43	43		
Nigeria	13	28	37	128	150		
Norway	36	66	83	83	83		
Paraguay	15	42	85	118	141		
Peru	14	64	72	84	91		
Philippines	89	304	415	712	710		
Poland	718	1,312	1,617	1,855	1,869	5	2.6
Portugal	78	98	164	242	236		
Romania	28	453	970	920	850		
Singapore	9	25	65	76	78		
South Africa	49	80	87	125	126		
Spain	147	468	1,115	1,789	1,850	6	2.6
Sweden	165	244	317	293	275		
Switzerland	83	201	273	270	266		
Thailand	60	210	265	337	340		
USSR (former)	1,002	4,638	5,223	6,600	6,200	3	8.8
United Kingdom	296	934	929	946	980		
United States	4,904	6,227	7,248	6,965	7,258	2	10.2
Uruguay	17	21	18	15	16		
Venezuela	16	46	76	99	101		
Vietnam	41	332	323	800	850		
Yugoslavia	151	525	789	817	815		

PAPER & PAPER BOARD

illion tonnes

	1961–65 av.	1970	1980	1990	1991	Rank	%
orld	86.7	128	170	239	243		
gentina	0.4	0.6	0.71	1	1		
stralia	0.6	1.1	1.43	2	2		
stria	0.6	1	1.62	2.9	3.1		
lgium	0.5	1	0.86	1.2	1.2		
azil	0.7	1.2	3.36	4.8	4.9		
algaria	0.1	0.2	0.4	0.3	0.2		
anada	8.6	11.3	13.49	16.5	16.6	4	6.8
ile	0.1	0.3	0.36	0.5	0.5		
hina	2.9	4.2	6.83	17.1	18.5	3	7.6
olombia	0.1	0.2	0.35	0.5	0.5		
zechoslovakia	0.7	1	1.19	1.3	1.1		
enmark	0.2	0.3	0.23	0.3	0.4		
nland	2.8	4.3	5.92	8.8	8.5	7	3.5
ance	3	4.1	5.15	7	7.4	9	3
ermany	4.7	7	8.82	13.2	13.5	5	5.6
reece	0.1	0.2	0.31	0.4	0.4		
ungary	0.2	0.3	0.44	0.4	0.4		
dia	0.5	1	0.96	2.3	2.4		
donesia	0.01	0.02	0.23	1.4	1.7		
aly	1.9	3.5	4.93	5.6	5.8	10	2.4
apan	6.4	13	18.09	28.1	29.1	2	12
orea, South	0.1	0.3	1.68	4.5	5		
exico	0.4	1	1.98	2.9	2.9		
etherlands	1.2	1.6	1.71	2.8	3		
ew Zealand	0.3	0.5	0.67	0.8	0.8		
orway	0.9	1.4	1.37	1.8	1.8		
eru	0.1	0.1	0.21	0.3	0.1		
hilippines	0.1	0.1	0.32	0.2	0.2		
oland	0.8	1	1.28	1.1	1.1		
ortugal	0.1	0.2	0.46	0.8	0.9		
omania	0.3	0.5	0.82	0.5	0.4		
South Africa	0.3	0.6	1.12	1.9	1.9		
Spain	0.5	1.3	2.57	3.4	3.6		
Sweden	2.7	4.4	6.18	8.4	8.4	8	3.5
Switzerland	0.6	0.7	0.91	1.3	1.2		
Taiwan	0.1	0.2	0.5	0.9	1		
Thailand	0.01	0.1	0.34	0.9	1.2		
Turkey	0.1	0.2	0.48	0.9	0.83		
USSR (former)	4	6.7	8.73	10.7	9.6	6	4
United Kingdom	4.2	5	3.79	4.9	5		
United States	34.1	46.1	56.84	72	72.7	1	30
Venezuela	0.1	0.3	0.5	0.6	0.6		
Yugoslavia	0.3	0.6	1.1	0.9	0.7		

PIGMEAT

thousand tonnes

	1950	1970	1980	1990	1991	Rank	%
World	16,389	38,619	54,581	69,883	70,852		
Argentina	151	221	258	216	216		
Australia	89	173	217	317	312		
Austria	125	263	438	439	429		
Belgium	177	455	669	825	900		
Brazil	351	763	953	1,150	1,160		
Bulgaria	69	160	315	406	366		
Burma	8	60	79	80	82		

POTATOES

thousand tonnes

	1950	1970	1980	1990	1991	Rank	%
World	247,443	275,758	258,465	268,107	261,162		
Algeria	212	253	540	809	1,000		
Argentina	1,169	2,212	1,836	2,500	2,600		
Australia	477	782	840	1,178	1,160		
Austria	2,270	2,787	1,356	794	791		
Bangladesh	111	842	942	1,066	800		
Belarus	...	...	...	...	8,958		
Belgium	2,127	1,631	1,468	1,750	1,950		
Bolivia	176	660	794	620	855		
Bosnia	...	...	...	...	340		
Brazil	699	1,557	2,002	2,219	2,214		
Bulgaria	240	378	376	433	503		
Canada	1,808	2,312	2,626	2,959	2,781		
Chile	461	707	894	829	844		
China	12,090	11,029	25,415	32,031	35,533	2	13.6
Colombia	506	871	1,931	2,464	2,372		
Croatia	...	...	...	...	620		
Czechoslovakia	7,055	4,864	3,388	2,534	2,713		
Denmark	117	845	913	1,483	1,511		
Ecuador	98	560	323	369	337		
Egypt	187	496	1,142	1,638	920		
Estonia	...	...	...	...	954		
Ethiopia	100	161	301	380	384		
Finland	1,442	906	629	881	672		
France	13,734	8,569	6,735	5,800	6,300	9	2.4
Georgia	...	...	...	...	294		
Germany	37,430	16,236	19,465	14,039	10,225	6	3.9
Greece	385	700	1,036	996	1,100		

	1950	1970	1980	1990	1991	Rank	%
Hungary	1,976	1,874	1,504	1,226	1,226		
India	1,547	4,482	9,377	14,770	15,254	5	5.8
Indonesia	27	99	217	559	500		
Iran	37	417	1,269	2,475	2,500		
Ireland	2,903	1,450	902	633	650		
Italy	2,732	3,632	2,941	2,309	2,227		
Japan	2,451	3,490	3,299	3,552	3,700		
Kazakhstan	...	...	...	...	1,783		
Kenya	190	206	392	260	300		
Korea, North	575	960	1,535	2,100	1,975		
Korea, South	302	598	452	371	416		
Kyrgyzstan	...	...	...	...	324		
Latvia	...	...	...	...	1,016		
Lithuania	...	...	...	...	1,508		
Madagascar	79	106	170	272	273		
Malawi	1	85	270	330	340		
Mexico	134	489	993	1,236	999		
Moldova	...	...	...	...	304		
Morocco	56	283	503	880	928		
Nepal	...	265	279	672	738		
Netherlands	4,679	5,367	6,329	7,036	6,735	7	2.6
New Zealand	130	284	209	303	300		
Norway	1,174	807	524	484	484		
Pakistan	28	213	412	831	750		
Peru	1,239	1,877	1,680	1,154	1,450		
Poland	29,641	45,012	39,508	36,313	29,038	3	11.1
Portugal	1,081	1,222	1,079	1,132	948		
Romania	1,661	2,671	4,381	3,186	1,900		
Russia	...	...	...	...	30,800		
Slovenia	...	...	...	...	385		
South Africa	230	583	747	1,247	1,250		
Spain	3,346	4,985	5,615	5,342	5,333	10	2
Sweden	1,814	1,221	1,191	1,186	1,048		
Switzerland	1,021	1,016	924	712	725		
Syria	34	62	279	398	295		
Turkey	605	1,984	2,957	4,300	4,600		
Ukraine	...	...	...	...	16,765		
USSR (former)	80,239	93,739	76,706	63,700	64,500	1	24.7
United Kingdom	9,443	7,359	6,601	6,504	6,700	8	2.6
United States	10,681	14,483	14,923	18,239	18,970	4	7.3
Uzbekistan	...	...	...	...	336		
Vietnam	2	103	710	365	281		
Yugoslavia	1,486	3,020	2,646	2,172	2,180		
Yugoslavia (Serbia)	...	...	...	...	800		

	1950	1970	1980	1990	1991	Rank
Ireland	28	32	52	93	95	
Israel	6	96	153	178	186	
Italy	57	619	1,007	1,104	1,105	8
Ivory Coast	4	9	27	46	48	
Jamaica	0.2	16	32	52	53	
Japan	10	494	1,115	1,418	1,417	5
Jordan	0.3	8	26	49	56	
Kenya	7	16	32	47	47	
Korea, North	8	20	32	47	48	
Korea, South	2	46	92	176	203	
Lebanon	2	21	46	55	59	
Libya	...	2	29	68	70	
Madagascar	12	35	55	86	88	
Malaysia	11	53	134	345	352	
Mexico	41	225	440	793	897	9
Morocco	16	30	80	125	130	
Netherlands	9	297	343	470	499	
New Zealand	3	17	35	58	58	
Nigeria	23	73	187	171	176	
Pakistan	27	14	46	157	182	
Peru	4	58	148	245	280	
Philippines	35	103	228	242	237	
Poland	33	141	417	332	310	
Portugal	7	54	131	129	131	
Puerto Rico	5	13	28	51	57	
Romania	45	128	413	370	350	
Saudi Arabia	...	8	46	265	275	
Singapore	3	27	66	66	67	
South Africa	21	107	233	384	394	
Spain	66	454	798	836	840	10
Sweden	13	27	44	44	45	
Syria	2	14	57	57	62	
Taiwan	10	22	51	88	90	
Thailand	28	64	373	661	717	
Tunisia	3	10	40	54	56	
Turkey	18	104	245	270	285	
USSR (former)	278	1,040	2,143	3,300	3,000	3
United Kingdom	95	574	751	1,026	1,112	7
United States	2,203	5,979	6,713	10,924	11,503	1
Venezuela	3	93	247	332	340	
Vietnam	...	70	135	161	168	
Yemen	0.9	2	7	57	55	
Yugoslavia	36	138	277	295	293	

POULTRY MEAT
thousand tonnes

	1950	1970	1980	1990	1991	Rank	%
World	...	17,760	27,245	38,160	39,870		
Algeria	14	28	46	65	69		
Argentina	33	182	321	369	391		
Australia	45	128	296	407	416		
Austria	3	47	71	87	81		
Bangladesh	...	61	90	74	58		
Belgium	29	116	133	187	190		
Brazil	87	360	1,345	2,417	2,614	4	6.6
Bulgaria	24	94	151	182	115		
Burma	23	16	70	80	83		
Canada	142	542	532	745	744		
Chile	12	52	105	124	140		
China	1,094	1,683	1,725	3,303	3,463	2	8.7
Colombia	27	46	107	248	257		
Cuba	5	40	74	91	92		
Czechoslovakia	24	109	192	245	210		
Denmark	23	76	100	131	135		
Dominican Rep.	...	28	61	131	138		
Ecuador	1	9	22	70	75		
Egypt	24	80	120	233	219		
Ethiopia	55	54	68	76	77		
France	248	631	1,131	1,384	1,394	6	3.5
Germany	67	344	531	618	602		
Greece	11	71	138	160	161		
Hong Kong	0.5	21	48	63	65		
Hungary	87	215	346	435	480		
India	45	83	111	334	368		
Indonesia	37	58	168	486	458		
Iran	18	53	180	270	275		
Iraq	1	16	56	192	156		

RAPESEED
thousand tonnes

	1950	1970	1980	1990	1991	Rank	%
World	2,820	6,617	11,093	24,416	27,217		
Algeria	...	...	34	87	93		
Argentina	...	2	16	7	80		
Australia	...	31	24	114	140		
Austria	5	8	7	97	125		
Bangladesh	95	132	225	240	210		
Belgium	5	1	1	18	26		
Canada	9	1,517	2,581	3,281	4,303	3	15.8
Chile	...	72	55	53	58		
China	782	996	2,952	6,958	7,436	1	27.3
Czechoslovakia	25	70	165	380	446	9	1.6
Denmark	9	30	204	793	734	8	2.7
Ethiopia	20	20	19	75	76		
Finland	6	9	68	117	95		
France	154	603	871	1,973	2,286	4	8.4
Germany	193	370	618	2,088	2,213	5	8.1
Hungary	4	46	71	106	120		
India	815	1,629	1,864	4,125	5,152	2	18.9
Italy	14	5	1	44	35		
Japan	129	54	4	2	2		
Korea, South	4	31	25	7	5		
Mexico	6	6	3	3	3		
Netherlands	33	22	28	26	25		
Norway	5	6	10	9	6		
Pakistan	175	249	249	233	228		
Poland	100	455	434	1,206	1,043	7	3.8
Romania	4	3	15	11	9		
Spain	4	5	15	30	17		
Sweden	146	218	313	401	350		
Switzerland	4	19	33	43	50		
Turkey	4	5	20	2	5		

	1950	1970	1980	1990	1991	Rank	%
SR (former)	63	4	17	506	355	10	1.3
ted Kingdom	3	10	274	1,231	1,330	6	4.9
ted States	1	1	1	44	89		
joslavia	5	13	75	72	40		

	1950	1970	1980	1990	1991	Rank	%
Philippines	1	19	66	185	201	6	4
Sri Lanka	102	150	137	113	102	8	2
Thailand	104	295	502	1,100	1,200	3	24
Vietnam	35	36	44	52	55	10	1
Zaire	10	43	21	10	10		

RICE

ousand tonnes

	1950	1970	1980	1990	1991	Rank	%
orld	169,575	311,469	396,259	521,703	519,869		
ghanistan	331	374	458	333	335		
gentina	137	347	288	467	347		
stralia	63	267	678	924	726		
ngladesh	10,000	16,540	20,125	26,778	28,575	4	6
azil	2,921	6,847	8,533	7,419	9,503	10	2
rma	5,481	8,107	12,637	13,969	13,201	7	3
mbodia	1,635	3,016	1,160	2,500	2,400		
ina	58,188	111,599	145,665	191,197	187,450	1	36
olombia	248	756	1,831	2,117	1,739		
aba	164	309	455	447	430		
uador	135	165	378	840	841		
jypt	971	2,567	2,376	3,167	3,152		
uinea	208	364	438	500	628		
dia	33,383	62,861	74,557	111,953	110,945	2	21
donesia	9,441	19,136	29,570	45,179	44,321	3	9
an	424	1,041	1,448	2,273	2,100		
aly	723	858	989	1,291	1,236		
ory Coast	104	335	438	687	690		
apan	12,736	16,281	13,320	13,124	12,005	8	2
azakhstan	...	...	...	...	579		
orea, North	1,158	2,329	4,733	5,300	5,100		
orea, South	3,385	5,573	6,780	7,732	7,478		
aos	530	870	1,025	1,491	1,400		
ladagascar	829	1,865	2,055	2,420	2,200		
lalaysia	631	1,689	2,053	1,655	1,550		
lexico	173	390	528	394	354		
epal	2,460	2,297	2,361	3,502	3,600		
igeria	250	352	1,027	2,500	3,185		
akistan	2,127	3,431	4,884	4,897	4,903		
eru	191	539	580	966	814		
hilippines	2,767	5,225	7,893	9,319	9,670	9	2
Russia	...	...	...	...	896		
Sierra Leone	274	474	504	504	386		
Spain	272	384	435	569	582		
Sri Lanka	479	1,463	2,093	2,538	2,397		
Taiwan	1,771	2,663	2,354	1,807	1,819		
Tanzania	62	172	251	740	664		
Thailand	6,846	13,475	16,967	17,300	20,040	5	4
JSSR (former)	202	1,272	2,558	2,473	2,200		
United States	1,925	3,953	6,968	7,080	7,006		
Uruguay	44	132	289	517	540		
Venezuela	41	208	638	401	608		
Vietnam	3,815	9,752	11,812	19,225	19,428	6	4

RUBBER - NATURAL

thousand tonnes

	1950	1970	1980	1990	1991	Rank	%
World	1,740	3,004	3,805	4,922	5,092		
Bolivia	1	3	5	4	4		
Brazil	22	24	28	33	35		
Burma	10	11	16	15	15		
Cambodia	16	20	7	38	30		
Cameroon	2	13	17	38	40		
China	5	5	116	264	280	5	6
Ghana	0.4	7	10	4	4		
Guatemala	8	10	11	18	18		
India	17	90	146	297	330	4	7
Indonesia	635	838	982	1,246	1,284	1	25
Ivory Coast	10	11	21	74	74	9	2
Liberia	31	78	81	40	9		
Malaysia	722	1,285	1,537	1,292	1,250	2	25
Nigeria	14	63	49	88	137	7	3
Papua New Guinea	2	6	4	4	6		

SHEEP

thousand head

	1950	1970	1980	1990	1991	Rank	%
World	773,843	1,076,956	1,087,985	1,215,633	1,202,920		
Afghanistan	14,000	18,900	18,667	13,500	13,500		
Albania	1,633	1,249	1,232	1,600	1,600		
Algeria	3,990	7,940	13,111	13,350	13,350		
Argentina	52,940	42,773	31,473	28,571	27,552		
Australia	111,485	177,491	134,871	170,297	162,774	1	14
Azerbaijan	...	...	...	...	5,258		
Bolivia	7,224	6,825	9,050	12,220	12,300		
Brazil	14,427	17,768	18,414	20,100	20,300		
Bulgaria	8,377	9,518	10,358	8,130	7,938		
Burkina Faso	590	1,657	1,855	3,150	3,339		
Cameroon	638	2,000	2,167	3,500	3,550		
Canada	1,176	635	729	759	780		
Chad	2,000	2,200	2,620	1,964	1,983		
Chile	5,789	6,179	6,059	6,650	6,650		
China	31,070	78,000	101,864	113,508	112,820	3	9
Colombia	1,153	1,935	2,399	2,690	2,745		
Ecuador	1,724	1,897	2,310	1,420	1,250		
Egypt	1,254	2,000	1,691	4,806	4,900		
Ethiopia	9,559	24,077	23,250	22,960	23,000		
Finland	1,102	963	107	61	57		
France	7,499	10,023	11,452	11,790	11,490		
Georgia	...	...	...	...	1,834		
Germany	3,231	2,534	3,147	4,136	3,240		
Ghana	443	1,324	1,942	2,224	2,500		
Greece	6,978	7,646	8,040	10,510	9,759		
Hungary	1,003	2,966	2,960	2,069	1,865		
India	36,824	40,657	44,987	54,588	55,700	5	5
Indonesia	2,038	3,169	4,124	5,900	5,750		
Iran	11,727	32,000	33,833	45,000	45,000	6	4
Iraq	10,000	12,000	10,399	9,600	7,800		
Ireland	2,419	4,092	2,374	5,782	6,001		
Italy	10,187	8,097	9,120	11,569	11,575		
Kazakhstan	...	...	...	...	36,223		
Kenya	7,240	3,935	5,100	6,516	6,550		
Kyrgyzstan	...	...	...	...	10,486		
Lesotho	1,561	1,610	1,183	1,460	1,470		
Libya	1,390	2,125	5,046	5,200	5,500		
Macedonia	...	...	...	...	2,297		
Mali	4,080	5,700	6,247	5,850	5,850		
Mauritania	1,065	4,427	5,098	4,200	4,200		
Mexico	5,041	8,687	6,484	5,846	6,003		
Moldova	...	...	...	...	1,282		
Mongolia	12,575	12,678	14,261	14,265	15,083		
Morocco	11,249	17,087	15,228	14,000	14,000		
Namibia	2,887	4,000	5,433	3,328	6,700		
Nepal	2,437	2,156	730	892	925		
Netherlands	404	579	856	1,702	1,800		
New Zealand	33,871	59,708	67,393	57,852	57,000	4	5
Niger	1,324	2,632	2,979	2,970	2,970		
Nigeria	5,200	8,083	9,000	22,104	24,000		
Norway	1,819	1,769	2,033	2,211	2,211		
Pakistan	8,000	13,096	22,580	29,239	30,160	9	3
Peru	17,515	16,698	14,565	12,257	11,250		
Poland	2,205	3,236	4,105	4,158	3,234		
Portugal	4,307	4,405	4,440	5,567	5,673		
Romania	10,519	13,964	15,766	15,435	14,062		
Russia	...	...	...	...	55,200		
Saudi Arabia	3,572	1,960	2,888	6,492	5,692		
Senegal	506	1,533	1,966	3,920	4,000		
Somalia	2,261	8,967	11,500	14,000	13,800		
South Africa	33,237	35,585	31,625	32,665	32,580	8	3
Spain	24,489	18,712	14,721	24,037	24,500		
Sudan	5,560	10,300	17,628	20,168	20,700		
Syria	2,968	5,843	9,311	14,509	15,321		
Tajikistan	...	...	...	...	3,359		
Tanzania	2,333	2,823	3,754	3,557	3,556		
Togo	264	589	592	1,200	1,220		
Tunisia	2,462	3,200	4,651	5,964	6,290		

	1950	1970	1980	1990	1991	Rank	%
Turkey	24,282	36,470	46,199	43,647	40,553	7	3
Turkmenistan	...	...	...	...	5,083		
Uganda	1,063	799	1,152	1,920	1,950		
Ukraine	...	...	...	...	8,419		
USSR (former)	76,879	136,434	142,591	138,000	134,000	2	11
United Kingdom	19,945	26,332	21,643	29,521	29,954	10	3
United States	31,565	20,501	12,670	11,364	11,200		
Uruguay	23,149	19,906	19,219	25,220	25,986		
Yemen	...	2,800	3,002	3,756	3,800		
Yugoslavia	10,493	9,136	7,359	7,596	7,431		
Yugoslavia (Serbia)	...	...	...	...	3,044		

	1950	1970	1980	1990	1991	Rank
Tunisia	19	27	23	38	40	
Turkey	52	226	253	304	303	6
Uganda	12	4	6	11	11	
USSR (former)	494	945	834	970	875	1 12
United Arab Em.	2	2	4	20	22	
United Kingdom	143	221	256	370	382	5
United States	283	250	143	165	165	
Uruguay	63	72	37	61	64	
Yemen	...	15	20	38	38	
Yugoslavia	34	50	59	67	66	

SHEEPMEAT
thousand tonnes

	1950	1970	1980	1990	1991	Rank	%
World	4,255	5,708	5,663	6,934	7,006		
Afghanistan	80	86	128	115	115		
Albania	18	16	17	16	15		
Algeria	34	40	61	71	71		
Argentina	194	181	119	88	85		
Australia	332	367	539	628	675	2	9.6
Belgium	2	7	6	8	8		
Bolivia	12	14	20	29	30		
Brazil	32	36	32	41	43		
Bulgaria	43	71	63	60	59		
Cameroon	4	9	8	14	15		
Canada	16	8	5	9	9		
Chad	9	7	11	8	3		
Chile	47	24	16	15	16		
China	220	350	237	548	572	3	8.2
Colombia	1	2	9	10	10		
Czechoslovakia	7	5	6	9	6		
Ecuador	3	11	8	5	5		
Egypt	36	29	22	67	69		
Ethiopia	75	80	82	82	82		
Finland	7	1	1	1	1		
France	82	113	170	168	167	10	2.4
Germany	55	21	43	50	47		
Ghana	3	4	5	6	7		
Greece	38	61	81	89	87		
Hungary	8	6	7	4	4		
Iceland	6	12	15	10	10		
India	272	112	115	162	166		
Indonesia	26	13	23	30	44		
Iran	90	145	229	231	240	7	3.4
Iraq	25	39	46	22	17		
Ireland	21	44	42	84	90		
Italy	47	49	65	81	79		
Jordan	5	5	4	6	6		
Kenya	1	13	18	26	26		
Kuwait	...	8	21	27	...		
Lebanon	2	11	8	11	11		
Libya	8	19	49	51	60		
Mali	26	18	24	20	20		
Mauritania	9	6	7	6	6		
Mexico	10	16	22	25	26		
Mongolia	150	69	96	112	106		
Morocco	60	47	56	55	55		
Namibia	2	12	17	11	50		
Nepal	16	7	2	3	3		
Netherlands	6	10	18	14	15		
New Zealand	324	563	567	535	550	4	7.9
Niger	18	4	12	13	13		
Nigeria	72	28	31	75	81		
Norway	15	17	20	24	25		
Pakistan	66	67	122	214	229	9	3.3
Peru	14	23	21	24	19		
Poland	7	22	19	29	20		
Portugal	16	19	19	25	25		
Romania	14	62	72	66	69		
Saudi Arabia	...	14	34	77	78		
Senegal	4	6	1	13	13		
Somalia	15	11	22	38	37		
South Africa	79	168	133	133	133		
Spain	78	123	152	217	230	8	3.3
Sudan	22	64	82	70	72		
Syria	43	40	80	90	91		
Tanzania	30	10	10	10	10		

SILK
tonnes

	1950	1970	1980	1990	1991	Rank
World	20,860	42,146	67,968	86,474	90,872	
Afghanistan	...	45	50	60	60	
Brazil	87	270	1,300	1,693	1,929	6
Bulgaria	100	253	199	150	150	
China	3,600	10,258	34,199	58,051	72,667	1 8
Greece	90	103	33	11	11	
India	927	2,245	4,926	11,000	11,900	2 1
Iran	176	145	383	537	537	9
Italy	1,452	321	20	2	2	
Japan	11,624	20,562	15,624	6,000	6,000	3
Korea, North	...	1,400	2,700	4,200	4,400	4
Korea, South	455	2,876	3,311	1,400	1,400	7
Lebanon	31	12	5	6	6	
Romania	100	106	120	150	150	
Spain	36	29	15	15	15	
Thailand	...	...	883	1,250	1,300	8
Turkey	150	146	233	270	270	
USSR (former)	1,855	3,009	3,625	4,094	4,100	5
Vietnam	...	233	246	500	500	10

SISAL
thousand tonnes

	1970	1980	1990	1991	Rank	%
World	312	527	377	386		
Angola	65	7	1	1		
Brazil	229	234	185	185	1	47.9
China	9	20	16	17	6	4.4
Cuba	2	5	7	7	10	1.8
Ethiopia	2	1	1	1		
Haiti	16	12	10	10	7	2.6
Indonesia	5	1	1	1		
Kenya	46	42	40	39	4	10.1
Madagascar	26	15	21	21	5	5.4
Mexico	50	86	39	45	2	11.7
Morocco	1	1	2	2		
Mozambique	28	11	1	1		
South Africa	8	6	7	8	9	2.1
Tanzania	198	80	38	40	3	10.4
Venezuela	12	6	8	9	8	2.3

SORGHUM
thousand tonnes

	1950	1970	1980	1990	1991	Rank	%
World	27,000	55,629	65,651	56,677	57,763		
Argentina	100	3,823	5,641	2,016	2,251	7	3.9
Australia	75	759	1,084	946	893	9	1.5
Benin	50	52	59	99	106		
Brazil	...	2	172	228	272		
Burkina Faso	370	528	620	751	1,113	8	1.9
Burundi	60	105	53	64	88		
Cameroon	...	...	301	350	400		

	1950	1970	1980	1990	1991	Rank	%
d	...	...	210	280	365		
a	...	8,607	7,034	5,777	5,615	3	9.7
mbia	20	153	488	777	738		
ot	...	...	641	630	655		
alvador	...	115	144	145	161163		
opia	150	827	1,149	787	805	10	1.4
ce	1	203	332	264	388		
na	79	147	140	136	241		
temala	12	46	80	87	80		
i	174	210	121	68	70		
duras	47	46	49	81	93		
a	5,981	8,516	11,380	11,878	10,800	2	18.7
	5	15	73	114	150		
ya	50	215	160	145	140		
ea, North	10	115	18	15	16		
otho	23	57	59	28	18		
awi	38	78	20	15	19		
i	...	...	341	531	729		
uritania	...	...	28	46	59		
xico	200	2,573	4,991	5,978	4,367	5	7.6
rocco	81	70	20	14	14		
zambique	140	202	181	175	155		
aragua	36	57	80	76	70		
er	215	262	347	286	472		
eria	1,500	3,632	3,341	4,185	4,800	4	8.3
istan	239	308	235	239	260		
anda	80	141	178	151	205		
udi Arabia	14	185	123	81	85		
negal	...	...	131	147	85		
malia	30	132	167	250	145		
uth Africa	180	376	540	275	251		
ain	4	168	181	86	108		
dan	601	1,525	2,361	1,180	2,941	6	5.1
nzania	250	156	543	368	480		
ailand	20	123	237	237	233		
go	...	...	87	115	106		
anda	240	337	312	360	380		
SSR (former)	56	62	103	150	155		
ited States	3,896	19,314	19,157	14,562	14,720	1	25.5
uguay	10	53	112	59	90		
nezuela	3	5	365	376	616		
men	...	878	616	441	132		
mbia	122	49	16	20	40		
nbabwe	100	98	71	91	68		

SOYABEANS

housand tonnes

	1950	1970	1980	1990	1991	Rank	%
orld	16,000	43,487	85,967	108,134	103,065		
rgentina	4	39	3,657	10,700	11,250	3	10.9
ustralia	...	5	85	77	70		
olivia	...	2	49	233	384		
azil	83	1,547	13,468	19,888	14,771	2	14.3
anada	86	257	651	1,292	1,406	7	1.4
hina	7,200	8,131	8,266	11,008	9,807	4	9.5
olombia	...	114	130	232	194		
cuador	...	2	32	167	169		
gypt	...	...	110	107	135		
rance	...	...	19	245	150		
dia	...	2	359	2,419	2,100	5	2
donesia	270	468	679	1,487	1,549	6	1.5
an	...	15	65	105	105		
aly	...	...	...	1,751	1,325	8	1.3
apan	376	128	192	220	260		
orea, North	...	255	340	455	460		
orea, South	136	228	243	233	183		
exico	...	252	580	575	718		
igeria	3	61	60	60	65		
araguay	...	46	616	1,795	1,304	9	1.3
omania	5	102	262	141	179		
outh Africa	...	...	32	94	126		
aiwan	15	65	26	8	8		
urkey	2	11	7	162	150		
JSSR (former)	166	400	494	880	760	10	0.7
Jnited States	7,312	31,174	54,861	52,416	54,039	1	52.4
ugoslavia	4	5	64	157	147		
imbabwe	...	...	86	110	97		

SUGAR

thousand tonnes

	1950	1970	1980	1990	1991	Rank	%
World	32,296	72,176	88,632	110,823	112,224		
Angola	47	74	31	25	32		
Argentina	638	985	1,584	1,351	1,594		
Australia	913	2,511	3,243	3,536	2,800		
Austria	104	315	450	451	462		
Bangladesh	...	90	595	200	262		
Barbados	168	146	113	70	67		
Belgium	330	711	994	1,120	905		
Belize	2	62	101	106	108		
Bolivia	1	120	250	271	355		
Brazil	1,649	5,161	8,191	7,835	8,675	3	7.7
Bulgaria	64	218	165	35	115		
Canada	122	130	112	147	152		
Chile	...	217	131	373	359		
China	986	3,878	4,160	7,197	7,836	4	7
Colombia	178	710	2,117	1,589	1,617		
Congo	...	78	13	40	40		
Costa Rica	26	160	214	230	250		
Cuba	5,786	6,388	7,510	8,445	7,623	5	6.7
Czechoslovakia	697	731	808	686	714		
Denmark	319	307	493	572	500		
Dominican Rep.	552	1,010	1,142	590	656		
Ecuador	56	258	402	311	319		
Egypt	196	564	666	971	1,064		
El Salvador	28	128	228	213	287		
Ethiopia	...	98	168	186	155		
Fiji	122	329	446	408	389		
Finland	20	60	104	168	174		
France	1,085	2,872	4,720	4,743	4,675	7	4.2
Germany	1,523	2,645	3,936	4,671	4,245	8	3.8
Greece	...	163	286	312	297		
Guadeloupe	73	154	86	26	53		
Guatemala	31	191	448	839	918		
Guyana	218	354	291	134	145		
Haiti	53	64	135	35	30		
Honduras	5	60	203	185	186		
Hungary	232	321	511	595	736		
India	1,316	4,188	13,487	11,168	12,528	1	11.2
Indonesia	287	760	1,587	2,218	2,334		
Iran	54	571	630	625	760		
Ireland	93	164	178	245	226		
Italy	598	1,271	1,956	1,584	1,640		
Ivory Coast	...	...	97	154	155		
Jamaica	279	383	247	209	237		
Japan	21	628	789	925	915		
Kenya	15	132	416	467	532		
Madagascar	16	103	115	118	116		
Malawi	...	32	140	189	195		
Martinique	40	29	6	6	7		
Mauritius	443	659	615	624	580		
Mexico	733	2,495	2,864	3,278	3,943	10	3.5
Morocco	...	168	364	638	675		
Mozambique	85	278	189	32	33		
Netherlands	364	769	1,000	1,337	1,060		
Nicaragua	27	147	204	201	225		
Pakistan	55	557	738	2,017	2,086		
Panama	16	78	184	97	128		
Paraguay	20	50	85	106	110		
Peru	496	782	586	601	550		
Philippines	827	1,859	2,318	1,810	1,780		
Poland	871	1,581	1,530	2,142	1,587		
Puerto Rico	1,157	383	158	62	67		
Réunion	116	220	247	191	237		
Romania	116	434	595	405	310		
St Christopher-N.	45	30	37	15	20		
South Africa	555	1,629	2,011	2,289	2,152		
Spain	315	882	934	1,043	1,037		
Sudan	...	85	166	421	470		
Swaziland	...	167	317	527	500		
Sweden	285	233	350	429	270		
Switzerland	27	65	119	160	132		
Taiwan	520	588	830	475	409		
Tanzania	10	100	124	108	116		
Thailand	34	436	2,134	3,506	4,006	9	3.6
Trinidad & Tobago	151	229	125	118	104		
Turkey	161	700	1,178	1,946	1,957		
Uganda	56	154	14	25	46		
USSR (former)	2,700	8,722	7,017	9,130	8,750	2	7.8

	1950	1970	1980	1990	1991	Rank	%
United Kingdom	626	1,033	1,215	1,349	1,292		
United States	2,785	5,215	5,342	6,273	6,531	6	5.8
Venezuela	60	448	351	499	556		
Vietnam	1	7	207	376	380		
Yugoslavia	132	440	798	934	663		
Zambia	...	37	105	147	152		
Zimbabwe	1	155	336	464	329		

This is raw sugar manufactured from beet and cane.

TEA

thousand tonnes

	1950	1970	1980	1990	1991	Rank	%
World	639	1,341	1,858	2,533	2,576		
Argentina	...	26	29	43	48	9	1.9
Bangladesh	22	25	38	39	38		
Bolivia	...	1	2	2	3		
Brazil	1	6	10	10	10		
Burundi	1	1	2	4	4		
Cameroon	...	1	2	3	3		
China	70	246	334	562	566	2	22
Ecuador	...	1	2	1	1		
India	273	416	558	715	730	1	28.3
Indonesia	39	65	104	149	158	5	6.1
Iran	5	18	32	44	45	10	1.7
Japan	41	91	101	90	90	8	3.5
Kenya	6	38	93	197	204	4	7.9
Malawi	7	18	31	39	41		
Malaysia	2	3	3	5	5		
Mauritius	...	4	5	6	6		
Mozambique	3	17	20	2	2		
Papua New Guinea	...	1	8	8	9		
Peru	...	2	2	3	3		
Rwanda		1	6	13	13		
South Africa	...	1	8	13	14		
Sri Lanka	140	215	203	238	241	3	9.4
Taiwan	11	28	24	22	21		
Tanzania	1	9	17	20	21		
Thailand	...	1	1	5	5		
Turkey	...	34	80	123	136	6	5.3
Uganda	2	18	2	7	8		
USSR (former)	21	65	128	136	118	7	4.6
Vietnam	6	10	21	31	32		
Zaire	...	8	6	3	3		
Zimbabwe	...	3	9	17	16		

TOBACCO

thousand tonnes

	1950	1970	1980	1990	1991	Rank	%
World	2,851	4,603	5,575	7,076	7,662		
Albania	2	12	18	15	12		
Algeria	20	5	4	4	5		
Argentina	30	60	61	68	94		
Australia	2	18	15	12	14		
Bangladesh	...	43	44	38	36		
Brazil	113	246	397	444	414	4	5.4
Bulgaria	45	113	138	77	74		
Burma	47	53	53	40	40		
Cambodia	5	12	5	13	14		
Canada	62	105	100	63	68		
Chile	7	7	6	14	15		
China	132	801	1,134	2,617	3,121	1	40.7
Colombia	21	42	52	33	40		
Cuba	32	31	32	44	44		
Czechoslovakia	8	6	5	5	5		
Dominican Rep.	18	22	41	19	25		
France	48	45	47	28	27		
Germany	24	8	12	10	7		
Greece	49	88	125	130	178	9	2.3
Guatemala	2	5	10	7	7		
Honduras	4	6	7	6	7		
Hungary	23	20	21	14	19		

	1950	1970	1980	1990	1991	Rank
India	247	353	458	550	560	3
Indonesia	64	73	105	150	159	10
Iran	12	18	24	25	25	
Iraq	3	15	10	4	2	
Italy	76	79	131	194	192	7
Japan	90	163	144	78	71	
Kenya	1	2	3	9	10	
Korea, North	12	40	45	65	66	
Korea, South	15	60	97	70	73	
Madagascar	4	5	3	4	4	
Malawi	13	21	53	101	125	
Malaysia	2	3	8	11	11	
Mexico	35	72	74	62	20	
Morocco	2	3	7	7	7	
Nepal	6	7	5	7	7	
Nigeria	11	13	13	9	9	
Pakistan	68	118	71	68	76	
Paraguay	8	20	19	5	5	
Philippines	21	58	57	82	79	
Poland	25	82	75	59	57	
Portugal	7	10	7	5	6	
Romania	17	26	35	32	34	
South Africa	23	35	37	34	35	
Spain	19	24	38	36	43	
Sri Lanka	3	9	15	10	11	
Syria	6	8	13	13	16	
Tanzania	2	12	17	14	14	
Thailand	27	77	78	71	71	
Turkey	91	157	204	288	247	5
Uganda	2	5	3	3	4	
USSR (former)	157	256	285	260	240	6
United States	959	819	813	738	753	2
Venezuela	10	12	16	15	12	
Vietnam	5	12	20	18	28	
Yemen	1	2	7	7	7	
Yugoslavia	24	46	65	46	46	
Zaire	3	5	7	4	4	
Zambia	3	6	4	4	5	
Zimbabwe	42	63	104	140	178	8

WHALING

number

	1970	1980	1988	1989	1
Minke whale					
World	...	11,828	421	334	
Brazil	...	902	0	...	
Greenland	...	...	119	73	
Japan	...	3,658	273	241	
Korea, South	...	925	0	...	
Norway	...	2,002	29	17	
USSR (former)	...	3,879	0	...	
Bryde's whale					
World	910	522	0	...	
Japan	...	307	0	...	
Sei whale					
World	10,466	102	10	2	
Iceland	...	100	10	...	
Fin whale					
World	4,547	472	77	78	
Iceland	...	236	68	68	
Denmark	...	...	9	...	
Spain	...	219	0	...	
Humpback whale					
Denmark	24	15	0	...	
Baleen whale					
World	...	217	173	198	19
United States	...	...	23	19	3
USSR (former)	...	178	150	179	16
Sperm whale					
World	22,904	2,210	8	...	
Japan	...	1,192	0	...	
Portugal	...	330...	...	...	
Longfin Pilot whale					
World	...	2,820	1,705	1,262	97
Faroe Is.	...	2,773	1,690	1,258	91
Killer whale					
World	...	971	0	9	
Japan	0	9	3		
Beluga whale					

	1970	1980	1988	1989	1990
-ld	...	1,909	13	1,356	1,283
ada	...	774	5	1,043	...
enland	...	889	0	50	1,000
SR (former)	...	236	8	27	44
vhal					
-ld	520	0	362	1,200	
enland	...	520	0	342	1,200
hed whale					
-ld	...	381	128,905	163,708	102,041
pan	...	...	48,816	52,930	41,414

WHEAT

ousand tonnes

	1950	1970	1980	1990	1991	Rank	%
rld	190,000	329,033	442,768	601,723	550,993		
hanistan	1,700	2,150	2,788	1,650	1,726		
ania	89	242	500	450	300		
eria	996	1,359	1,270	1,005	1,741		
entina	5,175	5,873	7,993	11,014	9,000		
menia	...	...	...	310	...		
stralia	5,161	9,014	14,486	15,402	9,633		
stria	348	912	1,025	1,404	1,341		
ngladesh	55	103	803	890	1,004		
gium	555	848	955	1,409	1,620		
snia	...	...	...	413	...		
azil	498	1,743	2,614	3,094	3,077		
lgaria	1,776	2,899	3,877	5,292	4,503		
nada	13,443	13,901	20,287	32,708	32,822	6	6
ile	942	1,296	882	1,718	1,589		
ina	16,000	31,005	57,965	98,232	95,003	1	17.2
oatia	...	...	...	1,495	...		
echoslovakia	1,493	3,436	4,507	6,707	6,205		
nmark	285	509	678	3,953	3,629		
ypt	1,111	1,509	1,834	4,268	4,483		
hiopia	460	643	470	867	890		
land	263	445	267	627	431		
ance	7,791	14,112	21,996	33,312	34,483	5	6.3
ermany	3,912	8,471	11,248	15,242	16,669	8	3
eece	894	1,867	2,703	1,965	2,750		
ungary	1,909	3,410	4,862	6,198	5,954		
dia	6,087	20,859	34,599	49,850	54,522	3	9.9
an	1,863	3,946	5,700	8,218	8,900		
aq	448	1,080	1,297	1,196	525		
eland	327	375	240	625	703		
aly	7,170	9,756	9,017	8,109	9,289		
apan	1,375	557	579	952	860		
azakhstan	...	...	...	16,200	...		
exico	534	2,141	2,771	3,931	4,115		
orocco	786	1,819	1,500	3,614	4,939		
epal	...	230	444	855	836		
etherlands	324	675	867	1,076	916		
ew Zealand	139	357	325	188	176		
akistan	3,630	6,796	10,698	14,316	14,505	9	2.6
oland	1,833	4,925	4,197	9,026	9,269		
ortugal	499	614	331	296	323		
omania	2,486	4,433	5,634	7,290	5,442		
ussia	...	...	...	49,600	...		
audi Arabia	16	111	150	3,600	4,000		
outh Africa	555	1,461	1,882	1,702	2,245		
pain	3,626	4,734	4,435	4,760	5,392		
udan	...	134	205	408	680		
weden	677	958	1,086	2,243	1,524		
witzerland	260	378	403	563	574		
yria	761	763	1,877	2,070	2,135		
unisia	452	520	837	1,122	1,786		
urkey	4,770	11,423	17,054	20,000	20,400	7	3.7
kraine	...	...	...	30,370	...		
JSSR (former)	35,759	92,804	92,131	109,600	80,000	2	14.5
United Kingdom	2,397	4,140	8,034	14,000	14,300	10	2.6
United States	31,065	40,034	66,242	74,475	53,915	4	9.8
Uruguay	469	379	377	539	136		
Yugoslavia	2,171	4,760	4,624	6,359	6,530		
Yugoslavia (Serbia)	...	...	...	4,109	...		

WINE

thousand tonnes

	1950	1970	1980	1990	1991	Rank	%
World	18,901	28,884	34,790	29,010	27,767		
Algeria	1,348	888	274	48	50		
Argentina	1,136	1,935	2,364	1,910	1,465	6	5.2
Australia	145	259	375	445	400		
Austria	92	239	265	317	300		
Brazil	102	179	258	311	311		
Bulgaria	248	436	455	293	293		
Canada	22	39	45	46	50		
Chile	313	443	591	398	390		
China	...	...	38	90	95		
Cyprus	13	45	54	60	60		
Czechoslovakia	31	100	139	142	134		
France	5,245	6,298	7,063	6,553	6,200	1	22.3
Germany	232	754	700	949	1,015	7	3.7
Greece	370	454	447	353	450		
Hungary	316	476	491	547	547		
Israel	6	33	18	13	13		
Italy	4,342	6,825	8,075	5,487	5,915	2	21.3
Japan	4	16	55	55	55		
Mexico	1	17	187	163	145		
Morocco	64	100	95	30	30		
New Zealand	3	18	44	49	49		
Portugal	817	959	1,127	1,097	991	8	3.6
Romania	402	584	880	598	600	10	2.2
South Africa	224	489	703	952	963	9	3.5
Spain	1,539	2,485	4,142	4,090	3,107	3	11.2
Switzerland	70	91	88	120	124		
Tunisia	74	79	60	27	41		
Turkey	15	44	17	24	24		
USSR (former)	277	2,630	3,200	1,570	1,800	4	6.5
United States	904	1,183	1,678	1,585	1,490	5	5.4
Uruguay	79	86	70	90	80		
Yugoslavia	414	603	727	517	500		

WOOD - CONIFEROUS*

million cubic metres

	1961–65 av.	1970	1980	1990	1991	Rank	%
World	959	1,081	1,190	1,400	1,295		
Afghanistan	1.7	2.3	2.4	2.4	2.5		
Algeria	0.7	0.8	1.1	1.5	1.5		
Argentina	0.5	0.6	0.9	2	2		
Australia	1.8	2.5	4.3	7.5	7.2		
Austria	9.4	10	12.1	15	14.2		
Belgium	1.4	1.5	1.5	4	3.4		
Brazil	16.9	26.1	38	46.4	46.7	5	3.6
Bulgaria	1.5	1.5	1.2	1.1	1		
Canada	89.9	111	145	167	164	3	12.6
Chile	2.2	3.7	8	11.4	11.5		
China	65.2	77.1	113	135	136	4	10.5
Czechoslovakia	10.2	10.6	14.3	14.1	12.9		
Denmark	0.9	1.3	1.2	1.5	1.5		
Ethiopia	1.8	2.4	2.3	2.8	2.8		
Finland	34.1	32.6	39.1	35.4	27.8	8	2.1
France	13.6	15	18.1	23.5	23.3	9	1.8
Germany	23.3	25.1	31	71	33	7	2.5
Guatemala	3.1	2.8	4.9	6.4	6.6		
Honduras	2.3	2.4	2.3	2.5	2.6		
India	3.5	4.3	8	10	10		
Ireland	0.2	0.3	0.3	1.6	1.6		
Italy	1.5	1.4	1.7	1.4	1.3		
Japan	34.7	26.8	21.4	19.5	19	10	1.5
Kenya	0.8	1	1.4	1.8	1.9		
Korea, North	2.7	3.1	2.4	2.7	2.8		
Korea, South	6.5	7.3	5.6	4.3	4.3		
Mexico	5.9	7.5	9.3	11.2	11.1		
Mongolia	1.1	2	2.2	2.2	2.2		
New Zealand	5.5	8.4	9.7	11.5	13.5		
Norway	8.4	7.7	8.3	10.7	10		
Pakistan	0.7	1	1	1.6	1.6		
Poland	14.1	15.3	16.8	13.8	12.7		
Portugal	4	4.5	5.5	6.7	6		

	1961–65 av.	1970	1980	1990	1991	Rank	%
Romania	6.4	7.3	7	6.3	5.6		
South Africa	2.5	4	6.3	7.2	6.7		
Spain	5.7	5.6	7.3	11.7	11.4		
Swaziland	0.4	0.8	1.4	1.6	1.6		
Sweden	40.5	53.3	41.7	45.5	44	6	3.4
Switzerland	2.8	3	3.1	5	3		
Turkey	5.8	10.4	14.2	9.4	9.4		
USSR (former)	301	321	298	321	291	2	22.4
United Kingdom	1.4	1.8	2.6	5.5	5.3		
United States	214	246	263	326	309	1	23.9
Yugoslavia	4.3	3.8	4.3	3.7	3.2		

*Statistics refer to roundwood which is timber as it is felled.

WOOD – NONCONIFEROUS*

million cubic metres

	1961–65 av.	1970	1980	1990	1991	Rank	%
World	1,162	1,315	1,632	1,970	1,993		
Afghanistan	3.5	4.2	3.9	4	4.2		
Albania	1.1	1.6	1.5	1.4	1.6		
Angola	5.9	7.3	4.3	5.4	5.5		
Argentina	10.4	11.2	7.3	7.4	7.4		
Australia	12.1	11	12.6	12.4	12		
Austria	1.6	1.8	2.3	2.5	2.5		
Bangladesh	7.8	9.5	23.8	31	31.7		
Benin	1.7	2.1	3.6	4.8	4.9		
Bhutan	...	...	3.2	1.5	1.6		
Bolivia	4.4	4.2	1.4	1.5	1.5		
Brazil	117	132.7	145.5	179	182	3	9.1
Bulgaria	3.9	3.6	2.9	3	2.7		
Burkina Faso	3.5	4.1	6.6	8.6	8.8		
Burma	13.4	15.6	18.2	23.2	23.6		
Burundi	0.7	0.8	3.1	4.1	4.3		
Cambodia	3.6	4	4.7	6	6.4		
Cameroon	6.4	7.6	10.2	13.3	13.5		
Canada	9.5	10.7	13.6	14.4	14.3		
Central Afr. Rep.	1.9	2.3	3	3.5	3.4		
Chad	2.9	3.3	1.2	1.5	1.5		
Chile	4.4	4	5.6	7	7.1		
China	81.4	95.2	121.2	145	146.7	5	7.4
Colombia	24.9	26.6	13.9	16.1	16.3		
Congo	1.7	2.1	2.3	3.7	3.7		
Costa Rica	2	2.8	3.4	4	4.1		
Cuba	2.2	1.8	2.8	2.6	2.6		
Czechoslovakia	2.7	4	4.5	3.7	3.6		
Dominican Rep.	1.7	1.8	0.5	0.6	0.6		
Ecuador	2.4	2.8	5.6	7.7	5.2		
Egypt	0.1	0.2	1.8	2.2	2.3		
El Salvador	2.7	2.4	3.7	4.4	4.5		
Ethiopia	18.6	20.8	30.1	38.3	39.4	9	2
Finland	12.1	12.5	8	8.2	6.3		
France	19.7	19.8	20.7	21.3	20.8		
Gabon	2.6	3	3.1	4.2	4.3		
Germany	10.2	10.4	12.3	13.8	11.8		
Ghana	9.6	10.1	10.6	14.5	12.6		
Greece	2.5	2.3	2	1.7	1.7		
Guatemala	0.6	4.2	1.1	1.4	1.4		
Guinea	2.3	2.8	3.2	3.9	4		
Haiti	3	3.4	4	4.8	5		
Honduras	1.3	1.7	2.6	3.6	3.7		
Hungary	3.7	4.8	5.8	5.6	5.6		
India	91.2	106.5	204	252.8	257.7	1	12.9
Indonesia	86	107.1	144.8	165.3	171.5	4	8.6
Iran	6.5	7	6.4	6.3	6.3		
Italy	9.8	13.7	7.3	6.6	7		
Ivory Coast	7.2	9	11.2	11.4	11.8		
Japan	26	23	13	10	9		
Kenya	8.8	10.3	15.7	22.6	23.4		
Korea, North	1.4	1.6	2	2	2		
Korea, South	2.9	3.3	3	2.1	2.1		
Laos	2.4	2.8	2.6	3.5	3.6		
Liberia	1.2	1.6	3.3	4	4		
Madagascar	3.7	5.3	6.1	8.1	8.3		
Malawi	3.5	4.2	5.8	8.1	8.4		
Malaysia	12.9	24.1	34	47.3	47	8	2.4
Mali	2.3	2.7	4.1	5.6	5.7		
Mexico	6.7	9	8.8	11.4	11.7		

	1961–65 av.	1970	1980	1990	1991	Rank
Morocco	1.8	2.2	0.9	1.1	1.60	
Mozambique	7.6	8.5	12.8	15.4	15.5	
Nepal	7.7	8.8	14	18	18.4	
Nicaragua	1.9	1.9	2.6	3.4	3.5	
Niger	1.9	2.3	3.6	5	5.1	
Nigeria	46.6	56.9	73	98.8	101.8	6
Pakistan	6.2	17.6	16.3	25	25.6	
Panama	1.6	1.4	1.8	2	2	
Papua New Guinea	3.8	4.7	7	8.1	8.1	
Paraguay	2.4	3.7	5.8	7.2	7.2	
Peru	4.7	5.7	8.1	7.7	8	
Philippines	24.9	33.7	34.8	38.4	38.7	10
Poland	2.6	3.2	4	3.8	4.3	
Portugal	1.9	2	3	4.5	5.1	
Romania	14.8	15	10.7	9.3	8.5	
Rwanda	3	3.7	4.8	5.6	5.6	
Senegal	2.1	2.5	3	4	4.1	
Sierra Leone	2.7	2.7	2.4	3	3.1	
Somalia	2.4	3	4.6	6.5	6.6	
South Africa	4.1	5.6	12.5	12.8	13	
Spain	9.2	8.1	5.1	5.8	5.5	
Sri Lanka	4	4.7	7.9	9	9.1	
Sudan	19.7	21	6.3	8.4	8.7	
Sweden	6	6.7	7.5	8	8	
Switzerland	...	1.2	1.5	1.2	1.1	
Tanzania	25.9	31.4	22.6	33	34.1	
Thailand	16	18.7	30.6	34	34.2	
Tunisia	1.2	1.4	1.7	2.1	2.2	
Turkey	5.2	6.4	8.4	6.3	6.3	
Uganda	11.5	14	10	14.2	14.8	
USSR (former)	65.9	64.4	58.9	65	65	7
United Kingdom	1.1	1.5	1.3	1.1	1.1	
United States	88.6	82	146.8	183.4	184	2
Uruguay	1	1	2.2	3	3	
Venezuela	5.6	7	1.2	1.3	1.3	
Vietnam	14.9	17.6	22.3	28.6	29.4	
Yugoslavia	13.3	12.5	8.8	9	8.2	
Zaire	12	14	26.7	36.2	37.2	
Zambia	3.8	4.7	5	6.7	7	
Zimbabwe	4.5	5.4	6	7.4	7.4	

*Statistics refer to roundwood which is timber as it is felled.

WOOL – GREASY

thousand tonnes

	1950	1970	1980	1990	1991	Rank	%
World	1,845	2,867	2,784	3,125	3,071		
Afghanistan	15	26	23	17	17		
Albania	2	2	3	3	2		
Algeria	4	13	20	49	51	10	1.
Argentina	186	169	152	130	115	5	3.
Armenia	...	...	...	3.3	...		
Australia	515	899	705	843	841	1	27.
Azerbaijan	...	...	...	11	...		
Bolivia	4	7	9	13	13		
Brazil	20	32	32	28	29		
Bulgaria	14	29	35	28	25		
Canada	4	2	1	1	1		
Chile	20	23	21	20	18		
China	45	60	173	239	241	4	7.8
Czechoslovakia	1	4	4	6	1		
Ecuador	0.3	2	3	2	2		
Egypt	2	3	2	2	2		
Ethiopia	12	12	12	12	12		
Falkland Is.	2	2	2	3	3		
France	20	20	22	22	22		
Georgia	...	...	...	6.4	...		
Germany	11	10	16	21	24		
Greece	8	8	10	10	10		
Hungary	4	10	12	7	7		
India	26	37	35	35	32		
Indonesia	2	5	12	17	17		
Iran	15	19	33	32	32		
Iraq	14	16	11	23	15		
Ireland	6	10	10.8	17	18		
Italy	15	12	13	14	14		
Jordan	...	3	2	3	3		
Kazakhstan	...	...	...	108	...		

	1950	1970	1980	1990	1991	Rank	%
yzstan	...	...	...	39	...		
tho	4	4	3	3	3		
a	2	4	8	8	8		
ico	6	8	7	5	5		
dova	...	...	...	3	...		
agolia	14	19	21	20	21		
occo	11	16	14	35	35		
iibia	7	4	5	2	2		
al	2	4	1	1	1		
herlands	...	4.5	2	4	4		
v Zealand	179	332	353	309	304	3	9.9
way	3	5	5	5	5		
stan	11	20	40	61	65	9	2.1
J	9	13	11	10	10		
ind	4	9	12	15	11		
tugal	10	9	9	9	8		
nania	16	30	37	38	40		
isia	...	...	...	227	...		
idi Arabia	...	4	3	3	3		
ith Africa	105	137	103	100	104	6	3.4
in	34	33	21	30	30		
Jan	5	10	15	18	19		
ia	8	14	20	36	38		
ikistan	...	...	...	4.6	...		
izania	...	...	4	4	4		
nisia	3	5	9	12	12		
key	33	47	61	43	50		
rkmenistan	...	...	...	16	...		
raine	...	...	...	30	...		
SR (former)	694	412	454	471	447	2	14.6
ited Kingdom	40	47	50	75	75	8	2.4
ited States	129	85	48	40	39		
iguay	79	81	68	93	101	7	3.3
men	...	4.4	3	4.1	4.1		
goslavia	15	12	10	10	10		
nbabwe	...	...	9	1	1		

MINERAL AND MANUFACTURED PRODUCTS

ALUMINIUM ORE (BAUXITE)

thousand tonnes

	1948	1970	1980	1990	1991	Rank	%
World	7,810	52,650	93,300	112,692	110,803		
Australia	6	3,294	27,179	41,391	40,503	1	36.6
Brazil	15	400	4,632	9,876	10,414	4	9.4
China	...	500	1,700	3,200	3,000	8	2.7
Dominican Rep.	0	1,086	511	85	7		
France	804	2,992	1,925	490	183		
Ghana	133	342	225	381	334		
Greece	44	2,283	3,259	2,496	2,134		
Guinea	0	2,642	13,911	17,524	17,054	2	15.4
Guyana	1,996	4,103	3,052	1,424	2,204	10	2
Haiti	–	673	461	0	0		
Hungary	478	2,022	2,950	2,559	2,037		
India	21	1,370	1,785	5,277	4,835	5	4.4
Indonesia	438	1,229	1,249	1,206	1,406		
Iran	0	0	0	93	140		
Italy	153	225	23	0	9		
Jamaica	–	12,106	11,978	10,937	11,609	3	10.5
Malaysia	0	1,139	920	398	376		
Romania	0	792	450	247	200		
Sierra Leone	0	443	674	1,445	1,288		
Surinam	1,983	6,011	4,893	3,267	3,136	7	2.8
Turkey	0	51	547	779	530		
USSR (former)	...	4,300	6,400	5,350	4,800	6	4.3
United States	1,752	2,562	1,559	495	50		
Venezuela	0	0	0	785	1,992		
Yugoslavia	144	2,099	3,138	2,951	2,542	9	2.3

YAMS

thousand tonnes

	1980	1990	1991	Rank	%
World	23,394	20,966	23,893		
enin	687	967	1,206	3	5
razil	179	215	215	9	0.9
urkina Faso	71	52	52		
ameroon	203	70	80		
entral African Republic	153	195	200		
had	163	240	248	8	1
olombia	143	28	41		
thiopia	276	260	261	7	1.1
iabon	80	110	110		
ihana	614	877	1,000	4	4.2
iuinea	64	100	106		
laiti	112	120	110		
vory Coast	2,079	2,528	2,559	2	10.7
amaica	142	161	186		
apan	144	171	174		
ligeria	17,000	13,624	16,000	1	67
'apua New Guinea	176	210	215	10	0.9
'hilippines	21	27	28		
Solomon Is.	18	22	22		
Sudan	114	95	128		
Togo	498	392	433	5	1.8
Tonga	34	33	33		
Venezuela	33	41	41		
Zaire	222	280	300	6	1.3

ASBESTOS

thousand tonnes

	1950	1970	1980	1990	1991	Rank	%
World	870	4,682	4,700	3,980	3,790		
Australia	1.3	1	92	...	...		
Brazil	1.5	340	170	232	233	3	6.1
Canada	650	1,508	1,323	725	643	2	16.7
China	...	170	132	160	160	5	4.2
Cyprus	8.1	29	36	30	–		
Finland	10.8	14	–	–	–		
Greece	–	–	–	73	–	9	1.9
India	0.1	10	34	35	35	7	0.9
Italy	13	119	158	20	–		
Japan	4.8	21	4	–	–		
Korea, South	–	2	10	–	...		
South Africa	42	287	268	148	145	6	3.8
Swaziland	29	33	33	35	...	10	0.9
Turkey	0.2	3	9	20	...		
USSR (former)	...	1,066	2,070	2,400	2,400	1	63.3
United States	34	114	80	20	33	8	0.9
Yugoslavia	2.3	12	11	7	7		
Zimbabwe	62	80	251	190	190	4	5

CARS

thousands

	1948	1970	1980	1990	1991	Rank	%
World	4,640	22,550	28,999	35,700	34,400		
Argentina	0	169	218	114	121		
Australia	29	391	316	361	311		
Belgium	...	734	891	1,160*	1,065*	10	3.1
Brazil	0	255	652	268	293		
Canada	167	923	847	941	890		
Colombia	0	8	32	36*	35*		
Czechoslovakia	18	143	186	191	176		

	1948	1970	1980	1990	1991	Rank	%
France	100	2,458	3,487	2,962	3,121	4	9.1
Germany	33	3,655	3,688	4,618	4,270	3	12.4
India	0	45	47	221	193		
Indonesia	...	...	43	57*	...		
Iran	0	33	...	...	...		
Ireland	14	47	45	...	...		
Italy	44	1,720	1,445	1,873	1,627	6	4.7
Japan	0.4	3,179	7,038	9,948	9,756	1	28.4
Korea, South	0	13	58	956	1,132	9	3.3
Malaysia	0	21	79	102*	152*		
Mexico	...	137	312	614	733		
Netherlands	2	85	80	124	85		
New Zealand	10	55	73	...	...		
Poland	0	65	352	266	167		
Portugal	0	55	22	60*	78*		
Romania	0	23	89	120	74		
South Africa	...	195	268	221*	...		
Spain	0.2	455	1,048	1,736	1,830	5	5.3
Sweden	...	272	257	336	269		
Taiwan	0	9	133	358	405		
Thailand	0	0	24	82*	76*		
Turkey	0	5	52	167*	197*		
USSR (former)	20	344	1,327	1,259	1,184	8	3.4
United Kingdom	335	1,641	924	1,296	1,278	7	3.7
United States	3,909	8,505	6,376	6,052	5,407	2	15.7
Venezuela	0	46	...	...	35		
Yugoslavia	0	109	187	292	218		

* Assembly only

	1948	1970	1980	1991	1992	Rank
Austria	3.3	3.7	2.9	2.5	2.5	
Bulgaria	4.1	28.9	29.9	29	28	
Canada	1.4	3.5	6	8	33	
China	...	...	9.3	119	90	4
Czechoslovakia	23.6	81.8	95.7	83	70	5
Denmark	2.4	0.1	0	0	0	
France	1.8	2.8	2.6	2	2	
Germany	177	369	388	279	242	2
Greece	0.1	7.7	23.5	53	60	7
Hungary	9.4	23.7	22.6	15	14.5	
India	0	3.5	4.5	16	16	
Italy	0.9	1.4	1.9	0.9	1.1	
New Zealand	1.9	1.9	0.2	0.1	0.2	
Poland	5	32.8	36.9	69	66.8	6
Romania	0.9	14.1	28.1	29	33.6	
Russia	...	...	...	130	123	
Spain	1.4	2.8	15.4	14	13	
Thailand	0	0.4	1.4	13	...	
Turkey	0.7	4.5	17	47	45	9
Ukraine	...	...	...	8.7	8.5	
USSR (former)	58.2	145	163	152	142	3
United States	2.8	5.4	43.4	298	295	1
Yugoslavia	9.7	27.8	46.6	71	39.3	10

COPPER ORE

thousand tonnes

metal content

	1948	1970	1980	1990	1991	Rank
World	2,120	6,320	7,900	9,040	9,112	
Albania	–	7	12	13.2	8	
Australia	13	142	244	327	320	8
Bolivia	7	9	2	0.2	0	
Botswana	0	0	16	20.6	20.6	
Brazil	–	4	...	36.5	37	
Bulgaria	1	43	62	32.9	47.2	
Burkina Faso	...	...	...	20.6	20.6	
Canada	223	610	716	794	798	4
Chile	445	711	1,068	1,588	1,814	1
China	...	100	165	360	350	7
Cuba	15	7	3	2	2	
Cyprus	11.4	17.3	4.8	0.5	0.2	
Czechoslovakia	...	10.7	9.3	3.6	2.6	
Finland	20	34	53	12.6	11.7	
Germany	6	10	12	3.6	0	
India	8	10	27	51.6	50.4	
Indonesia	–	–	59	170	212	
Iran	–	–	1	74.3	97	
Ireland	...	7.7	4.3	0	0	
Japan	26	120	53	13	12.4	
Korea, North	2	13	12	12	14	
Malaysia	–	–	27	24.3	25.6	
Mexico	59	61	175	291	267	10
Mongolia	–	–	44	124	120	
Morocco	–	3	8	15.3	14.2	
Namibia	8	23	39	32.5	33.9	
Norway	15	20	29	19.7	17.4	
Oman	–	–	–	13.7	13.5	
Papua New Guinea	...	...	147	170	205	
Peru	18	206	367	318	381	6
Philippines	2	160	305	181	151	
Poland	–	83	343	329	320	8
Portugal	...	...	1	158	158	
Romania	...	...	28	32	27	
South Africa	30	148	201	209	193	
Spain	4	10	48	15.3	10	
Sweden	15	26	43	73.5	79.9	
Turkey	11	22	21	39.8	35.5	
USSR (former)	...	925	1,130	900	840	3
United States	757	1,560	1,181	1,587	1,631	2
Yugoslavia	41	91	115	119	110	
Zaire	156	387	462	356	235	
Zambia	217	684	610	496	423	5
Zimbabwe	...	...	27	14.7	13.8	

Rank values (right column, partial): Australia 3; Canada 8; Chile 1; China 3; Mexico 2.9; Poland 3.5; Peru 4.2; USSR 9.2; United States 17.9; Zambia 4.6

COAL - BITUMINOUS

million tonnes

	1948	1970	1980	1991	1992	Rank	%
World	1,412	2,131	2,740	3,104	3,120		
Australia	15	44	78	166	180	5	5.8
Belgium	27	11	5.3	1.1	0.2		
Brazil	2	2.4	5.1	6.5	4.6		
Canada	15	12	31	60	32		
Chile	2	1.4	1	2.6	1.9		
China	32	360	590	921	1,095	1	35
Colombia	...	...	10	23	25		
Czechoslovakia	17	28	28	20	20		
France	43	37	18	13	11		
Germany	103	112	87	70	72	9	2.3
Hungary	1.2	4.2	3.1	2	1.3		
India	31	74	109	213	213	4	6.8
Indonesia	...	0.1	0.3	16	16		
Japan	34	40	18	8.3	7.6		
Kazakhstan	...	...	...	127	123		
Korea, North	2.1	24	19	48	50	10	1.6
Korea, South	0.8	12	19	15	12		
Mexico	...	...	5	13	13		
Netherlands	11	4.3	0	0	0		
Poland	70	140	193	140	132	7	4.2
Romania	2	6.4	9.7	4.4	3.2		
Russia	...	...	...	230	218		
South Africa	24	55	116	180	175	6	5.6
Spain	10	11	13	14	15		
Taiwan	1.6	4.5	2.6	0.4	0.3		
Turkey	2.7	5	6.6	5.6	5.6		
Ukraine	...	...	...	128	127		
USSR (former)	150	433	493	487	469	3	15
United Kingdom	213	145	130	96	87	8	2.8
United States	593	550	715	607	608	2	19.5
Vietnam	0.4	3	5.3	5.5	5.5		
Zimbabwe	1.7	3.4	3.1	5.2	5.2		

COAL - LIGNITE & BROWN

million tonnes

	1948	1970	1980	1991	1992	Rank	%
World	316	793	996	1,365	1,310		
Australia	6.8	24.3	32.9	48	51.1	8	3.9

DIAMONDS

thousand carats

	1948	1970	1980	1990	1991	Rank	%
World	10,270	47,634	42,000	106,700	99,200		
Angola	796	2,396	1,500	1,300	1,300	7	1.3
Australia	...	...	...	36,000	36,000	1	36.3
Botswana	...	464	5,146	17,300	16,500	3	16.6
Brazil	...	47	667	500	550	10	0.6
Central Afr. Rep.	119	494	342	500	500		
China	...	...	1,000	1,000	1,000	8	1
Ghana	786	2,550	1,149	200	200		
Guinea	80	74	38	100	100		
Guyana	37	61	10	8	20		
Liberia	...	826	298	300	300		
Namibia	201	1,865	1,560	800	1,400	6	1.4
Sierra Leone	466	2,050	592	700	600	9	0.6
South Africa	1,382	8,112	8,520	8,500	8,200	5	8.3
Tanzania	150	708	270	...	...		
USSR (former)	...	14,057	10,850	15,000	13,000	4	13.1
Venezuela	76	509	666	80	80		
Zaire	5,825	14,057	10,334	24,000	19,000	2	19.2

This table does not show synthetic diamond production.

FERTILIZERS - NITROGENOUS

thousand tonnes

	1970	1980	1990	1991	Rank	%
World	37,825	62,766	84,640	82,270		
Albania	36	73	80	73		
Algeria	50	24	88	80		
Australia	182	214	230	225		
Austria	230	300	230	227		
Bangladesh	92	161	678	654		
Belgium	641	743	678	725		
Brazil	78	384	748	737		
Bulgaria	523	730	926	915		
Canada	772	1,755	2,706	2,683	5	3.3
Chile	108	101	130	126		
China	2,245	10,286	14,515	14,915	1	18.1
Colombia	77	42	97	100		
Cuba	2	112	146	140		
Czechoslovakia	410	705	675	604		
Denmark	77	147	200	185		
Egypt	152	400	678	676		
Finland	243	266	278	268		
France	1,476	1,640	1,572	1,524	8	1.9
Germany	1,899	2,379	1,921	1,165		
Greece	240	311	407	396		
Hungary	374	651	591	470		
India	1,054	2,164	6,747	6,993	4	8.5
Indonesia	60	958	2,369	2,462	6	3
Iran	143	71	308	376		
Iraq	26	355	450	409		
Ireland	85	190	297	279		
Italy	1,046	1,335	1,169	762		
Japan	2,199	1,202	946	957		
Jordan	...	...	109	107		
Korea, North	230	553	660	660		
Korea, South	418	688	583	554		
Kuwait	270	218	386	204		
Libya	...	...	124	89		
Malaysia	31	35	249	211		
Mexico	356	739	1,498	1,366	9	1.7
Morocco	5	36	273	344		
Netherlands	1,217	1,624	1,848	1,875	7	2.3
Nigeria	...	...	272	284		
Norway	396	428	494	509		
Pakistan	274	580	1,156	1,120		
Philippines	55	34	127	121		
Poland	1,147	1,290	1,643	1,303	10	1.6
Portugal	150	172	133	126		
Qatar	...	286	350	343		
Romania	874	1,707	2,035	1,249		
Saudi Arabia	69	152	428	584		
South Africa	248	444	400	430		

	1970	1980	1990	1991	Rank	%
Spain	724	960	967	886		
Sweden	169	180	154	176		
Trinidad & Tobago	75	41	223	232		
Tunisia	...	47	206	202		
Turkey	145	672	700	947		
USSR (former)	6,533	10,155	14,272	13,094	3	15.9
United Arab Em.	...	...	266	228		
United Kingdom	751	1,167	1,070	980		
United States	8,433	11,825	12,576	13,552	2	16.5
Venezuela	10	145	370	337		
Yugoslavia	360	391	520	461		
Zimbabwe	58	72	72	83		

FERTILIZERS - PHOSPHATE

thousand tonnes

	1970	1980	1990	1991	Rank	%
World	23,673	34,515	39,733	38,906		
Algeria	38	31	45	50		
Australia	900	829	511	270		
Austria	139	105	85	70		
Bangladesh	...	33	67	51		
Belgium	780	590	333	353		
Brazil	278	1,582	1,109	1,057	6	2.7
Bulgaria	126	217	169	47		
Canada	738	724	440	348		
China	1,031	2,367	3,808	4,196	3	10.8
Colombia	40	46	39	40		
Czechoslovakia	334	361	320	290		
Denmark	97	135	136	81		
Egypt	116	106	217	182		
Finland	213	159	183	172		
France	1,611	1,351	1,025	921	7	2.4
Germany	1,395	1,056	595	294		
Greece	153	170	198	199		
Hungary	161	216	220	109		
India	330	859	1,834	2,089	4	5.4
Indonesia	...	220	551	589	9	1.5
Iran	62	30	50	81		
Iraq	...	...	415	207		
Ireland	136	44	...	...		
Israel	...	41	180	200		
Italy	500	447	266	222		
Japan	729	648	445	429		
Jordan	...	13	277	274		
Korea, North	105	127	137	137		
Korea, South	163	494	394	414		
Lebanon	42	103	15	34		
Mexico	217	201	448	498		
Morocco	154	177	934	1,180	5	3
Netherlands	351	328	378	357		
New Zealand	421	346	206	168		
Nigeria	...	5	44	50		
Norway	130	143	230	245		
Pakistan	8	58	105	105		
Philippines	42	37	191	199		
Poland	763	843	946	467		
Portugal	89	102	77	61		
Romania	313	687	648	387		
Senegal	...	25	28	50		
South Africa	340	480	375	380		
Spain	576	497	368	326		
Sweden	181	132	108	108		
Tunisia	194	408	754	657	8	1.7
Turkey	125	564	468	525	10	1.3
USSR (former)	2,784	6,023	9,015	8,961	2	23
United Kingdom	444	326	172	128		
United States	5,795	9,500	9,590	10,095	1	25.9
Venezuela	10	23	50	57		
Vietnam	42	33	55	66		
Yugoslavia	231	302	319	262		
Zimbabwe	38	42	38	41		

	1948	1970	1980	1990	1991	Rank
Venezuela	...	510	2,450	2,400	2,400	
Yugoslavia	183	1,377	2,668	2,628	1,428	
Zimbabwe	17	250	862	800	800	

GOLD

tonnes

metal content

	1948	1970	1980	1990	1991	Rank	%
World	698	1,483	1,220	1,744	1,782		
Australia	27.5	19.4	17	243	234	4	13.1
Brazil	4.1	5.6	13.8	84	80	7	4.5
Canada	110	74.9	50.6	167	177	5	9.9
Chile	5.1	2	6.8	33	33	9	1.9
China	...	...	45	95	110	6	6.2
Colombia	10.4	6.3	15.9	33	32	10	1.8
Dominican Rep.	0	0	11.5	6.5	...		
Ecuador	2.5	0.3	0.1	9.5	...		
Fiji	2.9	3.2	0.8	4.5	...		
Ghana	20.9	21.9	11	17	27		
India	5.6	3.2	2.5	1.8	1.8		
Indonesia	6.2	...	...	13	18		
Japan	3.1	3	3.2	7.5	6		
Korea, North	...	...	5	5	5		
Korea, South	0.1	1.6	1.3	12	12		
Mexico	11.4	6.2	6.1	9	9		
New Zealand	2.9	0.4	0.2	2.4	...		
Nicaragua	6.9	3.5	1.9	0.8	...		
Papua New Guinea	2.7	0.7	14.7	34	61	8	3.4
Peru	3.5	3	3.9	5.2	4		
Philippines	6.5	18.7	20	37	31		
South Africa	360	1002	673	605	601	1	33.7
Sweden	2.2	1.4	2	3.9	3.7		
Tanzania	1.8	0.2	0.3	0.2	...		
USSR (former)	...	195	260	280	242	3	13.6
United States	63	56.4	30.2	294	300	2	16.8
Yugoslavia	0.8	1.7	3.3	4.6	...		
Zaire	9.3	5.5	2.2	3.7	2.1		
Zimbabwe	16	15.6	11.4	15	15		

IRON AND FERRO-ALLOYS

thousand tonnes

	1948	1970	1980	1990	1991	Rank	%
World	113,000	436,416	520,000	543,000	500,000		
Algeria	...	409	669	1,500	1,500		
Argentina	17	847	1,095	2,100	2,000		
Australia	1,149	5,769	7,276	6,192	5,592		
Austria	613	2,970	3,493	3,444	3,400		
Belgium	3,929	10,950	9,845	9,360	8,520		
Brazil	552	4,334	14,774	21,120	23,424	6	4.7
Bulgaria	...	1,251	1,583	1,140	948		
Canada	2,140	8,424	11,185	7,344	8,268		
Chile	14	481	707	732	740		
China	...	17,060	39,014	64,548	69,480	3	13.9
Czechoslovakia	1,645	7,653	9,992	9,840	8,640		
Egypt	...	300	650	116	120		
Finland	90	1,164	2,072	2,280	2,328		
France	6,628	19,575	19,595	14,412	14,148	8	2.8
Germany	5,857	35,985	36,513	30,324	30,024	5	6
Hungary	384	1,837	2,227	1,692	1,308		
India	1,487	7,338	8,864	12,000	12,000	10	2.4
Italy	525	8,529	12,411	12,024	10,992		
Japan	836	69,728	88,907	81,360	81,144	2	16.2
Korea, North	105	2,400	5,470	6,570	7,000		
Korea, South	...	35	5,686	15,528	18,744	7	3.7
Luxembourg	2,624	4,814	3,568	2,724	2,450		
Mexico	176	2,353	5,330	3,840	3,228		
Netherlands	442	3,594	4,328	4,956	4,692		
Norway	202	1,251	1,991	900	864		
Peru	...	86	851	250	250		
Poland	1,134	7,111	11,682	8,664	6,516		
Portugal	...	314	577	336	252		
Romania	186	4,210	9,013	6,492	4,644		
South Africa	651	4,328	8,542	1,600	1,764		
Spain	537	4,278	6,725	5,748	5,400		
Sweden	804	2,842	2,612	2,736	2,808		
Turkey	100	1,176	2,048	4,824	4,500		
USSR (former)	13,742	85,933	102,960	110,796	90,948	1	18.2
United Kingdom	9,453	19,023	6,413	12,492	12,060	9	2.4
United States	56,166	85,303	63,748	54,924	48,504	4	9.7

IRON ORE

million tonnes

metal content

	1948	1970	1980	1990	1991	Rank
World	104	417	520	979	946	
Algeria	1	1.5	1.9	2.9	3	
Angola	–	3.8	–	–	–	
Argentina	–	...	...	0.8	0.7	
Australia	1.4	28.7	62.1	114	122	4	12.9
Austria	0.4	1.3	1	2.3	2	
Brazil	1.1	20.4	41.2	152	150	3	15.9
Bulgaria	–	0.8	0.5	1.1	0.6	
Canada	1.5	29.2	29.9	36.4	36.6	7	3.9
Chile	1.7	6.9	5.4	7.8	8.7	
China	...	24.2	32.5	169	176	2	18.6
Colombia	–	0.5	0.2	0.6	0.6	
Czechoslovakia	0.4	0.4	0.5	1.8	1.8	
Egypt	...	0.2	0.8	1.2	...	
Finland	...	...	0.6	–	–	
France	7.6	17.8	9	8.7	7.5	
Germany	1.8	1.8	0.5	–	–	
India	1.5	19.7	25.8	53.7	54.7	6	5.8
Iran	...	...	...	5.5	5.5	
Italy	0.3	0.4	–	–	–	
Japan	0.3	0.9	0.3	...	...	
Korea, North	–	4	3.7	9.5	9.5	
Liberia	–	15.4	12.5	3	1.2	
Luxembourg	1	1.6	0.3	–	–	
Malaysia	...	0.5	0.3	0.3	...	
Mauritania	...	5.9	5.6	11.4	10	
Mexico	0.2	2.6	5.2	8.3	7.8	
Morocco	0.7	0.5	0.1	...	...	
New Zealand	...	...	...	1.3	1.3	
Norway	0.1	2.6	2.5	2.1	2.3	
Peru	–	6.1	3.4	3.5	3.8	
Poland	0.2	0.7	0.1	...	...	
Romania	0.1	0.9	0.6	0.6	0.3	
Sierra Leone	0.6	1.4	0.2	...	...	
South Africa	0.7	5.9	16.4	30.3	28.9	8	3.1
Spain	0.8	3.5	4.4	3	3.9	
Swaziland	...	1.5	–	–	–	
Sweden	8.2	19.8	17	19.9	19.3	10	2
Tunisia	0.4	0.4	0.2	...	...	
Turkey	0.1	1.7	1.4	6.2	5.4	
USSR (former)	16.2	106	148	236	198	1	20.9
United Kingdom	3.9	3.4	0.3	–	–	
United States	50.9	53.3	43.9	56.4	55.5	5	5.9
Venezuela	–	14.1	10.4	20.1	19.9	9	2.1
Yugoslavia	0.4	1.3	1.6	4.1	2.6	
Zimbabwe	0.2	0.3	0.9	0.6	0.6	

LEAD ORE

thousand tonnes

metal content

	1948	1970	1980	1990	1991	Rank	%
World	1,370	3,400	3,600	3,345	3,341		
Algeria	1.2	8.4	2.1	1.1	4		
Argentina	17.8	36	33	23.4	24.2		
Australia	220	459	397	561	579	1	17.3
Austria	3.5	6	5	1.5	1.2		
Bolivia	25.6	26	17	19.9	20.8		
Brazil	...	18	22	9.2	8.6		
Bulgaria	12.9	96	100	45.2	40.6		
Burma	–	4	6	2.3	2.7		
Canada	172	358	297	241	278	5	8.3
Chile	6.2	1	0	1.1	1.1		
China	...	100	160	315	320	4	9.6
Congo	2.7	...	2.5	–	–		

	1948	1970	1980	1990	1991	Rank	%
hoslovakia	...	7	3	3	3.4		
ce	7.7	29	29	1.2	1.7		
nany	22.4	41	32	8.6	7.3		
ce	1.2	10	22	26.2	31.7		
nland	–	...	30	16.7	–		
duras	0.1	15	14	4.2	8.7		
a	0.4	3	14	25.9	27.8		
	...	23	12	9.3	15.1		
nd	...	63	58	35.3	39.9		
	30.4	35	24	15.6	14		
an	6.7	64	43	18.7	18.3		
ea, North	...	70	100	70	80	10	2.4
ea, South	0.3	11	11	18.7	15		
ico	193	177	145	187	168	7	5
occo	28.8	85	115	66.9	71.2		
ibia	33.6	71	48	19.4	16.1		
way	0.3	3	2	3	3.5		
u	48.5	157	189	188	200	6	6
and	14.5	157	189	45.4	47		
nania	4	42	23	24.7	16.2		
th Africa	0.1	...	86	69.4	76.3		
in	31.2	60	87	61.5	49.2		
eden	23.6	78	72	84.2	87	8	2.6
iland	–	1	11	22	16.7		
isia	13.2	22	9	1.8	0.8		
key	2.6	5	8	12.3	15.3		
SR (former)	...	450	580	490	460	3	13.8
ted States	2.3	4	4	...	...		
ited States	354	519	550	497	477	2	14.3
goslavia	62.3	127	121	83	84.5	9	2.5
mbia	13.2	33	14	11.5	9.8		

	1948	1970	1980	1990	1991	Rank	%
Germany	...	68	190	–	–		
Italy	1,318	1,530	3	–	–		
Japan	50	58	222	–	–		
Mexico	165	1,043	145	735	720	3	19.7
Spain	782	1,570	1,721	962	52	7	1.4
Turkey	1	324	154	47	25	10	0.7
USSR (former)	...	1,655	1,800	1,400	1,200	1	32.9
United States	496	941	1,058	500	40	8	1.1
Yugoslavia	377	533	–	37	35	9	1

NATURAL GAS

*thousand terajoules**

	1970	1980	1990	1991	1992	Rank	%
World	38,455	53,938	74,806	76,275	76,600		
Afghanistan	95	102	110	...	...		
Algeria	64	759	1,615	1,714	1,750	7	2.3
Argentina	209	326	793	886	925		
Australia	56	359	784	908	922		
Austria	77	78	46	48	52		
Azerbaijan	...	...	323	280	260		
Bahrain	14	114	201	202	163		
Bangladesh	0	45	165	174	186		
Bolivia	1	80	107	107	100		
Brazil	3	41	147	146	155		
Brunei	8	399	414	425	433		
Burma	2.2	13.3	90	85	...		
Canada	2,113	2,790	4,114	4,370	4,760	3	6.2
Chile	48.1	27.1	9.3	7.6	...		
China	144	555	593	599	601		
Colombia	55.2	151	275	279	275		
Egypt	3	41	240	275	297		
France	271	289	111	139	134		
Germany	479	774	530	613	572		
Hungary	114	237	183	184	173		
India	19	51	441	519	520		
Indonesia	46	607	1,578	1,819	1,900	6	2.5
Iran	45	278	934	999	961		
Iraq	30.5	50	392	61.1	...		
Ireland	–	34	92	95	93		
Italy	498	477	648	646	638		
Japan	10	85	84	88	89		
Kazakhstan	...	...	240	260	180		
Kuwait	80	133	498	19	97		
Libya	79.6	134	225	220	230		
Malaysia	3	10	502	626	667		
Mexico	451	1,035	955	948	1,000		
Netherlands	1,116	3,205	2,286	2,286	2,301	4	3
New Zealand	4	39	192	207	222		
Nigeria	4	52	145	111	120		
Norway	–	1,065	1,121	1,134	1,150	9	1.5
Pakistan	96	246	490	523	543		
Poland	186	193	134	130	126		
Qatar	39.1	176	260	310	...		
Romania	990	1,455	959	989	880		
Russia	...	...	21,000	21,000	20,900		
Saudi Arabia	...	49	1,101	1,452	1,500	8	2
Thailand	...	–	234	254	315		
Trinidad & Tobago	73	146	215	242	242		
Turkmenistan	...	...	2,800	2,800	2,000		
Ukraine	...	...	925	800	680		
USSR (former)	6,670	15,148	26,600	26,500	25,500	1	33.3
United Arab Em.	8.9	471	1840	1920	...		
United Kingdom	434	1,454	1,903	1,955	1,972	5	2.6
United States	22,860	19,256	19,373	19,509	19,322	2	25.2
Uzbekistan	...	...	1,300	1,400	1,400		
Venezuela	382	643	955	1,053	1,050	10	1.4
Yugoslavia	39	75	82	60	59		

* A terajoule is a measure of energy equivalent to 23.88 tonnes of oil or 34.12 tonnes of coal.

MANGANESE ORE

onnes

	1948	1970	1980	1990	1991	Rank	%
orld	2,100	7,400	12,786	24,000	22,000		
ngola	0	9	–	–	–		
gentina	1	10	2	2	...		
ustralia	2	397	969	2,300	1,450	6	6.6
otswana	–	16	–	–	–		
azil	79	830	1,027	1,850	2,000	4	9.1
ile	11	11	11	30	30		
ina	...	300	480	2,700	2,700	3	12.3
echoslovakia	...	14	0	0	...		
abon	...	729	1,073	2,200	1,800	5	8.2
hana	314	191	100	260	320	8	1.5
ungary	20	35	25	80	80	10	0.4
dia	255	616	592	1,300	1,300	7	5.9
aly	7	15	3	9	...		
apan	19	79	28	...	...		
exico	24	99	161	450	250	9	1.1
orocco	85	60	65	30	30		
hilippines	12	3	1	1	...		
omania	18	27	18	65	65		
outh Africa	116	1,182	4,743	3,795	3,200	2	14.5
pain	7	4	–	–	...		
hailand	...	8	24	8	...		
urkey	4	6	17	7	...		
USA	69	47	21	4	...		
JSSR (former)	...	...	6,000	9,000	8,000	1	36.4
anuatu	–	12	–	–	...		
ugoslavia	4	5	10	40	40		
aire	6	156	3	...	...		

MERCURY

tonnes

	1948	1970	1980	1990	1991	Rank	%
World	3,250	8,810	6,818	5,514	3,652		
Algeria	0	0	841	637	431	4	11.8
China	...	690	800	930	1,000	2	27.4
Czechoslovakia	–	17	159	126	75	5	2.1
Finland	...	3	75	140	74	6	2

NICKEL ORE

thousand tonnes

metal content

	1948	1970	1980	1990	1991	Rank	%
World	144	651	738	881	871		
Albania	...	...	4.8	8.5	4		
Australia	–	18	74.3	67	69	4	7.9
Botswana	–	–	15.4	19.7	20.4	10	2.3
Brazil	–	2.9	4.3	13	13.5		
Canada	120	278	185	196	197	2	22.6
China	–	–	11	26	25	9	2.9
Colombia	–	–	–	18.4	20.2		
Cuba	2.1	35.2	38.2	40.8	33.3	6	3.8
Dominican Rep.	–	–	18	28.7	29.1	7	3.3
Finland	...	6.7	6.4	11.5	9.1		
Germany	...	...	2.7	0.9	–		
Greece	–	–	13.9	18.5	18		
Indonesia	–	18	40.5	68.6	66.1	5	7.6
New Caledonia	3.6	138	86.6	85	99.7	3	11.4
Norway	–	–	0.6	2.2	2.3		
Philippines	...	...	34.9	15.8	13.8		
Poland	–	2	1.1	–	–		
South Africa	0.5	11.6	25.7	30	29	8	3.3
USSR (former)	17.5	109	143	212	200	1	23
United States	0.8	17	10.2	0.3	5.5		
Yugoslavia	–	–	0.5	4.9	3.2		
Zimbabwe	0	10.9	14.3	12.6	12.4		

OIL - CRUDE

million tonnes

	1948	1970	1980	1990	1991	1992	Rank	%
World	469	2,244	2,829	3,158	3,133	3,170		
Algeria	–	51.2	50.6	55.2	56.4	57		
Angola	–	4.5	7.5	24.1	25	27		
Argentina	3.3	19.1	24.2	24	24	27.9		
Australia	–	8.7	18.9	28.5	27.2	24.7		
Azerbaijan	...	...	...	12.5	12	11.9		
Bahrain	–	3.8	2.4	2.1	2.1	1.9		
Brazil	–	8	9.1	33	32.7	32.5		
Brunei	2.7	7.4	11.5	7	8	9		
Cameroon	–	0.1	2.9	7.9	7.5	7		
Canada	1.7	62.9	70.3	93.7	93.9	98.2	10	3.1
China	0.1	24.9	106	138	139	142	6	4.5
Colombia	3.3	10.7	6.2	21.9	21.2	22.2		
Congo	–	–	2.8	7.6	7.5	8		
Denmark	–	–	0.3	5.9	7.4	7.8		
Ecuador	0.3	0.2	11.1	15	15.5	16.7		
Egypt	2.1	16.3	29.7	45.5	46	46.1		
France	0.1	2.3	1.3	3	2.8	2.9		
Gabon	–	5.4	9	13.6	14.8	14.7		
Germany	0.6	7.3	4.5	3.6	3.4	3.2		
India	0.3	6.9	9.1	33.9	31.9	28.7		
Indonesia	4.3	42.5	78.5	70.1	72.9	74.3		
Iran	25.3	166	73	155	162	172	4	5.4
Iraq	3.4	77.1	131	98.2	11.3	23.6		
Italy	–	1.5	1.8	4.8	4.4	4.6		
Kazakhstan	–	–	27	27	28	27		
Kuwait	6.4	136	68.8	51.8	4.4	45.6		
Libya	–	165	88.9	64.8	72.2	73		
Malaysia	–	–	14.3	30.6	32.1	32.6		
Mexico	8.4	21.4	95.4	142	149	155	5	4.9
Netherlands	0.5	1.8	1.2	3.9	3.6	3.3		
Nigeria	–	53.9	102	87.8	93.6	91.6		
Norway	–	–	26.3	81.9	93.4	107	9	3.4
Oman	–	16.6	14.1	34.1	35.3	36.1		
Pakistan	–	0.5	0.5	2.9	3.5	3.5		
Peru	1.9	3.6	9.5	7	6	6		
Qatar	–	18	23.5	21.2	20.5	22.6		
Romania	4.1	13.4	12.4	7.9	6.5	6.6		
Russia	...	...	582	544	485	396		
Saudi Arabia	19.1	177	480	326	419	428	2	13.5
Syria	–	4.1	8.2	21	24.5	25.2		
Trinidad & Tobago	2.9	7	10.5	7.4	7.3	7.2		
Tunisia	–	4.4	5.5	4.5	5.1	5.3		
Turkey	–	3.4	2.2	3.8	4.4	4.3		
USSR (former)	29.2	353	603	570	515	450	1	
United Arab Em.	–	96.7	85.1	109	124	118	8	
United Kingdom	0.2	0.1	80.6	91.6	91.6	94.2		
United States	273	480	427	420	424	417	3	
Venezuela	71.7	185	108	123	136	129	7	
Vietnam	–	–	–	2.5	3.8	5.4		
Yemen	–	–	4.2	9.5	10.9	9.1		
Yugoslavia	–	2.9	4.2	3.1	2.9	...		

PETROLEUM PRODUCTS*

million tonnes

	1970	1980	1990	1991	Rank	%
World	2,032	2,762	3,500	3,400		
Algeria	2.3	13	38	38		
Argentina	19.4	23.7	18.6	18.8		
Australia	22.1	28.2	26.1	25.8		
Austria	5.5	8.8	7.4	7.2		
Bahamas	2.3	8.3	...	...		
Bahrain	11.2	10.6	11	11		
Belgium	26	29.5	22.6	25.8		
Brazil	23.5	47.7	44	41.9		
Bulgaria	5.8	11.7	10	10		
Canada	57.4	98.3	64	61.6	9	
Chile	3.6	5	5.4	5.5		
China	21.8	64.2	84.5	87.8	4	
Colombia	6.2	7.7	10	10.8		
Cuba	4.2	5.5	6.5	6.5		
Czechoslovakia	8.7	16.1	9.7	8.5		
Denmark	9.4	6.2	7.2	7.6		
Ecuador	1.1	4.5	5.8	5.9		
Egypt	3.2	13.4	21.7	22.3		
Finland	7	10.9	8.7	9.2		
France	88.5	103	63.1	21.2		
Germany	105.1	115.8	82.2	83	5	2
Greece	4.6	13.1	14.7	13.3		2
Hungary	5	8.9	6	5.8		
India	14.3	19.4	37.2	36.9		
Indonesia	10.4	23.8	31.5	32.2		
Iran	24.2	32.9	33.5	35.7		
Iraq	3.3	8.2	15.8	11.9		
Israel	5	5.6	7	7		
Italy	104	85.4	76.5	77.4	7	2
Japan	...	185	137	147	3	4
Korea, South	8.8	22	33.2	44.5		
Kuwait	17	17.8	24	5		
Libya	0.4	5.3	12.3	12.5		
Malaysia	4	5.6	8.9	8.9		
Mexico	21.1	56.1	58	60.8	10	1
Morocco	1.4	3.8	4.5	4.4		
Netherlands	51.6	51.9	43.3	46.2		
Neths. Antilles	45.6	26.1	10	10		
New Zealand	2.7	2.7	3.6	3.4		
Nigeria	0.9	6.2	11.6	11.3		
Norway	5.5	7.5	11.3	10.7		
Pakistan	4	3.9	5.1	5.9		
Peru	4.1	7.2	7.5	7.5		
Philippines	8.1	8.8	9.9	9.3		
Poland	6.1	12.8	9.8	9.3		
Portugal	3.3	7.1	9.4	8.5		
Puerto Rico	9.4	10.2	4.5	4.5		
Romania	14	24.6	19.6	12.4		
Saudi Arabia	25.5	36.9	62.9	65.6	8	1.9
Singapore	10.7	25.1	30	30		
South Africa	7.7	12.7	14	14		
Spain	29.3	44.2	42.1	43.7		
Sweden	10.4	16.7	15.6	13.9		
Switzerland	4.9	4.4	2.7	4.2		
Syria	1.7	5.1	10.8	11.2		
Taiwan	5.9	20.3	20	20		
Thailand	3.2	7.2	12	12		
Trinidad & Tobago	21.7	11.5	4.3	5.3		
Turkey	6.8	11.4	19.2	19		
USSR (former)	246	396	450	450	2	13.2
United Arab Em.	0	...	15	13		
United Kingdom	90.6	77.6	75.8	78.8	6	2.3
United States	496	677	572	571	1	16.8
US Virgin Is.	13.1	22.5	11	11		
Venezuela	60.6	46.3	44.1	48.7		

	1970	1980	1990	1991	Rank	%
...men	6.3	1.9	3.5	3.5		
...oslavia	6.4	13.7	11	9.5		

...he principal products are aviation gasolene, fuel oils, diesel oil, jet fuel, ...osene liquefied petroleum gas, motor gasolene and residual fuel oil.

	1948	1970	1980	1990	1991	Rank	%
United Kingdom	1,176	1,237	244	284	265		
United States	126	338	558	18	63		
Yugoslavia	6	393	123	798	691	6	4.3

RUBBER - SYNTHETIC

...ousand tonnes

	1960	1970	1980	1990	1991	Rank	%
...rld	2,439	5,055	6,515	7,300	7,000		
...gentina	...	39	33.4	57.6	44.76		
...stralia	11.4	41.9	46.2	41	37		
...lgium	0	50	115	125	114		
...azil	10.1	96.4	287	252	232	8	3.3
...lgaria	0	6	30	...	...		
...nada	168	218	256	213	160		
...ina	...	...	250	315	335	5	4.8
...echoslovakia	0	64.2	79.3	69	43		
...nland	...	...	...	29	30		
...ance	17.5	343	528	520	469	4	6.7
...ermany	218	442	540	524	504	3	7.2
...dia	0	30.3	22.5	52	55		
...aly	67	155	250	300	300	6	4.3
...apan	18.6	760	1,161	1,426	1,368	2	19.5
...orea, South	0	5.1	75.5	184	181	10	2.6
...exico	43.7	90.8	132	119	107		
...etherlands	12	200	212	240	223	9	3.2
...oland	20.2	61.7	118	103	79		
...omania	...	61.2	150	102	61		
...outh Africa	0	28.6	38.7	46	36		
...pain	...	38.6	81.1	66	63		
...weden	...	7.8	13.2	...	...		
...urkey	0	0	23	39	34		
...nited Kingdom	138	345	227	298	274	7	3.9
...nited States	1,757	2,436	2,302	2,114	2,190	1	31.3
...ugoslavia	0	6.2	7.4	...	...		

SILVER

tonnes

metal content

	1948	1970	1980	1990	1991	Rank	%
World	5,000	9,393	11,101	14,834	14,241		
Argentina	212	64	73	76	70		
Australia	313	855	767	1,143	1,180	6	8.3
Bolivia	235	186	190	311	337	9	2.4
Brazil	...	11	45	60	50		
Bulgaria	...	...	24	54	37.3		
Burma	14	17	30	3.4	5.3		
Canada	529	1,376	1,070	1,502	1,338	4	9.4
Chile	27	74	299	655	674	8	4.7
China	...	25	60	150	180		
Czechoslovakia	...	...	35	26	28		
Dominican Rep.	...	...	48	22.9	22		
Finland	5	23	48	30	30.3		
France	15	150	74	20.5	23.6		
Germany	94	205	85	28	7.2		
Greece	1	...	60	63	70		
Honduras	100	119	22	31	43		
India	0.4	2	11	32.2	31.9		
Indonesia	...	9	22	67	80		
Iran	...	...	...	38	48		
Ireland	...	62	20	8.8	10.5		
Italy	21	33	43	11	13.6		
Japan	94	343	268	150	171		
Korea, North	...	22	290	280	300	10	2.1
Korea, South	1	53	63	16.4	3		
Malaysia	...	...	22	12.6	13.4		
Mexico	1,789	1,332	1,557	2,399	2,290	1	16.1
Morocco	15	21	98	241	234		
Namibia	12	38	105	93	92		
New Zealand	7	...	23	4.8	11		
Nicaragua	...	7	16	1.1	1		
Papua New Guinea	1	1	37	115	125		
Peru	289	1,239	1,315	1,781	1,769	3	12.4
Philippines	6	53	61	45.1	34.9		
Poland	...	...	766	832	867	7	6.1
Portugal	...	...	2	43	42.6		
Romania	20	25	28	24	17		
South Africa	36	110	232	161	171		
Spain	11	51	178	270	208		
Sweden	35	123	166	225	253		
Thailand	...	...	...	20.5	20		
USSR (former)	...	1,182	1,550	1,380	1,270	5	8.9
United States	1,220	1,400	1,006	2,125	1,848	2	13
Yugoslavia	47	106	149	105	92		
Zaire	118	53	79	84	50		
Zambia	5	48	24	18.5	14.2		
Zimbabwe	3	2	30	21.2	20.3		

SHIPS

Merchant vessels launched

thousand gross registered tons

	1948	1970	1980	1990	1991	Rank	%
World	2,308	21,690	15,397	14,680	15,897		
Argentina	0	18	60	37	53		
Australia	9	54	8	30	15		
Belgium	52	155	99	110	120		
Brazil	0	100	615	698	669	8	4.2
Bulgaria	...	53	152	129	132		
Canada	102	33	80	1	15		
China	...	...	...	340	495		
Denmark	99	514	227	108	82		
Egypt	...	9	6	20	11		
Finland	7	222	198	350	314		
France	138	960	328	182	155		
Germany	...	2,021	802	502	780	4	4.9
Greece	...	73	22	19	21		
India	...	29	74	144	147		
Indonesia	...	...	...	15	67		
Ireland	0	28	7	...	...		
Italy	112	598	168	826	680	7	4.3
Japan	...	10,476	7,288	5,030	5,245	1	33
Korea, South	...	...	629	1,795	2,422	2	15.2
Netherlands	142	461	125	137	105		
Norway	47	639	319	111	99		
Peru	...	35	17	14	15		
Poland	5	463	395	425	603	10	3.8
Portugal	4	16	167	24	96		
Romania	...	...	31	...	1,033	3	6.5
Singapore	...	6	27	102	97		
Spain	22	524	509	482	651	9	4.1
Sweden	246	1,711	338	40	41		
Taiwan	0	217	572	1,211	741	5	4.7
Turkey	...	11	14	207	205		

STEEL

thousand tonnes

	1948	1970	1980	1991	1992	Rank	%
World	155,800	593,791	690,000	730,000	710,000		
Argentina	122	1,859	2,556	2,976	2,700		
Australia	1,245	6,874	7,895	6,216	6,456		
Austria	648	4,079	4,624	4,404	3,900		
Belgium	6,373	12,609	12,321	11,292	10,332		
Brazil	483	5,390	7,940	22,608	23,904	9	3.4
Bulgaria	0	1,800	2,565	1,620	1,600		
Canada	2,903	11,198	15,901	23,844	25,992	7	3.7
Chile	30	547	695	804	810		
China	800	17,790	37,120	70,560	82,000	4	11.5
Czechoslovakia	2,621	11,480	15,225	12,072	10,900		
Denmark	...	...	734	636	588		
Egypt	0	304	500	2,600	2,500		

	1948	1970	1980	1991	1992	Rank	%
Finland	103	1,167	2,509	2,892	3,084		
France	7,236	23,773	23,176	18,432	18,000		
Germany	5,866	5,093	51,146	38,784	36,876	5	5.2
Greece	...	435	935	984	1,000		
Hungary	770	3,108	3,766	1,860	1,560		
India	1,277	6,286	9,427	16,392	18,100	10	2.5
Indonesia	...	...	360	3,000	3,100		
Iran	...	...	565	2,200	2,900		
Italy	2,125	17,277	26,501	25,032	24,800	8	3.5
Japan	1,715	93,322	111,395	109,644	98,100	2	13.8
Korea, North	115	2,200	3,500	7,000	7,000		
Korea, South	8	481	5,760	26,808	27,800	6	3.9
Luxembourg	2,624	5,462	4,620	3,384	3,072		
Mexico	292	3,846	7,003	7,716	8,400		
Netherlands	334	5,042	4,959	5,172	5,436		
Norway	74	869	853	444	456		
Poland	1,955	11,750	18,648	10,440	11,000		
Portugal	...	...	382	576	600		
Romania	353	6,517	13,175	7,116	5,300		
Saudi Arabia	...	...	50	1,800	1,900		
South Africa	596	4,674	8,976	8,940	9,200		
Spain	624	7,394	12,563	12,564	12,600		
Sweden	1,276	5,494	4,231	4,236	4,416		
Switzerland	120	524	929	1,000	1,000		
Taiwan	18	607	3,651	11,000	10,800		
Turkey	102	1,312	1,700	9,300	10,344		
USSR (former)	18,639	115,889	147,941	139,920	112,000	1	15.8
United Kingdom	15,116	28,316	11,277	16,632	16,100		
United States	80,413	119,309	101,456	87,444	91,596	3	12.9
Venezuela	...	927	1,784	3,108	3,400		
Yugoslavia	368	2,228	2,306	4,500	4,500		
Zimbabwe	9	250	804	1,000	1,000		

URANIUM

tonnes

metal content

	1970	1980	1991	1992	Rank	
World	24,000	52,000	62,000	60,000		
Argentina	50	242	10	10		
Australia	299	1,561	3,500	3,750	3	
Belgium	...	...	40	20		
Bulgaria	...	...	400	100		
Canada	3,639	6,739	8,200	9,250	1	15
China	...	...	1,250	1,250	10	2
Czechoslovakia	...	...	1,750	1,500	8	2
France	1,476	2,845	2,500	2,100	5	3
Gabon	472	1,034	700	500		
Germany	0	41	1,100	250		
Hungary	...	...	400	425		
India	0	150	210	220		
Namibia	0	4,036	2,450	1,500	8	2
Niger	54	4,132	3,000	3,000	4	
Portugal	95	68	60	40		
Romania	...	...	100	200		
South Africa	3,737	6,186	1,700	1,750	6	2
Spain	60	167	200	175		
USSR (former)	...	...	10,000	8,200	2	13.
United States	11,538	16,800	3,000	1,750	7	2

TIN ORE

thousand tonnes

metal content

	1948	1970	1980	1990	1991	Rank	%
World	154	186	236	209	179		
Argentina	0.3	2.3	0.4	0.1	–		
Australia	1.9	8.9	11.6	7.4	5.7	9	3.2
Bolivia	38	30.1	27.5	17.3	16.8	5	9.3
Brazil	0.2	4.3	6.9	39.1	29.3	3	16.4
Burma	1.2	0.3	1.1	0.5	0.5		
Canada	0.3	0.1	6.9	3.8	4.5	10	2.5
China	4.9	...	16	35.8	33.7	1	18.8
Czechoslovakia	...	0.2	0.2	0.3	–		
Germany	0.2	...	1.8	1.8	–		
Indonesia	31.1	19.1	32.5	30.2	30.1	2	16.8
Japan	0.1	0.8	0.5	–	–		
Laos	0	1.4	0.6	0.3	0.2		
Malaysia	45.5	73.8	61.4	28.5	20.7	4	11.6
Mexico	0.2	0.5	0.1	–	–		
Mongolia	0	0	0	0.2	0.3		
Namibia	0.1	1	1	0.9	–		
Nigeria	9.4	8	2.7	0.2	0.2		
Peru	0.1	0	1.1	5.1	6.6	8	3.7
Portugal	0.7	0.4	0.3	1.4	3.1		
Rwanda	1.4	1.3	1.6	0.7	0.7		
South Africa	0.5	2	2.9	1.1	1		
Spain	0.3	0.4	0.4	0.1	–		
Thailand	4.3	21.8	33.7	14.6	10.9	7	6.1
USSR (former)	...	...	16	13	11	6	6.1
United Kingdom	0.9	1.7	3.3	3.4	2.3		
United States	...	...	16	0.1	0.1		
Vietnam	...	...	0.4	0.8	0.8		
Zaire	11.7	6.5	3.2	1.6	–		
Zimbabwe	0.1	0.6	0.9	0.8	0.8		

ZINC ORE

thousand tonnes

metal content

	1948	1970	1980	1990	1991	Rank	%
World	1,790	5,520	6,192	7,366	7,513		
Algeria	6	17	8	4	3.5		
Argentina	13	39	34	38.7	39.1		
Australia	194	496	495	939	1,048	2	13.9
Austria	3	16	22	16.7	14.8		
Bolivia	21	47	50	108	130		
Brazil	...	12	70	113	103		
Bulgaria	9.7	76	89	34.7	29.1		
Canada	252	1,239	1,059	1,203	1,148	1	15.3
Chile	...	1	1	25.1	31		
China	...	106	180	619	710	4	9.5
Czechoslovakia	...	...	7	7.4	7.8		
Finland	8	69	58	51.7	55.5		
France	6	19	37	23.9	27.1		
Germany	29	127	121	58.1	54		
Greece	3	9	27	26.7	30		
Greenland	0	0	86	48	...		
Honduras	...	5	16	29.3	38.3		
India	...	8	32	70	105		
Iran	...	58	30	14.8	31.1		
Ireland	...	97	229	167	188	10	2.5
Italy	74	110	57	42.4	37.1		
Japan	33	280	238	127	133		
Korea, North	13	130	130	195	215	9	2.9
Korea, South	...	23	56	22.8	22.6		
Mexico	179	266	243	307	317	7	4.2
Morocco	2	16	6	18.4	23.6		
Namibia	12	46	32	37.7	33.1		
Norway	6	10	28	16.7	18.9		
Peru	59	321	468	584	628	5	8.4
Philippines	0	3	9	...	...		
Poland	96	242	217	155	145		
Romania	...	...	40	35.6	25.9		
South Africa	...	...	82	74.8	64.4		
Spain	47	98	179	258	261	8	3.5
Sweden	36	93	167	160	158		
Thailand	...	0.5	1	80.8	86.9		
Tunisia	2	12	9	7.3	5.1		
Turkey	2	24	23	39.1	32.5		
USSR (former)	...	610	1,000	870	800	3	10.6
United States	572	485	349	543	547	6	7.3
Vietnam	...	...	10	10	15		
Yugoslavia	37	101	95	76	74		
Zaire	47	104	67	61.8	45		
Zambia	23	66	43	35.4	24.8		

WORLD
ALMANAC

PHYSICAL DIMENSIONS

Each topic list is divided into continents and within a continent the items are listed in order of size. T sequence of the continents is Europe, Asia, Africa, Australasia, North America and South Ameri All major features are listed. The world top ten are shown in square brackets; in the case of mountains t has not been done because the world top 30 are all in Asia. The figures are rounded as appropriate.

WORLD, CONTINENTS, OCEANS

	km²	miles²	%
The World	509,450,000	196,672,000	–
Land	149,450,000	57,688,000	29.3
Water	360,000,000	138,984,000	70.7
Asia	44,500,000	17,177,000	29.8
Africa	30,302,000	11,697,000	20.3
North America	24,241,000	9,357,000	16.2
South America	17,793,000	6,868,000	11.9
Antarctica	14,100,000	5,443,000	9.4
Europe	9,957,000	3,843,000	6.7
Australia & Oceania	8,557,000	3,303,000	5.7
Pacific Ocean	179,679,000	69,356,000	49.9
Atlantic Ocean	92,373,000	35,657,000	25.7
Indian Ocean	73,917,000	28,532,000	20.5
Arctic Ocean	14,090,000	5,439,000	3.9

SEAS

Pacific	km²	miles²
South China Sea	2,974,600	1,148,500
Bering Sea	2,268,000	875,000
Sea of Okhotsk	1,528,000	590,000
East China & Yellow	1,249,000	482,000
Sea of Japan	1,008,000	389,000
Gulf of California	162,000	62,500
Bass Strait	75,000	29,000

Atlantic	km²	miles²
Caribbean Sea	2,766,000	1,068,000
Mediterranean Sea	2,516,000	971,000
Gulf of Mexico	1,543,000	596,000
Hudson Bay	1,232,000	476,000
North Sea	575,000	223,000
Black Sea	462,000	178,000
Baltic Sea	422,170	163,000
Gulf of St Lawrence	238,000	92,000

Indian	km²	miles²
Red Sea	438,000	169,000
The Gulf	239,000	92,000

MOUNTAINS

Europe		m	ft
Mont Blanc	France/Italy	4,807	15,771
Monte Rosa	Italy/Switzerland	4,634	15,203
Dom	Switzerland	4,545	14,911
Weisshorn	Switzerland	4,505	14,780
Matterhorn/Cervino	Italy/Switzerland	4,478	14,691
Mt Maudit	France/Italy	4,465	14,649
Finsteraarhorn	Switzerland	4,274	14,022
Aletschhorn	Switzerland	4,182	13,720
Jungfrau	Switzerland	4,158	13,642
Barre des Ecrins	France	4,103	13,461
Schreckhorn	Switzerland	4,078	13,380
Gran Paradiso	Italy	4,061	13,323

		m	ft
Piz Bernina	Italy/Switzerland	4,049	13,284
Ortles	Italy	3,899	12,792
Monte Viso	Italy	3,841	12,602
Grossglockner	Austria	3,797	12,457
Wildspitze	Austria	3,774	12,382
Weisskügel	Austria/Italy	3,736	12,257
Balmhorn	Switzerland	3,709	12,169
Dammastock	Switzerland	3,630	11,909
Tödi	Switzerland	3,620	11,877
Presanella	Italy	3,556	11,667
Monte Adamello	Italy	3,554	11,660
Mulhacén	Spain	3,478	11,411
Pico de Aneto	Spain	3,404	11,168
Posets	Spain	3,375	11,073
Marmolada	Italy	3,342	10,964
Etna	Italy	3,340	10,958
Musala	Bulgaria	2,925	9,596
Olympus	Greece	2,917	9,570
Gerlachovka	Slovak Republic	2,655	8,711
Galdhöpiggen	Norway	2,469	8,100
Pietrosul	Romania	2,305	7,562
Hvannadalshnúkur	Iceland	2,119	6,952
Narodnaya	Russia	1,894	6,214
Ben Nevis	UK	1,343	4,406

Asia		m	ft
Everest	China/Nepal	8,848	29,029
Godwin Austen (K2)	China/Kashmir	8,611	28,251
Kanchenjunga	India/Nepal	8,598	28,208
Lhotse	China/Nepal	8,516	27,939
Makalu	China/Nepal	8,481	27,824
Cho Oyu	China/Nepal	8,201	26,906
Dhaulagiri	Nepal	8,172	26,811
Manaslu	Nepal	8,156	26,758
Nanga Parbat	Kashmir	8,126	26,660
Annapurna	Nepal	8,078	26,502
Gasherbrum	China/Kashmir	8,068	26,469
Broad Peak	China/Kashmir	8,051	26,414
Gosainthan	China	8,012	26,286
Disteghil Sar	Kashmir	7,885	25,869
Nuptse	Nepal	7,879	25,849
Masherbrum	Kashmir	7,821	25,659
Nanda Devi	India	7,817	25,646
Rakaposhi	Kashmir	7,788	25,551
Kanjut Sar	India	7,760	25,459
Kamet	India	7,756	25,446
Namcha Barwa	China	7,756	25,446
Gurla Mandhata	China	7,728	25,354
Muztag	China	7,723	25,338
Kongur Shan	China	7,719	25,324
Tirich Mir	Pakistan	7,690	25,229
Saser	Kashmir	7,672	25,170
K'ula Shan	Bhutan/China	7,543	24,747
Pik Kommunizma	Tajikistan	7,495	24,590
Aling Gangri	China	7,314	23,996
Elbrus	Russia	5,642	18,501
Demavend	Iran	5,604	18,386
Ararat	Turkey	5,165	16,945
Gunong Kinabalu	Malaysia (Borneo)	4,101	13,455
Yu Shan	Taiwan	3,997	13,113
Fuji-san	Japan	3,776	12,388
Rinjani	Indonesia	3,726	12,224
Mt Rajang	Philippines	3,364	11,037
Pidurutalagala	Sri Lanka	2,524	8,281

~ica		m	ft
~manjaro	Tanzania	5,895	19,340
. Kenya	Kenya	5,199	17,057
wenzori	Uganda/Zaïre	5,109	16,762
s Dashan	Ethiopia	4,620	15,157
~ru	Tanzania	4,565	14,977
risimbi	Rwanda/Zaïre	4,507	14,787
: Elgon	Kenya/Uganda	4,321	14,176
tu	Ethiopia	4,307	14,130
~na	Ethiopia	4,231	13,882
~ubkal	Morocco	4,165	13,665
~il Mgoun	Morocco	4,071	13,356
: Cameroon	Cameroon	4,070	13,353
~nba Ferit	Ethiopia	3,875	13,042
~ide	Spain (Tenerife)	3,718	12,198
~abana Ntlenyana	Lesotho	3,482	11,424
~ni Kussi	Chad	3,415	11,204
t aux Sources	Lesotho/S. Africa	3,282	10,768
~t Piton	Réunion	3,069	10,069

~ceania		m	ft
~ncak Jaya	Indonesia	5,029	16,499
~ncak Trikora	Indonesia	4,750	15,584
~ncak Mandala	Indonesia	4,702	15,427
~t Wilhelm	Papua New Guinea	4,508	14,790
~auna Kea	USA (Hawaii)	4,205	13,796
~auna Loa	USA (Hawaii)	4,170	13,681
~t Cook	New Zealand	3,753	12,313
~t Balbi	Solomon Is.	2,439	8,002
~rohena	Tahiti	2,241	7,352
~t Kosciusko	Australia	2,237	7,339

~lorth America		m	ft
~t McKinley	USA (Alaska)	6,194	20,321
~t Logan	Canada	5,959	19,551
~itlaltepetl	Mexico	5,700	18,701
~t St Elias	USA/Canada	5,489	18,008
~opocatepetl	Mexico	5,452	17,887
~t Foraker	USA (Alaska)	5,304	17,401
~xtaccihuatl	Mexico	5,286	17,342
~ucania	Canada	5,227	17,149
~t Steele	Canada	5,073	16,644
Mt Bona	USA (Alaska)	5,005	16,420
Mt Blackburn	USA (Alaska)	4,996	16,391
Mt Sanford	USA (Alaska)	4,940	16,207
Mt Wood	Canada	4,848	15,905
Nevado de Toluca	Mexico	4,670	15,321
Mt Fairweather	USA (Alaska)	4,663	15,298
Mt Whitney	USA	4,418	14,495
Mt Elbert	USA	4,399	14,432
Mt Harvard	USA	4,395	14,419
Mt Rainier	USA	4,392	14,409
Blanca Peak	USA	4,372	14,344
Long's Peak	USA	4,345	14,255
Nevado de Colima	Mexico	4,339	14,235
Mt Shasta	USA	4,317	14,163
Tajumulco	Guatemala	4,220	13,845
Gannett Peak	USA	4,202	13,786
Mt Waddington	Canada	3,994	13,104
Mt Robson	Canada	3,954	12,972
Chirripó Grande	Costa Rica	3,837	12,589
Pico Duarte	Dominican Rep.	3,175	10,417

South America		m	ft
Aconcagua	Argentina	6,960	22,834
Illimani	Bolivia	6,882	22,578
Bonete	Argentina	6,872	22,546
Ojos del Salado	Argentina/Chile	6,863	22,516
Tupungato	Argentina/Chile	6,800	22,309
Pissis	Argentina	6,779	22,241
Mercedario	Argentina/Chile	6,770	22,211
Huascaran	Peru	6,768	22,204
Llullaillaco	Argentina/Chile	6,723	22,057
Nudo de Cachi	Argentina	6,720	22,047
Yerupaja	Peru	6,632	21,758
N. de Tres Cruces	Argentina/Chile	6,620	21,719
Incahuasi	Argentina/Chile	6,600	21,654
Ancohuma	Bolivia	6,550	21,489
Sajama	Bolivia	6,542	21,463
Coropuna	Peru	6,425	21,079
Ausangate	Peru	6,384	20,945
Cerro del Toro	Argentina	6,380	20,932
Ampato	Peru	6,310	20,702
Chimborasso	Ecuador	6,267	20,561
Cotopaxi	Ecuador	5,896	19,344
S. Nev. de S. Marta	Colombia	5,800	19,029
Cayambe	Ecuador	5,796	19,016
Pico Bolivar	Venezuela	5,007	16,427

Antarctica	m	ft
Vinson Massif	4,897	16,066
Mt Kirkpatrick	4,528	14,855
Mt Markham	4,349	14,268

OCEAN DEPTHS

Atlantic Ocean	m	ft	
Puerto Rico (Milwaukee) Deep	9,220	30,249	[7]
Cayman Trench	7,680	25,197	[10]
Gulf of Mexico	5,203	17,070	
Mediterranean Sea	5,121	16,801	
Black Sea	2,211	7,254	
North Sea	660	2,165	
Baltic Sea	463	1,519	
Hudson Bay	258	846	

Indian Ocean	m	ft
Java Trench	7,450	24,442
Red Sea	2,635	8,454
Persian Gulf	73	239

Pacific Ocean	m	ft	
Mariana Trench	11,022	36,161	[1]
Tonga Trench	10,882	35,702	[2]
Japan Trench	10,554	34,626	[3]
Kuril Trench	10,542	34,587	[4]
Mindanao Trench	10,497	34,439	[5]
Kermadec Trench	10,047	32,962	[6]
Peru-Chile Trench	8,050	26,410	[8]
Aleutian Trench	7,822	25,662	[9]
Middle American Trench	6,662	21,857	

Arctic Ocean	m	ft
Molloy Deep	5,608	18,399

LAND LOWS

		m	ft
Caspian Sea	Europe	-28	-92
Dead Sea	Asia	-403	-1,322
Lake Assal	Africa	-156	-512
Lake Eyre North	Oceania	-16	-52
Death Valley	N. America	-86	-282
Valdés Peninsula	S. America	-40	-131

RIVERS

Europe		km	miles
Volga	Caspian Sea	3,700	2,300
Danube	Black Sea	2,850	1,770
Ural	Caspian Sea	2,535	1,575
Dnepr	Volga	2,285	1,420
Kama	Volga	2,030	1,260
Don	Volga	1,990	1,240

		km	miles	
Petchora	Arctic Ocean	1,790	1,110	
Oka	Volga	1,480	920	
Belaya	Kama	1,420	880	
Dnister	Black Sea	1,400	870	
Vyatka	Kama	1,370	850	
Rhine	North Sea	1,320	820	
N. Dvina	Arctic Ocean	1,290	800	
Desna	Dnepr	1,190	740	
Elbe	North Sea	1,145	710	
Vistula	Baltic Sea	1,090	675	
Loire	Atlantic Ocean	1,020	635	
W. Dvina	Baltic Sea	1,019	633	

Asia

		km	miles	
Yangtze	Pacific Ocean	6,380	3,960	[3]
Yenisey-Angara	Arctic Ocean	5,550	3,445	[5]
Huang He	Pacific Ocean	5,464	3,395	[6]
Ob-Irtysh	Arctic Ocean	5,410	3,360	[7]
Mekong	Pacific Ocean	4,500	2,795	[9]
Amur	Pacific Ocean	4,400	2,730	[10]
Lena	Arctic Ocean	4,400	2,730	
Irtysh	Ob	4,250	2,640	
Yenisey	Arctic Ocean	4,090	2,540	
Ob	Arctic Ocean	3,680	2,285	
Indus	Indian Ocean	3,100	1,925	
Brahmaputra	Indian Ocean	2,900	1,800	
Syrdarya	Aral Sea	2,860	1,775	
Salween	Indian Ocean	2,800	1,740	
Euphrates	Indian Ocean	2,700	1,675	
Vilyuy	Lena	2,650	1,645	
Kolyma	Arctic Ocean	2,600	1,615	
Amudarya	Aral Sea	2,540	1,575	
Ural	Caspian Sea	2,535	1,575	
Ganges	Indian Ocean	2,510	1,560	
Si Kiang	Pacific Ocean	2,100	1,305	
Irrawaddy	Indian Ocean	2,010	1,250	
Tarim-Yarkand	Lop Nor	2,000	1,240	
Tigris	Indian Ocean	1,900	1,180	
Angara	Yenisey	1,830	1,135	
Godavari	Indian Ocean	1,470	915	
Sutlej	Indian Ocean	1,450	900	
Yamuna	Indian Ocean	1,400	870	

Africa

		km	miles	
Nile	Mediterranean	6,670	4,140	[1]
Zaïre/Congo	Atlantic Ocean	4,670	2,900	[8]
Niger	Atlantic Ocean	4,180	2,595	
Zambezi	Indian Ocean	3,540	2,200	
Oubangi/Uele	Zaïre	2,250	1,400	
Kasai	Zaïre	1,950	1,210	
Shaballe	Indian Ocean	1,930	1,200	
Orange	Atlantic Ocean	1,860	1,155	
Cubango	Okavango Swamps	1,800	1,120	
Limpopo	Indian Ocean	1,600	995	
Senegal	Atlantic Ocean	1,600	995	
Volta	Atlantic Ocean	1,500	930	
Benue	Niger	1,350	840	

Australia

		km	miles
Murray-Darling	Indian Ocean	3,750	2,330
Darling	Murray	3,070	1,905
Murray	Indian Ocean	2,575	1,600
Murrumbidgee	Murray	1,690	1,050

North America

		km	miles	
Mississippi-Missouri	G. of Mexico	6,020	3,740	[4]
Mackenzie	Arctic Ocean	4,240	2,630	
Mississippi	Gulf of Mexico	3,780	2,350	
Missouri	Mississippi	3,780	2,350	
Yukon	Pacific Ocean	3,185	1,980	
Rio Grande	Gulf of Mexico	3,030	1,880	
Arkansas	Mississippi	2,340	1,450	
Colorado	Pacific Ocean	2,330	1,445	
Red	Mississippi	2,040	1,270	
Columbia	Pacific Ocean	1,950	1,210	
Saskatchewan	Lake Winnipeg	1,940	1,205	

		km	miles
Snake	Columbia	1,670	1,040
Churchill	Hudson Bay	1,600	990
Ohio	Mississippi	1,580	980
Brazos	Gulf of Mexico	1,400	870
St Lawrence	Atlantic Ocean	1,170	730

South America

		km	miles	
Amazon	Atlantic Ocean	6,450	4,010	[2]
Paraná-Plate	Atlantic Ocean	4,500	2,800	
Purus	Amazon	3,350	2,080	
Madeira	Amazon	3,200	1,990	
São Francisco	Atlantic Ocean	2,900	1,800	
Paraná	Plate	2,800	1,740	
Tocantins	Atlantic Ocean	2,750	1,710	
Paraguay	Paraná	2,550	1,580	
Orinoco	Atlantic Ocean	2,500	1,550	
Pilcomayo	Paraná	2,500	1,550	
Araguaia	Tocantins	2,250	1,400	
Juruá	Amazon	2,000	1,240	
Xingu	Amazon	1,980	1,230	
Ucayali	Amazon	1,900	1,180	
Maranón	Amazon	1,600	990	
Uruguay	Plate	1,600	990	
Magdalena	Caribbean Sea	1,540	960	

LAKES

Europe

		km²	miles²
Lake Ladoga	Russia	17,700	6,800
Lake Onega	Russia	9,700	3,700
Saimaa system	Finland	8,000	3,100
Vänern	Sweden	5,500	2,100
Rybinsk Reservoir	Russia	4,700	1,800

Asia

		km²	miles²	
Caspian Sea	Asia	371,800	143,550	[1]
Aral Sea	Kazakh./Uzbek.	36,000	13,900	[6]
Lake Baykal	Russia	30,500	11,780	[9]
Tonlé Sap	Cambodia	20,000	7,700	
Lake Balkhash	Kazakhstan	18,500	7,100	
Dongting Hu	China	12,000	4,600	
Ysyk Köl	Kyrgyzstan	6,200	2,400	
Lake Urmia	Iran	5,900	2,300	
Koko Nur	China	5,700	2,200	
Poyang Hu	China	5,000	1,900	
Lake Khanka	China/Russia	4,400	1,700	
Lake Van	Turkey	3,500	1,400	
Ubsa Nur	China	3,400	1,300	

Africa

		km²	miles²	
Lake Victoria	E. Africa	68,000	26,000	[3]
Lake Tanganyika	C. Africa	33,000	13,000	[7]
Lake Malawi/Nyasa	E. Africa	29,600	11,430	[10]
Lake Chad	C. Africa	25,000	9,700	
Lake Turkana	Ethiopia/Kenya	8,500	3,300	
Lake Volta	Ghana	8,500	3,300	
Lake Bangweulu	Zambia	8,000	3,100	
Lake Rukwa	Tanzania	7,000	2,700	
Lake Mai-Ndombe	Zaïre	6,500	2,500	
Lake Kariba	Zambia/Zimbabwe	5,300	2,000	
Lake Mobutu	Uganda/Zaïre	5,300	2,000	
Lake Nasser	Egypt/Sudan	5,200	2,000	
Lake Mweru	Zambia/Zaïre	4,900	1,900	
Lake Cabora Bassa	Mozambique	4,500	1,700	
Lake Kyoga	Uganda	4,400	1,700	
Lake Tana	Ethiopia	3,630	1,400	
Lake Kivu	Rwanda/Zaïre	2,650	1,000	
Lake Edward	Uganda/Zaïre	2,200	850	

Australia

		km²	miles²
Lake Eyre	Australia	8,900	3,400
Lake Torrens	Australia	5,800	2,200
Lake Gairdner	Australia	4,800	1,900

h America		km²	miles²	
Superior	Canada/USA	82,350	31,800	[2]
Huron	Canada/USA	59,600	23,010	[4]
Michigan	USA	58,000	22,400	[5]
at Bear Lake	Canada	31,800	12,280	[8]
at Slave Lake	Canada	28,500	11,000	
Erie	Canada/USA	25,700	9,900	
Winnipeg	Canada	24,400	9,400	
Ontario	Canada/USA	19,500	7,500	
Nicaragua	Nicaragua	8,200	3,200	
Athabasca	Canada	8,100	3,100	
allwood Reservoir	Canada	6,530	2,520	
adeer Lake	Canada	6,400	2,500	
Winnipegosis	Canada	5,400	2,100	
illing Lake	Canada	5,500	2,100	
Nipigon	Canada	4,850	1,900	
Manitoba	Canada	4,700	1,800	

th America		km²	miles²
e Titicaca	Bolivia/Peru	8,300	3,200
e Poopo	Peru	2,800	1,100

ISLANDS

ope		km²	miles²	
eat Britain	UK	229,880	88,700	[8]
land	Atlantic Ocean	103,000	39,800	
and	Ireland/UK	84,400	32,600	
vaya Zemlya (N.)	Russia	48,200	18,600	
Spitzbergen	Norway	39,000	15,100	
vaya Zemlya (S.)	Russia	33,200	12,800	
ily	Italy	25,500	9,800	
rdinia	Italy	24,000	9,300	
E. Spitzbergen	Norway	15,000	5,600	
rsica	France	8,700	3,400	
ete	Greece	8,350	3,200	
aland	Denmark	6,850	2,600	

ia		km²	miles²	
orneo	S.E. Asia	744,360	287,400	[3]
umatra	Indonesia	473,600	182,860	[6]
onshu	Japan	230,500	88,980	[7]
elebes	Indonesia	189,000	73,000	
va	Indonesia	126,700	48,900	
zon	Philippines	104,700	40,400	
indanao	Philippines	101,500	39,200	
okkaido	Japan	78,400	30,300	
akhalin	Russia	74,060	28,600	
ri Lanka	Indian Ocean	65,600	25,300	
aiwan	Pacific Ocean	36,000	13,900	
yushu	Japan	35,700	13,800	
ainan	China	34,000	13,100	
mor	Indonesia	33,600	13,000	
hikoku	Japan	18,800	7,300	
almahera	Indonesia	18,000	6,900	
eram	Indonesia	17,150	6,600	

		km²	miles²	
Sumbawa	Indonesia	15,450	6,000	
Flores	Indonesia	15,200	5,900	
Samar	Philippines	13,100	5,100	
Negros	Philippines	12,700	4,900	
Bangka	Indonesia	12,000	4,600	
Palawan	Philippines	12,000	4,600	
Panay	Philippines	11,500	4,400	
Sumba	Indonesia	11,100	4,300	
Mindoro	Philippines	9,750	3,800	
Buru	Indonesia	9,500	3,700	
Bali	Indonesia	5,600	2,200	
Cyprus	Mediterranean	3,570	1,400	
Wrangel Is.	Russia	2,800	1,000	

Africa		km²	miles²	
Madagascar	Indian Ocean	587,040	226,660	[4]
Socotra	Indian Ocean	3,600	1,400	
Réunion	Indian Ocean	2,500	965	
Tenerife	Atlantic Ocean	2,350	900	
Mauritius	Indian Ocean	1,865	720	

Oceania		km²	miles²	
New Guinea	Indon./Pap. NG	821,030	317,000	[2]
New Zealand (S.)	New Zealand	150,500	58,100	
New Zealand (N.)	New Zealand	114,700	44,300	
Tasmania	Australia	67,800	26,200	
New Britain	Papua NG	37,800	14,600	
New Caledonia	Pacific Ocean	19,100	7,400	
Viti Levu	Fiji	10,500	4,100	
Hawaii	Pacific Ocean	10,450	4,000	
Bougainville	Papua NG	9,600	3,700	
Guadalcanal	Solomon Is.	6,500	2,500	
Vanua Levu	Fiji	5,550	2,100	
New Ireland	Papua NG	3,200	1,200	

North America		km²	miles²	
Greenland	Greenland	2,175,600	839,800	[1]
Baffin Is.	Canada	508,000	196,100	[5]
Victoria Is.	Canada	212,200	81,900	[9]
Ellesmere Is.	Canada	212,000	81,800	[10]
Cuba	Cuba	110,860	42,800	
Newfoundland	Canada	110,680	42,700	
Hispaniola	Atlantic Ocean	76,200	29,400	
Banks Is.	Canada	67,000	25,900	
Devon Is.	Canada	54,500	21,000	
Melville Is.	Canada	42,400	16,400	
Vancouver Is.	Canada	32,150	12,400	
Somerset Is.	Canada	24,300	9,400	
Jamaica	Caribbean Sea	11,400	4,400	
Puerto Rico	Atlantic Ocean	8,900	3,400	
Cape Breton Is.	Canada	4,000	1,500	

South America		km²	miles²
Tierra del Fuego	Argentina/Chile	47,000	18,100
Falkland Is. (E.)	Atlantic Ocean	6,800	2,600
South Georgia	Atlantic Ocean	4,200	1,600
Galapagos	Pacific Ocean	2,250	870

THE EARTH

The most widely accepted theory about the origins of the Earth is that it was formed from a solar cloud consisting mainly of hydrogen 4,600 million years ago. The cloud condensed, forming the planets. The lighter elements floated to the surface of the Earth, where they cooled to form a crust; the inner material remained hot and molten. The first rocks were formed over 3,500 million years ago, but the Earth's surface has since been constantly altered.

The Earth has an oblate spheroid or solid shape, with an equatorial diameter of 12,756.28 km [7,926.38 mls] and a polar diameter of 12,713.51 km [7,899.81 mls]. The equatorial circumference is 40,075.02 km [24,906.46 mls] and is divided into 360 degrees of longitude, which is measured degrees, minutes and seconds east or west the Greenwich meridian. North and south the Equator, distance is measured in degre minutes and seconds of latitude (the Equa lies at 0°, the North Pole at 90°N, the Sou Pole at 90°S, the Tropic of Cancer at 23° 2€ and the Tropic of Capricorn at 23° 26'S).

The surface area of the Earth is made of 70.92% water and 29.08% land. Bene the surface area are three layers: the crust, mantle and the core.

The crust: This accounts for about 1.5% the Earth's volume and consists of a britt low-density material varying from 5–50 k [3–31 mls] in depth (it is thickest beneath t continents and thinnest beneath the ocean The material is a combination of silica a aluminium and is known as sial. Below the s is a denser basaltic layer, composed of sili and magnesium, known as sima. Separating t crust and the next layer, the mantle, is a boun ary called the Mohorovičić Discontinuity.

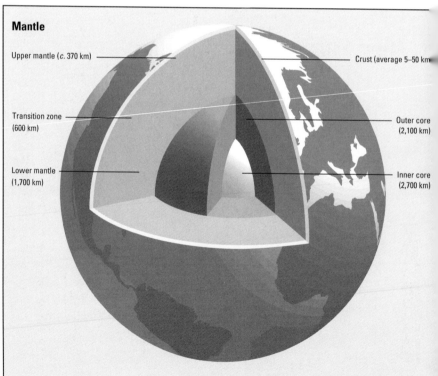

Mantle

Upper mantle (c. 370 km)

Transition zone (600 km)

Lower mantle (1,700 km)

Crust (average 5–50 km

Outer core (2,100 km)

Inner core (2,700 km)

PLATE TECTONICS

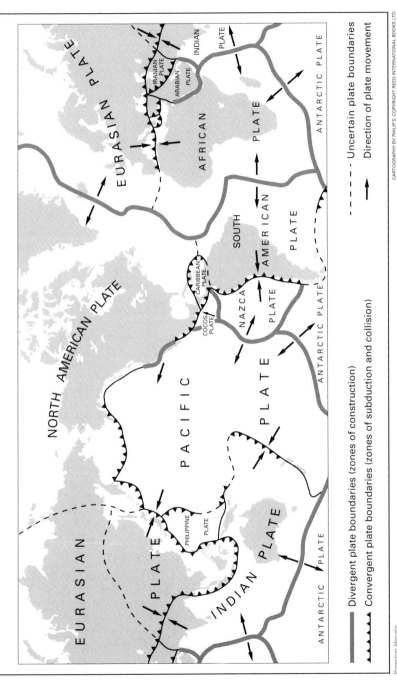

PLATE TECTONICS

NORTH AMERICAN PLATE

EURASIAN PLATE

EURASIAN PLATE

ANTARCTIC PLATE

AFRICAN PLATE

IRANIAN PLATE

ARABIAN PLATE

INDIAN PLATE

PACIFIC PLATE

PHILIPPINE PLATE

INDIAN PLATE

ANTARCTIC PLATE

CARIBBEAN PLATE

COCOS PLATE

NAZCA PLATE

SOUTH AMERICAN PLATE

ANTARCTIC PLATE

——— Divergent plate boundaries (zones of construction)

▲▲▲ Convergent plate boundaries (zones of subduction and collision)

– – – – Uncertain plate boundaries

→ Direction of plate movement

Projection: Mercator

The mantle: The upper mantle (including the transition zone) is about 1,000 km [600 mls] deep and is rich in iron and magnesium silicates. It is a rigid layer and temperatures can reach as much as 1,600°C [2,915°F]. Below this layer, the lower mantle is more viscous and is about 1,700 km [1,050 mls] deep. **The core:** The core has two parts. The outer core, measuring about 2,100 km [1,300 mls], consists of molten iron and nickel at between 2,100°C [3,800°F] and 5,000°C [9,000°F]. About 5,000 km [3,000 mls] below the surface is a liquid transition zone, below which is the solid inner core, about 2,700 km [1,700 mls] in depth and with rock about three times as dense as the crust, probably consisting mostly of iron. The temperature at the centre of the Earth is thought to be 5,000°C [9,000°F].

CONTINENTAL DRIFT

The jigsaw-puzzle-like fit of the Atlantic coasts led to the theory of continental drift proposed by Alfred Wegener in 1915. He suggested that an ancient supercontinent, called Pangaea, incorporating all the Earth's land masses, gradually split up to form the six geographic continents we know today. By 180 million years ago, Pangaea had split into two major continents; a northern one, Laurasia, and a southern one, Gondwanaland, separated by a long narrow ocean known as Tethys. Gondwanaland began to break up, with India and Antarctica-Australia becoming isolated. To form today's pattern, India 'collided' with Asia (crumpling up sediments to form the Himalayas); South America rotated and moved west to connect with North America; Australia separated from Antarctica and moved north; and the familiar gap developed between Greenland and Europe.

PLATE TECTONICS

The continental drift theory led to the idea of plate tectonics. The discovery that the continents are carried along on the top of slowly-moving crustal plates (which float on heavier liquid material – the lower mantle) provided the mechanism for the drift theories to work. There are 15 plates of various sizes (usually combining both oceanic and continental crust) which converge and diverge along margins marked by seismic and volcanic activity.

Plates diverge from mid-ocean ridges whe molten lava pushes up and forces the pla apart at a rate of up to 40 mm [1.6 in] a ye converging plates form either a trench (whe the oceanic plates sink below the lighter con nental rock) or mountain ranges (where tv continents collide). Most of the world's mou tain building, earthquakes and volcanic eru tions take place along plate boundaries ■

OCEANS

Over 360 million sq km [140 millic sq mls] of the Earth's surface is covere by oceans and seas; this is equivalent t over 70% of the Earth's surface. In a stric geographical sense there are only three tru oceans: the Atlantic, Pacific and Indian wit an average depth of 3,900 m [12,900 ft]. Th Pacific Ocean alone accounts for nearly 36% of the total surface of the Earth and almos 50% of the sea area. Gravity holds in aroun 1,400 million cubic km [335 million cubi mls] of water, of which over 97% is saline.

OCEAN PROFILE

The continental shelf: This is geologically still part of the land mass and drops gently to about 200 m [660 ft] below sea level. Thi area is home to most sea life, particularly the sunlit upper layer. In this surface zone huge energies are exchanged between the oceans and the atmosphere above. The oceans absorb large quantities of carbon dioxide and partially exchange it for oxygen, largely by way of the phytoplankton, tiny plants that photosynthesize solar energy and form the base of the marine food chain. Light and colour fade with depth and by 200 m [660 ft] there is only a dim twilight.

The continental slope: Here the sea bed falls away suddenly at 3° to 6°. There is then a more gradual descent to the ocean floor, known as the continental rise, with gradients between 1 in 100 and 1 in 700. At these depths temperature and light are minimal, and at a depth of about 1,000 m [3,000 ft] there occurs a temperature change almost as rupt as the transition between the air and ter above. Below this thermocline, at a ar-stable 3°C [37.4°F], the waters are un-oved by the winds at the surface and circu-e very slowly, often remaining in the same ace for thousands of years. The pressure is mense, touching 1,000 atmospheres in the epest trenches. Some life is supported here d the water also serves as a storehouse for at and assorted atmospheric chemicals.

he abyssal plains: These are found at tween 2,500 m and 6,000 m [8,200 ft and ,000 ft]. From these plains rise volcanoes or example, Mauna Kea on Hawaii reaches ,203 m [33,468 ft], although only 4,205 m 3,796 ft] is visible above sea level) and nderwater mountain chains up to 1,000 km 00 mls] across, whose peaks sometimes pear above sea level as islands such as eland and Tristan da Cunha.

Ocean trenches may cut into the sea ottom, extending the depth of the ocean. hese are found particularly in the Pacific cean, where six trenches reach more than 0,000 m [33,000 ft] below sea level, in-luding the Mariana Trench, at 11,022 m 36,161 ft] below sea level.

OCEAN CURRENTS

Moving immense quantities of energy as well s billions of tonnes of water every hour, he ocean currents are a vital part of the eat engine that drives the Earth's climate. They themselves are produced by a twofold mechanism. At the surface, winds push huge masses of water before them; in the deep cean, below the abrupt temperature gradient, density variations cause slow vertical move-ments. The pattern of circulation of the great surface currents is determined by the dis-placement known as the Coriolis effect. As the Earth turns beneath a moving object, it appears to be deflected to one side. The deflection is most obvious near the Equator, where the Earth's surface is spinning east-wards at about 1,700 km/h [1,050 mph]; currents moving polewards are curved clock-wise in the northern hemisphere and anti-clockwise in the southern hemisphere.

The result is a system of spinning circles known as gyres. The Coriolis effect piles up water on the left of each gyre, creating a nar-row, fast-moving stream that is matched by a slower, broader returning current on the right. North and south of the Equator, the fastest currents are located in the west and in the east respectively. In each case, warm water moves from the Equator and cold water returns from it. Cold currents often bring an upwelling of old nutrients with them, supporting the world's most economically important fisheries.

Depending on the prevailing winds, some currents on or near the Equator may reverse their direction in the course of a year – a seasonal variation on which Asian monsoon rains depend, and whose occasional failure can bring disaster to millions of people ▪

GEOLOGICAL TIME

A scheme of age classification has been evolved for geological time extending back hundreds of million of years. Geologists devised their timescale on the basis of relative, not calendar, ages. Accurate dating was impossible and estimates were often bitterly disputed, but the order in which the rocks were formed could be deduced from careful observation. The use of radioactive dating – culminating in the 1950s with the develop-ment of a mass spectrometer capable of measuring tiny quantities of isotopes – appears to have settled most of the arguments.

The years since the formation of the Earth are divided in the timescale into four great eras, further split into periods and, in the case of the most recent era, epochs. The present era is the Cainozoic (from the Greek meaning 'new life'), extending backwards through the Mesozoic ('middle life') and Palaeozoic ('ancient life') to the Pre-Cambrian, named after the Latin word for Wales, the location of some of the earliest known fossils.

Most of the Earth's geological history is encompassed by the Pre-Cambrian: though traces of ancient life have since been found (for example, algae and bacteria), it was largely the proliferation of fossils from the beginning of the Palaeozoic era onwards, some 570 million years ago, which first allowed

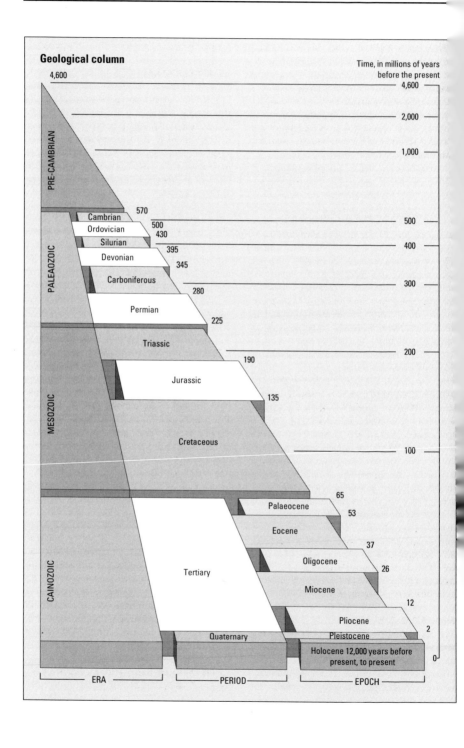

Geological column

4,600

Time, in millions of years
before the present

PRE-CAMBRIAN

4,600

2,000

1,000

Cambrian — 570
Ordovician — 500
Silurian — 430
Devonian — 395
Carboniferous — 345
Permian — 280
Triassic — 225
Jurassic — 190
Cretaceous — 135

PALEOZOIC

500

400

300

200

MESOZOIC

100

Palaeocene — 65
Eocene — 53
Oligocene — 37
Miocene — 26
Tertiary
Pliocene — 12
Quaternary
Pleistocene — 2
Holocene 12,000 years before
present, to present — 0

CAINOZOIC

ERA — PERIOD — EPOCH

ecise subdivisions to be made. Like the ambrian, most are named after regions exemifying a period's geology. Others – the arboniferous ('coal-bearing'), for example, or e Cretaceous ('chalk-bearing') – are more rectly descriptive. During the Mesozoic era ant reptiles, marsupial mammals and the rliest known species of bird all appeared. ogether with coniferous trees and flowering ants, the birds and mammals all survived to the next era (Cainozoic) ■

TIME MEASUREMENT

Time is measured in terms of the rotation of the Earth about its axis (rotational ime) or in terms of periodic phenomena ccurring within atoms (atomic time). The arious forms of rotational time and the relaionship between them and atomic time are explained below.

SOLAR TIME
The time taken for the Earth to complete one rotation on its axis, relative to the Sun, is a solar day. Because the Earth moves round the Sun in an ellipse rather than in a circle, and its speed is not constant along its orbit, the length of day or apparent solar day is not constant throughout the year (it becomes shorter than average at the equinoxes and longer at the solstices). The mean solar day averages out the differences over a period of one year. Mean solar time observed on the meridian of the telescope at the Royal Observatory at Greenwich, in England, is called Greenwich Mean Time (GMT). GMT, also known as Universal time, is the basis of standard time throughout the world and is of particular use in navigation and astronomy.

SIDEREAL TIME
The time taken for the Earth to complete one rotation on its axis, with reference to a point in the heavens called the First Point of Aries, is a sidereal (or 'star') day. Because of the precession of the Earth's axis (which makes the length of the sidereal day shorter than the real

period of rotation by 0.008 seconds) and various oscillations, astronomers use a mean sidereal time with these fluctuations evened out.

EPHEMERIS TIME
A detailed study of the motions of the Sun, Moon and planets relative to the Earth has shown that there are irregularities in the Earth's rotation. A table giving the apparent daily positions of the Sun, planets and Moon is called an ephemeris; the method of time measurement based on bringing the ephemeris into agreement with observed values is ephemeris time.

ATOMIC TIME
Time can be measured to a high degree of accuracy using the interval between energy changes (quantum transitions) within an atom. When an atom of a element moves from one energy level to another higher or lower one, electromagnetic radiation of a particular frequency is given out. Hydrogen, rubidium and caesium atoms have been used for this purpose. Since 1967, the SI unit of time is now the 'second' as defined in terms of a specified transition within the caesium atom. SI stands for Système International d'Unités – an international system of units devised in 1960 to meet all known needs for measurement in science and technology.

Relationship between rotational and atomic time: Because of variations in the speed of rotation of the Earth, the mean solar second (1/86,400 of the mean solar day) is unsatisfactory for precision measurements. In 1955 the International Astronomical Union defined the second of ephemeris time as 1/31,566,925.9747 of the tropical year for 1 January 1900 at 12 hours ephemeris time. In 1956 this definition was accepted by the General Conference of Weights and Measures. In 1964 the Conference also defined an ephemeris second as 9,192,631,770 periods of radiation of a particular transition of the caesium-133 atom. This definition was adopted as the sole definition of the SI unit of time in 1967.

BRITISH SUMMER TIME AND BRITISH STANDARD TIME (BST)
During World War I an Act of Parliament

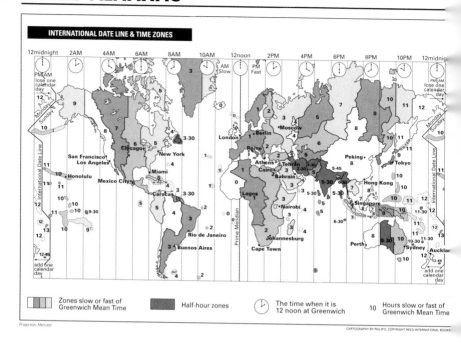

INTERNATIONAL DATE LINE & TIME ZONES

| | Zones slow or fast of Greenwich Mean Time | | Half-hour zones | | The time when it is 12 noon at Greenwich | 10 | Hours slow or fast of Greenwich Mean Time |

Projection: Mercator

CARTOGRAPHY BY PHILIP'S. COPYRIGHT REED INTERNATIONAL BOOKS

decreed that during the summer months in Britain the legal time should be one hour in advance of GMT. During World War II the duration of summer time was extended, and in 1914–45 and again in 1947 double summer time (two hours in advance of GMT) was introduced. In 1968 the British

BRITISH SUMMER TIME

Year	Begins	Ends
1995	26 March	22 October
1996	24 March	20 October
1997	30 March	19 October

Standard Time Act put the legal time one hour ahead of GMT for the whole year to bring Britain into line with Central European Time. As from 31 October 1971 Parliament restored the concept of summer time, to operate one hour in advance of GMT between 0200 hr GMT on the day following the third Saturday in March and 0200 hr GMT on the day following the fourth Saturday in October.

TIME AROUND THE WORLD

The Earth rotates through 360° in 24 hours and therefore moves 15° every hour. In 1883 a system for dividing the world into separate longitudinal time zones was internationally agreed, thereby replacing local time in different areas with standard time to cover wider areas. The world was divided into 24 standard time zones (see the map above), each being approximately 15° of latitude wide, with the Greenwich meridian at the centre of the first zone. These zones are based on Greenwich Mean Time, time in each zone usually differing from GMT by a whole number of hours. All places to the west of Greenwich are one hour behind for every zone and places to the east are ahead by one hour for every zone. Some large countries have several time zones because they stretch through so many degrees of longitude; the United States, Canada and Russia, for example, are divided into zones approximately 7.5° of latitude wide on each side of central meridians. Zone boundaries are often adjusted to follow local boundaries or to avoid separating cities and towns from neighbours by a time difference. To relate work and leisure more closely to sun time or daylight,

standard zone time can be adjusted for
rt of the year; summer time is an example
this.

When it is 12 noon at the Greenwich
eridian, 180° east the day is only just begin-
ng. To overcome this, the International Date
ine was established, an imaginary line run-
ing more or less along the 180th meridian
although the line is adjusted locally so that it
oes not divide countries or groups of islands).
Vest of the date line, the date is one day ahead
f that east of the line. For example, if you
ravelled westwards from Samoa (170° West)
Japan (140° East) you would pass from
unday morning into Sunday night ■

THE CALENDAR

A calendar is a method of reckoning time
for regulating religious, commercial and
civil life, and for dating events. Calendars have
been in use from earliest times – the Ancient
Egyptians had a system based on the movement of the star Sirius and on the seasons
(determined by the fluctuations of the River
Nile). Like all calendars this was based on
the astronomical motions of the Earth, Moon
and Sun. In modern times, the rotation of
the Earth gives us the day, the lunar cycle the
month, and the solar cycle the changing
seasons and the year. The units of time used
in calendar reckoning are thus the day, the
month and the year.

THE DAY

The day is the time taken for the Earth to
make one complete turn on its axis. In modern
calendars the day is reckoned from midnight
to midnight and is divided into 24 hours.
The hours are counted in two sections: the
first from midnight to 12 noon (when the
Sun crosses the meridian), which are known
as a.m. (ante meridian), and the second from
12 noon to midnight, which are known as p.m.
(post meridian). The 24-hour clock disregards
a.m. and p.m. and is simply counted from 0 to
23. The hours of daylight vary throughout the
year. They also vary with latitude; the further
north one gets the greater is the difference
between daylight hours and hours of darkness.
The subdivision of the day into hours, minutes
and seconds is arbitrary and only for our
convenience.

THE MONTH

The month is the time taken for the Moon
to complete one full revolution around the
Earth. There are different ways of defining
this period; the one used in calendars is the
synodic month, which is the time between
successive new moons – a period of 29.53059
days. The month is used because it is a convenient number of days to count, and because
the changes in the Moon's shape are easily
recognized. The timing of many religious festivals, such as Easter, is based on the Moon.
The week probably owes its origin to the four
phases of the Moon.

Phases of the Moon: The Moon rises and
sets as a result of the Earth's rotation and,
in addition, it shows characteristic phases

DAYS OF THE WEEK

The seven days that make up a *week* have names derived from Old English translations
or adaptations of their Roman names.

	Old English	Roman
Sunday	Sun	Sol
Monday	Moon	Luna
Tuesday	Tiw/Tbr (God of War)	Mars
Wednesday	Woden/Odin	Mercury
Thursday	Thor	Jupiter
Friday	Frigga/Freyja (Goddess of Love)	Venus
Saturday	Saeternes	Saturn

because of its movement around the Earth. At different points in its orbit, different parts of the illuminated half are visible. At new moon the part illuminated by the Sun is hidden from the Earth and the Moon's disc is completely dark. In a lunar cycle the visible part grows (waxes) from a thin crescent, through a half moon (first quarter), to reach a full moon when the disc is completely illuminated. It then diminishes (wanes) through a second half moon (the last quarter) back to a new moon again. When the moon is between a half moon and a full moon it is said to be gibbous. The full moon nearest to the autumnal equinox (22 September) is often called a harvest moon; the following full moon, in October, is a hunter's moon.

The tides: The Moon and, to a lesser extent, the Sun cause tides by their gravitational pull on the water of the oceans. The effect of the Moon's attraction is to raise the water level at a point on the Earth closest to the Moon, thus distorting the Earth's water mass and producing a similar 'bulge' on the opposite side of the Earth. These places have high tide; points on the 'sides' of the Earth have low tides.

As the Earth rotates different places have high tides; most places have two tides every day separated by approximately 12 hours. The precise times of tides depend on the relative positions of the Moon and the Sun, and also on ocean currents. Each month there are two particularly high tides occurring at full and new moon, where the Sun and the Moon are acting in the same direction. These are known as spring tides. Midway between these two are the neap tides, with lowest rise and fall, when the Sun and Moon act in opposite directions.

THE YEAR

The year is the time taken for the Earth to complete one revolution around the Sun. Again there are different ways of defining it; the one used in calendars is the tropical year, which is the time taken for the Sun to complete a full cycle of its apparent motion north and south of the Equator. The tropical year is 365.242199 days.

The seasons occur because the Earth's axis is not at right-angles to a line between the Earth and the Sun, but is tilted at a constant angle 66.5°. At one part of the orbit the

THE SEASONS

The seasons are arbitrary divisions of the year into four periods. The generally accepted dates in Europe are:

Spring   21 March to 21 June
Summer   22 June to 22 September
Autumn   23 September to 22 December
Winter   23 December to 20 March

northern hemisphere is tilted towards the Sun. At these times it is summer in the northern hemisphere, the hours of daylight exceed the hours of darkness, and the Sun is north of the Equator. As the Earth moves to the opposite side of the orbit, six months later, the northern hemisphere is tilted away from the Sun. It is then winter, the hours of darkness exceed the hours of daylight, and the Sun is south of the Equator.

Equinoxes and solstices: The equinoxes occur when the Sun crosses the Equator on its apparent journey north or south. At these times the Sun is directly overhead at the Equator and the hours of daylight equal the hours of darkness at all points on the Earth. The vernal equinox occurs when the Sun is moving northwards, about 21 March. The autumnal equinox occurs on about 22 September, when the Sun is moving southwards.

Midway between the equinoxes are the solstices, which occur when the Sun is at the extremes of its apparent motion north and south of the Equator. In the northern hemisphere the summer solstice occurs on about 21 June, when the Sun is furthest north and this is the longest day of the year. The winter solstice, on about 22 December, is the shortest day in the northern hemisphere and occurs when the Sun is furthest south.

Eclipses: When the Moon passes between the Sun and the Earth it causes either a partial eclipse of the Sun (if the Earth passes through the Moon's outer shadow), or a total eclipse (if the inner cone shadow crosses the Earth's surface). In a lunar eclipse, the Earth's shadow crosses the Moon and, again, provides either a partial or total eclipse. Eclipses of the Sun and Moon do not occur every month because of the 5° difference between the plane the Moon's orbit and the plane in which the Earth moves. In the 1990s only 14 lunar eclipses are possible, seven partial and seven total; each is visible only from certain, and variable, parts of the world. In the same period there are 13 solar eclipses, six partial and seven total.

QUARTER DAYS

Quarter days are four days marking quarters of the year. They fall close to the equinoxes and solstices; note that Midsummer day is not the longest day of the year. In England, Wales and Northern Ireland, the quarter days are:

Lady day	25 March
Midsummer day	24 June
Michaelmas	29 September
Christmas day	25 December

In Scotland, the quarter days are:

Candlemas	2 February
Whit Sunday	movable
Lammas	1 August
Martinmas	11 November

THE MODERN CALENDAR

The main difficulty in compiling a calendar is that the day, the month and the year are not commensurate – the month is not an exact number of days and the year is not an exact number of months. For convenience, months and years are assigned a whole number of days, and extra days (called intercalations) are added at intervals to compensate. Thus the year, which is about 365.25 days, is taken to be 365 days. As time goes by the seasons get out of step with the dates – the solstices and equinoxes occur one day later every four years. To compensate, an extra day (29 February) is added every four years (the so-called leap years, or bissextiles in the Roman calendar).

The calendar used at the present time is the Gregorian calendar, which is a modification of the earlier Julian calendar.

The Julian calendar: This was introduced by Julius Caesar in the first century BC and came from an earlier Roman system based on the Moon. The Julian calendar abandoned any attempt to keep the calendar months in step with the Moon's phases; as a result, the months became arbitrary divisions of time and full moon did not occur on the same day of the month every year. The calendar was based on a year of 365.25 days with an extra day every four years added to February. The calendar was modified by Augustus, who changed the lengths of the months to the number of days they now have.

The Gregorian calendar: The value of 365.25 days of the Julian calendar is slightly longer (about 11 minutes) than the true value and over the years the error mounted up. By 1582 there was a difference of 10 days between the solstices and their original dates. In this year a papal bull (edict) issued by Pope Gregory XIII corrected the discrepancy by making 5 October into 15 October. The bull also modified the rule for leap years, introducing the rule that the first year of a century (1600, 1700 and so on) is a leap year only if it is divisible by 400 (thus 1600 was a leap year but 1700 was not).

The Gregorian system was not adopted immediately in all countries, in particular in Protestant countries. It was introduced in Italy, France, Spain and Portugal in 1582, but not until 1752 was it introduced in England, when it was adopted by dating the day following 2 September 1752 as 14 September. In addition the start of the year was fixed at 1 January in 1752; from the 14th century the year had been reckoned from 25 March (the feast of the Annunciation).

The Gregorian calendar is often called the New Style calendar, to distinguish it from the Julian, or Old Style, calendar. In converting dates between New and Old Styles it is necessary to subtract or add 11 days, to take into account the different starting dates for the year, and the fact that 1700 was a leap year in the Julian calendar but not in the Gregorian calendar.

Leap years: The modern rule for determining leap years is that leap years are divisible by four without remainder unless they are centennial years, in which case they are only a leap year if they are divisible by 400 except for the year 4000 and its multiples. These will not be leap years. Thus the year 2000 will be a leap year but 3000 and 4000 will not ■

RELIGIOUS CALENDARS

Religious calendars are cycles of festivals and seasons marking events or rituals of special significance. Often they are based on the Moon and do not follow the civil calendar. Nevertheless, they have a wider importance – movable feasts such as Easter and Whitsuntide, in the Christian faith, are also national holidays.

THE CHRISTIAN CALENDAR

This developed from the Jewish calendar, which was based on a lunar cycle. The festival of Easter developed from the Jewish Passover; Christmas was introduced later to be celebrated at the time of the winter solstice, which had long been marked by such pagan festivals as the Saturnalia.

The Christian year is set by the governing bodies of individual Churches and inevitably there are differences in practice – in particular, there are differences between the Eastern and Western Churches. The festivals dated here are those currently used in the Western Roman Catholic and Anglican Churches. There are two cycles of important dates: one of saints' days and other fixed dates, the other of movable feasts based on Easter.

The dates of the principal movable festivals are calculated as follows: Shrove Tuesday is the day before Ash Wednesday; Palm Sunday is the Sunday before Easter Sunday; Maundy Thursday and Good Friday are the Thursday and Friday before Easter Sunday. Corpus Christi (RC) occurs on the Thursday after Trinity Sunday. Rogation Sunday is five wee after Easter. The Festival of Christ the Ki (RC) is the Last Sunday after Pentecost. T Baptism of Christ is the first Sunday aft Epiphany (6 January).

THE JEWISH CALENDAR

This is based on lunar and solar cycles. Yea are dated from the creation, supposed to be the time of the autumnal equinox in 3760 B and designated AM (anno mundi). The Jewi year runs from September to Septembe AD 1 January 1995 occurred in 5756 AM.

JEWISH FESTIVALS 1995

Purim	16 March
Passover	15 April
Jewish New Year	25 September
Day of Atonement	4 October
Feast of Tabernacles	9 October

Normal years (called a Common Regula year) are divided into 12 months which start a about the time of the new moon: these month have 30 and 29 days alternately, leading to a year of 354 days. In order to keep the month roughly in step with the seasons, an extra month is included in certain years and change are also made in the number of days in some months. Jewish fasts and festivals occur on fixed dates in the Jewish calendar, which means they are movable in the civil calendar.

THE MUSLIM CALENDAR

This is a purely lunar calendar consisting of 12 months alternating between 30 or 29 days. An extra day is added to the last month at

MOVABLE CHRISTIAN FEASTS

	1995	1996	1997	1998
Ash Wednesday	March	21 February	12 February	25 February
Easter Sunday	16 April	7 April	30 March	12 April
Ascension Day	25 May	16 May	8 May	21 May
Whit Sunday	4 June	26 May	18 May	31 May
Trinity Sunday	11 June	2 June	24 May	7 June
Advent Sunday	3 December	1 December	30 November	29 November

tervals to keep the months in step with the new moon, which occurs about the beginning of each month. The months do not keep in step with the seasons. The main date in the Muslim calendar is the Hejira, the flight of the Prophet Muhammed from Mecca to Medina; this corresponds to AD 16 July 622 in the Julian calendar. Hejira years (AH) are used in Iran, Turkey, Egypt, some Arab countries and in some parts of India and Malaysia.

THE HINDU CALENDAR

This is also a lunar calendar, consisting of 12 months of 29 days, 12 hours each. Each month is made up of a light fortnight and a dark fortnight, based on the waxing and waning of the Moon. The new year begins in the month of Chiatra (March/April). When necessary a 'leap' month is added to the Hindu calendar to make up the difference between the Hindu (360 days) and the solar (365 days) years ■

IMPORTANT DATES

The table below gives the dates of some of the main religious and secular anniversaries and festivals during the course of the year. The saints' days here marked as 'RC' are mainly celebrated in the Roman Catholic calendar; those marked 'Ang' are in the Anglican Book of Common Prayer; unmarked saints are common to both. The saints' days are always fixed – that is, they invariably fall on the designated date irrespective of the day of the week.

In the majority of countries, Independence Day (otherwise known as National Day) is also fixed, although sometimes a government moves it to avoid it falling on a particular day (such as a Sunday) ■

IMPORTANT DATES

RELIGIOUS	SECULAR
January	
1 Circumcision: Solemnity of the BV Mary (RC)	Sudan: Independence Day
3 St Genevieve (RC)	
6 Twelfth Night	
7 St John the Baptist (RC); Orthodox Christmas	
8 St Lucian (Ang)	
10 St Gregory (RC)	
17 St Anthony (RC)	
18 St Prisca (Ang)	
20 St Fabian (Ang)	
21 St Agnes	
22 St Vincent	
24 St Francis de Sales (RC)	
25 Conversion of St Paul	
26 SS Timothy and Titus (RC)	Australia: Australia Day; India: Republic Day
27 St Devoté (Monaco)	
28 St Thomas Aquinas (RC)	
30 St Basil (RC)	
31 St John Bosco (RC)	
February	
2 Purification of the Virgin Mary	
3 St Blasius (Ang)	

RELIGIOUS		SECULAR
5	St Agatha	
6		New Zealand: Treaty of Waitangi
10	St Scholastica (RC)	
14	St Valentine; SS Cyril and Methodius (RC)	
24	St Matthias	
29		Leap Year Day
March		
1	St David	
2	St Chad (Ang)	
3		Bulgaria: End of Ottoman Rule; Morocco: Accession of Hassan II
7	St Perpetua (Ang)	
12	St Gregory (Ang)	
15		Hungary: National day
17	St Patrick (RC)	Ireland: St Patrick's Day
18	St Edward (Ang)	
19	St Joseph (RC)	
20		Tunisia: Independence Day
21	St Benedict (Ang)	Vernal equinox
23		Pakistan: Republic Day
25	The Annunciation of the Virgin Mary	Greece: Independence Day; Lady Day (Quarter Day)
26		Bangladesh: Independence Day
April		
1		All Fool's Day; Iran: Islamic Republic Day
3	St Richard (Ang)	
4	St Ambrose (Ang)	
5		Fiscal year ends
16		Denmark: Birthday of HM Queen
17		Syria: National day
18		Zimbabwe: Independence Day
19	St Alphege (Ang)	
21	St Anslem (RC)	
23	St George	
25	St Mark	
27		Afghanistan: Anniversary of Saur Revolution
29	St Catherine	
30		Netherlands: National Day
May		
1	SS Philip and James	
3	St Athanasius (RC); Invention of the Cross	
6	Martyrdom of St John the Evangelist (RC)	
14	St Matthias (RC)	
17		Norway: Independence Day
19	St Dunstan (Ang)	
20		Cameroon: National Day
24		Commonwealth Day
25	St Bede	

RELIGIOUS	SECULAR
26 St Philip Neri (RC); St Augustine (Ang)	
27 St Augustine (RC); St Bede (Ang)	
31 The Visitation of our Blessed Lady (RC)	South Africa: Republic Day
June	
1 St Justine (RC); St Nicomede (Ang)	
2	Italy: Republic Day
3 SS Charles Lwanga and Companions (RC)	
5 St Boniface (Ang)	
6	Sweden: National day
10	Portugal: National day
11 St Barnabas	
13 St Anthony (RC)	
17 St Alban (Ang)	
20 St Alban (RC)	
21 St Aloysius (RC)	Summer solstice: longest day
22 SS John Fisher and Thomas More (RC)	
24 St John the Baptist	Midsummer Day (Quarter Day)
25	Mozambique: Independence Day
28 St Irenaeus (RC)	
29 St Peter and Paul (RC); St Peter (Ang)	
July	
1	Canada: National day
2 Visitation of the Blessed Virgin Mary (Ang)	
4	USA: Independence Day
10	Argentina: Independence Day
11 St Benedict (RC)	
14	France: Fall of the Bastille
15 St Bonaventure (RC); St Swithian	
17	Iraq: Military Revolution
20 St Margaret (Ang)	Colombia: Independence Day
21	Barbados: Independent Kingdom Day
22 St Mary Magdalene	Poland: National Day
23	Egypt: Anniversary of Revolution
25 St James	
26 SS Joachim and Anne (RC); St Anne (Ang)	
28	Peru: Independence Day
29 St Martha (RC)	
August	
1 St Alphonsus (RC); Lammas Day	Switzerland: National Day
4 St John Vianney (RC)	
6 Transfiguration of Jesus	
7 Name of Jesus	
8 St Dominic (RC)	
9	Singapore: Independence Day
10 St Laurence	
11 St Clare (RC)	Chad: Independence Day
15 The Assumption of Mary (RC)	North Korea, South Korea: Independence Day
20 St Bernard	
24 St Bartholomew	

RELIGIOUS	SECULAR
27 St Monica (RC)	
28 St Augustine of Hippo (Ang)	
29 St John the Baptist	
31	Malaysia: Independence Day

September

1	St Giles (Ang)	
3	St Gregory (RC)	
7	St Evurtius (Ang)	Brazil: Independence Day
8	Nativity of the Virgin Mary	
12		Ethiopia: People's Revolution Day
13	St John Chrysostom (RC)	
14	Holy Cross Day	
15	Our Lady of Sorrows (RC)	El Salvador: Independence Day
16	SS Cornelius and Cyprian (RC)	Mexico: National Day
17	St Lambert (Ang)	
18		Chile: Independence Day
21	St Matthew	
22		Autumnal equinox
23		Saudi Arabia: Unification of the Kingdom
26	St Cyprian (Ang)	
27	St Vincent de Paul (RC)	
29	SS Michael, Gabriel and Raphael (RC); St Michael and all Angels (Ang)	Michaelmas Day (Quarter Day)
30	St Jerome	Botswana: Independence Day

October

1	St Teresa of the Child Jesus (RC); St Remigius (Ang)	China: Proclamation of People's Republic; Nigeria: Republic Day
4	St Francis (RC)	
6	St Faith (Ang)	
9	St Denys (Ang)	
10		Taiwan: Republic Day
12	Our Lady Fiesta Day (Spain)	Spain: Discovery of America Day
13	St Edward the Confessor	
15	St Teresa of Avila (RC)	
17	St Ignatius (RC); St Ethelreda (Ang)	
18	St Luke	
25	St Crispin	
26		Austria: Proclamation of Neutrality
28	SS Simon and Jude	
29		Turkey: Republic Day
31	Hallowe'en	

November

1	All Saints' Day	Algeria: Revolution Day
2	All Souls' Day	
4	St Charles (RC)	
5		UK: Guy Fawkes' Day
10	St Leo (RC)	
11	St Martin	Angola: Independence Day
13	St Britius (Ang)	

RELIGIOUS		SECULAR
15	St Machutus (Ang)	
17	St Elizabeth of Hungary (RC)	
18	St Hugh (Ang)	
20	St Edmund (Ang)	
22	St Cecilia	
23	St Clement (Ang)	
24		Zaïre: Anniversary of Second Republic; USA: Thanksgiving Day
25	St Catherine (Ang)	
28		Albania: Independence Day
30	St Andrew	
December		
3	St Francis Xavier (RC)	
6	St Nicholas (Netherlands)	
7	St Ambrose	
8	Immaculate Conception	
12		Kenya: Independence Day
13	St Lucy (Lucia)	
14	St John of the Cross (RC)	
21	St Thomas	
22		Winter solstice: shortest day
23		Japan: the Emperor's Birthday
25	Christmas Day	Quarter Day

INTERNATIONAL ORGANIZATIONS

ARAB LEAGUE

Founded in 1945 to promote economic, social, political and military co-operation between its members. (Also known as League of Arab States.)

Members: Algeria, Bahrain, Comoros, Djibouti, Egypt, Iraq, Jordan, Kuwait, Lebanon, Libya, Mauritania, Morocco, Oman, Palestine Liberation Organization, Qatar, Saudi Arabia, Somalia, Sudan, Syria, Tunisia, United Arab Emirates, Yemen.

ASSOCIATION OF SOUTH-EAST ASIAN NATIONS (ASEAN)

Founded in Thailand in 1967 to hasten the development (economic, social and cultural) of member countries and to encourage co-operation and unity between them.

Members: Brunei, Indonesia, Malaysia, Philippines, Singapore, Thailand.

CARIBBEAN COMMUNITY AND COMMON MARKET (CARICOM)

Founded in 1973, the aim of CARICOM is to strengthen economic co-operation through the Caribbean Common Market, to co-ordinate foreign policy and encourage functional co-operation in common services, such as education, health and industrial relations.

Members: Antigua and Barbuda, Bahamas, Barbados, Belize, Dominica, Grenada, Guyana, Jamaica, Montserrat, St Christopher and Nevis, St Lucia, St Vincent and the Grenadines, Trinidad and Tobago.

COLOMBO PLAN

Founded in 1950 as the Colombo Plan for Co-operative Economic and Social Development in Asia and the Pacific to aid developing countries in the region.

Members: Afghanistan, Australia, Bangladesh, Bhutan, Burma, Cambodia, Canada, Fiji, India, Indonesia, Iran, Japan, Laos, Malaysia, Maldives, Nepal, New Zealand, Pakistan, Papua New Guinea, Philippines, Singapore, South Korea, Sri Lanka, Thailand, UK, USA.

COMMONWEALTH OF INDEPENDENT STATES (CIS)

Formed in 1991, the CIS co-ordinates foreign defence and economic policies in its member states and provides a forum for addressing matters arising from the break-up of the USSR, which formally ceased to exist on 26 December 1991.

Members: Armenia, Azerbaijan, Belarus, Georgia, Kazakhstan, Kyrgyzstan, Moldova, Russia, Tajikistan, Turkmenistan, Ukraine, Uzbekistan.

COMMONWEALTH OF NATIONS

Evolved from the British Empire, with foundations in the 1926 Imperial Conference, the Commonwealth is a free grouping of the UK and most of its former dependencies. It was formed to further international co-operation and strengthen economic, technical and educational links. The countries in the Commonwealth comprise 16 nations recognizing the British monarch as head of state, 30 republics and five indigenous monarchies.

Members: Antigua and Barbuda, Australia, Bahamas, Bangladesh, Barbados, Belize, Botswana, Brunei, Canada, Cyprus, Dominica, The Gambia, Ghana, Grenada, Guyana, India, Jamaica, Kenya, Kiribati, Lesotho, Malawi, Malaysia, Maldives, Malta, Mauritius, Namibia, Nauru (special member), New Zealand, Nigeria, Pakistan, Papua New Guinea, St Christopher and Nevis, St Lucia, St Vincent and the Grenadines, Seychelles, Sierra Leone, Singapore, Solomon Islands, South Africa, Sri Lanka, Swaziland, Tanzania, Tonga, Trinidad and Tobago, Tuvalu (special member), Uganda, UK, Vanuatu, Western Samoa, Zambia, Zimbabwe.

CONFERENCE ON SECURITY AND CO-OPERATION IN EUROPE (CSCE)

Formed in 1975 under the Helsinki Final Act, the CSCE is a group of countries with the common aim of strengthening co-operation and security in Europe. It also covers co-operation on scientific, technological and environmental matters. In November 1990 a Charter of Paris for a New Europe was signed, following the demise of the Cold War. The charter covers human rights, democracy and a rule of law. In July 1992

the member nations set up an armed peace keeping force.

Members: Albania, Armenia, Austria, Azerbaijan, Belgium, Belarus, Bosnia-Herzegovina, Bulgaria, Canada, Croatia, Cyprus, Czech Republic, Denmark, Estonia, Finland, France, Georgia, Germany, Greece, Hungary, Iceland, Ireland, Italy, Kazakhstan, Kyrgyzstan, Latvia, Liechtenstein, Lithuania, Luxembourg, Malta, Moldova, Monaco, Netherlands, Norway, Poland, Portugal, Romania, Russia, San Marino, Slovak Republic, Slovenia, Spain, Sweden, Switzerland, Tajikistan, Turkey, Turkmenistan, Ukraine, UK, USA, Uzbekistan, Vatican City, Yugoslavia (suspended since July 1992).

EUROPEAN UNION (EU)

Formed in three separate stages: the European Coal and Steel Community was founded in 1951 by the Treaty of Paris, followed by the European Economic Community (the EEC) and the European Atomic Energy Community in 1957 by the Treaty of Rome. The executive and decision-making bodies of these three merged in 1967 to form the European Community. In 1992 the Single European Market was established, removing duties, tariffs and quotas on trade between member countries and allowing a freer movement of people, money and goods within the community. Economic and monetary union may happen sometime in the future. The Maastricht Treaty, which came into effect on 1 November 1993, established the European Union, composed of three pillars: the European Community; a pillar concerned with foreign and security policy; and a pillar to co-ordinate justice and interior affairs. On 1 January 1995, Austria, Finland and Sweden joined the EU following referenda.

Members: Austria, Belgium, Denmark, Finland, France, Germany, Greece, Ireland, Italy, Luxembourg, Netherlands, Portugal, Spain, Sweden, UK.

EUROPEAN FREE TRADE ASSOCIATION (EFTA)

Formed in 1960 to eliminate tariffs between members on industrial goods, enabling free trade. Part of the aim was to achieve a single West European market and increase world

de; to this end, most internal tariffs on
dustrial goods were abolished by the end
1966 and the EC and EFTA created a
uropean Economic Area in 1993. Denmark
d Britain left EFTA in 1972 to join the EC,
rtugal in 1986 and Austria, Finland and
veden in 1995, leaving only four members.
embers: Iceland, Liechtenstein, Norway,
vitzerland.

ATIN AMERICAN INTEGRATION
SSOCIATION (LAIA)
eplaced the Latin American Free Trade
ssociation in 1980, to continue working
wards a Latin American common market,
ntred around the removal of tariffs and the
couragement of trade.
Members: Argentina, Bolivia, Brazil, Chile,
olombia, Ecuador, Mexico, Paraguay, Peru,
ruguay, Venezuela.
Costa Rica, Cuba, Dominican Republic,
l Salvador, Guatemala, Honduras, Italy,
icaragua, Panama, Portugal and Spain have
bserver membership.

NORTH ATLANTIC TREATY
ORGANIZATION (NATO)
ormed in 1949 as a collective defence
lliance, where an attack against one member
ountry is seen as an attack against them all.
t has continued despite the winding up in
991 of the Warsaw Pact (Eastern European
Mutual Assistance Treaty), the former Eastern
loc's equivalent of NATO.
Members: Belgium, Canada, Denmark,
France, Germany, Greece, Iceland, Italy,
Luxembourg, Netherlands, Norway, Portugal,
Spain, Turkey, UK, USA.

ORGANIZATION OF AFRICAN UNITY
(OAU)
Formed in 1963 to promote unity and co-
operation, and to eliminate colonialism and
apartheid from Africa. Its 53 members repre-
sent over 94% of Africa's total population.
Members: Algeria, Angola, Benin, Botswana,
Burkina Faso, Burundi, Cameroon, Cape
Verde, Central African Republic, Chad,
Comoros, Congo, Djibouti, Egypt, Equatorial
Guinea, Eritrea, Ethiopia, Gabon, The
Gambia, Ghana, Guinea, Guinea-Bissau,
Ivory Coast, Kenya, Lesotho, Liberia, Libya,

Madagascar, Malawi, Mali, Mauritania,
Mauritius, Mozambique, Namibia, Niger,
Nigeria, Rwanda, São Tomé and Príncipe,
Senegal, Seychelles, Sierra Leone, Somalia,
South Africa, Sudan, Swaziland, Tanzania,
Togo, Tunisia, Uganda, Western Sahara,
Zaïre, Zambia, Zimbabwe.

ORGANIZATION OF AMERICAN
STATES (OAS)
Founded in 1948 to promote unity and co-
operation between the developed nations of
North America and the developing nations of
Latin America, and to defend the sovereignty
of its members.
Members: Antigua and Barbuda, Argentina,
Bahamas, Barbados, Belize, Bolivia, Brazil,
Canada, Chile, Colombia, Costa Rica, Cuba
(suspended since 1962), Dominica, Domin-
ican Republic, Ecuador, El Salvador, Grenada,
Guatemala, Guyana, Haiti, Honduras,
Jamaica, Mexico, Nicaragua, Panama, Para-
guay, Peru, St Christopher and Nevis, St
Lucia, St Vincent and the Grenadines, Suri-
nam, Trinidad and Tobago, USA, Uruguay,
Venezuela.

ORGANIZATION FOR ECONOMIC
CO-OPERATION AND DEVELOPMENT
(OECD)
Founded in 1961 as a replacement for
the Organization for European Economic
Co-operation (OEEC). The OECD aims to
stimulate progress in member countries and
direct aid to developing countries.
Members: Australia, Austria, Belgium,
Canada, Denmark, France, Finland, Germany, Greece, Iceland, Ireland, Italy, Japan,
Luxembourg, Mexico, Netherlands, New
Zealand, Norway, Portugal, Spain, Sweden,
Switzerland, Turkey, UK, USA, Yugoslavia
(suspended since 1992).
The 'G7' (Group of Seven) is its 'inner
group', comprising Canada, France, Germany, Italy, Japan, UK and USA, whose
heads of government meet to discuss economic, monetary and political matters.

ORGANIZATION OF PETROLEUM
EXPORTING COUNTRIES (OPEC)
Founded in 1960 in Iraq to co-ordinate the
production and sale of petroleum by its mem-

ber countries. It controls about three-quarters of the world's oil supply.

Members: Algeria, Gabon, Indonesia, Iran, Iraq, Kuwait, Libya, Nigeria, Qatar, Saudi Arabia, United Arab Emirates, Venezuela.

UNITED NATIONS

Formed in 1945 to promote peace, international co-operation and security, and to help solve economic, social, cultural and humanitarian problems. Other aims include the promotion of human rights and freedom. There were 51 original members; this has now risen to 185. The UN is the world's largest political organization and has six principal organs:

The General Assembly: The forum at which member nations discuss moral and political issues affecting world development, peace and security. The Assembly meets every September under a newly-elected President.

The Security Council: The primary instrument for maintaining international peace, by attempting to settle disputes between nations.

The Economic and Social Council: The largest UN executive, it instructs the many UN agencies to implement Assembly decisions and co-ordinates their work.

The Secretariat: The staff of the UN, who administer the policies and programmes.

The Trusteeship Council: Administers trust territories with the aim of promoting their advancement. The Council remains despite the fact that its last charge, the Trust Territory of the Pacific Islands (Palau), became fully independent (of the US) in 1994.

The International Court of Justice: The judicial organ of the UN. (Also known as the World Court.)

Examples of some of the UN social and humanitarian programmes include:

United Nations Development Programme (UNDP): Plans and funds projects to help developing countries make better use of resources and raw materials.

United Nations International Children's Fund (UNICEF): Created in 1945 to help children after World War II, it now provides basic healthcare and aid worldwide.

Food and Agriculture Organization (FAO): Aims to raise living standards and nutrition levels in rural areas by improving food production and distribution.

There are also agencies involved in ma aspects of international trade, safety a security. These include:

International Labour Organization (ILC Seeks to improve labour conditions a promote productive employment with the a of raising living standards.

International Maritime Organizati (IMO): Promotes unity amongst mercha shipping, especially in regard to safety, mari. pollution and standardization.

World Trade Organization (WTO): R placed the General Agreement on Tariffs a Trade (GATT) on 1 January 1995. It spo sores negotiations on international trade ar advocates a common code of conduct.

The **World Bank** comprises three U agencies:

International Monetary Fund (IMF): cult vates international monetary co-operation ar the expansion of trade.

International Bank for Reconstructio and Development (IBRD): Provides fund and assistance to developing countries.

International Finance Corporation (IFC Encourages the growth of productive priva enterprise in less developed countries.

Recent additions to the United Nation include Andorra, Bosnia-Herzegovina, Mol dova, Palau, San Marino and the Sloval Republic. There are seven independent state which are not members — Kiribati, Nauru Switzerland, Taiwan, Tonga, Tuvalu and the Vatican City ∎

UN CONTRIBUTIONS

In 1994, the top ten contributors to the UN budget, which in 1994–5 was $2.6 billion, were as follows:

1	USA	25.0 %
2	Japan	12.5 %
3	Germany	8.9 %
4	Russia	6.7 %
5	France	6.0 %
6	UK	5.0 %
7	Italy	4.3 %
8	Canada	3.1 %
9	Spain	2.0 %
10	Brazil	1.6 %

INDEX

The number in bold type which follows each name in the index refers to the number of the map page where that feature or place will be found. This is usually the largest scale on which the place or feature appears.
Rivers have been indexed to their mouth or to where they join another river.
All river names are followed by the symbol →
A solid square ■ follows the name of a country, while an open square □ refers to a first-order administrative area.
The geographical co-ordinates which follow the place name are sometimes only approximate, but are close enough for the place name to be located.

M